Lecture Notes in Computer Science 8931

Advanced Research in Computing and Software Science

Subline of Lectures Notes in Computer Science

Deepak D'Souza Akash Lal
Kim Guldstrand Larsen (Eds.)

Verification, Model Checking, and Abstract Interpretation

16th International Conference, VMCAI 2015
Mumbai, India, January 12-14, 2015
Proceedings

Springer

Volume Editors

Deepak D'Souza
Indian Institute of Science
Department of Computer Science and Automation
Bangalore, India
E-mail: deepakd@csa.iisc.ernet.in

Akash Lal
Microsoft Research India
Bangalore, India
E-mail: akashl@microsoft.com

Kim Guldstrand Larsen
Aalborg University
Department of Computer Science
Aalborg East, Denmark
E-mail: kgl@cs.aau.dk

ISSN 0302-9743 e-ISSN 1611-3349
ISBN 978-3-662-46080-1 e-ISBN 978-3-662-46081-8
DOI 10.1007/978-3-662-46081-8
Springer Heidelberg New York Dordrecht London

Library of Congress Control Number: 2014958456

LNCS Sublibrary: SL 1 – Theoretical Computer Science and General Issues

Typesetting: Camera-ready by author, data conversion by Scientific Publishing Services, Chennai, India

Printed on acid-free paper

Springer is part of Springer Science+Business Media (www.springer.com)

Preface

This volume contains the papers presented at the 16th International Conference on Verification, Model Checking, and Abstract Interpretation (VMCAI 2015), held during January 12–14, 2015, in Mumbai, India.

This edition of the conference attracted 53 competitive submissions from 22 countries across the world. Each submission was reviewed by at least three Program Committee members. The Committee decided to accept 24 papers. The program also included four invited talks.

We would like to thank our invited speakers Supratik Chakraborty, Rustan Leino, Antoine Miné, and Jean-François Raskin for readily agreeing to share their insights with us through their talks and articles contributed to the conference. We would like to thank all the Program Committee members and reviewers for their diligent reviews that helped maintain the high standards of VMCAI. Like many other conferences, we are indebted to EasyChair for providing us with an excellent conference management system. We are grateful to Alfred Hofmann and Anna Kramer of Springer for their close cooperation in publishing these proceedings.

Finally, we would to thank ACM SIGPLAN-SIGACT and the local organizers, especially Sriram Rajamani and Paritosh Pandya, for the excellent infrastructural support to VMCAI.

November 2014

Deepak D'Souza
Akash Lal
Kim Guldstrand Larsen

Organization

Program Committee

Erika Abraham	RWTH Aachen University, Germany
S. Akshay	IIT Bombay, India
Aws Albarghouthi	University of Toronto, Canada
Patricia Bouyer	ENS Cachan, France
Alessandro Cimatti	Fondazione Bruno Kessler, Trento, Italy
Agostino Cortesi	Università Ca' Foscari di Venezia, Italy
Deepak D'Souza	Indian Institute of Science, Bangalore, India
Thomas Dillig	University of Texas, Austin, USA
Constantin Enea	Université Paris, Diderot, France
William Harris	University of Wisconsin-Madison, USA
Ranjit Jhala	University of California, San Diego, USA
Barbara Jobstmann	Verimag, Grenoble, France
Daniel Kroening	University of Oxford, UK
Akash Lal	Microsoft Research, Bangalore, India
Kim Larsen	Aalborg University, Denmark
Francesco Logozzo	Microsoft Research, Redmond, USA
Ken Mcmillan	Cadence Berkeley Labs, USA
David Monniaux	Verimag, Grenoble, France
David Parker	University of Birmingham, UK
Matthew Parkinson	Microsoft Research, Cambridge, UK
Ruzica Piskac	Yale University, USA
Andreas Podelski	University of Freiburg, Germany
Pavithra Prabhakar	IMDEA Software Institute
Xiaokang Qiu	Massachusetts Institute of Technology, USA
Sriram Sankaranarayanan	University of Colorado, Boulder, USA
Thomas Wies	New York University, USA

Additional Reviewers

Bogomolov, Sergiy
Bollig, Benedikt
Calzavara, Stefano
Chakraborty, Supratik
Chen, Xin
Christ, Juergen
Corzilius, Florian
Coughlin, Devin
D'Silva, Vijay
Dang, Thao
Delahaye, Benoît
Deshmukh, Jyotirmoy
Dodds, Mike
Dragoi, Cezara
Emmi, Michael
Ferrara, Pietro

Ganty, Pierre
Gonnord, Laure
Griesmayer, Andreas
Griggio, Alberto
Guha, Shibashis
Hamza, Jad
Harris, William
Hoenicke, Jochen
Irfan, Ahmed
Joshi, Saurabh
Kapinski, James
Kinder, Johannes
Kirchner, Florent
Koskinen, Eric
Kremer, Gereon
Kuncak, Viktor
Maiza, Claire
Mastroeni, Isabella
Micheli, Andrea
Misailovic, Sasa
Mover, Sergio
Murano, Aniello
Niksic, Filip
Norman, Gethin
Parlato, Gennaro
Potet, Marie-Laure
Ramalingam, Ganesan
S., Krishna
Sampath, Prahaladavaradan
Schupp, Stefan
Sharma, Subodh
Song, Fu
Sousa, Marcelo
Srivathsan, B.
Stückrath, Jan
Summers, Alexander J.
Suter, Philippe
Tautschnig, Michael
Tiezzi, Francesco
Trivedi, Ashutosh
Zufferey, Damien

Abstracts

AstréeA: A Static Analyzer for Large Embedded Multi-Task Software

Antoine Miné

CNRS & École Normale Supérieure
45, rue d'Ulm
75005 Paris, France
mine@di.ens.fr

Embedded critical systems, such as planes and cars, cannot be easily fixed during missions and any error can have catastrophic consequences. It is thus primordial to ensure the correctness of their controlling software before they are deployed. At the very least, critical embedded software must be exempt from runtime errors, including ill-defined operations according to the specification of the language (such as arithmetic or memory overflows) as well as failure of programmer-inserted assertions. Sound and approximate static analysis can help, by providing tools able to analyze the large codes found in the industry in a fully automated way and without missing any real error. Sound and scalable static analyzers are sometimes thought to be too imprecise and report too many false alarms to be of any use in the context of verification. This claim was disproved when, a decade ago [2], the Astrée static analyzer [1] successfully analyzed the runtime errors in several Airbus control flight software, with few or no false alarm. This result could be achieved by employing abstract interpretation [4], a principled framework to define and compose modular sound-by-construction and parametric abstractions, but also by adopting a design-by-refinement development strategy. Starting from an efficient and easy to design, but rather coarse, fully flow- and context-sensitive interval analyzer, we integrated more complex abstractions (carefully chosen from the literature, such as octagons [10], adapted from it, such as trace partitioning [9], or specifically invented for our needs, such as digital filter domains [6]) to remove large sets of related false alarms, until we reached our precision target.

In this presentation, we discuss our *on-going* efforts towards a similar goal: the efficient and precise sound verification of the absence of run-time errors, but targeting another, more complex class of software: *shared-memory concurrent embedded C software*. Such software are already present in critical systems and will likely become the norm with the generalization of multi-core processors in embedded systems, leading to new challenging demands in verification. Our analyzer is named AstréeA [5], in reference to Astrée on which it takes its inspiration and on the code base of which it elaborates. AstréeA's specialization target is a family of several embedded avionic codes, each featuring a small fixed set of a dozen threads, more than 1.5 Mlines of C code, implicit communication through the shared memory, and running under a real-time OS based on the ARINC 653 specification.

One major challenge is that a concurrent program execution does not follow a fixed sequential order, but one of many interleavings of executions from different tasks chosen by the scheduler. A sound analysis must consider all possible interleavings in order to cover every corner case and race condition. As it is impractical to build a fully flow-sensitive analysis by enumerating explicitly all interleavings, we took inspiration from *thread-modular* methods: we analyze each thread individually, in an environment consisting of (an abstraction of) the effect of the other threads. This is a form of *rely-guarantee* reasoning [8], but in a fully automatic static analysis settings formalized as abstract interpretation. Contrary to Jones' seminal rely-guarantee proof method or its more recent incarnations [7], our method does not require manual annotations: thread interferences are automatically inferred by the analysis (including which variables are actually shared and their possible values). Following the classic methodology of abstract interpretation [4, 3], a thread-modular static analysis is now viewed as a computable abstraction of a *complete* concrete thread-modular semantics. This permits a fine control between precision and efficiency, and opens the way to analysis specialization: any given safety property of a given program can be theoretically inferred given the right abstract domain.

Following the design-by-refinement principle of Astrée, our first prototype AstréeA [11] used a very coarse but efficient flow-insensitive and non-relational notion of thread interference: it gathered independently for each variable and each thread an interval abstraction of the values the thread can store into the variable along its execution, and injected these values as non-deterministic writes into other threads. This abstraction allowed us to scale up to our target applications, in efficiency (a few tens of hours of computation) if not in precision (a few tens of thousands alarms).

This presentation will describe our subsequent work in improving the precision of AstréeA by specialization on our target applications, and the interesting abstractions we developed along the way. For instance, we developed new interference abstractions enabling a limited but controllable (for efficiency) degree of relationality and flow-sensitivity [12]. We also designed abstractions able to exploit our knowledge of the real-time scheduler used in the analysis target: *i.e.*, it schedules tasks on a single core and obeys a strict priority scheme.[1] The resulting analysis is less general, but more precise on our target applications, which was deemed necessary as the correctness of the applications relies on these hypotheses on the scheduler.[2] Finally, not all false alarms are caused by our abstraction of concurrency; we also developed numeric and memory domains to handle more

[1] The scheduler remains fully preemptive: a low-priority thread may be interrupted at any point by a higher-priority thread whose request to an external resource has just been granted, resulting in a large number of possible thread interleavings.

[2] It is important not to confuse here specialization with restriction: the scheduler abstraction is optional and can be omitted to achieve a more general, but less specialized analysis.

precisely some programming patterns which we did not encounter in our previous experience with Astrée and for which no stock abstract domain was available.

The end-result is a more precise analyzer on our target applications, with currently around a thousand alarms. We stress that AstréeA is a work in progress and that its results, although they are not yet as impressive as those of Astrée, are likely to improve through further specialization. We also believe that, thanks to the intrinsic modularity of the abstract interpretation framework, the analysis performed by AstréeA can be adapted to other settings (other families of applications, other schedulers, other concurrency models) by developing new abstractions, while the abstractions we designed along the journey may also be of use in similar or different static analyses.

References

1. Blanchet, B., Cousot, P., Cousot, R., Feret, J., Mauborgne, L., Miné, A., Monniaux, D., Rival, X.: The Astrée static analyzer, `http://www.astree.ens.fr`
2. Blanchet, B., Cousot, P., Cousot, R., Feret, J., Mauborgne, L., Miné, A., Monniaux, D., Rival, X.: A static analyzer for large safety-critical software. In: PLDI 2013, pp. 196–207. ACM (2003)
3. Cousot, P., Cousot, R.: Invariance proof methods and analysis techniques for parallel programs. In: Automatic Program Construction Techniques, ch. 12, pp. 243–271. Macmillan, New York (1984)
4. Cousot, P., Cousot, R.: Abstract interpretation frameworks. Journal of Logic and Computation 2(4), 511–547 (1992)
5. Cousot, P., Cousot, R., Feret, J., Miné, A., Rival, X.: The AstréeA static analyzer, `http://www.astreea.ens.fr`
6. Feret, J.: Static analysis of digital filters. In: Schmidt, D. (ed.) ESOP 2004. LNCS, vol. 2986, pp. 33–48. Springer, Heidelberg (2004)
7. Flanagan, C., Freund, S.N., Qadeer, S.: Thread-Modular Verification for Shared-Memory Programs. In: Le Métayer, D. (ed.) ESOP 2002. LNCS, vol. 2305, pp. 262–277. Springer, Heidelberg (2002)
8. Jones, C.B.: Tentative steps toward a development method for interfering programs. ACM TOPLAS 5, 596–619 (1983)
9. Mauborgne, L., Rival, X.: Trace Partitioning in Abstract Interpretation Based Static Analyzers. In: Sagiv, M. (ed.) ESOP 2005. LNCS, vol. 3444, pp. 5–20. Springer, Heidelberg (2005)
10. Miné, A.: The octagon abstract domain. Higher-Order and Symbolic Computation 19(1), 31–100 (2006)
11. Miné, A.: Static analysis of run-time errors in embedded critical parallel C programs. In: Barthe, G. (ed.) ESOP 2011. LNCS, vol. 6602, pp. 398–418. Springer, Heidelberg (2011)
12. Miné, A.: Relational thread-modular static value analysis by abstract interpretation. In: McMillan, K.L., Rival, X. (eds.) VMCAI 2014. LNCS, vol. 8318, pp. 39–58. Springer, Heidelberg (2014)

Word-Level Quantifier Elimination

Supratik Chakraborty

Department of Computer Science & Engineering
Indian Institute of Technology Bombay

A first order theory $\mathcal{T}$ is said to admit *quantifier elimination* if every $\mathcal{T}$-formula of the form $Qx.\,\varphi(x, y_1, \ldots y_n)$, where $\varphi(x, y_1, \ldots y_n)$ is quantifier-free and Q is either $\exists$ or $\forall$, is $\mathcal{T}$-equivalent to a quantifier-free formula of the form $\widehat{\varphi}(y_1, \ldots y_n)$. The process of systematically deriving $\widehat{\varphi}(y_1, \ldots y_n)$ from $\varphi(x, y_1, \ldots y_n)$ is called "quantifier elimination".

Quantifier elimination is an important operation in several verification, synthesis and analysis tasks. When reasoning about hardware and software with finite precision arithmetic, the theory $\mathcal{T}$ of relevance is that of fixed-width bit-vectors (or words). Since each variable in this theory has a fixed finite domain, the theory is easily seen to admit quantifier elimination via expansion of quantified variables. This naive approach, however, does not translate to a practical algorithm for eliminating quantifiers, since the domain of a variable is exponential in its bit-width. Therefore, the formula resulting from expansion of quantified variables blows up exponentially, rendering the naive approach infeasible in practice. Approaches based on bit-blasting $\varphi(x, y_1, \ldots y_n)$, followed by quantifier elimination techniques for quantified propositional formulas are not very useful either, since the result obtained via such approaches have no word-level structure at all. This makes it difficult to apply further word-level reasoning on the formula resulting from quantifier elimination. It is therefore important to develop *word-level quantifier elimination* algorithms that avoid variable expansion and bit-blasting as much as possible, and instead reason directly at the level of bit-vectors (or words).

The importance of word-level quantifier elimination in several application domains has spurred a lot of interesting work in this area in the recent past. This talk surveys these techniques, and discusses in more depth some quantifier elimination algorithms for linear word-level constraints, developed in our research group. Since the output of each word-level quantifier elimination technique is a word-level formula, it is indeed possible to harness the power of multiple techniques in a co-operative manner to quantify a set of variables. The talk concludes with an overview of sub-problems that still remain to be addressed satisfactorily in our quest for word-level quantifier elimination techniques for real-world verification, synthesis and analysis problems.

Early Verification

K. Rustan and M. Leino

Microsoft Research, Redmond, WA, USA
leino@microsoft.com

Abstract. Technology that accurately models, analyzes, and verifies software has come a long way since its conception several decades ago. One mode of using such technology is to look for defects in software that has already left the hands of developers. Another mode is to integrate the technology into the process of software authoring (see, for example, [2,1,5,3,4]). The advantage of this mode is that it lends analytical power to the developer's thinking. To be used in this way, the technology must be packaged in a way that is understandable, unobtrusive, and responsive. In this talk, I showcase an integrated development environment that supports reasoning and verification, trying to provide an aid to the developer earlier during the software development process.

References

[1] Abrial, J.-R.: Modeling in Event-B: System and Software Engineering. Cambridge University Press (2010)

[2] Bourdoncle F.: Abstract debugging of higher-order imperative languages. In: Cartwright, R. (ed.) Proceedings of the ACM SIGPLAN 1993 Conference on Programming Language Design and Implementation (PLDI), pp. 46–55. ACM (June 1993)

[3] Leino, K.R.M.: Dafny: An automatic program verifier for functional correctness. In: Clarke, E.M., Voronkov, A. (eds.) LPAR-16 2010. LNCS, vol. 6355, pp. 348–370. Springer, Heidelberg (2010)

[4] Logozzo, F., Barnett, M., Fähndrich, M., Cousot, P., Cousot, R.: A semantic integrated development environment. In: Leavens, G.T. (ed.) Conference on Systems, Programming, and Applications: Software for Humanity, SPLASH 2012. ACM (October 2012)

[5] Reif, W.: The KIV system: Systematic construction of verified software. In: Kapur, D. (ed.) CADE 1992. LNCS, vol. 607, pp. 753–757. Springer, Heidelberg (1992)

Variations on the Stochastic Shortest Path Problem*

Mickael Randour[1], Jean-François Raskin[2], and Ocan Sankur[2]

[1] LSV, CNRS & ENS Cachan, France
[2] Département d'Informatique, Université Libre de Bruxelles (U.L.B.), Belgium

Abstract. In this invited contribution, we revisit the stochastic shortest path problem, and show how recent results allow one to improve over the classical solutions: we present algorithms to synthesize strategies with multiple guarantees on the distribution of the length of paths reaching a given target, rather than simply minimizing its expected value. The concepts and algorithms that we propose here are applications of more general results that have been obtained recently for Markov decision processes and that are described in a series of recent papers.

1 Introduction

Markov decision processes (MDP) [18] are natural models for systems that exhibit both non-deterministic and stochastic evolutions. An MDP is executed in rounds. In each round, the MDP is in a give state and an action is chosen by a controller (this is the resolution of non-determinism). Once this action has been fixed then the next state is determined following a probability distribution associated to the current state and the action that has been chosen by the controller. A controller can thus be considered as a *strategy* (a.k.a. *policy*) that determines which action to choose according to the history of the execution so far. MDPs have been studied intensively and there are algorithms to synthesize strategies that enforce a large variety of objectives like omega-regular objectives [9], PCTL objectives [1], or quantitative objectives [18].

One Philosophy, Three Variants. The classical strategy synthesis setting often considers a single objective to be optimized such as the reachability probability, or the expected cost to target. Such simple objectives are not always sufficient to describe the properties required from an efficient controller. Indeed, on the one hand, one often has several measures of performance, and several objectives to satisfy, so the desired strategies have to settle for trade-offs between these. On the other hand, the strategies computed in the classical setting are tailored for the precise probabilities given in the MDP, which often correspond to the *average behavior* of the system in hand. This approach is not satisfactory if one is also interested in giving some formal guarantees under several scenarios,

* Work partially supported by ERC starting grant inVEST (FP7-279499) and European project CASSTING (FP7-ICT-601148).

D. D'Souza et al. (Eds.): VMCAI 2015, LNCS 8931, pp. 1–18, 2015.

say, under normal conditions (i.e., average behavior), but also a minor failure, and a major failure. In this paper, we summarize recent results that we have obtained in this direction with the common goal of improving the strategies that can be synthesized for probabilistic systems. They were presented in three recent publications [5,20,19]. All three models that we studied share a common philosophy which is to provide a framework for the synthesis of strategies ensuring *richer performance guarantees* than the traditional models. The three problems we tackle can be summarized as follows.

First, in [5], we study a problem that is at the crossroad between the analysis of two-player zero-sum quantitative graph games and of quantitative MDPs. In the former, we want strategies for the controller that ensure a given minimal performance against *all* possible behaviors of its environment: we ask for strict guarantees on the *worst-case* performance. In the latter, the controller plays against a stochastic environment, and we want strategies that ensure a good expected performance, with no guarantee on individual outcomes. Both models have clear weaknesses: strategies that are good for the worst-case may exhibit suboptimal behaviors in probable situations while strategies that are good for the expectation may be terrible in some unlikely but possible situations. The *beyond worst-case synthesis problem* asks to construct strategies that provide both worst-case guarantees and guarantees on the expected value against a particular stochastic model of the environment given as input. We have considered both the mean-payoff value problem and the shortest path problem.

Second, in [19], we study multi-dimensional weighted MDPs, which are useful for modeling systems with multiple objectives. Those objectives may be conflicting, and so the analysis of trade-offs is important. To allow the analysis of those trade-offs, we study a general form of *percentile queries*. Percentile queries are as follows: given a multi-dimensional weighted MDP and a quantitative payoff function f (such as mean-payoff or truncated sum), quantitative thresholds v_i (one per dimension), and probability thresholds α_i, we show how to compute a *single* strategy that enforces that for all dimensions i, the probability that an outcome ρ satisfies $f_i(\rho) \geq v_i$ is at least α_i. We have obtained several new complexity results on the associated decision problems and established efficient algorithms to solve these problems.

Third, in [20], we introduce *multi-environment* MDPs (MEMDPs) which are MDPs with a *set* of probabilistic transition functions. The goal in an MEMDP is to synthesize a single controller with guaranteed performances against *all* environments of this set even though the environment is unknown a priori. While MEMDPs can be seen as a special class of partially observable MDPs, several verification problems that are undecidable for partially observable MDPs, are decidable for MEMDPs and sometimes even allow for efficient solutions.

Stochastic Shortest Path. To illustrate those results in a uniform manner, we consider the *stochastic shortest path problem*, SSP problem, and study several variations. The *shortest path* problem is a classical optimization problem that asks, given a weighted graph, to find a path from a starting state to a target state such that the sum of weights along edges used in the path is minimized.

Table of Contents

Stochastic variants consider edges with probabilistic distributions on destinations and/or on weights. We revisit here some of those variants at the light of the results that we have obtained in the contributions described above.

Structure of the Paper. Our paper is organized as follows. In Sect. 2, we recall some elementary notions about MDPs. In Sect. 3, we define two classical stochastic variations on the SSP problem: the first one asks to minimize the expected length of paths to target, and the second one asks to force short paths with high probability. In Sect. 4, we apply the *beyond worst-case analysis* to the shortest path problem and summarize our results presented in [5]. In Sect. 5, we consider a multi-dimension version of the shortest path problem where edges both have a length and a cost. We illustrate how *percentile queries*, that we have studied in [19], are natural objectives for the study of trade-offs in this setting. In Sect. 6, we study a version of the SSP where the stochastic information is given by several probabilistic transition relations instead of one, so we apply the *multi-environment* MDP analysis introduced in [20] on this variant. Throughout Sect. 4-6, we also give a summary of our general results on the corresponding models, as well as additional pointers to the literature.

2 Preliminaries

Markov Decision Processes. A (finite) *Markov decision process* (MDP) is a tuple $D = (S, s_{\mathsf{init}}, A, \delta)$ where S is a finite set of *states*, $s_{\mathsf{init}} \in S$ is the initial state, A is a finite set of *actions*, and $\delta \colon S \times A \to \mathcal{D}(S)$ is a partial function called the *probabilistic transition function*, where $\mathcal{D}(S)$ denotes the set of rational probability distributions over S. The set of actions that are available in a state $s \in S$ is denoted by $A(s)$. We use $\delta(s, a, s')$ as a shorthand for $\delta(s, a)(s')$. A *weighted* MDP $D = (S, s_{\mathsf{init}}, A, \delta, w)$ is an MDP with a *d-dimension integer weight function* $w \colon A \to \mathbb{Z}^d$. For any dimension $i \in \{1, \ldots, d\}$, we denote by $w_i \colon A \to \mathbb{Z}$ the projection of w to the i-th dimension, i is omitted when there is only one dimension.

We define a *run* ρ of D as a finite or infinite sequence $\rho = s_1 a_1 \ldots a_{n-1} s_n \ldots$ of states and actions such that $\delta(s_i, a_i, s_{i+1}) > 0$ for all $i \geq 1$. We denote the prefix of ρ up to state s_i by $\rho(i)$. A run is called *initial* if it starts in the initial state s_{init}. We denote the set of runs of D by $\mathcal{R}(D)$ and its set of *initial* runs by $\mathcal{R}_{s_{\mathsf{init}}}(D)$. Finite runs that end in a state are also called *histories*, and denoted by $\mathcal{H}(D)$ and $\mathcal{H}_{s_{\mathsf{init}}}(D)$, respectively.

Strategies. A *strategy* σ is a function $\mathcal{H}(D) \to \mathcal{D}(A)$ such that for all $h \in \mathcal{H}(D)$ ending in s, we have $\mathsf{Supp}(\sigma(h)) \in A(s)$, where Supp denotes the support of the probability distribution. The set of all possible strategies is denoted by Σ. A strategy is *pure* if all histories are mapped to *Dirac distributions*. A strategy σ can be encoded by a *stochastic Moore machine*, $(\mathcal{M}, \sigma_a, \sigma_u, \alpha)$ where $\mathcal{M}$ is a finite or infinite set of memory elements; $\sigma_a \colon S \times \mathcal{M} \to \mathcal{D}(A)$ the *next action function* where $\mathsf{Supp}(\sigma(s, m)) \subseteq A(s)$ for any $s \in S$ and $m \in \mathcal{M}$; $\sigma_u : A \times S \times \mathcal{M} \to \mathcal{D}(\mathcal{M})$ the *memory update function*; and α the *initial distribution on* $\mathcal{M}$. We say that σ is *finite-memory* if $|\mathcal{M}| < \infty$, and K-*memory* if $|\mathcal{M}| = K$; it is memoryless if $K = 1$, thus only depends on the last state of the history. We define such strategies as functions $s \mapsto \mathcal{D}(A(s))$ for all $s \in S$. Otherwise a strategy is *infinite-memory*.

Markov Chains. A weighted *Markov chain* (MC) is a tuple $M = (S, d_{\mathsf{init}}, \Delta, w)$ where S is a (non-necessarily finite) set of *states*, $d_{\mathsf{init}} \in \mathcal{D}(S)$ is the initial distribution, $\Delta\colon S \to \mathcal{D}(S)$ is the *probabilistic transition function*, and $w\colon S \times S \to \mathbb{Z}^d$ is a *d-dimension weight function*. Markov chains are essentially MDPs where for all $s \in S$, we have that $|A(s)| = 1$.

We define a *run* of M as a finite or infinite sequence $s_1 s_2 \ldots s_n \ldots$ of states such that $\Delta(s_i, s_{i+1}) > 0$ for all $i \geq 1$. A run is called *initial* if it starts in the initial state s such that $d_{\mathsf{init}}(s) > 0$. Runs of M are denoted by $\mathcal{R}(M)$, and its set of *initial* runs by $\mathcal{R}_{d_{\mathsf{init}}}(M)$.

Markov Chains Induced by a Strategy. An MDP $D = (S, s_{\mathsf{init}}, A, \delta)$ and a strategy σ encoded by $(\mathcal{M}, \sigma_a, \sigma_u, \alpha)$ determine a Markov chain $M = D^\sigma$ defined on the state space $S \times \mathcal{M}$ as follows. The initial distribution is such that for any $m \in \mathcal{M}$, state (s_{init}, m) has probability $\alpha(m)$, and 0 for other states. For any pair of states (s, m) and (s', m'), the probability of the transition $((s, m), a, (s', m'))$ is equal to $\sigma_a(s, m)(a) \cdot \delta(s, a, s') \cdot \sigma_u(s, m, a)(m')$. So, a *run* of D^σ is a finite or infinite sequence of the form $(s_1, m_1), a_1, (s_2, m_2), a_2, \ldots$ where each $((s_i, m_i), a_i, (s_{i+1}, m_{i+1}))$ is a transition with non-zero probability in D^σ, and $s_1 = s_{\mathsf{init}}$. In this case, the run $s_1 a_1 s_2 a_2 \ldots$, obtained by projection to D, is said to be *compatible with* σ.

In an MC M, an *event* is a measurable set of runs $\mathcal{E} \subseteq \mathcal{R}_{d_{\mathsf{init}}}(M)$. Every event has a uniquely defined probability [24] (Carathodory's extension theorem induces a unique probability measure on the Borel σ-algebra over $\mathcal{R}_{d_{\mathsf{init}}}(M)$). We denote by $\mathbb{P}_M(\mathcal{E})$ the probability that a run belongs to $\mathcal{E}$ when the initial state is chosen according to d_{init}, and M is executed for an infinite number of steps. Given a measurable function $f\colon \mathcal{R}(M) \to \mathbb{R} \cup \{\infty\}$, we denote by $\mathbb{E}_M(f)$ the *expected value* or *expectation* of f over initial runs in M. When considering probabilities of events in D^σ, for D an MDP and σ a strategy on D, we often consider runs defined by their projection on D. Thus, given $\mathcal{E} \subseteq \mathcal{R}(D)$, we denote by $\mathbb{P}^\sigma_D[\mathcal{E}]$ the probability of the runs of D^σ whose projections to D are in $\mathcal{E}$.

3 The Stochastic Shortest Path Problem

The *shortest path problem* in a weighted graph is a classical problem that asks, given a starting state s and a set of target states T, to find a path from s to a state $t \in T$ of minimal length (i.e., that minimizes the sum of the weights along the edges in the path). See for example [8]. There have been several stochastic variants of this classical graph problem defined and studied in the literature, see for example [18]. We recall here two main variants of this problem, other new variants are defined and studied in the subsequent sections.

Let $D = (S, s_{\mathsf{init}}, A, \delta, w)$ be an MDP with a *single-dimensional* weight function $w\colon A \to \mathbb{N}_0$ that assigns to each action $a \in A$ a strictly positive integer. Let $T \subseteq S$ be a set of target states. Given an initial run $\rho = s_1 s_2 \ldots s_i \ldots$ in the MDP, we define its *truncated sum* up to T to be $\mathsf{TS}^T(\rho) = \sum_{j=1}^{n-1} w(a_j)$ if s_n is the first visit of a state in $T \subseteq S$ within ρ; otherwise if T is never reached, then we set $\mathsf{TS}^T(\rho) = \infty$. The function TS^T is measurable, and so this function has an expected value in a weighted MC and sets of runs defined from TS^T are measurable. The following two problems have been considered in the literature.

Minimizing the Expected Length of Paths to Target. Given a weighted MDP, we may be interested in strategies (choices of actions) that minimize the expected length of paths to target. This is called the *stochastic shortest path expectation* problem, SSP-E for short, and it is defined as follows.

Definition 1 (SSP-E problem). *Given a single-dimensional weighted MDP $D = (S, s_{\mathsf{init}}, A, \delta, w)$ and a threshold $\ell \in \mathbb{N}$, decide if there exists σ such that $\mathbb{E}^{\sigma}_{D}(\mathsf{TS}^T) \leq \ell$.*

Theorem 1 ([2]). *The SSP-E problem can be decided in polynomial time. Optimal pure memoryless strategies always exist and can be constructed in polynomial time.*

There are several algorithms proposed in the literature to solve this problem. We recall a simple one based on linear programming (LP). For other solutions based on *value iteration* or *strategy iteration*, we refer the interested reader to, e.g., [2,10]. To apply the reduction to LP, we must make the hypothesis that, for each state $s \in S$ of the MDP, there is a path from s to the target set T. It is clear that the expectation of states that are not connected to the target set T by a path is infinite. So, we will assume that all such states have first been removed from the MDP. This can easily be done in linear time. Also, it is clear that for all states in T, the expected length of the shortest path is trivially equal to 0. So, we restrict our attention to states in $S \setminus T$. For each state $s \in S \setminus T$, we consider one variable x_s, and we define the following LP:

$$\max \sum_{s \in S \setminus T} x_s$$

under the constraints

$$x_s \leq w(a) + \sum_{s' \in S \setminus T} \delta(s, a, s') \cdot x_{s'} \qquad \text{for all } s \in S \setminus T, \text{ for all } a \in A(s).$$

It can be shown (e.g., in [2]) that the optimal solution $\mathbf{v}$ for this LP is such that $\mathbf{v}_s$ is the expectation of the length of the shortest path from s to a state in T under an optimal strategy. Such an optimal strategy can easily be constructed from the optimal solution $\mathbf{v}$. The following pure memoryless strategy $\sigma^{\mathbf{v}}$ is optimal:

$$\sigma^{\mathbf{v}}(s) = \arg \min_{a \in A(s)} \left[w(a) + \sum_{s' \in S \setminus T} \delta(s, a, s') \cdot \mathbf{v}_{s'} \right].$$

Forcing Short Paths with High Probability. As an alternative to the expectation, given a weighted MDP, we may be interested in strategies that maximize the probability of short paths to target. This is called the *stochastic shortest path percentile* problem, SSP-P for short, and provides a preferable solution if we are risk-averse. The problem is defined as follows.

Definition 2 (SSP-P problem). *Given a single-dimensional weighted MDP* $D = (S, s_{\mathsf{init}}, A, \delta, w)$*, value* $\ell \in \mathbb{N}$*, and probability threshold* $\alpha \in [0,1] \cap \mathbb{Q}$*, decide if there exists a strategy* σ *such that* $\mathbb{P}^{\sigma}_{D}\big[\{\rho \in \mathcal{R}_{s_{\mathsf{init}}}(D) \mid \mathsf{TS}^{T}(\rho) \leq \ell\}\big] \geq \alpha$.

Theorem 2. *The* SSP-P *problem can be decided in pseudo-polynomial time, and it is* PSPACE*-hard. Optimal pure strategies with pseudo-polynomial memory always exist and can be constructed in pseudo-polynomial time.*

The PSPACE-hardness result was recently proved in [15]. An algorithm to solve this problem can be obtained by a (pseudo-polynomial-time) reduction to the *stochastic reachability problem*, SR for short.

Given an unweighted MDP $D = (S, s_{\mathsf{init}}, A, \delta)$, a set of target states $T \subseteq S$, and a probability threshold $\alpha \in [0,1] \cap \mathbb{Q}$, the SR problem asks to decide if there is a strategy σ that ensures, when played from s_{init}, to reach the set T with a probability that exceeds the threshold α. The SR problem can also be solved in polynomial time by a reduction to linear programming. Here is a description of the LP. For all states $s \in S$, we consider a variable x_s in the following LP:

$$\min \sum_{s \in S} x_s$$

under the constraints

$$\begin{array}{ll} x_s = 1 & \forall s \in T, \\ x_s = 0 & \forall s \in S \text{ which cannot reach } T, \\ x_s \geq \sum_{s' \in S} \delta(s,a,s') \cdot x_{s'} & \forall a \in A(s). \end{array}$$

The optimal solution $\mathbf{v}$ for this LP is such that $\mathbf{v}_s$ is the maximal probability to reach the set of targets T that can be achieved from s. From the optimal solution $\mathbf{v}$, we can define a pure memoryless strategy $\sigma^{\mathbf{v}}$ which achieve $\mathbf{v}_s$ when played from s, we define it for all states $s \notin T$ that can reach T:

$$\sigma^{\mathbf{v}}(s) = \arg \max_{a \in A(s)} \left[\sum_{s' \in S} \delta(s,a,s') \cdot x_{s'} \right].$$

We are now ready to define the reduction from the SSP-P problem to the the SR problem. Given a weighted MDP $D = (S, s_{\mathsf{init}}, A, \delta, w)$, a set of targets $T \subseteq S$, a value $\ell \in \mathbb{N}$, and a probability threshold $\alpha \in [0,1] \cap \mathbb{Q}$, we construct an MDP D_ℓ. D_ℓ is constructed from D and contains an additional information in its state space: it records the sum of the weights encountered so far. Formally, $D_\ell = (S', s'_{\mathsf{init}}, A', \delta', w')$ where:

- S' is the set of states, each one being a pair (s, v), where $s \in S$ and $v \in \{0, 1, \ldots, \ell\} \cup \{\bot\}$. Intuitively v records the running sum along an execution in D ($\bot > \ell$ by convention);

- its initial state s'_{init} is equal to $(s_{\mathsf{init}}, 0)$;
- the set of actions is A and the weight function is unchanged, i.e., $A' = A$ and $w' = w$;
- the transition relation is as follows: for all pairs $(s, v), (s', v') \in S'$, and actions $a \in A$, we have that $\delta((s, v), a)(s', v') = \delta(s, a)(s')$ if $v' = v + w(a) \leq \ell$, $\delta((s, v), a)(s', v') = \delta(s, a)(s')$ if $v' = \bot$ and $v + w(a) > \ell$, and $\delta((s, v), a)(s', v') = 0$ otherwise.

The size of D_ℓ is proportional to the size of D and the value ℓ, i.e., it is thus *pseudo-polynomial* in the encoding of the SSP-P problem. The SR objective in D_ℓ is to reach $T' = \{(s, v) \mid s \in T \wedge v \leq \ell\}$ with a probability at least α.

Runs that satisfy the reachability objective in D_ℓ are in bijection with runs that reach T in D with a truncated sum at most ℓ. So if there is a strategy that enforces reaching T' in D_ℓ with probability $p \geq \alpha$, then there is a strategy in D to ensure that T is reached with a path of length at most ℓ with probability $p \geq \alpha$ (the strategy that is followed in D_ℓ can be followed in D if we remember what is the sum of weights so far). The converse also holds. As for a reachability objective, memoryless strategies are optimal, we deduce that pseudo-polynomial-size memory is sufficient (and is sometimes necessary) in the SSP-P problem, and the problem can be solved in pseudo-polynomial time. As the problem has been shown to be PSPACE-Hard, this pseudo-polynomial-time solution is essentially optimal, see [15] for details.

Illustration. We illustrate the concepts of this paper on a running example that we have introduced in [5] and that we extend in the subsequent sections. The MDP of Fig. 1 models the choices that an employee faces when he wants to reach work from home. He has the choice between taking the train, driving or biking. When he decides to bike, he reaches his office in 45 minutes. If he decides to take his car, then the journey depends on traffic conditions that are modeled by a probabilistic distribution between light, medium and heavy traffic. The employee can also try to catch a train, which takes 35 minutes to reach work. But trains can be delayed (potentially multiple times): in that case, the employee decides if he waits or if he goes back home (and then take his car or his bike). We consider two scenarios that correspond to the two problems defined above.

If the employee wants to minimize the expected duration of his journey from home to work, we need to solve a SSP-E problem. By Theorem 1, we know that pure memoryless strategies suffice to be optimal. It turns out that in our example, taking the car is the strategy that minimizes the expected time to work: this choice gives an expectation equal to 33 minutes.

Observe that taking the car presents some risk: if the traffic is heavy, then work is only reached after 71 minutes. This can be unacceptable for the employee's boss if it happens too frequently. So if the employee is *risk-averse*, optimizing the expectation may not be the best choice. For example, the employee may want to reach work within 40 minutes with high probability, say 95%. In this case, we need to solve a SSP-P problem. First, observe that taking the train ensures to reach work within 40 minutes in 99% of the runs. Indeed, if the train is not delayed, we reach work with 37 minutes, and this happens with probability 9/10.

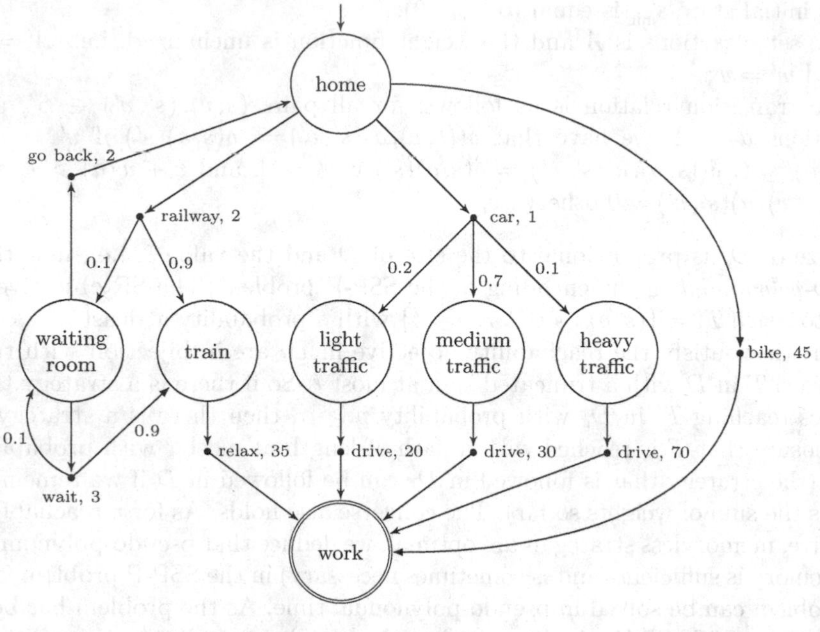

Fig. 1. An everyday life application of stochastic shortest path problems: choosing a mean of transport to go from home to work. Actions (black dots) are labeled with durations in minutes, and stochastic transitions are labeled with their probability.

Now, if the train is late and the employee decides to wait, the train arrives in the next 3 minutes with probability 9/10: in that case, the employee arrives at work within 40 minutes. So, the strategy consisting in going to the railway station and waiting for the train (as long as needed) gives us a probability 99/100 to reach work within 40 minutes, fulfilling our objective. Second, it is easy to see that both bicycle and car are excluded in order to satisfy the SPP-P problem. With bicycle we reach work in 45 minutes with probability one, and with the car we reach work in 71 minutes with probability 1/10, hence we miss the constraint of 40 minutes too often.

Related Work. The SPP-P problem was studied in MDPs with either all non-negative or all non-positive weights in [17,22]. The related notion of *quantile queries* was studied in [23]: such queries are essentially equivalent to minimizing the value ℓ inside the constraint of an SSP-P problem such that there still exists a satisfying strategy for some fixed α. It has been recently extended to *cost problems* [15], which can handle arbitrary Boolean combinations of inequalities over the truncated sum instead of only $\mathsf{TS}^T(\rho) \leq \ell$. All those works only study single-dimensional MDPs. For the SPP-E problem, extensions to multi-dimensional MDPs have been considered in [14].

4 Good Expectation under Acceptable Worst-Case

Worst-Case Guarantees. Assume now that the employee wants a strategy to go from home to work such that work is *guaranteed* to be reached within 60 minutes (e.g., to avoid missing an important meeting with his boss). It is clear that both optimal (w.r.t. problems SSP-E and SSP-P respectively) strategies of Sect. 3 are excluded: there is the possibility of heavy traffic with the car (and a journey of 71 minutes), and trains can be delayed indefinitely in the *worst case*.

To ensure a strict upper bound on the length of the path, an adequate model is the *shortest path game problem*, SP-G for short. In a shortest path game, the uncertainty becomes adversarial: when there is some uncertainty about the outcome of an action, we do not consider a probabilistic model but we let an *adversary* decide the outcome of the action. So, to model a shortest path game based on an MDP $D = (S, s_{\mathsf{init}}, A, \delta, w)$, we modify the interpretation of the transition relation as follows: after some history h that ends up in state s, if the strategy chooses action $a \in A(s)$, then the adversary chooses the successor state within $\mathsf{Supp}(\delta(s,a))$ without taking into account the actual values of the probabilities. With this intuition in mind, if we fix a strategy σ (for the controller), then the set of possible *outcomes* in D, noted $\mathsf{Out}^{\sigma}_{D}$, is the set of initial runs that are compatible with σ, i.e., $\mathsf{Out}^{\sigma}_{D} = \{\rho \in \mathcal{R}_{s_{\mathsf{init}}}(D) \mid \forall i \geq 0 \colon\ a_i \in \mathsf{Supp}(\sigma(\rho(i)))\}$. Now, we can define the SP-G problem as follows.

Definition 3 (SP-G **problem**). *Given single-dimensional weighted MDP $D = (S, s_{\mathsf{init}}, A, \delta, w)$, set of target states $T \subseteq S$, and value $\ell \in \mathbb{N}$, decide if there exists a strategy σ such that for all $\rho \in \mathsf{Out}^{\sigma}_{D}$, we have that $\mathsf{TS}^{T}(\rho) \leq \ell$.*

Theorem 3 ([16]). *The* SP-G *problem can be decided in polynomial time. Optimal pure memoryless strategies always exist and can be constructed in polynomial time.*

Under the hypothesis that actions in D have strictly positive weight, the controller has no interest in forming cycles, and if he cannot avoid to close cycles (before reaching T), then there will be outcomes that will never reach T, yielding an infinite truncated sum. As a consequence, the only option for the controller is to win within $|S| = n$ steps. So, to solve the SP-G problem, we compute for each state s and for each i, $0 \leq i \leq n$, the value $\mathbb{C}(s,i)$, representing the lowest bound on the length to the target T from s that the controller can ensure, if the game is played for i steps. Those values can be computed using *dynamic programming* as follows: for all $s \in T$, $\mathbb{C}(s,0) = 0$, and for all $s \in S \setminus T$, $\mathbb{C}(s,0) = +\infty$. Now, assume that $0 < i < n$ and that we have already computed $\mathbb{C}(s, i-1)$ for all $s \in S$. Then for i steps, we have that

$$\mathbb{C}(s,i) = \min\left[\mathbb{C}(s,i-1),\ \min_{a \in A(s)} \max_{s' \in \mathsf{Supp}(\delta(s,a))} w(a) + \mathbb{C}(s', i-1)\right].$$

So, $\mathbb{C}(s_{\mathsf{init}}, n)$ can be computed in polynomial time, and we have that the controller can force to reach T from s_{init} with a path of length at most ℓ if and only if $\mathbb{C}(s_{\mathsf{init}}, n) \leq \ell$.

Related Work. For results about the SP-G problem when weights can also be negative, we refer the interested reader to [3] where a pseudo-polynomial-time algorithm has been designed and to [11] where complexity issues are discussed (see Theorem 8 in that reference). In multi-dimensional MDPs with both positive and negative weights, it follows from results on total-payoff games that the SP-G problem is undecidable [7].

Illustration. If we apply this technique on the example of Fig. 1, it shows that taking bicycle is a safe option to ensure the strict 60 minutes upper bound. However, the expected time to reach work when following this strategy is 45 minutes, which is far from the optimum of 33 minutes that can be obtained when we neglect the worst-case constraint.

In answer to this, we may be interested in synthesizing a strategy that minimizes the expected time to work under the constraint that work is reached within 60 minutes in the worst case. We claim that the optimal strategy in this case is the following: try to take the train, if the train is delayed three times consecutively, then go back home and take the bicycle. This strategy is safe as it always reaches work within 58 minutes and its expectation is $\approx 37,34$ minutes (so better than taking directly the bicycle). Observe that it is pure but requires finite memory, in contrast to the case of problems SSP-E and SSP-G.

Beyond Worst-Case Synthesis. In [5,4], we study the synthesis of strategies that ensure, *simultaneously*, a worst-case threshold (when probabilities are replaced by adversarial choices), and a good expectation (when probabilities are taken into account). We can now recall the precise definition of the problem.

Definition 4 (SSP-WE problem). *Given a single-dimensional weighted MDP $D = (S, s_{\mathsf{init}}, A, \delta, w)$, a set of target states $T \subseteq S$, and two values $\ell_1, \ell_2 \in \mathbb{N}$, decide if there exists a strategy σ such that:*

1. $\forall \rho \in \mathsf{Out}^{\sigma}_{D}\colon\ \mathsf{TS}^{T}(\rho) \leq \ell_1$,
2. $\mathbb{E}^{\sigma}_{D}(\mathsf{TS}^{T}) \leq \ell_2$.

While the SP-G problem and the SSP-E problem are both solvable in polynomial time and pure memoryless strategies suffice in both cases, the SSP-WE problem proves to be inherently harder.

Theorem 4 ([5]). *The* SSP-WE *problem can be decided in pseudo-polynomial time and is* NP*-hard. Pseudo-polynomial memory is always sufficient and in general necessary, and satisfying strategies can be constructed in pseudo-polynomial time.*

The algorithm proposed in [5] to solve the SSP-WE problem can be summarized as follows. First, construct the MDP D_ℓ as for solving the SSP-P problem. States of D_ℓ are pairs (s, v) where $s \in S$ is a state of D and v is the sum of weights of edges traversed so far. Consider the target $T' = \{(s, v) \mid s \in T \wedge v \leq \ell\}$. Second, compute for each state (s, v) what are the *safe actions*, noted $\mathbb{A}(s, v)$, that ensure to reach T' in D_ℓ no matter how the adversary resolves non-determinism. $\mathbb{A}(s, v)$ can be computed inductively as follows: we start with $\mathbb{A}_0(s, v) = A(s)$ if $v \leq \ell$

and $\mathbb{A}_0(s, v) = \emptyset$ if $v = \perp$, i.e., a priori, all the actions are good in states that have not yet exceeded the sum ℓ while states that have exceeded ℓ are hopeless and none of the actions are good. Assume that we have computed $\mathbb{A}_i(s, v)$, for $i \geq 0$, then $\mathbb{A}_{i+1}(s, v) = \{a \in \mathbb{A}_i(s, v) \mid \forall (s', v') \in \mathsf{Supp}(\delta((s, v), a)) \colon \mathbb{A}_i(s, v) \neq \emptyset\}$. As the set of good actions is finite and is decreasing, it is easy to see that this process ends after a finite number of steps that is polynomial in the size of D_ℓ. We note $D_\ell^{\mathbb{A}}$, the MDP D_ℓ limited to the safe actions. Then, it remains to solve the SSP-E on $D_\ell^{\mathbb{A}}$. The overall complexity of the algorithm is pseudo-polynomial, and the NP-hardness result established in [5] implies that we cannot hope to obtain a truly-polynomial-time algorithm unless P = NP.

Additional Results. In [5,4], we also study the so-called beyond worst-case synthesis for models with the *mean-payoff* function instead of the truncated sum. Mean-payoff games [12] are infinite-duration, two-player zero-sum games played on weighted graphs. In those games, the controller wants to maximize the long-run average of the weights of the edges traversed during the game while the adversary aims to minimize this long-run average. Given a mean-payoff game and a stochastic model of the adversary, their product defines an MDP on which we study the problem MP-WE, the mean-payoff analogue of problem SSP-WE. We have shown that it is in NP $\cap$ coNP for *finite-memory* strategies, essentially matching the complexity of the simpler problem MP-G of solving mean-payoff games without considering the expected value. We have also established that pure strategies with pseudo-polynomial-memory are sufficient. Our synthesis algorithm is much more complex than for SSP-WE, and requires to overcome several technical difficulties to prove NP $\cap$ coNP-membership.

5 Percentile Queries in Multi-Dimensional MDPs

Illustration. Consider the MDP D depicted in Fig. 2. It gives a simplified choice model for commuting from home to work, but introduces two-dimensional weights: each action is labeled with a duration, in minutes, and a cost, in Euro. Multi-dimensional MDPs are useful to analyze systems with *multiple objectives* that are potentially conflicting and make necessary the analysis of trade-offs. For instance, we may want a choice of transportation that gives us high probability to reach work in due time but also limits the risk of an expensive journey. Since faster options are often more expensive, trade-offs have to be considered.

Recall the SSP-P problem presented in Def. 2: it asks to decide the existence of strategies satisfying a *single percentile constraint*. This problem can only be applied to single-dimensional MDPs. For example, one may look for a strategy that ensures that 80% of compatible initial runs take at most 40 minutes (constraint C1), *or* that 50% of them cost at most 10 Euro (C2). A good strategy for C1 would be to take the taxi, which guarantees that work is reached within 10 minutes with probability $0.99 > 0.8$. For C2, taking the bus is a good option, because already 70% of the runs will reach work for only 3 Euro. Note that taking the taxi does not satisfy C2, nor does taking the bus satisfy C1.

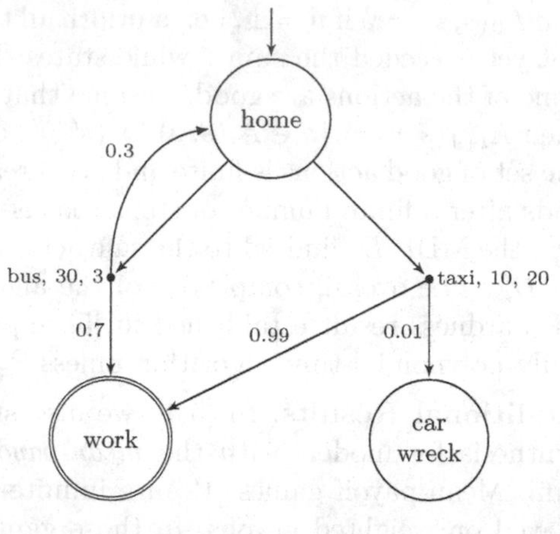

Fig. 2. Multi-percentile queries can help when actions both impact the duration of the journey (first dimension) and its cost (second dimension): trade-offs have to be considered

In practice, a desirable strategy should be able to satisfy *both* C1 and C2. This is the goal of our model of *multi-constraint percentile queries*, introduced in [19]. For example, an appropriate strategy for the conjunction (C1 $\wedge$ C2) is to try the bus once, and then take the taxi if the bus does not depart. Indeed, this strategy ensures that work is reached within 40 minutes with probability larger than 0.99 thanks to runs home·bus·work (probability 0.7 and duration 30) and home·bus·home·taxi·work (probability 0.297 and duration 40). Furthermore, it also ensures that more than half the time, the total cost to target is at most 10 Euro, thanks to run home·bus·work which has probability 0.7 and cost 3. Observe that this strategy requires *memory*. In this particular example, it is possible to build another acceptable strategy which is memoryless but requires *randomness*. Consider the strategy that flips an unfair coin in home to decide if we take the bus or the taxi, with probabilities 3/5 and 2/5 respectively. Constraint C1 is ensured thanks to runs home·bus·work (probability 0.42) and home·taxi·work (probability 0.396). Constraint C2 is ensured thanks to runs $(\text{home}\cdot\text{bus})^n\cdot\text{work}$ with $n = 1, 2, 3$: they have probabilities 0.42, ≥ 0.07 and ≥ 0.01 respectively, totaling to ≥ 0.5, while they all have cost at most $3 \cdot 3 = 9 < 10$. As we will see, percentile queries in general require strategies that both use memory *and* randomness, in contrast to the previous problems which could forgo randomness.

Percentile Queries. In [19], we study the synthesis of strategies that enforce percentile queries for the shortest path.

Definition 5 (SSP-PQ **problem).** *Given a d-dimensional weighted MDP* $D = (S, s_{\mathsf{init}}, A, \delta, w)$, *and* $q \in \mathbb{N}$ *percentile constraints described by sets of target states* $T_i \subseteq S$, *dimensions* $k_i \in \{1, \ldots, d\}$, *value thresholds* $\ell_i \in \mathbb{N}$ *and probability thresholds* $\alpha_i \in [0,1] \cap \mathbb{Q}$, *where* $i \in \{1, \ldots, q\}$, *decide if there exists a strategy* σ *such that*

$$\forall i \in \{1, \ldots, q\},\ \mathbb{P}^{\sigma}_{D}\big[\mathsf{TS}^{T_i}_{k_i} \leq \ell_i\big] \geq \alpha_i,$$

where $\mathsf{TS}^{T_i}_{k_i}$ *denotes the truncated sum on dimension* k_i *and w.r.t. target set* T_i.

Our algorithm is able to solve the problem for queries with multiple constraints, potentially related to different dimensions of the weight function and to different target sets: this offers great flexibility which is useful in modeling applications.

Theorem 5 ([19]). *The* SSP-PQ *problem can be decided in exponential time in general, and pseudo-polynomial time for single-dimension single-target* *multi-contraint queries. The problem is* PSPACE*-hard even for single-constraint queries. Randomized exponential-memory strategies are always sufficient and in general necessary, and satisfying strategies can be constructed in exponential time.*

The first step to solve an SSP-PQ problem on MDP D is to build a new MDP D_ℓ similarly to what was defined for the SSP-P problem, but with $\ell = \max_i \ell_i$, and adapting the construction to multi-dimensional weights. In particular, we observe that a run can only be disregarded when the sum on each of its dimensions exceeds ℓ. Essentially, some runs may satisfy only a subset of constraints and still be interesting for the controller, as seen in the example above. Still, the size of D_ℓ can be maintained to a *single*-exponential by defining a suitable equivalence relation between states (pseudo-polynomial for single-dimensional MDPs and single-target queries). Precisely, the states of D_ℓ are in $S \times (\{0, \ldots, \ell\} \cup \{\bot\})^d$. Now, for each constraint i, we compute a set of target states R_i in D_ℓ that exactly captures all runs satisfying the inequality of the constraint.

We are left with a *multiple reachability problem* on D_ℓ: we look for a strategy σ_ℓ that ensures that each of these sets R_i is reached with probability α_i. This is a generalization of the SR problem defined above. It follows from [13] that this multiple reachability problem can be answered in time polynomial in $|D_\ell|$ but exponential in the number of sets R_i, i.e., in q. The complexity can be reduced for single-dimensional MDPs and queries with a unique target T: in that case, sets R_i can be made absorbing, and the multiple reachability problem can be answered in time polynomial in D_ℓ through linear programming. Overall, our algorithm thus requires pseudo-polynomial time in that case. It is clear that σ_ℓ can be easily translated to a good strategy σ in D and conversely.

The PSPACE-hardness result already holds for the single-constraint case, i.e., the SSP-P problem (Theorem 2), following results of [15]. Hence the SSP-PQ framework offers a wide extension for basically no price in computational complexity.

Additional Results. In [19], we establish that the SSP-PQ problem becomes undecidable if we allow for both negative and positive weights in multi-dimensional MDPs, even with a unique target set.

Furthermore, in [19], we study the concept of percentile queries for a large range of classical payoff functions, not limited to the truncated sum: *sup*, *inf*, *limsup*, *liminf*, *mean-payoff* and *discounted sum*. In all cases, the complexity for the most general setting - multi-dimensional MDPs, multiple constraints - is at most exponential, better in some cases. Interestingly, when the query size is fixed, all problems except for the discounted sum can be solved in polynomial time. Note that in most applications, the query size can be reasonably bounded while the model can be very large, so this framework is ideally suited. In many cases, we show how to reduce the complexity for single-dimensional queries, and for single-constraint queries. We also improve the knowledge of the multiple reachability problem sketched above by proving its PSPACE-hardness and identifying the subclass of queries with nested targets as solvable in polynomial time.

Related Work. As mentioned in Sect. 3, there are several works that extend the SSP-P problem in different directions. In particular, *cost problems*, recently introduced in [15], can handle arbitrary Boolean combinations of inequalities φ over the truncated sum inside an SSP-P problem: it can be written as $\mathbb{P}^{\sigma}_{D}[\mathsf{TS}^{T} \models \varphi] \geq \alpha$. Observe that this is orthogonal to our percentile queries. Cost problems are studied on single-dimensional MDPs and all the inequalities relate to the same target T, in contrast to our setting which allows both for multiple dimensions and multiple target sets. The single probability threshold bounds the probability of the whole event φ whereas we analyze each event independently. Both settings are in general incomparable (see [19]), but they share the SSP-P problem as a common subclass.

6 Multiple Environments

The probabilities in a stochastic process represent a model of the *environment.* For instance, in Fig. 1, the probability of a train coming when we wait in the train station is a simplified model of the behavior of the train network. Clearly, this behavior can be significantly different on some particular days, for instance, when there is a strike. In this section, we consider the problem of synthesizing strategies in probabilistic systems with guarantees against a finite number of different *environments.*

Illustration. Let us consider again the problem of commuting to work, and assume that some days there may be an unannounced strike (S) in the train service, and an accident (A) in the highway. Thus, four settings are possible: (), (A), (S), (AS). When there is a strike, there is no train service; and when there is an accident, the highway is blocked. We assume that we are not informed of the strike or the accident in advance. Our goal is to synthesize a strategy with guarantees against these four environments with *no prior knowledge* of the situation we are in.

Consider the MDP D of Fig. 3, which models the *normal conditions* without strike or accident. We will define three different MDPs from D on the same state space to model the three other environments, by modifying the probabilities of dotted edges. For each environment $E \in \{(A), (S), (AS)\}$, we define MDP D^{E} from D as follows.

1. For $D^{(S)}$, action wait from state stat deterministically leads back to stat.
2. For $D^{(A)}$, action go from state h_2 deterministically leads back to h_2.
3. For $D^{(AS)}$, we apply both items 1 and 2.

Note that if strikes and accidents have small probabilities, instead of creating separate models, one could integrate their effect in a single model by adjusting the probabilities in D, for instance, by reducing the probability of moving forward in the highway. Such an approach may be useful (and simpler) for an *average analysis.* However, we are interested here in giving guarantees against each scenario rather than optimizing a global average. Our formulation can rather be

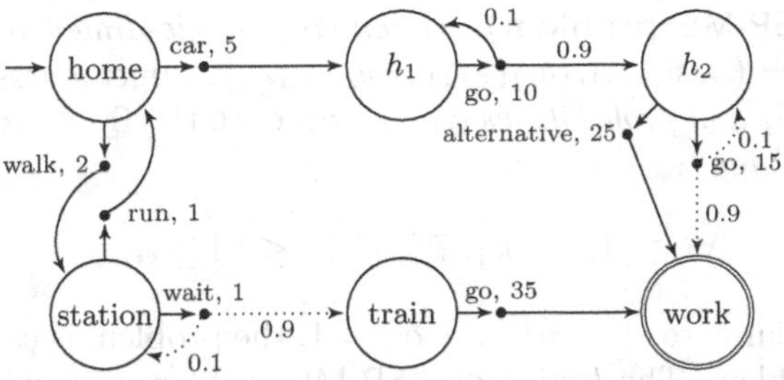

Fig. 3. Commuting to work. States h_1, h_2 represent sections of the highway. After h_1, one may take an alternative road which is longer but not affected by traffic.

modeled by *partially observable* MDPs since the strategy is not aware of the state of the system. However, most problems are undecidable in this setting [6].

Our objective is to get to work with high probability within reasonable time. More precisely, we would like to make sure to be at work, with probability 0.95 in all cases: in 40 minutes if there is no strike, in 50 minutes if there is a strike but no accident, and 75 minutes if there is a strike and an accident. More formally, we would like to synthesize a *single* strategy σ such that:

- $\mathbb{P}^{\sigma}_{D}[\mathsf{TS}^T \leq 40] \geq 0.95$,
- $\mathbb{P}^{\sigma}_{D(A)}[\mathsf{TS}^T \leq 40] \geq 0.95$,
- $\mathbb{P}^{\sigma}_{D(S)}[\mathsf{TS}^T \leq 50] \geq 0.95$,
- $\mathbb{P}^{\sigma}_{D(SA)}[\mathsf{TS}^T \leq 75] \geq 0.95$.

Solution. We will describe a strategy that satisfies our objective. First, note that we shouldn't take the car right away since even if we take the alternative road, we will be at work in 40 minutes only with probability 0.90 (even if there is no accident, we may spend 20 minutes in h_1). Our strategy is the following. We first walk to the train station, and wait there at most twice. Clearly, if there is no strike, we get to work in less than 40 minutes with probability at least 0.99. Otherwise, we run back home, and take the car. Note that we already spent 5 minutes at this point. Our strategy on the highway is the following. We take the alternative road if, and only if we failed to make progress twice by taking action go (e.g., we observed $h_1 \cdot \mathrm{go} \cdot h_1 \cdot \mathrm{go} \cdot h_2 \cdot \mathrm{go} \cdot h_2$).

We already saw that in the absence of strike, this strategy satisfies our objective. If there is a strike but no accident, we will surely take the car. Then the history ending with $h_1 \cdot \mathrm{go} \cdot h_2 \cdot \mathrm{go} \cdot \mathrm{work}$ has probability 0.81 and takes 30 minutes. The histories ending with $h_1 \cdot \mathrm{go} \cdot h_1 \cdot \mathrm{go} \cdot h_2 \cdot \mathrm{go} \cdot \mathrm{work}$ and $h_1 \cdot \mathrm{go} \cdot h_2 \cdot \mathrm{go} \cdot h_2 \cdot \mathrm{go} \cdot \mathrm{work}$ have each probability 0.081 and take 40 and 45 minutes respectively. Overall, with probability at least 0.97 we get to work in at most 50 minutes. If there is a strike and an accident, then the history $h_2 \cdot \mathrm{go} \cdot \mathrm{work}$ is never observed. In this case, the history ending with $h_1 \cdot \mathrm{go} \cdot h_2 \cdot \mathrm{go} \cdot h_2 \cdot \mathrm{go} \cdot h_2 \cdot \mathrm{alternative}$ has probability 0.90 and takes 75 minutes, and history $h_1 \cdot \mathrm{go} \cdot h_1 \cdot \mathrm{go} \cdot h_2 \cdot \mathrm{go} \cdot h_2 \cdot \mathrm{alternative}$ has probability 0.09 and takes 75 minutes. Hence we ensure the constraint with probability 0.99.

Algorithms. Formally, we define a *multi-environment MDP* as a tuple $D = (S, s_{\mathsf{init}}, A, (\delta_i)_{1 \leq i \leq k}, (w_i)_{1 \leq i \leq k})$, where each $(S, s_{\mathsf{init}}, A, \delta_i, w_i)$ is an MDP, corresponding to a different environment.

Definition 6 (SSP-ME problem). *Given any single-dimensional multi-environment MDP $D = (S, s_{\mathsf{init}}, A, (\delta_i)_{1\leq i\leq k}, (w_i)_{1\leq i\leq k})$, target states $T \subseteq S$, thresholds $\ell_1, \ldots, \ell_k \in \mathbb{N}$, and probabilities $\alpha_1, \ldots, \alpha_k \in [0,1] \cap \mathbb{Q}$, decide if there exists a strategy σ satisfying*

$$\forall i \in \{1, \ldots, k\},\ \mathbb{P}^{\sigma}_{D_i}[\mathsf{TS}^T \leq \ell_i] \geq \alpha_i.$$

For the particular case of $\alpha_1 = \ldots = \alpha_k = 1$, the problem is called the *almost-sure* SSP-ME problem. The *limit-sure* SSP-ME problem asks whether the SSP-ME problem has a solution for *all* probability vectors $(\alpha_1, \ldots, \alpha_k) \in]0,1[^k$. If the limit-sure problem can be satisfied, the almost-sure case can be approximated arbitrarily closely. Note that in some multi-environment MDPs, the limit-sure SSP-ME problem has a solution although the almost-sure one does not.

Theorem 6 ([20]). *The almost-sure and limit-sure* SSP-ME *problems can be solved in pseudo-polynomial time for a fixed number of environments. Finite memory suffices for the almost-sure case, and a family of finite-memory strategies that witness the limit-sure problem can be computed.*

We analyze the structure of the MDPs to identify *learning components* in which one can almost-surely (resp. limit-surely) determine the current environment. Once these are identified, one can transform the MDPs into simpler forms on which known algorithms on (single-environment) MDPs are applied [21].

For an example of a *learning component*, consider two states s, t and action a, with $\delta_1(s,a,t) = 0.9, \delta_1(s,a,s) = 0.1$, and $\delta_1(t,a,s) = 1$ for the first environment, and $\delta_2(s,a,t) = 0.1, \delta_2(s,a,s) = 0.9$, and $\delta_2(t,a,s) = 1$ for the second environment. Now, at state s, repeating the action a a large number of times, and looking at the generated history, one can guess with arbitrarily high confidence the current environment. However, no strategy can guess the environment with certainty. If, we rather set $\delta_1(s,a,t) = 1$, and $\delta_2(s,a,s) = 1$, then an observed history uniquely determines the current environment.

For the general SSP-ME problem, there is an algorithm for an *approximate* version of the above problem, namely the ε-gap problem. For any $\varepsilon > 0$, a procedure for the *ε-gap* SSP-ME *problem* answers Yes if the SSP-ME problem has a solution; it answers No if the SSP-ME problem has no solution when each α_i is replaced with $\alpha_i - \varepsilon$; and answers either Yes or No otherwise. Intuitively, such a procedure gives a correct answer on positive instances, and on instances that are clearly too far (by ε) to be satisfiable. However, there is an uncertainty zone of size ε on which the answer is not guaranteed to be correct. The algorithm is based on a reduction to the first order theory of the reals (see [20]).

Theorem 7. *The* SSP-ME *problem and the ε-gap* SSP-ME *are NP-hard. For any $\varepsilon > 0$, there is a procedure for the ε-gap* SSP-ME *problem.*

Additional Results. In [21], we restricted our study to MDPs with *two* environments, and considered reachability, safety, and parity objectives. We proved these problems to be decidable in polynomial time for almost-sure and limit-sure conditions. The general quantitative case, i.e., arbitrary satisfaction probabilities is shown to be NP-hard already for two environments and MDPs with no cycles other than self-loops. We gave a doubly exponential-space procedure to solve the ε-gap problem for reachability. We are currently studying the exact complexity of the case of arbitrary number of environments.

7 Conclusion

Through this paper, we gave an overview of classical approaches to the quantitative evaluation of strategies in MDPs, and presented three recent extensions that increase the modeling power of that framework. We chose to illustrate them through application to the stochastic shortest path problem. We hope this helps in understanding and comparing the different approaches. Let us sum up.

Given a weighted MDP modeling a stochastic shortest path problem, a first natural question is to find a strategy that minimizes the *expected* sum of weights to target. This is the SSP-E problem. Optimizing the average behavior of the controller is interesting if the process is to be executed a great number of times, but it gives no guarantee on individual runs, which may perform very badly. For a risk-averse controller, it may be interesting to look at the SSP-P problem, which asks to maximize the *probability* that runs exhibit an acceptable performance. When one really wants to ensure that no run will have an unacceptable performance, it is useful to resort to the SSP-G problem, which asks to optimize the *worst-case* performance of the controller.

In recent works, we introduced three related models that may be used to synthesize strategies with richer performance guarantees. First, if one reasons using the SSP-G problem, he may obtain a strategy which is sub-optimal on average while using the SSP-E problem gives no worst-case guarantee. With the framework of *beyond worst-case synthesis*, developed in [5,4], and presented here as the SSP-WE problem, we can build strategies that provide *both* worst-case guarantees and good expectation. Second, we are interested in describing rich constraints on the performance profile of strategies in multi-dimensional MDPs. To that end, we extended the SSP-P problem to the SSP-PQ problem, which handles multi-constraint *percentile queries* [19]. Those queries are particularly useful to characterize trade-offs between, for example, the length of a journey and its cost. Third and finally, we have discussed another extension of the SSP-P problem that models some uncertainty about the stochastic model of the environment which is defined in the MDP through the transition function. With the SSP-ME problem, we are able to analyze *multi-environment* MDPs and synthesize strategies with guarantees against all considered environments [21,20].

References

1. Baier, C., Katoen, J.-P.: Principles of model checking. MIT Press (2008)
2. Bertsekas, D.P., Tsitsiklis, J.N.: An analysis of stochastic shortest path problems. Mathematics of Operations Research 16(3), 580–595 (1991)
3. Brihaye, T., Geeraerts, G., Haddad, A., Monmege, B.: To reach or not to reach? Efficient algorithms for total-payoff games. CoRR, abs/1407.5030 (2014)

4. Bruyère, V., Filiot, E., Randour, M., Raskin, J.-F.: Expectations or guarantees? I want it all! A crossroad between games and MDPs. In: Proc. of SR. EPTCS, vol. 146, pp. 1–8 (2014)
5. Bruyère, V., Filiot, E., Randour, M., Raskin, J.-F.: Meet your expectations with guarantees: Beyond worst-case synthesis in quantitative games. In: Proc. of STACS. LIPIcs, vol. 25, pp. 199–213. Schloss Dagstuhl - LZI (2014)
6. Chatterjee, K., Chmelik, M., Tracol, M.: What is decidable about partially observable Markov decision processes with omega-regular objectives. In: Proc. of CSL. LIPIcs, vol. 23, Schloss Dagstuhl - LZI (2013)
7. Chatterjee, K., Doyen, L., Randour, M., Raskin, J.-F.: Looking at mean-payoff and total-payoff through windows. In: Van Hung, D., Ogawa, M. (eds.) ATVA 2013. LNCS, vol. 8172, pp. 118–132. Springer, Heidelberg (2013)
8. Cherkassky, B.V., Goldberg, A.V., Radzik, T.: Shortest paths algorithms: Theory and experimental evaluation. Math. Programming 73(2), 129–174 (1996)
9. Courcoubetis, C., Yannakakis, M.: The complexity of probabilistic verification. J. ACM 42(4), 857–907 (1995)
10. de Alfaro, L.: Computing minimum and maximum reachability times in probabilistic systems. In: Baeten, J.C.M., Mauw, S. (eds.) CONCUR 1999. LNCS, vol. 1664, pp. 66–81. Springer, Heidelberg (1999)
11. Filiot, E., Gentilini, R., Raskin, J.-F.: Quantitative languages defined by functional automata. In: Koutny, M., Ulidowski, I. (eds.) CONCUR 2012. LNCS, vol. 7454, pp. 132–146. Springer, Heidelberg (2012)
12. Ehrenfeucht, A., Mycielski, J.: Positional strategies for mean payoff games. International Journal of Game Theory 8, 109–113 (1979)
13. Etessami, K., Kwiatkowska, M.Z., Vardi, M.Y., Yannakakis, M.: Multi-objective model checking of Markov decision processes. LMCS 4(4) (2008)
14. Forejt, V., Kwiatkowska, M., Norman, G., Parker, D., Qu, H.: Quantitative multi-objective verification for probabilistic systems. In: Abdulla, P.A., Leino, K.R.M. (eds.) TACAS 2011. LNCS, vol. 6605, pp. 112–127. Springer, Heidelberg (2011)
15. Haase, C., Kiefer, S.: The odds of staying on budget. CoRR, abs/1409.8228 (2014)
16. Khachiyan, L., Boros, E., Borys, K., Elbassioni, K.M., Gurvich, V., Rudolf, G., Zhao, J.: On short paths interdiction problems: Total and node-wise limited interdiction, pp. 204–233 (2008)
17. Ohtsubo, Y.: Optimal threshold probability in undiscounted markov decision processes with a target set. Applied Math. and Computation 149(2), 519–532 (2004)
18. Puterman, M.L.: Markov Decision Processes: Discrete Stochastic Dynamic Programming, 1st edn. John Wiley & Sons, Inc., New York (1994)
19. Randour, M., Raskin, J.-F., Sankur, O.: Percentile queries in multi-dimensional Markov decision processes. CoRR, abs/1410.4801 (2014)
20. Raskin, J.-F., Sankur, O.: Multiple-environment Markov decision processes. CoRR, abs/1405.4733 (2014)
21. Raskin, J.-F., Sankur, O.: Multiple-environment Markov decision processes. In: Proc. of FSTTCS. LIPIcs, Schloss Dagstuhl - LZI (2014)
22. Sakaguchi, M., Ohtsubo, Y.: Markov decision processes associated with two threshold probability criteria. Journal of Control Theory and Applications 11(4), 548–557 (2013)
23. Ummels, M., Baier, C.: Computing quantiles in Markov reward models. In: Pfenning, F. (ed.) FOSSACS 2013. LNCS, vol. 7794, pp. 353–368. Springer, Heidelberg (2013)
24. Vardi, M.: Automatic verification of probabilistic concurrent finite state programs. In: Proc. of FOCS, pp. 327–338. IEEE Computer Society (1985)

Abstracting Induction by Extrapolation and Interpolation

Patrick Cousot

Courant Institute of Mathematical Sciences, New York University
pcousot@cims.nyu.edu
cims.nyu.edu/~pcousot

Abstract. We introduce a unified view of induction performed by automatic verification tools to prove a given program specification This unification is done in the abstract interpretation framework using extrapolation (widening/dual-widening) and interpolation (narrowing, dual-narrowing, which are equivalent up to the exchange of the parameters). Dual-narrowing generalizes Craig interpolation in First Order Logic pre-ordered by implication to arbitrary abstract domains. An increasing iterative static analysis using extrapolation of successive iterates by widening followed by a decreasing iterative static analysis using interpolation of successive iterates by narrowing (both bounded by the specification) can be further improved by a increasing iterative static analysis using interpolation of iterates with the specification by dual-narrowing until reaching a fixpoint and checking whether it is inductive for the specification.

Keywords: Abstract induction, Abstract interpretation, Dual-narrowing, Dual-widening, Extrapolation, Interpolation, Narrowing, Static analysis, Static checking, Static verification, Widening.

1 Introduction

Program analysis, checking, and verification require some form of induction on program steps [41, 62], fixpoints [64], program syntactic structure [47, 65], program data [6], or more generally segmentation hierarchies [26]. Whichever form of induction is chosen, the difficulties boil down to the basic case of a proof that $\mathbf{lfp}^{\subseteq} F \subseteq S$ where $S \in \mathcal{D}$ is a specification in a concrete poset $\langle \mathcal{D}, \subseteq, \bot, \cup \rangle$ and $F \in \mathcal{D} \mapsto \mathcal{D}$ is a transformer given by the program semantics, or dually[1,2]. Hypotheses on F like monotony, [co-]continuity, contraction, *etc.* ensure the existence of the least fixpoint $\mathbf{lfp}^{\subseteq} F$ for partial order $\subseteq$.

Since the concrete domain $\mathcal{D}$ is in general not machine-representable, the problem is abstracted in an abstract domain $\overline{\mathcal{D}}$ which is a pre-order[3] $\langle \overline{\mathcal{D}}, \sqsubseteq, \overline{\bot}, \overline{\sqcup} \rangle$ with increasing concretization $\gamma \in \overline{\mathcal{D}} \mapsto \mathcal{D}$. An example is the pre-order $\langle \mathsf{FOL}, \Rightarrow, \mathsf{ff}, \vee \rangle$ of

[1] $\mathbf{lfp}^{\subseteq}_{D} F$ is the $\subseteq$-least fixpoint of F $\subseteq$-greater than or equal D, if any. The least fixpoint of F, if any, is $\mathbf{lfp}^{\subseteq} F \triangleq \mathbf{lfp}^{\subseteq}_{\bot} F$ where $\bot$ is the infimum of $\mathcal{D}$. $\mathbf{gfp}^{\subseteq}_{D} F \triangleq \mathbf{lfp}^{\supseteq}_{D} F$ is dual.

[2] A variant, as found in strictness analysis [61] is $\mathbf{lfp}^{\sqsubseteq} F \subseteq S$ where the computational order $\sqsubseteq$ is different from the approximation order/logical implication $\subseteq$ can be handled in a way similar to that proposed in this paper, see [23].

[3] The pre-order $\sqsubseteq$ is reflexive and transitive. Additionally, a partial order is antisymmetric.

D. D'Souza et al. (Eds.): VMCAI 2015, LNCS 8931, pp. 19–42, 2015.

first-order formulæ FOL preordered by implication $\Rightarrow$. The concretization is the interpretation of formulae in a given set-theoretic structure. This is an abstraction since not all set-theoretic properties are expressible in first order logic, a problem which is at the origin of the incompleteness of Hoare logic [47, 17].

The concrete transformer F is abstracted by an abstract transformer $\overline{F} \in \overline{\mathcal{D}} \mapsto \overline{\mathcal{D}}$ satisfying the pointwise semi-commutation property $F \circ \gamma \,\dot{\sqsubseteq}\, \gamma \circ \overline{F}$ (or dually). Abstract iterates $\overline{X}^0 \triangleq \bot, \ldots, \overline{X}^{n+1} \triangleq \overline{F}(\overline{X}^n), \ldots$, are designed to converge to a limit $\overline{I} \in \overline{\mathcal{D}}$, which is an inductive abstract property, that is $\overline{F}(\overline{I}) \sqsubseteq \overline{I}$ (*e.g.* $\overline{I}$ is an inductive invariant [41, 62]).

For abstract specifications $\overline{S} \in \overline{\mathcal{D}}$, the program verification consists in checking that $\overline{I} \sqsubseteq \overline{S}$. By semi-commutation and fixpoint induction [66], this implies $\mathbf{lfp}^{\subseteq} F \subseteq \gamma(\overline{S})$. The abstraction is always meant to be sound (a proof in the abstract is valid in the concrete, $\overline{I} \sqsubseteq \overline{S} \Rightarrow \mathbf{lfp}^{\subseteq} F \subseteq \gamma(\overline{S})$) and sometimes complete (a valid concrete property $\gamma(\overline{S})$ can be proved in the abstract *i.e.* $\mathbf{lfp}^{\subseteq} F \subseteq \gamma(\overline{S}) \Rightarrow \overline{I} \sqsubseteq \overline{S}$). A very simple example of a complete abstraction is the FIRST of a context-free grammar [25].

When using finite domains $|\overline{\mathcal{D}}| \in \mathbb{N}$ (which was shown in [18] to be strictly equivalent to predicate abstraction [43]) or Noetherian domains (*i.e.*, with no infinite ascending and/or descending chain), the induction is done implicitly by repeated joins (or dually meets) in the abstract domain. By the finiteness hypothesis, the abstract iterates always converge in finitely many steps to a fixpoint limit.

This is more difficult for static analysis using infinitary abstract domains not satisfying ascending/descending chain conditions. Successive joins/meets for successive fixpoint iterations may diverge. It is therefore necessary to make an induction on the iterates and to pass to the limit. Under appropriate conditions like [co-]continuity this limit does exist and is unique. Abstract interpretation theory has introduced increasing iterations with widening extrapolation followed by a decreasing iteration with narrowing interpolation (and there duals) to over/under-approximate the limit in finitely many steps [13, 20]. When the specification cannot be verified after these two phases, we propose to use a further increasing iteration phase by interpolation with respect to this specification by dual-narrowing. The whole process can be repeated if necessary. In the particular case where the abstract domain $\overline{\mathcal{D}}$ is the set $\langle$FOL, $\Rightarrow$, ff, $\vee\rangle$ of first-order logical sentences over the program variables and symbols, often quantifier-free, pre-ordered by implication, the additional phase is comparable to program verification using Craig interpolants [56].

We recall and show the following results.

- In **Sect. 2**, we recall known facts on iteration and fixpoints.
- In **Sect. 3**, we briefly recall basic static analysis methods in infinite abstract domains by extrapolation with widening/dual-widening and interpolation with narrowing/dual-narrowing.
- In **Sect. 4**, we explain why a terminating [dual-]widening (enforcing the convergence of iterations by extrapolation with [dual-]widening) cannot be increasing in its first parameter. It follows that static analyzers (like Astrée [28]) which proceed by induction on the program syntax cannot assume that the abstract transformers $\overline{F}[\![\mathtt{C}]\!]$ of commands C are increasing since loop components of C may involve non-increasing [dual-]widenings.

- After expressing soundness conditions on widening and its dual with respect to the concrete in **Sect. 5**, we show in **Sect. 6** that iteration with widening extrapolation is sound for non-increasing abstract transformers $\overline{F}$ by referring to the concrete fixpoint iterations for an increasing transformer F. Similarly, soundness conditions on narrowing and its dual are expressed in the concrete in **Sect. 7** In **Sect. 8**, iterations with narrowing interpolation for non-increasing abstract transformers are shown to be sound with respect to the concrete iterations for a increasing concrete transformer F.
- In **Sect. 9**, we study dual-narrowing, which is shown to be a narrowing with inverted arguments, and inversely. Graig interpolation [37] in the abstract domain $\langle \mathsf{FOL}, \Rightarrow, \mathsf{ff}, \vee \rangle$ of first-order formulæ pre-ordered by logical implication is an example of dual-narrowing. Static analysis based on Graig interpolation and SMT solvers [55] has limitations [1], including to be only applicable to $\langle \mathsf{FOL}, \Rightarrow, \mathsf{ff}, \vee \rangle$, that can be circumvented by appropriate generalization to dual-narrowing in arbitrary abstract domains.
- In **Sect. 10**, we discuss terminating extrapolators and interpolators.
- In **Sect. 11**, we show that after an increasing abstract iteration using extrapolation of successive iterates by widening which converges to a post-fixpoint followed by a decreasing abstract iteration using interpolation of successive iterates by narrowing to an abstract fixpoint, it is no longer possible to improve this imprecise abstract fixpoint by repeated applications of the abstract transformer. Nevertheless, it is still possible to improve the over-approximation of the concrete fixpoint by an increasing abstract iteration using interpolation of iterates by dual-narrowing with respect to this imprecise abstract fixpoint. This can be repeated until an inductive argument is found implying the specification or no further improvement is possible.
- In **Sect. 12**, we compare static verification, checking, and analysis. In **Sect. 13**, we discuss different utilizations of extrapolation and interpolation. We conclude in **Sect. 14**

2 Iteration and Fixpoints

We recall results on the iteration of transformers on posets. We let $\mathbb{O}$ be the class of all ordinals. We have [14]:

Lemma 1 (Increasing sequences in posets are ultimately stationary). *Any $\preceq$-increasing*[4] *transfinite sequence $\langle X^\delta,\ \delta \in \mathbb{O}\rangle$ of elements of a poset $\langle \mathcal{P},\ \preceq\rangle$ is ultimately stationary (i.e. $\exists \epsilon \in \mathbb{O} : \forall \delta \geqslant \epsilon : X^\delta = X^\epsilon$. The smallest such ϵ is the rank of the sequence.).* □

Definition 2 (Upper-bounded iterates). *Let $F \in \mathcal{D} \mapsto \mathcal{D}$ be an transformer on a poset $\langle \mathcal{D},\ \sqsubseteq\rangle$ and $D \in \mathcal{D}$. By* upper-bounded iterates *of F from D we mean a transfinite sequence $\langle X^\delta,\ \delta \in \mathbb{O}\rangle$ of elements of $\mathcal{D}$ such that $X^0 \triangleq D$, $X^{\delta+1} \triangleq F(X^\delta)$, and for limit ordinals λ, $\forall \delta < \lambda : X^\delta \sqsubseteq X^\lambda$.* □

Definition 3 (Least-upper-bounded iterates). *Least-upper-bounded iterates (or lub-iterates) are upper-bounded iterates in* **Def. 2** *such that for limit ordinals λ, X^λ is the least element such that $\forall \delta < \lambda : X^\delta \sqsubseteq X^\lambda$ i.e. $\forall Y : \forall \delta < \lambda : X^\delta \sqsubseteq Y \Rightarrow X^\lambda \sqsubseteq Y$.* □

[4] A map $f \in P \mapsto Q$ of pre-order $\langle P, \sqsubseteq\rangle$ into pre-order $\langle Q, \leqslant\rangle$ is *increasing* if and only if $\forall x, y \in P : x \sqsubseteq y \Rightarrow f(x) \leqslant f(y)$. In particular, a sequence $\langle X^\delta,\ \delta \in \mathbb{O}\rangle$, considered as a map $X \in \mathbb{O} \mapsto \mathcal{D}$ where $X^\delta \triangleq X(\delta)$, is *increasing* when $\beta \leqslant \delta \Rightarrow X^\beta \sqsubseteq X^\delta$. It is then called an increasing chain.

Lemma 4 (Increasing fixpoint iterates). *Let $\langle X^\delta,\ \delta \in \mathbb{O}\rangle$ be the iterates of a transformer $F \in \mathfrak{D} \mapsto \mathfrak{D}$ on a poset $\langle \mathfrak{D},\ \subseteq\rangle$ from $D \in \mathfrak{D}$.*

(a) *If F is extensive (i.e. $\forall X \in \mathfrak{D} : X \subseteq F(X)$) and the iterates are upper-bounded then they are increasing and F has a fixpoint $\subseteq$-greater than of equal to D.*

(b) *If F is increasing, D a prefix-point of F (i.e. $D \subseteq F(D)$), and the iterates are upper-bounded (resp. least-upper-bounded) then they are increasing and F has a fixpoint $\subseteq$-greater than of equal to D (resp. least fixpoint $\mathbf{lfp}_D^{\subseteq} F$).*

(c) *In case* (b) *of lub-iterates, $\forall Y \in \mathfrak{D} : (D \subseteq Y \wedge F(Y) \subseteq Y) \Rightarrow (\mathbf{lfp}_D^{\subseteq} F \subseteq Y)$.* □

Lem. 4.(b)–(c) is often used with the extra assumption that $D = \bot$ is the infimum of a cpo $\langle \mathfrak{D},\ \subseteq,\ \bot\rangle$, but the least upper bound (lub) needs only to exist for the iterates, not for all increasing chains (increasing ω-chains when F is assumed to be continuous) of the cpo. For example, $\langle$FOL, $\Rightarrow$, ff, $\vee\rangle$ has no infinite lubs in general, but specific iterates may or may not have a lub.

Even when X^λ is chosen to be a minimal upper bound of the previous iterates for limit ordinals λ (*i.e.* $\forall \delta < \lambda : X^\delta \subseteq X^\lambda \wedge \forall Y \in \mathfrak{D} : (\forall \delta < \lambda : X^\delta \subseteq Y) \Rightarrow Y \not\subseteq X^\lambda$), F may have no minimal fixpoint, as shown by the following counter-example

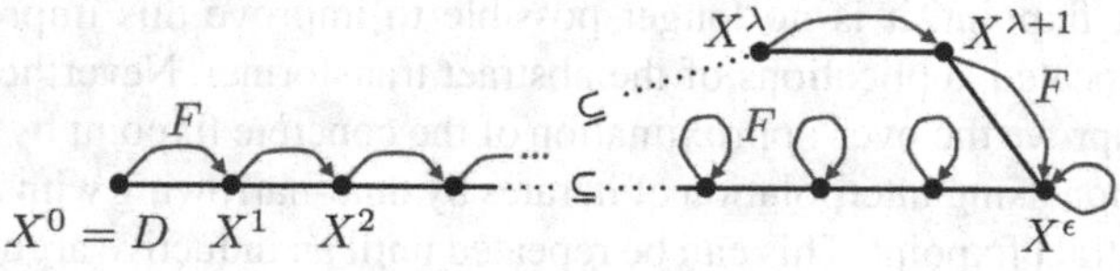

3 Iterative Static Analysis by Extrapolation and Interpolation

3.1 Mathematical Iteration with Induction

To calculate a solution $\overline{I}$ to a system of constraints $\overline{F}(X) \sqsubseteq X$ on a poset $\langle \overline{\mathfrak{D}},\ \sqsubseteq\rangle$, a mathematician (i) will start from an initial approximation $\overline{I}^0 = \overline{D}$ for some initial guess $\overline{D}$, (ii) calculate the first iterates $\overline{I}^1 = \overline{F}(\overline{I}^0)$, $\overline{I}^2 = \overline{F}(\overline{I}^1)$, *etc.* to help her guess a recurrence hypothesis $\overline{I}^n = \mathcal{I}(\overline{I}^0, \overline{F}, \overline{S}, \sqsubseteq, n)$, (iii) prove that the recurrence hypothesis is inductive $\overline{I}^{n+1} = \overline{F}(\overline{I}^n) = \overline{F}(\mathcal{I}(\overline{I}^0, \overline{F}, \overline{S}, \sqsubseteq, n)) = \mathcal{I}(\overline{I}^0, \overline{F}, \overline{S}, \sqsubseteq, n+1)$ so that, by recurrence, $\forall n \in \mathbb{N} : \overline{I}^n = \mathcal{I}(\overline{I}^0, \overline{F}, \overline{S}, \sqsubseteq, n)$), and (iv) pass to the limit $\overline{I} = \lim_{n\to\infty} \mathcal{I}(\overline{I}^0, \overline{F}, \overline{S}, \sqsubseteq, n)$. Static analysis must do a similar induction in the abstract.

3.2 Abstract Iteration in Noetherian Domains

In abstract interpretation with finite abstract domains (which has been shown to be strictly equivalent to predicate abstraction [18]) and, more generally, with Noetherian domains, the induction, which consists in joining/(dually intersecting) the successive abstract properties $\mathcal{I}(\overline{I}^0, \overline{F}, \overline{S}, \sqsubseteq, n+1) = \bigsqcup_{k \leqslant n} (\mathcal{I}(\overline{I}^0, \overline{F}, \overline{S}, \sqsubseteq, k))$, is pre-encoded in the join/(dually meet) operations of the abstract domain. They are ensured to converge in finitely many steps to a fixpoint limit.

3.3 Abstract Iteration in Non-Noetherian Domains with Convergence Acceleration

In abstract interpretation with infinitary non-Noetherian abstract domains extra machinery is needed to discover inductive hypotheses and pass to the limit. For example extrapolators like terminating widening [12] and dual-widening [20] can enforce convergence of increasing iterations after finitely many steps as illustrated in **Fig. 1**. Instead of applying the function as in **Def. 2** or 3, its derivative is used to accelerate convergence and ultimately reach a post-fixpoint which over-approximates the least fixpoint [66]. A similar widening is implicitly used in [36].

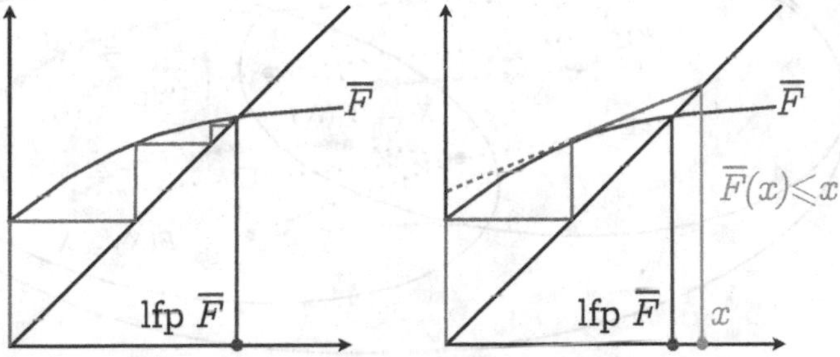

Fig. 1. Convergence acceleration by extrapolation with widening

3.4 Extrapolators (Widening, Dual-Widening) and Interpolators (Narrowing, Dual-Narrowing)

The convergence acceleration operators used in abstract interpretation are of two distinct kinds. The widening [12] and dual-widening [20] are extrapolators. They are used to find abstract properties outside the range of known abstract properties. The narrowing [13] and dual-narrowing [20] are interpolators. They are used to find abstract properties within the range of known abstract properties. The objective is to over-approximate or under-approximate the limit of increasing or decreasing fixpoint iterations, so that the various possibilities of using the convergence acceleration operators of **Table 1** are illustrated in **Fig. 2**. Notice that their are four distinct notions since widening and narrowing (as well as dual-widening and dual-narrowing) are definitely *not* order-dual concepts. Of course widening and dual-widening (as well as narrowing and dual-narrowing) *are* order-dual concepts. In [11], the approximation properties of extrapolators are considered separately from their convergence properties. For example, their approximation properties are useful to approximate missing or costly lattice join/meet operations. Independently, their convergence properties are useful to ensure termination of iterations for fixpoint approximation.

4 Terminating (Dual) Widenings Are Not Increasing

An iteration sequence with widening in a poset $\langle \overline{\mathcal{D}}, \sqsubseteq \rangle$ has the form $\overline{X}^0 \triangleq \overline{D}$, where $\overline{D} \in \overline{\mathcal{D}}$ is some initial approximation, and $\overline{X}^{k+1} \triangleq \overline{X}^k \mathbin{\nabla} \overline{F}(\overline{X}^k)$, $k \in \mathbb{N}$ where $\overline{F}$ can be

Table 1. Extrapolators ($\nabla, \widetilde{\nabla}$) and interpolators ($\Delta, \widetilde{\Delta}$)

	Convergence above the limit	Convergence below the limit
Increasing iteration	Widening ∇	Dual-narrowing $\widetilde{\Delta}$
Decreasing iteration	Narrowing Δ	Dual-widening $\widetilde{\nabla}$

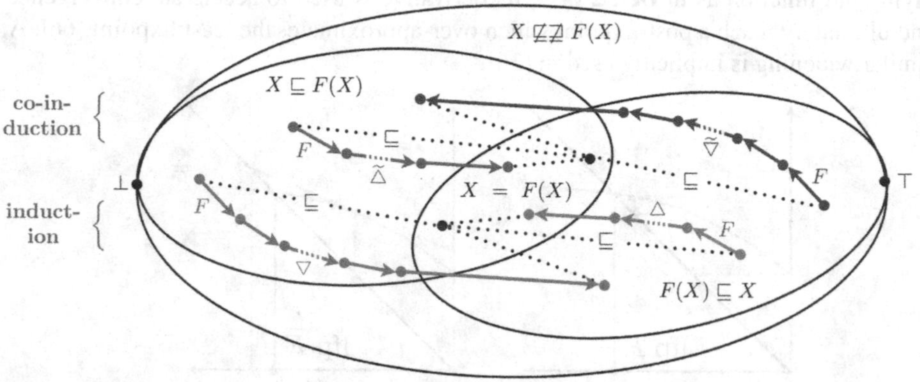

Fig. 2. Fixpoint iteration approximation

assumed to be extensive on the iterates[5]. It follows that the iterates $\langle \overline{X}^k, k \in \mathbb{N}\rangle$ form a $\sqsubseteq$-increasing chain[6].

The widening $\nabla \in \overline{\mathcal{D}} \times \overline{\mathcal{D}} \mapsto \overline{\mathcal{D}}$ should have the following properties.

(∇.a) $\forall \overline{X}, \overline{Y} \in \overline{\mathcal{D}} : \overline{Y} \sqsubseteq \overline{X} \nabla \overline{Y}$.

Requiring the widening to be extensive in its second parameter, that is an extrapolator, ensures that $\overline{F}(\overline{X}^k) \sqsubseteq \overline{X}^{k+1}$, which guarantees convergence to an over-approximation of the limit $\lim\limits_{k \to +\infty} \overline{F}^k(D)$ of the exact iterates $\overline{F}^0(\overline{X}) = \overline{X}$ and $\overline{F}^{n+1}(\overline{X}) = \overline{F}(\overline{F}^n(\overline{X}))$.[7]

(∇.b) $\forall \overline{X}, \overline{Y} \in \overline{\mathcal{D}} : (\overline{Y} \sqsubseteq \overline{X}) \Rightarrow (\overline{X} \nabla \overline{Y} = \overline{X})$.

This condition (∇.b) guarantees that the iterations with widening do stop as soon as a solution $\overline{X}^n$ to the constraint problem of finding $\overline{X}$ such that $\overline{F}(\overline{X}) \sqsubseteq \overline{X}$ has been found. If $\overline{F}(\overline{X}^n) \sqsubseteq \overline{X}^n$, then ($\nabla$.b) ensures that the next iterate is $\overline{X}^{n+1} \triangleq \overline{X}^n \nabla \overline{F}(\overline{X}^n) = \overline{X}^n$.

[5] *i.e.*, $\forall k \in \mathbb{N} : \overline{X}^k \sqsubseteq \overline{F}(\overline{X}^k)$. This is also the case when $\overline{D} \sqsubseteq \overline{F}(\overline{D})$ and $\overline{F}$ is increasing, *i.e.*, $\forall \overline{X}, \overline{Y} \in \overline{\mathcal{D}} : (\overline{X} \sqsubseteq \overline{Y}) \Rightarrow \overline{F}(\overline{X}) \sqsubseteq \overline{F}(\overline{Y})$. It is always possible to use $\lambda \overline{X} \bullet \overline{X} \sqcup \overline{F}(\overline{X})$ when the join $\sqcup$ exists in the abstract domain $\overline{\mathcal{D}}$.

[6] If $\overline{F}$ is not extensive, one can assume that $\forall \overline{X}, \overline{Y} \in \overline{\mathcal{D}} : \overline{X} \sqsubseteq \overline{X} \nabla \overline{Y}$ in which case $\forall i \in \mathbb{N} : \overline{X}^i \sqsubseteq \overline{X}^{i+1}$.

[7] Besides extrapolation, widenings are also as an over-approximation/upper-bound in posets missing least upper bounds. In that case, in addition to (∇.a), it is also required $\forall \overline{X}, \overline{Y} \in \overline{\mathcal{D}} : \overline{X} \sqsubseteq \overline{X} \nabla \overline{Y}$. Such widenings can be generalized to sets of infinitely many parameters $\nabla \in \wp(\overline{\mathcal{D}}) \mapsto \overline{\mathcal{D}}$ such that $\forall \mathcal{X} \in \wp(\overline{\mathcal{D}}) : \forall P \in \mathcal{X} : P \sqsubseteq \nabla \mathcal{X}$.

($\triangledown$.c) $\triangledown$ is *terminating* that is for any increasing chain $\langle \overline{X}^k \in \overline{\mathcal{D}}, k \in \mathbb{N}\rangle$ and arbitrary sequence $\langle \overline{Y}^k \in \overline{\mathcal{D}}, k \in \mathbb{N}\rangle$ such that $\forall k \in \mathbb{N} : \overline{X}^k \sqsubseteq \overline{Y}^k$, the sequence $\langle \overline{X}^k \triangledown \overline{Y}^k, k \in \mathbb{N}\rangle$ is ultimately stationary (*i.e.* $\exists n \in \mathbb{N} : \forall k \geqslant n : \overline{X}^k \triangledown \overline{Y}^k = \overline{X}^n$).

This condition ($\triangledown$.c) guarantees the convergence of the iterates with widening where $\langle \overline{Y}^k, k \in \mathbb{N}\rangle$ stands for $\langle \overline{F}(\overline{X}^k), k \in \mathbb{N}\rangle$ so that $\forall k \in \mathbb{N} : \overline{X}^k \sqsubseteq \overline{Y}^k$ since $\overline{F} \in \overline{\mathcal{D}} \mapsto \overline{\mathcal{D}}$ is extensive but is otherwise unknown. Because $\overline{X}^k \sqsubseteq \overline{F}(\overline{X}^k) \sqsubseteq \overline{X}^k \triangledown \overline{F}(\overline{X}^k) \triangleq \overline{X}^{k+1}$, $\langle \overline{X}^k, k \in \mathbb{N}\rangle$ is a $\sqsubseteq$-increasing chain.

Example 5 (Interval widenings). The basic widening on the abstract domain of integer intervals $\mathbb{I} \triangleq \{\emptyset\} \cup \{[a, b] \mid -\infty \leqslant a \leqslant b \leqslant +\infty \wedge a \neq +\infty \wedge b \neq -\infty\}$ was defined in [19] as $\emptyset \triangledown X = X \triangledown \emptyset \triangleq X$, $[a, b] \triangledown [c, d] \triangleq [(\!| c < a \mathbin{?} -\infty \mathbin{:} a |\!), (\!| d > b \mathbin{?} +\infty \mathbin{:} b |\!)]$[8]. This basic widening may yield static analyzes which are less precise than the sign analysis. For example $[2, +\infty] \triangledown [1, +\infty] = [-\infty, +\infty]$ whereas the sign is $[0, +\infty]$. This is why the interval widening was refined in [16] into $[a, b] \triangledown [c, d] \triangleq [(\!| 0 \leqslant c < a \mathbin{?} 0 \parallel c < a \mathbin{?} -\infty \mathbin{:} a |\!), (\!| d > b \geqslant 0 \mathbin{?} 0 \parallel d > b \mathbin{?} +\infty \mathbin{:} b |\!)]$. This can be further improved by using static thresholds in addition to zero [28] or even dynamic thresholds chosen during the static analysis [52]. In all cases, these widenings are not increasing in their first parameter $[0, 1] \sqsubseteq [0, 2]$ but $[0, 1] \triangledown [2, 2] = [0, +\infty] \not\sqsubseteq [0, 2] = [0, 2] \triangledown [2, 2]$. □

Counter-example 6 (Top widening). The top widening $X \triangledown_{\top} Y \triangleq \top$ is terminating, increasing in its first parameter, but does not satisfy ($\triangledown$.b). A solution $\overline{F}(\overline{X}^k) \sqsubseteq \overline{X}^k$ is degraded to $\overline{X}^{k+1} = \overline{X}^k \triangledown \overline{F}(\overline{X}^k) = \top$. This imprecision can be avoided by choosing $X \triangledown Y \triangleq (\!| Y \sqsubseteq X \mathbin{?} X \mathbin{:} \top |\!)$, which is more accurate but not increasing. If $X_1 \sqsubset Y \sqsubset X_2 \sqsubset T$ then $X_1 \triangledown Y = \top \not\sqsubseteq X_2 \triangledown Y = X_2$. □

Theorem 7 (Non-monotonicity of terminating [dual] widening). *Let* $\langle \overline{\mathcal{D}}, \sqsubseteq\rangle$ *be a poset and* $\triangledown \in \overline{\mathcal{D}} \times \overline{\mathcal{D}} \mapsto \overline{\mathcal{D}}$ *be a widening satisfying* ($\triangledown$.a), ($\triangledown$.b), *and* ($\triangledown$.c). *Then* $\triangledown$ *cannot be increasing in its first parameter. The dual holds for the dual-widening* $\overline{\triangledown}$ *satisfying the order-dual* ($\overline{\triangledown}$.a), ($\overline{\triangledown}$.b), *and* ($\overline{\triangledown}$.c) *of conditions* ($\triangledown$.a), ($\triangledown$.b) *and possibly* ($\triangledown$.c).

Proof. By reflexivity, $\overline{Y} \sqsubseteq \overline{Y}$ so ($\triangledown$.b) implies $\overline{Y} \triangledown \overline{Y} = \overline{Y}$. By reductio ad absurdum, if $\triangledown$ is increasing in its first parameter then $\overline{X} \sqsubseteq \overline{Y}$ implies $\overline{X} \triangledown \overline{Y} \sqsubseteq \overline{Y} \triangledown \overline{Y} = \overline{Y} \sqsubseteq \overline{X} \triangledown \overline{Y}$ by ($\triangledown$.a) which implies that $\overline{X} \triangledown \overline{Y} = \overline{Y}$ by antisymmetry. By ($\triangledown$.c), $\forall k \geqslant n, \overline{X}^{n+k} = \overline{X}^k \triangledown \overline{Y}^k = \overline{X}^k = \overline{X}^n$. By hypothesis $\overline{X}^k \sqsubseteq \overline{Y}^k$ so $\overline{X}^k \triangledown \overline{Y}^k = \overline{Y}^k$ which implies $\forall k \geqslant n : \overline{Y}^k = \overline{X}^n$, in contradiction with the fact that $\langle \overline{Y}^k, k \in \mathbb{N}\rangle$ is an arbitrary sequence of elements of $\overline{\mathcal{D}}$, hence in general not ultimately stationary. □

When $D \sqsubseteq \overline{F}(D)$ and $\overline{F}$ is continuous, hence increasing and such that $\lim_{k\to+\infty} \overline{F}^k(D) = \mathbf{lfp}^{\sqsubseteq}_{D} \overline{F}$, the intuition for **Th. 7** is that applications of $\overline{F}$ and $\triangledown$ from below this fixpoint would remain below the fixpoint, making any over-approximation impossible. The jump over the least fixpoint must be extensive but cannot be increasing (dually decreasing hence monotone in general).

[8] The conditional expression is $(\!| \text{tt} \mathbin{?} a \mathbin{:} b |\!) \triangleq a$ and $(\!| \text{ff} \mathbin{?} a \mathbin{:} b |\!) \triangleq b$.

Many non-Noetherian static analyzes of infinite-state systems proceed by successive analyzes in different abstract domains $\langle \overline{\mathcal{D}}_i, \sqsubseteq_i \rangle$, $i = 1, \ldots, n$, *e.g.* by refinement. A comparison of the successive iterative analyzes performed in these domains is possible by concretizing to the most precise one (or their reduced product). Then **Th. 7** shows that there is no guarantee of precision improvement. This problem is soundly taken into account by [54, Sect. 7] and [59, Sect. 5.1], but is otherwise too often completely ignored.

When transformers $\overline{F}[\![\mathsf{C}]\!]$ are defined by structural induction on the syntax of the command C as in Astrée [28], this command C may involve loops, which abstract semantics is defined by fixpoint iterations with terminating widenings, hence may be non-increasing. In the worst case, $\mathbf{lfp}^{\sqsubseteq} \overline{F}[\![\mathsf{C}]\!]$ may simply not exist.

Example 8 (Non-increasing transformer). Consider the program `while (TRUE) {if (x == 0) {x = 1} else {x = 2}}`. To ensure termination of the static analysis, the forward transformer for this program is $\overline{F}_{\mathtt{while}}(I) = \mathbf{lfp}^{\sqsubseteq} \lambda X \bullet X \,\overline{\nabla}\, (I \sqcup \overline{F}_{\mathtt{if}}(X))$ where $\overline{\nabla}$ is the basic widening of *Ex. 5* and $\overline{F}_{\mathtt{if}}(X) = (\!| 0 \in X \;?\; [1,1] \;:\; \emptyset |\!) \sqcup (\!| \exists x \in X : x \neq 0 \;?\; [2,2] \;:\; \emptyset |\!)$ is the transformer for the conditional.

The iterates for $\overline{F}_{\mathtt{while}}([0,0])$ are $\overline{X}^0 = \emptyset$, $\overline{X}^1 = \overline{X}^0 \,\overline{\nabla}\, \overline{F}_{\mathtt{if}}(\overline{X}^0) = [0,0]$, and $\overline{X}^2 = \overline{X}^1 \,\overline{\nabla}\, \overline{F}_{\mathtt{if}}(\overline{X}^1) = [0,0] \,\overline{\nabla}\, ([0,0] \sqcup ([1,1] \sqcup \emptyset)) = [0, +\infty]$ such that $\overline{F}_{\mathtt{if}}(\overline{X}^2) \sqsubseteq \overline{X}^2$. The iterates for $\overline{F}_{\mathtt{while}}([0,2])$ are $\overline{Y}^0 = \emptyset$, $\overline{Y}^1 = \overline{Y}^0 \,\overline{\nabla}\, \overline{F}_{\mathtt{if}}(\overline{Y}^0) = [0,2]$, and $\overline{Y}^2 = \overline{Y}^1 \,\overline{\nabla}\, \overline{F}_{\mathtt{if}}(\overline{Y}^1) = [0,2] \,\overline{\nabla}\, ([0,0] \sqcup ([1,1] \sqcup [2,2])) = [0,2]$ such that $\overline{F}_{\mathtt{if}}(\overline{Y}^2) \sqsubseteq \overline{Y}^2$.

So the transformer $\overline{F}_{\mathtt{while}}$ is *not* increasing since $[0,0] \sqsubseteq [0,2]$ but $\overline{F}_{\mathtt{while}}([0,0]) \not\sqsubseteq \overline{F}_{\mathtt{while}}([0,2])$. It follows that the transformer of any program containing this `while` command will be a composition of transformers involving $\overline{F}_{\mathtt{while}}$ and so will not, in general, be increasing. □

5 Hypotheses on Widening, Dual-Widening, and Correspondence

Widening and dual-widening are extrapolators in that their result is outside the range of their parameters.

5.1 Widening

Soundness conditions on widenings are usually expressed in the abstract domain (such as ($\overline{\nabla}$.a)) but can be weakened into conditions expressed in the concrete domain, as follows:

Hypotheses 9 (Sound widening for concretization γ)

(a) • for $\overline{\nabla} \in \overline{\mathcal{D}} \times \overline{\mathcal{D}} \mapsto \overline{\mathcal{D}}$, $\quad \forall \overline{P}, \overline{Q} \in \overline{\mathcal{D}} : \gamma(\overline{P}) \subseteq \gamma(\overline{P} \,\overline{\nabla}\, \overline{Q}) \wedge \gamma(\overline{Q}) \subseteq \gamma(\overline{P} \,\overline{\nabla}\, \overline{Q})$

(a′) $\quad \forall \overline{P}, \overline{Q} \in \overline{\mathcal{D}} : \overline{P} \sqsubseteq (\overline{P} \,\overline{\nabla}\, \overline{Q}) \wedge \overline{Q} \sqsubseteq (\overline{P} \,\overline{\nabla}\, \overline{Q})$

(b) • for $\overline{\nabla} \in \wp(\overline{\mathcal{D}}) \mapsto \overline{\mathcal{D}}$, $\quad \forall \mathfrak{X} \in \wp(\overline{\mathcal{D}}) : \forall \overline{P} \in \mathfrak{X} : \gamma(\overline{P}) \subseteq \gamma(\overline{\nabla} \mathfrak{X})$ □

Widenings have to be defined for each specific abstract domains like intervals [19], polyhedra [30, 2], *etc.* or combinations of abstract domains like reduced product, powerset domains [3], cofibred domains [68], *etc.* It follows that the Galois calculus to define abstract interpretations [27] can be extended to widening and more generally to all interpolators and extrapolators.

5.2 Dual-Widening

The dual-widening $\widetilde{\nabla}$ satisfies the order dual of **Hyp. 9** hence the dual of the following theorem **Th. 10** reformulating [11, Ch. 4, Th. 4.1.1.0.3 & Th. 4.1.1.0.9]. This is useful to under-approximate greatest fixpoints *e.g.* [7].

6 Over-Approximating Increasing Abstract Iterates by Extrapolation with Widening

We reformulate the abstract static analysis by iteration with widening of **Sect. 4** for non-increasing transformers. Soundness proofs can no longer be done in the abstract. They can be done instead with respect to an increasing concrete semantics (**Th. 10**).

6.1 Increasing Iteration with Widening

We have the following reformulation of [11, Ch. 4, Th. 4.1.1.0.2 & Th. 4.1.1.0.6].

Theorem 10 (Over-approximation of increasing abstract iterates by widening). *Let* $\langle X^\delta,\ \delta \in \mathbb{O}\rangle$ *be the least upper bound iterates of the increasing transformer* $F \in \mathfrak{D} \mapsto \mathfrak{D}$ *on a concrete poset* $\langle \mathfrak{D},\ \subseteq\rangle$ *from* $D \in \mathfrak{D}$ *such that* $D \subseteq F(D)$*. By* **Lem. 4** (b), $\langle X^\delta,\ \delta \in \mathbb{O}\rangle$ *is therefore increasing and ultimately stationary at* $X^\epsilon = \mathsf{lfp}_D^\subseteq F$.

Let $\overline{\mathfrak{D}}$ *be the abstract domain,* $\gamma \in \overline{\mathfrak{D}} \mapsto \mathfrak{D}$ *be the concretization,* $\overline{F} \in \overline{\mathfrak{D}} \mapsto \overline{\mathfrak{D}}$ *be the abstract transformer,* $\nabla \in \overline{\mathfrak{D}} \times \overline{\mathfrak{D}} \mapsto \overline{\mathfrak{D}}$ *be a widening satisfying* **Hyp. 9** (a) *and* $\nabla \in \wp(\overline{\mathfrak{D}}) \mapsto \overline{\mathfrak{D}}$ *be a widening satisfying* **Hyp. 9** (b) *for all* $\mathfrak{X} = \{\overline{X}^\delta \mid \delta < \lambda \wedge \lambda \in \mathbb{O}$ *is a limit ordinal*$\}$ *where the abstract iterates are the transfinite sequence* $\langle \overline{X}^\delta \in \overline{\mathfrak{D}},\ \delta \in \mathbb{O}\rangle$ *defined such that* $\overline{X}^{\delta+1} \triangleq \overline{X}^\delta\ \nabla\ \overline{F}(\overline{X}^\delta)$ *and* $\overline{X}^\lambda \triangleq \underset{\beta<\lambda}{\nabla} \overline{X}^\beta$ *for limit ordinals* λ*. Then*

(a) *The concretization* $\langle \gamma(\overline{X}^\delta),\ \delta \in \mathbb{O}\rangle$ *of the abstract iterates* $\langle \overline{X}^\delta,\ \delta \in \mathbb{O}\rangle$ *is increasing and ultimately stationary with limit* $\gamma(\overline{X}^\varepsilon)$.

Moreover, if $D \subseteq \gamma(\overline{X}^0)$ *and the semi-commutation condition* $\forall \delta \in \mathbb{O} : F \circ \gamma(\overline{X}^\delta) \subseteq \gamma \circ \overline{F}(\overline{X}^\delta)$ *holds, then*

(b) $\forall \delta \in \mathbb{O} : X^\delta \subseteq \gamma(\overline{X}^\delta)$ *(so, in particular* $X^\epsilon \subseteq \gamma(\overline{X}^\varepsilon)$*).*

Moreover if the abstract domain $\langle \overline{\mathfrak{D}},\ \sqsubseteq\rangle$ *is a pre-order* ($\sqsubseteq$ *is reflexive and transitive, but not necessarily antisymmetric*) *and the concretization* $\gamma \in \overline{\mathfrak{D}} \mapsto \mathfrak{D}$ *is increasing* ($\overline{X} \sqsubseteq \overline{Y} \Rightarrow \gamma(\overline{X}) \subseteq \gamma(\overline{Y})$)*, then*

(c) $\forall \delta \in \mathbb{O} : F(\gamma(\overline{X}^\delta)) \subseteq \gamma(\overline{X}^\delta) \Rightarrow \mathsf{lfp}_D^\subseteq F \subseteq \gamma(\overline{X}^\delta)$.

(d) *Moreover, if* ∇ *is terminating i.e. the iterates are ultimately stationary at some rank* $n \in \mathbb{N}$ *then* $\overline{F}(\overline{X}^n) \nabla \overline{X}^n = \overline{X}^n$ *so* $\gamma(\overline{F}(\overline{X}^n)) \subseteq \gamma(\overline{X}^n)$, $F(\gamma(\overline{X}^n)) \subseteq \gamma(\overline{X}^n)$, *and* $\mathbf{lfp}^{\subseteq}_{D} F \subseteq \gamma(\overline{X}^n)$.
(e) *Moreover, if the terminating widening satisfies* ∇ *satisfies* **Hyp. 9** (a′) *then* $\exists n \in \mathbb{N} : \overline{F}(\overline{X}^n) \sqsubseteq \overline{X}^n$ *so* $\mathbf{lfp}^{\subseteq}_{D} F \subseteq \gamma(\overline{X}^n)$. □

Condition **Th. 10**.(c) is a sufficient condition for stopping the abstract iteration, always applicable by **Th. 10**.(d) for terminating widenings, and in case **Hyp. 9** (a′) checkable with the abstract pre-order $\sqsubseteq$ by **Th. 10**.(e). Note that in **Th. 10**.(d), the abstract domain is a pre-order, maybe not antisymmetric, so that the widening must avoid the problem of iterating within an equivalence class under equivalence $(X \equiv Y) \triangleq (X \sqsubseteq Y \wedge X \sqsupseteq Y)$. Interesting examples are given in [42].

Remark 11. Notice that in **Th. 10**, F is assumed to be increasing but $\overline{F}$ is <u>not</u> assumed to be either $\sqsubseteq$-extensive or increasing because, in case $\overline{F}$ is defined by structural induction, it might depend upon widenings that are not increasing, see *Ex. 8* and **Th. 7**. Nevertheless, the limit of the abstract iterates over-approximate that of the concrete iterates. This may not be the case with the hypotheses of **Lem. 4**.(a). In the following counter-example, F is extensive but not increasing. Both concrete and abstract iterates have limits but $X^{\epsilon} \not\subseteq \gamma(\overline{X}^{\varepsilon})$.

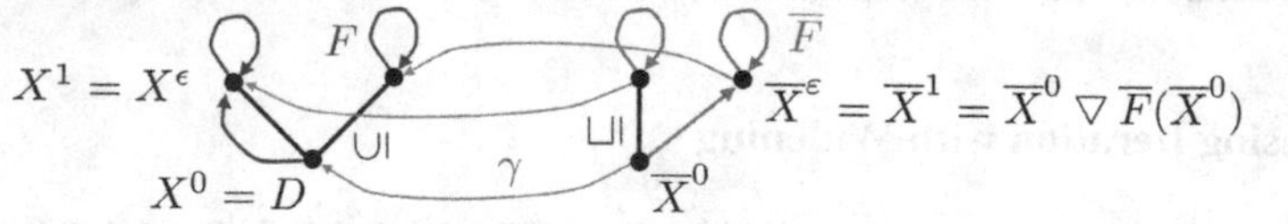

□

Remark 12. If in **Th. 10** (d) the widening ∇ satisfies **Hyp. 9** (b) but not **Hyp. 9** (a′) then there may exist no $\delta \in \mathbb{O}$ such that $\overline{F}(\overline{X}^{\delta}) \sqsubseteq \overline{X}^{\delta}$. Here is a counter-example where ∇ is the lub.

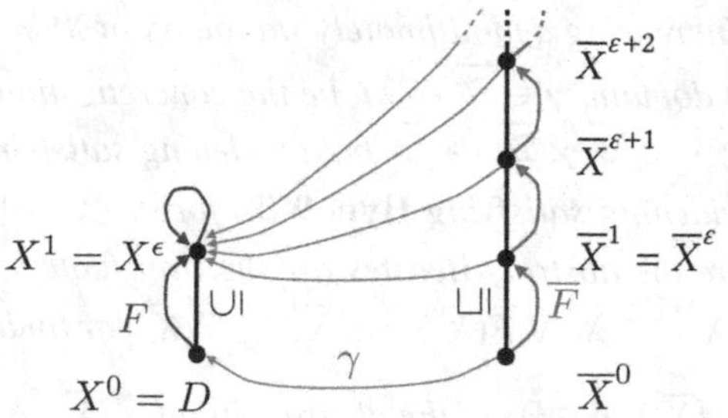

□

6.2 Parameterized Widening

The abstract iterates with widening in **Th. 10** can be generalized to widenings including additional parameters such the iteration rank δ, a list of thresholds T, possibly depending on the rank $T(\delta)$, the abstract transformer $\overline{F}$, all previous iterates $\langle \overline{X}^{\beta}, \beta \leqslant \delta \rangle$ and their transformation $\langle \overline{F}(\overline{X}^{\beta}), \beta \leqslant \delta \rangle$, *etc*, so that $\overline{X}^{\delta+1} \triangleq \nabla(\delta, T(\delta), \overline{F}, \langle \overline{X}^{\beta}, \beta \leqslant \delta \rangle, \langle \overline{F}(\overline{X}^{\beta}), \beta \leqslant \delta \rangle)$. The idea applies to all other extrapolators and interpolators.

Example 13 (Parameterized [dual-]widenings). Delayed widening [28] is an example of parameterized widening $\nabla(\delta)$ where a join or a standard widening is performed depending on the iteration rank parameter δ (often counted as the number of iterations in a loop).

n-bounded abstract model checking [4] for universal properties implicitly uses an iteration $\overline{X}^{k+1} \triangleq \overline{X}^{k} \;\overline{\nabla}_{(k)}\; \overline{F}(\overline{X}^{k})$ with an parameterized widening $\overline{X} \;\overline{\nabla}_{(k)}\; \overline{Y} \triangleq (\!| k \leqslant n \;?\; \overline{Y} \;\text{:}\; \overline{\top} |\!)$ where $\overline{\top}$ is the abstract supremum: $\forall X \in \mathfrak{D} : P \subseteq \gamma(\overline{\top})$. For existential properties, n-bounded abstract model checking implicitly uses a dual-widening $\overline{X} \;\widetilde{\overline{\nabla}}_{(k)}\; \overline{Y} \triangleq (\!| k \leqslant n \;?\; \overline{Y} \;\text{:}\; \overline{\bot} |\!)$. Unreachability after n steps is a correct under-approximation of the executions that do go on. It follows in both cases that everything is known exactly before n steps and completely unknown beyond n steps. This is an abstract interpretation of the concrete trace semantics, even when $\overline{\mathfrak{D}} = \mathfrak{D}$ and $\overline{F} = F$, since in both cases concrete traces are abstracted by the identity for the first n steps and by $\top$ (resp. $\bot$) for the remaining steps.

ESC/Java™ [39] implicitly uses a dual-widening which unrolls loops twice (and outs assume false, *i.e.* $\overline{\bot}$). This under-approximates the loop semantics which is unsound for checking invariance properties.

An extreme example avoiding any iteration is the so called *abstract acceleration* for specific abstract domains and programs where $\overline{\nabla}(\overline{\sqsubseteq}, \overline{D}, \overline{F}) = \overline{X}^{\varepsilon}$ so that the abstract solution can be computed exactly from the program text abstraction $\overline{F}$ [50], may be including a few iterations for iterative constraint solving methods.

Between these extreme examples, parameterized widenings can smoothly be made less and less precise over successive iterations (*e.g.* by widening to less and less given or program-dependent thresholds [28]). □

7 Hypotheses on Narrowing, Dual-Narrowing, and Correspondence

Narrowing and dual-narrowing are interpolators in that their result is within the range of their parameters.

7.1 Narrowing

A narrowing $\overline{\Delta} \in \overline{\mathfrak{D}} \times \overline{\mathfrak{D}} \mapsto \overline{\mathfrak{D}}$ is an interpolation of its parameters, $\forall \overline{P}, \overline{Q} \in \overline{\mathfrak{D}} : \overline{Q} \;\overline{\sqsubseteq}\; \overline{P} \Rightarrow \overline{Q} \;\overline{\sqsubseteq}\; \overline{P} \;\overline{\Delta}\; \overline{Q} \;\overline{\sqsubseteq}\; \overline{P}$. We can also define $\overline{\Delta} \in \wp(\overline{\mathfrak{D}}) \mapsto \overline{\mathfrak{D}}$ such that $\forall \mathfrak{X} \in \wp(\overline{\mathfrak{D}}) : \forall \overline{P} \in \overline{\mathfrak{D}} : (\forall \overline{Q} \in \mathfrak{X} : \overline{P} \;\overline{\sqsubseteq}\; \overline{Q}) \Rightarrow \overline{P} \;\overline{\sqsubseteq}\; \overline{\Delta}\mathfrak{X}$. Otherwise stated, the narrowing $\overline{\Delta}\mathfrak{X}$ over-approximate any lower bound of X (hence its greatest lower bound if it exists).

These conditions expressed in the abstract domain can be weakened into conditions expressed in the concrete domain, as follows:

Hypotheses 14 (Sound narrowing for concretization γ)

- for $\overline{\Delta} \in \overline{\mathfrak{D}} \times \overline{\mathfrak{D}} \mapsto \overline{\mathfrak{D}}$,

(a) $\quad \forall \overline{P}, \overline{Q} \in \overline{\mathfrak{D}} : (\gamma(\overline{Q}) \subseteq \gamma(\overline{P})) \Rightarrow (\gamma(\overline{Q}) \subseteq \gamma(\overline{P} \;\overline{\Delta}\; \overline{Q}) \subseteq \gamma(\overline{P}))$

(a′) $\quad \forall \overline{P}, \overline{Q} \in \overline{\mathfrak{D}} : (\gamma(\overline{Q}) \subseteq \gamma(\overline{P})) \Rightarrow (\overline{Q} \;\overline{\sqsubseteq}\; (\overline{P} \;\overline{\Delta}\; \overline{Q}) \;\overline{\sqsubseteq}\; \overline{P})$

(a″) $\forall \overline{P}, \overline{Q} \in \overline{\mathfrak{D}} : (\overline{Q} \sqsubseteq \overline{P}) \Rightarrow (\overline{Q} \sqsubseteq (\overline{P} \mathbin{\overline{\Delta}} \overline{Q}) \sqsubseteq \overline{P})$

- for $\overline{\Delta} \in \wp(\overline{\mathfrak{D}}) \mapsto \overline{\mathfrak{D}}$,

(b) $\forall P \in \mathfrak{D} : \forall \mathfrak{X} \in \wp(\overline{\mathfrak{D}}) : (\forall \overline{Q} \in \mathfrak{X} : P \subseteq \gamma(\overline{Q})) \Rightarrow (P \subseteq \gamma(\overline{\Delta}\mathfrak{X}) \subseteq \gamma(\overline{Q}))$ □

Example 15 (Interval narrowing). The narrowing of [13, 20] for integer intervals $\mathbb{I}$ was $\emptyset \mathbin{\Delta} X \triangleq X \mathbin{\Delta} \emptyset = \emptyset$ for the infimum $\overline{\bot} = \emptyset$. Otherwise, $[a, b] \mathbin{\Delta} [c, d] \triangleq [\llparenthesis\, a = -\infty \mathbin{?} c \mathbin{:} \min(a, c)\,\rrparenthesis, \llparenthesis\, b = +\infty \mathbin{?} d \mathbin{:} \max(b, d)\,\rrparenthesis]$ improves infinite bounds only. □

7.2 Dual-Narrowing

The dual-narrowing $\widetilde{\Delta}$ satisfies the order dual of **Hyp. 14** hence the dual of **Th. 22** reformulating [11, Ch. 4, Th. 4.1.1.0.12].

Example 16 (Interval dual-narrowing). If $[a, b] \subseteq [c, d]$ then $c \leqslant a \leqslant b \leqslant d$ so we can define $[a, b] \mathbin{\widetilde{\Delta}} [c, d] \triangleq [\llparenthesis\, c = -\infty \mathbin{?} a \mathbin{:} \lfloor (a + c)/2 \rfloor\,\rrparenthesis, \llparenthesis\, d = \infty \mathbin{?} b \mathbin{:} \lceil (b + d)/2 \rceil\,\rrparenthesis]$ where $\lfloor x \rfloor$ is the largest integer not greater than real x and $\lceil x \rceil$ is the smallest integer not less than real x since $c \leqslant \lfloor (a + c)/2 \rfloor \leqslant a \leqslant b \leqslant \lceil (b + d)/2 \rceil \leqslant d$ and therefore $[a, b] \subseteq ([a, b] \mathbin{\widetilde{\Delta}} [c, d]) \subseteq [c, d]$. □

Example 17 (Bounded interval dual-narrowing). If $[a, b] \subseteq [c, d] \subseteq [\ell, h]$ (*e.g.* ℓ = `min_int`, h = `max_int` for machine integers) then $[a, b] \mathbin{\widetilde{\Delta}} [c, d] \triangleq [\lfloor (a + c)/2 \rfloor, \lceil (b + d)/2 \rceil] \subseteq [\ell, h]$. □

Example 18 (Craig interpolation). Craig's interpolation theorem [31] implies that for all first-order formulæ $\varphi, \psi \in \mathsf{FOL}$ such that $\neg(\varphi \wedge \psi)$ there exist a first-order formula ρ, called an interpolant, such that $\psi \Rightarrow \rho$, $\neg(\rho \wedge \psi)$, and $\mathsf{Vars}[\![\rho]\!] \subseteq (\mathsf{Vars}[\![\varphi]\!] \cap \mathsf{Vars}[\![\psi]\!])$. Letting $\psi' \triangleq \neg\psi$ this means that if $\varphi \Rightarrow \psi'$ then there exists an interpolant ρ such that $\varphi \Rightarrow \rho \Rightarrow \psi'$. So a dual-narrowing can be defined as $\varphi \mathbin{\widetilde{\Delta}} \psi' \triangleq \rho$ on the abstract domain $\langle \mathsf{FOL}, \Rightarrow \rangle$ of first-order formulæ pre-ordered by implication $\Rightarrow$, the concretization of a formula being its interpretation in a given domain of discourse. The interpolant is in general not unique, may contain exponentially more logical connectives than φ, and successive interpolations may not terminate. So arbitrary choices have to be done, for example, to compute quantifier-free interpolants with a minimal number of components and symbols [48].

[35, Sect. 5.2, page 145] recognized that Craig interpolation is a narrowing (in fact a dual-narrowing, see **Lem. 19** just below) without the syntactic constraints of Craig interpolation because the lattice is not necessarily constructed from formulae. In Boolean lattices, this coincide with McMillan's use of Craig interpolation [56], which is called separation, mapping a pair satisfying $A \sqcap B \sqsubseteq \bot$ to I such that $A \sqsubseteq I \wedge I \sqcap B \sqsubseteq \bot$ [44, p. 447].

Interpolants in the style of [57] require that abstract domains are or can be complemented [10]. When the interpolation cannot be directly applied to the representation of abstract properties A, B in the abstract domain $\overline{\mathfrak{D}}$, it can be applied to their concretization into a pair of formulæ $\langle \gamma(A), \gamma(B) \rangle$ in $\langle \mathsf{FOL}, \Rightarrow \rangle$ and the interpolant $\gamma(A) \mathbin{\widetilde{\nabla}} \gamma(B)$ constructed from a refutation proof *e.g.* by an SMT solver [49] can be abstracted back to the abstract domain $\alpha(\gamma(A) \mathbin{\widetilde{\nabla}} \gamma(B))$, a technique is used *e.g.* to generate abstract transformers [67], which can also be used during the static analysis. □

7.3 Correspondence between Narrowing and Dual-Narrowing

The **Hyp. 14** are not self dual. Nevertheless, the narrowing and dual-narrowing are essentially the same notion up to the inversion of their parameters: $X \mathbin{\Delta} Y = X \mathbin{\widetilde{\Delta}^{-1}} Y \triangleq Y \mathbin{\widetilde{\Delta}} X$ and $X \mathbin{\widetilde{\Delta}} Y = X \mathbin{\Delta^{-1}} Y \triangleq Y \mathbin{\Delta} X$[9].

Lemma 19 (dual-narrowing as inverse narrowing and dually). *If* Δ *is a narrowing satisfying* **Hyp. 14** (a) *then* Δ^{-1} *is a dual-narrowing satisfying the order-dual of* **Hyp. 14** (a). *Reciprocally, the inverse* $\widetilde{\Delta}^{-1}$ *of a dual-narrowing* $\widetilde{\Delta}$ *is a narrowing.* □

The interpretation of **Lem. 19** in the context of **Table 1** is that if a narrowing is used for decreasing iterates in **Th. 22** then its inverse can be used for increasing iterates in the dual of **Th. 22**.

Example 20 (Interval narrowing). The inverse of the dual-narrowing of *Ex. 16* is the narrowing $[c, d] \mathbin{\Delta} [a, b] \triangleq [(\!| c = -\infty \mathbin{?} a \mathbin{8} \lfloor (a + c)/2 \rfloor |\!), (\!| d = \infty \mathbin{?} b \mathbin{8} \lceil (b + d)/2 \rceil |\!)]$ which is more precise than the narrowing of [13, 20] in *Ex. 15*. Convergence in **Th. 22** is guaranteed but much slower. □

Example 21 (Polyhedral narrowing). By *Ex. 18*, Craig interpolation is a dual-narrowing, hence by **Lem. 19** and parameter inversion, a narrowing. For example, Craig interpolation for linear arithmetic over the rationals [8] should yield a narrowing $P \mathbin{\Delta} Q$ for polyhedral static analysis [30] when there is a difference in the variables appearing in both systems of constraints P and Q[10]. □

8 Over-Approximating Decreasing Abstract Iterates by Interpolation with Narrowing

A static analysis by increasing iteration with widening can be improved by any iterate of a decreasing iteration with narrowing. The narrowing cannot make downwards extrapolations which might jump over the least fixpoint. So the narrowing can only do interpolations which prevent jumping below any fixpoint (hence the least one which cannot be simply distinguished from the other fixpoints). We have the following reformulation of [11, Ch. 4, Th. 4.1.1.0.16].

Theorem 22 (Over-approximation of decreasing iterates with narrowing). *By the dual of* **Def. 3**, *let* $\langle Y^\delta, \delta \in \mathbb{O} \rangle$ *be the greatest lower bound iterates of the increasing transformer* $F \in \mathcal{D} \mapsto \mathcal{D}$ *on a concrete poset* $\langle \mathcal{D}, \sqsubseteq \rangle$ *from* $D \in \mathcal{D}$ *such that* $F(D) \sqsubseteq D$. *By the dual of* **Lem. 4** (b), $\langle Y^\delta, \delta \in \mathbb{O} \rangle$ *is therefore decreasing and ultimately stationary at* $Y^\epsilon = \mathsf{gfp}_D^{\sqsubseteq} F$.

Let the abstract domain $\langle \overline{\mathcal{D}}, \overline{\sqsubseteq} \rangle$ *be a pre-order, the concretization* $\gamma \in \overline{\mathcal{D}} \mapsto \mathcal{D}$ *be increasing, the abstract transformer be* $\overline{F} \in \overline{\mathcal{D}} \mapsto \overline{\mathcal{D}}$, $\Delta \in \overline{\mathcal{D}} \times \overline{\mathcal{D}} \mapsto \overline{\mathcal{D}}$ *be a narrowing*

9 We use $^{-1}$ to denote the exchange of parameters as in the inverse of relations $r^{-1}(x, y) = r(y, x)$, not as the inverse image of a function $f^{-1}(x, y) = \{z \mid f(z) = \langle x, y \rangle\}$.

10 Thanks to reviewer 7 for pointing out that the semantic notions of amalgamation might be more adequate than the purely syntactic notion of Craig interpolation in this context. This (together with the related Robinson joint consistency property) remains to be explored [60].

satisfying **Hyp. 14** (a) *and* $\Delta \in \wp(\overline{\mathcal{D}}) \mapsto \overline{\mathcal{D}}$ *satisfies* **Hyp. 14** (b) *for* $\mathcal{X} = \{\overline{Y}^{\delta} \mid \delta < \lambda \wedge \lambda \in \mathbb{O}$ *is a limit ordinal*$\}$, *where the abstract iterates are the transfinite sequence* $\langle \overline{Y}^{\delta} \in \overline{\mathcal{D}}, \delta \in \mathbb{O}\rangle$ *such that* $D \subseteq \gamma(\overline{Y}^{0})$, $\overline{Y}^{\delta+1} \triangleq \overline{Y}^{\delta} \Delta \overline{F}(\overline{Y}^{\delta})$, $\overline{Y}^{\lambda} \triangleq \Delta_{\beta<\lambda} \overline{Y}^{\beta}$ *for limit ordinals* λ, *and do satisfy the semi-commutation condition* $\forall \delta \in \mathbb{O} : F \circ \gamma(\overline{Y}^{\delta}) \subseteq \gamma \circ \overline{F}(\overline{Y}^{\delta})$.

If the abstract transformer $\overline{F} \in \overline{\mathcal{D}} \mapsto \overline{\mathcal{D}}$ *is reductive on the abstract iterates* $\langle \overline{Y}^{\delta}, \delta \in \mathbb{O}\rangle$ (*i.e.* $\forall \delta \in \mathbb{O} : \gamma(\overline{F}(\overline{Y}^{\delta})) \subseteq \gamma(\overline{Y}^{\delta})$[11]) *then their concretization* $\langle \gamma(\overline{Y}^{\delta}), \delta \in \mathbb{O}\rangle$ *is decreasing and ultimately stationary with limit* $\gamma(\overline{Y}^{\varepsilon})$ *such that* $\forall \delta \in \mathbb{O} : \mathbf{gfp}_{D}^{\subseteq} F = Y^{\epsilon} \subseteq \gamma(\overline{Y}^{\varepsilon}) \subseteq \gamma(\overline{Y}^{\delta})$. □

Lemma 23 (Traditional soundness requirement for narrowing). *The more traditional hypotheses that* $(P \sqsubseteq Q) \Rightarrow (P \sqsubseteq P \Delta Q \sqsubseteq Q)$, $\forall i \in \Delta : (P \sqsubseteq Q_i) \Rightarrow (P \sqsubseteq \Delta_{j \in \Delta} Q_j \sqsubseteq Q_i)$, *the initial iterate is* $\overline{F}(\overline{Y}^{0}) \sqsubseteq \overline{Y}^{0}$, *and* $\overline{F}$ *is increasing imply that* $\overline{F}$ *is reductive on the iterates.* □

9 Over-Approximating Bounded Increasing Abstract Iterates by Interpolation with Dual-Narrowing

When the upper bound $\gamma(\overline{Y}^{n})$ of the concrete least fixpoint can no longer be improved in the decreasing abstract iterates with narrowing interpolation of **Sect. 8**, *i.e.* $\overline{F}(\overline{Y}^{n}) \sqsubseteq \overline{Y}^{n+1} = \overline{Y}^{n} \Delta \overline{F}(\overline{Y}^{n}) = \overline{Y}^{n}$, the upper bound $\overline{Y}^{n}$ can still be further improved by computing increasing abstract iterates with dual-narrowing interpolation bounded by the *bound specification* $\overline{S} \triangleq \overline{Y}^{n}$.

9.1 Bounded Increasing Iteration with Dual-Narrowing

Let us now consider increasing iterates bounded by a given specification.

Theorem 24 (Over-approximation of bounded increasing iterates with dual-narrowing). *Let* $\langle Z^{\delta}, \delta \in \mathbb{O}\rangle$ *be the least upper bound iterates of the increasing transformer* $F \in \mathcal{D} \mapsto \mathcal{D}$ *on a concrete poset* $\langle \mathcal{D}, \subseteq\rangle$ *from* $D \in \mathcal{D}$ *such that* $D \subseteq F(D)$. *By* **Lem. 4** (b), $\langle Z^{\delta}, \delta \in \mathbb{O}\rangle$ *is therefore increasing and ultimately stationary at* $Z^{\epsilon} = \mathbf{lfp}_{D}^{\subseteq} F$.

Let $\overline{\mathcal{D}}$ *be the abstract domain,* $\gamma \in \overline{\mathcal{D}} \mapsto \mathcal{D}$ *be the concretization,* $\overline{S} \in \overline{\mathcal{D}}$ *be the bound specification,* $\overline{F} \in \overline{\mathcal{D}} \mapsto \overline{\mathcal{D}}$ *be the abstract transformer,* $\widetilde{\Delta} \in \overline{\mathcal{D}} \times \overline{\mathcal{D}} \mapsto \overline{\mathcal{D}}$ *be the dual-narrowing satisfying the order dual of* **Hyp. 14** (a), *and* $\widetilde{\Delta} \in \wp(\overline{\mathcal{D}}) \mapsto \overline{\mathcal{D}}$ *be the dual-narrowing satisfying the order dual of* **Hyp. 14** (b) *for* $\mathcal{X} \triangleq \{\overline{Z}^{\lambda} \mid \delta < \lambda \wedge \lambda \in \mathbb{O}$ *is a limit ordinal*$\}$ *where the abstract iterates are the transfinite sequence* $\langle \overline{Z}^{\delta} \in \overline{\mathcal{D}}, \delta \in \mathbb{O}\rangle$ *such that* $D \subseteq \gamma(\overline{Z}^{0}) \subseteq \gamma(\overline{S})$, $\overline{Z}^{\delta+1} \triangleq [\![\gamma(\overline{F}(\overline{Z}^{\delta})) \subseteq \gamma(\overline{S}) \; ? \; \overline{F}(\overline{Z}^{\delta}) \widetilde{\Delta} \overline{S} \; : \; \overline{S}]\!]$, $\overline{Z}^{\lambda} \triangleq \widetilde{\Delta}_{\beta<\lambda} \overline{Z}^{\beta}$ *for limit ordinals* λ, *which are assumed to satisfy the semi-commutation condition* $\forall \delta \in \mathbb{O} : F \circ \gamma(\overline{Z}^{\delta}) \subseteq \gamma \circ \overline{F}(\overline{Z}^{\delta})$. *Then*

11 Since γ is increasing this is implied by $\forall \delta \in \mathbb{O} : \overline{F}(\overline{Y}^{\delta}) \sqsubseteq \overline{Y}^{\delta}$.

(a) *The concretization* $\langle \gamma(\overline{Z}^{\delta}),\ \delta \in \mathbb{O}\rangle$ *of the abstract iterates* $\langle \overline{Z}^{\delta},\ \delta \in \mathbb{O}\rangle$ *is such that* $\forall \delta \in \mathbb{O} : (Z^{\delta} \subseteq \gamma(\overline{S})) \Rightarrow (Z^{\delta} \subseteq \gamma(\overline{Z}^{\delta}) \subseteq \gamma(\overline{S}))$;

(b) *Moreover, if* $\langle \overline{\mathcal{D}}, \overline{\sqsubseteq}\rangle$ *is a pre-order and the concretization* $\gamma \in \overline{\mathcal{D}} \mapsto \mathcal{D}$ *is increasing, then* $\forall \delta \in \mathbb{O}$, *if* $\gamma(\overline{F}(\overline{Z}^{\delta})) \subseteq \gamma(\overline{Z}^{\delta})$ *then* $\mathbf{lfp}^{\subseteq}_{D}\, F = Z^{\delta} \subseteq \gamma(\overline{Z}^{\delta}) \subseteq \gamma(\overline{S})$. □

Note 25. In case (b), the definition $\overline{Z}^{\delta+1} \triangleq \llparenthesis\, \gamma(\overline{F}(\overline{Z}^{\delta})) \subseteq \gamma(\overline{S}) \mathrel{?} \overline{F}(\overline{Z}^{\delta})\, \widetilde{\Delta}\, \overline{S} \mathrel{\wr} \overline{S} \,\rrparenthesis$ of the next iterate can be over-approximated by $\overline{Z}^{\delta+1} \triangleq \llparenthesis\, \overline{F}(\overline{Z}^{\delta}) \mathrel{\overline{\sqsubseteq}} \overline{S} \mathrel{?} \overline{F}(\overline{Z}^{\delta})\, \widetilde{\Delta}\, \overline{S} \mathrel{\wr} \overline{S} \,\rrparenthesis$.

Note 26. In case (b), if $\overline{F}$ is extensive or $\overline{Z}^{0} \mathrel{\overline{\sqsubseteq}} \overline{F}(\overline{Z}^{0})$ and $\overline{F}$ is increasing then the abstract iterates $\langle \overline{Z}^{\delta}, \delta \in \mathbb{O}\rangle$ in **Th. 24** form an increasing chain, but this is not necessarily the case in general. □

Note 27. In the definition of the abstract iterates $\langle \overline{Z}^{\delta},\ \delta \in \mathbb{O}\rangle$ in **Th. 24**, the dual-narrowing $\widetilde{\Delta}$ in $\overline{Z}^{\delta+1} \triangleq \llparenthesis\, \gamma(\overline{F}(\overline{Z}^{\delta})) \subseteq \gamma(\overline{S}) \mathrel{?} \overline{F}(\overline{Z}^{\delta})\, \widetilde{\Delta}\, \overline{S} \mathrel{\wr} \overline{S} \,\rrparenthesis$ does not use the information provided by $\overline{Z}^{\delta}$. It would be more informative to use a ternary dual-narrowing with $\overline{Z}^{\delta+1} \triangleq \llparenthesis\, \gamma(\overline{F}(\overline{Z}^{\delta})) \subseteq \gamma(\overline{S}) \mathrel{?} \widetilde{\Delta}(\overline{Z}^{\delta}, \overline{F}(\overline{Z}^{\delta}), \overline{S}) \mathrel{\wr} \overline{S} \,\rrparenthesis$ such that $\overline{P} \mathrel{\overline{\sqsubseteq}} \overline{Q} \mathrel{\overline{\sqsubseteq}} \overline{S}$ implies $\overline{Q} \mathrel{\overline{\sqsubseteq}} \widetilde{\Delta}(\overline{P}, \overline{Q}, \overline{S}) \mathrel{\overline{\sqsubseteq}} \overline{S}$. □

Example 28. A variant of *Ex. 17* where $[a, b] \subseteq [c, d] \subseteq [\ell, h] = \overline{S}$ would be $\widetilde{\Delta}([a, b], [c, d], \overline{S}) \triangleq [\llparenthesis\, \lfloor(3c - 2a + \ell)\,2\rfloor > \ell \mathrel{?} \lfloor(3c - 2a + \ell)\,2\rfloor \mathrel{\wr} \ell \,\rrparenthesis, \llparenthesis\, \lceil(3d - 2b + h)/2\rceil < h \mathrel{?} \lceil(3d - 2b + h)/2\rceil \mathrel{\wr} h \,\rrparenthesis]$ which doubles the growth of $[a, b]$ to $[c, d]$. Another example is the widening "up-to" of [46] for polyhedra. □

9.2 Bounded Widening versus Dual-Narrowing

A widening $\nabla_{\overline{S}}$ is bounded by $\overline{S} \in \overline{\mathcal{D}}$ if and only if it satisfies **Hyp. 9** (a′) and $\forall \overline{P}, \overline{Q} : \overline{P}\ \nabla_{\overline{S}}\ \overline{Q} \mathrel{\overline{\sqsubseteq}} \overline{S}$. An example is the interval widening on machine integers bounded by [`min_int`, `max_int`] which can be generalized to any interval bound $[\ell, h]$.

Then, continuing *Note 27*, $\widetilde{\Delta}(\overline{P}, \overline{Q}, \overline{S}) \triangleq \overline{P}\, \nabla_{\overline{S}}\, \overline{Q}$ is a dual-narrowing since if $\overline{P} \mathrel{\overline{\sqsubseteq}} \overline{Q} \mathrel{\overline{\sqsubseteq}} \overline{S}$ then by **Hyp. 9** (a′), $\overline{Q} \mathrel{\overline{\sqsubseteq}} \overline{P}\ \nabla_{\overline{S}}\ \overline{Q}$ and $\overline{P}\ \nabla_{\overline{S}}\ \overline{Q} \mathrel{\overline{\sqsubseteq}} \overline{S}$ since the widening is bounded so that $\overline{Q} \mathrel{\overline{\sqsubseteq}} \widetilde{\Delta}(\overline{P}, \overline{Q}, \overline{S}) \mathrel{\overline{\sqsubseteq}} \overline{S}$.

Reciprocally, if $\widetilde{\Delta}$ is a dual-narrowing then $\overline{P}\ \nabla_{\overline{S}}\ \overline{Q} \triangleq\ \widetilde{\Delta}\,(\overline{P}, \overline{Q}, \overline{S})$ may not satisfy **Hyp. 9** (a′) in case $\overline{P} \mathrel{\overline{\not\sqsubseteq}} \overline{P}\ \nabla_{\overline{S}}\ \overline{Q}$. However, in case $\overline{F}$ is increasing or extensive in **Th. 10**, the widening is used only when $\overline{P} \mathrel{\overline{\sqsubseteq}} \overline{Q}$ in which case **Hyp. 9** (a′) holds.

In conclusion, although widenings and dual-narrowing are different concepts, they are equivalent in the specific contexts considered in this **Sect. 9.2**.

Example 29. Observe that $\widetilde{\Delta}([a, b], [c, d], \overline{S})$ in *Ex. 28* is a bounded widening. □

10 Terminating Extrapolators and Interpolators

Extrapolators/interpolators $\boxtimes \in \{\nabla, \widetilde{\nabla}, \Delta, \widetilde{\Delta}\}$ over/under-approximate the limit of increasing/decreasing chains by abstract induction. *Terminating* operators also enforce termination.

Enforcing Termination by Extrapolators/Interpolators. For terminating extrapolators/ interpolator, the abstract iterates $\overline{X}^0, \ldots, \overline{X}^{i+1} \triangleq \overline{X}^i \boxtimes \overline{F}(\overline{X}^i), \ldots$ must be ultimately stationary at some rank $n \in \mathbb{N}$. Let us say that the widening ∇ and dual-narrowing $\widetilde{\Delta}$ are *increasing* (since they operate on increasing chains $\langle \gamma(\overline{X}^i), i \in \mathbb{N} \rangle$) and, dually that the dual-widening $\widetilde{\nabla}$ and narrowing Δ are *decreasing* (since they operate on decreasing chains $\langle \gamma(\overline{X}^i), i \in \mathbb{N} \rangle$). Since we don't want to make hypotheses on the abstract transformer $\overline{F}$, we can consider abstract iterates of the form $\overline{X}^0, \ldots, \overline{X}^{i+1} \triangleq \overline{X}^i \boxtimes \overline{Y}^i, \ldots$ where $\langle \gamma(\overline{X}^i), i \in \mathbb{N} \rangle$ is a chain and $\langle \overline{Y}^i, i \in \mathbb{N} \rangle$ is arbitrary.

Definition 30 (Terminating extrapolator/interpolator). *An increasing (resp. decreasing) extrapolator/interpolator* $\boxtimes \in \{\nabla, \widetilde{\nabla}, \Delta, \widetilde{\Delta}\}$ *such that* $\boxtimes \in \overline{\mathcal{D}} \times \overline{\mathcal{D}} \mapsto \overline{\mathcal{D}}$ *is* terminating *whenever for any chain* $\langle \overline{X}^i \in \overline{\mathcal{D}}, i \in \mathbb{N} \rangle$ *increasing (resp. decreasing) in the concrete and arbitrary sequence* $\langle \overline{Y}^i \in \overline{\mathcal{D}}, i \in \mathbb{N} \rangle$*, the sequence* $\overline{X}^0, \ldots, \overline{X}^{i+1} \triangleq \overline{X}^i \boxtimes \overline{Y}^i, \ldots$ *is ultimately stationary at some rank* $n \in \mathbb{N}$. □

The interval widenings of *Ex. 5* and narrowing of *Ex. 15* are all terminating.

Definition 31 (Terminating bounded interpolation operator). *An increasing (resp. decreasing) interpolator* $\boxtimes \in \{\Delta, \widetilde{\Delta}\}$ *such that* $\boxtimes \in \overline{\mathcal{D}} \times \overline{\mathcal{D}} \times \overline{\mathcal{D}} \mapsto \overline{\mathcal{D}}$ *is* terminating *whenever for any chain* $\langle \overline{Y}^i \in \overline{\mathcal{D}}, i \in \mathbb{N} \rangle$ *increasing (resp. decreasing) in the concrete and bound* $\overline{S} \in \overline{\mathcal{D}}$*, the sequence* $\overline{X}^0 = \overline{Y}^0, \ldots, \overline{X}^{i+1} = \boxtimes(\overline{X}^i, \overline{Y}^i, \overline{S})$[12]*, … is ultimately stationary at some rank* $n \in \mathbb{N}$. □

Example 32. The dual-narrowing of *Ex. 16* bounded by $[-\infty, h]$ or $[\ell, +\infty]$ is not terminating. The bounded interval dual-narrowing of *Ex. 17* is terminating but convergence may be slow. □

11 Fixpoint Over-Approximation Strategy

Given a concrete fixpoint $\mathbf{lfp}^{\subseteq}_{\perp} F$ of a concrete increasing operator $F \in \mathcal{D} \mapsto \mathcal{D}$ on a partially ordered concrete domain $\langle \mathcal{D}, \subseteq, \perp, \cup \rangle$ such that $\mathbf{lfp}^{\subseteq}_{\perp} F = \bigcup_{\delta \in \mathbb{O}} F^{\delta}(\perp)$ does exist, the static analysis problem is to effectively compute an over approximation of this fixpoint. The abstraction method consists in designing a pre-ordered abstract domain $\langle \overline{\mathcal{D}}, \sqsubseteq, \overline{\perp}, \sqcup \rangle$, an abstract transformer $\overline{F} \in \overline{\mathcal{D}} \mapsto \overline{\mathcal{D}}$, and an increasing concretization function $\gamma \in \overline{\mathcal{D}} \mapsto \mathcal{D}$ satisfying the semi-commutation condition $F \circ \gamma \,\dot{\subseteq}\, \gamma \circ \overline{F}$, pointwise. We obtain the fixpoint over-approximation by the following successive over-approximations, the first two ones (A) and (B) being classical, as illustrated in **Fig. 3**.

Algorithm 33 (Fixpoint over-approximation by successive extrapolations and interpolations). Input $\overline{F} \in \overline{\mathcal{D}} \mapsto \overline{\mathcal{D}}$ and $\overline{D} \in \overline{\mathcal{D}}$ on a pre-order $\langle \overline{\mathcal{D}}, \sqsubseteq \rangle$. Define $\overline{X} \equiv \overline{Y} \triangleq \overline{X} \sqsubseteq \overline{Y} \wedge \overline{X} \sqsupseteq \overline{Y}$.

---

12 $\overline{X}^{i+1} = \overline{Y}^i \boxtimes \overline{S}$ for binary interpolators $\boxtimes \in \overline{\mathcal{D}} \times \overline{\mathcal{D}} \mapsto \overline{\mathcal{D}}$.

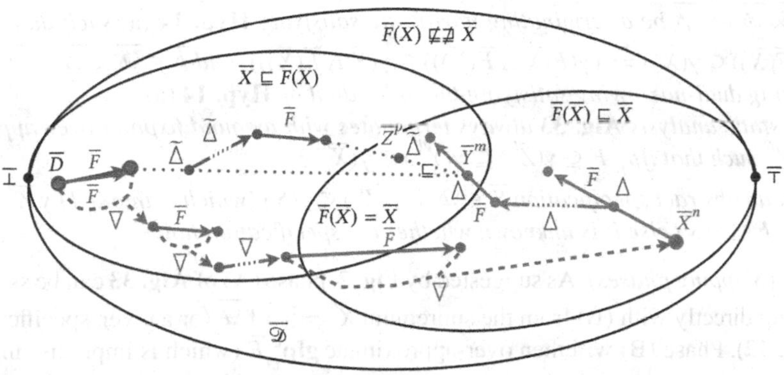

Fig. 3. Successive extrapolations and interpolations

(A) Using a terminating widening $\nabla \in \overline{\mathcal{D}} \times \overline{\mathcal{D}} \mapsto \overline{\mathcal{D}}$, compute the iterates $\overline{X}^0 \triangleq \overline{D}, \ldots, \overline{X}^{k+1} \triangleq \overline{X}^k \nabla \overline{F}(\overline{X}^k)$ until convergence $\overline{X}^{n+1} \equiv \overline{X}^n$ at some rank n[13, 14]

(B) If $\overline{F}(\overline{X}^n) \not\equiv \overline{X}^n$ then compute the iterates $\overline{Y}^0 \triangleq \overline{X}^n, \ldots, \overline{Y}^{k+1} \triangleq \overline{Y}^k \Delta \overline{F}(\overline{Y}^k)$ with terminating narrowing $\Delta \in \overline{\mathcal{D}} \times \overline{\mathcal{D}} \mapsto \overline{\mathcal{D}}$, until convergence $\overline{Y}^{m+1} \equiv \overline{Y}^m$ at some rank m.
Otherwise $\overline{F}(\overline{X}^n) \equiv \overline{X}^n$ so skip this step (B) with $\overline{Y}^m \triangleq \overline{X}^n$.

(C) Using a terminating dual-narrowing $\widetilde{\Delta} \in \overline{\mathcal{D}} \times \overline{\mathcal{D}} \mapsto \overline{\mathcal{D}}$, compute the iterates $\overline{Z}^0 \triangleq \overline{D}, \ldots, \overline{Z}^{k+1} \triangleq \overline{F}(\overline{Z}^k) \widetilde{\nabla} \overline{Y}^m$ until reaching $\overline{Z}^{p+1} \equiv \overline{Z}^p$ at some rank p.

Optionally, if $F(\gamma(\overline{Z}^p)) \subseteq \gamma(\overline{Z}^p)$ and $\overline{Z}^p \not\equiv \overline{Y}^m$, repeat the interpolation steps (B) and (C) from $\overline{X}'^n \triangleq \overline{Z}^p \Delta' \overline{Y}^m$ (where Δ' is a terminating narrowing satisfying **Hyp. 14** (a)) until convergence to $\overline{Z}^p \Delta' \overline{Y}^m \equiv \overline{Y}^m$[15]. If $F(\gamma(\overline{Z}^p)) \subseteq \gamma(\overline{Z}^p)$ then return $\overline{Z}^p$ else $\overline{Z}^p \triangleq \overline{Y}^m$ (no improvement). □

Theorem 34 (Soundness and termination of Alg. 33). *Let $\langle \mathcal{D}, \subseteq, \cup \rangle$ be a poset, $F \in \mathcal{D} \mapsto \mathcal{D}$ be increasing, $D \in \mathcal{D}$ be such that $D \subseteq F(D)$, and the concrete iterates $X^0 \triangleq D$, $X^{\delta+1} \triangleq F(X^\delta)$ for successor ordinals, and $X^\lambda \triangleq \bigcup_{\beta<\lambda} X^\beta$ for limit ordinals λ, be well defined in the poset $\langle \mathcal{D}, \subseteq, \cup \rangle$ (i.e. the lubs $\bigcup$ do exist).*

Let the abstract domain $\langle \overline{\mathcal{D}}, \sqsubseteq \rangle$ be a pre-order, the concretization $\gamma \in \overline{\mathcal{D}} \mapsto \mathcal{D}$ be increasing, the abstract transformer be $\overline{F} \in \overline{\mathcal{D}} \mapsto \overline{\mathcal{D}}$ satisfying the pointwise semi-commutation condition $F \circ \gamma \dot{\subseteq} \gamma \circ \overline{F}$.

Let $\overline{D} \in \overline{\mathcal{D}}$ be such that $D \subseteq \gamma(\overline{D})$ and $\forall \overline{X} \in \overline{\mathcal{D}} : (\gamma(\overline{D}) \subseteq \gamma(\overline{X}) \wedge \gamma(\overline{F}(\overline{X})) \subseteq \gamma(\overline{X})) \Rightarrow (\gamma(\overline{D}) \subseteq \gamma(\overline{F}(\overline{X})))$, $\nabla \in \overline{\mathcal{D}} \times \overline{\mathcal{D}} \mapsto \overline{\mathcal{D}}$ be a terminating widening satisfying **Hyp. 9** *(a),*

13 As shown by **Fig. 3**, checking that $\overline{F}(\overline{F}(\overline{X}^n)) \sqsubseteq \overline{F}(\overline{X}^n)$ might sometimes avoid a last useless widening but **Alg. 33** (A) follows the classical iteration method [20].

14 The traditional termination condition of reaching a post-fixpoint $\overline{F}(\overline{X}^n) \sqsubseteq \overline{X}^n$ is obtained by $\overline{X} \nabla' \overline{Y} \triangleq (\!| \overline{Y} \sqsubseteq \overline{X} \;?\; \overline{X} \;\wr\; \overline{X} \nabla \overline{Y} |\!)$.

15 In case of static checking (**Sect. 12**) of a specification $\overline{S}$, one can stop as soon as $\overline{Z}^p \sqsubseteq \overline{S}$. Otherwise, one can also restart at (A) with the new specification $\overline{S} \triangleq \overline{Z}^p$, see **Th. 36**.

$\Delta \in \overline{\mathcal{D}} \times \overline{\mathcal{D}} \mapsto \overline{\mathcal{D}}$ *be a terminating narrowing satisfying* **Hyp. 14** (a) *such that* $\forall \overline{X} \in \overline{\mathcal{D}} : (\gamma(\overline{F}(\overline{X})) \subseteq \gamma(\overline{X})) \Rightarrow (\gamma(\overline{F}(\overline{X}\,\Delta\,\overline{F}(\overline{X}))) \subseteq \gamma(\overline{X}\,\Delta\,\overline{F}(\overline{X})))$, *and* $\widetilde{\Delta} \in \overline{\mathcal{D}} \times \overline{\mathcal{D}} \mapsto \overline{\mathcal{D}}$ *be a terminating dual-narrowing satisfying the order dual of* **Hyp. 14** (a).

Then static analysis **Alg. 33** *always terminates with a sound fixpoint over-approximation* $\overline{Z}^p$ *such that* $\mathbf{lfp}^{\subseteq}_{D} F \subseteq \gamma(\overline{Z}^p) \subseteq \gamma(\overline{Y}^m) \subseteq \gamma(\overline{X}^n)$.

Given an abstract specification $\overline{S} \in \overline{\mathcal{D}}$, *if* $\gamma(\overline{Z}^p) \subseteq \gamma(\overline{S})$ *(which is implied by* $\overline{Z}^p \sqsubseteq \overline{S}$*) then* $\mathbf{lfp}^{\subseteq}_{D} F \subseteq \gamma(\overline{S})$ *else it is unknown whether the specification holds.* □

Note 35 (Skipping phases). As suggested by **Fig. 2**, phase (A) of **Alg. 33** can be skipped by starting directly with (B) from the supremum $\overline{X}^n = \overline{\top}$ of $\overline{\mathcal{D}}$ (or a given specification, see **Sect. 12**). Phase (B) will then over-approximate $\mathbf{gfp}^{\sqsubseteq}_{\overline{\top}} \overline{F}$ (which is imprecise in general). Phase (A) of **Alg. 33** is useful to provide an initial over-approximation of $\mathbf{gfp}^{\sqsubseteq}_{\overline{X}^n} \overline{F}$, which, in general, is below $\mathbf{gfp}^{\sqsubseteq}_{\overline{\top}} \overline{F}$. The narrowing iteration (B) of **Alg. 33** can also be skipped by choosing $Y \,\Delta\, X \triangleq X$. Both phases (A) and (B) of **Alg. 33** can be skipped by starting (C) with an abstract specification $\overline{S} \in \overline{\mathcal{D}}$. □

12 Static Verification, Checking, and Analysis

The static inductive proof $\exists \overline{I} \in \overline{\mathcal{D}} : \overline{F}(\overline{I}) \sqsubseteq \overline{I} \wedge \overline{I} \sqsubseteq \overline{S}$ can be done in various forms.

(a) In *static verification* by deductive verification methods, the induction hypothesis $\overline{I}$ is provided by the end-user so that the problem is to generate and check the verification condition $\overline{F}(\overline{I}) \sqsubseteq \overline{I} \wedge \overline{I} \sqsubseteq \overline{S}$.
(b) In *static checking*, the induction hypothesis $\overline{I}$ must be automatically inferred from the transformer $\overline{F}$ and the specification $\overline{S}$ (and also checked to satisfy the verification condition $\overline{F}(\overline{I}) \sqsubseteq \overline{I} \wedge \overline{I} \sqsubseteq \overline{S}$).
(c) In *static analysis*, the induction hypothesis $\overline{I}$ must be automatically inferred from the transformer $\overline{F}$ (independently of a particular specification $\overline{S}$) and checked to satisfy the verification $\overline{F}(\overline{I}) \sqsubseteq \overline{I}$. Then later, when a specification $\overline{S}$ is given, it remains to check that $\overline{I} \sqsubseteq \overline{S}$.

Of course static verification (a) such as Boogie [5], ESC/Java [39, 40], Dafny [53], *etc* is a sub-problem of static checking/analysis since it consists in proving an implication only.

There is no essential difference between static analysis (c) and static checking (b).

- Static analysis (c) is static checking (b) where the specification $\overline{S} = \overline{\top}$ is the always true *i.e.* $\forall \overline{I} : \overline{I} \sqsubseteq \overline{\top}$.
- Static checking (b) is static analysis (c) in the abstract domain $\overline{\mathcal{D}}' \triangleq \{P \in \overline{\mathcal{D}} \mid P \sqsubseteq \overline{S}\}$. The idea is therefore to assume that the specification $\overline{S}$ does hold and to calculate by **Alg. 33** a more precise inductive fixpoint over-approximation $\overline{Z}^p$ in $\overline{\mathcal{D}}'$. Upon termination it remains to check that the fixpoint over-approximation $\overline{Z}^p$ is inductive and stronger than the specification $\overline{S}$ in $\overline{\mathcal{D}}$.

The following **Th. 36** shows that static checking can be reduced to a static analysis by **Alg. 33** using a widening and transformers bounded by the specification (so that the specification is assumed to hold), to infer a conditionally sound invariant, and then checking that the invariant is inductive.

Theorem 36 (Static checking). *Assume the hypotheses of* **Th. 34**. *Let* $\overline{S} \in \overline{\mathfrak{D}}$ *be a (non-inductive) abstract specification, define* $\overline{\mathfrak{D}}' \triangleq \{P \in \overline{\mathfrak{D}} \mid \gamma(P) \subseteq \gamma(\overline{S})\}$, *and let* $\overline{D} \in \overline{\mathfrak{D}}'$ *such that* $D \subseteq \gamma(\overline{D}) \subseteq \gamma(\overline{S})$ *and* $\gamma(\overline{F}(\overline{S})) \nsubseteq \gamma(\overline{S})$[16]. *Let* $\overline{Z}'^{p}$ *be the result of* **Alg. 33** *applied to the restriction* $\overline{F}'(\overline{X}) \triangleq \llparenthesis \gamma(\overline{F}(\overline{X})) \subseteq \gamma(\overline{S}) \mathrel{?} \overline{F}(\overline{X}) \mathrel{;} \overline{S} \rrparenthesis$ *of* $\overline{F}$ *to* $\overline{\mathfrak{D}}'$, *with bounded widening* $\overline{X} \mathbin{\nabla'} \overline{Y} \triangleq \llparenthesis \overline{X} \mathbin{\nabla} \overline{Y} \sqsubseteq \overline{S} \mathrel{?} \overline{X} \mathbin{\nabla} \overline{Y} \mathrel{;} \overline{S} \rrparenthesis$ *restricting widening* ∇ *satisfying* **Hyp. 9** (a) *to* $\overline{\mathfrak{D}}'$, *and same narrowing satisfying* **Hyp. 14** (a) *and same dual-narrowing satisfying the dual of* **Hyp. 14** (a). *If* $F(\gamma(\overline{Z}'^{p})) \subseteq \gamma(\overline{Z}'^{p})$ *(which is implied by* $\overline{F}(\overline{Z}'^{p}) \sqsubseteq \overline{Z}'^{p}$*) then* $\textbf{lfp}^{\subseteq}_{D} F \subseteq \gamma(\overline{S})$. □

13 Discussion

The proposal of [45] is to iterate the widening (A) and narrowing (B) phases of **Alg. 33** to get a sequence of results $\overline{Y}_i^{m_i}$, $i = 1, \ldots, k$ and to return their intersection $\bigsqcap_{i=1}^{k} \overline{Y}_i^{m_i}$. After each widening/narrowing phase, the result $\overline{Y}_i^{m_i}$ is heuristically perturbated (after observing the origin of the imprecision of the widening) to get a $\sqsubseteq$-smaller value $\overline{D}$ used to restart with the next widening/narrowing phase. One such heuristic perturbation can be done by considering the dual-narrowing $(\bigsqcap_{j=1}^{i-1} \overline{Y}_j^{m_j}) \mathbin{\widetilde{\Delta}} \overline{Y}_i^{m_i}$ with the intersection of the previous iterates, which in general will not be one of the already explored iterates $\overline{Y}_j^{m_j}$, $j = 1, \ldots, i$. However, by **Th. 7**, the widening is not increasing, so that, in contrast to the dual-narrowing phase (C) of **Alg. 33**, there is no guarantee of improvement after a perturbation, whichever perturbation method is chosen.

If ∇ is a widening and $\widetilde{\Delta}$ is a dual-narrowing on an abstract pre-ordered domain $\langle \overline{\mathfrak{D}}, \sqsubseteq \rangle$, and the widening overshoots the specification, then $P \mathbin{\nabla'} Q \triangleq Q \mathbin{\widetilde{\Delta}} (P \mathbin{\nabla} Q)$ is a more precise widening (although termination might be lost). This is the essence of [44] where the dual-narrowing is by interpolation.

Following [58], let us compare widening (extrapolation) versus interpolation (narrowing/dual-narrowing), more precisely, **Alg. 33** (A) and (B) on any abstract domain $\overline{\mathfrak{D}}$ versus **Alg. 33** (C) alone on the abstract domain $\langle \mathsf{FOL}, \Rightarrow \rangle$ of first-order predicates pre-ordered FOL by implication $\Rightarrow$ with Craig interpolation as dual-narrowing.

- It can be argued that **Alg. 33** (A) and (B) uses a weak/inexpressive abstract domain with efficient representations and small search space while **Alg. 33** (c) uses a strong/expressive abstract domain $\langle \mathsf{FOL}, \Rightarrow \rangle$ with generic representations and large search space. In fact both approaches rely on an abstract domain, with loss of information, and this choice is independent of the chosen iteration method. For example [29] shows that combinations of theories in SMT solvers are reduced products of abstract domains (just lacking extrapolation and interpolation operators). Some theories in SMT solvers rely on specific internal representations for efficiency (like affine inequalities).
- The transformers F (and $\overline{F}$) can be weakest pre- or strongest post-conditions (and their abstraction). The fact that the equivalence formalized in the concrete by the Galois

[16] If $D \nsubseteq \gamma(\overline{S})$ the problem has no solution and if $\gamma(\overline{F}(\overline{S})) \subseteq \gamma(\overline{S})$ so $F(\gamma(\overline{S})) \subseteq \gamma(\overline{S})$ by semi-commutativity, it is solved, two cases without any interest.

connection $\langle \mathcal{D}, \subseteq\rangle \underset{\mathsf{post}[\tau]}{\overset{\widetilde{\mathsf{pre}}[\tau]}{\longleftrightarrow}} \langle \mathcal{D}, \subseteq\rangle$ is preserved in the abstract depends on the abstract domain not on the convergence acceleration method (widening, narrowing, and duals).

– The decision to abstract to (relational) invariants or sets of computation histories is part of the choice of the abstract domain. For example trace-based abstraction [21, 9] and trace partitioning [63] can lift any abstraction to reason by case analysis on computation histories.

– Incompleteness comes from the choice of the abstract domain and the extrapolation/interpolation operators. The abstraction is fundamentally incomplete by undecidability. Extrapolation itself is not necessarily non-terminating and incomplete. A counter-example is *abstract acceleration* where the abstract fixpoint can be computed exactly [50].

– Ockham's razor (*lex parsimoniae*) can be made part of the definition of the abstract transformer and the extrapolation/interpolation operators. As pointed out in [24], it is always possible to introduce simplification heuristics *e.g.* by using $\lambda X \cdot X \mathbin{\nabla} \overline{F}(X)$ or it's n-unrolling version $\lambda X \cdot (\ldots((X \mathbin{\nabla} \overline{F}(X)) \mathbin{\nabla} \overline{F}^2(X)) \ldots \mathbin{\nabla} \overline{F}^n(X))$ where the local widening ∇ performs heuristic simplifications or to approximate the transformer based on interpolation *e.g.* by using $\lambda X \cdot \overline{F}(X) \mathbin{\widetilde{\Delta}} \overline{S}$ as proposed in [56]. Notice that the main contribution to get a simplified transformer $\overline{F} \in \overline{\mathcal{D}} \mapsto \overline{\mathcal{D}}$ is through the careful design of the abstract domain $\overline{\mathcal{D}}$ (and, up to the machine representation of abstract properties in $\overline{\mathcal{D}}$, one can always perform exactly the same static analysis in the concrete domain $\mathcal{D}$ using a widening on $\mathcal{D}$ [22]).

14 Conclusion

The unifying of apparently diverging points of view on extrapolation and interpolation in the abstract interpretation theory leaves opened the question of which part of the fixpoint over-approximation strategy of **Sect. 11** should be used. Obviously. using only one phase is imprecise while iterating three successive phases in **Alg. 33** will be costly. In our opinion this depends on how close the specification $\overline{S}$ is from the inductive argument $\overline{I}$ to be calculated to do the proof $\overline{F}(\overline{I}) \sqsubseteq \overline{I} \sqsubseteq \overline{S}$ in the abstract. In [51, Sect. 2.5], James H. Morris and Ben Wegbreit observed that subgoal induction (which is a relational backward deductive positive induction method as shown in [15]) "can often be used to prove a loop's correctness directly from its input-output specification without the use of an invariant." or " with weaker-than-normal inductive assertions inside the loops.". Looking at their examples, one sees that the induction hypothesis $\overline{I}$ (is or is a very simple variant of) the specification $\overline{S}$ itself. This was also exploited by Dijsktra for calculational program design [32, 33], and more recently in program checking by interpolation [56] and abductive inference [34]. Of course this favorable situation is more frequent for tiny programs than very large ones, in particular when the specification is very far from the inductive invariant.

Such a challenging example is the automatic inference of an interval in the following filter program, intervals being usually considered to be a very simple property.

```
typedef enum {FALSE = 0, TRUE = 1} BOOLEAN; BOOLEAN INIT; float P, X;
void filter () { static float E[2], S[2];
   if (INIT) {S[0] = X; P = X; E[0] = X;}
   else { P= (((((0.5*X)-(E[0]*0.7))+(E[1]*0.4))+(S[0]*1.5))-(S[1]*0.7));}
   E[1] = E[0]; E[0] = X; S[1] = S[0]; S[0]= P;
   /* S[0], S[1] in [l, h] */ }
void main () { X = 0.2*X+5; INIT = TRUE;  /* simulated filter input */
   while (1) { X= 0.9*X+35; filter (); INIT = FALSE; } }
```

The problem is to infer automatically maximal `l` and minimal `h` bounds such that `S[0]`, `S[1] ∈ [l, h]` is invariant in the program. Because `l` and `h` are unknown in the invariant `S[0], S[1] ∈ [l, h]`, neither static verification nor static checking methods can be helpful. The full burden of finding the bounds, which is not easy, is entirely put by these methods on the end-users. But static analyzers, like ASTRÉE [28, 38], automatically infer that `[l, h] ⊆ [-1418.3753, 1418.3753]`, with no user hint or interaction. This is challenging in purely syntactic domains such as ⟨FOL, ⇒⟩.

Acknowledgements. Work supported by NSF Expeditions in Computing CMACS, award 0926166.

References

[1] Albarghouthi, A., Li, Y., Gurfinkel, A., Chechik, M.: UFO: A framework for abstraction- and interpolation-based software verification. In: Madhusudan, P., Seshia, S.A. (eds.) CAV 2012. LNCS, vol. 7358, pp. 672–678. Springer, Heidelberg (2012)

[2] Bagnara, R., Hill, P.M., Ricci, E., Zaffanella, E.: Precise widening operators for convex polyhedra. Sci. Comput. Program. 58(1-2), 28–56 (2005)

[3] Bagnara, R., Hill, P.M., Zaffanella, E.: Widening operators for powerset domains. STTT 9(3-4), 413–414 (2007)

[4] Biere, A., Cimatti, A., Clarke, E., Zhu, Y.: Symbolic model checking without BDDs. In: Cleaveland, W.R. (ed.) TACAS/ETAPS 1999. LNCS, vol. 1579, pp. 193–207. Springer, Heidelberg (1999)

[5] Böhme, S., Leino, K.R.M., Wolff, B.: HOL-Boogie — An interactive prover for the Boogie program-verifier. In: Mohamed, O.A., Muñoz, C., Tahar, S. (eds.) TPHOLs 2008. LNCS, vol. 5170, pp. 150–166. Springer, Heidelberg (2008)

[6] Burstall, R.M.: Program proving as hand simulation with a little induction. In: IFIP Congress, pp. 308–312 (1974)

[7] Chakarov, A., Sankaranarayanan, S.: Expectation invariants for probabilistic program loops as fixed points. In: Müller-Olm, M., Seidl, H. (eds.) SAS 2014. LNCS, vol. 8723, pp. 85–100. Springer, Heidelberg (2014)

[8] Cimatti, A., Griggio, A., Sebastiani, R.: Efficient generation of Craig interpolants in satisfiability modulo theories. ACM Trans. Comput. Log. 12(1), 7 (2010)

[9] Colby, C., Lee, P.: Trace-based program analysis. In: POPL, pp. 195–207. ACM (1996)

[10] Cortesi, A., Filé, G., Giacobazzi, R., Palamidessi, C., Ranzato, F.: Complementation in abstract interpretation. ACM TOPLAS 19(1), 7–47 (1997)

[11] Cousot, P.: Méthodes itératives de construction et d'approximation de points fixes d'opérateurs monotones sur un treillis, analyse sémantique de programmes. Thèse d'État ès sciences mathématiques, Université Joseph Fourier, Grenoble, France (March 21, 1978)

[12] Cousot, P., Cousot, R.: Static verification of dynamic type properties of variables. Research Report R.R. 25, Laboratoire IMAG, Université Joseph Fourier, Grenoble, France (November 1975)
[13] Cousot, P., Cousot, R.: Static determination of dynamic properties of programs. In: Proc. Secont Int. Symp. on Programming, pp. 106–130. Dunod, Paris (1976)
[14] Cousot, P., Cousot, R.: Constructive versions of Tarski's fixed point theorems. Pacific J. of Math. 82(1), 43–57 (1979)
[15] Cousot, P., Cousot, R.: Induction principles for proving invariance properties of programs. In: Tools & Notions for Program Construction: An Advanced Course, pp. 75–119. Cambridge University Press (August 1982)
[16] Cousot, P.: Semantic foundations of program analysis. In: Program Flow Analysis: Theory and Applications, ch. 10, pp. 303–342. Prentice-Hall (1981)
[17] Cousot, P.: Methods and logics for proving programs. In: Handbook of Theoretical Computer Science, Volume B: Formal Models and Sematics (B), pp. 841–994. Elsevier, North-Holland (1990)
[18] Cousot, P.: Verification by abstract interpretation. In: Dershowitz, N. (ed.) Verification: Theory and Practice. LNCS, vol. 2772, pp. 243–268. Springer, Heidelberg (2004)
[19] Cousot, P., Cousot, R.: Vérification statique de la cohérence dynamique des programmes. Rapport du contrat IRIA SESORI No 75-035, Laboratoire IMAG, Université Joseph Fourier, Grenoble, France, 125 p. (Septembr 23, 1975)
[20] Cousot, P., Cousot, R.: Abstract interpretation: A unified lattice model for static analysis of programs by construction or approximation of fixpoints. In: POPL, pp. 238–252. ACM (1977)
[21] Cousot, P., Cousot, R.: Systematic design of program analysis frameworks. In: POPL, pp. 269–282. ACM (1979)
[22] Cousot, P., Cousot, R.: Comparing the Galois connection and widening/narrowing approaches to abstract interpretation. In: Bruynooghe, M., Wirsing, M. (eds.) PLILP 1992. LNCS, vol. 631, pp. 269–295. Springer, Heidelberg (1992)
[23] Cousot, P., Cousot, R.: Galois connection based abstract interpretations for strictness analysis. In: Bjorner, D., Broy, M., Pottosin, I.V. (eds.) FMP&TA 1993. LNCS, vol. 735, pp. 98–127. Springer, Heidelberg (1993)
[24] Cousot, P., Cousot, R.: Formal language, grammar and set-constraint-based program analysis by abstract interpretation. In: FPCA, pp. 170–181. ACM (1995)
[25] Cousot, P., Cousot, R.: Grammar semantics, analysis and parsing by abstract interpretation. TCS 412(44), 6135–6192 (2011)
[26] Cousot, P., Cousot, R.: An abstract interpretation framework for termination. In: POPL, pp. 245–258. ACM (2012)
[27] Cousot, P., Cousot, R.: A Galois connection calculus for abstract interpretation. In: POPL, pp. 3–4. ACM (2014)
[28] Cousot, P., Cousot, R., Feret, J., Mauborgne, L., Miné, A., Rival, X.: Why does Astrée scale up? Formal Methods in System Design 35(3), 229–264 (2009)
[29] Cousot, P., Cousot, R., Mauborgne, L.: Theories, solvers and static analysis by abstract interpretation. J. ACM 59(6), 31 (2012)
[30] Cousot, P., Halbwachs, N.: Automatic discovery of linear restraints among variables of a program. In: POPL, pp. 84–96. ACM (1978)
[31] Craig, W.: Three uses of the Herbrand-Gentzen theorem in relating model theory and proof theory. Journal of Symbolic Logic 22(3), 269–285 (1957)
[32] Dijkstra, E.W.: Heuristics for a calculational proof. Inf. Process. Lett. 53(3), 141–143 (1995)
[33] Dijkstra, E.W., Scholten, C.S.: Predicate calculus and program semantics. Texts and monographs in computer science. Springer (1990)

[34] Dillig, I., Dillig, T., Li, B., McMillan, K.L.: Inductive invariant generation via abductive inference. In: OOPSLA, pp. 443–456. ACM (2013)
[35] D'Silva, V., Haller, L., Kroening, D.: Abstract satisfaction. In: POPL, pp. 139–150. ACM (2014)
[36] Esparza, J., Kiefer, S., Luttenberger, M.: Newtonian program analysis. J. ACM 57(6), 33 (2010)
[37] Feferman, S.: Harmonious logic: Craig's interpolation theorem and its descendants. Synthese 164(3), 341–357 (2008)
[38] Feret, J.: Static analysis of digital filters. In: Schmidt, D. (ed.) ESOP 2004. LNCS, vol. 2986, pp. 33–48. Springer, Heidelberg (2004)
[39] Flanagan, C., Leino, K.R.M., Lillibridge, M., Nelson, G., Saxe, J.B., Stata, R.: Extended static checking for Java. In: PLDI, pp. 234–245. ACM (2002)
[40] Flanagan, C., Leino, K.R.M., Lillibridge, M., Nelson, G., Saxe, J.B., Stata, R.: PLDI 2002: Extended static checking for Java. SIGPLAN Notices 48(4S), 22–33 (2013)
[41] Floyd, R.: Assigning meaning to programs. In: Proc. Symposium in Applied Mathematics, vol. 19, pp. 19–32. Amer. Math. Soc. (1967)
[42] Gange, G., Navas, J.A., Schachte, P., Søndergaard, H., Stuckey, P.J.: Abstract interpretation over non-lattice abstract domains. In: Logozzo, F., Fähndrich, M. (eds.) SAS 2013. LNCS, vol. 7935, pp. 6–24. Springer, Heidelberg (2013)
[43] Graf, S., Saïdi, H.: Construction of abstract state graphs with PVS. In: Grumberg, O. (ed.) CAV 1997. LNCS, vol. 1254, pp. 72–83. Springer, Heidelberg (1997)
[44] Gulavani, B.S., Chakraborty, S., Nori, A.V., Rajamani, S.K.: Automatically refining abstract interpretations. In: Ramakrishnan, C.R., Rehof, J. (eds.) TACAS 2008. LNCS, vol. 4963, pp. 443–458. Springer, Heidelberg (2008)
[45] Halbwachs, N., Henry, J.: When the decreasing sequence fails. In: Miné, A., Schmidt, D. (eds.) SAS 2012. LNCS, vol. 7460, pp. 198–213. Springer, Heidelberg (2012)
[46] Halbwachs, N., Proy, Y., Roumanoff, P.: Verification of real-time systems using linear relation analysis. FMSD 11(2), 157–185 (1997)
[47] Hoare, C.A.R.: An axiomatic basis for computer programming. C. ACM 12(10), 576–580 (1969)
[48] Hoder, K., Kovács, L., Voronkov, A.: Playing in the grey area of proofs. In: POPL, pp. 259–272. ACM (2012)
[49] Huang, G.: Constructing Craig interpolation formulas. In: Li, M., Du, D.-Z. (eds.) COCOON 1995. LNCS, vol. 959, pp. 181–190. Springer, Heidelberg (1995)
[50] Jeannet, B., Schrammel, P., Sankaranarayanan, S.: Abstract acceleration of general linear loops. In: POPL, pp. 529–540. ACM (2014)
[51] Morris Jr., J.H., Wegbreit, B.: Subgoal induction. C. ACM 20(4), 209–222 (1977)
[52] Lakhdar-Chaouch, L., Jeannet, B., Girault, A.: Widening with thresholds for programs with complex control graphs. In: Bultan, T., Hsiung, P.-A. (eds.) ATVA 2011. LNCS, vol. 6996, pp. 492–502. Springer, Heidelberg (2011)
[53] Leino, K.R.M., Wüstholz, V.: The Dafny integrated development environment. F-IDE. EPTCS 149, 3–15 (2014)
[54] Logozzo, F., Lahiri, S.K., Fähndrich, M., Blackshear, S.: Verification modulo versions: Towards usable verification. In: PLDI, p. 32. ACM (2014)
[55] McMillan, K.L.: Interpolation and SAT-based model checking. In: Hunt Jr., W.A., Somenzi, F. (eds.) CAV 2003. LNCS, vol. 2725, pp. 1–13. Springer, Heidelberg (2003)
[56] McMillan, K.L.: Applications of Craig interpolants in model checking. In: Halbwachs, N., Zuck, L.D. (eds.) TACAS 2005. LNCS, vol. 3440, pp. 1–12. Springer, Heidelberg (2005)
[57] McMillan, K.L.: An interpolating theorem prover. TCS 345(1), 101–121 (2005)
[58] McMillan, K.L.: Widening and interpolation. In: Yahav, E. (ed.) SAS 2011. LNCS, vol. 6887, p. 1. Springer, Heidelberg (2011)

[59] Venet, A.: Abstract cofibered domains: Application to the alias analysis of untyped programs. In: Cousot, R., Schmidt, D.A. (eds.) SAS 1996. LNCS, vol. 1145, pp. 366–382. Springer, Heidelberg (1996)

[60] Metcalfe, G., Montagna, F., Tsinakis, C.: Amalgamation and interpolation in ordered algebras. J. of Algebra 402, 21–82 (2014)

[61] Mycroft, A.: The theory and practice of transforming call-by-need into call-by-value. In: Salinesi, C., Pastor, O. (eds.) CAiSE Workshops 2011. LNCS, vol. 83, pp. 269–281. Springer, Heidelberg (2011)

[62] Naur, P.: Proofs of algorithms by general snapshots. BIT 6, 310–316 (1966)

[63] Rival, X., Mauborgne, L.: The trace partitioning abstract domain. TOPLAS 29(5) (2007)

[64] Scott, D.S.: Continuous lattices. In: Toposes, Algebraic Geometry and Logic. LNM, vol. 274, Springer (1972)

[65] Scott, D., Strachey, C.: Towards a mathematical semantics for computer languages. Technical Report PRG-6, Oxford University Computer Laboratory (August 1971)

[66] Tarski, A.: A lattice theoretical fixpoint theorem and its applications. Pacific J. of Math. 5, 285–310 (1955)

[67] Thakur, A., Elder, M., Reps, T.: Bilateral algorithms for symbolic abstraction. In: Miné, A., Schmidt, D. (eds.) SAS 2012. LNCS, vol. 7460, pp. 111–128. Springer, Heidelberg (2012)

[68] Venet, A.: Abstract cofibered domains: Application to the alias analysis of untyped programs. In: Cousot, R., Schmidt, D.A. (eds.) SAS 1996. LNCS, vol. 1145, pp. 366–382. Springer, Heidelberg (1996)

Path Sensitive Cache Analysis Using Cache Miss Paths

Kartik Nagar and Y.N. Srikant

Indian Institute of Science,
Bangalore, India
{kartik.nagar,srikant}@csa.iisc.ernet.in

Abstract. Cache analysis plays a very important role in obtaining precise Worst Case Execution Time (WCET) estimates of programs for real-time systems. While Abstract Interpretation based approaches are almost universally used for cache analysis, they fail to take advantage of its unique requirement: it is not necessary to find the guaranteed cache behavior that holds across all executions of a program. We only need the cache behavior along one particular program path, which is the path with the maximum execution time. In this work, we introduce the concept of cache miss paths, which allows us to use the worst-case path information to improve the precision of AI-based cache analysis. We use Abstract Interpretation to determine the cache miss paths, and then integrate them in the IPET formulation. An added advantage is that this further allows us to use infeasible path information for cache analysis. Experimentally, our approach gives more precise WCETs as compared to AI-based cache analysis, and we also provide techniques to trade-off analysis time with precision to provide scalability.

1 Introduction

Real time systems need a safe estimate of the execution time of a program, which should never be exceeded by any of the program's actual runs. Modern architectures use caches, out-of-order pipelines and all kinds of speculation to make programs run faster, and this has a significant impact on their execution times. The Worst Case Execution Time (WCET) of a program on a particular architecture is defined as the maximum execution time of the program across all its possible runs on that architecture. Ideally, we would like to find this WCET, but theoretically, it is not possible. Timing analysis techniques try to find an upper bound on the WCET of programs. Since the scheduler in a real-time system is likely to assign computational resources such as the processor to a program for the entire duration of its estimated WCET, it is desirable that the upper bound be as close as possible to the actual WCET to avoid wastage.

Caches have a major impact on execution time of programs, because of the huge difference in cache access latency and main memory latency in current architectures. The execution time of a memory-accessing instruction can change by a factor of 100, depending on whether the access hits the cache or goes to the

D. D'Souza et al. (Eds.): VMCAI 2015, LNCS 8931, pp. 43–60, 2015.

main memory. Cache analysis techniques try to find the accesses in a program which will hit the cache, so that the cache latency can be used for those accesses while finding the WCET.

The cache behavior of an instruction depends on the sequence of accesses made to the cache by the program before the instruction, which in turn depends on the program path taken to reach the instruction. Since we want to find the WCET, we would be interested only in the worst-case (WC) program path, which is the program path with the maximum execution time. If the WC path is known, then this information can be used to determine the accurate cache behavior of the accesses along it. However, this results in a 'boot-strapping' problem, because to find the WC path, we must know its execution time, which requires knowledge of the cache hits along the path. But, cache hits along the worst-case path cannot be accurately estimated unless we know the path leading to the cache accesses.

One way to solve this problem is to find the accesses which hit the cache irrespective of the program path taken to reach them. This is the approach taken by the almost universally used Abstract Interpretation (AI) based cache analysis [1], which finds the guaranteed cache hits in a program. All the accesses which are not guaranteed to hit the cache are classified as misses, and the resulting hit-miss classification is used to determine the latency of memory-accessing instructions. Once the execution time of each individual instruction is determined, the Implicit Path Enumeration Technique (IPET) [2] can be used to find the worst-case path in the program. IPET generates an Integer Linear Program (ILP), whose optimal solution encodes the worst-case path.

In our work, we target those accesses which will hit the cache along the worst-case path, but not necessarily along all other paths. To do this, we integrate a limited amount of cache analysis into the IPET formulation, thus taking advantage of the knowledge about the worst-case path to classify certain cache accesses. We propose the concept of cache miss paths of an access, *which are simply those program paths along which the access will suffer a cache miss.* We concentrate on the accesses which are not classified as hit by AI-based cache analysis, and find the cache miss paths of these accesses. We then integrate the miss paths into the IPET formulation to ensure that a cache access will be considered a miss only if the worst-case path contains a miss path of the access. Previously, we have used a similar concept of cache hit paths, to determine the effect of shared cache interference on cache hits [6].

There are many advantages of integrating cache analysis into the IPET formulation. Most of the imprecision of AI-based cache analysis stems from the fact it requires an access to hit the cache along all paths leading to the access. However, an access can be safely classified as hit, if it experiences a cache hit along the worst-case path. This will only happen if the worst-case path does not contain a miss path of the access.

Moreover, some programs have infeasible paths, which generally take the form of conflicting basic blocks, which will never be executed together. Information about infeasible paths can be obtained separately using abstract execution [3], SMT solvers [5], model checking [7], etc. and is part of the program flow analysis stage. This stage generally occurs before timing analysis, and is primarily used to determine the program CFG, loop bounds, etc. A number of works have integrated infeasible path information into the IPET formulation, ensuring that infeasible paths will be ignored while finding the worst-case path in the program ([4], [5]). Since we integrate cache miss paths into the IPET formulation, our approach will have the added advantage of utilizing infeasible path information for cache analysis. Previous works ([7], [8]) have shown that substantial precision improvement in the WCET can be achieved by utilizing infeasible path information during cache analysis.

Experimentally, we found that our approach gave lower WCETs for 9 out of 27 Mälardalen benchmarks [15], as compared to AI-based cache analysis, with an average precision improvement of 22.54 % and with negligible increase in analysis time. Another advantage of our analysis is that it subsumes persistence analysis, which is used to classify accesses inside loops as First-Miss. Since our approach adds some portion of cache analysis to the IPET formulation and thus increases the size of the generated ILP and hence the time required to solve it, we also provide two methods to control the analysis time. Since the number of extra variables/constraints added to the ILP depend on the size and total number of cache miss paths, we allow user-controlled upper bounds on these values. We experimented with different bounds, and found that substantial precision improvement can be obtained even with very low bounds on the size of cache miss paths. We also propose a CEGAR-like strategy which introduces cache miss paths of accesses into the ILP one access at a time, by selecting the cache access which suffers a hit along the worst case path, but has the maximum number of cache misses in the ILP. This allows us to stop the refinement of the WCET at any iteration of the CEGAR loop, and thus trade-off precision with analysis time.

2 Related Work

Few works have looked at the impact of infeasible paths on cache analysis ([7], [8]). However, none of these works have directly integrated cache analysis with the IPET formulation. In [7], the authors instrument the code by introducing variables to count the number of cache misses suffered by accesses which are not classified as Hit by AI-based analysis, and then use model checking to verify assertions on these variables. This approach requires code instrumentation, and is also known to have very high analysis time [8]. There is no way to reuse infeasible path information, which may already have been determined separately during the program flow analysis stage. Moreover, no information about the worst-case path is used to refine the cache analysis, and hence the approach will work only when there are actual infeasible paths (and model checking can identify them).

[8] modifies the AI-based approach for cache analysis, by annotating cache states with logic formulae, corresponding to the partial path along which the cache state would be realized. However, their work can only handle limited types of infeasible paths. In particular, they only consider a maximum of two conflicting

basic blocks, and because of their abstract lattice, the conflicting basic blocks must be close to each other in the program CFG (there cannot be more than one join between two conflicting basic blocks). Moreover, they also ignore the worst-case path information and consider only the impact of infeasible paths on cache analysis.

There have also been previous efforts in performing complete cache analysis using the ILP-based IPET formulation, most notably, the CSTG-based approach proposed by Lee et al. [9]. In this work, the authors first generate the cache state transition graph (CSTG), whose nodes are all possible cache states generated during execution, and edges show the transition between the cache states. Integer variables are introduced in the IPET ILP for all the edges in the CSTG, and these variables are then used to provide an upper bound on the number of hits experienced by accesses. However, as has been noted by [10], this approach introduces an exponentially large number of variables, and significantly increases the size of the ILP, rendering it non-practical even for small programs.

In our approach, we also introduce new variables for a cache access and their miss paths, but only for those accesses which are not classified as Hit by the AI-based cache analysis. In [9], the authors essentially find cache hit paths in the CSTG, constrain the number of cache hits using the variables in the CSTG, and then link these variables with the basic block counts in the CFG. In our case, we directly find the cache miss paths in the CFG, using an AI-based approach, and hence do not need to generate the CSTG.

3 Foundations

Caches store a small subset of main memory closer to the processor, and provide fast access to its contents. To take advantage of spatial locality of memory accesses, all data transfer between the main memory and cache takes place in equal-sized chunks called memory blocks (or cache blocks). To enable fast lookup, caches are further divided into cache sets. For an $A - way$ set associative cache, each cache set can contain maximum of A cache blocks. Given an access to a cache block, the cache subsystem first finds the unique cache set containing the accessed cache block, searches for it among the (at most) A cache blocks in the cache set, and if it is not present, brings it from the main memory.

Since the total number of cache blocks mapped to a cache set will usually be much greater than the associativity (A), the cache replacement policy decides which cache block should be evicted, if the cache set is full and a new cache block has to be brought in. The Least Recently Used (LRU) policy orders all cache blocks in a cache set according to their most recent accesses, and evicts the cache block which was accessed farthest in the past. We will assume LRU replacement policy in our work. We also assume a timing anomaly-free architecture.

Must Analysis [1] for caches produces abstract cache states at each program point, which contains those cache blocks which are guaranteed to be in the actual cache at the program point across all executions of the program. It is used to classify accesses as cache hits. Similarly, May analysis produces abstract cache states which contain cache blocks which may be present in the actual cache during some execution. It is used to classify accesses as cache misses.

4 Cache Miss Paths

To keep things simple, we will now assume a single-level instruction cache. However, our approach can in general be applied to any level in a multi-level instruction cache hierarchy. First we formally define cache miss paths.

Given an instruction a which accesses the cache block m mapped to cache set s, a path π in the CFG of the program is called a **cache miss path** of a if

1. π ends with instruction a and has no other accesses to m other than a, and
2. either the number of distinct cache blocks mapped to s and accessed by instructions in π is equal to $A+1$ (where A is the cache associativity), or π begins from the start of the program.

Note that there are only two possible ways that an instruction a can suffer a cache miss: the accessed cache block m has not been brought into the cache at all from the start of the program, or it was brought but then evicted before a. Both these scenarios are captured in the definition of cache miss path. If miss path π begins from the start of the program, then since a is the only instruction which accesses m, m will not be brought into the cache along the path π, before a. Otherwise, if π contains accesses to $A+1$ distinct cache blocks, then the instructions of π before a must have accessed A distinct cache blocks different from m. Hence, by the time a is executed, m is guaranteed to be not present in the cache. Since the cache miss paths consider both the reasons for a cache miss, this shows that an access suffers a cache miss if and only if execution passes through a miss path of the access.

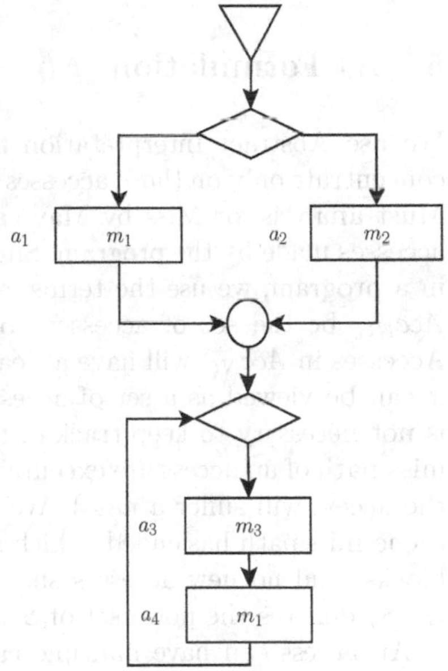

Fig. 1.

Consider the example program in Figure 1, which shows four cache accesses a_1, a_2, a_3, a_4, accessing cache blocks m_1, m_2, m_3, m_1 respectively. Assume the cache has an associativity of 2, and also assume that m_1, m_2, m_3 map to the same cache set. Let us concentrate on the access a_4, which accesses cache block m_1, and consider the program paths leading to this access.

The path $\triangleright - a_2 - a_3 - a_4$ begins from the start of the program, and does not access m_1 until a_4. Hence, this is a cache miss path of a_4. On the other hand, the path $a_1 - a_3 - a_4$ begins with an access to m_1, and accesses only 2 distinct cache blocks. Execution along this path will result in a cache hit for a_4, and hence it is not a cache miss path. The path $a_4 - a_3 - a_4$ lies entirely within the loop, and is again not a cache miss path, as it accesses only 2 distinct cache blocks. Hence, a_4 does not have a cache miss path entirely within the loop, and so is guaranteed to be a cache hit for all iterations except the first. In addition, it will be a cache hit in the first iteration if the worst-case path passes through a_1.

The miss path of an access can be determined by traversing backward in the CFG starting from the access and keeping track of the cache blocks encountered along different paths. If the number of distinct cache blocks encountered along a path (without encountering the accessed cache block) becomes greater than cache associativity, the path can be deemed as a miss path and further accounting of cache blocks along the path can be stopped. On the other hand, if the accessed cache block itself is encountered on a path, then such paths can be discarded, as they cannot become cache miss paths of the access. For accesses inside loops, we may have to take the back-edges (in the reverse direction) more than once to find all cache miss-paths.

5 AI Formulation

We use Abstract Interpretation to find the cache miss paths of accesses. We concentrate only on those accesses which are not classified as Hit by the AI-based Must analysis, or Miss by May cache analysis. Let Acc be the set of all cache accesses made by the program. Since cache accesses are made by the instructions in a program, we use the terms 'access' and 'instruction' interchangeably . Let Acc_{NC} be the set of accesses not classified as Hit or Miss ($Acc_{NC} \subseteq Acc$). Accesses in Acc_{NC} will have at least one cache-miss path. Each cache-miss path π can be viewed as a set of accesses which satisfies the required properties (it is not necessary to keep track of their sequence, because if all instructions in a miss path of an access are executed, then irrespective of their order of execution, the access will suffer a miss). We use the special symbol $\dashv$ to indicate that the cache-miss path has ended, which means that it has accessed $A+1$ distinct cache blocks, and no new accesses should be added to it. Hence $\pi \in \mathcal{P}(Acc \cup \{\dashv\})$. ($\mathcal{P}(S)$ denotes the powerset of S).

An access can have multiple cache-miss paths, and hence we maintain a set of miss paths for every access in Acc_{NC}. Our abstract lattice is the set of functions $F = \{f | f : Acc_{NC} \rightarrow \mathcal{P}(\mathcal{P}(Acc \cup \{\dashv\}))\}$. For $f_1, f_2 \in F$, we say that $f_1 \preccurlyeq f_2$ if and only if $\forall a \in Acc_{NC}, f_1(a) \subseteq f_2(a)$. This is the standard power-set lattice formulation, with the join being defined as point-wise union: $(f_1 \sqcup f_2)(a) = f_1(a) \cup f_2(a)$.

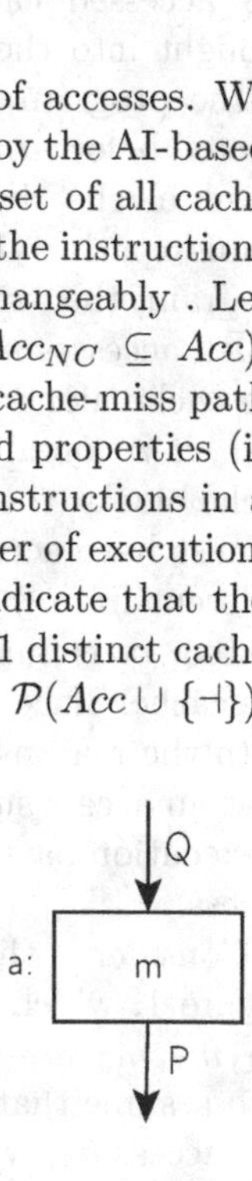

Fig. 2.

We now define the transfer function. Let $cb(a)$ and $cs(a)$ denote the cache block and cache set accessed by instruction a respectively. Given a set of instructions, π, $dist\_blocks(\pi)$ gives the number of distinct cache blocks accessed by instructions in π. Hence, $dist\_blocks(\pi) = |\{cb(a) | a \in \pi\}|$. The direction of the analysis will be backward, assigning an empty set of cache-miss paths initially for all accesses in Acc_{NC}. Since all miss-paths of an access end with the access itself, as soon as an access in Acc_{NC} is encountered, the collection of its miss-paths will begin. As shown in Figure 2, suppose instruction a accesses cache block m mapped to cache set s. The transfer function $\mathcal{T}_{PQ}$ for this instruction takes as input function $f_P \in F$, and outputs function f_Q:

$$f_Q(a') = \begin{cases} \{\{a\}\} \cup \{\pi : \pi \in f_P(a) \wedge \dashv \in \pi\}, & \text{if } a = a', \\ \{\pi : \pi \in f_P(a') \wedge \dashv \in \pi\}, & \text{else if } m = cb(a') \\ \{\pi \cup \{a\} : \pi \in f_P(a') \wedge \dashv \notin \pi \wedge dist\_blocks(\pi \cup \{a\}) \leq A\} & \\ \cup \{\pi \cup \{a, \dashv\} : \pi \in f_P(a') \wedge \dashv \notin \pi \wedge dist\_blocks(\pi \cup \{a\}) > A\} & \\ \cup \{\pi : \pi \in f_P(a') \wedge \dashv \in \pi\}, & \\ & \text{else if } cs(a) = cs(a') \\ f_P(a') & \text{otherwise} \end{cases}$$

First, we consider the miss paths of the access a itself (if $a \in Acc_{NC}$). We add the singleton path $\{a\}$ to start the collection of miss paths of a, while any existing paths of a which have been already been ended are retained. An existing path of a will be present in $f_P(a)$ when a is inside a loop, and it has already been encountered once during an earlier AI iteration. If an existing path of a has not ended, then it would have accessed at most A distinct cache blocks (including m). The access a will bring m to the cache, but there would not be enough cache blocks in this path to evict m before the next access by a. Such a path will never be a cache-miss path of a, and hence must be discarded.

In the second case, we consider the paths of those instructions a' which access the same cache block m. Since this is a backward analysis, any existing path of a' which reaches a would indicate that there is a path from a to a'. Since a brings cache block m into the cache, any path from a to a' will be a cache miss path only if there are enough cache blocks accessed on it to evict m. In this case, only the existing paths which have already been ended will be retained, while all other paths of a' will be discarded. This is because any path which has already been ended would have accessed $A + 1$ distinct cache blocks, or A distinct cache blocks other than m. Hence, m would have been evicted by the time a' is executed. On the other hand, any path which has not been ended will not have accessed enough cache blocks to evict m.

In the third case, we consider the paths of instruction a' which access a different cache block $cb(a')$, mapped to the same cache set $cs(a)$. In this case, cache block m will conflict with $cb(a')$ and therefore the access a should be added to any existing path of a'. In addition, if the number of distinct cache blocks accessed along a path (after adding a) becomes greater than A, such a path would now become a cache-miss path and hence can be ended. Also, miss paths which have already ended are retained without any modification. Finally, in the last case, paths of instructions which do not access the cache set $cs(a)$ are not modified.

It is easy to see that the transfer function is monotonic, as it operates separately on every path of a cache access. It either adds a new path, discards existing paths or adds new accesses to a path, but this depends solely on the properties of the access or the path itself. We also give a formal proof in Section 7. Moreover, the abstract lattice F is finite, and hence termination of the analysis is guaranteed. All the cache-miss paths of accesses in Acc_{NC} will be gathered at the start of the program in the fixpoint solution.

6 ILP Formulation

We now integrate the cache-miss paths into the IPET formulation [2]. We introduce new integer variables for every access in Acc_{NC}, as well as for each cache-miss path of these accesses. The number of cache misses suffered along a cache-miss path will be constrained by the execution counts of the accesses along the path.

Table 1. Notation

Symbol	Explanation
y_i	Integer variable storing the execution count of basic block b_i
x_{ij}	Integer variable storing the total number of cache misses suffered by instruction a_{ij}
x_{ij}^{π}	Integer variable storing the number of cache misses of instruction a_{ij} along cache-miss path π
w_{ij}	Integer variable storing the execution count of edge between basic blocks b_i and b_j
e_i	Execution time of basic block b_i assuming NC-instructions as cache hits
c_p	Cache miss penalty

Let $b_1, \ldots, b_n$ be the basic blocks of the program, and let $a_{i1}, \ldots, a_{il_i}$ be the instructions in b_i which are not classified (NC) as Hit or Miss. Table 1 contains all the notations used in the ILP. Note that e_i is the estimated execution time of b_i obtained by using the AI-based cache hit-miss classification, and assuming cache hit latency for all instructions classified as NC. Let $BB(a)$ denote the index of the basic block containing instruction a.

We first give a brief description of the IPET formulation. For each basic block b_i, y_i stores the execution count of this basic block on the worst-case path. For an edge between basic blocks b_i and b_j in the CFG, the variable w_{ij} stores the number of times execution passes from b_i to b_j on the worst case path. The objective is to find the worst-case path, i.e. the execution counts of basic blocks which maximizes the execution time of the program. The execution counts are constrained by the program structure, which basically places the restriction that the number of times execution enters a basic block (through an incoming edge in the CFG) must be the same as the number of times execution leaves the basic block (through an outgoing edge), and this will also be the execution count of the basic block. Hence, the sum of the w variables for all incoming edges to a basic block will be the same as the sum of w variables for all outgoing edges. Following is our proposed ILP, which is based on the IPET formulation:

$$\text{Maximize} \sum_{i=1}^{n}(e_i y_i + \sum_{j=1}^{l_i} c_p x_{ij}) \tag{1}$$

subject to

$$\forall i, \quad y_i = \sum_{j \in pred(b_i)} w_{ji} = \sum_{k \in succ(b_i)} w_{ik} \tag{2}$$

$$\forall i \forall j, \quad x_{ij} \leq y_i \tag{3}$$

$$\forall i \forall j, \quad x_{ij} \leq \sum_{\text{all miss paths } \pi \text{ of } a_{ij}} x_{ij}^{\pi} \tag{4}$$

$\forall i \forall j \forall \pi$ where π is a miss path of $x_{ij}, \pi = \{a_{\pi 1}, a_{\pi 2}, \ldots, a_{\pi k}\}$

$$x_{ij}^{\pi} \leq y_{BB(a_{\pi 1})} \tag{5}$$

$$\vdots$$

$$x_{ij}^{\pi} \leq y_{BB(a_{\pi k})}$$

Loop Constraints ...

Infeasible path constraints ...

The product $e_i y_i$ is the contribution of b_i to the execution time of the program, assuming that all NC-instructions are cache hits. The variable x_{ij} accounts for the cache misses suffered by access a_{ij}. Each cache miss causes an additional execution time of c_p. Hence, the objective function is the sum of the total execution times of all basic blocks on the worst-case path (Equation 1). Equation 2 encodes the flow constraint for each basic block. The maximum number of misses suffered by an access will be the execution count of the basic block containing the access, and this gives a trivial upper bound on x_{ij} (Equation 3). For each miss path π of a_{ij}, the variable x_{ij}^{π} counts the number of misses suffered by a_{ij} along π.

For a_{ij} to experience a miss along miss path π, all the accesses in the miss-path should happen. Hence, x_{ij}^{π} is upper-bounded by the execution counts of all the basic blocks which contain the instructions present in π (Equation 5 onwards). If an access has multiple cache miss paths, then it can suffer a miss along any of its miss paths. Moreover, for an access inside a loop, multiple cache-miss paths of the access may be executed (for example, in different iterations). Hence, the total number of misses suffered by an access (x_{ij}) is bounded by the sum of its x_{ij}^{π} variables (Equation 4). Since the two notions of an access suffering a cache miss, and its cache-miss path being executed are equivalent, and the AI-based approach will determine all the cache miss paths, the above ILP is guaranteed to account for all the cache misses suffered by an access.

In addition to loop constraints, which will bound the execution count of loop headers, infeasible path constraints can also be provided in the above ILP. An infeasible path generally takes the form of a set of conflicting basic blocks, which will never be executed together. The constraints will place an upper bound on the sum of the execution counts (y_i) of conflicting basic blocks. By appending them to the above ILP, we not only guarantee that the worst case path will not contain the infeasible path, but also that no cache miss will be caused due to it. If the cache miss path of an access is infeasible, then the contribution of cache misses along such a path would become zero.

Multi-level Cache Hierarchy: Our technique can be applied at any level in a multi-level cache hierarchy. To apply the technique at level x in a cache hierarchy with L levels, Acc will consist of all accesses which may reach level x, while Acc_{NC} will consist of accesses which are not classified as Hit at level x. The AI-based approach to find the cache miss paths can be directly applied, except that a miss-path of an access can be discarded in the transfer function, only when there is a guaranteed access to the same cache block, and the miss-path has not ended. Similarly, the same ILP formulation can also be used, except that the cache miss penalty (c_p) of an access will now depend on whether it hits any cache level beyond x, or if it has to go to the main memory.

7 Scalability

Previous approaches [9] at integrating cache analysis into the IPET formulation have struggled with the exponential increase in the size of the ILP due to the addition of extra variables and constraints. However, these approaches did not perform any prior cache analysis, and hence relied solely on the ILP for the hit-miss classification of all cache accesses made by the program. In our case, we are weeding out the cache accesses classified as Hit or Miss by the AI-based cache analysis, and only rely upon the ILP for the remaining accesses.

However, we are also introducing extra variables for each cache-miss path of NC accesses, and extra constraints for each basic block present in a cache-miss path. In general, the number of cache miss paths, and their sizes can be exponentially large in the size of the program. Even though a cache-miss path will access at most $A+1$ distinct cache blocks, this does not place any restrictions on its size, as multiple instructions could access the same cache block. Hence, we propose two changes in the original AI-formulation to limit the size of generated cache-miss paths and hence the size of the final ILP. *We note that this is main advantage of using cache miss paths, as more abstractions can be used to speed up the analysis time, at the cost of precision, but without jeopardizing the safety requirements of cache analysis.* There could be other ways in which cache miss paths can be combined/ignored without under-estimating the number of cache misses, to tradeoff precision with analysis time.

We first modify the transfer function to limit the size of each miss-path to a maximum threshold (T). For miss path π of access a, let $|\pi|$ denote its size, i.e., the number of accesses present in π, excluding the access a. Referring back to the original transfer function defined in Section 5, an access a was added to a miss-path of access a' if they accessed different cache blocks mapped to the same cache set and the miss-path had not ended. In the new transfer function, we will add a new access to an existing miss-path only if the size of the expanded miss-path does not exceed T. A miss-path will be ended when its size reaches T, even though the number of distinct cache blocks accessed on the path may not have reached $A + 1$. The following equation shows the only change in the transfer function $\mathcal{T}_{PQ}$ of an access a, proposed in Section 5:

$$f_Q(a') = \begin{cases} \{\pi \cup \{a\} : \pi \in f_P(a') \wedge \dashv \notin \pi \wedge dist\_blocks(\pi \cup \{a\}) \leq A \ \wedge |\pi \cup \{a\}| < T\} \\ \cup \{\pi \cup \{a, \dashv\} : \pi \in f_P(a') \wedge \dashv \notin \pi \wedge (dist\_blocks(\pi \cup \{a\}) > A \vee |\pi \cup \{a\}| = T)\} \\ \cup \{\pi : \pi \in f_P(a') \wedge \dashv \in \pi\} \\ \qquad \text{if } cb(a) \neq cb(a') \text{ and } cs(a) = cs(a') \end{cases}$$

The new transfer function ends a miss-path either when its size becomes equal to the threshold, or if it accesses more than A distinct cache blocks. Note that there is no restriction on the threshold T, and it can take any value. It is possible that paths determined using above restriction may not actually be cache miss paths. However, we will not lose any actual cache miss paths, because if the length of any actual miss path is greater than T, then its sub-path of length T will be considered as a miss-path by the analysis. This is safe in the context of the ILP as well, since an upper bound on the number of cache misses along a miss path, obtained using the entire path, will be smaller than the upper bound obtained using only its sub-path. Hence, we will only be overestimating the number of misses along the shortened miss-path.

The analysis will lose precision with lower values of T, as more paths which access less than $A + 1$ distinct cache blocks may be treated as cache miss-paths, and the upper bound on the number of cache misses along the more shortened paths will also not be precise. In our experiments, we were able to achieve good precision by setting T to be twice the cache associativity. By limiting the maximum size of cache-miss path, we also decrease the number of cache-miss paths of an access.

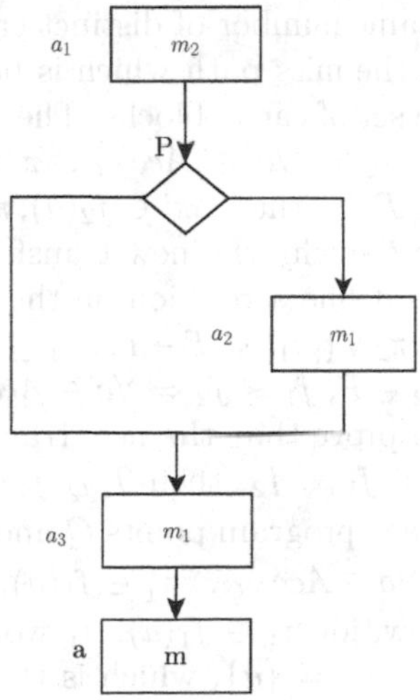

Fig. 3.

The other modification is made to the join in the abstract lattice. In the original formulation, at the join points, we simply took the union of the incoming miss paths for every cache access. However, some miss paths may be entirely contained in other miss paths, and in such a scenario, it is safe to discard the larger miss paths, if they access the same number of distinct cache blocks as the smaller miss paths present inside them.

For example, consider the program fragment shown in Figure 3 which shows cache accesses a, a_1, a_2 and a_3 all accessing the same cache set. Assume that the cache associativity is 2. We concentrate on the miss paths of the access a to cache block m. While finding the fixpoint (in the backward direction), at program point P, we will get two different paths of a, $\pi_1 = \{a_3, a\}$ and $\pi_2 = \{a_2, a_3, a\}$. Clearly $\pi_1 \subseteq \pi_2$, and both paths access the same number of distinct cache blocks. In this case, it is safe to discard π_2 during the join, because if π_2 were to eventually become a cache miss-path by adding some accesses (for example, by adding a_1), then the same accesses will also make π_1 a cache miss-path. Moreover, in the ILP formulation, $x_a^{\pi_1} \geq x_a^{\pi_2}$. Hence, the contribution of cache misses along π_2 will be accounted for by the path π_1.

Experimentally, we have found that such scenarios occur very often in benchmarks, and using the modified join can substantially decrease the number of miss-paths. Moreover, this also has a positive impact on the ILP, as we will not count the same cache miss multiple times along different miss paths. In the example, the access a suffer a cache miss along both the miss paths $\{a_1, a_3, a\}$ and $\{a_1, a_2, a_3, a\}$. In actual execution, a will only suffer one cache miss, but if we did not discard π_2, then we would have counted two misses along both the miss-paths in the ILP. We now give a formal definition of the join. Given $f_1, f_2 \in F$, we define $f_1 \sqcup f_2$ as follows:

$$\begin{aligned}\forall a \in Acc_{NC}, (f_1 \sqcup f_2)(a) = (f_1(a) \cup f_2(a)) \setminus \{\pi \in (f_1(a) \cup f_2(a)) : |\pi| < T - 1 \\ \wedge (\exists \pi' \in (f_1(a) \cup f_2(a)) \setminus \{\pi\}, (\pi' \subsetneq \pi) \\ \wedge (dist\_blocks(\pi) = dist\_blocks(\pi')))\}\end{aligned}$$

From the pointwise union of miss paths from f_1 and f_2, we remove those miss paths which contain less than $T-1$ accesses and for which a sub-path accessing the same number of distinct cache blocks is also present in the union. Note that both the miss path which is being removed and its subpath will also access the same set of cache blocks. The ordering relation $\preccurlyeq$ in the lattice F now becomes: $f_1 \preccurlyeq f_2 \Leftrightarrow \forall a \in Acc_{NC}, \forall \pi \in f_1(a)$, if $|\pi| \geq T-1$, then $\pi \in f_2(a)$, and if $|\pi| < T-1$ then $\exists \pi' \in f_2(a), \pi' \subseteq \pi$ and $dist\_blocks(\pi) = dist\_blocks(\pi')$.

To see why the new transfer function remains monotonic with the new join, let us define a relation on the miss paths, $\sqsubseteq$. For $\pi_1, \pi_2 \in 2^{Acc \cup \{\dashv\}}$, $\pi_1 \sqsubseteq \pi_2 \Leftrightarrow \pi_1 = \pi_2 \vee (|\pi_1| < T-1 \wedge \pi_2 \subsetneq \pi_1 \wedge dist\_blocks(\pi_1) = dist\_blocks(\pi_2))$. Then, for $f_1, f_2 \in F$, $f_1 \preccurlyeq f_2 \Leftrightarrow \forall a \in Acc_{NC}, \forall \pi_1 \in f_1(a), \exists \pi_2 \in f_2(a)$, such that $\pi_1 \sqsubseteq \pi_2$.

To prove that the new transfer function $\mathcal{T}_{PQ}$ is monotonic, we have to show that if $f_1 \preccurlyeq f_2$, then $\mathcal{T}_{PQ}(f_1) \preccurlyeq \mathcal{T}_{PQ}(f_2)$. Assume that the access a' happens between program points Q and P. Let $\mathcal{T}_{PQ}(f_x) = \hat{f}_x$, $x = 1, 2$. We have to show that $\forall a \in Acc_{NC}, \forall \pi_1' \in \hat{f}_1(a), \exists \pi_2' \in \hat{f}_2(a)$, such that $\pi_1' \sqsubseteq \pi_2'$.

Now, for $\pi_1' \in \hat{f}_1(a)$, π_1' would have been obtained from some $\pi_1 \in f_1$. Otherwise, $\pi_1' = \{a\}$, which is the singleton miss-path added when $a = a'$. In this case, $\{a\}$ would be present in $\hat{f}_2(a)$ as well.

The transfer function will add the new access a' and possibly end the miss-path to obtain $\pi_1' \in \hat{f}_1(a)$ from π_1. We know that there exists $\pi_2 \in f_2(a)$ such that $\pi_1 \sqsubseteq \pi_2$. Suppose $\pi_1 = \pi_2$, then $\pi_1 \in f_2(a)$. Hence, $\pi_1' \in \hat{f}_2(a)$. For the original transfer function and join defined in Section 5, this proof will be sufficient to prove that $\mathcal{T}_{PQ}$ is monotonic.

On the other hand, suppose $|\pi_1| < T - 1$, and $\exists \pi_2 \in f_2(a)$ such that $\pi_2 \subsetneq \pi_1$ and $dist\_blocks(\pi_1) = dist\_blocks(\pi_2)$. Since $|\pi_1| < T - 1$, even if the transfer function adds the new access a' to π_1, its length will not reach the threshold T. Let $\pi'_2 \in \hat{f}_2(a)$ be the miss-path obtained from π_2. Since $|\pi_2| < |\pi_1|$, adding a new access to π_2 will also not violate the threshold. Also, if $\pi'_1 = \pi_1 \cup \{a'\}$, then $\pi'_2 = \pi_2 \cup \{a'\}$, because both π_1 and π_2 access the same number of distinct cache blocks. Similarly, if $\pi'_1 = \pi_1 \cup \{a', \dashv\}$ then $\pi'_2 = \pi_2 \cup \{a', \dashv\}$. This shows that $\pi'_2 \subsetneq \pi'_1$, with $dist\_blocks(\pi'_1) = dist\_blocks(\pi'_2)$. Hence, $\pi'_1 \sqsubseteq \pi'_2$.

8 Experimental Results

We have implemented our approach for path sensitive cache analysis in the Chronos framework [14]. Chronos performs AI-based Must and May cache analysis, and classifies cache accesses as one of Hit, Miss, or NC. In addition, Chronos also provides the option of performing persistence cache analysis to further improve the classification of NC-cache accesses to Persistent (PS). We use *lp_solve* to solve the generated ILPs. Our experiments were conducted on a 4-core Intel i5 CPU with 4 GB memory.

If a cache access is classified as PS, then the accessed cache block will never get evicted during execution. This means that such accesses can experience at most one cache miss. PS classification is very useful for accesses inside loops, where the first iteration will bring the accessed block into the cache, and the block will stay in the cache for subsequent iterations. In our terminology, it would mean that the access has a cache-miss path which begins outside the loop, but has no cache-miss path entirely within the loop itself. Hence, our approach can identify persistent cache accesses, and make persistence analysis redundant.

For the experiments, we assume a 1 KB L1 instruction cache with block size 32 bytes and associativity 4. The L1 hit latency is 1 cycle, while the miss latency is 30 cycles. We use Must and May cache analysis as our baseline cache analysis. We apply our approach for all NC-accesses. We restrict the threshold value (i.e. the maximum miss-path length) to 8 (twice the cache associativity). Further, if the number of cache miss paths of an access exceeds 100, then we ignore all the miss-paths and simply classify the access as a cache miss. We experimented on 27 benchmarks from the Mälardalen WCET benchmark suite [15], and found that our approach was able to improve the WCET estimate for 9 benchmarks, with an average precision improvement of 22.54 %, compared to the WCET obtained using the baseline cache analysis.

Some of the precision improvement would be due to persistent cache blocks, and to find their contribution, we compare the WCETs obtained using Persistence analysis with our approach. Figure 4 compares the precision improvement obtained by performing persistence analysis and the improvement obtained using our approach. It can be seen that our approach gives higher precision improvement for 8 out of the 9 benchmarks, and is very close to persistence analysis for *cover*. Our approach works better because apart for identifying persistent accesses, it also takes into account the worst-case path information while classifying accesses as cache misses. Note that this precision improvement is obtained without adding any infeasible path information.

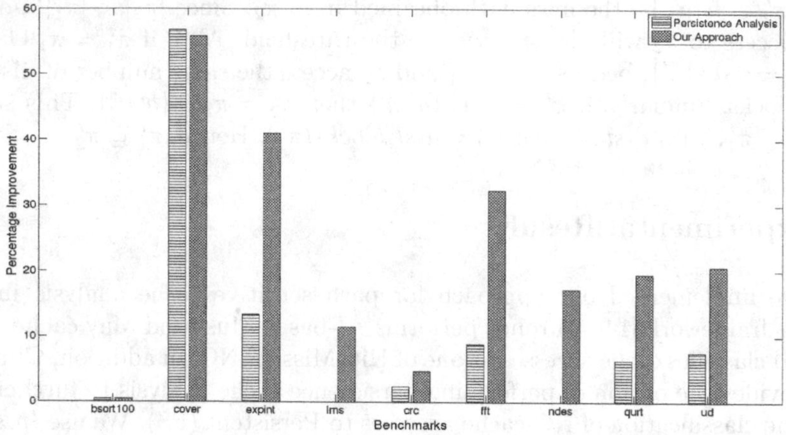

Fig. 4. Graph showing percentage improvement of WCET obtained using (1) Persistence analysis and (2) Our approach, over baseline cache analysis

The total time taken to determine the WCET (including the time to solve the ILP) was less than 1 second for all 27 benchmarks except *nsichneu* and *statemate*. For *statemate*, the AI analysis took 3.16 seconds, while solving the ILP required 0.6 seconds. For *nsichneu*, the AI analysis took 63.87 seconds, while solving the ILP required 3 seconds. For both these benchmarks, neither persistence analysis nor our approach showed any precision improvement. For most of the accesses in *nsichneu*, the number of cache miss paths were greater than 100, and hence these accesses were classified as cache misses. Note that *nsichneu* has a large number of program paths.

In general, there is no correlation between the effectiveness of our approach, and factors such program size, number of accesses, number of program paths, etc. However, in almost all the benchmarks programs where our approach was successful, there were accesses inside loops which had small number of cache miss paths, whose classification was refined by our approach. If an access has large number of cache miss paths, then it is highly likely that the worst-case path will contain one of them, and such accesses will not benefit from our approach. As the program size increases, the number of cache accesses will also increase, which in turn will increase size of the ILP and the time required to solve it. It is not necessary to find the cache miss paths of all accesses which are classified as NC. Accesses which are more likely to affect the WCET (for example, accesses inside loops) can be selected for miss-path based analysis, while the rest of the accesses can be simply considered as cache misses.

CEGAR-Like Approach: To test the effectiveness of our approach when applied only on selected cache accesses, we used a strategy similar to Counterexample guided Abstraction refinement (CEGAR) [12]. We start with IPET ILP (with no cache miss path information) and solve it to obtain the worst-case (WC) path. Then we determine the actual cache states along this path, to find the accesses which were considered as cache misses in the ILP but actually hit the cache along the WC path. Among such accesses, we pick the access with the maximum number of cache misses in the ILP (this is the counter-example), and find the cache miss paths of this access. This is equivalent to an abstraction refinement for this access, as we will now take into account its cache behavior along different paths. These miss paths are then integrated into the (current) ILP to find the new WCET (and possibly the new WC path), and the process is repeated again in the next iteration.

Since the selected cache access was actually hitting the cache along the WC path (of that iteration), no cache miss path of the access will be contained in the WC path. Hence, by integrating the cache miss path information of this access into the ILP, we would be forcing the ILP to either classify the access as a hit, or to find a new WC path which contains a miss path of the access. The new WCET is guaranteed to be less than or equal to the previous WCET. At each iteration, the size of the ILP will increase, as new cache miss path information will be added (note that the miss path information added during earlier iterations is retained). An important advantage of this approach is that the refinement process can be stopped at any time, and the WCET that was obtained after the last completed iteration can be safely used.

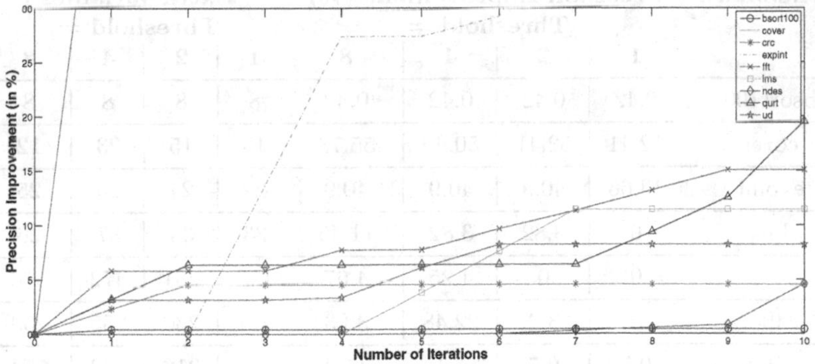

Fig. 5. Graph showing precision improvement in WCET obtained at different iterations of our CEGAR-like approach, over baseline cache analysis

Figure 5 shows the precision improvement in WCET of 9 benchmarks over the baseline cache analysis, obtained after different number of iterations of the above approach, ranging from 1 to 10. Most of the benchmarks start showing lower WCETs from the first iteration itself, with increasing precision improvement as the number of iterations increase. For 5 benchmarks, the maximum precision improvement is achieved within 10 iterations, while the other benchmarks continue to show precision improvement after the first 10 iterations. This demonstrates that our approach is useful even when applied to limited number of cache accesses, if they are selected appropriately.

Note that we continue to use a threshold of 8 on the size of cache miss paths. The above strategy is motivated by a similar CEGAR-like strategy used for WCET estimation in [13], in which the accesses for abstraction refinement are selected in a similar manner. However, for the refinement itself, [13] uses AI-based Must and May cache analysis on the cache set containing the selected access. Hence, the information about the worst-case path is still ignored during the refinement process.

Decreasing the Threshold: Restricting the length of the miss paths is another avenue for trading off precision with analysis time, since this will decrease both the time required to find the miss paths and the size of the ILP. We experimented with different thresholds for the maximum miss path length, noting the number of extra variables in the final ILP (as compared to the ILP generated by IPET), and the precision improvement of WCET. Table 2 shows the precision improvement in WCET, and the extra number of variables, for each of the 9 benchmarks of Figure 4, with different threshold values, ranging from 1 to 8. Note that in this experiment, we find and integrate miss paths of all NC-accesses into the ILP.

Table 2. Effect of different thresholds of miss path length on size of ILP and WCET

Benchmark	Precision Improvement (%) Threshold =				Extra variables Threshold =			
	1	2	4	8	1	2	4	8
bsort100	0.42	0.42	0.42	0.42	8	8	8	8
cover	52.41	52.41	50.49	55.78	15	15	23	12
expint	13.66	40.9	40.9	40.9	22	24	25	25
lms	0	3.82	3.82	11.45	33	34	37	26
crc	0	0	4.25	4.67	186	231	472	576
fft	2	3.2	22.48	33.3	211	230	255	259
ndes	0.7	0.7	6.1	17.3	312	316	543	574
qurt	9.7	9.7	19.38	25.28	329	328	366	500
ud	5	5	5	20.6*	323	390	972	897*

Concentrating on the precision improvement, it is interesting to see that even with low thresholds, several benchmarks show considerable precision improvement. With a threshold of 2 (half the cache associativity), all benchmarks except *crc* experience non-zero precision improvement, while for a threshold value equal to the cache associativity, all benchmarks show improvement. For all the benchmarks, the maximum precision improvement is obtained at the highest threshold value (8). The caveat with increasing the maximum miss path length is the increase in the size of the ILP. For most of the benchmarks, the maximum number of extra variables are added at the maximum threshold. Note that for these benchmarks, the number of added variables is still small enough for *lp_solve* to solve it very fast. variables decrease when the threshold is increased from 4 to 8. However, the precision improvement is still higher.

For some benchmarks, (e.g. *cover*, *lms*) the number of variables decrease on increasing the threshold value from 4 to 8. The reason is that some of the miss paths determined with a threshold of 4 would not be actual cache miss paths, but the analysis does not recognize this due to the restriction on length. Once the allowable length is increased, the analysis will be able to determine this, and discard them, thus decreasing the number of variables. It should be noted that for the benchmark *nsichneu*, for a threshold of upto 4, all the accesses had less than 100 miss paths. The number of extra variables in the ILP for *nsichneu* with a threshold of 4 were 2832, with 52 seconds required to compute the miss paths, and 4 seconds required to solve the ILP (970 extra variables were required for thresholds of 1 and 2). In general, the above results suggest that by lowering the threshold on the length of miss-paths, the size of the ILP can be controlled. Also, even with a low threshold, it is possible to improve the precision of the WCET using our approach.

While we have not experimented with the impact of infeasible paths on cache analysis, we note that previous techniques which integrate infeasible path information into the IPET ILP ([4], [5]) can be directly applied on our modified ILP which has cache miss path information added to it. We have only concentrated on instruction caches, because although it is possible to use cache miss paths for data caches with few modifications, it may not have the same impact on improving the precision. Address analysis for data caches is highly imprecise, and may only estimate a set of cache blocks (instead of a single cache block) accessed by an instruction. Hence, while finding cache miss paths, we may quickly exceed A distinct cache blocks, which may result in short and imprecise miss paths.

9 Conclusion

In this work, we have presented a new approach to cache analysis which does not completely rely on Abstract interpretation, but instead uses AI to obtain path-sensitive information about cache accesses, in the form of cache miss paths. This information is then integrated into the IPET ILP, thus allowing us to take advantage of the worst-case path information and find the cache behavior of accesses along this path. Since our AI-based analysis is path-sensitive to a limited extent, to control the size of the ILP, we also provide user-defined thresholds and a CEGAR-like approach to trade-off analysis time with precision. Experimentally, our approach provides lower WCETs for 9 out of 27 Mälardalen benchmarks, with an average precision improvement 22.5 %, with a negligible increase in analysis time. Our approach also provides the opportunity to use already available infeasible path information for cache analysis.

Acknowledgements. This work was supported by Microsoft Corporation and Microsoft Research India under the Microsoft Research India PhD Fellowship Award. We would also like to thank the anonymous reviewers for their suggestions.

References

1. Ferdinand, C., Wilhelm, R.: Efficient and precise cache behavior prediction for real-time systems. Real-Time Systems 17(2-3), 131–181 (1999)
2. Li, Y.T.-S., Malik, S., Wolfe, A.: Efficient microarchitecture modeling and path analysis for real-time software. In: 16th IEEE Real-Time Systems Symposium, pp. 298–307 (1995)
3. Gustafsson, J., Ermedahl, A., Sandberg, C., Lisper, B.: Automatic Derivation of Loop Bounds and Infeasible Paths for WCET Analysis Using Abstract Execution. In: 27th IEEE Real-Time Systems Symposium, pp. 57–66 (December 2006)
4. Engblom, J., Ermedahl, A.: Modeling complex flows for worst-case execution time analysis. In: 21st IEEE Real-Time Systems Symposium, pp. 163–174 (2000)
5. Blackham, B., Liffiton, M., Heiser, G.: Trickle:automated infeasible path detection using all minimal unsatisfiable subsets. In: 20th IEEE Real-time and Embedded Technology and Applications Symposium (2014)
6. Nagar, K., Srikant, Y.N.: Precise shared cache analysis using optimal interference placement. In: 20th IEEE Real-time and Embedded Technology and Applications Symposium (2014)
7. Chattopadhyay, S., Roychoudhury, A.: Scalable and Precise Refinement of Cache Timing Analysis via Model Checking. In: 32nd IEEE Real-Time Systems Symposium, pp. 193–203 (2011)
8. Banerjee, A., Chattopadhyay, S., Roychoudhury, A.: Precise micro-architectural modeling for WCET analysis via AI+SAT. In: 19th IEEE Real-Time and Embedded Technology and Applications Symposium, pp. 87–96 (2013)
9. Li, Y.T.-S., Malik, S., Wolfe, A.: Cache modeling for real-time software: beyond direct mapped instruction caches. In: 17th IEEE Real-Time Systems Symposium, pp. 254–263 (1996)
10. Wilhelm, R.: Why AI + ILP Is Good for WCET, but MC Is Not, Nor ILP Alone. In: Steffen, B., Levi, G. (eds.) VMCAI 2004. LNCS, vol. 2937, pp. 309–322. Springer, Heidelberg (2004)
11. Huynh, B.K., Ju, L.: Roychoudhury, A.: Scope-Aware Data Cache Analysis for WCET Estimation. In: 17th IEEE Real-Time and Embedded Technology and Applications Symposium, pp. 203–212 (2011)
12. Clarke, R., Grumberg, O., Jha, S., Lu, Y., Veith, H.: Counterexample-guided abstraction refinement for symbolic model checking. J. ACM 50(5), 752–794 (2003)
13. Cerny, P., Henzinger, T., Radhakrishna, A.: Quantitative abstraction refinement. In: Proceedings of the 40th Annual ACM SIGPLAN-SIGACT Symposium on Principles of Programming Languages (POPL), pp. 115–128 (2013)
14. Li, X., Liang, Y., Mitra, T., Roychoudhury, A.: Chronos: A Timing Analyzer for Embedded Software. Science of Computer Programming 69(1-3), 56–67 (2007)
15. WCET Projects / Benchmarks, `http://www.mrtc.mdh.se/projects/wcet/benchmarks.html`

Datacentric Semantics for Verification of Privacy Policy Compliance by Mobile Applications

Agostino Cortesi[1,2], Pietro Ferrara[1], Marco Pistoia[1], and Omer Tripp[1]

[1] IBM Thomas J.Watson Research Center, USA
[2] Università Ca' Foscari Venezia, Italy

Abstract. We introduce an enhanced information-flow analysis for tracking the amount of confidential data that is possibly released to third parties by a mobile application. The main novelty of our solution is that it can explicitly keep track of the footprint of data sources in the expressions formed and manipulated by the program, as well as of transformations over them, yielding a lazy approach with finer granularity, which may reduce false positives with respect to state-of-the-art information-flow analyses.

Keywords: Abstract Interpretation, Privacy, Information-flow Analysis.

1 Introduction

Mobile applications typically ask for permission to access personal (i.e. relevant with respect to privacy) information stored on the device. However, even in non-malicious applications, once these permissions are granted it is often the case that data concerning gender, sex, age, GPS location, smartphone ID, etc. is managed in a way that partially releases it to third parties (e.g. for advertising, profiling, analytics and social computing), with or without some degree of obfuscation, leaving the user unaware of how much confidential information actually leaked [29,36]. Most systems, in fact, are designed to allow users to configure access control (e.g., by setting permissions), without enabling them to monitor the actual information flow of confidential data. In reality, users may trust an application to manage their personal information, but might be concerned about the obfuscation degree applied to that information before it is passed to other (possibly untrusted) actors. The key issue is to keep track of (and possibly restrict) the amount of confidential information that is released by an app, without compromising the usability of the app itself by enforcing overly conservative constraints.

In this challenging context, the aim of this work is to define a theoretical framework to support the design of tools that provide developers as well as end users with better control of how the values managed by the applications reveal confidential data stored on the device.

1.1 Background

Preserving confidentiality of sensitive information in software systems is a subject of intensive research. Various language-based information-flow security analyses were

D. D'Souza et al. (Eds.): VMCAI 2015, LNCS 8931, pp. 61–79, 2015.

proposed [18,21,32,35]. Most of these works are based on the non-interference notion that says that a variation of confidential data given as input to a program does not cause any variation of publicly observable data [12]. The approaches are different (type systems [28,32,34], dependence graphs [18,22], slicing [2,6,21,35], etc.), and apply to different languages including imperative, object-oriented, functional and structured query languages [17,18,21,30]. Recent works address in particular data protection from permission-hungry Android applications [4,7,15,19,24,40], and data-leakage aggregation due to undesired inter-application dataflows [31].

However, in the scenario depicted above the crucial point is not just to discover if sensitive data is confined to private variables, but also to keep control of how the authorized access to confidential data is compliant with respect to a privacy policy, expressed in terms of minimal degree of obfuscation that should be applied to sensitive data in the exposed values. In this respect, the information-flow approach of the mentioned works yields overly conservative results, as the granularity of public/private variables is too coarse, just like the tampered/untampered granularity [1] assigned to data when declassification mechanisms are introduced for relaxing confidentiality policies [5].

1.2 Contribution

This work extends taint analysis, which is a popular variant of information-flow analysis [37,38,39] in order to trace the dependence flow of confidential information from data sources to data sinks. A finer granularity of the analysis is obtained by explicitly keeping track of the footprint of data sources in the expressions managed by the program, as well as of the obfuscation impact of the program operators. As the analysis is defined as an instance of the Abstract Interpretation framework [10], the tradeoff between accuracy and efficiency can be tuned by a suitable choice of the concrete domain abstraction.

The main contributions of this paper can be summarized as follows:

- We design an enhanced concrete semantics that makes explicit the dependence of values on local data sources.
- We define the notion of "confidentiality value of an expression" in terms of min/-max confidentiality degree of its sources and of min/max obfuscation degree of the operators that are used to generate it.
- We lift the enhanced concrete semantics to (computable) abstract semantics according to the Abstract Interpretation framework.
- We show how a static analysis based on this framework can be used to verify the satisfaction of privacy policies.
- We provide practical evidence of the effectiveness of our approach.

In concrete implementations, tracking indirect information flows negatively impacts the effectiveness of the analysis due to the presence of exceptions. Therefore, our approach disregards them. However, the treatment of implicit flows can be further incorporated into our framework by infusing relational operators' footprint in the different conditional statements' branches.

```
1 public class IMBanner {
2  public void loadBanner() {
3   UserInfo user = new UserInfo();
4   user.updateInfo ();
5   BannerView banner = new BannerView(user);
6   banner.loadNewAd();
7   show(banner);
8  }
9 }
10
11 public class BannerView {
12  private UserInfo user;
13  BannerView(UserInfo user) {
14   this.user = user;
15  }
16  void loadNewAd() {
17   String url = "http :// www.inmobi.com/...?id="
18     + user.id + "&lang="+user.language+
19     "&country=" + user.country + "&loc=" + user.loc;
20   //open an http connection with url
21   //update the new ad to display
22  }
23 }
25 public class UserInfo {
26  String language;
27  String country;
28  String id;
29  Location loc;
30
31  void updateInfo() {
32   Locale localLocale = Locale.getDefault ();
33   language = localLocale.getLanguage();
34   country = localLocale.getCountry();
35   String androidId = Settings.Secure.getAndroidId();
36   id = MessageDigest.hashSHA1(androidId);
37   loc = LocationManager.getLastKnownLocation();
38  }
39 }
```

Fig. 1. Code Snippet from the `Inmobi` Library

1.3 Structure of the Paper

The rest of paper is structured as follows: Section 2 presents some examples that motivate the main novelties of our approach. Sections 3, 4, and 5 describe the syntax, and the enhanced concrete and abstract semantics, respectively. Section 6 introduces the notion of confidentiality and obfuscation values for sources and operators. Section 7 shows how this framework can be applied to the verification of privacy compliance policies. Section 8 discusses related work, while Section 9 concludes.

2 Motivating Examples

2.1 `Inmobi`

Consider the motivating example in Figure 1. This code is extracted from the `Inmobi` library.[1] `Inmobi` is among the three most popular advertisement engines for Android apps [3]. This code sketches the main steps performed by the `Inmobi` library when loading an advertisement banner. This is performed by method `IMBanner.loadBanner()`, that first creates and updates a `UserInfo` object (lines 3-4), then creates and loads the advertisement banner view passing the information about the user (lines 5-6), and finally displays the banner (line 7). Even though, at a first glance, this method does not seem to access any confidential information, `user.updateInfo()` collects and transforms various pieces of information about the user and the device, and in particular (i)

[1] This library is obfuscated, and some parts (and in particular `BannerView.loadNewAd()`) cannot be decompiled. For the sake of readability, we represented the main components of the library in this code snippet.

the language and country of the user from the default `Locale` object (lines 32-34), (ii) the hashing of the Android ID (lines 35-36)[2], and (iii) the last known location (line 37). When a `UserInfo` object is passed to the constructor of `BannerView`, it is stored in a local field. The information contained in this field is then concatenated in the URL (lines 17-19) used to retrieve the advertisement banner. In this way, the data collected by `UserInfo.updateInfo()` is leaked to the advertisement server. This data aggregates various sources (language and country from the `Locale`, the android ID, and the location).

This example shows that we need to track complex flows of information. For instance, with a standard taint analysis [39] an alarm would be raised upon any flow from a source to a sink. In this particular example, we expect that it would be fine to release to the advertisement server some of the sources (e.g., the country and the language, but not the Android ID), so taint analysis could raise a false alarm in this scenario. Indeed, we are interested in computing the global amount of data that is released (that is, country, language, Android ID, and location), and to raise an alarm only if this amount exceeds a specified threshold. In addition, one needs to specify if the transformation performed on the confidential data (e.g., hashing the Android ID) is obfuscating the value sufficiently or not. For instance, the hashing of the ID might be used to track a user or device if the hash clashing is quite rare, and therefore the level of obfuscation performed by this transformation might be insufficient.

2.2 IMSI

The following code snippet is extracted from internal Android library `com.android.internal.telephony.cdma.RuimRecords`:

```
String mImsi = telephonyManager.getDeviceId();
log("IMSI:" + mImsi.substring (0, 6) + "xxxxxxxxx");
```

It leaks a portion of the device identifier through the log. The fundamental question here is whether the first 6 characters of the International Mobile Subscriber Identity (IMSI) code contain confidential information that the user does not want to leak outside. The IMSI code is usually made by 15 characters, where the first 3 characters identify the country, the following 2 or 3 characters identify the mobile network, and the rest is used to identify the device.[3] Therefore, we assume that the first 6 characters do not contain confidential information.

3 Syntax

At the lowest level of the language, we consider expressions on strings ($s \in \mathbb{S}$), integers ($n \in \mathbb{Z}$), and Boolean values ($b \in \mathbb{B}$). We denote by $bexp$ and $nexp$ Boolean

[2] The Android ID is "randomly generated when the user first sets up the device and should remain constant for the lifetime of the user's device". Therefore, it is used to track a specific user (rather than a device) by advertisement engines. We simplify the API call to make the code more readable.

[3] `http://en.wikipedia.org/wiki/International_mobile_subscriber_identity`.

and numerical expressions, respectively. In addition to basic numerical, textual, and Boolean expressions, we introduce label constants (that refer to datastore entries). Let `Lab` be the set of labels. We denote by ℓ, possibly subscripted, labels identifiers in `Lab`. Our language support a statement $read(\ell)$ that returns the value read from the datastore corresponding to the label ℓ. We define string expressions by $sexp ::= s \mid sexp_1 \circ sexp_2 \mid encrypt(sexp, k) \mid sub(sexp, nexp_1, nexp_2) \mid hash(sexp) \mid read(lexp)$ where $\circ$ denotes the concatenation of two strings, k denotes a key used to encrypt a textual value, $sub(s, n_1, n_2)$ computes the substring of s from the n_1-th to the n_2-th character, and $hash(s)$ computes the hash value of s. For the sake of simplicity, we focus our formalization on this minimal representative language, and on operations over strings. Our approach can be extended straigthforwardly to support other operations and types.

Finally, we define a standard minimal imperative set of statements. In particular, we support string assignment (x := $sexp$), concatenation ($c_1; c_2$), conditional `if` (`if` $bexp$ `then` c_1 `else` c_2), and `while` loops (`while` $bexp$ do c). In addition, we have a special statement $send(sexp)$ that leaks a string value.

4 Collecting Semantics

4.1 Domain

First of all, we define atomic data expressions by $\mathbb{D} = \{\langle \ell_i, L_i \rangle : i \in I\}$. Given a set of data labels, which identify the locations of the *read-only*[4] datastore a program interacts with, an atomic data expression $adexp$ is a set of elements $\langle \ell_i, \{(op_j, \ell'_j) : j \in J\}\rangle$. An element $\langle \ell_i, \{(op_j, \ell'_j) : j \in J\}\rangle$ in $adexp$ says that the value of $adexp$ has been obtained from the datum stored in the location ℓ_i by combining it with data coming from the locations ℓ'_j through the corresponding operations op_j. In other words, an atomic data expression keeps track, for each source of the expression value, of the set of other data sources that were used to get that value from it. We denote by $\mathbb{D}$ the domain of atomic data.

We focus our collecting semantics on the variables referring to values coming from the datastore. Therefore, we define a data environment mapping local variables in `Var` to atomic data expressions (D : `Var` $\longrightarrow \wp(\mathbb{D})$). Note that each variable may contain data about different sources (e.g., the concatenation of the strings representing the Android identifier and the location), and therefore each variable is related to a set of atomic data expressions. In addition, the concrete state tracks value information as well (V : `Var` $\longrightarrow (\mathbb{Z} \cup \mathbb{S})$). Formally, $\Sigma = D \times V$.

We then introduce a concrete datastore that contains all the possible atomic data that may be read by a program, where the special label $\star$ is used to represent data coming either from the input of the program or from the constant set of the program itself, i.e. data that is not contained in the datastore.

Definition 1 (Concrete Datastore). *A concrete datastore* C *is a set* $\{\langle \ell_i, \emptyset \rangle\} : i \in I\} \subseteq \mathbb{D}$ *such that* $\forall i, j \in I : i \neq j \Rightarrow \ell_i \neq \ell_j$, *and* $\ell_i \neq \star\}$.

[4] We restrict our focus to a read-only datastore, for the sake of simplicity. Extending the model to the general case brings about the problem of aliasing that should be studied further.

$$
\begin{aligned}
S_A[\![x]\!](a,v) &= a(x)\\
S_A[\![read(lexp)]\!](a,v) &= \{\langle S_L[\![lexp]\!](a,v),\emptyset\rangle\}\\
S_A[\![encrypt(sexp,k)]\!](a,v) &= \{\langle \ell_1, L_1 \cup \{([encrypt,k],\ell_1)\}\rangle : \langle \ell_1, L_1\rangle \in S_A[\![sexp]\!](a,s,n)\}\\
S_A[\![s]\!](a,v) &= \{\langle \star,\emptyset\rangle\}\\
S_A[\![sexp_1 \circ sexp_2]\!](a,v) &= \{\langle \ell_1, L_1 \cup \{(\circ,\ell_2)\}\rangle, \langle \ell_2, L_2 \cup \{(\circ,\ell_1)\}\rangle :\\
&\qquad \langle \ell_1, L_1\rangle \in S_A[\![sexp_1]\!](a,v), \langle \ell_2, L_2\rangle \in S_A[\![sexp_2]\!](a,v)\}\\
S_A[\![sub(sexp,k_1,k_2)]\!](a,v) &= \{\langle \ell_1, L_1 \cup \{([sub,k_1,k_2],\ell_1)\}\rangle : \langle \ell_1, L_1\rangle \in S_A[\![sexp]\!](a,v)\}\\
S_A[\![hash(sexp)]\!](a,v) &= \{\langle \ell_1, L_1 \cup (hash,\ell_1)\rangle : \langle \ell_1, L_1\rangle \in S[\![sexp]\!](a,v)\}
\end{aligned}
$$

Fig. 2. Semantics of Expressions on Atomic Data

$$
\begin{aligned}
S[\![x := sexp]\!](a,v) &= (a[x \mapsto S_A[\![sexp]\!](a,v)], v[x \mapsto S_S[\![sexp]\!](v)])\\
S[\![send(sexp)]\!](a,v) &= (a,v)\\
S[\![c_1; c_2]\!](a,v) &= S[\![c_2]\!](S[\![c_1]\!](a,v)))\\
S[\![\text{if } bexp \text{ then } c_1 \text{ else } c_2]\!](a,v) &= \begin{cases} S[\![c_1]\!](a,v) & \text{if } S_B[\![bexp]\!](v)\\ S[\![c_2]\!](a,v) & \text{otherwise}\end{cases}\\
S[\![\text{while } bexp \text{ do } c]\!](a,v) &= S[\![\text{ if } (bexp) \text{ (c; while } bexp \text{ do c)}]\!](a,v)
\end{aligned}
$$

Fig. 3. Concrete Semantics of Statements

Given a program p, we will denote the concrete datastore associated with this program by C_p.

Example Consider the `Inmobi` example from Section 2. Method `updateInfo` accesses various data coming from the datastore. We represent by (i) $\langle$`Language`$, \emptyset\rangle$ the language returned by the `Default` object (line 30), (ii) $\langle$`Country`$, \emptyset\rangle$ the country returned by the `Default` object (line 31), and (iii) $\langle$`AndroidId`$, \emptyset\rangle$ the Android identifier. These three data sources are stable, that is, they always return the same values. For the locations (that is, line 34) it may be the case that different calls of `getLastKnownLocation` retrieves different locations. Therefore, the concrete datastore contains $\langle \texttt{Location}_i, \emptyset\rangle : i \in \mathbb{N}$ as well. Instead, for the `IMSI` example we have only one datum $\langle$`IMSI`$, \emptyset\rangle$.

4.2 Semantics

We suppose that a standard concrete evaluation of numerical ($S_N : nexp \times V \to \mathbb{Z}$) and string ($S_S : sexp \times V \to \mathbb{S}$) expressions is provided, as well as the evaluation of Boolean conditions ($S_B : bexp \times V \to \{\mathsf{true}, \mathsf{false}\}$). In addition, we suppose that the semantic evaluation of label expressions ($S_L : lexp \times \Sigma \to \texttt{Lab}$) returns a data label given a label expression.

The evaluation of the expressions on atomic data $S_A : sexp \times \Sigma \to \wp(\mathbb{D})$ is defined in Fig. 2. Observe that this enhanced concrete semantics of expressions can be seen as an abstract representation of partial execution traces, where each expression tree is projected to the data associated to the labels in `Lab`.

Once the semantics of expression is formalized, the (concrete enhanced) semantics of statements can be expressed as depicted in Figure 3.

Example. Consider again the `Inmobi` example of Section 2. After the execution of `updateInfo` (line 4) we have that (i) `user.language` $\mapsto$ $\{\langle$`Language`$, \emptyset\rangle\}$,

(ii) $\texttt{user.country} \mapsto \{\langle\texttt{Country}, \emptyset\rangle\}$, (iii) $\texttt{user.id} \mapsto \{\langle\texttt{AndroidId}, \{(\texttt{hash.Android-Id})\}\rangle\}$, and (iv) $\texttt{user.loc} \mapsto \{\langle\texttt{Location}_1, \emptyset\rangle\}$. We then concatenate all this data in a string stored in `url` at line 17. Therefore, we obtain the following atomic data expression with label `AndroidId`:

$\langle\texttt{AndroidId}, \{(\texttt{hash}, \texttt{AndroidId}), (\circ, \texttt{Language}), (\circ, \texttt{Country}), (\circ, \texttt{Location}_1)\}\rangle$ while for $\texttt{Location}_1$ we obtain $\langle\texttt{Location}_1, \{(\circ, \texttt{AndroidId})\}\rangle$ since this is the last element concatenated when building `url`. For the `IMSI` example, we obtain that the data expression leaked at line 2 is $\langle\texttt{IMSI}, \{([sub, 0, 6], \texttt{IMSI})\}\rangle$.

4.3 Canonical Form of Atomic Data

The definition of atomic data does not impose any constraint on the number of elements. In particular, the same source label can appear several times in an atomic datum, when its data have multiple impact on the expression's value. However, if we are just interested to observe the sources of an expression, and the set of operators applied to each source, a more compact representation of atomic data can be given, where each source label appears at most once.

Given an atomic datum $d = \{\langle\ell_j, L_j\rangle : j \in J\}$, we denote by $\texttt{src}(d)$ its source set $\{\ell_j : j \in J\}$. Moreover, given a label ℓ and an atomic datum d, we denote by $\texttt{links}(\ell, d)$ the links set of ℓ in d if $\ell \in \texttt{src}(d)$, and $\emptyset$ otherwise.

Definition 2. *We say that an atomic datum d is in* canonical form *if every label in* $\texttt{src}(d)$ *occurs as a source label exactly once in d. Given an atomic datum, its canonical form can be obtained by applying the following unary source collapse operator* ρ*:*

$$\rho(d) = \{\langle\ell, \cup\texttt{links}(\ell, d)\rangle : \ell \in \texttt{src}(d)\}$$

5 Abstract Semantics

There are two main ways to get abstractions of the concrete semantics defined so far: abstracting values, and abstracting labels. The abstract elements should be an overapproximation of the concrete values assigned to variables in the concrete computation steps.

5.1 Values Abstraction

Values can be abstracted by means of well-known either relational or non-relational domains for numerical and textual values [9,26]. Therefore, we suppose that a value abstract domain V^a is provided, and it is equipped with the standard lattice and semantic operators.

5.2 Labels Abstraction

Labels can be abstracted by any abstract domain for categorical data, like a flat constant propagation domain. Observe that when dealing with data stored in relational form, i.e. by means of bi-dimensional tables, a relational abstract domain for array representation can be adopted, as defined in [11].

Example. In the `Inmobi` example of Section 2, we do not need to apply any abstraction on `Language`, `Country`, and `AndroidId`, since these are persistent throughout the execution. Instead, we need to apply abstraction to the locations $\texttt{Location}_i : i \in \mathbb{N}$, since the statement at line 37 may produce many values. Therefore, we abstract together all the locations produced by the same program point pp with $\texttt{Location}^{\text{pp}}$. In our example, this means that we abstract the data source at line 37 with $\texttt{Location}^{37}$.

5.3 Atomic Data Abstraction

We are now in position to formalize the atomic data abstract domain $\mathbb{AD}$.

Definition 3 (Abstract Atomic Data). *Given a set of atomic data, an abstract element will be a set of tuples* $\{\langle \ell^a_j, L^{a\sqcap}_j, L^{a\sqcup}_j \rangle : j \in J\} \in \mathbb{AD}$, *where*

- ℓ^a_j *is an element of an abstract domain that abstracts labels in* `Lab`
- $L^{a\sqcap}_j = \{(op^a_{ij}, \ell^a_{ij}) : i \in I\}$ *is an under-approximation of the set of operators applied to the sources represented by* ℓ^a_j *with values coming from sources represented by* ℓ^a_{ij}
- $L^{a\sqcup}_j = \{(op^a_{ij}, \ell^a_{ij}) : i \in I'\}$ *is an over-approximation of the set of operators applied to the sources represented by* ℓ^a_j *with values coming from sources represented by* ℓ^a_{ij}
- $L^{a\sqcap}_j \subseteq L^{a\sqcup}_j$.

The order on the abstract elements is given by the order on the Cartesian product of the components' domain, and the least upper bound and greatest lower bound operators are defined accordingly.

Definition 4 (Partial Order on Abstract Atomic Data). *Given two abstract atomic data* $d_1 = \{\langle \ell^a_{1i}, L^{a\sqcap}_{1i}, L^{a\sqcup}_{1i} \rangle : i \in I_1\}$ *and* $d_2 = \{\langle \ell^a_{2i}, L^{a\sqcap}_{2i}, L^{a\sqcup}_{2i} \rangle : i \in I_2\}$ *on the same abstract domains for values and labels,*

$$d_1 \sqsubseteq d_2 \Leftrightarrow \forall i \in I_1 \exists j \in I_2 : \ell^a_{1i} = \ell^a_{2j},\ L^{a\sqcap}_{1i} \supseteq L^{a\sqcap}_{2j},\ L^{a\sqcup}_{1i} \subseteq L^{a\sqcup}_{2j}$$

Given an abstract atomic datum $\{\langle \ell^a_j, L^{a\sqcap}_j, L^{a\sqcup}_j \rangle : j \in J\}$, we denote by $\texttt{src}(d)$ its source set $\{\ell^a_j : j \in J\}$.

Definition 5 (Least Upper bound of Abstract Atomic Data). *Given two abstract atomic data* $d_1 = \{\langle \ell^a_{1i}, L^{a\sqcap}_{1i}, L^{a\sqcup}_{1i} \rangle : i \in I_1\}$ *and* $d_2 = \{\langle \ell^a_{2i}, A, L^{a\sqcap}_{2i}, L^{a\sqcup}_{2i} \rangle : i \in I_2\}$ *on the same abstract domains for values and labels, the least upper bound of* d_1 *and* d_2 *is the atomic datum*

$$d_1 \sqcup d_2 = \bigcup_{\ell^a \in \texttt{src}(d_1) \cup \texttt{src}(d_2)} \left\{ \begin{array}{ll} \langle \ell^a, L^{a\sqcap}_1, L^{a\sqcup}_1 \rangle & \textit{if } \ell^a \in \texttt{src}(d_1) \setminus \texttt{src}(d_2) \\ \langle \ell^a, L^{a\sqcap}_2, L^{a\sqcup}_2 \rangle & \textit{if } \ell^a \in \texttt{src}(d_2) \setminus \texttt{src}(d_1) \\ \langle \ell^a, L^{a\sqcap}_1 \cap L^{a\sqcap}_2, L^{a\sqcup}_1 \cup L^{a\sqcup}_2, \rangle & \textit{otherwise} \end{array} \right\}$$

Let $\texttt{Lab}^a$ and $\texttt{A}$ be complete lattices featuring Galois Connections with the concrete domains of labels and values, respectively. Let $(\gamma_{\texttt{Lab}}, \alpha_{\texttt{Lab}}), (\gamma_{\texttt{A}}, \alpha_{\texttt{A}})$ be the corresponding concretization and abstraction functions. When applied to a set of links $\{(op_i, \ell_i) : i \in I\}$, the function $\alpha_{\texttt{Lab}}$ returns the set $\{(op^a_i, \alpha_{\texttt{Lab}}(\ell_i)) : i \in I\}$, where op^a_i is the abstract operator that safely approximates op_i in the abstract domain $\texttt{A}$.

Definition 6 (Abstraction function). *The abstraction function $\alpha : \wp(\mathbb{D}) \longrightarrow \mathbb{AD}$ is first defined on singletons and then extended to sets by applying the least upper bound operator.*

$$\alpha_s(\{\langle \ell_i, L_i \rangle : i \in I\}) = \{\langle \alpha_{\mathtt{Lab}}(\ell_i), \alpha_{\mathtt{Lab}}(L_i), \alpha_{\mathtt{Lab}}(L_i) \rangle : i \in I\}$$
$$\alpha(\{d_j \in \mathbb{D} : j \in J\}) = \bigsqcup_{j \in J} \alpha_s(d_j).$$

Notice that in the definition above, when considering a single atomic datum, in its abstract representation the under- and over-approximations of the link sets are equal. The gap among these sets is introduced in fact by the least upper bound operator.

Definition 7 (Concretization function). *The concretization of abstract atomic data is defined as an adjoint of the abstraction function: $\gamma(ad) = \{d \in \mathbb{D} : \alpha(d) \sqsubseteq ad\}$*

Theorem 1 (Galois Connection). *The functions α and γ defined above form a Galois Connection between $\wp(\mathbb{D})$ and $\mathbb{AD}$, i.e.:*

i) α and γ are monotone,
ii) $\forall ad \in \mathbb{AD} : \alpha(\gamma(ad)) \sqsubseteq_{\mathbb{AD}} ad$
iii) $\forall S \subseteq \mathbb{D} : S \subseteq \gamma(\alpha(S))$.

Proof. $\mathbb{AD}$ is the Cartesian product of abstract domains featuring Galois Connections with the concrete domain $\wp(\mathbb{D})$, and the functions α and γ are defined in canonical way w.r.t. the Cartesian product [8].

We define by $AD^a : \mathtt{Var} \mapsto \wp(\mathbb{AD})$ the component of the abstract domain tracking information on atomic data expressions. The partial order, the upper bound and the concretization function are defined as pointwise application of the operators defined on $\mathbb{AD}$.

5.4 Abstract Domain

Our abstract domain is the Cartesian product of the Atomic Data abstract domain (AD^a), and the value domain (V^a).

5.5 Data-Store Abstraction

The analysis of a program P aimed at verifying that it satisfies a given confidentiality policy with respect to data stored in devices running P can be defined either as a "datastore-aware" analysis, i.e. running the analysis on the actual data contained in the device, or in a "datastore-unaware" way, i.e. running the analysis on a generic datastore that represents the actual datastores under a suitable abstraction of labels and values.

A "datastore-aware" analysis has the advantage of being in general more accurate, as it allows to deal with the actual values that are leaked by the program. However, this scenario requires the analysis being applied only once the program is installed on the device, as an app that runs on the device itself or on a third-party verifier that should be given access permission to the device's datastore.

The accuracy of a "datastore-unaware" analysis heavily relies on the datastore abstraction, but it has the advantage of being applicable to the program with no need to access the actual confidential data when running the analysis itself.

$$\begin{aligned}
S^a[\![x := sexp]\!](a^a, v^a) &= (a^a, S^a_v[\![x := sexp]\!](v^a)) \\
S^a[\![send(sexp)]\!](a^a, v^a) &= (a^a, v^a) \\
S^a[\![c_1; c_2]\!](a^a, v^a) &= S^a[\![c_2]\!](S^a[\![c_1]\!](a^a, v^a)) \\
S^a[\![\text{if } bexp \text{ then } c_1 \text{ else } c_2]\!](a^a, v^a) &= S^a[\![c_1]\!](a^a, S^a_B[\![bexp]\!](v^a)) \sqcup S^a[\![c_2]\!](a^a, S^a_B[\![\neg bexp]\!](v^a)) \\
S^a[\![\text{while } bexp \text{ do } c]\!](a^a, v^a) &= fix(S^a[\![\text{ if } (bexp) \text{ (while } bexp \text{ do } c)]\!](a^a, v^a))
\end{aligned}$$

Fig. 4. (Abstract) Semantics of Statements

Definition 8 (Abstract Datastore). *Given a Galois connection between $\wp(\mathbb{D})$ and $\mathbb{AD}$, an abstract datastore is a set $D^a = \{\{\langle \ell^a_j, \emptyset, \emptyset\rangle\} : j \in J\} \subseteq \mathbb{AD}$ such that $\forall i, j \in J : i \neq j \Rightarrow \ell^a_i \neq \ell^a_j$.*

An abstract datastore $D^a = \{\{\langle \ell^a_j, \emptyset, \emptyset\rangle\} : j \in J\}$ is an abstraction of all concrete datastores $D = \{\{\langle \ell_i, \emptyset\rangle\} : i \in I\}$ that satisfies the following conditions: $\bigcup_{i \in I}\{\alpha(\ell_i)\} = \bigcup_{j \in J}\{\ell^a_j\}$, and $\forall i \in I\ \exists! j \in J$ such that $\ell_i \in \gamma_{\mathtt{Lab}}(\ell^a_j)$.

Example. Consider the `Inmobi` example introduced in Section 2. In particular, we have the following atomic data expressions: $\langle$`Language`$, \emptyset, \emptyset\rangle$, $\langle$`Country`$, \emptyset, \emptyset\rangle$, and $\langle$`AndroidId`$, \emptyset, \emptyset\rangle$. The only case that is slightly different regards `Location` since we abstract with $\langle \mathtt{Location}^{37}, \emptyset, \emptyset\rangle$ all the concrete data expressions in $\langle \mathtt{Location}_i, \emptyset\rangle : i \in \mathbb{N}$. Similarly, for the `IMSI` example we have $\langle$`IMSI`$, \emptyset, \emptyset\rangle$.

5.6 Abstract Semantics of Statements

Figure 4 depicts the abstract semantics of statements[5]. We omit the abstract semantics of expressions, as it can be easily formalized by mimicking the concrete semantics, the only difference being that (1) every operation has impact on both link sets associated to an abstract label, and (2) abstract atomic data are kept in canonical form by systematically applying the following normalization operator in presence of multiple occurrences of the same label in the source set of an abstract atomic datum: $\rho(ad) = \{\langle \ell^a, \cap\mathtt{links}(\ell^a, ad), \cup\mathtt{links}(\ell^a, ad)\rangle : \ell^a \in \mathtt{src}(ad)\}$

Example. The abstract semantics of the `Inmobi` example does not substantially differ from the concrete semantics for the the example of Section 2. After the execution of `updateInfo` (line 4), we have the same information described in Section 4.2, the only difference being that the abstract label for the location is $\mathtt{Location}^{37}$ instead of the concrete label $\mathtt{Location}_1$[6]. The same consideration applies to the results of the concatenation at line 17.

For the `IMSI` example, the abstract semantics tracks that we log the abstract datum $\langle \mathtt{IMSI}, \{([sub, 0, 6], \mathtt{IMSI})\}, \{([sub, 0, 6], \mathtt{IMSI})\}\rangle$.

The following theorem formalizes the soundness of the analysis.

[5] Observe that this semantics does not capture indirect information flow.

[6] For the sake of simplicity, we ignore the issues related with heap abstraction. It has been demonstrated [16] that value domains (like AD^a and V^a) can be combined with heap abstractions relying on standard operators of value domains.

Theorem 2. *The abstract semantics of a program P with an abstract datastore D^a is a conservative (sound) over-approximation of the enhanced concrete semantics of P with a concrete datastore $D \in \gamma(D^a)$.*

Proof. By induction on the lenght of the trace as in [23], by lifting the local correctness of the operations to the Cartesian product [8].

We observe in particular that for each execution of P with input $\mathtt{I}$, if a value assigned to a variable v in the store is obtained from values coming from local data stored in ℓ through operations in R, then there is a corresponding abstract trace of P with input $\alpha(\mathtt{I})$, assigning v an abstract atomic datum ad such that (i) $\ell^a \in \mathtt{src}(ad)$, and (ii) $R \subseteq \{\mathtt{op} : (\mathtt{op}^a, \ell^a_j) \in \mathtt{links}(\ell^a, ad)\}$ (where $\ell^a = \alpha(\ell)$ is the label in the abstract datastore representing ℓ).

6 Confidentiality and Obfuscation

So far, we made no distinctions among data contained in the data-store, with respect to their confidentiality level. In general, we can consider a lattice of confidentiality levels $\mathtt{S}$, and we can associate to each label ℓ in $\mathtt{Lab}$ an element $s_\ell \in \mathtt{S}$. Confidentiality levels are assigned to labels, and values corresponding to these labels will inherit from them the same confidentiality level.

On the operation side, we introduce the notion of *obfuscation degree*. The intuitive idea is that if you know which operation has been applied to get an expression, and the expression itself, you can look at the amount of information which is necessary to recover the sources the operation applied to. This leads us to assume the existence of a partial-order relation among operations that captures their different obfuscation impact.

This can be seen as a generalization of the all-or-nothing tainting approach [37,39], where only declassification operators (e.g., encryption) are tracked.

The obfuscation degree of an operator can be seen as a measure of the complexity of the brute-force analysis needed by an external observer in order to detect the actual source data when knowing just the result of the operation and the applied operator.

Definition 9 (Obfuscation Degree). *Consider a complete lattice $(\mathtt{O}, \sqsubseteq_{\mathtt{O}})$, and a map $\zeta : Op \to \mathtt{O}$, such that $\zeta(op_1) \sqsubseteq_{\mathtt{O}} \zeta(op_2)$ if the obfuscation power of op_1 is smaller than the obfuscation power of op_2. We say that the obfuscation degree of an operator $op \in Op$ is $\zeta(op)$.*

Example. The string operators of $sexp$ introduced in Section 3 have different obfuscation degrees. For instance, $encrypt$ obfuscates more that $hash$, while the power of obfuscation of $substring$ may depend on the indexes used to compute the substring, and the particular information contained in the string. For instance, in the `IMSI` example of Section 2 the `substring` operator at line 2 has a high obfuscation degree, but this relies on the value information tracked on the indexes passed to `substring`.

6.1 Confidentiality of Atomic Data

Given an atomic datum, a confidentiality value can be assigned to it by considering an under- and over-approximation of the confidentiality levels of source data, and by considering an under- and over- approximation of obfuscation power of the operations applied to them.

We first define it at a concrete level, on top of our instrumented atomic data semantics, and then we can lift this notion to the abstract case.

Definition 10 (Confidentiality of Atomic Data for Monotonic Operators). *Let* S *be a lattice representing confidentiality levels of labels. Let* O *be a lattice representing the obfuscation power of operators. Finally, let* η *and* ζ *be functions assigning confidentiality/obfuscation values in* S *and* O *to labels and operators, respectively.*

If the combination of operators in $\bigcup_{i \in I} L_i$ *is monotonic with respect to the obfuscation order in the lattice* O*, the confidentiality value of an atomic datum* $\{\langle \ell_i, L_i \rangle : i \in I\}$ *with respect to* (η, ζ) *is the tuple* $(sc_{min}, sc_{max}, lc_{min}, lc_{max})$*, where:*

$$sc_{min} = \sqcap_{\mathtt{D}}\{\eta(\ell_i) : i \in I\} \qquad lc_{min} = \sqcap_{\mathtt{O}}\{\zeta(op_{ij}) : (op_{ij}, \ell_j) \in L_i, i \in I\}$$
$$sc_{max} = \sqcup_{\mathtt{D}}\{\eta(\ell_i) : i \in I\} \qquad lc_{max} = \sqcup_{\mathtt{O}}\{\zeta(op_{ij}) : (op_{ij}, \ell_j) \in L_i, i \in I\}$$

Example. Imagine that we have L $<$ M $<$ H as both the confidentiality and obfuscation lattice. We then establish that *encrypt* has H obfuscation level, and *hash* has level M, whereas the obfuscation level of substring depends on the parameters: $[sub, k_1, k_2]$ has level L if $k_1 = 6$ and $k_2 = 9$, it has level M if $6 < k_1 + k_2 < 15$, and it has level H if $k_1 + k_2 \leq 6$. Consider then the concrete labels of the `Inmobi` example introduced in Section 4.1. We define as L both `Language` and `Country`, since they do not contain particularly confidential information. Instead, we define as H `AndroidId`, since this datum allows to uniquely identify our Android account, and track our activity. Finally, $\mathtt{Location}_i : i \in \mathbb{N}$ are all M, since these locations allow to identify our geographical location at a given point, but do not uniquely identify us. For the `IMSI` example, we obtain that for the data expression leaked at line 2, i.e. $\langle \mathtt{IMSI}, \{([sub, 0, 6], \mathtt{IMSI})\}\rangle$, we get $sc_{min} = sc_{max} =$ H and $lc_{min} = lc_{max} =$ H. This says that even if sensitive data items are leaked, a powerful obfuscation is definitely applied to them before releasing them.

Notice that Definition 10 is explicitly restricted to the case of operators whose combination is monotonic with respect to the obfuscation order in O. If we are interested to consider also programs where the combination of operators is non-monotonic, we just need to give an obfuscation value to sets of operators instead of singletons.

Definition 11 (Confidentiality of Atomic Data - General Case). *Let* S *be a lattice representing confidentiality levels of labels. Let* O *be a lattice representing the obfuscation power of operators. Finally, let* η *be a function assigning confidentiality values in* S *to labels, and let* ζ *be a function assigning to each set of operators an interval in* O $\times$ O *representing its min and max obfuscation power.*

The confidentiality value of an atomic datum $\{\langle \ell_i, L_i \rangle : i \in I\}$ *with respect to* (η, ζ) *is the tuple* $(sc_{min}, sc_{max}, lc_{min}, lc_{max})$*, where:*

$$sc_{min} = \sqcap_{\mathtt{D}}\{\eta(\ell_i) : i \in I\} \qquad lc_{min} = \sqcap_{\mathtt{O}}\{\pi_1(\zeta(\{op_{ij} : (op_{ij}, \ell_j) \in L_i\})) : i \in I\}$$
$$sc_{max} = \sqcup_{\mathtt{D}}\{\eta(\ell_i) : i \in I\} \qquad lc_{max} = \sqcup_{\mathtt{O}}\{\pi_2(\zeta(\{op_{ij} : (op_{ij}, \ell_j) \in L_i\})) : i \in I\}$$

where π_1 *and* π_2 *denote the on the min and max element of the interval, respectively.*

Notice that keeping track of mimimal confidentaility and maximal obfuscation allows us (when they are equal to maximal confidentiality and minimal obfuscation, respctively) to be aware of the precision of these values.

6.2 Confidentiality of Abstract Atomic Data

In order to define the confidentiality value of abstract atomic data, we need to assign a confidentiality value to abstract labels. As abstract labels may represent concrete labels with different confidentiality values, the confidentiality function η^a returns an interval min/max of values in $\mathsf{S} \times \mathsf{S}$ instead of a single value. On the obfuscation side, we just lift the value, as we can assume there is a always a one-to-one correspondence between concrete and abstract operators.

As in the concrete setting, we distinguish the case in which all operator combinations behave monotonically with respect to the obfuscation order, from the general case, that takes into account non-monotonic behaviors, the price to pay being to assign obfuscation values to sets of operators instead of single ones.

Definition 12 (Confidentiality Value of Abstract Atomic Data - Monotonic Operators). *Let* S *and* O *be the lattices representing the labels' confidentiality and the obfuscation power of operators, respectively. Let* η *and* ζ *be functions assigning confidentiality/obfuscation values in* S *and* O *to (concrete) labels and operators, respectively. Let* $\eta^a : \mathsf{Lab^a} \to \mathsf{S} \times \mathsf{S}$ *such that* $\eta^a(\ell^a) = [\sqcap\{\eta(\ell) : \ell \in \gamma(\ell^a)\}, \sqcup\{\eta(\ell) : \ell \in \gamma(\ell^a)\}]$. *Let* ζ^a *be the function assigning to each abstract operator the same obfuscation value assigned by* ζ *to the concrete operator it corresponds.*

If the combination of operators in Op *appearing in* $\bigcup_{i \in I} L_i^{a\sqcup}$ *is monotonic with respect to the obfuscation order in* O*, then the confidentiality value of an abstract atomic datum* $\{\langle \ell_i^a, val_i^a, A_i, L_i^{a\sqcap}, L_i^{a\sqcup}\rangle : i \in I\}$ *is a tuple* $(sc^a_{min}, sc^a_{max}, lc^a_{min}, lc^a_{max})$*, where:*

$$sc^a_{min} = \sqcap_{\mathsf{S}}\{\pi_1(\eta^a(\ell_i^a)) : i \in I\} \quad lc^a_{min} = \sqcap_{\mathsf{O}}\{\zeta^a(op^a_{ij}) : (op^a_{ij}, \ell^a_j) \in L_i^{a\sqcap}, i \in I\}$$
$$sc^a_{max} = \sqcup_{\mathsf{S}}\{\pi_2(\eta^a(\ell_i^a)) : i \in I\} \quad lc^a_{max} = \sqcup_{\mathsf{O}}\{\zeta^a(op^a_{ij}) : (op^a_{ij}, \ell^a_j) \in L_i^{a\sqcup}, i \in I\}$$

where π_1 *and* π_2 *denote the min and max element of the interval, respectively.*

Observe that lc^a_{min} is obtained as the greatest lower bound of the obfuscation values corresponding to operators that are surely applied to compute the value, while lc^a_{max} is obtained as the least upper bound of the obfuscation values corresponding to operators that are possibly applied to compute the value. As $L_i^{a\sqcap} \subseteq L_i^{a\sqcup}$ for each $i \in I$, we get that $lc^a_{min} \sqsubseteq_{\mathsf{O}} lc^a_{max}$.

Definition 13 (Confidentiality Value of Abstract Atomic Data - General Case). *Let* S *and* O *be the lattices representing the labels' confidentiality and the obfuscation power of operators, respectively. Let* η *and* ζ *be functions assigning confidentiality/obfuscation values in* S *and* O *to (concrete) labels and operators, respectively. Let* $\eta^a : \mathsf{Lab^a} \to \mathsf{S} \times \mathsf{S}$ *such that* $\eta^a(\ell^a) = [\sqcap\{\eta(\ell) : \ell \in \gamma(\ell^a)\}, \sqcup\{\eta(\ell) : \ell \in \gamma(\ell^a)\}]$. *Finally, let* ζ^a *be a function assigning to each set of (abstract) operators an interval in* $\mathsf{O} \times \mathsf{O}$ *representing the min and max obfuscation power.*

The confidentiality value of an abstract atomic datum $\{\langle \ell_i^a, val_i^a, A_i, L_i^{a\sqcap}, L_i^{a\sqcup}\rangle : i \in I\}$ *is a tuple* $(sc^a_{min}, sc^a_{max}, lc^a_{min}, lc^a_{max})$*, where:*

$$sc^a_{min} = \sqcap_{\mathsf{S}}\{\pi_1(\eta^a(\ell_i^a)) : i \in I\} \quad lc^a_{min} = \sqcap_{\mathsf{O}}\{\pi_1(\zeta^a(S)) : S \subseteq \{op^a_{ij} : (op^a_{ij}, \ell^a_j) \in L_i^{a\sqcup}\}, i \in I\}$$
$$sc^a_{max} = \sqcup_{\mathsf{S}}\{\pi_2(\eta^a(\ell_i^a)) : i \in I\} \quad lc^a_{max} = \sqcup_{\mathsf{O}}\{\pi_2(\zeta^a(S)) : S \subseteq \{op^a_{ij} : (op^a_{ij}, \ell^a_j) \in L_i^{a\sqcup}\}, i \in I\}$$

where π_1 *and* π_2 *denote the on the min and max element of the interval, respectively.*

Notice that lc^a_{min} and lc^a_{max} in the general case are both obtained as the greatest lower bound and least upper bound, respectively, of the obfuscation values corresponding to operators that are possibly applied to compute the value. This conservative approach guarantees the soundness of the result also in presence of operators whose combination does not behave monotonically with respect to obfuscation, i.e. the monotonicity of confidentiality with respect to the partial order in the domain of abstract atomic data.

7 Privacy Compliance Policies

Definition 14 (Confidentiality Policy). *Given the set of data source labels* Lab*, and the confidentiality/obfuscation lattices* S *and* O *for labels and operations, respectively, a confidentiality policy is a tuple* $\pi = (\eta, \zeta, \kappa_{sc\_max}, \kappa_{lc\_min})$ *such that*

- η, ζ *assign each label and each operator a corresponding value in the confidentiality lattices* S *and* O*, respectively.*
- κ_{sc_max} *is a source confidentiality threshold (the max confidentiality level allowed for sources).*
- κ_{lc_min} *is an obfuscation threshold (the min obfuscation level required for operators).*

Given a program P, let X be the set of concrete/abstract atomic data P generated as an output. We say that P satisfies the confidentiality policy $\pi = (\eta, \zeta, \kappa_{sc\_max}, \kappa_{lc\_min})$ if:

$\forall d \in X$, if $(sc_{min}, sc_{max}, lc_{min}, lc_{max})$ is the confidentiality value of d with respect to (η, ζ), then, $sc_{max} \sqsubseteq_{\mathtt{S}} \kappa_{sc\_max}$ and $lc_{min} \sqsupseteq_{\mathtt{O}} \kappa_{lc\_min}$.

Theorem 3. *Consider a program* P*, an abstract datastore* A*, and a confidentiality policy* $\pi = (\eta, \zeta, \kappa_{sc\_max}, \kappa_{lc\_min})$*. If the program* P *terminates, and the output of the analysis on* P *and* A *satisfies* π*, then any actual execution of program* P *on a concrete datastore in* $\gamma(A)$ *satisfies the confidentiality policy* π*.*

Proof. By Theorem 2, and by the monotonicity of confidentiality values with respect to the partial order on the domain of abstract atomic data.

Example. A reasonable privacy policy for the `Inmobi` example of Section 2 may be that a datum can be released only if its obfuscation level is equal or higher than its confidentiality level. This program satisfies this model for `Country` and `Language` (whose confidentiality level is `L` and they are released without any obfuscation), but not for `Location`$_i$ (with confidentiality level `M` and released without any obfuscation) and `AndroidId` (whose confidentiality level is `H` and it is released after invoking *hash*, that is, with obfuscation level `M`).

7.1 Sources' Confidentiality Policies

The definition of confidentiality policy of atomic data discussed in the previous sections allows to capture the min and max levels of confidentiality/obfuscation carried by the values returned by a program, or shared with other applications.

As an orthogonal approach, we may define (at the concrete level) a confidentiality policy as a propositional formula that captures constraints on the allowed releasing levels of confidential data in the datastore, and verify if the atomic data returned by the concrete execution of the program satisfy that formula.

Let Lab denote as usual the set of data source labels, and Op denote the set of operators in the program. Consider a set of propositional variables V (with empty intersection with the set of program variables), and a function λ that maps elements of V into either labels or links.

$$\lambda : \mathtt{V} \longrightarrow \mathtt{Lab} \cup \{(op, \ell) : op \in \mathtt{Op}, \ell \in \mathtt{Lab}\}$$

A *policy formula* is a positive propositional formula on V, i.e. a propositional formula using only $\wedge$, $\vee$ and $\leftrightarrow$ logical operators[7].

Example. For instance, we can express the fact that we can leak the Android ID if encrypted and the location, or the hashed Android ID, or the first six characters of the IMSI, by means of the formula $\varphi = (x \wedge y) \vee z \vee w$, where $\lambda(x) = ([encrypt, k], \mathtt{AndroidId})$, $\lambda(y) = \mathtt{Location}$, and $\lambda(z) = (hash, \mathtt{AndroidId})$, $\lambda(w) = ([sub, 0, 6], \mathtt{AndroidId})$.

Given a set of atomic data S, a set of propositional variables V and an assignment λ on V, we say that S satisfies the policy formula φ on V if $S, \lambda \models \varphi$, as defined inductively as follows:

$$\begin{array}{lll} S, \lambda \models v \in \mathtt{V} & \Leftrightarrow & \begin{cases} \lambda(v) \in \bigcup_{d \in S} \mathtt{src}(d) & \text{if } \lambda(v) \in \mathtt{Lab} \\ \lambda(v) \in \bigcup_{d \in S} \mathtt{links}(d) & \text{otherwise.} \end{cases} \\ S, \lambda \models \varphi_1 \vee \varphi_2 & \Leftrightarrow & S, \lambda \models \varphi_1 \text{ or } S, \lambda \models \varphi_2 \\ S, \lambda \models \varphi_1 \wedge \varphi_2 & \Leftrightarrow & S, \lambda \models \varphi_1 \text{ and } S, \lambda \models \varphi_2 \\ S, \lambda \models \varphi_1 \leftrightarrow \varphi_2 & \Leftrightarrow & S, \lambda \models \varphi_1 \text{ iff } S, \lambda \models \varphi_2. \end{array}$$

Observe that, by construction, if the data resource denoted by $\lambda(x)$ contributes to any of the values represented by the atomic data S, then $S, \lambda \models x$.

Example The formula φ in the Example above is satisfied by the data expressions leaked by either Inmobi and IMSI as described in the Example in Section 3.2.

Observe that checking the policy reduces to checking the satisfiability of the propositional assignment [42].

When we lift to the abstract setting, three-valued models of propositional formulas should be used in order to preserve soundness. Let S^a be a set of abstract atomic data, and $\lambda^a : \mathtt{V} \longrightarrow \mathtt{Lab^a} \cup \{(op^a, \ell^a) : op \in \mathtt{Op}, \ell^a \in \mathtt{Lab^a}\}$ be a function mapping propositional variables into abstract labels and links. Consider the three value assignment

[7] The advantage of using positive formulas, i.e. formulas that are satisfied by assigning true to all its propositional variables, is that they well capture monotonic behaviors [42].

$assign(S^a, \lambda) : \mathtt{V} \mapsto \{\mathtt{true}, \mathtt{false}, \top\}$ defined by

$$assign(S^a, \lambda^a)(v) = \begin{cases} \mathtt{true} & \text{if } \lambda^a(v) \in \mathtt{Lab^a} \text{ and } \lambda^a(v) \in \bigcup_{d \in S} \mathtt{links\_lab}(\mathtt{L}_d^{\sqcap}) \\ & \text{or} \\ & \text{if } \lambda^a(v) \notin \mathtt{Lab^a} \text{ and } \lambda^a(v) \in \bigcup_{d \in S} \mathtt{L}^{\sqcap}(d) \\ \mathtt{false} & \text{if } \lambda^a(v) \in \mathtt{Lab^a} \text{ and } \lambda^a(v) \notin \bigcup_{d \in S} \mathtt{src}(d) \\ & \text{or} \\ & \text{if } \lambda^a(v) \notin \mathtt{Lab^a} \text{ and } \lambda^a(v) \notin \bigcup_{d \in S} \mathtt{L}^{\sqcup}(d) \\ \top & \text{otherwise} \end{cases}$$

(where $\mathtt{L}^{\sqcap}(d)$ and $\mathtt{L}^{\sqcup}(d)$ denote the last two components of d, respectively), and consider the logical operators extended to the top value $\top$ by:

$\wedge$	true	false	$\top$
$\top$	$\top$	false	$\top$

$\vee$	true	false	$\top$
$\top$	true	$\top$	$\top$

$\leftrightarrow$	true	false	$\top$
$\top$	$\top$	$\top$	$\top$

Theorem 4. *Let φ be a positive formula on a set* $\mathtt{V}$ *of propositional variables, S^a be a set of abstract atomic data, and $\lambda^a : \mathtt{V} \longrightarrow \mathtt{Lab^a} \cup \{(op^a, \ell^a) : op \in \mathtt{Op}, \ell^a \in \mathtt{Lab^a}\}$ be a function mapping propositional variables into abstract labels and links. If $assign(S, \lambda)(\varphi) = \mathtt{true}$, then there is a set of atomic data $S \subseteq \bigcup_{d \in S^a} \gamma(d)$ and a function λ satisfying $\forall v \in \mathtt{V} : \lambda(v) \in \gamma_{\mathtt{Lab}}(\lambda^a(v))$, such that $S, \lambda \models \varphi$.*

Proof. By structural induction on the formula φ, and by Theorem 1.

8 Related Work

In this section, we discuss in details how our work compares to some similar approaches in the area in addition to the high-level overview on the state of the art of Section 1.1.

Quantitative Information Flow (QIF) [25] is aimed at measuring the quantity of information that is leaked by a program. A given confidential datum might be manipulated by the program, that at the end releases only partial information. Then, the analysis checks if the quantity of released information is below a given threshold. Our approach shares with QIF the intuition that is crucial to estimates the quantity of information revealed, since ofter it is necessary to partially disclose a part of the information. Nevertheless, instead of measuring a quantity, our approach tracks the set of operators that have been applied to the datum before its release, and then we check if this matches what specified on the policy. We believe that QIF can be seen as an abstraction of a concrete semantics tracking the exact order of operators applied to a datum (instead of a set of operators as we do). In addition, QIF can track implicit flows, while we explicitly ignored these flows as we believe they lead to many false alarms.

Declassification-based approaches [33] suppose that a list of declassifier operators is given, and as soon as one of these operators is applied to a datum, then it can be sent to a sink. Our analysis can represent declassifiers through a policy stating that it is allowed to release the data on which at least one of these operators has been applied.

Decentralized Information Flow Control [20,27] systems represent a finer grained and more expressive model, in which each process can declassify information, rather than a central authority as in centralized system and classical declassification-based approaches. Nevertheless, our analysis can support this more complex scenarios by defining specific policies per process.

Another approach that has gained relevant results recently is Differential Privacy [13,14]. Given a data store, the goal of Differential Privacy is to discover if the variation of a query over the data set stays below a given threshold when an entry is added. Usually, some statistical noise is added in order to ensure differential privacy. Our approach may track how the data from the data set is aggregated and noise added, and this may be a first step towards proving differential privacy. However, how to relate this information on the operators applied to data and ϵ-differential privacy is not straightforward at all, and it requires further investigation.

9 Conclusion

Our semantic framework for fine-grained information-flow analysis captures how the values released by an application may partially reveal confidential data stored on the device through different levels of obfuscation. The enhanced concrete semantics and the generic abstract domain we presented provide a workbench for (static) analysis of mobile apps that can be tuned by setting a few parameters: the domain representing values, the domain representing data locations, and the confidentiality and obfuscation values for data and operators. This data-centric approach may be utilized to refine existing tools like [15,41,40] aimed at enforcing privacy policies, providing the user with more accurate privacy control.

The problem of formalizing how the semantics of operations reflects on the corresponding obfuscation values, as well as the problem of assisting the user in the definition of privacy compliance policies remain of course, as there is a tradeoff between the amount of sensitive information that she allows the device to release and the accuracy and efficiency of some functionalities.

Aknowledgments. Work partially supported by PRIN "Security Horizons".

References

1. Alvim, M.S., Scedrov, A., Schneider, F.B.: When not all bits are equal: Worth-based information flow. In: Abadi, M., Kremer, S. (eds.) POST 2014. LNCS, vol. 8414, pp. 120–139. Springer, Heidelberg (2014)
2. Amtoft, T., Banerjee, A.: A logic for information flow analysis with an application to forward slicing of simple imperative programs. Science of Compututer Programming 64, 3–28 (2007)
3. AppBrain. Adnetwork stats, `http://www.appbrain.com/stats/libraries/ad`
4. Arzt, S., Rasthofer, S., et al.: Flowdroid: Precise context, flow, field, object-sensitive and lifecycle-aware taint analysis for android apps. In: PLDI. ACM (2014)
5. Askarov, A., Myers, A.: A semantic framework for declassification and endorsement. In: Gordon, A.D. (ed.) ESOP 2010. LNCS, vol. 6012, pp. 64–84. Springer, Heidelberg (2010)
6. Cavadini, S.: Secure slices of insecure programs. In: ASIACCS. ACM Press (2008)
7. Chaudhuri, A.: Language-based security on android. In: PLAS. ACM (2009)

8. Cortesi, A., Costantini, G., Ferrara, P.: A survey on product operators in abstract interpretation. EPTCS 129, 325–336 (2013)
9. Costantini, G., Ferrara, P., Cortesi, A.: Static analysis of string values. In: Qin, S., Qiu, Z. (eds.) ICFEM 2011. LNCS, vol. 6991, pp. 505–521. Springer, Heidelberg (2011)
10. Cousot, P., Cousot, R.: Abstract interpretation: Past, present and future. In: CSL-LICS. ACM (2014)
11. Cousot, P., Cousot, R., Logozzo, F.: A parametric segmentation functor for fully automatic and scalable array content analysis. In: POPL. ACM (2011)
12. Denning, D.E.: A lattice model of secure information flow. Communications of the ACM 19, 236–243 (1976)
13. Dwork, C.: Differential privacy: A survey of results. In: Agrawal, M., Du, D.-Z., Duan, Z., Li, A. (eds.) TAMC 2008. LNCS, vol. 4978, pp. 1–19. Springer, Heidelberg (2008)
14. Ebadi, H., Sands, D., Schneider, G.: Differential privacy: Now it's getting personal. In: POPL. ACM (2015)
15. Enck, W., Gilbert, P., et al.: Taintdroid: An information flow tracking system for real-time privacy monitoring on smartphones. Comm. of the ACM 57(3), 99–106 (2014)
16. Ferrara, P.: Generic combination of heap and value analyses in abstract interpretation. In: McMillan, K.L., Rival, X. (eds.) VMCAI 2014. LNCS, vol. 8318, pp. 302–321. Springer, Heidelberg (2014)
17. Halder, R., Zanioli, M., Cortesi, A.: Information leakage analysis of database query languages. In: SAC. ACM (2014)
18. Hammer, C., Snelting, G.: Flow-sensitive, context-sensitive, and object-sensitive information flow control based on program dependence graphs. International Journal of Information Security 8, 399–422 (2009)
19. Hornyack, P., Han, S., Jung, J., Schechter, S.E., Wetherall, D.: These aren't the droids you're looking for: retrofitting android to protect data from imperious applications. In: CCS. ACM (2011)
20. Krohn, M.N., Tromer, E.: Noninterference for a practical DIFC-based operating system. In: IEEE S&P. IEEE (2009)
21. Li, B.: Analyzing information-flow in java program based on slicing technique. SIGSOFT Softw. Eng. Notes 27, 98–103 (2002)
22. Lochbihler, A., Snelting, G.: On temporal path conditions in dependence graphs. Journal of Automated Software Engineering 16, 263–290 (2009)
23. Logozzo, F.: Class invariants as abstract interpretation of trace semantics. Computer Languages, Systems & Structures 35, 100–142 (2009)
24. Lu, L., Li, Z., Wu, Z., Lee, W., Jiang, G.: Chex: statically vetting android apps for component hijacking vulnerabilities. In: CCS. ACM (2012)
25. McCamant, S., Ernst, M.D.: Quantitative information flow as network flow capacity. In: PLDI. ACM (2008)
26. Miné, A.: The octagon abstract domain. Higher-Order and Symbolic Computation 19(1), 31–100 (2006)
27. Myers, A.C., Liskov, B.: A decentralized model for information flow control. In: SOSP. ACM (1997)
28. Nanevski, A., Banerjee, A., Garg, D.: Dependent type theory for verification of information flow and access control policies. ACM TOPLAS 35(2), 6:1–6:41 (2013)
29. Omoronyia, I., Cavallaro, L., et al.: Engineering adaptive privacy: on the role of privacy awareness requirements. In: ICSE. IEEE/ACM (2013)
30. Pottier, F., Simonet, V.: Information flow inference for ml. ACM Transactions on Programming Languages and Systems 25, 117–158 (2003)
31. Rasthofer, S., Lovat, E., Bodden, E.: Droid force: Enforcing complex, data-centric, system-wide policies in android. In: ARES (2014)

32. Sabelfeld, A., Myers, A.C.: Language-based information-flow security. IEEE Journal on Selected Areas in Communications 21, 5–19 (2003)
33. Sabelfeld, A., Sands, D.: Declassification: Dimensions and principles. Journal of Computer Security 17, 517–548 (2009)
34. Smith, G.: Principles of secure information flow analysis. In: Christodorescu, M., et al. (eds.) Malware Detection. Advances in Information Security, vol. 27, pp. 291–307. Springer (2007)
35. Smith, S.F., Thober, M.: Refactoring programs to secure information flows. In: PLAS. ACM (2006)
36. Spiekermann, S., Cranor, L.F.: Engineering privacy. IEEE Trans. Software Eng. 35(1), 67–82 (2009)
37. Sridharan, M., Artzi, S., Pistoia, M., Guarnieri, S., Tripp, O., Berg, R.: F4f: Taint analysis of framework-based web applications. In: OOPSLA. ACM (2011)
38. Tripp, O., Ferrara, P., Pistoia, M.: Hybrid security analysis of web javascript code via dynamic partial evaluation. In: ISSTA. ACM (2014)
39. Tripp, O., Pistoia, M., Fink, S.J., Sridharan, M., Weisman, O.: Taj: Effective taint analysis of web applications. In: PLDI. ACM (2009)
40. Tripp, O., Rubin, J.: A bayesian approach to privacy enforcement in smartphones. In: USENIX Security (2014)
41. Xiao, X., Tillmann, N., Fähndrich, M., de Halleux, J., Moskal, M.: User-aware privacy control via extended static-information flow analysis. In: ASE. ACM (2012)
42. Zanioli, M., Ferrara, P., Cortesi, A.: Sails: Static analysis of information leakage with sample. In: SAC. ACM (2012)

Induction for SMT Solvers

Andrew Reynolds and Viktor Kuncak*

École Polytechnique Fédérale de Lausanne (EPFL), Switzerland
{firstname.lastname}@epfl.ch

Abstract. Satisfiability modulo theory solvers are increasingly being used to solve quantified formulas over structures such as integers and term algebras. Quantifier instantiation combined with ground decision procedure alone is insufficient to prove many formulas of interest in such cases. We present a set of techniques that introduce inductive reasoning into SMT solving algorithms that is sound with respect to the interpretation of structures in SMT-LIB standard. The techniques include inductive strengthening of conjecture to be proven, as well as facility to automatically discover subgoals during an inductive proof, where subgoals themselves can be proven using induction. The techniques have been implemented in CVC4. Our experiments show that the developed techniques have good performance and coverage of a range of inductive reasoning problems. Our experiments also show the impact of different representations of natural numbers and quantifier instantiation techniques on the performance of inductive reasoning. Our solution is freely available in the CVC4 development repository. In addition its overall effectiveness, it has an advantage of accepting SMT-LIB input and being integrated with other SMT solving techniques of CVC4.

1 Introduction

One of the strengths of satisfiability modulo theory (SMT) solvers [3,10] lies in their efficient handling of many useful theories arising in software verification. These theories often model ubiquitous data types, such as integers, bitvectors, arrays, algebraic data types, sets, or maps. The theories of many of these data types can be naturally thought of as statements that hold in certain concrete structures (for example, integers), or families of structures [20] (for example, lists instantiated into lists of integers). Such semantics is also supported by the SMT-LIB standard's definition of theories [1], meaning that the satisfiability of such formulas is determined by its interpretation in these structures, whether or not the satisfiability problem is easily axiomatizable in first-order logic, or whether it is decidable.

From the early days, many SMT solvers and their predecessors have been supporting satisfiability of not only quantifier-free but also universally *quantified* formulas, typically using quantifier instantiation strategies [11], which have become increasingly more robust over time [12,13,24]. Quantifiers together with uninterpreted functions and theory-specific symbols give great modeling power to the input language.

* This work is supported in part by the European Research Council (ERC) Project *Implicit Programming*.

D. D'Souza et al. (Eds.): VMCAI 2015, LNCS 8931, pp. 80–98, 2015.

Unfortunately, the use of quantifier instantiation alone for such problems is highly incomplete, not only in a theoretical sense (the problem is not even recursively enumerable), but also in a very concrete practical sense. Namely, current solvers cannot solve any statements requiring non-trivial use of induction! This is an acknowledged fact in the SMT community. For example, the Z3 tutorial [2] clarifies explicitly that *"The ground decision procedures for recursive datatypes don't lift to establishing inductive facts. Z3 does not contain methods for producing proofs by induction."* Similarly, CVC4 (until now) did not contain a method to perform induction, nor did most other competitive SMT solvers of which we are aware.

Automating induction is a considered very difficult for automated provers [5,9]. Recent progress has been made in several tools [7, 16, 17], with which we make detailed comparison in Section 4. Interactive theorem provers heavily use inductive proofs, but have largely avoided to automate induction within their tactics, suggesting that this is among the most difficult tasks to automate. A notable exception is the ACL2 prover, which has early been recognized for its sophisticated inductive reasoning [19]. However, these tools miss an opportunity to fully benefit from efficient theory reasoning: they encode most values using algebraic data types, and need to prove from scratch theory lemmas, which could be handled more efficiently with an SMT approach.

It is worthwhile mentioning that program analysis and verification tools implicitly incorporate inductive reasoning into their algorithms. In fact, it could be argued that the current division of tasks between program analyzers (including software model checkers and verifiers) delegates non-inductive reasoning to SMT solvers, and performs induction in a specialized manner. We do not claim that the techniques we propose will replace such verification techniques, often specialized for the meaning of non-deterministic programs. Instead, we expect that they will complement them, in similar ways that algebraic reasoning of SMT solvers complements fixpoint reasoning of abstract interpretation and software model checking engines. Note that for infinite-state systems, the form of invariants inferred by these tools is often of a particular form, either given by an abstract domain, or given by a class of formulas such as linear constraints [26], or constraint satisfying certain templates [14, 15, 18, 23]. Thefore, especially in cases when invariants themselves may contain recursive functions, it seems desirable to incorporate inductive reasoning into an SMT solver. In fact, Rustan Leino has proposed a pre-processing of formulas to incorporate inductive reasoning, which already proved very helpful for a program verifier based on an SMT solver [22].

In this paper, we present the first technique and implementation of inductive reasoning *within* an SMT solver. Among the advantages of this approach are not only convenience and, in some cases, performance, but also the ability to exploit the internal state of the solver to automatically discover subgoals that themselves need to be proved by induction, which is essential to be able to prove more difficult conjectures.

Contributions. This paper makes the following contributions:

- We describe an approach for supporting inductive reasoning inside an SMT solver that integrates well with existing approaches for handling quantified formulas in SMT. The starting point of this approach is inductively strengthening existentially quantified conjectures.

- We present techniques that help to infer relevant subgoals used in inductive proofs. The generation of subgoals is based on introduction of splitting lemmas into the DPLL(T) framework. The automatically discovered lemmas are generated by enumerating potential equalities while applying the following filtering techniques:
  - limiting the generalization to terms that refer to variables in the conjecture being proven;
  - inferring universally quantified identities that allow us to remove subgoals that are found to be equivalent to others;
  - removing subgoals that are contradicted by ground facts in the current context.
- We provide a set of 933 benchmarks in the SMT-LIB2 syntax, which are publicly available at `http://lara.epfl.ch/~reynolds/VMCAI2015-ind`. This is the first set of SMT-LIB2 benchmarks targeting inductive reasoning, and includes several previously used benchmark sets used to exercise inductive theorem provers.
- We demonstrate that our implementation in the SMT solver CVC4 performs well on this set of benchmarks, in particular through the use of newly developed techniques for inductive reasoning described in this paper. We show our approach is competitive with existing tools for automating induction, comparing favorably against these tools in many cases.

2 Skolemization with Inductive Strengthening

To determine the T-satisfiability of an input set of ground clauses F for some background theory T, a DPLL(T)-based SMT solver first consults a SAT solver for finding a subset of its literals M (which we will call a *context*) that propositionally entails F. If successful, the ground decision procedure for theory T determines the satisfiability of M, adding additional clauses to F as necessary when M is found to be T-unsatisfiable. When extending SMT to quantified formulas, the input F (and likewise a context M) may contain literals whose atoms are universally quantified formulas $\forall x.\ P(x)$.

SMT solvers commonly handle universally quantified formulas $\forall x.P(x)$ from M using instantiation-based techniques, and handle existentially quantified formulas[1] $\neg\forall x.\ P(x)$ from M by *skolemization*. In the latter case, they infer the lemma $(\forall x.\ P(x)) \vee \neg P(k)$, where k is a fresh constant, which is then added to F. We will refer to $\neg P(k)$ as the skolemization of $\neg\forall x.\ P(x)$, and k as the skolem constant for $\neg\forall x.\ P(x)$. Assuming $P(k)$ is quantifier-free, the aforementioned lemma enables a ground decision procedure to reason about the satisfiability of $\neg P(k)$. Unfortunately, SMT solvers have limited ability to prove the unsatisfiability of $\neg P(k)$ in cases when inductive reasoning is required, as in the following example.

Example 1. Assume an axiomatization of the length function $len : List \rightarrow Int$:

$$len(nil) \approx 0 \qquad (A_1)$$
$$\forall xy.\ len(cons(x,y)) \approx 1 + len(y) \qquad (A_2)$$

[1] Informally, we refer to $\neg\forall x.\ P(x)$ as an existentially quantified formula, since it is equivalent to $\exists x.\ \neg P(x)$.

and the conjecture $\psi := \forall x.\ len(x) \geq 0$. To determine the satisfiability of $F := \{A_1, A_2, \neg\psi\}$, the SMT solver by skolemization will add the clause $(\psi \vee \neg len(k) \geq 0)$ to F for fresh constant k, after which we find a context $M := \{A_1, A_2, \neg\psi, \neg len(k) \geq 0\}$ that propositionally entails it. The (combined) decision procedure for inductive datatypes and linear arithmetic will determine the satisfiability of the ground porition of this context, $\{A_1, \neg len(k) \geq 0\}$, where it will find a model where $k \approx cons(head(k), tail(k))$ and $len(k) \approx -1$. By instantiation, the solver may add $(\neg A_2 \vee len(cons(head(k), tail(k))) \approx 1 + len(tail(k)))$ to F. In turn, the solver will find a context M' that in addition to M now contains the right disjunct above. The ground portion of M' is satisfied, for instance, by a model where $len(k) \approx -1$ and $len(tail(k)) \approx -2$. Again by instantiation, the solver may add $(\neg A_2 \vee len(cons(head(tail(k)), tail(tail(k)))) \approx 1 + len(tail(tail(k))))$ to F, and this loop will continue indefinitely. This is not a coincidence: there exist, in fact, a non-standard model of the axioms used to decide the ground theory of algebraic data types, in which the conjecture is false. In other words, the theory axioms implicitly used within the solver are inadequate for our purpose. □

The aforementioned example can be solved using inductive reasoning. In particular, we may assume without loss of generality that our skolem constant k is the smallest such list that satisfies the property $\neg len(k) \geq 0$, thereby allowing us to assume in particular that $len(tail(k)) \geq 0$. More generally, we may strengthen a conjecture for a variable of sort T when we have a well-founded ordering R over terms of sort T. The general scheme for strengthening our skolemization according to such an R is:

$$(\forall x.\ P(x)) \vee (\neg P(k) \wedge \forall x.\ (R(x, k) \Rightarrow P(x))) \quad (1)$$

where k is a fresh constant. We call $\forall x.\ (R(x, k) \Rightarrow P(x))$ the *inductive strengthening* of $\neg P(k)$ based on R. Note that conjoining the formula (1) with the initial input formula F does not affect the outcome of the satisfiability of F. The intuition is that if a universal statement does not hold, then there exists the least counterexample with respect to R.

Remark 1. Let φ be the formula (1) for well-founded relation R. The formula $\exists k.\ \varphi$ holds in all interpretations.

Proof: Consider any interpretation for symbols other than k. If $\forall x.\ P(x)$ holds in this interpretation, then the first disjunct of φ holds in this interpretation. We show that otherwise the second disjunct holds. Consider the set S of all elements y of sort T in this structure such that $\neg P(y)$. Let y_0 any element in S, which exists because $\forall x.\ P(x)$ does not hold. If we consider an arbitrary maximal sequence $y_0, y_1, \ldots \in S$ such that $R(y_{i+1}, y_i)$ for all i, then this sequence must be finite and stop at some y_n, because R is well founded. Let us interpret the fresh constant k as y_n. Then $\neg P(k)$ holds because $y_n \in S$. Because y_n is the last element of the sequence, k also satisfies $\forall x.\ R(x, k) \Rightarrow P(x)$, so the second disjunct of φ holds. ■

Two examples of well-founded relations R in the context of SMT solving are structural induction for inductive datatypes where $R(s, t)$ if and only if s is a subterm of t, and natural number induction on integers where $R(s, t)$ if and only $0 \leq s < t$. Both of these refer to forms of *strong induction*, where a conjecture is assumed for all terms less than k according to a transitive relation R. Alternatively, we may apply forms of *weak induction*, where for inductive datatypes $R(s,t)$ if and only if s is a direct subterm of t, and for integers $R(s,t)$ if and only if $0 \leq s = t-1$. The advantage of the weak form for induction is that, in the case of inductive datatypes, $R(s,t)$ can be encoded without introducing a subterm relation, which is not supported natively by the solver.

Example 2. The skolemization with inductive strengthening of the negated conjecture $\neg\forall x.\ len(x) \geq 0$ in Example 1 based on weak structural induction is:

$$\neg len(k) \geq 0 \wedge \forall y.(k \approx cons(head(k), tail(k)) \wedge y \approx tail(k)) \Rightarrow len(y) \geq 0)$$

The right conjunct in the formula above simplifies to $k \approx cons(head(k), tail(k)) \Rightarrow len(tail(k)) \geq 0$. With this constraint, the original conjecture can be solved immediately, noting that the length of $tail(k)$ is forced to be non-negative in the case where $k \approx cons(head(k), tail(k))$. □

For quantification over multiple variables, we consider induction schemes that are limited to lexicographic orderings. As a result, we skolemize variables one at a time and independently, starting from the outermost variable. Thus a formula $\neg\forall xy.\ P(x,y)$ is skolemized as: $\forall xy.\ P(x,y) \vee (\neg\forall y.P(k,y) \wedge \forall xy.\ R(x,k) \Rightarrow P(x,y))$. The first conjunct in the conclusion, $\neg\forall y.P(k,y)$, can then be skolemized in the same manner if and when it is necessary to do so. It is also important to note that the variable y is universally quantified in the rightmost conjunct, meaning that $P(x,y)$ can be assumed for any y assuming we choose an x that is smaller k according to R.

For some problems requiring inductive reasoning, it is challenging to determine which variable to apply induction on first. In our approach, the SMT solver is capable of applying induction for different variable orders simultaneously. For instance, in the case of a quantified formula over x and y and induction on y is necessary, this can be done simply by inferring: $\forall xy.P(x,y) \vee \neg\forall yx.P(x,y)$. Subsequently, we will apply induction based on y if and when skolemization is applied to $\neg\forall yx.P(x,y)$.

Our approach is closely related to the approach used in the Dafny tool [22], where (non-negated) conjectures are inductively weakened in an intermediate language before being sent to an SMT solver. Here, we advocate an approach where this transformation is pushed within the core of the SMT solver. This gives several advantages over external approaches. First, the SMT solver may have insight into how and when to invoke inductive strengthening, performing this step lazily or with multiple induction schemes as necessary. Second, certain benchmarks require the skolemization of existentially quantified formulas during the search procedure when a new quantified formula is created or becomes asserted. This may occur, for instance, when instantiating quantified formulas with nested existentially quantified formulas, or in the case when the SMT solver itself introduces an existentially quantified formula of interest, as we will see in the next section. Our approach enables the SMT solver to inductively strengthen its assertions for each such skolemization, which otherwise would not be possible if done externally.

3 Subgoal Generation

A majority of the complexity in inductive reasoning lies in discovering intermediate lemmas, or subgoals, that are required for proving the overall conjecture. A variety of tools, including [7,16,17], have focused on inferring such subgoals automatically in the context of automated theorem proving. In context of software verification, a subgoal corresponds to a necessary loop invariant or adequate post-condition describing the input/output behavior of a function that is required for a proof to succeed. Tools for this purpose that analyze functional programs include [21,23,25].

In this section, we use the following as a running example.

Example 3. Consider the (combined) theory T of equality and inductively defined datatypes Nat and $List$ whose signature Σ contains the functions $plus$, app, rev, and sum, representing natural number addition, list append and reverse, and summing the elements of list respectively. Let $\mathcal{A}$ be the axiomatization of app, rev, and sum where for the latter, $\mathcal{A}$ contains:

$$sum(nil) \approx Z \quad \forall xy.\ sum(cons(x, y)) \approx plus(x, sum(y))$$

Now, consider the conjecture $\psi := \forall x.\ sum(rev(x)) \approx sum(x)$. Showing the validity of this conjecture requires, for instance, discovering the intermediate subgoals $\varphi_1 := \forall xy.\ sum(app(x, y)) \approx plus(sum(x), sum(y))$ and $\varphi_2 := \forall xy.\ plus(x, y) \approx plus(y, x)$. Even more so, proving φ_1 itself requires induction and the intermediate subgoal $\varphi_3 := \forall xyz.\ plus(x, plus(y, z)) \approx plus(plus(x, y), z)$. As we will see in our evaluation, theory reasoning capabilities of the SMT solver can preempt the need for discovering the latter two subgoals φ_2 and φ_3, by enabling the solver to assume that various properties of the builtin integer operator for addition $+$ also hold for applications of the function $plus$. Even so, the solver will not succeed in showing the validity of ψ until it has first discovered and proven φ_1, or some other sufficient subgoal. □

A naive approach for subgoal generation is to enumerate candidate subgoals according to a fair strategy until a set of sufficient subgoals is discovered. In Example 3, we could enumerate all well-typed equalities between Σ-terms built from variables, constructors of sort $List$ and Nat, $plus$, app, rev, and sum up to a particular size until the subgoal φ_1 is discovered. However, an exhaustive enumeration of subgoals is not scalable even for cases where the signature and necessary subgoals are small. It is thus crucial to avoid enumeration of a vast majority of candidate subgoals φ, either by determining that φ is not relevant, redundant, or does not hold.

In this section, we present a design and implementation of an additional component of an SMT solver, which we will refer to as the *subgoal generation module*, whose aim is to discover subgoals that are relevant for proving a given conjecture. We first describe our scheme for basic operation of the subgoal generation module in relation to the rest of the SMT solver, and then describe several heuristics for how it determines which subgoals are likely to be relevant. In particular, these heuristics will make use of the information maintained at the core of a DPLL(T)-based SMT solver. Conceptually, our approach is similar to that of subgoal generation in the Quickspec tool [8], which enumerates candidate subgoals in a principled fashion that can in turn be used within a theorem prover [7]. Like their approach, here we limit ourselves to equality subgoals only. Unlike Quickspec, however, we benefit from integration into a DPLL(T) engine.

```
proc check(F)
  M := findSatAssignment(F)
  if M = fail
    return "unsat"
  else
    C := getTConflict(M)
    if C = fail
      I := quantInst(M) ∪ subgoalGen(M)
      return check(F ∪ I)
    else
      return check(F ∪ ¬C)
```

Fig. 1. The method check, giving the interaction of components within an SMT solver, for an input set of clauses F. The SAT solver (method findSatAssignment), when possible, returns a set of literals M that propositionally entails F. The ground decision procedure(s) (method getTConflict), when possible, returns a subset $C \subseteq M$ that is inconsistent according to the background theory. The quantifier instantiation and subgoal generation modules (methods quantInst and subgoalGen) return a set of clauses I based on M.

3.1 Subgoal Generation in DPLL(T)

To prove the conjecture ψ in Example 3, the solver must (1) determine that φ_1 is a relevant subgoal, (2) prove that φ_1 holds, and (3) prove the original conjecture ψ under the assumption φ_1. The DPLL(T) search procedure used by SMT solvers enables a straightforward scheme for accomplishing both (2) and (3). If the subgoal generation module determines that $\forall x.t \approx s$ is a relevant subgoal, it adds $(\neg \forall x.t \approx s) \vee \forall x.t \approx s$, which we refer to as a *splitting lemma*, to the set of clauses currently known by the solver, and additionally may set its decision heuristic to explore the branch $\neg \forall x.t \approx s$ first. A subgoal may be proven by induction, since the skolemization of the assertion $\neg \forall x.\, t \approx s$ can in turn be inductively strengthened according to the method described in Section 2. Subsequently, the solver will backtrack and assert $\forall x.t \approx s$ positively if and only if the standard conflict analysis mechanism of the SMT solver causes $\neg \forall x.\ t \approx s$ to be backtracked during the search. In terms of Example 3, the solver will succeed in proving ψ only after it does so for such a $\forall x.t \approx s$ that entails φ_1. Notice that this behavior is managed entirely by a combination of the SAT solver, ground decision procedures and quantifier instantiation mechanism of the SMT solver, and requires no further intervention from the subgoal generation module, thus enabling it to focus its attention solely on its choice of which subgoals to introduce. This scheme also allows conjecturing multiple candidate subgoals to the system at once, and as needed, during the search, which plays to the advantage of an SMT solver, which is capable of handling inputs having a large number of clauses.

Figure 1 gives the overall interaction between the ground solver, quantifier instantiation, and subgoal generation modules. Notice that the quantifier instantiation and subgoal generation both run after the SAT solver finds a context M which propositionally entails F that is T-consistent according to ground decision procedure(s). Both modules add additional clauses I to F in the form of instances of quantified formulas and splitting lemmas for candidate subgoals respectively. It remains to be shown which subgoals are chosen by the subgoal generation module, i.e. the subgoals in the splitting lemmas returned by the method subgoalGen(M) for context M.

As mentioned, a naive approach for subgoal generation amounts to a fair enumeration of candidate subgoals. At its core, our approach performs such an enumeration, but discards all candidates that it determines are not useful. For enumerating candidate subgoals in a fair manner, our approach considers subgoals that are smaller than larger ones according to the following measure. Let *size* of a term t be the number of function applications occurring in t plus the number of duplicated variables. For instance, the size of $f(g(x, y))$ is 2, and the the size of $g(x, f(x))$ is 3. The size of a subgoal of the form $\forall x.\ t \approx s$ is the maximum of the size of t and the size of s. Thus, the size of the subgoal φ_1 from Example 3 has size 3. Given a fixed signature Σ, we enumerate the set of all subgoals $\mathcal{S}_n$ of size n, starting with $n = 0$. We will call this the set of *candidate subgoals of size* n. For each n, we heuristically determine a subset $\mathcal{S}_n^R \subseteq \mathcal{S}_n$ of these subgoals, which we will call *relevant*; all others we say are *filtered*. The method subgoalGen returns splitting lemmas corresponding to a subset of the subgoals $\mathcal{S}_n^R$, where the total number of splitting lemmas it returns does not exceed some fixed number (typically ≤ 3). We continue constructing relevant subgoals for increasing values of n until this limit is reached. In the rest of this section, we will focus on three effective techniques for determining which subgoals are relevant, and which should be filtered.

3.2 Filtering Candidate Subgoals

Filtering Based on Active Conjectures. Consider the conjecture $\psi := \neg\forall x.\ sum(rev(x)) \approx sum(x)$ from Example 3, and its corresponding skolemization $\neg sum(rev(k)) \approx sum(k)$. An implicit side effect of this skolemization is that a new function symbol k (not occurring in func(Σ)) is introduced, thus requiring the solver to determine the satisfiability of constraint in a signature Σ' that extends Σ with k. Assuming all functions in Σ are axiomatized as terminating functions in our axiomatization, $\mathcal{A}$, the introduction of k into our constraint is in fact the very reason why inductive reasoning is required, since now the solver cannot reason about Σ'-constraints simply based on a combination of ground theory reasoning and unfolding function definitions by quantifier instantiation. Based on this observation, our first form of filtering is to generate candidate subgoals that state properties about terms that generalize Σ'-terms only, in particular, ones that are not entailed to be equivalent to Σ-terms in the current context.

We thus say a term t is inactive if $M \models_T t \approx s$ for some Σ-term s, and active otherwise.[2] An existentially quantified formula is *inactive in context* M if and only if its skolem constant is inactive in M, and active otherwise. For instance in Example 3, if $k \approx nil \in M$, then k and ψ are inactive in M, indicating that inductive reasoning is not required for reasoning about the skolemization of ψ in M. Indeed, $k \approx nil, \neg sum(rev(k)) \approx sum(k)$ imply $\neg sum(rev(nil)) \approx sum(nil)$, and determining the satisfiability of $\mathcal{A} \wedge \neg sum(rev(nil)) \approx sum(nil)$ can be done by a ground decision procedure and quantifier instantiation for unfolding function definitions.

[2] Determining if term t is active in M can be accomplished when t is an inductive datatype, since our decision procedure for inductive datatypes [4] infers all entailed equalities.

We say that a term $f(t_1, \ldots, t_n)$ occurring in M is *ground-relevant in* M if and only if at least one of $t_1, \ldots, t_n$ is active in M. We say a Σ-term t is *relevant in* M if and only if it generalizes a ground-relevant term s from M, that is, M entails $(t \approx s)\sigma$ for some grounding substitution over $FV(t)$, the free variables of t. Notice that since s contains symbols from Σ', all relevant terms are necessarily non-ground. For context M, the subgoal generation module will only consider subgoals $\forall \boldsymbol{x}.t \approx s$ where t is relevant in M, and $FV(s) \subseteq FV(t)$.

Example 4. Assume a context $M = \{sum(k) \approx Z, sum(rev(k)) \approx S(Z), rev(k) \approx nil\}$. The term $sum(x)$ is relevant in context M since it generalizes the term $sum(k)$, which is ground-relevant since k is active. The term $sum(rev(x))$ is not relevant in context M since it only generalizes $sum(rev(k))$, which is not ground-relevant. As a result, in context M, the subgoal generation module will filter out all candidate subgoals of the form $\forall x.\ sum(rev(x)) \approx s$. □

To generate the set of all candidate subgoals of size n, we first generate the set $\mathcal{R}_n$ of terms (unique up to variable renaming) of size at most n that are relevant in M, which will be set of terms used on the left-hand side of all candidate subgoals. The set $\mathcal{R}_n$ can be efficiently computed by a branching procedure whose states are an (initially empty) sequence of substitutions of the form $(\{x_1 \mapsto t_n\}, \ldots, \{x_n \mapsto t_n\})$ where for each $j = 1, \ldots, n$, either $t_j = x_i$ for some $i \leq j$ or t_j is a well-typed term of the form $f(x_{k+1}, \ldots, x_{k+n})$, where $FV(t_1, \ldots, t_{j-1}) = \{x_1, \ldots, x_k\}$ for $k > j$. Let $term((\sigma_1, \ldots, \sigma_n))$ denote the term $(\ldots(x_1\sigma_1)\ldots)\sigma_n$. Intuitively, appending σ_{n+1} to a state $s = (\sigma_1, \ldots, \sigma_n)$ corresponds to deciding on the form of the subterm x_{n+1} of $term(s)$, either it is a variable or a function applied to new variables not occurring in $term(s)$. We do not explore states s where $term(s)$ has size greater than n, or if $term(s)$ does not generalize an active term from M. Then, $\mathcal{R}_n$ is the set $\{term(s) \mid s \in S\}$ where S is the set of states reached by this procedure.

After several iterations of the loop from Figure 1 on the axiomatization and conjecture from Example 3, we obtain a context M where there are on the order of 20 relevant terms of size 2, and on the order of 100 relevant terms of size 3 that are unique up to variable renaming. Overall in the signature Σ, there are > 40 terms of size at most 2 and > 200 terms of size at most 3 unique up to variable renaming, indicating that this form of filtering determines over half of Σ-terms do not generalize an active term. Notice when Σ contains functions not occurring in the conjecture ψ, the percentage of potential terms this filtering eliminates is even higher.

Filtering Based on Canonicity. SMT solvers contain efficient methods for reasoning about conjunctions of ground equalities and disequalities, in particular through the use of data structures for maintaining equivalence classes of ground terms, and performing congruence closure over these terms. Note that all inferences (reflexivity, symmetry, transitivity, and congruence) either implicitly or explicitly made by a standard procedure for congruence closure extend to universal equalities as well. Thus, such data structures can be lifted without modification to maintain equivalence classes of non-ground terms that are entailed to be equivalent in a context M.

In detail, say we have a set of equalities $U \subseteq M$ between (possibly) non-ground Σ-terms, corresponding to function definitions from our axiomatization, and the set of subgoals we have proven thus far. The subgoal generation module maintains a congruence closure U^* over the set U, where each equivalence class $\{t_1, \ldots, t_n\}$ in U^* is such that M entails $\forall[FV(t_i) \cup FV(t_j)].\ t_i \approx t_j$ for each $i, j \in \{1, \ldots, n\}$. The structure U^* can be used to avoid considering multiple conjectures that are equivalent. Each equivalence class in U^* is associated with one of its terms, which we call its *representative term*. We say a term is *canonical in* U^* if and only if it is a representative of an equivalence class in U^*, and *non-canonical in* U^* if and only if it exists in U^* and is not canonical. In our approach, we choose the term in an equivalence class with the smallest size to be its representative term. While enumerating candidate subgoals, we discard all subgoals that contain at least one non-canonical subterm.

Determining whether a subgoal φ is canonical involves adding an equality $t \approx t$ to U for each subterm t of φ not occurring in U^*, and then recomputing U^*. For the purposes of increasing the frequency when a term such as t is found to be non-canonical, we may infer additional equalities between t and terms from U^*, which is based on the following. If $t = s\sigma$ for some substitution σ where s is a term from U^*, and moreover if $s \approx r \in U^*$ and $r\sigma$ is a term from U^*, then we add the equality $t \approx r\sigma$ to U^*, noting that $(s \approx r)\sigma$ is a consequence of $s \approx r$ by instantiation. This allows us to merge the equivalence classes of t and $r\sigma$ in U^*, forcing one of them to be non-canonical, as demonstrated in the following example.

Example 5. Say our context M is $\{\forall x.\ app(x, nil) \approx x\}$. Our set U is $\{app(x, nil) \approx x\}$, and U^* contains the equivalence classes $\{x, app(x, nil)\}$ and $\{nil\}$. Consider a candidate subgoal $\varphi := \forall x.\ rev(app(rev(x), nil))) \approx x$. We recompute U^*, now including all subterms of this conjecture, after which it will additionally contain the equivalence classes $\{rev(x)\}$, $\{app(rev(x), nil)\}$ and $\{rev(app(rev(x), nil))\}$. Since $app(rev(x), nil)) = app(x, nil)\sigma$ for substitution $\sigma := \{x \mapsto rev(x)\}$, and $app(x, nil) \approx x \in U^*$, and since $x\sigma = rev(x)$, our procedure will merge the equivalence classes $\{rev(x)\}$ and $\{app(rev(x), nil)\}$ to obtain one having $rev(x)$ as its representative term. This indicates that the subgoal $\forall x.\ rev(app(rev(x), nil))) \approx x$ is *redundant* in context M, since it contains the non-canonical subterm $app(rev(x), nil)$. We are justified in filtering this subgoal since the above reasoning has determined that it is equivalent to $\forall x.\ rev(rev(x))) \approx x$, which the subgoal generation module may choose to generate instead, if necessary. □

This technique is particularly useful in our approach for subgoal generation in DPLL(T), since our ability to filter candidate subgoals is refined whenever a new subgoal becomes proven. In the previous example, learning $\forall x. app(x, nil) \approx x$ allows us to filter an entire class of candidate subgoals, namely that contains a subterm of the form $app(t, nil)$ for any term t. This gives us a constant factor of improvement in our ability to filter future subgoals *for each* subgoal that we prove during the DPLL(T) search.

Filtering Based on Ground Facts. As mentioned, DPLL(T)-based SMT solvers maintain a context of ground facts M that represent the current satisfying assignment for the set of clauses F. A straightforward method for determining whether a candidate subgoal $\forall \boldsymbol{x}.\ t \approx s$ does not hold (in M) is to determine if one of its instances is *falsified* by M. In other words, if M entails $\neg(t \approx s)\sigma$, where σ is a grounding substitution over $\boldsymbol{x}$, then clearly $\forall \boldsymbol{x}.\ t \approx s$ does not hold in context M.

Example 6. Assume our context M is $\{\ k \approx nil, sum(cons(Z, k)) \approx sum(k), sum(k) \approx Z\ \}$, and a candidate subgoal $\varphi := \forall x.\ sum(cons(Z, x)) \approx S(Z)$. We have that M entails $\neg(sum(cons(Z, x)) \approx S(Z))\{x \mapsto nil\}$, indicating that φ does not hold in context M. □

Notice that the fact that φ has a counterexample in context M does not imply that φ will always be filtered out, since the solver may later find a different context that does not contain $sum(k) \approx Z$. Conversely, we may filter candidate subgoals $\forall \boldsymbol{x}.\ t \approx s$ if none (or fewer than a constant number) of its instances are entailed in M, that is, M does not entail $(t \approx s)\sigma$ for any grounding substitution over $\boldsymbol{x}$. Note the following example.

Example 7. Assume our context M is $\{\ sum(cons(Z, k)) \approx plus(Z, sum(k)), plus(Z, sum(k)) \approx sum(k)\ \}$, and a candidate subgoal $\varphi := \forall x.\ sum(x) \approx S(Z)$. Although no ground instance of φ is falsified, neither is any ground instance of φ entailed. Thus, we may choose to filter out φ. □

When the above two forms of filtering are enabled, our implementation also introduces additional ground terms, initially 40 per function symbol, which are subsequently incorporated into contexts and may be evaluated as a result of our quantifier instantiation heuristics. This both increases the likelihood that witnesses are found that falsify candidate subgoals, and can ensure that at least one ground instance of candidate subgoals is confirmed.

To give a rough and informal idea of the overall number of subgoals that are filtered by these techniques, consider the axiomatization and conjecture ψ from Example 3. We found there were approximately 33800 well-typed equalities between Σ-terms that met the basic syntactic requirements of being a candidate subgoal[3]. We measured the average number of relevant subgoals for contexts M obtained after several iterations of the loop from Figure 1. With filtering based on active conjectures alone, there were on average approximately 11200 relevant subgoals of size at most 3, with filtering based on canonicity alone (given only the set of axioms in $\mathcal{A}$), there were approximately 23400, and with filtering based on ground facts alone, there were approximately 2100. With all three filtering techniques enabled, there were approximately 450 relevant subgoals of size at most 3, reducing the space of conjectures well over fifty times. Furthermore, filtering based on the canonicity of the candidate subgoal is refined whenever a new subgoal becomes proven. We thus found that, once the solver proves the commutativity and right identity of $plus$, as well as the right identity of *app*, the number of relevant subgoals of size at most 3 decreased to around 260 on average. After proving the associativity of $plus$ and *app*, this further decreases to 70, making the discovery of the sufficient subgoal φ_1 in this example much less daunting from a practical perspective.

4 Evaluation

We have implemented the techniques described in this paper in the SMT solver CVC4 [3]. We evaluate the implementation on a library of 933 benchmarks, which we

[3] Namely, for a subgoal $\forall \boldsymbol{x}.\ t \approx s$, we require $FV(s) \subseteq FV(t)$, and t must be an application of an uninterpreted function.

constructed from several sources, including previous test suites for tools that specifically target induction (Isaplanner, Clam, Hipspec), as well as verification conditions from the Leon verification system. The benchmarks in SMT-LIB2 format can be retrieved from `http://lara.epfl.ch/~reynolds/VMCAI2015-ind`.

Isaplanner. We considered 85 benchmarks from the test suite for automatic induction introduced by the authors of the Isaplanner system [17]. These benchmarks contain conjectures involving lists, natural numbers, and binary trees. A handful of these benchmarks involved higher-order functions on lists, such as map, which we encoded using an auxiliary uninterpreted function as input (the function to be mapped) for each instance of map in a conjecture.

Clam. We considered 86 benchmarks used for evaluating the CLAM prover [16]. Of the 86 benchmarks, 50 are conjectures designed such that subgoal generation is likely necessary for the proof to succeed, 12 are generalizations of these conjectures, and 24 are subgoals that were discovered by CLAM during its evaluation. These benchmarks involve lists, natural numbers, and sets.

Hipspec. We considered benchmarks based on three examples from [7], which included intermediate subgoals used by the HipSpec theorem prover for proving various conjectures. The first example states that list reverse is equivalent to its tail-recursive version, the second example states that rotating a list by its length returns the original list, and the third example states that the sum of the first n cubes is the nth triangle number squared. Between the three examples, there are a total of 26 benchmarks, 16 of which are reported to require subgoals.

Leon. We considered three sets of benchmarks for programs taken from Leon, a system for verification and synthesis of Scala programs (`http://lara.epfl.ch/w/leon`). We considered these benchmarks since they involve more sophisticated data structures (such as queues, binary trees and heaps), and are representative of properties seen when verifying simple functional programs. In the first set, we conjecture the correctness of various operations on amortized queues, in particular that enqueue and pop behave analogously to a corresponding implementation on lists. In the second set, we conjecture the correctness of some of the more complex operations on binary search trees, in particular that membership lookup according to binary search is correct if the tree is sorted, and the correctness of removing an element from a tree.

4.1 Encodings

For our evaluation, we considered three encodings of the aforementioned benchmarks into SMT-LIB2 syntax. In the first encoding, which we will refer to as **dt**, all functions were encoded as uninterpreted functions over inductive datatypes. In particular, natural numbers were encoded as an inductive datatype with constructors S and Z, and sets were represented using the same datatype for lists, where its constructors $cons$ and nil represented insertion and the empty set respectively.

Direct Translation to Theory. For the purposes of leveraging the decision procedures of the SMT solver for reasoning about the behavior of built-in functions, we considered an alternative encoding, which we will refer to as **dtt**. This encoding is obtained as a result of replacing all occurrences of certain datatypes with builtin sorts. For instance, we replace all occurrences of Nat (the datatype for natural numbers) with Int (the built-in type for integers) according to the following steps. First, all occurrences of f-applications are replaced by f_i-applications where f_i is an uninterpreted function whose sort is obtained from the sort of f by replacing all occurrences of Nat by Int. All variables of sort Nat in quantified formulas are replaced by variables of sort Int. All occurrences of $S(t)$ are replaced by $1 + t$ (where $+$ is the built-in operator for integer addition), and all occurrences of Z were replaced by the integer numeral 0. Second, to preserve the semantics of natural numbers, all quantified formulas of the form $\forall x.\varphi$ where x is of type Int are replaced with $\forall x.x \geq 0 \Rightarrow \varphi$ (indicating a pre-condition for the function/conjecture), and for all functions $f_i : S_1 \times \ldots \times S_n \to Int$, the quantified formula $\forall x_1, \ldots, x_n.f_i(x_1, \ldots, x_n) \geq 0$ was added (indicating a post-condition for the function). Finally, constraints are added, wherever possible, stating the equivalence between uninterpreted functions from Σ and a corresponding built-in functions supported by the SMT solver if one existed. For instance, we add the quantified formulas $\forall xy.\ (x \geq 0 \wedge y \geq 0) \Rightarrow plus(x, y) = x+y$ and $\forall xy.\ (x \geq 0 \wedge y \geq 0) \Rightarrow less(x, y) \Leftrightarrow x < y$.[4] Since CVC4 has recently added support for a native theory for sets, a similar translation was done for set operations as well, so insertion and empty data structure are replaced by $\{x\} \cup y$ and $\emptyset$, respectively.

Datatype to Theory Isomorphism. We considered a third encoding, which we will refer to **dti**, that is intended to capitalize on the advantages of both encodings **dt** and **dtt**. In this encoding, we use the signature Σ, axioms for function definitions, and all conjectures as for **dtt**, and introduce uninterpreted functions to map between certain datatypes and builtin types. For instance, we introduce an uninterpreted function $f_{Nat} : Nat \to Int$ mapping natural numbers as algebraic data type into the built-in integer type. We add constraints to all benchmarks for its definition, also stating that f_{Nat} is an injection to non-negative integers:

$$f_{Nat}(Z) \approx 0 \qquad \forall x.\ f_{Nat}(S(x)) \approx 1 + f_{Nat}(x)$$
$$\forall x.\ f_{Nat}(x) \geq 0 \quad \forall xy.\ f_{Nat}(x) \approx f_{Nat}(y) \Rightarrow x \approx y$$

We then add constraints for the uninterpreted functions from Σ that correspond to built-in functions involving Int that are supported by the solver. For instance, we add the constraints $\forall xy.\ f_{Nat}(plus(x, y)) \approx f_{Nat}(x) + f_{Nat}(y)$ and $\forall xy.\ less(x, y) \Leftrightarrow f_{Nat}(x) < f_{Nat}(y)$. A similar mapping was introduced between lists and sets, where constraints were added for each basic set operation.

4.2 Results

In our results, we evaluate the performance of our implementation in the SMT solver CVC4 on all benchmarks in each of the three encodings. To measure the number of benchmarks that can be solved without inductive reasoning, we ran the SMT solver Z3 [10], as well as CVC4 without the inductive reasoning module enabled (as indicated by the configuration **cvc4**).[5] We then ran two configurations of CVC4 with inductive reasoning.

[4] We did not provide this constraint for multiplication $mult$, since it introduces non-linear arithmetic, which SMT solvers only have limited support for.

[5] Note these two configurations were only run to measure the number of benchmarks that did not require inductive reasoning, and not to be considered as competitive.

		Isaplanner	Clam+sg	Clam	Hipspec+sg	Hipspec	Leon+sg	Total
Encoding	Config	85	86	50	26	16	46	311
dt	z3	16	11	0	2	0	6	35
	cvc4	15	4	0	3	0	7	29
	cvc4+i	68	72	7	25	3	29	204
	cvc4+ig	75	79	40	24	8	34	260
dtt	z3	35	19	4	4	1	9	72
	cvc4	34	14	2	4	1	8	63
	cvc4+i	64	57	5	14	3	37	180
	cvc4+ig	67	61	16	14	4	39	201
dti	z3	35	22	3	5	1	9	75
	cvc4	34	16	3	5	1	9	68
	cvc4+i	76	78	14	25	6	41	240
	cvc4+ig	80	83	38	25	9	42	277

Fig. 2. Number of solved benchmarks. All experiments run with a 300 second timeout. The suffix $+sg$ indicates classes where subgoals were explicitly provided. All benchmarks in the **Clam** and **Hipspec** classes are reported to require subgoals. The **Isaplanner** class contains a mixture of benchmarks, some of which require subgoals.

The first, configuration **cvc4+i** is identical to the behavior of CVC4, except that it applies skolemization with inductive strengthening as described in Section 2. The second configuration **cvc4+ig** additionally enables the subgoal generation scheme as described in Section 3. In both configurations, inductive strengthening is applied to all inductive datatype skolem variables based on weak structural induction, and to all integer skolem variables based on weak natural number induction. All configurations of CVC4 used newly developed quantifier instantiation techniques that prioritize instantiations that lead to ground conflicts [24].

Figure 2 shows the results for the four configurations on each of the three encodings. For isolating the benchmarks where subgoal generation is reported to be necessary, we divide the results for the Clam and Hipspec classes into two columns. The first (columns **Clam+sg** and **Hipspec+sg**) explicitly provide all necessary subgoals (if any) as indicated by the sources of the benchmarks in [16] and [7] as theorems. The second (columns **Clam** and **Hipspec**) includes only the benchmarks where subgoals were required, and does not explicitly provide these subgoals. The Leon benchmarks were considered sequentially: to prove k^{th} conjecture, the previous $k-1$ conjectures were assumed as theorems for the next conjecture, whether they were needed or not. Therefore, these benchmarks contain many quantified assumptions.

As expected, a majority of the benchmarks over all classes in the base encoding **dt** require inductive reasoning, as Z3 and CVC4 solve 35 and 29 respectively (around 10% of the benchmarks overall). Encodings that incorporate theory reasoning eliminated the need for inductive reasoning for approximately an additional 10% of the benchmarks, as Z3 and CVC4 solve 72 and 63 respectively on benchmarks in the **dtt** encoding, and 75 and 68 respectively in the **dti** encoding.

Our results show that the basic configuration of inductive reasoning **cvc4+i** has a relatively high success rate for classes where subgoal generation is reported to be unnecessary (**Clam+sg**, **Hipspec+sg** and **Leon+sg**). Over these three sets, **cvc4+i** solves 126 (80%) of the benchmarks in the **dt** encoding, 108 (68%) in the **dtt** encoding, and 144 (91%) in the **dti** encoding. We found that 4 of the heapsort benchmarks from **Leon+sg** likely require an induction scheme based on induction on the size of a heap, consequently **cvc4+i** (as well as **cvc4+ig**) was unable to solve them. Our results confirm that subgoal generation is necessary for a majority of benchmarks in the **Clam** and **Hipspec** classes, as **cvc4+i** solves only 10 out of 66 total in these sets. [6] However, note that **cvc4+i** solves twice as many of these benchmarks (20) simply by leveraging theory reasoning, as seen in the results for **Clam** and **Hipspec** in the **dti** encoding.

With subgoal generation enabled, CVC4 was able to solve an additional 114 benchmarks over all classes and encodings. In total, CVC4 automatically inferred subgoals sufficient for proving conjectures in 123 cases that were otherwise unsolvable without subgoal generation. This improvement was most noticeable on the benchmarks from the **dt** encoding, where **cvc4+ig** solved 56 more than **cvc4+i** (260 vs. 204). This can be attributed to the fact that many of the subgoals it discovered related to simple facts related to arithmetic functions, such as the commutatitivity and associativity of $plus$, whereas in the other two encodings these facts are inherent consequences of theory reasoning. The performance of the subgoal generation module was the least noticeable on benchmarks from the **dtt** encoding, which we attribute to the fact that the techniques from Section 3 are not well suited for signatures that contain theory symbols. In the **dti** encoding, subgoal generation led to **cvc4+ig** solving 37 more benchmarks than **cvc4+i** (277 vs. 240). The techniques for filtering candidate subgoals from Section 3.2 were critical for these cases. We found that only 1 of these 37 benchmarks was solved in a configuration identical to **cvc4+ig** but where all filtering techniques were disabled.

The majority of subgoals found by **cvc4+ig** were small, the largest for a given benchmark typically having size at most three. Nevertheless, we remark that **cvc4+ig** was able to discover and prove several interesting subgoals. For the conjecture $\forall nx.\ count(n,x) \approx count(n, sort(x))$ from the **Isaplanner** class, stating the number of times n occurs in a list is the same after an insertion sort, we first determined by paper-and-pencil analysis this would need two subgoals (also from the Isaplanner set):

$$\forall nx.\ count(n, insert(n,x)) \approx S(count(n,x)), \text{ and}$$
$$\forall nmx.\ \neg n \approx m \Rightarrow count(n, insert(m,x)) \approx count(n,x)$$

However, CVC4's subgoal generation module found and proved a single subgoal $\forall nmx.\ count(n, insert(m,x)) \approx count(n, cons(m,x))$, which by itself was sufficient to prove the original conjecture. CVC4 was thus able to fully automatically find a simpler proof than we found by hand.

On most of the benchmarks we considered, the subgoal generation module has only a small overhead in performance for benchmarks where subgoal generation is not required. In only 30 cases **cvc4+ig** took more than twice as long to solve a benchmark than **cvc4+i** (for benchmarks that took **cvc4+ig** more than a second to solve), and in only 9 cases **cvc4+ig** was unable to solve a benchmark that **cvc4+i** solved.

[6] These 10 benchmarks are solved by CVC4 without subgoal generation, despite being described in literature as requiring subgoals. In some cases, the reason is that CVC4 chose a different variable to apply induction to. For instance, the conjecture $rotate(S(n), rotate(m, xs)) \approx rotate(S(m), rotate(n, xs))$ is said to be proven by Hipspec by induction on xs after discovering the subgoal $rotate(n, rotate(m, xs)) \approx rotate(m, rotate(n, xs))$. Instead, CVC4 proved this conjecture by induction on n using no subgoals.

Id	Property	Solved only by
47	$\forall t.\ height(mirror(t)) = height(t)$	CVC4, HipSpec, Zeno
50	$\forall x.\ butlast(x) = take(minus(len(x), S(Z)), x)$	CVC4, Zeno
54	$\forall mn.\ minus(plus(m, n), n) = m$	CVC4, HipSpec, Zeno
56	$\forall nmx.\ drop(n, drop(m, x)) = drop(plus(n, m), x)$	CVC4, HipSpec, Zeno
66	$\forall x.\ leq(len(filter(x)), len(x))$	CVC4, ACL2, Zeno
67	$\forall x.\ len(butlast(x)) = minus(len(x), S(Z))$	CVC4, HipSpec, Zeno
68	$\forall xl.\ leq(len(delete(x, l)), len(l))$	CVC4, ACL2, Zeno
81	$\forall nmx.\ take(n, drop(m, x)) = drop(m, take(plus(n, m), x))$	CVC4, HipSpec, Zeno
83	$\forall xyz.\ zip(app(x, y), z) = app(zip(x, take(len(x), z)), zip(y, drop(len(x), z)))$	CVC4, HipSpec, Zeno
84	$\forall xyz.\ zip(x, app(y, z)) = app(zip(take(len(y), x)y), zip(drop(len(y), x), z))$	CVC4, HipSpec, Zeno
72	$\forall ix.\ rev(drop(i, x)) = take(minus(len(x), i)rev(x))$	Hipspec
73	$\forall x.\ rev(filter(x)) = filter(rev(x))$	HipSpec, Zeno
74	$\forall ix.\ rev(take(i, x)) = drop(minus(len(x), i)rev(x))$	Hipspec
78	$\forall l.\ sorted(sort(l))$	ACL2, Zeno
85	$\forall xy.\ len(x) = len(y) \Rightarrow zip(rev(x), rev(y)) = rev(zip(x, y))$	

Fig. 3. Isaplanner benchmarks that cannot be solved by either a competing inductive prover, or using CVC4 with its inductive mode with subgoal generation on the **dti** encoding. The first part shows benchmarks solved by our approach but not by one of the competing provers. Zeno excels at these benchmarks, but note that, e.g., CVC4 solves 21 Clam benchmarks that Zeno cannot.

Overall, the results show that the performance of all configurations is the best for benchmarks in the **dti** encoding. While the **dtt** encoding enables the SMT solver to leverage the decision procedure for linear integer arithmetic when reasoning about inductive conjectures, it degrades performance for many benchmarks, often leading to conjectures being unsolved. We attribute this to several factors. Firstly, the **dtt** encoding complicates the operation of the matching-based heuristic for quantifier instantiation. For instance, finding ground terms that modulo equality match a pattern $f(1+x)$ is less straightforward than finding terms that match a pattern $f(S(x))$. Secondly, as opposed to the other two encodings, the **dtt** encoding relies heavily on decisions made by the theory solver for linear integer arithmetic. For a negated conjecture $\neg P_i(k_i)$ for integer k_i, a highly optimized Simplex decision procedure for linear integer arithmetic will find a satisfying assignment, which may or may not choose to explore useful values of k_i. On the other hand, given a negated conjecture $\neg P(k)$ for natural number k, in the absence of conflicts, the decision procedure for inductive datatypes will first case-split on whether k is zero. We believe the behavior of the decision procedure for inductive datatypes has more synergy with the quantifier instantiation mechanism in CVC4 for our axiom sets, since its case splitting naturally corresponds with the case splitting in the definition of recursive functional programs. As a result, the **dti** encoding is the best of the three, as it allows the solver to effectively consult the integer solver for making theory-specific inferences as needed, without affecting the interaction between the ground solver and quantifier instantiation mechanism.

Comparison with Inductive Theorem Provers. By comparing to reported results of inductive provers, we find that tools perform well on their own benchmark sets, but, unsurprisingly, less well on benchmarks used to evaluate competing tools. Although no tool dominates, **cvc4+ig** performs well across all benchmark sets. Combined with the convenience of using the standardized SMT-LIB2 format and the benefits of other SMT techniques, CVC4 becomes an attractive choice for inductive proofs.

For the 85 benchmarks in Isaplanner set, **cvc4+ig** solves a total of 80 benchmarks in the **dti** encoding. These benchmarks have been translated into the native formats supported by a number of tools. As points of comparison, as reported in [27], Zeno solves a total of 82 benchmarks, 2 that **cvc4+ig** cannot. Hipspec [7] solves a total of 80 benchmarks, 3 that **cvc4+ig** cannot, while **cvc4+ig** solves 3 benchmarks that Hipspec cannot. ACL2 [6] solves a total of 73 benchmarks, 1 that **cvc4+ig** cannot, while **cvc4+ig** solves 8 that ACL2 cannot. We list all benchmarks that either CVC4, Zeno, Hipspec, or ACL2 does not solve in Figure 3. Isaplanner [17] and Dafny [22] solve 47 and 45 benchmarks respectively, the latter of which does not incorporate techniques for automatically generating subgoals. Interestingly, we found one property in the original set of benchmarks from [17], $\forall xyz.\ less(x, y) \Rightarrow mem(x, insert(y, z)) \approx mem(x, z)$ is true, although it is cited in later sources as not a theorem, and excluded from the evaluation of the other tools. We found that CVC4 was able to prove this property, both by enabling theory reasoning (**cvc4+i** on the **dtt** and **dti** encodings) and by enabling subgoal generation (**cvc4+ig** on the **dt** encoding).

For the original 50 benchmarks from the Clam set (which include 38 benchmarks from **Clam** class in Figure 2 that require subgoals and 12 benchmarks from **Clam+sg** that do not), **cvc4+ig** solves a total of 39 benchmarks in the **dti** encoding. A version of Hipspec solves a total of 47 of these benchmarks, 10 that **cvc4+ig** cannot, while **cvc4+ig** solves 2 benchmarks that Hipspec cannot (which were solved due to the use of CVC4's native support for sets). Zeno solves a total of 21 benchmarks, 3 that **cvc4+ig** cannot, while **cvc4+ig** solves 21 that Zeno cannot. The Clam tool itself solves 41 fully automatically, 7 that **cvc4+ig** cannot, while **cvc4+ig** solves 5 that Clam cannot.

5 Conclusion

We have presented a method for incorporating inductive reasoning within a DPLL(T)-based SMT solver. We have shown an implementation that has a high success rate for benchmarks taken from inductive theorem proving and software verification sources, and is competitive with state-of-the-art tools for automating induction. We have provided a larger and unified set of benchmarks in a standard SMT-LIB2 format, which will make future comparisons more feasible. Our evaluation indicates the inductive reasoning capabilities in our approach benefit from an encoding where theory reasoning can be consulted using a mapping between datatypes and builtin types, allowing the solver to leverage inferences made by its ground decision procedures. Our evaluation shows that our approach for subgoal generation is feasible for automatically inferring subgoals that are relevant to proving a conjecture. The scalability of our approach is made possible by several powerful techniques for filtering out irrelevant candidate subgoals based on the information the solver knows about its current context. Future work includes incorporating further induction schemes, inferring subgoals containing propositional symbols, and improvements to the heuristics used for filtering candidate subgoals.

Acknowledgments. We thank Ravichandhran Madhavan for an initial version of the Leon benchmarks and Cesare Tinelli for discussions about SMT-LIB semantics.

References

1. SMT-LIB theories (2014), `http://smtlib.cs.uiowa.edu/theories.shtml`.
2. Z3 will not prove inductive facts (September 2014), `http://rise4fun.com/z3/tutorial`.
3. Barrett, C., Conway, C.L., Deters, M., Hadarean, L., Jovanović, D., King, T., Reynolds, A., Tinelli, C.: CVC4. In: Gopalakrishnan, G., Qadeer, S. (eds.) CAV 2011. LNCS, vol. 6806, pp. 171–177. Springer, Heidelberg (2011)
4. Barrett, C., Shikanian, I., Tinelli, C.: An abstract decision procedure for satisfiability in the theory of recursive data types. Electronic Notes in Theoretical Computer Science (2007)
5. Bundy, A.: The automation of proof by mathematical induction. In: Handbook of Automated Reasoning. vol. 1, ch. 13, Elsevier and The MIT Press (2001)
6. Chamarthi, H.R., Dillinger, P., Manolios, P., Vroon, D.: The ACL2 Sedan theorem proving system. In: Abdulla, P.A., Leino, K.R.M. (eds.) TACAS 2011. LNCS, vol. 6605, pp. 291–295. Springer, Heidelberg (2011)
7. Claessen, K., Johansson, M., Rosén, D., Smallbone, N.: Automating inductive proofs using theory exploration. In: Bonacina, M.P. (ed.) CADE 2013. LNCS (LNAI), vol. 7898, pp. 392–406. Springer, Heidelberg (2013)
8. Claessen, K., Smallbone, N., Hughes, J.: QUICKSPEC: Guessing formal specifications using testing. In: Fraser, G., Gargantini, A. (eds.) TAP 2010. LNCS, vol. 6143, pp. 6–21. Springer, Heidelberg (2010)
9. Comon, H.: Inductionless induction. In: Handbook of Automated Reasoning, vol. 1, ch. 14. Elsevier and The MIT Press (2001)
10. de Moura, L., Bjørner, N.S.: Z3: An efficient SMT solver. In: Ramakrishnan, C.R., Rehof, J. (eds.) TACAS 2008. LNCS, vol. 4963, pp. 337–340. Springer, Heidelberg (2008)
11. Detlefs, D., Nelson, G., Saxe, J.B.: Simplify: A theorem prover for program checking. J. ACM 52(3), 365–473 (2005)
12. Flanagan, C., Joshi, R., Saxe, J.B.: An explicating theorem prover for quantified formulas. Technical Report HPL-2004-199, HP Laboratories Palo Alto (2004)
13. Ge, Y., Barrett, C.W., Tinelli, C.: Solving quantified verification conditions using satisfiability modulo theories. In: Pfenning, F. (ed.) CADE 2007. LNCS (LNAI), vol. 4603, pp. 167–182. Springer, Heidelberg (2007)
14. Grebenshchikov, S., Lopes, N.P., Popeea, C., Rybalchenko, A.: Synthesizing software verifiers from proof rules. In: PLDI, pp. 405–416 (2012)
15. Gupta, A., Popeea, C., Rybalchenko, A.: Solving recursion-free Horn clauses over LI+UIF. In: Yang, H. (ed.) APLAS 2011. LNCS, vol. 7078, pp. 188–203. Springer, Heidelberg (2011)
16. Ireland, A.: Productive use of failure in inductive proof. J. Autom. Reasoning 16(1-2), 79–111 (1996)
17. Johansson, M., Dixon, L., Bundy, A.: Case-analysis for rippling and inductive proof. In: Kaufmann, M., Paulson, L.C. (eds.) ITP 2010. LNCS, vol. 6172, pp. 291–306. Springer, Heidelberg (2010)
18. Kahsai, T., Ge, Y., Tinelli, C.: Instantiation-based invariant discovery. In: Bobaru, M., Havelund, K., Holzmann, G.J., Joshi, R. (eds.) NFM 2011. LNCS, vol. 6617, pp. 192–206. Springer, Heidelberg (2011)
19. Kaufmann, M., Manolios, P., Moore, J.S. (eds.): Computer-Aided Reasoning: An Approach. Kluwer Academic Publishers (2000)
20. Krstić, S., Goel, A., Grundy, J., Tinelli, C.: Combined satisfiability modulo parametric theories. In: Grumberg, O., Huth, M. (eds.) TACAS 2007. LNCS, vol. 4424, pp. 602–617. Springer, Heidelberg (2007)

21. Ledesma-Garza, R., Rybalchenko, A.: Binary reachability analysis of higher order functional programs. In: Miné, A., Schmidt, D. (eds.) SAS 2012. LNCS, vol. 7460, pp. 388–404. Springer, Heidelberg (2012)
22. Leino, K.R.M.: Automating induction with an SMT solver. In: Kuncak, V., Rybalchenko, A. (eds.) VMCAI 2012. LNCS, vol. 7148, pp. 315–331. Springer, Heidelberg (2012)
23. Madhavan, R., Kuncak, V.: Symbolic resource bound inference for functional programs. In: Biere, A., Bloem, R. (eds.) CAV 2014. LNCS, vol. 8559, pp. 762–778. Springer, Heidelberg (2014)
24. Reynolds, A., Tinelli, C., Moura, L.D.: Finding conflicting instances of quantified formulas in SMT. In: Formal Methods in Computer-Aided Design (FMCAD) (2014)
25. Rondon, P.M., Kawaguchi, M., Jhala, R.: Liquid types. In: PLDI, pp. 159–169 (2008)
26. Rümmer, P., Hojjat, H., Kuncak, V.: Disjunctive interpolants for Horn-clause verification. In: Sharygina, N., Veith, H. (eds.) CAV 2013. LNCS, vol. 8044, pp. 347–363. Springer, Heidelberg (2013)
27. Sonnex, W., Drossopoulou, S., Eisenbach, S.: Zeno: An automated prover for properties of recursive data structures. In: Flanagan, C., König, B. (eds.) TACAS 2012. LNCS, vol. 7214, pp. 407–421. Springer, Heidelberg (2012)

Automatic Synthesis of Piecewise Linear Quadratic Invariants for Programs*

Assalé Adjé and Pierre-Loïc Garoche

Onera, the French Aerospace Lab, France
Université de Toulouse, Toulouse, France
{firstname.lastname}@onera.fr

Abstract. Among the various critical systems that are worth to be formally analyzed, a wide set consists of controllers for dynamical systems. Those programs typically execute an infinite loop in which simple computations update internal states and produce commands to update the system state. Those systems are yet hardly analyzable by available static analysis method, since, even if performing mainly linear computations, the computation of a safe set of reachable states often requires quadratic invariants.

In this paper we consider the general setting of a piecewise affine program; that is a program performing different affine updates on the system depending on some conditions. This typically encompasses linear controllers with saturations or controllers with different behaviors and performances activated on some safety conditions.

Our analysis is inspired by works performed a decade ago by Johansson et al, and Morari et al, in the control community. We adapted their method focused on the analysis of stability in continuous-time or discrete-time settings to fit the static analysis paradigm and the computation of invariants, that is over-approximation of reachable sets using piecewise quadratic Lyapunov functions.

Keywords: formal verification, static analysis, piecewise affine systems, piecewise quadratic lyapunov functions.

1 Introduction

With the success of Astrée [BCC+11], static analysis in general and abstract interpretation in particular are now seriously considered by industrials from the critical embedded system community, and more specifically by the engineers developing and validation controllers. The certification norms concerning the V&V of those software have also evolved and now enable the use of such methods in the development process.

These controller software are meant to perform an infinite loop in which values of sensors are read, a function of inputs and internal states is computed,

* This work has been partially supported by an RTRA/STAE BRIEFCASE project grant, the ANR projects INS-2012-007 CAFEIN, and ASTRID VORACE.

D. D'Souza et al. (Eds.): VMCAI 2015, LNCS 8931, pp. 99–116, 2015.

and the value of the result is sent to actuators. In general, in the most critical applications, the controllers used are based on a simple linear update with minor non linearities such as saturations, i.e. enforcing bounds, or specific behaviors when some conditions are met. The controlled systems range from aircraft flight commands, guidance algorithms, engine control from any kind of device optimizing performance or fuel efficiency, control of railway infrastructure, fan control in tunnels, etc.

It is therefore of outmost importance to provide suitable analyses to verify these controllers. One of the approach is to rely on quadratic invariants, such as the digital filters abstract domain of Feret [Fer04], since, according to Lyapunov theorem, any globally asymptotically stable linear system admits a quadratic Lyapunov function. This theorem does not hold in presence of disjunction, such as saturations.

In static analysis, dealing with disjunction is an import concern. When the join of two abstract element is imprecise, one can consider the disjunctive completion of the domain [FR94]. This process enriches the set of abstract elements with new ones, but the cost, i.e. the number of new elements, could be exponential in the number of initial elements. Concerning relation abstract domains, one should mention the tropical polyhedra of Allamigeon [All09] in which an abstract element characterizes a finite disjunction of zones [Min01]. However concerning quadratic properties, no static analysis actually performs the automatic computation of disjunctive quadratic invariants.

The goal of this paper is to propose such a computation: produce a disjunctive quadratic invariant as a sub-level of a piecewise quadratic Lyapunov function.

Related works. Most relational abstractions used in the static analysis community rely on a linear representation of relationship between variables, e.g. polyhedra [CH78], octagons [Min06], zonotopes [GGP09] are not join-complete. Integrating constraints in invariants generation was developed in [CSS03] but for computing linear invariants. As mentioned above, the tropical polyhedra domain [All09] admits some disjunctions since it characterizes a family of properties encoded as finite disjunction of zones.

Concerning non linear properties, the need for quadratic invariant was addressed a decade ago with ellipsoidal abstract domains for simple linear filters [Fer04] and more recently for non linear template domains [CS11] and policy iteration based static analysis [GSA+12].

More recently, techniques used in the control community have been used to synthesize appropriate quadratic templates using SDP solvers and Lyapunov functions [RJGF12].

The proposed technique addresses a family of systems well beyond the ones handled by the mentioned methods. In general, a global quadratic invariant is not enough to bound the reachable value of the considered systems, hence none of these could succeed.

On the control community side, Lyapunov based analysis are typically used to show the good behavior of a controlled system: it is globally asymptotically stable (GAS), i.e. when time goes to infinity the trajectories of the system goes to 0. Since about a decade SDP solvers, i.e. convex optimization algorithms for semi-definite programming, have reached a level of maturity that enable their use to compute quadratic Lyapunov functions. On the theory side, variants of quadratic Lyapunov functions such as the papers motivating our work – Johansson and Rantzer [RJ00, Joh03] as well as Mignone, Ferrari-Trecate and Morari [MFTM00] – addressed the study of piecewise linear systems for proving the GAS property.

In general, computing a safe superset of reachable states as needed when performing static analysis, is not a common question for control theorist. They would rather address the related notions of controllabilty or stability under perturbations. In most case, either the property considered, or the technique used, relies on the existence of a such a bound over reachable state; which we aim to compute in static analysis.

Contributions. Our contribution is threefold and based on the method of Johansson and Mignone used to prove the GAS property of a piecewise linear system:

- we detailed the method in the discrete setting, computing a piecewise quadratic Lyapunov function of a *discrete-time system*;
- we adapted it to compute an invariant over reachable states of the analyzed system;
- we showed the applicability of the proposed method to a wide set of generated examples.

Organization of the paper. The paper is structured as follow. Section 2 introduces the kind of programs considered. Section 3 details our version of the piecewise quadratic Lyapunov function as well as the characterization of invariant sets. Section 4 presents the experimentations while Section 5 concludes and opens future direction of research.

2 Problem Statement

The programs we consider here are composed of a single loop with possibly a complicated switch-case type loop body. Our switch-case loop body is supposed to be written as a nested sequence of *ite* statements, or a *switch* $c1 \to$ *inst*$1; c2 \to$ *instr*$2; c3 \to$ *instr*3. Moreover, we suppose that the analyzed programs are written in affine arithmetic. Consequently, the programs analyzed here can be interpreted as piecewise affine discrete-time systems. Finally, we reduce the problem to compute automatically an overapproximation of the reachable states of a piecewise affine discrete-time system. The term piecewise affine means that there exists a polyhedral partition $\{X^i, i \in I\}$ of the state-input space $\mathcal{X} \subseteq \mathbb{R}^{d+m}$ such that for all $i \in I$, the dynamic of the system is affine and represented by the following relation for all $k \in \mathbb{N}$:

$$\text{if } (x_k, u_k) \in X^i,\ x_{k+1} = A^i x_k + B^i u_k + b^i, k \in \mathbb{N} \tag{1}$$

where A^i is a $d \times d$ matrix, B^i a $d \times m$ matrix and b^i a vector of $\mathbb{R}^d$. The variable $x \in \mathbb{R}^d$ refers to the state variable and $u \in \mathbb{R}^m$ refers to some input variable.

For us, a polyhedral partition is a family of convex polyhedra which partitions the state-input space i.e. $\mathcal{X} = \bigcup_{i \in I} X^i \subseteq \mathbb{R}^{d+m}$ such that $X^i \cap X^j = \emptyset$ for all $i, j \in I, i \neq j$. From now on, we call X^i *cells*. Cells $\{X^i\}_{i \in I}$ are convex polyhedra which can contain both strict and weak inequalities. Cells can be represented by a $n_i \times (d+m)$ matrix T^i and c^i a vector of $\mathbb{R}^{n_i}$. We denote by $\mathbb{I}_i^s$ the set of indices which represent strict inequalities for the cell X^i, denote by T_s^i and c_s^i the parts of T^i and c^i corresponding to strict inequalities and by T_w^i and c_w^i the one corresponding to weak inequalities. Finally, we have the matrix representation given by Formula (2).

$$X^i = \left\{ \begin{pmatrix} x \\ u \end{pmatrix} \in \mathbb{R}^{d+m} \middle| T_s^i \begin{pmatrix} x \\ u \end{pmatrix} \ll c_s^i,\ T_w^i \begin{pmatrix} x \\ u \end{pmatrix} \leq c_w^i \right\} \tag{2}$$

We use the following notation: $y \ll z$ means that for all coordinates l, $y_l < z_l$ and $y \leq z$ means that for all coordinates l, $y_l \leq z_l$.

We will need homogeneous versions of laws and thus introduce the $(1+d+m) \times (1+d+m)$ matrices F^i defined as follows:

$$F^i = \begin{pmatrix} 1 & 0_{1 \times d} & 0_{1 \times m} \\ b^i & A^i & B^i \\ 0 & 0_{m \times d} & \mathrm{Id}_{m \times m} \end{pmatrix} \tag{3}$$

The system defined in Equation (1) can be rewritten as $(1, x_{k+1}, u_{k+1})^\intercal = F^i(1, x_{k+1}, u_k)$. Note that we introduce a "virtual" dynamic law $u_{k+1} = u_k$ on the input variable in Equation (3). In the point of view of set invariance computation, we will see that it remains to consider such dynamic law. Indeed we suppose that the input is bounded and we write $u_k \in \mathcal{U}$ for all $k \in \mathbb{N}$ with $\mathcal{U}$ is a nonempty compact set (polytope).

We are interested in proving that the reachable states $\mathcal{R}$ is bounded and a proof of this statement can be expressed by directly computing $\mathcal{R}$ that is:

$$\mathcal{R} = \{y \in \mathbb{R}^d \mid \exists\, k \in \mathbb{N},\ \exists\, i \in I,\ \exists\, (x_k, u_k) \in X^i,\ y = A^i x_k + B^i u_k + b^i\} \cup \{x_0\}$$

and prove that this set is bounded. We can also compute an overapproximation of $\mathcal{R}$ from a set $\mathcal{S} \subseteq \mathbb{R}^{d+m}$ such that $(x_0, u_0) \in \mathcal{S}$, $\mathcal{R} \times \mathcal{U} \subseteq \mathcal{S}$ and $\mathcal{S}$ is an inductive invariant in the sense of, for all $i \in I$:

$$(x, u) \in \mathcal{S} \cap X^i \implies (A^i x + B^i u + b^i, u) \in \mathcal{S}.$$

Indeed, by induction since (x_0, u_0) belongs to $\mathcal{S}$, $(x_k, u_k) \in \mathcal{S}$ for all $k \in \mathbb{N}$. Since every image of the dynamic of the system stays in $\mathcal{S}$, a reachable state (y, u) belongs to $\mathcal{S}$. Finally, if we prove that $\mathcal{S}$ is bounded then $\mathcal{R}$ is also bounded.

Working directly on sets can be difficult and usually invariant sets are computed as a sublevel of some function to find. For (convergent) discrete-time linear systems, it is classical to compute ellipsoidal overapproximation of reachable states. Indeed, sublevel sets of Lyapunov functions are invariant set for the analyzed linear system and to compute an ellipsoid containing the initial states provides an overapproximation of reachable states. Initially, Lyapunov functions are used to prove quadratic asymptotic stability. In this paper, we use an analogue of Lyapunov functions for piecewise affine systems to compute directly an overapproximation of reachable states.

Example 1 (Running example). Let us consider the following program. It is constituted by a single while loop with two nested conditional branches in the loop body.

```
(x,y)∈ [−9,9] × [−9,9];
while(true)
   ox=x;
   oy=y;
   read(u); \\u ∈ [−3,3]
   if (−9*ox+7*y+6*u<5){
      if(−4*ox+8*oy−8*u<4){
         x=0.4217*ox+0.1077*oy+0.5661*u;
         y=0.1162*ox+0.2785*oy+0.2235*u−1;
         }
      else { \\4*ox−8*oy+8*u<−4
         x=0.4763*ox+0.0145*oy+0.9033*u;
         y=0.1315*ox+0.3291*oy+0.1459*u+9;
         }
      }
   else { \\9*ox−7*y−6*u<−5
      if(−4*ox+8*oy−8*u<4){
         x=0.2618*ox+0.1107*oy+0.0868*u−4;
         y=0.4014*ox+0.4161*oy+0.6320*u+4;
         }
      else { \\4*ox−8*oy+8*u<−4
         x=0.3874*ox+0.00771*oy+0.5153*u+10;
         y=0.2430*ox+0.4028*oy+0.4790*u+7;
         }
      }
```

The initial condition of the piecewise affine systems is $(x, y) \in [-9, 9] \times [-9, 9]$ and the polytope where the input variable u lives is $\mathcal{U} = [-3, 3]$.

We can rewrite this program as a piecewise affine discrete-time dynamical systems using our notations. We give details on the matrices T_s^i and T_w^i and vectors c_s^i and c_w^i (see Equation (2)) which characterize the cells and on the matrices F^i representing the homogeneous version (see Equation (3)) of affine laws in the cell X^i.

$$F^1 = \begin{pmatrix} 1 & 0 & 0 & 0 \\ 0 & 0.4217 & 0.1077 & 0.5661 \\ -1 & 0.1162 & 0.2785 & 0.2235 \\ 0 & 0 & 0 & 1 \end{pmatrix}, \begin{cases} T_s^1 = \begin{pmatrix} -9 & 7 & 6 \\ -4 & 8 & -8 \end{pmatrix} \\ c_s^1 = (5\ 4)^\intercal \end{cases}, \begin{cases} T_w^1 = \begin{pmatrix} 0 & 0 & 1 \\ 0 & 0 & -1 \end{pmatrix} \\ c_w^1 = (3\ 3)^\intercal \end{cases}$$

$$F^2 = \begin{pmatrix} 1 & 0 & 0 & 0 \\ 0 & 0.4763 & 0.0145 & 0.9033 \\ 9 & 0.1315 & 0.3291 & 0.1459 \\ 0 & 0 & 0 & 1 \end{pmatrix}, \left\{ \begin{array}{l} T_s^2 = (-9\ 7\ 6) \\ c_s^2 = 5 \end{array} \right., \left\{ \begin{array}{l} T_w^2 = \begin{pmatrix} 4 & -8 & 8 \\ 0 & 0 & 1 \\ 0 & 0 & -1 \end{pmatrix} \\ c_w^2 = (-4\ 3\ 3)^\intercal \end{array} \right.$$

$$F^3 = \begin{pmatrix} 1 & 0 & 0 & 0 \\ -4 & 0.2618 & 0.1177 & 0.0868 \\ 4 & 0.4014 & 0.4161 & 0.6320 \\ 0 & 0 & 0 & 1 \end{pmatrix}, \left\{ \begin{array}{l} T_s^3 = (-4\ 8\ -8) \\ c_s^3 = 4 \end{array} \right., \left\{ \begin{array}{l} T_w^3 = \begin{pmatrix} 9 & -7 & -6 \\ 0 & 0 & 1 \\ 0 & 0 & -1 \end{pmatrix} \\ c_w^2 = (-5\ 3\ 3)^\intercal \end{array} \right.$$

$$F^4 = \begin{pmatrix} 1 & 0 & 0 & 0 \\ 10 & 0.3874 & 0.0771 & 0.5153 \\ 7 & 0.2430 & 0.4028 & 0.4790 \\ 0 & 0 & 0 & 1 \end{pmatrix}, \left\{ \begin{array}{l} T_w^4 = \begin{pmatrix} 9 & -7 & -6 \\ 4 & -8 & 8 \\ 0 & 0 & 1 \\ 0 & 0 & -1 \end{pmatrix} \\ c_w^4 = (-5\ -4\ 3\ 3)^\intercal \end{array} \right.$$

3 Invariant Computation

In [Joh03, MFTM00], the authors propose a method to prove stability of piecewise affine dynamical discrete-time systems. The method is a generalization of Lyapunov stability equations in the case where affine laws defining the system depend on the current state. Let A be a $d \times d$ matrix and let $x_{k+1} = Ax_k$, $k \in \mathbb{N}$, $x_0 \in \mathbb{R}^d$ be a linear dynamical system. We recall that L is a quadratic Lyapunov function iff there exists a $d \times d$ symmetric matrix P such that $L(x) = x^\intercal Px$ for all $x \in \mathbb{R}^d$ and $P \succ 0$ and $P - A^\intercal PA \succ 0$. The notation $P \succ 0$ means that P is positive definite i.e. $x^\intercal Px > 0$ for all $x \in \mathbb{R}^d$, $x \neq 0$ and 0 for $x = 0$. We will denote by $Q \succeq 0$ when Q is positive semidefinite i.e. $x^\intercal Px \geq 0$ for all $x \in \mathbb{R}^d$. Positive definite matrices characterize square of norm on $\mathbb{R}^d$. A Lyapunov function allows to prove the stability by the latter fact : the norm (associated to the Lyapunov function) of the states x_k decreases along the time. In switched system, similarly to the classical case, we exhibited a positive matrix (square norm) to prove that the trajectories decrease along the time. The main difficulty in the switched case is the fact that we change the laws and we must decrease whenever a transition from one cell to other is fired. Moreover, we only require the norm to be local i.e. positive only where the law is used.

3.1 Quadratization of Cells

We recall that for us local means that true on a cell and thus true on a polyhedron. Using the homogeneous version of a cell, we can define local positiveness on a polyhedral cone. Let Q be a $d \times d$ symmetric matrix and M be a $n \times d$ matrix.

Local positivity in our case means that $My \geq 0 \implies y^\intercal Qy \geq 0$. The problem will be to write the local positivity as a constraint without implication. The problem is not new (e.g. the survey paper [IS00]). The paper [MJ81] proves that local positivity is equivalent, when M has a full row rank, to $Q - M^\intercal CM \succeq 0$ where C is a copositive matrix i.e. $x^\intercal Cx \geq 0$ if $x \geq 0$. First in general (when the rank of M is not necessarily equal to its number of rows), note that if $Q - M^\intercal CM \succeq 0$ for some copositive matrix C then Q satisfies $My \geq 0 \implies y^\intercal Qy \geq 0$. Secondly every matrix C with nonnegative entries is copositive. Since copositivity seems to be as difficult as local positivity to handle, we will restrict copositive matrices to be matrices which nonnegative entries. The idea is instead of using cells as polyhedral cones, we use a quadratization of cells by introducing nonnegative entries and we will define the quadratization of a cell X^i by:

$$\overline{X^i} = \left\{ \begin{pmatrix} x \\ u \end{pmatrix} \in \mathbb{R}^{d+m} \;\middle|\; \begin{pmatrix} 1 \\ x \\ u \end{pmatrix}^\intercal E^{i\intercal} W^i E^i \begin{pmatrix} 1 \\ x \\ u \end{pmatrix} \geq 0 \right\} \tag{4}$$

where W^i is a $(1+n_i) \times (1+n_i)$ symmetric matrix with nonnegative entries and $E^i = \begin{pmatrix} E_s^i \\ E_w^i \end{pmatrix}$ with $E_s^i = \begin{pmatrix} 1 & 0_{1\times(d+m)} \\ c_s^i & -T_s^i \end{pmatrix}$ and $E_w^i = \begin{pmatrix} c_w^i & -T_w^i \end{pmatrix}$. Recall that n_i is the number of rows of T^i. The matrix E^i is thus of the size $n_i + 1 \times (1+d+m)$. The goal of adding the row $(1, 0_{1\times(d+m)})$ is to avoid to add the opposite of a vector of X^i in $\overline{X^i}$. Indeed without this latter vector $\overline{X^i}$ would be symmetric. We illustrate this fact at Example 2. Note that during optimization process, matrices W^i will be decision variables.

Example 2 (The reason of adding the row $(1, 0_{1\times(d+m)})$). Let us take the polyhedra $X = \{x \in \mathbb{R} \mid x \leq 1\}$. Using our notations, we have $X = \{x \mid M(1\ x)^\intercal \geq 0\}$ with $M = (1\ -1)$. Let us consider two cases, the first one without adding the row and the second one using it.

Without any modification, the quadratization of X relative to a nonnegative real W is $X' = \{x \mid (1\ x)M^\intercal WM(1\ x)^\intercal \geq 0\}$. But $(1\ x)M^\intercal WM(1\ x)^\intercal = W(1\ x)(1\ -1)^\intercal(1\ -1)(1\ x)^\intercal = 2W(1-x)^2$. Hence $X' = \mathbb{R}$ for all nonnegative real W.

Now let us take $E = \begin{pmatrix} 1 & 0 \\ 1 & -1 \end{pmatrix}$. The quadratization as defined by Equation (4) relative to a 2×2 symmetric matrix W with nonnegative coefficients is $\overline{X} = \{x \mid (1\ x)E^\intercal WE(1\ x)^\intercal \geq 0\}$. We have:

$$(1\ x)\begin{pmatrix} 1 & 1 \\ 0 & -1 \end{pmatrix}\begin{pmatrix} w_1 & w_3 \\ w_3 & w_2 \end{pmatrix}\begin{pmatrix} 1 & 0 \\ 1 & -1 \end{pmatrix}(1\ x)^\intercal = w_1 + 2w_3(1-x) + w_2(1-x)^2 \ .$$

To take a matrix W such that $w_2 = w_1 = 0$ and $w_3 > 0$ implies that $\overline{X} = X$.

Now we introduce an example of the quadratization of the cell X^1 for our running example.

Example 3. Let us consider the running example and the cell X^1. We recall that X^1 is characterized by the matrices and vectors:

$$\begin{cases} T_s^1 = \begin{pmatrix} -9 & 7 & 6 \\ -4 & 8 & -8 \end{pmatrix} \\ c_s^1 = (5\ 4)^\intercal \end{cases}, \begin{cases} T_w^1 = \begin{pmatrix} 0 & 0 & 1 \\ 0 & 0 & -1 \end{pmatrix} \\ c_w^1 = (3\ 3)^\intercal \end{cases} \text{ and } E^1 = \begin{pmatrix} 1 & 0 & 0 & 0 \\ 5 & 9 & -7 & -6 \\ 4 & 4 & -8 & 8 \\ 3 & 0 & 0 & -1 \\ 3 & 0 & 0 & 1 \end{pmatrix}$$

As suggested we have added the row $(1, 0_{1\times 3})$. Take for example the matrix:

$$W^1 = \begin{pmatrix} 63.0218 & 0.0163 & 0.0217 & 12.1557 & 8.8835 \\ 0.0163 & 0.0000 & 0.0000 & 0.0267 & 0.0031 \\ 0.0217 & 0.0000 & 0.0000 & 0.0094 & 0.0061 \\ 12.1557 & 0.0267 & 0.0094 & 4.2011 & 59.5733 \\ 8.8835 & 0.0031 & 0.0061 & 59.5733 & 3.0416 \end{pmatrix}$$

We have $\overline{X^1} = \{(x, y, u) \mid (1, x, y, u)E^1 W^1 E^1 (1, x, y, u)^\intercal \geq 0\} \supseteq X^1$. In Section 4, we will come back on the generation of W^1.

Local positivity of quadratic forms will also be used when a transition from a cell to an other is fired . For the moment, we are interested in the set of (x, u) such that $(x, u) \in X^i$ and whose the image is in X^j and we denote by X^{ij} the set:

$$\left\{ \begin{pmatrix} x \\ u \end{pmatrix} \in \mathbb{R}^{d+m} \;\middle|\; \begin{pmatrix} x \\ u \end{pmatrix} \in X^i \text{ and } (A^i x + B^i u + b^i, u) \in X^j \right\}$$

for all pairs $i, j \in I$. Note that in [MFTM00], the authors take into account all pairs (i, j) such that there exists a state x_k at moment k in X^i and the image of x_k that is x_{k+1} is in X^j. We will discuss in Subsection 3.2 the computation or a reduction to possible switches using linear programming as suggested in [BGLM05]. To construct a quadratization of X^{ij}, we use the same approach than before by introducing a $(1 + n_i + n_j) \times (1 + n_i + n_j)$ symmetric matrix U^{ij} with nonnegative entries to get a set $\overline{X^{ij}}$ defined as:

$$\overline{X^{ij}} = \left\{ \begin{pmatrix} x \\ u \end{pmatrix} \in \mathbb{R}^{d+m} \;\middle|\; \begin{pmatrix} 1 \\ x \\ u \end{pmatrix}^\intercal E^{ij\intercal} U^{ij} E^{ij} \begin{pmatrix} 1 \\ x \\ u \end{pmatrix} \geq 0 \right\} \tag{5}$$

where $E^{ij} = \begin{pmatrix} E_s^{ij} \\ E_w^{ij} \end{pmatrix}$ with

$$E_s^{ij} = \begin{pmatrix} 1 & 0_{1\times(d+m)} \\ c_s^i & -T_s^i \\ c_s^j - T_s^j \begin{pmatrix} b^i \\ 0 \end{pmatrix} & -T_s^j \begin{pmatrix} A^i & B^i \\ 0_{d\times m} & \mathrm{Id}_{m\times m} \end{pmatrix} \end{pmatrix}$$
$$\text{and} \tag{6}$$
$$E_w^{ij} = \begin{pmatrix} c_w^i & -T_w^i \\ c_w^j - T_w^j \begin{pmatrix} b^i \\ 0 \end{pmatrix} & -T_w^j \begin{pmatrix} A^i & B^i \\ 0_{d\times m} & \mathrm{Id}_{m\times m} \end{pmatrix} \end{pmatrix}$$

3.2 Switching Cells

We have to manage another constraint which comes from the cell switches. After applying the available law in cell X^i, we have to specify the reachable cells i.e. the cells X^j such that there exists (x, u) satisfying:

$$(x, u) \in X^i \text{ and } (A^i x + B^i u + b^i, u) \in X^j$$

We say that a switch from i to j is fireable iff:

$$\left\{ (x, u) \in \mathbb{R}^{d+m} \left| \begin{array}{l} T_s^i (x, u)^\intercal \ll c_s^i \\ T_s^j (A^i x + B^i u + b^i, u)^\intercal \ll c_s^j \\ T_w^i (x, u)^\intercal \leq c_w^i \\ T_w^j (A^i x + B^i u + b^i, u)^\intercal \leq c_w^j \end{array} \right. \right\} \neq \emptyset \tag{7}$$

We will denote by $i \to j$ if the switch from i to j is fireable. Recall that the symbol $<$ means that we can deal with both strict inequalities and inequalities. Problem (7) is a linear programming feasibility problem with both strict and weak inequalities. However, we only check whether the system is solvable and we can detect infeasibility by using Motzkin transposition theorem [Mot51]. Motkin's theorem is an alternative type theorem, that is we oppose two linear systems such that exactly one of the two is feasible. To describe the alternative system, we have to separate strict and weak inequalities and use the matrices E_s^{ij} and E_w^{ij} defined at Equation (6). Problem (7) is equivalent to check whether the set $\{y = (z, x, u) \in \mathbb{R}^{1+d+m} \mid E_w^{ij} y \geq 0,\ E_s^{ij} y \gg 0\}$ is empty or not. To detect feasibility we test the infeasibility of the alternative system defined as:

$$\begin{cases} (E_s^{ij})^\intercal p^s + (E_w^{ij})^\intercal p = 0 \\ \sum_{k \in \mathbb{I}} p_k^s = 1 \\ p_k^s \geq 0,\ \forall k \in \mathbb{I} \\ p_i \geq 0,\ \forall i \notin \mathbb{I} \end{cases} \tag{8}$$

From Motzkin's transposition theorem [Mot51], we get the following proposition.

Proposition 1. *Problem* (7) *is feasible iff Problem* (8) *is not.*

However reasoning directly on the matrices can allow unfireable switches. For certain initial conditions, for all $k \in \mathbb{N}$, the condition $(x_k, u_k) \in X^i$ and $(A^i x_k + B^i u + b^i, u) \in X^j$ does not hold whereas Problem (7) is feasible. To avoid it, we must know all the possible trajectories of the system (which we want to compute) and remove all inactivated switches. A sound way to underapproximate unfireable transitions is to identify unsatisfiable sets of linear constraints.

Example 4. We continue to detail our running example. More precisely, we consider the possible switches. We take for example the cell X^2. To switch from cell X^2 to cell X^1 is possible if the following system of linear inequalities has a solution:

$$\begin{aligned} -9x+7y+6u &< 5 \\ -0.8532x+2.5748y-10.4460 &< -68 \\ -3.3662x+2.1732y-1.1084u &< -58 \\ 4x-8y+8u &\leq -4 \\ u &\leq 3 \\ -u &\leq 3 \end{aligned} \tag{9}$$

The two first consists in constraining the image of (x,y,u) to belong to X^1 and the four last constraints correspond to the definition of X^2. The representation of these two sets (X^2 and the preimage of X^1 by the law defined in X^2) is given at Figure 1. We see at Figure 1 that the system of inequalities defined at

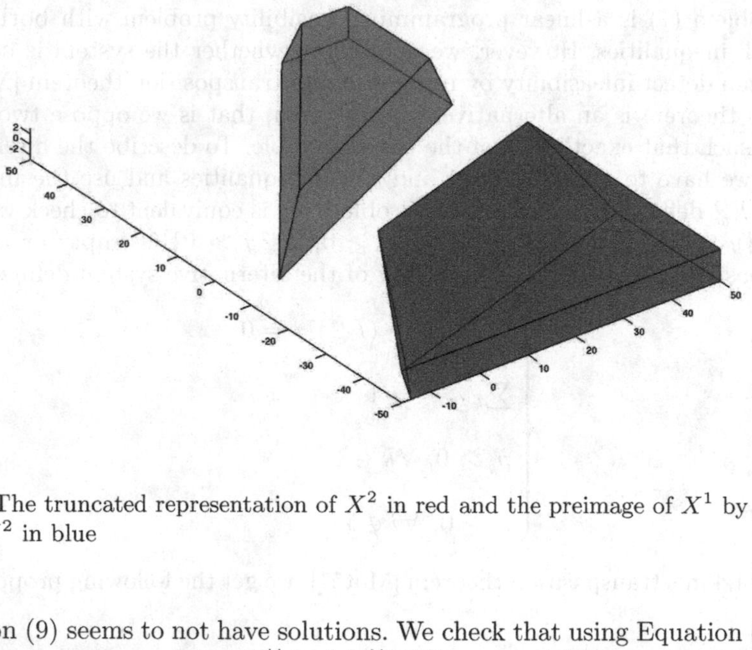

Fig. 1. The truncated representation of X^2 in red and the preimage of X^1 by the law inside X^2 in blue

Equation (9) seems to not have solutions. We check that using Equation (8) and Proposition 1. The matrices E_s^{ij} and E_w^{ij} of Equation (8) are in this example:

$$E_s^{21} = \begin{pmatrix} 5 & 9 & -7 & -6 \\ -68 & 0.8532 & -2.5748 & 10.446 \\ -58 & 3.3662 & -2.1732 & 1.1084 \end{pmatrix} \text{ and } E_w^{21} = \begin{pmatrix} -4 & -4 & 8 & -8 \\ 3 & 0 & 0 & -1 \\ 3 & 0 & 0 & 1 \end{pmatrix}$$

We thus solve the linear program defined in Equation (8) (with Matlab and Linprog) and we found $p=(0.8735, 0.0983, 0.0282)^\intercal$ and $q=(0.3325, 14.2500, 7.8461)^\intercal$. This means that the alternative system is feasible and consequently the initial is not from Proposition 1. Finally the transition from X^2 to X^1 is not possible.

3.3 Piecewise Quadratic Lyapunov Functions to Compute Invariant Sets

Now we adapt the work of Rantzer and Johansson [Joh03] and the work of Mignone et al [MFTM00] to compute of an invariant set for switched systems i.e. a subset $\mathcal{S}$ such that $(x_k, u) \in \mathcal{S}$ implies $(x_{k+1}, u) \in \mathcal{S}$. These works are instead focused on deciding whether a piecewise affine system is global asymptotic convergent or not. Even if the problem is undecidable [BBK⁺01] the latter authors prove a stronger property on the system: there exists a piecewise Lyapunov functions for the piecewise affine systems. Rantzer and Johansson [Joh03] and Mignone et al [MFTM00] suggest to compute a piecewise quadratic function as Lyapunov function in the case of discrete-time piecewise affine systems to prove GAS property. Recall that a piecewise quadratic function on $\mathbb{R}^d$ is a function defined on a polyhedric partition of $\mathbb{R}^d$ which is quadratic on each polyhedron of the partition. In this paper, we propose to compute a (weaker) piecewise Lyapunov function to characterize an invariant set for our piecewise affine systems. In this section, we will denote by V this function. The pieces are given by the cells of the piecewise affine system and thus V is defined as:

$$\begin{aligned} V(x,u) &= V^i(x,u), \text{ if } \begin{pmatrix} x \\ u \end{pmatrix} \in X^i \\ &= \begin{pmatrix} x \\ u \end{pmatrix}^\intercal P^i \begin{pmatrix} x \\ u \end{pmatrix} + 2{q^i}^\intercal \begin{pmatrix} x \\ u \end{pmatrix}, \text{ if } \begin{pmatrix} x \\ u \end{pmatrix} \in X^i \end{aligned}$$

The function V^i is thus a local function only defined on X^i.

A sublevel set S_α of V of level $\alpha \in \mathbb{R}$ is represented as:

$$\begin{aligned} S_\alpha &= \bigcup_{i\in I} S_{i,\alpha} \\ &= \bigcup_{i\in I} \left\{ \begin{pmatrix} x \\ u \end{pmatrix} \in X^i \mid \begin{pmatrix} x \\ u \end{pmatrix}^\intercal P^i \begin{pmatrix} x \\ u \end{pmatrix} + 2{q^i}^\intercal x \le \alpha \right\} \\ &= \bigcup_{i\in I} \left\{ \begin{pmatrix} x \\ u \end{pmatrix} \in X^i \mid \begin{pmatrix} 1 \\ x \\ u \end{pmatrix}^\intercal \begin{pmatrix} -\alpha & {q^i}^\intercal \\ q^i & P^i \end{pmatrix} \begin{pmatrix} 1 \\ x \\ u \end{pmatrix} \le 0 \right\}. \end{aligned}$$

The set $S_{i,\alpha}$ is thus the local sublevel set of V^i associated to the level α.

So we are looking a family of pairs of a matrix and a vector $\{(P^i, q^i)\}_{i\in I}$ and a real $\alpha \in \mathbb{R}$ such that S_α is invariant by the piecewise affine system. To obtain invariance property, we have to constraint S_α to contain initial conditions of the system. Finally, to prove that the reachable set is bounded, we have to constraint S_α to be bounded.

Before deriving the semi-definite constraints, let us first state a useful result in Proposition 2. This result allows to encode implications into semi-definite constraint in a safe way safe. The implication must involve quadratic inequalities on both sides.

Proposition 2. *Let A, B, C be $d \times d$ matrices. Then $C + A + B \succeq 0$ holds implies that the implication $(y^\intercal Ay \le 0 \wedge\ y^\intercal By \le 0) \implies y^\intercal Cy \ge 0$ holds.*

Proof. Suppose that $C+A+B \succeq 0$. It is equivalent to say $y^\intercal(C+A+B)y \geq 0$ for all $y \in \mathbb{R}^d$. Now pick $z \in \mathbb{R}^d$ such that $z^\intercal Az \leq 0$ and $z^\intercal Bz \leq 0$. Since $z^\intercal Cz \geq -z^\intercal Az - z^\intercal Bz$, we conclude that $z^\intercal Cz \geq 0$ and the implication is true.

Writing Invariance as Semi-definite Constraints . We assume that $(x,u) \in X^i \cap S_{i,\alpha}$ (this index i is unique). Invariance means that if we apply the available law to (x,u) and suppose that the image of (x,u) belongs to some cell X^j (notation $i \to j$), then the image of (x,u) belongs to $S_{j,\alpha}$. Note that $(x,u) \in X^i$ and its image is supposed to be in X^j then $(x,u) \in X^{ij}$. Let $(i,j) \in I^2$ such that $i \to j$, invariance translated in inequatilities and implication gives :

$$\begin{pmatrix} x \\ u \end{pmatrix} \in X^{ij} \wedge \begin{pmatrix} x \\ u \end{pmatrix} \in S_{i,\alpha} \Longrightarrow \begin{pmatrix} A^i x + B^i u + b^i \\ u \end{pmatrix} \in S_{j,\alpha} \tag{10}$$

We can use the relaxation of Subsection 3.1 as representation of cells and use matrix variables W^i and U^{ij} to encode their quadratization. We get, for $(i,j) \in I^2$ such that $i \to j$:

$$\begin{aligned} &\begin{pmatrix} 1 \\ x \\ u \end{pmatrix}^\intercal E^{ij\intercal} U^{ij} E^{ij} \begin{pmatrix} 1 \\ x \\ u \end{pmatrix} \geq 0 \wedge \begin{pmatrix} 1 \\ x \\ u \end{pmatrix}^\intercal \begin{pmatrix} -\alpha & q^{i\intercal} \\ q^i & P^i \end{pmatrix} \begin{pmatrix} 1 \\ x \\ u \end{pmatrix} \leq 0 \\ \Longrightarrow &\begin{pmatrix} 1 \\ x \\ u \end{pmatrix}^\intercal \left(F^{i\intercal} \begin{pmatrix} -\alpha & q^{j\intercal} \\ q^j & P^j \end{pmatrix} F^i \right) \begin{pmatrix} 1 \\ x \\ u \end{pmatrix} \leq 0 \end{aligned} \tag{11}$$

where E^{ij} is the matrix defined at Equation (5) and F^i is defined at Equation (3).

Finally, we obtain a stronger condition by considering semi-definite constraint such as Equation (12). Proposition 2 proves that if $(P^i, P^j, q^i, q^j, U^{ij})$ is a solution of Equation (12) then $(P^i, P^j, q^i, q^j, U^{ij})$ satisfies Equation (11). For $(i,j) \in I^2$ such that $i \to j$:

$$-F^{i\intercal} \begin{pmatrix} 0 & q^{j\intercal} \\ q^j & P^j \end{pmatrix} F^i + \begin{pmatrix} 0 & q^{i\intercal} \\ q^i & P^i \end{pmatrix} - E^{ij\intercal} U^{ij} E^{ij} \succeq 0 \ . \tag{12}$$

Note that the symbol $-\alpha$ is cancelled during the computation.

Integrating Initial Conditions . To complete invariance property, invariant set must contain initial conditions. Suppose that initial condition is a polyhedron $X^0 = \{(x,u) \in \mathbb{R}^{d+m} \mid T_w^0(x,u) \leq c_w^0,\ T_s^0(x,u) \ll c_s^0\}$. We must have $X^0 \subseteq S_\alpha$. But X^0 is contained in the union of X^i. Hence X^0 is the union over $i \in I$ of the sets $X^0 \cap X^i$. If, for all $i \in I$, the set $X^0 \cap X^i$ is contained in $S_{i,\alpha}$ then $X^0 \subseteq S_\alpha$. We can use the same method as before to express that all sets $S_{i,\alpha}$ such that $X^0 \cap X^i \neq \emptyset$ must contain $X^0 \cap X^i$. In term of implications, it can be rewritten as for all $i \in I$ such that $X^0 \cap X^i \neq \emptyset$:

$$(x,u) \in X^0 \cap X^i \implies (x,u)P^i(x,u)^\intercal + 2(x,u)q^i \leq \alpha \tag{13}$$

Since $X^0 \cap X^i$ is a polyhedra, it admits some quadratization that is: $\overline{X^0 \cap X^i} = \{(x,u) \in \mathbb{R}^{d+m} \mid (1,x,u)E^{0i\intercal}Z^i E^{0i}(1,x,u)^\intercal \geq 0\}$ where $E^{0i} = \begin{pmatrix} E_s^{0i} \\ E_w^{0i} \end{pmatrix}$ with:

$$E_w^{0i} = \begin{pmatrix} c_w^0 & -T_w^0 \\ c_w^i & -T_w^i \end{pmatrix} \text{ and } E_s^{0i} = \begin{pmatrix} 1 & 0_{1\times(d+m)} \\ c_s^0 & -T_s^0 \\ c_s^i & -T_s^i \end{pmatrix}$$

and Z^i is some symmetric matrix whose coefficients are nonnegative.

For all $i \in I$ such that $X^0 \cap X^i \neq \emptyset$, we obtain a stronger notion by introducing semi-definite constraints:

$$-\begin{pmatrix} -\alpha & q^{i\intercal} \\ q^i & P^i \end{pmatrix} - E^{0i\intercal} Z^i E^{0i} \succeq 0 \tag{14}$$

Proposition 2 proves that if (P^i, q^i, Z^i) is a solution of Equation (14) then (P^i, q^i, Z^i) satisfies Equation (13).

Note since $X^0 \cap X^i$ is a polyhedron then its emptyness can be decided by checking the feasibility of the linear problem (15) and by using of same argument than Proposition 1.

$$\begin{cases} (E_s^{0i})^\intercal p^s + (E_w^{0i})^\intercal p = 0 \\ \sum_{k\in\mathbb{I}} p_k^s = 1 \\ p_k^s \geq 0, \ \forall k \subset \mathbb{I} \\ p_i \geq 0, \ \forall i \notin \mathbb{I} \end{cases} \tag{15}$$

Linear program (15) is feasible iff $X^0 \cap X^i = \emptyset$.

Writing Boundedness as Semi-Definite Constraints . The sublevel S_α is bounded if and only if for all $i \in I$, the sublevel $S_{i,\alpha}$ is bounded The boundedness constraint in term of implications is, for all $i \in I$, there exists $\beta \geq 0$:

$$(x,u) \in X^i \wedge \begin{pmatrix} x \\ u \end{pmatrix} \in S_{i,\alpha} \implies \|(x,u)\|_2^2 \leq \beta \tag{16}$$

where $\|\cdot\|_2$ denotes the Euclidian norm of $\mathbb{R}^{d+m}$.

As invariance, we use the quadratization of X^i and the definition of $S_{i,\alpha}$. We use the fact that $\|(x,u)\|_2^2 = \begin{pmatrix} x \\ u \end{pmatrix}^\intercal \mathrm{Id}_{(d+m)\times(d+m)} \begin{pmatrix} x \\ u \end{pmatrix}$ and we get for all $i \in I$:

$$\begin{pmatrix} 1 \\ x \\ u \end{pmatrix}^\intercal E^{i\intercal} W^i E^i \begin{pmatrix} 1 \\ x \\ u \end{pmatrix} \geq 0 \text{ and } \begin{pmatrix} 1 \\ x \\ u \end{pmatrix}^\intercal \begin{pmatrix} -\alpha & q^{i\intercal} \\ q^i & P^i \end{pmatrix} \begin{pmatrix} 1 \\ x \\ u \end{pmatrix} \leq 0$$
$$\implies \begin{pmatrix} 1 \\ x \\ u \end{pmatrix}^\intercal \begin{pmatrix} -\beta & 0_{1\times(d+m)} \\ 0_{(d+m)\times 1} & \mathrm{Id}_{(d+m)\times(d+m)} \end{pmatrix} \begin{pmatrix} 1 \\ x \\ u \end{pmatrix} \leq 0 \tag{17}$$

where E^i is defined in Equation (4).

Finally, as invariance we obtain a stronger condition by considering semi-definite constraint such as Equation (18). Proposition 2 proves that (P^i, q^i, W^i) is a solution of Equation (18) the (P^i, q^i, W^i) satisfies Equation (17). For all $i \in I$:

$$-E^{i\intercal} W^i E^i + \begin{pmatrix} -\alpha & q^{i\intercal} \\ q^i & P^i \end{pmatrix} + \begin{pmatrix} \beta & 0_{1\times(d+m)} \\ 0_{(d+m)\times 1} & -\mathrm{Id}_{(d+m)\times(d+m)} \end{pmatrix} \succeq 0 \qquad (18)$$

Method to Compute Invariant Set for Piecewise Affine Systems and Prove the Boundedness of Its Reachable Set. To compute a piecewise ellipsoidal invariant set for a piecewise affine systems of the form (1) whose initial conditions is a polyhedron, we can proceed as follows:

1. Define a matrix L of size $I \times I$ following Equation (7): set $L(i,j) = 1$ if Problem (8) is not feasible and $L(i,j) = 0$ otherwise;
2. Define the real variables α, β;
3. For $i \in I$, compute the matrix E^i of Equation (4) define the variable P^i as a symmetric matrix of size $(d+m) \times (d+m)$, the variable matrix W^i with nonnegative coefficients of size ($\sharp$ lines of E^i) $\times$ ($\sharp$ lines of E^i) and add the constraint (18). If Problem (15) is not feasible, add Constraint (14);
4. For all $(i,j) \in I^2$, if $L(i,j) = 1$ construct the matrix E^{ij} defined by Equation (5) and define the symmetric matrix variable $U^{i,j}$ of the size ($\sharp$ lines of E^{ij}) $\times$ ($\sharp$ lines of E^{ij}) with nonnegative coefficients and add the constraint (12);
5. Add as linear objective function the sum of α and β to minimize;
6. Solve the semi-definite program;
7. If there exists a solution then the set $\bigcup_{i\in I}\{(x,u) \in X^i \mid (x,u)P^i_{opt}(x,u)^\intercal + 2(x,u)q^i_{opt} \leq \alpha_{opt}\}$ is a bounded invariant of system (1) and the norm $\|(x,u)\|$ is less than β_{opt} for all the reachable (x,u) of the system.

3.4 Solution

The method is implemented in Matlab and the solution is given by a semi-definite programming solver in Matlab. For our running example, Matlab returns the following the values:

$$\alpha_{opt} = 242.0155$$
$$\beta_{opt} = 2173.8501$$

This means that $\|(x,y,u)\|_2^2 = x^2+y^2+u^2 \leq \beta_{opt}$. We can conclude, for example, that the values taken by the variables x are between $[-46.6154, 46.6154]$. The value α_{opt} gives the level of the invariant sublevel of our piecewise quadratic Lyapunov function where the local quadratic functions are characterized by the following matrices and vectors:

$$P^1 = \begin{pmatrix} 1.0181 & -0.0040 & -1.1332 \\ -0.0040 & 1.0268 & -0.5340 \\ -1.1332 & -0.5340 & -13.7623 \end{pmatrix} \text{ and } q^1 = (0.1252, 1.3836, -29.6791)^\intercal$$

$$P^2 = \begin{pmatrix} 9.1540 & -7.0159 & -2.6659 \\ -7.0159 & 9.5054 & -2.4016 \\ -2.6659 & -2.4016 & -8.9741 \end{pmatrix} \text{ and } q^2 = (-21.3830, -44.6291, 114.2984)^\intercal$$

$$P^3 = \begin{pmatrix} 1.1555 & -0.3599 & -2.6224 \\ -0.3599 & 2.4558 & -2.8236 \\ -2.6224 & -2.8236 & -2.3852 \end{pmatrix} \text{ and } q^3 = (-5.3138, 6.7894, -40.5537)^\intercal$$

$$P^4 = \begin{pmatrix} 3.7314 & -3.4179 & -3.1427 \\ -3.4179 & 6.1955 & 0.9499 \\ -3.1427 & 0.9499 & -10.6767 \end{pmatrix} \text{ and } q^4 = (28.5011, -73.5421, 48.2153)^\intercal$$

Finally, for conciseness reason, we only give the matrix certificates for the cell X^1. First we give the matrix W^1 which encodes the quadratization of the guard X^1. Recall that this matrix ensures that $(x, u) \mapsto \alpha - (x, u)P^1(x, u)^\intercal - 2(x, u)q^i$ is nonnegative on X^1.

$$W^1 = \begin{pmatrix} 63.0218 & 0.0163 & 0.0217 & 12.1557 & 8.8835 \\ 0.0163 & 0.0000 & 0.0000 & 0.0267 & 0.0031 \\ 0.0217 & 0.0000 & 0.0000 & 0.0094 & 0.0061 \\ 12.1557 & 0.0267 & 0.0094 & 4.2011 & 59.5733 \\ 8.8835 & 0.0031 & 0.0061 & 59.5733 & 3.0416 \end{pmatrix}$$

Secondly, we give the matrices U^{1j} which encodes the quadratization of polyhedron X^{1j}. Recall that those matrices ensure that the image of $(1, x, u)$ by F^1 belongs to the set $S_{j,\alpha}$ for all $(1, x, u)$ such that $F^1(1, x, u) \in X^j$.

$$U^{11} = \begin{pmatrix} 0.0004 & 0.0000 & 0.0000 & 0.0000 & 0.0000 & 0.0000 & 0.0001 \\ 0.0000 & -0.0000 & -0.0000 & -0.0000 & -0.0000 & -0.0000 & -0.0000 \\ 0.0000 & -0.0000 & -0.0000 & -0.0000 & -0.0000 & 0.0000 & -0.0000 \\ 0.0000 & -0.0000 & -0.0000 & -0.0000 & -0.0000 & -0.0000 & -0.0000 \\ 0.0000 & -0.0000 & -0.0000 & -0.0000 & -0.0000 & 0.0000 & -0.0000 \\ 0.0000 & -0.0000 & 0.0000 & -0.0000 & 0.0000 & 0.0000 & 0.0000 \\ 0.0001 & -0.0000 & -0.0000 & -0.0000 & -0.0000 & 0.0000 & 0.0001 \end{pmatrix}$$

$$U^{12} = \begin{pmatrix} 2.1068 & 0.4134 & 0.0545 & 1.4664 & 0.1882 & 2.3955 & 2.4132 \\ 0.4134 & 0.0008 & 0.0047 & 0.0009 & 0.0819 & 0.5474 & 0.0484 \\ 0.0545 & 0.0047 & 0.0050 & 0.0147 & 0.0097 & 0.1442 & 0.2316 \\ 1.4664 & 0.0009 & 0.0147 & 0.0041 & 0.3383 & 0.8776 & 0.0999 \\ 0.1882 & 0.0819 & 0.0097 & 0.3383 & 0.0675 & 0.4405 & 0.4172 \\ 2.3955 & 0.5474 & 0.1442 & 0.8776 & 0.4405 & 8.1215 & 9.6346 \\ 2.4132 & 0.0484 & 0.2316 & 0.0999 & 0.4172 & 9.6346 & 0.9532 \end{pmatrix}$$

$$U^{13} = \begin{pmatrix} 0.3570 & 0.2243 & 0.0031 & 0.0050 & 0.1431 & 0.0388 & 0.7675 \\ 0.2243 & 0.0201 & 0.0023 & 0.0050 & 0.1730 & 0.0494 & 0.1577 \\ 0.0031 & 0.0023 & 0.0001 & 0.0001 & 0.0071 & 0.0006 & 0.0088 \\ 0.0050 & 0.0050 & 0.0001 & 0.0002 & 0.3563 & 0.0009 & 0.0168 \\ 0.1431 & 0.1730 & 0.0071 & 0.3563 & 0.0527 & 0.2689 & 0.8979 \\ 0.0388 & 0.0494 & 0.0006 & 0.0009 & 0.2689 & 0.0137 & 0.1542 \\ 0.7675 & 0.1577 & 0.0088 & 0.0168 & 0.8979 & 0.1542 & 0.2747 \end{pmatrix}$$

$$U^{14} = \begin{pmatrix} 1.3530 & 0.1912 & 0.0280 & 0.1178 & 2.9171 & 0.7079 & 1.4104 \\ 0.1912 & 0.0512 & 0.0068 & 0.0326 & 1.7179 & 0.3764 & 0.6045 \\ 0.0280 & 0.0068 & 0.0022 & 0.0048 & 0.1396 & 0.0264 & 0.0679 \\ 0.1178 & 0.0326 & 0.0048 & 0.0409 & 0.5231 & 0.1204 & 0.2390 \\ 2.9171 & 1.7179 & 0.1396 & 0.5231 & 15.0992 & 5.1148 & 14.3581 \\ 0.7079 & 0.3764 & 0.0264 & 0.1204 & 5.1148 & 0.5102 & 1.6230 \\ 1.4104 & 0.6045 & 0.0679 & 0.2390 & 14.3581 & 1.6230 & 1.2985 \end{pmatrix}$$

We remark that U^{11} has negative coefficients whereas in our method, we are looking for a nonnegative coefficients matrix. It is due to the interior point method which is used to solve the semi-definite programming problems. Interior point methods returns ϵ-optimal solution i.e. a solution which belongs to the ball of radius ϵ centered at an optimal solution. Hence, the solution furnished by the solver can slightly violate the constraints of the semi-definite program. We are aware of that and the projection of the returned solution on the feasible set should be studied as a future work.

4 Experimentations

To illustrate the applicability of our method to a wide set of examples, we generated about a thousand of dynamical systems with at most 4 partition cells, 4 state variables and a single input.

In [BBK+01], the authors show (Theorem 2) that to determine the stability a piecewise affine dynamical system is undecidable. In order to generated more stable examples, we restricted the class of program generated. Each partition cell affine semantics would be (i) generated with small coefficients, since big coefficients are usually avoided in controllers and, (ii) enforced locally stable when needed by updating the values of the coefficients using the spectral radius.

Our example synthesis still does not guaranty to obtain globally stable system, but, with these required properties of local stability and small coefficients, it is more likely that switching from one cell to the other would not break stability and therefore boundedness of the reachable states. The intuition behind is that when we pass from a cell to another cell, we multiply a vector by a small number then all the coordinates of the vector image are strictly smaller than the ones of initial vector.

About 300 of such 1000 examples are automatically shown to be bounded using our technique while the class of program considered is unlikely to be analyzable with other static analysis tools the author are aware of, including the previous analyzes proposed [RG13]. A typical run of the analysis, including the time to generate the problem instance, is about 20s.

All the computation have been performed within Matlab, including the synthesis of the examples. The source code of the analysis as well a document summarizing the examples and their analysis is available at`https://cavale.enseeiht.fr/vmcai15/`.

5 Conclusion

The presented approach is able, considering a piecewise affine system, to compute a piecewise quadratic invariant able to bound the set of reachable state.

The technique extends the classical quadratic Lyapunov function synthesis using SDP solvers by formulating a more complex set of constraints to the SDP solver. This new formulation accounts the definition of the partitioning and encodes within the SDP constraints the relationship between partitions.

In practice our technique has been applied to a wide set of generated examples and was able to bound their reachable state space while a global quadratic invariant was proven not computable.

Our future work will consider the combination of this technique with other formal methods. A first direction will rely on the computed piecewise quadratic form as a template domain, bounding its value on some code using either Kleene iterations [CC77] or policy iteration [GSA+12]. This will require to extend the existing algorithms to fit this piecewise description of the template.

A second direction is to ease the applicability of the method and to integrate the technique in a more common analysis framework. A requirement for the presented work is to obtain a global representation of the program, as matrix updates and conditions. Existing static analysis [RG13] used for policy iteration extracts such a graph with the appropriate representation. We plan to integrate the two frameworks to ease the applicability on more realistic programs in an automated fashion.

Acknowledgement. We thank the anonymous referees for their useful comments regarding the paper.

References

[All09] Allamigeon, X.: Static analysis of memory manipulations by abstract interpretation — Algorithmics of tropical polyhedra, and application to abstract interpretation. PhD thesis, École Polytechnique, Palaiseau, France (November 2009)

[BBK+01] Blondel, V., Bournez, O., Koiran, P., Papadimitriou, C., Tsitsiklis, J.: Deciding stability and mortality of piecewise affine dynamical systems. Theoretical Computer Science A 1–2(255), 687–696 (2001)

[BCC+11] Bertrane, J., Cousot, P., Cousot, R., Feret, J., Mauborgne, L., Miné, A., Rival, X.: Static analysis by abstract interpretation of embedded critical software. ACM SIGSOFT Software Engineering Notes 36(1), 1–8 (2011)

[BGLM05] Biswas, P., Grieder, P., Löfberg, J., Morari, M.: A Survey on Stability Analysis of Discrete-Time Piecewise Affine Systems. In: IFAC World Congress, Prague, Czech Republic (July 2005)

[CC77] Cousot, P., Cousot, R.: Abstract interpretation: A unified lattice model for static analysis of programs by construction or approximation of fixpoints. In: Conference Record of the Fourth Annual ACM SIGPLAN-SIGACT Symposium on Principles of Programming Languages, Los Angeles, California, pp. 238–252. ACM Press, New York (1977)

[CH78] Cousot, P., Halbwachs, N.: Automatic discovery of linear restraints among variables of a program. In: Aho, A., Zilles, S., Szymanski, T. (eds.) POPL, pp. 84–96. ACM Press (1978)

[CS11] Colón, M.A., Sankaranarayanan, S.: Generalizing the template polyhedral domain. In: Barthe, G. (ed.) ESOP 2011. LNCS, vol. 6602, pp. 176–195. Springer, Heidelberg (2011)

[CSS03] Colón, M.A., Sankaranarayanan, S., Sipma, H.B.: Linear invariant generation using non-linear constraint solving. In: Hunt Jr., W.A., Somenzi, F. (eds.) CAV 2003. LNCS, vol. 2725, pp. 420–432. Springer, Heidelberg (2003)

[Fer04] Feret, J.: Static analysis of digital filters. In: Schmidt, D. (ed.) ESOP 2004. LNCS, vol. 2986, pp. 33–48. Springer, Heidelberg (2004)

[FR94] Filé, G., Ranzato, F.: Improving abstract interpretations by systematic lifting to the powerset. In: Logic Programming, Proc. of the 1994 International Symposium, Ithaca, New York, USA, November 13-17, pp. 655–669 (1994)

[GGP09] Ghorbal, K., Goubault, E., Putot, S.: The zonotope abstract domain taylor1+. In: Bouajjani, A., Maler, O. (eds.) CAV 2009. LNCS, vol. 5643, pp. 627–633. Springer, Heidelberg (2009)

[GSA+12] Gawlitza, T., Seidl, H., Adjé, A., Gaubert, S., Goubault, E.: Abstract interpretation meets convex optimization. J. Symb. Comput. 47(12), 1416–1446 (2012)

[IS00] Ikramov, K.D., Savel'eva, N.V.: Conditionally definite matrices. Journal of Mathematical Sciences 98(1), 1–50 (2000)

[Joh03] Johansson, M.: On modeling, analysis and design of piecewise linear control systems. In: Proc. of the 2003 International Symposium on Circuits and Systems, ISCAS 2003, vol. 3, pp. III–646–III–649 (May 2003)

[MFTM00] Mignone, D., Ferrari-Trecate, G., Morari, M.: Stability and stabilization of piecewise affine and hybrid systems: An lmi approach. In: Proc. of the 39th IEEE Conference on Decision and Control, vol. 1, pp. 504–509 (2000)

[Min01] Miné, A.: A new numerical abstract domain based on difference-bound matrices. In: Danvy, O., Filinski, A. (eds.) PADO-II 2001. LNCS, vol. 2053, pp. 155–172. Springer, Heidelberg (2001)

[Min06] Miné, A.: The octagon abstract domain. Higher-Order and Symbolic Computation 19(1), 31–100 (2006)

[MJ81] Martin, D.H., Jacobson, D.H.: Copositive matrices and definiteness of quadratic forms subject to homogeneous linear inequality constraints. Linear Algebra and its Applications 35(0), 227–258 (1981)

[Mot51] Motzkin, T.S.: Two consequences of the transposition theorem on linear inequalities. Econometrica 19(2), 184–185 (1951)

[RG13] Roux, P., Garoche, P.-L.: Integrating policy iterations in abstract interpreters. In: Van Hung, D., Ogawa, M. (eds.) ATVA 2013. LNCS, vol. 8172, pp. 240–254. Springer, Heidelberg (2013)

[RJ00] Rantzer, A., Johansson, M.: Piecewise linear quadratic optimal control. IEEE Transactions on Automatic Control 45(4), 629–637 (2000)

[RJGF12] Roux, P., Jobredeaux, R., Garoche, P.-L., Feron, E.: A generic ellipsoid abstract domain for linear time invariant systems. In: Dang, T., Mitchell, I. (eds.) HSCC, pp. 105–114. ACM (2012)

Distributed Markov Chains

Ratul Saha[1], Javier Esparza[2], Sumit Kumar Jha[3,⋆],
Madhavan Mukund[4,⋆⋆], and P.S. Thiagarajan[1,⋆⋆⋆]

[1] National University of Singapore, Singapore
{ratul,thiagu}@comp.nus.edu.sg
[2] Technische Universität München, Germany
esparza@in.tum.de
[3] University of Central Florida, USA
jha@eecs.ucf.edu
[4] Chennai Mathematical Institute, India
madhavan@cmi.ac.in

Abstract. The formal verification of large probabilistic models is challenging. Exploiting the concurrency that is often present is one way to address this problem. Here we study a class of communicating probabilistic agents in which the synchronizations determine the probability distribution for the next moves of the participating agents. The key property of this class is that the synchronizations are deterministic, in the sense that any two simultaneously enabled synchronizations involve disjoint sets of agents. As a result, such a network of agents can be viewed as a succinct and distributed presentation of a large global Markov chain. A rich class of Markov chains can be represented this way.

We use partial-order notions to define an interleaved semantics that can be used to efficiently verify properties of the global Markov chain represented by the network. To demonstrate this, we develop a statistical model checking (SMC) procedure and use it to verify two large networks of probabilistic agents.

We also show that our model, called distributed Markov chains (DMCs), is closely related to deterministic cyclic negotiations, a recently introduced model for concurrent systems [10]. Exploiting this connection we show that the termination of a DMC that has been endowed with a global final state can be checked in polynomial time.

1 Introduction

We present here a class of distributed probabilistic systems called distributed Markov chains (DMCs). A DMC is a network of probabilistic transition

⋆ Sumit Kumar Jha acknowledges support from the National Science Foundation under projects CCF-1438989 and CCF-1422257, Air Force Research Lab under contract #CA0116UCF2013, and the Oak Ridge National Laboratory under contract #4000126570.

⋆⋆ Partially supported by a grant from Infosys Foundation.

⋆⋆⋆ P.S. Thiagarajan acknowledges support from the Singapore Ministry of Education grant T1 251RES1115.

D. D'Souza et al. (Eds.): VMCAI 2015, LNCS 8931, pp. 117–134, 2015.

systems that synchronize on common actions. The information that the agents gain through a synchronization determines the probability distribution for their next moves. Internal actions correspond to synchronizations involving only one agent. The synchronizations are deterministic in the sense that, at any global state, if two synchronizations are enabled then they will involve disjoint set of agents. We capture this syntactically by requiring that at a local state of an agent, the synchronizations that the agent is willing to engage in will all involve the same set of partners. In many distributed probabilistic systems, the communication protocols are naturally deterministic in this sense, or can be designed to be so. As our two case studies in Section 7 show, the determinacy restriction is less limiting than may appear at first sight while permitting a considerable degree of concurrency.

We define an interleaved semantics where one synchronization action is executed at a time, followed by a probabilistic move by the participating agents. Except in the trivial case where there is no concurrency, the resulting transition system will *not* be a Markov chain. Hence, defining a probability measure over interleaved runs, called *trajectories*, is a technical challenge. We address this by noting that there is a natural independence relation on local actions—two actions are independent if they involve disjoint sets of agents. Using this relation, we partition the trajectories in the usual way into equivalence classes that correspond to partially ordered executions. We then use the maximal equivalence classes to form a trajectory space that is a counterpart to the path space of a Markov chain.

To endow this trajectory space with a probability measure, we exploit the fact that, due to determinacy of synchronizations, any two actions enabled at a global state will be independent. Hence, by executing all the enabled actions simultaneously, followed by probabilistic moves by all the agents involved, one obtains a finite state Markov chain that captures the global behavior of the DMC under this "maximally parallel" execution semantics.

Using Mazurkiewicz trace theory [8], we then embed the trajectory space into the path space of this Markov chain and use this embedding to induce a probability measure over the trajectory space. Consequently, the global behavior of this Markov chain can be verified efficiently using the interleaved semantics.

We then demonstrate on two fronts that the DMC model possesses a good of modeling power while considerably easing the task of analyzing the global behavior of the network. First we formulate a statistical model checking (SMC) procedure for DMCs in which the specifications consist of Boolean combinations of local bounded linear temporal logic (BLTL) [4] formulas. We then use the sequential probability ratio test (SPRT) based SMC technique [21,22] to analyze the global behavior of a DMC.

Our two case studies show that one can easily construct DMC models of a variety of distributed probabilistic systems [7]. Both the systems we study exhibit a considerable degree of concurrency. Further, the performance and scalability of our interleaved semantics based verification techniques is significantly better than the SMC procedure of PLASMA [6].

The second front we briefly explore demonstrates that the determinacy restriction adds a considerable amount of analysis power. Specifically, we show that the DMC model constitutes the probabilistic version of the deterministic cyclic negotiations model [10]. As a result one readily obtains a polynomial time algorithm to verify that a DMC that has been endowed with a global final (goal) state almost certainly terminates. This suggests that by using the DMC model one can efficiently analyze the termination properties of a range of goal-oriented distributed stochastic processes such as communication protocols and stochastic distributed algorithms.

To summarize, our main contributions are: (i) establishing that deterministic synchronizations are a fruitful restriction for distributed stochastic systems, (ii) showing that the space of partially ordered runs of such systems can be endowed with a probability measure due to the clean combination of concurrent and stochastic dynamics, (iii) constructing an SMC procedure in this distributed stochastic setting and, (iv) establishing a connection to the model of deterministic negotiations, and thereby deriving a polynomial time algorithm to check for termination of DMCs endowed with global final states.

In what follows we will mainly present proof sketches of the main results. The details can be found in the full paper [19].

Related Work. Our work is in line with partial order based methods for Markov Decision Processes (MDPs) [12] where, typically, a partial commutation structure is imposed on the actions of a *global* MDP. For instance, in [5], partial order reduction is used to identify "spurious" nondeterminism arising out of the interleaving of concurrent actions, in order to determine when the underlying behavior corresponds to a Markov chain. In contrast, in a DMC, deterministic communication ensures that local behaviors always generate a global Markov chain. The independence of actions is directly given by the local state spaces of the components. This also makes it easier to model how components influence each other through communications.

The interplay between concurrency and stochasticity has also been explored in the setting of event structures [2,20]. In these approaches, the global behaviour — which is not a Markov chain — is endowed with a probability measure. Further, probabilistic verification problems are not formulated and studied. Markov nets, studied in [3] can be easily modeled as DMCs. However, in [3], the focus is on working out a probabilistic event structure semantics rather than on developing a model checking procedure based on the interleaved semantics, as we do here.

Our model is formulated as a sub-class of probabilistic asynchronous automata [14], where we require synchronizations to be deterministic. This restriction allows us to develop a probability measure over the (infinite) trajectory space, which in turn paves the way for carrying out formal verification based on probabilistic temporal logic specifications. In contrast, the work reported in [14] is language-theoretic, with the goal of generalizing Zielonka's theorem [23] to a probabilistic setting. Moreover, in the model of [14], conflicting actions may be enabled at a global state and it is difficult to see how one can formulate a σ-algebra over the runs with a well-defined probability measure.

2 The Distributed Markov Chain (DMC) Model

We fix n agents $\{1, 2, \ldots, n\}$ and set $[n] = \{1, 2, \ldots, n\}$. For convenience, we denote various $[n]$-indexed sets of the form $\{X_i\}_{i \in [n]}$ as just $\{X_i\}$. We begin with some notation for distributed state spaces.

Definition 1. *For $i \in [n]$, let S_i be a finite set of local states, where $\{S_i\}$ are pairwise disjoint.*

- $S = \bigcup_i S_i$ *is the set of* local states.
- *For nonempty $u \subseteq [n]$, $\mathbf{S}_u = \prod_{i \in u} S_i$ is the set of u-states.*
- $\mathbf{S}_{[n]}$ *is the set of* global states, *typically denoted $\mathbf{S}$.*
- *For a state $\mathbf{v} \in \mathbf{S}_u$ and $w \subseteq u$, $\mathbf{v}_w$ denotes the projection of $\mathbf{v}$ to $\mathbf{S}_w$.*
- *For $u = \{i\}$, we write $\mathbf{S}_i$ and $\mathbf{v}_i$ rather than $\mathbf{S}_{\{i\}}$ and $\mathbf{v}_{\{i\}}$, respectively.*

Our model is a restricted version of probabilistic asynchronous automata [14].

Definition 2. *A* probabilistic asynchronous system *is a structure* $(\{S_i\}, \{s_i^{in}\}, A, loc, en, \{\pi^a\}_{a \in A})$ *where:*

- *S_i is a finite set of local states for each i and $\{S_i\}$ is pairwise disjoint.*
- *$s_i^{in} \in S_i$ is the initial state of agent i.*
- *A is a set of synchronization actions.*
- *$loc : A \to 2^{[n]} \setminus \emptyset$ specifies the agents that participate in each action a.*
  - *For $a \in A$, we write $\mathbf{S}_a$ instead of $\mathbf{S}_{loc(a)}$ and call it the set of a-states.*
- *For each $a \in A$, $en_a \subseteq \mathbf{S}_a$ is the subset of a-states where a is enabled.*
- *With each $a \in A$, we associate a probabilistic transition function $\pi^a : en_a \to (\mathbf{S}_a \to [0,1])$ such that, for every $\mathbf{v} \in en_a$, $\sum_{\mathbf{u} \in \mathbf{S}_a} \pi^a(\mathbf{v})(\mathbf{u}) = 1$.*

The action a represents a synchronization between the agents in $loc(a)$ and it is enabled at the global state $\mathbf{s}$ if $\mathbf{s}_a \in en_a$. When a occurs at $\mathbf{s}$, only the components in $loc(a)$ are involved in the move to the new global state $\mathbf{s}'$; the new a-state $\mathbf{s}'_a$ is chosen probabilistically according to the distribution $\pi^a(\mathbf{s}_a)$. On the other hand, for every $j \notin loc(a)$, $\mathbf{s}_j = \mathbf{s}'_j$.

We would like to lift the probabilities associated with individual moves to a probability measure over the runs of the system. This is difficult to achieve because of the combination of nondeterminism, concurrency and probability in the model. This motivates us to restrict the nondeterminism in the model.

For an agent i and a local state $s \in S_i$, we define the set of actions that i can participate in at s to be $act(s) = \{a \mid i \in loc(a), s = \mathbf{v}_i \text{ for some } \mathbf{v} \in en_a\}$. Using this notion we define the DMC model as follows.

Definition 3. *A* distributed Markov chain (DMC) *is a probabilistic asynchronous system $\mathcal{D} = (\{S_i\}, \{s_i^{in}\}, A, loc, en, \{\pi^a\}_{a \in A})$ in which (i) for each local state $s \in S$, if $a, b \in act(s)$ then $loc(a) = loc(b)$, and (ii) if $a, b \in A$, $a \neq b$ and $loc(a) = loc(b)$, then $en_a \cap en_b = \emptyset$.*

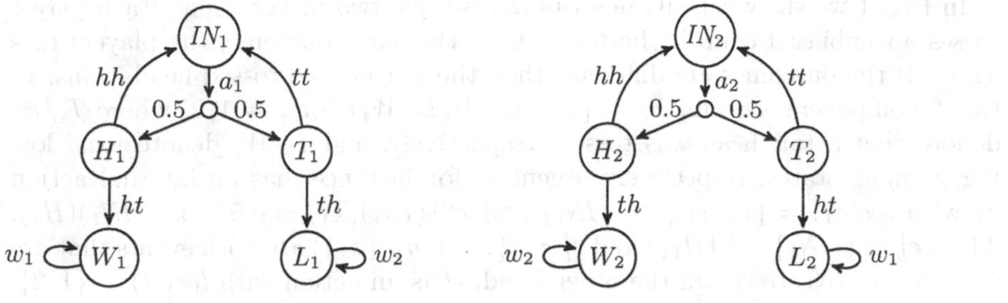

Fig. 1. The DMC model for the two players coin toss game

By (i), the set of partners that an agent can synchronize with is fixed deterministically by its current local state. Typically an agent will be willing to engage in a *set* of actions at a local state. But by (ii), at most one of these actions will be enabled in any global state.

Events. Events will play a crucial role in defining the dynamics of a DMC. Let $\mathcal{D}$ be a DMC. An *event* of $\mathcal{D}$ is a triple $e = (\mathbf{v}, a, \mathbf{v}')$ where $\mathbf{v}, \mathbf{v}' \in \mathbf{S}_a$, $\mathbf{v} \in en_a$ and $\pi^a(\mathbf{v})(\mathbf{v}') > 0$. We define $loc((\mathbf{v}, a, \mathbf{v}'))$ to be $loc(a)$.

Suppose $e = (\mathbf{v}, a, \mathbf{v}')$ is an event and $p = \pi^a(\mathbf{v})(\mathbf{v}')$. Then e represents an occurrence of the synchronization action a followed by a joint move by the agents in $loc(a)$ from $\mathbf{v}$ to $\mathbf{v}'$ with probability p. Again, components outside $loc(e)$ are unaffected by this move.

Let Σ denote the set of events of $\mathcal{D}$ and $e, e', \ldots$ range over Σ. With the event $e = (\mathbf{v}, a, \mathbf{v}')$ we associate the probability $p_e = \pi^a(\mathbf{v})(\mathbf{v}')$.

The Interleaved Semantics. We now associate a global transition system with $\mathcal{D}$ based on event occurrences.

Recall that $\mathbf{S}$ is the set of global states. The event $e = (\mathbf{v}, a, \mathbf{v}')$ is *enabled* at $\mathbf{s} \in \mathbf{S}$ iff $\mathbf{v} = \mathbf{s}_a \in en_a$. The transition system of $\mathcal{D}$ is $TS = (\mathbf{S}, \Sigma, \rightarrow, \mathbf{s}^{in})$, where $\mathbf{s}^{in}$ is the global initial state with $\mathbf{s}_i^{in} = s_i^{in}$ for each i. The transition relation $\rightarrow \subseteq \mathbf{S} \times (\Sigma \times (0,1]) \times \mathbf{S}$ is given by $\mathbf{s} \xrightarrow{e,p_e} \mathbf{s}'$ iff $e = (\mathbf{v}, a, \mathbf{v}')$ is enabled at $\mathbf{s}$, $\mathbf{s}'_a = \mathbf{v}'$ and $\mathbf{s}_j = \mathbf{s}'_j$ for every $j \notin loc(e)$.

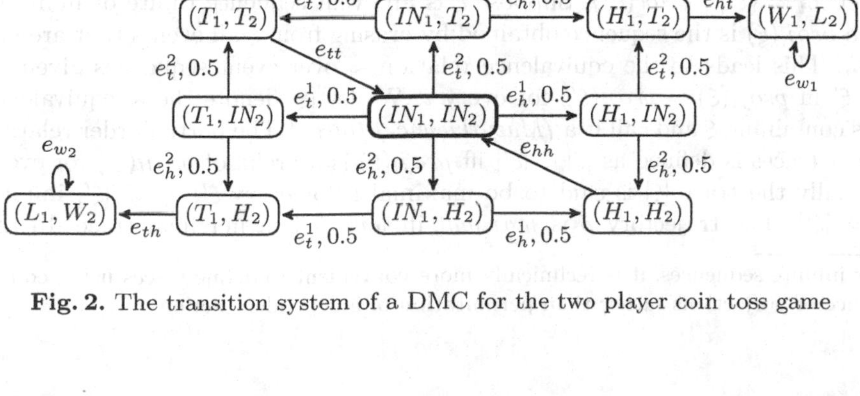

Fig. 2. The transition system of a DMC for the two player coin toss game

In Fig. 1 we show a DMC describing a simple two player game. Each player tosses an unbiased coin. If the tosses have the same outcome, the players toss again. If the outcomes are different, then the player who tossed heads wins. In this 2-component system, $S_i = \{IN_i, T_i, H_i, L_i, W_i\}$ for $i = 1, 2$, where T_i/H_i denote that a tail/head was tossed, respectively, and L_i/W_i denote local losing/winning states, respectively. Agent 1, for instance, has an internal action a_1 with $loc(a_1) = \{1\}$, $en_{a_1} = \{IN_1\}$ and $\pi^{a_1}(IN_1)(T_1) = 0.5 = \pi^{a_1}(IN_1)(H_1)$. Thus, $e_h^1 = (\{IN_1\}, a_1, \{H_1\})$ and $e_t^1 = (\{IN_1\}, a_1, \{T_1\})$ are both events that are enabled at (IN_1, IN_2). On the other hand, tt is an action with $loc(tt) = \{1, 2\}$, $en_{tt} = \{(T_1, T_2)\}$. There will be an event $e_{tt} = (\{T_1, T_2\}, tt, \{IN_1, IN_2\})$ with $\pi^{tt}((T_1, T_2))((IN_1, IN_2)) = 1$. To aid readability, such an action with a unique event (with probability 1) as its only outcome is shown without any probability value. In this simple example, all the actions except a_1 and a_2 are of this type.

The Trace Alphabet (Σ, I). The independence relation $I \subseteq \Sigma \times \Sigma$ given by $e\ I\ e'$ iff $loc(e) \cap loc(e') = \emptyset$. Clearly I is irreflexive and symmetric and hence (Σ, I) is a Mazurkiewicz trace alphabet [8].

3 The Trajectory Space

Let TS be the transition system associated with a DMC $\mathcal{D}$. To reason about the probabilistic behaviour of $\mathcal{D}$ using TS, one must build a σ-algebra over the paths of this transition system and endow it with a probability measure. The major difficulty is that, due to the mix of concurrency and stochasticity, TS is not a Markov chain (except in trivial cases where there is no concurrency). In Fig. 2, for instance, the sum of the probabilities of the transitions originating from the state (IN_1, IN_2) is 2. To get around this, we first filter out concurrency by working with equivalence classes of paths.

We shall refer to paths in TS as *trajectories*. A finite *trajectory* of TS from $\mathbf{s} \in \mathbf{S}$ is a sequence of the form $\mathbf{s}_0 e_0 \mathbf{s}_1 \ldots \mathbf{s}_{k-1} e_{k-1} \mathbf{s}_k$ such that $\mathbf{s}_0 = \mathbf{s}$ and, for $0 \leq \ell < k$, $\mathbf{s}_\ell \xrightarrow{e_\ell, p_{e_\ell}} \mathbf{s}_{\ell+1}$. Infinite trajectories are defined as usual.

For the trajectory $\rho = \mathbf{s}_0 e_0 \mathbf{s}_1 \ldots \mathbf{s}_{k-1} e_{k-1} \mathbf{s}_k$, we define $ev(\rho)$ to be the event sequence $e_0 e_1 \ldots e_{k-1}$. Again, this notation is extended to infinite trajectories in the natural way. Due to concurrency, one can have infinite trajectories that are not maximal, so we proceed as follows.

Let $\Sigma_i = \{e \mid i \in loc(e)\}$. Suppose ξ is an event sequence (finite or infinite). Then $proj_i(\xi)$ is the sequence obtained by erasing from ξ all events that are not in Σ_i. This leads to the equivalence relation $\approx$ over event sequences given by $\xi \approx \xi'$ iff $proj_i(\xi) = proj_i(\xi')$ for every i. We let $[\xi]$ denote the $\approx$-equivalence class containing ξ and call it a *(Mazurkiewicz) trace.* [1] The partial order relation $\sqsubseteq$ over traces is defined as $[\xi] \sqsubseteq [\xi']$ iff $proj_i(\xi)$ is a prefix of $proj_i(\xi')$ for every i. Finally the trace $[\xi]$ is said to be maximal if for every ξ', $[\xi] \sqsubseteq [\xi']$ implies $[\xi] = [\xi']$. The trajectory ρ is *maximal* iff $[ev(\rho)]$ is a maximal trace. In the

[1] For infinite sequences, it is technically more convenient to define traces using equivalence of projections rather than permutation of independent actions.

transition system of Fig. 2, $(IN_1, IN_2)e_h^1(H_1, IN_2)e_T^2(H_1, T_2)e_{ht}((W_1, L_2)e_{w_1})^\omega$ is a maximal infinite trajectory. In fact, in this example all the infinite trajectories are maximal.

The σ-Algebra of Trajectories. We denote by $Trj_{\mathbf{s}}$ the set of maximal trajectories from $\mathbf{s}$. Two trajectories can correspond to interleavings of the same partially ordered execution of events. Hence, one must work with equivalence classes of maximal trajectories to construct a probability measure. The equivalence relation $\simeq$ over $Trj_{\mathbf{s}}$ that we need is defined as $\rho \simeq \rho'$ if $ev(\rho) \approx ev(\rho')$. As usual $[\rho]$ will denote the equivalence class containing the trajectory ρ.

Let ρ be finite trajectory from $\mathbf{s}$. Then $\uparrow\rho$ is the subset of $Trj_{\mathbf{s}}$ satisfying $\rho' \in \uparrow\rho$ iff ρ is a prefix of ρ'. We now define $BC(\rho)$, the basic trj-cylinder at $\mathbf{s}$ generated by ρ, to be the least subset of $Trj_{\mathbf{s}}$ that contains $\uparrow\rho$ and satisfies the closure property that if $\rho' \in BC(\rho)$ and $\rho' \simeq \rho''$ then $\rho'' \in BC(\rho)$. In other words, $BC(\rho) = \{[\rho'] \mid \rho' \in Trj_{\mathbf{s}}, [ev(\rho)] \sqsubseteq [ev(\rho')]\}$.

It is worth noting that we could have $BC(\rho) \cap BC(\rho') \neq \emptyset$ without having $\rho \simeq \rho'$. For instance, in Fig. 2, let $\rho = (IN_1, IN_2)e_h^1(H_1, IN_2)$ and $\rho' = (IN_1, IN_2)e_t^2(IN_1, T_2)$. Then $BC(\rho)$ and $BC(\rho')$ will have common maximal trajectories of the form $(IN_1, IN_2)e_h^1(H_1, IN_2)e_t^2(H_1, T_2)\ldots$.

We now define $\widehat{SA}(\mathbf{s})$ to be the least σ-algebra that contains the basic trj-cylinders at $\mathbf{s}$ and is closed under countable unions and complementation (relative to $Trj_{\mathbf{s}}$).

To construct the probability measure $\widehat{P} : \widehat{SA}(\mathbf{s}) \to [0,1]$ we are after, a natural idea would be to assign a probability to each basic trj-cylinder as follows. Let $BC(\rho)$ be a basic trj-cylinder with $\rho = \mathbf{s}_0 e_0 \mathbf{s}_1 \ldots \mathbf{s}_{k-1} e_{k-1} \mathbf{s}_k$. Then $\widehat{P}(BC(\rho)) = p_0 \cdot p_1 \cdot \ldots \cdot p_{k-1}$, where $p_\ell = p_{e_\ell}$, for $0 \leq \ell < k$. This is inspired by the Markov chain case in which the probability of a basic cylinder is defined to be the product of the probabilities of the events encountered along the common finite prefix of the basic cylinder. However, showing directly that this extends uniquely to a probability measure over $\widehat{SA}_{\mathbf{s}}$ is very difficult.

We get around this by associating a Markov chain $\mathcal{M}$ with $\mathcal{D}$ and then embed $\widehat{SA}_{\mathbf{s}}$ into $SA_{\mathbf{s}}$, the σ-algebra generated by the infinite paths in $\mathcal{M}$ starting from $\mathbf{s}$. The standard probability measure over $SA_{\mathbf{s}}$ will then induce a probability measure over $\widehat{SA}_{\mathbf{s}}$.

4 The Markov Chain Semantics

We associate a Markov chain with a DMC using a "maximal parallelism" based semantics. A *nonempty* set of events $u \subseteq \Sigma$ is a *step* at $\mathbf{s}$ if each $e \in u$ is enabled at $\mathbf{s}$ and, for every distinct pair of events $e, e' \in u$, $e\ I\ e'$. We say u is a *maximal* step at $\mathbf{s}$ if u is a step at $\mathbf{s}$ and $u \cup \{e\}$ is not a step at $\mathbf{s}$ for any $e \notin u$. In Fig. 2, $\{e_h^1, e_h^2\}$, $\{e_h^1, e_t^2\}$, $\{e_t^1, e_h^2\}$ and $\{e_t^1, e_t^2\}$ are maximal steps at the initial state (IN_1, IN_2).

Let u be a maximal step at $\mathbf{s}$. Then $\mathbf{s}'$ is the u-successor of $\mathbf{s}$ if the following conditions are satisfied: (i) For each $e \in u$, if $e = (\mathbf{v}, a, \mathbf{v}')$ and $i \in loc(e)$ then $\mathbf{s}'_i = \mathbf{v}'_i$, and (ii) $\mathbf{s}_j = \mathbf{s}'_j$ if $j \notin loc(u)$, where $loc(u) = \bigcup_{e \in u} loc(e)$.

Suppose u is a maximal step at $\mathbf{s}$ and $i \in loc(u)$. Then, because events in a step are independent, it follows that there exists a unique $e \in u$ such that $i \in loc(e)$, so the u-successor of $\mathbf{s}$ is unique. We say $\mathbf{s}'$ is a *successor* of $\mathbf{s}$ if there exists a maximal step u at $\mathbf{s}$ such that $\mathbf{s}'$ is the u-successor of $\mathbf{s}$. From the definition of a DMC, it is easy to see that if $\mathbf{s}'$ is a successor of $\mathbf{s}$ then there exists a unique maximal step u at $\mathbf{s}$ such that $\mathbf{s}'$ is the u-successor of $\mathbf{s}$. Finally, we say that $\mathbf{s}$ is a *deadlock* if no event is enabled at $\mathbf{s}$.

Definition 4. *The Markov chain $\mathcal{M} : \boldsymbol{S} \times \boldsymbol{S} \to [0,1]$ generated by $\mathcal{D}$ is given by:*

- *If $\boldsymbol{s} \in \boldsymbol{S}$ is a deadlock then $\mathcal{M}(\boldsymbol{s},\boldsymbol{s}) = 1$ and $\mathcal{M}(\boldsymbol{s},\boldsymbol{s}') = 0$ for $\boldsymbol{s} \neq \boldsymbol{s}'$.*
- *Suppose $\boldsymbol{s} \in \boldsymbol{S}$ is not a deadlock. Then $\mathcal{M}(\boldsymbol{s},\boldsymbol{s}') = p$ if there exists a maximal step u at $\boldsymbol{s}$ such that $\boldsymbol{s}'$ is the u-successor of $\boldsymbol{s}$ and $p = \prod_{e\in u} p_e$.*
- *If $\boldsymbol{s}$ is not a deadlock and $\boldsymbol{s}'$ is not a successor of $\boldsymbol{s}$ then $\mathcal{M}(\boldsymbol{s},\boldsymbol{s}') = 0$.*

It follows that $\mathcal{M}(\mathbf{s},\mathbf{s}') \in [0,1]$ for every $\mathbf{s},\mathbf{s}' \in \mathbf{S}$. In addition, if u and u' are two maximal steps at $\mathbf{s}$ then $loc(u) = loc(u')$ and $|u| = |u'|$. Using these facts, it is easy to verify that $\mathcal{M}$ is indeed a finite state Markov chain. The initial state of $\mathcal{M}$ is $\mathbf{s}^{in} = (s_1^{in}, s_2^{in}, \ldots, s_n^{in})$.

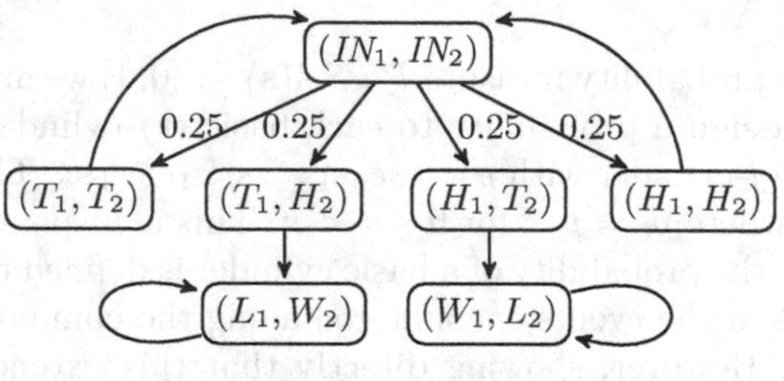

Fig. 3. Markov chain for the DMC in Fig. 2

In Fig. 3 we show the Markov chain of the DMC whose transition system was shown in Fig. 2. Again, unlabelled transitions have probability 1.

Suppose u is a maximal step at $\mathbf{s}$ with $|u| = m$ and $|S_i| = k$ for each $i \in loc(u)$. In $\mathcal{M}$ there will be, in general, k^m transitions at $\mathbf{s}$. In contrast there will be at most $k \cdot m$ transitions at $\mathbf{s}$ in TS. Hence—assuming that we do not explicitly construct $\mathbf{S}$—there can be substantial computational gains if one can verify the properties of $\mathcal{D}$ by working with TS instead of $\mathcal{M}$. This will become clearer when we look at some larger examples in Section 7.

The Path Space of $\mathcal{M}$. Let $\mathcal{M}$ be the Markov chain associated with a DMC $\mathcal{D}$. The path space and a probability measure over this space is obtained in the usual way. A finite path in $\mathcal{M}$ from $\mathbf{s}$ is a sequence $\tau = \mathbf{s}_0\mathbf{s}_1 \ldots \mathbf{s}_m$ such that $\mathbf{s}_0 = \mathbf{s}$ and $\mathcal{M}(\mathbf{s}_\ell, \mathbf{s}_{\ell+1}) > 0$, for $0 \leq \ell < m$. The notion of an infinite path starting from $\mathbf{s}$ is defined as usual. $Path_{\mathbf{s}}$ and $Path_{\mathbf{s}}^{fin}$ denote the set of infinite and finite paths starting from $\mathbf{s}$, respectively.

For $\tau \in Paths_{\mathbf{s}}^{fin}$, $\uparrow\tau \subseteq Paths_{\mathbf{s}}$ is the set of infinite paths that have τ as a prefix. $\Upsilon \subseteq Paths_{\mathbf{s}}$ is a basic cylinder at $\mathbf{s}$ if $\Upsilon = \uparrow\tau$ for some $\tau \in Paths_{\mathbf{s}}^{fin}$. The σ-algebra over $Paths_{\mathbf{s}}$, denoted $SA(\mathbf{s})$, is the least family that contains the basic cylinders at $\mathbf{s}$ and is closed under countable unions and complementation (relative to $Paths_{\mathbf{s}}$). $P_{\mathbf{s}} : SA(\mathbf{s}) \to [0, 1]$ is the usual probability measure that assigns to each basic cylinder $\uparrow\tau$, with $\tau = \mathbf{s}_0\mathbf{s}_1 \ldots \mathbf{s}_m$, the probability $p = p_0 \cdot p_1 \cdots p_{m-1}$, where $\mathcal{M}(\mathbf{s}_\ell, \mathbf{s}_{\ell+1}) = p_\ell$, for $0 \leq \ell < m$.

5 The Probability Measure for the Trajectory Space

To construct a probability measure over the trajectory space we shall associate infinite paths in $\mathcal{M}$ with maximal trajectories in TS. The Foata normal form from Mazurkiewicz trace theory will help achieve this. Let $\xi \in \Sigma^\star$. A standard fact is that $[\xi]$ can be canonically represented as a "step" sequence of the form $u_1u_2 \ldots u_k$. More precisely, the Foata normal form of the finite trace $[\xi]$, denoted $FN([\xi])$, is defined as follows [8].

- $FN([\epsilon]) = \epsilon$.
- Suppose $\xi = \xi' e$ and $FN([\xi']) = u_1u_2 \ldots u_k$. If there exists $e' \in u_k$ such that $(e', e) \notin I$ then $FN([\xi]) = u_1u_2 \ldots u_k\{e\}$. If not, let ℓ be the least integer in $\{1, 2, \ldots, k\}$ such that $e\ I\ e'$ for every $e' \in \bigcup_{\ell \leq m \leq k} u_m$. Then $FN([\xi]) = u_1 \ldots u_{\ell-1}(u_\ell \cup \{e\})u_{\ell+1} \ldots u_m$.

For the example shown in Fig. 2, $FN(e_h^1\ e_t^2\ e_{ht}\ e_{w_1}\ e_{w_1}) = \{e_h^1, e_t^2\}\ \{e_{ht}\}\ \{e_{w_1}\}\ \{e_{w_1}\}$. This notion is extended to infinite traces in the obvious way. Note that $\xi \approx \xi'$ iff $FN(\xi) = FN(\xi')$.

Conversely, we can extract a (maximal) step sequence from a path in $\mathcal{M}$. Suppose $\mathbf{s}_0\mathbf{s}_1 \ldots$ is a path in $Paths_{\mathbf{s}}$. There exists a unique sequence $u_1u_2 \ldots$ such that u_ℓ is a maximal step at $\mathbf{s}_{\ell-1}$ and $\mathbf{s}_\ell$ is the u_ℓ-successor of $\mathbf{s}_{\ell-1}$ for every $\ell > 0$. We let $st(\tau) = u_1\,u_2 \ldots$ and call it the step sequence induced by τ.

This leads to the map $tp : Trj_{\mathbf{s}} \to Paths_{\mathbf{s}}$ given by $tp(\rho) = \tau$ iff $FN(ev(\rho)) = st(\tau)$. It is easy to check that tp is well-defined. As usual, for $X \subseteq Trj_{\mathbf{s}}$ we define $tp(X) = \{tp(\rho) \mid \rho \in X\}$. It turns out that tp maps each basic cylinder in the trajectory space to a finite union of basic cylinders in the path space. As a result, tp maps every measurable set of trajectories to a measurable set of paths. Consequently, one can define the probability of a measurable set of trajectories X to be the probability of the measurable set of paths $tp(X)$.

To understand how tp acts on the basic cylinder $BC(\rho)$, let $FN(ev(\rho)) = u_1u_2 \ldots u_k$. We associate with ρ the set of finite paths $paths(\rho) = \{\pi \mid st(\pi) = U_1U_2 \ldots U_k$ and $u_\ell \subseteq U_\ell$, for $1 \leq \ell \leq k\}$. In other words $\pi \in paths(\rho)$ if it extends each step in $FN(ev(\rho))$ to a maximal step. Then, tp maps $BC(\rho)$ to the (finite) union of the basic cylinders generated by the finite paths in $paths(\rho)$. These observations and their main consequence, namely, the construction of a probability measure over the trajectory space, can be summarized as:

Lemma 5. *(i) Let $B = BC(\rho)$ be a basic trj-cylinder from* $\mathbf{s}$*, with* $FN(ev(\rho)) = u_1u_2 \ldots u_k$*. Then* $tp(B)$ *is a finite union of basic cylinder sets in* $SA(\mathbf{s})$

and is hence a member of $SA(\mathbf{s})$. *Furthermore* $P(tp(B)) = \prod_{1 \leq \ell \leq k} p_\ell$ *where* $p_\ell = \prod_{e \in u_\ell} p_e$ *for* $1 \leq \ell \leq k$.

(ii) If $B \in \widehat{SA}(\mathbf{s})$ *then* $tp(B) \in SA(\mathbf{s})$.

(iii) Define $\widehat{P} : \widehat{SA}(\mathbf{s}) \to [0,1]$ *as* $\widehat{P}(B) = P(tp(B))$. *Then* $\widehat{P}$ *is a probability measure over* $\widehat{SA}(\mathbf{s})$.

Proof sketch. Let $BC(\rho)$ be the basic trj-cylinder from $\mathbf{s}$ generated by $\rho \neq \epsilon$ and $FN(ev(\rho)) = u_1 u_2 \ldots u_k$. Suppose $\tau \in Paths_{\mathbf{s}}$. Then, using the semantic definitions, it is tedious but straightforward to show that $\tau \in tp(BC(\rho))$ iff $u_i \subseteq st(\tau)(\ell)$, for $1 \leq \ell \leq k$. (Here, $st(\tau)(\ell)$ is the maximal step appearing in position ℓ of the sequence $st(\tau)$.) It will then follow that $tp(BC(\rho))$ is a finite union of basic cylinder sets in $SA(\mathbf{s})$ and is hence a member of $SA(\mathbf{s})$. Furthermore, one can argue that $P(tp(BC(\rho)) = \prod_{1 \leq \ell \leq k} p_\ell$.

For the other two parts, we first establish easily that if $B \in \widehat{SA}(\mathbf{s})$, $\rho \in B$ and $\rho \simeq \rho'$ then $\rho' \in B$ as well. Next, it is straightforward to show that if $B, B' \in \widehat{SA}(\mathbf{s})$ with $B \cap B' = \emptyset$ then $tp(B) \cap tp(B') = \emptyset$ too. Finally, one can also show tp is onto. Using these facts, the second and third parts of the lemma can be easily established. □

Note that while a finite path in $\mathcal{M}$ always induces a maximal step sequence, a finite trajectory, in general, does not have this structure. Some components can get ahead of others by an arbitrary amount. The lemma above states that, despite this, any finite trajectory defines a finite set of of basic cylinders whose overall probability can be easily computed, by taking the product of the probabilities of the events encountered along the trajectory. This helps considerably when verifying the properties of $\mathcal{M}$. In particular, local reachability properties can be checked by exercising only those components that are relevant.

Going back to our running example, let $\rho_t = (IN_1, IN_2)e_t^1(T_1, IN_2)$, and $X_t = \uparrow\rho_t$. Let $\rho_t' = (IN_1, IN_2)e_t^2(IN_1, T_2)$, and $X_t' = \uparrow\rho_t$. Assume ρ_h, X_h, ρ_h' and X_h' are defined similarly. Then $\widehat{P}(X_t) = \widehat{P}(X_h') = 0.5$, while $\widehat{P}(X_h \cup X_t) = 1$. On the other hand, due to the fact that e_h^1 and e_h^2 are independent, we have $\widehat{P}(X_h \cup X_h') = 0.75$.

6 A Statistical Model Checking Procedure for DMCs

To bring out the applicability of the DMC formalism and its interleaved semantics, we formulate a statistical model checking procedure. The specification logic $PBLTL^{\otimes}$ (product $PBLTL$) is a simple generalization of probabilistic bounded linear time temporal logic ($PBLTL$) [15] that captures Boolean combinations of local properties of the components. The logic can express interesting global reachability properties as well since the Boolean connectives can capture -in a limited fashion- the way the components influence each other.

We assume a collection of pairwise disjoint sets of atomic propositions $\{AP_i\}$. As a first step, the formulas of $BLTL^{\otimes}$ are given as follows.

(i) $ap \in AP_i$ is a $BLTL^{\otimes}$ formula and $type(ap) = \{i\}$.
(ii) If φ and φ' are $BLTL^{\otimes}$ formulas with $type(\varphi) = type(\varphi') = \{i\}$ then so is $\varphi \mathbf{U}_i^t \varphi'$ where t is a positive integer. Further, $type(\varphi \mathbf{U}_i^t \varphi') = \{i\}$. As usual, $F^t\varphi$ abbreviates $(true\mathbf{U}^t\varphi)$ and $G^t\varphi$ is defined as $\neg F^t \neg\varphi$.
(iii) If φ and φ' are $BLTL^{\otimes}$ formulas then so are $\neg\varphi$ and $\varphi \vee \varphi'$ with $type(\neg\varphi) = type(\varphi)$ and $type(\varphi \vee \varphi') = type(\varphi) \cup type(\varphi')$.

The formulas of $PBLTL^{\otimes}$ are given by:

(i) Suppose φ is a $BLTL^{\otimes}$ formula and γ a rational number in the open interval $(0,1)$. Then $Pr_{\geq\gamma}(\varphi)$ is a $PBLTL^{\otimes}$ formula.
(ii) If ψ and ψ' are $PBLTL^{\otimes}$ formulas then so are $\neg\psi$ and $\psi \vee \psi'$.

To define the semantics, we project each trajectory to its components. For $\mathbf{s} \in \mathbf{S}$ and $i \in [n]$ we define $Proj_i : Trj_{\mathbf{s}}^{fin} \to S_i^+$ inductively.

(i) $Proj_i(\mathbf{s}) = \mathbf{s}_i$.
(ii) Suppose $\rho = \mathbf{s}_0 e_0 \mathbf{s}_1 \ldots \mathbf{s}_m e_m \mathbf{s}_{m+1}$ is in $Trj_{\mathbf{s}}^{fin}$ and $\rho' = \mathbf{s}_0 e_0 \mathbf{s}_1 \ldots \mathbf{s}_m$. If $i \in loc(e_m)$ then $Proj_i(\rho) = Proj_i(\rho')(\mathbf{s}_{m+1})_i$. Otherwise $Proj_i(\rho) = Proj_i(\rho')$.

We lift $Proj_i$ to infinite trajectories in the obvious way—note that $Proj_i(\rho)$ can be a finite sequence for the infinite trajectory ρ. We assume a set of local valuation functions $\{V_i\}$, where $V_i : S_i \to 2^{AP_i}$. Let φ be a $BLTL^{\otimes}$ formula with $type(\varphi) = \{i\}$. We begin by interpreting such formulas over sequences generated by the alphabet S_i. For $\varrho \subset S_i^+ \cup S_i^{\omega}$, the satisfaction relation $\varrho, k \models_i \varphi$, with $0 \leq k \leq |\varrho|$, is defined as follows.

(i) $\varrho, k \models_i ap$ for $ap \in AP_i$ iff $ap \in V_i(\varrho(k)(i))$, where $\varrho(k)(i)$ is the S_i-state at position k of the sequence ϱ.
(ii) $\neg$ and $\vee$ are interpreted in the usual way.
(iii) $\varrho, k \models_i \varphi_1 \mathbf{U}_i^t \varphi_2$ iff there exists ℓ such that $k \leq \ell \leq max(k+t, |\varrho|)$ with $\varrho, \ell \models_i \varphi_2$, and $\varrho, m \models_i \varphi_1$, for $k \leq m < \ell$.

As usual, $\varrho \models_i \varphi$ iff $\varrho, 0 \models_i \varphi$. Next, suppose φ is a $BLTL^{\otimes}$ formula and $\rho \in Paths_{\mathbf{s}}$. Then the relation $\rho \models_{\mathbf{s}} \varphi$ is defined as follows.

(i) If $type(\varphi) = \{i\}$ then $\rho \models_{\mathbf{s}} \varphi$ iff $Proj_i(\rho) \models_i \varphi$.
(ii) Again, $\neg$ and $\vee$ are interpreted in the standard way.

Given a formula φ in $BLTL^{\otimes}$ and a global state $\mathbf{s}$, we define $Trj_{\mathbf{s}}(\varphi)$ to be the set of trajectories $\{\rho \in Trj_{\mathbf{s}} \mid \rho \models_s \varphi\}$.

Lemma 6. *For every formula φ, $Trj_{\mathbf{s}}(\varphi)$ is a member of $\widehat{SA}(\mathbf{s})$.*

Proof sketch. If we interpret the formulas over $\mathcal{M}$, we easily derive that $Paths_{\mathbf{s}}(\varphi)$ is a member of $SA(\mathbf{s})$ for every φ. We then use Lemma 5 to obtain this result. □

The semantics of $PBLTL^{\otimes}$ is now given by the relation $\mathcal{D} \models_{\mathbf{s}}^{trj} \psi$, defined as:

(i) Suppose $\psi = Pr_{\geq\gamma}(\varphi)$. Then $\mathcal{D} \models^{trj}_{\mathbf{s}} \psi$ iff $\widehat{P}(Path_{\mathbf{s}}(\varphi)) \geq \gamma$.
(ii) Again, the interpretations of $\neg$ and $\vee$ are the standard ones.

For the example in Fig. 1, one can assert $Pr_{\geq 0.99}((F^7(L_1) \wedge F^7(W_2)) \vee (F^7(W_1) \wedge F^7(L_2)))$. Here, the local states also serve as the atomic propositions. Hence, the formula says that with probability ≥ 0.99, a winner will be decided within 7 rounds.

We write $\mathcal{D} \models^{trj} \psi$ for $\mathcal{D} \models^{trj}_{\mathbf{s}^{in}} \psi$. The model checking problem is to determine whether $\mathcal{D} \models^{trj} \psi$. We shall adapt the SMC procedure developed in [22] to solve this problem approximately.

6.1 The Statistical Model Checking Procedure

We note that in the Markov chain setting, given a BLTL formula and a path in the chain, there is a bound k that depends only on the formula such that we can decide whether the path is a model of the formula by examining just a prefix of the path of length k [15]. By the same reasoning, for a $BLTL^{\otimes}$ formula φ, we can compute a vector of bounds $(k_1, k_2, \ldots, k_n)$ that depends only on φ such that for any trajectory ρ starting from $\mathbf{s}^{in}$, we only need to examine a finite prefix ρ' of ρ that satisfies $|Proj_i(\rho')| \geq k_i$, for $1 \leq i \leq n$. The complication in our setting is that it is not guaranteed that one can generate such a prefix with bounded effort. This is due to the mix of concurrency and stochasticity in DMCs. More precisely, at a global state $\mathbf{s}$, one may need to advance the history of the agent i but this may require first executing an event $e = (\mathbf{v}, a, \mathbf{v}')$ at $\mathbf{s}$ that does not involve the agent i. However, there could also be another event $e' = (\mathbf{v}, a, \mathbf{u})$ enabled at $\mathbf{s}$. Since one must randomly choose one of the enabled events according to the underlying probabilities, one may repeatedly fail to steer the computation towards a global state in which the history of i can be advanced. A second complication is that starting from the current global state it may be impossible to reach a global state at which some event involving i is enabled.

To cope with this, we maintain a count vector $(c_1, c_2, \ldots, c_n)$ that records how many times each component has moved along the trajectory ρ that has been generated so far. A simple reachability analysis will reveal whether a component is *dead* in the current global state — that is, starting from the current state, there is no possibility of reaching a state in which an event involving this agent can be executed. If this is the case for the agent i or the c_i is already the required bound then remove it from the current set of active agents. If the current set of active agents is not empty, we execute, one by one, all the enabled actions — using a fixed linear order over the set of actions — followed by one move by each of the participating agents, according to the underlying probabilities. Recall that action a is enabled at $\mathbf{s}$ iff $\mathbf{s}_a \in en_a$. Due to the determinacy of synchronizations, the global state thus reached will depend only on the probabilistic moves chosen by the participating agents. We then update the count vector to $(c'_1, c'_2, \ldots, c'_n)$ and mark the new dead components. It is not difficult to prove that, continuing in this manner, with probability 1 we will eventually generate a finite trajectory $\widehat{\rho}$ and reach a global state $\mathbf{s}$ with no active agents. We then check if $\widehat{\rho}$ satisfies φ and update the score associated with the statistical test described below.

The parameters for the test are δ, α, β, where δ is the size of the indifference region and (α, β) is the strength of the test, with α bounding the Type I errors (false positives) and β bounding the Type II errors (false negatives). These parameters are to be chosen by the user. We generate finite i.i.d. sample trajectories sequentially. We associate a Bernoulli random variable x_ℓ with the sample ρ_ℓ and set $x_\ell = 1$ if $\rho_\ell \in Trj_{\mathbf{s}^{in}}(\varphi)$ and set $x_\ell = 0$ otherwise. We let $c_m = \sum_\ell x_\ell$ and compute the score $SPRT$ via

$$SPRT = \frac{(\gamma^-)^{c_m}(1-\gamma^-)^{n-c_m}}{(\gamma^+)^{c_m}(1-\gamma^+)^{n-c_m}}$$

Here $\gamma^+ = \gamma + \delta$ and $\gamma^- = \gamma - \delta$. If $SPRT \leq \frac{\beta}{1-\alpha}$, we declare $\mathcal{D} \models^{trj} \widehat{P}_{\geq r}\varphi$. If $SPRT \geq \frac{1-\beta}{\alpha}$, we declare $\mathcal{D} \not\models^{trj} \widehat{P}_{\geq \gamma}\varphi$. Otherwise, we draw one more sample and repeat.

This test is then extended to handle formulas of the form $\neg\psi$ and $\psi_1 \vee \psi_2$ in the usual way [15]. It is easy to establish the correctness of this statistical model checking procedure.

7 Experimental Results

We have tested our SMC procedure on two probabilistic distributed algorithms: (i) a leader election protocol for a unidirectional ring of anonymous processes by Itai and Rodeh [11,13] and (ii) a randomized solution to the dining philosophers problem [18]. Both these algorithms -for large instances- exhibit a considerable degree of concurrency since any two agents that do not share a neighbor can execute independently. We focused on approximately verifying termination properties of these algorithms to bring out the scalability and the performance features of our SMC technique. We also compared our results with the corresponding ones obtained using the tool PLASMA [6].

In the leader election protocol, each process randomly chooses an identity from $\{1, 2, \ldots, N\}$, and passes it on to its neighbor. If a process receives an identity lower than its own, the message is dropped. If the identity is higher than its own, the process drops out of the election and forwards the message. Finally, if the identity is the same as its own, the process forwards the message, noting the identity clash. If an identity clash is recorded, all processes with the highest identity choose a fresh identity and start another round.

Since the initial choice of identity for the N processes can be done concurrently, in the global Markov chain, there will be N^N possible moves. However, correspondingly in the interleaved semantics, there will be N^2 transitions from the initial state.

We have built a DMC model of this system in which each process and channel is an agent. Messages are transferred between processes and channels via synchronizations while ensuring this is done using a deterministic protocol. For simplicity, all channels in our implementation have capacity 1. We can easily construct higher capacity channels by cascading channels of capacity 1 while staying within the DMC formalism.

The challenge in modeling the dining philosophers problem as a DMC is to represent the forks between philosophers, which are typically modeled as shared variables. We use a deterministic round robin protocol to simulate these shared variables. The same technique can be used for a variety of other randomized distributed algorithms presented as case studies for PLASMA.

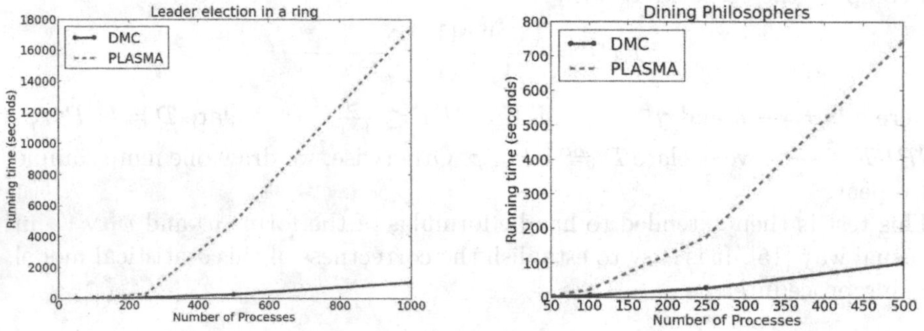

Fig. 4. Comparison of simulation times in DMC and PLASMA

We ran our trajectories based SPRT procedure written in Python programming language on a Linux server (Intel Xeon 2.30 GHz, 16 core, 72GB RAM). For the first example, we verified that a leader is elected with probability above 0.99 within K rounds, for a ring of N processes for various values of N up to 1000. For each N, it turned out that $K = N$ is a good choice for K as explained below.

The termination property was specified as follows. Let L_i denote the boolean variable which evaluate to true iff in the current global state, node i has been elected as the leader. Then for N processes with $K = N$, the specification is:

$$Pr_{\geq 0.99}(\bigvee_{i=1}^{n}[F^N(\neg L_1)\wedge\cdots\wedge F^N(\neg L_{i-1})\wedge F^N(L_i)\wedge F^N(\neg L_{i+1})\wedge\cdots\wedge F^N(\neg L_n)])$$

For the dining philosophers, we verified that with probability above 0.95 every philosopher eventually eats, up to $N = 500$ philosophers. In both the experiments, we set the bound on both the Type I and Type II errors to be 0.01 and the indifference region to be 0.01. We tested the same properties with the same statistical parameters using the PLASMA model. PLASMA supports parallel execution and multithreading. Since our DMC implementation is currently sequential, we restricted PLASMA to single-threaded sequential execution for a meaningful comparison.

In Fig. 4, we have compared the running time for SPRT model-checking in the DMC model with that for PLASMA. The x-axis is the number of processes in the system and the y-axis is the running time, in seconds. We have not been able to determine from the literature how PLASMA translates the model into a DTMC. Consequently we could only compare the simulation times at the system level while treating the PLASMA tool as a black box. In the case of PLASMA, the specifications use time bounds which we took it to imply the number of time steps for which the model is simulated. We found that for $N = 1000$, PLASMA verifies the termination property to be true if the time bound is set to be 10,000. Further, increasing the bound does not cause the simulation times to change. Hence we fixed the time bound to be 10,000 for all choices of N in the PLASMA setting. In the DMC setting we found that setting $K = N$ caused our implementation to verify the termination property to be true. Again, increasing this to larger number of rounds does not change the simulation times. For this reason we fixed $K = N$ for each N.

The experiments show that as the model size increases, the running time increase for the DMC approach is almost linear whereas for PLASMA it is more rapid. The results also show the significant performance and scalability advantages of using the interleaved semantics approach based on DMC models. We expect further improvements to be easily achieved via a parallel implementation.

8 DMCs with Global Final States

The preceding section demonstrates the applicability of the DMC model and the scalability of the interleaved semantics based SMC procedure. Here we wish to show that the "determinacy of synchronizations" restriction brings a considerable amount of analysis power. To bring this out we augment the DMC model with a global final state. For convenience, we shall refer to this extended model also as a DMC in this section. This is a natural extension since in many situations — including distributed algorithms, protocols and task executions in uncertain environments — the goal is to reach a desired final state instead of executing forever.

Accordingly, we work here with the formalism $\widehat{\mathcal{D}} = (\mathcal{D}, \{s_i^f\}, F, en_F, \pi_F)$ where $\mathcal{D} = (\{S_i\}, \{s_i^{in}\}, A, loc, \{en_a\}_{a \in A}, \{\pi^a\}_{a \in A})$ is as before, while $s_i^f \in S_i$ is the final state for each agent i. It is a final state in the sense no action in A is enabled at $\mathbf{s}^f$ where $\mathbf{s}^f$, the global final state, is given by $\mathbf{s}^f(i) = s_i^f$ for every i. Further, $F \notin A$ is a synchronization action with $loc(F) = [n]$ and $en_F = \{\mathbf{s}^f\}$. Finally, π_F is given by: $\pi_F(\mathbf{s}^f)(\mathbf{s}^f) = 1$. Thus F is enabled only at the global final state $\mathbf{s}^f$ and when the system reaches this state, it loops at this state with probability 1. For technical convenience, we have assumed a unique global final state. Our arguments can be easily extended to multiple final states.

The key property to explore here is termination. To define this notion we assume that $\widehat{TRJ}$ be the set of maximal trajectories of $\widehat{\mathcal{D}}$ defined in the obvious way. We note that if $\rho \in \widehat{TRJ}$ encounters the state $\mathbf{s}^f$ then all the subsequent states encountered will also be $\mathbf{s}^f$. We next define $\widehat{TRJ}_f \subseteq \widehat{TRJ}$ via: $\rho \in \widehat{TRJ}_f$ iff $\mathbf{s}^f$ appears in ρ. Since each element in $\widehat{TRJ}_f$ will have a finite prefix in which $\mathbf{s}^f$ appears for the first time we are assured that $\widehat{TRJ}_f$ is a countable set and hence measurable. We now say that $\widehat{\mathcal{D}}$ *terminates* iff $Pr(\widehat{TRJ}_f) = 1$. Our main observation here is as follows:

Theorem 7. *Whether $\widehat{\mathcal{D}}$ terminates can be decided in polynomial time.*

This result can be proved by translating $\mathcal{D}$ into a deterministic cyclic negotiation (DCN) model [10]. We explain this translation with the help of the coin toss example, whose DCN representation is shown in Fig. 5. To avoid clutter, we do not show the mild changes to the DMC model to incorporate a global final state — we have assumed that the system will transit to this global final state as soon as (L_1, W_2) or (W_1, L_2) is reached. The corresponding actions will have a single associated event with probability 1 while the self-looping actions w_1 and w_2 are removed.

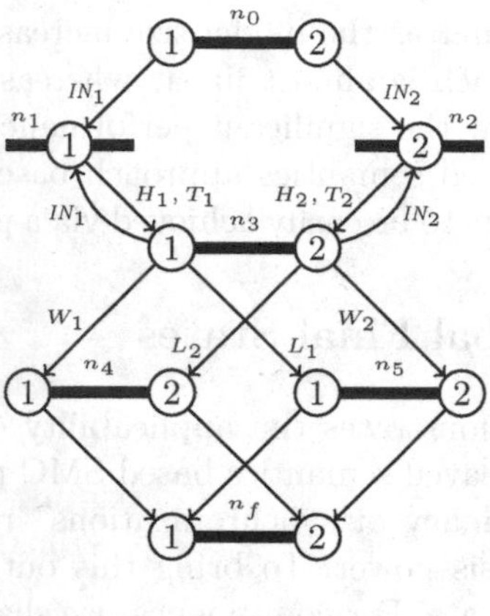

Fig. 5. Negotiation for coin toss

We briefly recall that a DCN consists of atoms called negotiations, each involving a set of agents, a set of outcomes, and a transformation associated with each outcome that non-deterministically transforms the internal states of the agents participating in the negotiation into a new tuple of internal states. To comply with the notion of deterministic negotiations, we gather together actions to form negotiations as follows. For $a \in A$ we first define $pre(a) \subseteq S$: $s \in pre(a)$ iff there exists $i \in loc(a)$ and $\mathbf{v} \in en_a$ such that $\mathbf{v}_i = s$. For $a \in A$ we then define $cl(a)$ to be the least subset of A that contains a and satisfies: if $b \in cl(a)$ then $act(pre(b)) \subseteq cl(a)$. It is easy to check that $\{cl(a)\}_{a \in A}$ is a partition of A. We associate a negotiation with each block in this partition. We then construct the transformation functions using the transition relation defining the interleaved semantics of $\mathcal{D}$. For instance, in the coin toss example, $cl(tt) = \{tt, th, ht, hh\}$, and these actions are grouped together into the single negotiation n_3 with a single outcome that will transform (T_1, T_2) into (IN_1, IN_2) and transform (T_1, H_2) into (L_1, W_2) etc. Similarly, there will be a negotiation n_1 corresponding to the action a_1 with two outcomes, one of which will transform IN_1 into T_1, while the other one will transform IN_1 into H_1. On the other hand, $cl(w_1) = \{w_1\}$ and $cl(w_2) = \{w_2\}$. We note that the transformation function will mimic the effects of events which, by definition, will have a non-zero probability. It is now straightforward to show that this translation yields a deterministic cyclic negotiation. Further, the DMC will terminate iff the corresponding negotiation model is *sound* in the sense defined in [1]. Using a finite set of reduction rules it has been shown that soundness can be checked for deterministic cyclic negotiations in polynomial time [10]. This at once implies theorem 7.

9 Conclusion

We have formulated a distributed probabilistic system model called DMCs. Our model achieves a clean mix of concurrency and probabilistic dynamics by restricting synchronizations to be deterministic. Our key technical contribution is the construction of a probability measure over the σ-algebra generated by the (interleaved) trajectories of a DMC. This opens the door to using partial order reduction techniques to efficiently verify the dynamic properties of a DMC. As a first step we have developed a SPRT based statistical model checking procedure for the logic $PBLTL^{\otimes}$. Our experiments suggest that our method can handle systems of significant sizes.

The main partial order concept we have used is to group trajectories into equivalence classes. One can also explore how ample sets [16] and related notions can be used to model check properties specified in logics such as PCTL [4]. Another possibility is to see if the notion of finite unfoldings from Petri net theory can be applied in the setting of DMCs [9,17].

In our two case studies, the specification has a global character in that it mentions every agent in the system. In many specifications, only a few agents will be mentioned. If the system is loosely coupled, we can check whether the required property is fulfilled without having to exercise all the agents. This will lead to additional computational gains.

In many of the benchmark examples in [7], the probabilistic moves are local. On the other hand, DMCs allow synchronous probabilistic moves where the probability distribution is influenced by information obtained through communication. It will be interesting to exploit this feature to model and analyze applications arising in embedded control systems.

We currently allow agents to gain complete information about the state of the agents they synchronize with. In practice, only a part of this state may/should be exposed. We are also encouraged by the close relationship between DMCs and deterministic negotiations. Here, we have exploited the powerful reduction rules based analysis technique for deterministic negotiations to check the termination of DMCs with final states. There could be other ways to fruitfully transfer results across the two formalisms.

References

1. van der Aalst, W.M.P., van Hee, K.M., ter Hofstede, A.H.M., Sidorova, N., Verbeek, H.M.W., Voorhoeve, M., Wynn, M.T.: Soundness of workflow nets: Classification, decidability, and analysis. Form. Asp. Comp. 23(3), 333–363 (2011)
2. Abbes, S., Benveniste, A.: True-concurrency probabilistic models: Branching cells and distributed probabilities for event structures. Info. and Comp. 204(2), 231–274 (2006)

3. Abbes, S., Benveniste, A.: True-concurrency probabilistic models: Markov nets and a law of large numbers. Theor. Comput. Sci. 390(2-3), 129–170 (2008)
4. Baier, C., Katoen, J.-P.: Principles of Model Checking. The MIT Press (2008)
5. Bogdoll, J., Ferrer Fioriti, L.M., Hartmanns, A., Hermanns, H.: Partial order Methods for statistical model checking and simulation. In: Bruni, R., Dingel, J. (eds.) FMOODS/FORTE 2011. LNCS, vol. 6722, pp. 59–74. Springer, Heidelberg (2011)
6. Boyer, B., Corre, K., Legay, A., Sedwards, S.: PLASMA-lab: A Flexible, sistributable statistical model checking library. In: Joshi, K., Siegle, M., Stoelinga, M., D'Argenio, P.R. (eds.) QEST 2013. LNCS, vol. 8054, pp. 160–164. Springer, Heidelberg (2013)
7. PRISM: Case studies, `http://www.prismmodelchecker.org/casestudies/`
8. Diekert, V., Rozenberg, G.: The book of traces. World Scientific (1995)
9. Esparza, J., Heljanko, K.: Unfoldings: A Partial-Order Approach to Model Checking, 1st edn. Springer Publishing Company (2008)
10. Esparza, J., Desel, J.: On negotiation as concurrency primitive II: Deterministic cyclic negotiations. In: Muscholl, A. (ed.) FOSSACS 2014. LNCS, vol. 8412, pp. 258–273. Springer, Heidelberg (2014)
11. Fokkink, W.: Variations on Itai-Rodeh leader election for anonymous rings and their analysis in PRISM. J. UCS, 12 (2006)
12. Groesser, M., Baier, C.: Partial order reduction for Markov decision processes: A survey. In: de Boer, F.S., Bonsangue, M.M., Graf, S., de Roever, W.-P. (eds.) FMCO 2005. LNCS, vol. 4111, pp. 408–427. Springer, Heidelberg (2006)
13. Itai, A., Rodeh, M.: Symmetry breaking in distributed networks. Info. and Comp. 88(1), 60–87 (1990)
14. Jesi, S., Pighizzini, G., Sabadini, N.: Probabilistic asynchronous automata. Math. Systems Theory 29(1), 5–31 (1996)
15. Jha, S.K., Clarke, E.M., Langmead, C.J., Legay, A., Platzer, A., Zuliani, P.: A Bayesian approach to model checking biological systems. In: Degano, P., Gorrieri, R. (eds.) CMSB 2009. LNCS, vol. 5688, pp. 218–234. Springer, Heidelberg (2009)
16. Clarke Jr., E.M., Grumberg, O., Peled, D.A.: Model Checking. The MIT Press, Cambridge (1999)
17. McMillan, K.L., Probst, D.K.: A technique of state space search based on unfolding. Form. Method. Syst. Des. 6(1), 45–65 (1995)
18. Pnueli, A., Zuck, L.D.: Verification of multiprocess probabilistic protocols. Distributed Computing 1(1), 53–72 (1986)
19. Saha, R., Esparza, J., Jha, S.K., Mukund, M., Thiagarajan, P.S.: Distributed Markov chains. Technical report (2014), `http://www.comp.nus.edu.sg/~ratul/public/dmc_vmcai.pdf`
20. Varacca, D., Völzer, H., Winskel, G.: Probabilistic event structures and domains. In: Gardner, P., Yoshida, N. (eds.) CONCUR 2004. LNCS, vol. 3170, pp. 481–496. Springer, Heidelberg (2004)
21. Wald, A.: Sequential tests of statistical hypotheses. Ann. Math. Statist., 117–186
22. Lorens, H., Younes, S.: Verification and Planning for Stochastic Processes with Asynchronous Events. PhD thesis, Carnegie Mellon University, Pittsburgh, PA, USA (2004)
23. Zielonka, W.: Notes on finite asynchronous automata. ITA 21(2), 99–135 (1987)

Analysis of Infinite-State Graph Transformation Systems by Cluster Abstraction*

Peter Backes and Jan Reineke

Universität des Saarlandes, Saarbrücken, Germany
{rtc,reineke}@cs.uni-saarland.de

Abstract. Analysis of distributed systems with message passing and dynamic process creation is challenging because of the unboundedness of the emerging communication topologies and hence the infinite state space. We model such systems as graph transformation systems and use abstract interpretation to compute a finite overapproximation of the set of reachable graphs. To this end, we propose cluster abstraction, which decomposes graphs into small overlapping clusters of nodes. Using `astra`, our implementation of cluster abstraction, we are for the first time able to prove several safety properties of the merge protocol. The merge protocol is a coordination mechanism for car platooning where the leader car of one platoon passes its followers to the leader car of another platoon, eventually forming one single merged platoon.

Keywords: graph transformation, abstract interpretation, parameterized verification, shape analysis, distributed message-passing systems.

1 Introduction

Distributed message-passing systems such as car platoons and drone swarms consist of an unbounded and dynamically changing number of agents. These agents act in a coordinated fashion using wireless ad-hoc networks to achieve common goals. For this purpose, they assume different roles in a logical communication topology that is established on top of the physical communication medium. These communication topologies, which consist of unidirectional channels between pairs of agents, are formed by distributed protocols that all agents execute concurrently.

The purpose of our analysis is to determine the emerging topologies, which can then be used to evaluate safety properties, ensuring that the system will never reach a state with an undesired topology.

We model such systems by graph transformation systems, i.e., graphs modified by transformation rules. Graph transformation is a lingua franca with a broad

* This work was partially supported by the German Research Council (DFG) as part of the Transregional Collaborative Research Center "Automatic Verification and Analysis of Complex Systems" (SFB/TR 14 AVACS). See `http://www.avacs.org/` for more information.

D. D'Souza et al. (Eds.): VMCAI 2015, LNCS 8931, pp. 135–152, 2015.

range of applications in systems modeling, all of which become potential use cases for our method. Many domain-specific models can be translated automatically into graph transformation systems.

In the graph transformation framework, we represent agents as labeled nodes and communication channels and message queues as labeled, directed edges of a graph. We model the dynamics of the system, like agents sending and receiving messages, detecting each other's presence and setting up and closing communication channels, as transformation rules that are applied to the graphs. Those rules match subgraph patterns in a graph, optionally restricted by application conditions, and replace them by modified subgraphs.

The main challenges with respect to the analysis of the systems under consideration are the unboundedness of the graphs, caused by the unboundedness of the number of agents, and the concurrency of the computations of the participating agents. In particular, the state space of such systems is infinite, and naive state-space exploration cannot be used for our purpose. Instead, we use abstract interpretation, overapproximating the graphs by abstract representations of bounded size.

To compute this overapproximation, we lift rule application to the abstract level, reducing the infinite concrete state space to a finite abstract one: We match the rules on the abstract representation, partly undo the abstraction, just enough to apply the rule, and restore abstraction on the result. By fixed-point iteration, we end up with one final abstract topology, an overapproximation of all graphs the system may produce.

The crucial idea of our abstraction is to decompose graphs into overlapping, simultaneously evolving *clusters*, one per node of the graph—*cluster abstraction*. Each cluster consists of a *core node*, corresponding to the specific node under consideration, and *peripheral nodes*, corresponding to the immediate neighborhood of the core node, i.e., its adjacent nodes. We keep the edges between peripheral nodes and the core node, as well as the core node itself, completely concrete. The neighborhood of a node may be unbounded, e.g., in some protocols a leader may have an unbounded number of followers. To arrive at a finite abstract domain, we use approximated counting: two or more neighborhood nodes that are similar become one summary node in the periphery. By a three-valued abstraction, we preserve information about the neighborhood edges where possible.

We have implemented cluster abstraction in a tool called `astra`. In addition to benchmarks from the literature, ranging from red-black trees to firewalls, we successfully apply `astra` to the merge protocol. The merge protocol is a coordination mechanism for car platooning that could not be fully analyzed with previous approaches.

Outline. In Section 2, we describe the graph transformation framework our work is based upon. Section 3 introduces cluster abstraction and the computation of the corresponding abstract transformer. In Section 4 we present our tool implementation `astra` and experimental results. After discussing related work in Section 5, we conclude the paper in Section 6.

2 Background

2.1 Graph Preliminaries

Our framework is based on directed graphs with edge and node labels. We allow several edges between the same pair of nodes, but only as long as their direction or edge label differ.

Definition 1 (Graph). *Let $\mathcal{V}$ be a set of node names, $\mathcal{N}$ a set of node labels and $\mathcal{E} = \{\beta_1, \ldots, \beta_{|\mathcal{E}|}\}$ a set of edge labels. A* graph *G is a tuple $(V_G, E_G^{\beta_1}, \ldots, E_G^{\beta_{|\mathcal{E}|}}, \ell_G)$ where $V_G \subseteq \mathcal{V}$ is the set of nodes, $\ell_G : V_G \to \mathcal{N}$ is the node label assignment and $E_G^{\beta} \subseteq V_G \times V_G$ is the set of edges with label $\beta \in \mathcal{E}$.*

For simplicity, we assume a globally unique set $\mathcal{V}$ of node names, plus a globally unique set of node labels $\mathcal{N}$ and edge labels $\mathcal{E}$. Note the difference between node names and node labels: Nodes may share the same node label and nodes from different graphs may share the same node name, but nodes from the same graph always have different node names. We use mappings over node names to relate nodes of different graphs. We denote the set of graphs as $\mathcal{G}$.

Graph morphisms map the nodes of one graph to the nodes of another graph such that the node labels agree and all edges are preserved. The existence of a graph morphism means that one graph is a subgraph of another.

Definition 2 (Partial and total graph morphism, subgraph relation). *Let G and H be graphs. An injective partial function $h : V_G \rightharpoonup V_H$ is a* partial graph morphism *iff $\ell_G \cap (\mathrm{def}(h) \times \mathcal{N}) = h \circ \ell_H$ and for all $\beta \in \mathcal{E}$, $h(E_G^{\beta}) \subseteq E_H^{\beta}$. We call h a* (total) graph morphism *iff it is a total function, i.e., $h : V_G \to V_H$. If an injective graph morphism exists, G is a* subgraph *of H, denoted by $G \lesssim_h H$.*

For the purpose of abstraction, we will later need to consider *spokes* between nodes, not merely individual edges. Spokes represent the configuration of edges, i.e., direction and edge label of edges between two given nodes.

Definition 3 (Spoke). *Let G be a graph and $v, v' \in V_G$. Then the* spoke *between v and v' in G is the pair $SP_G(v, v') := (\{\beta \in \mathcal{E} \mid (v, v') \in E_G^{\beta}\}, \{\beta \in \mathcal{E} \mid (v', v) \in E_G^{\beta}\})$ We denote the set of all spokes $2^{\mathcal{E}} \times 2^{\mathcal{E}}$ by $\mathcal{SP}$. An alternative notation for the empty spoke $(\emptyset, \emptyset)$ shall be $\emptyset$.*

2.2 Graph Transformation Systems

Graph transformation systems rewrite graphs according to transformation rules, starting with some initial graph. Rule application can be restricted via negative application conditions. In this paper, we consider negative application conditions specified by partner constraints. A partner constraint prohibits incident edges with a specific direction and label to an adjacent node with a specific label.

Definition 4 (Partner constraint). *A* partner constraint *is a tuple $(d, \beta, l) \in \mathcal{PC} = \{in, out\} \times \mathcal{E} \times \mathcal{N}$ where d is a direction, β an edge label and l a node label.*

Transformation rules consist of a left hand side graph matched against the host graph, a right hand side graph by which the left hand side graph is replaced, and a mapping that describes node correspondence between the left and the right hand side graph. Additionally, for each left hand side node, an optional set of partner constraints can be specified.

Definition 5 (Graph transformation rule). *A graph transformation rule is a tuple (L, h, p, R) where L (the* left hand side*) and R (the* right hand side*) are graphs, $h : V_L \rightharpoonup V_R$ is an injective partial mapping from the left to the right hand side and $p : V_L \rightharpoonup 2^{\mathcal{PC}}$ specifies the partner constraints.*

For simplicity, in the following, we assume one globally unique set of graph transformation rules $\mathcal{R}$ and an initial graph I, which, together with node and edge labels, form the graph transformation system $\mathcal{S} := (\mathcal{N}, \mathcal{E}, I, \mathcal{R})$. We further assume for simplicity that in each rule, either all or none of its right hand side nodes are newly created.

For a rule to match, its left hand side must be a subgraph of the host graph and all negative application conditions need to be satisfied: We check each partner constraint against the matched node and its neighborhood.

Definition 6 (Match, partner constraint satisfaction). *Let $r = (L, h, p, R)$ be a rule, G a graph and $m : V_L \to V_G$. Then m is a* match *from r to G iff $L \lesssim_m G$ such that the partner constraints p are satisfied: For each $v \in \text{def}(p)$ and $\beta \in \mathcal{E}$, we have $p(v) \cap E = \emptyset$, where*

$$E = \{(out, \beta, \ell_G(u')) \mid (m(v), u') \in E_G^\beta\} \\ \cup \{(in, \beta, \ell_G(u')) \mid (u', m(v)) \in E_G^\beta\})\}$$

Rule application requires that the left hand side matches the host graph. A result graph is the host graph with labels of matched nodes changed as specified by h, nodes and edges of the left hand side removed and nodes and edges of the right hand side added as specified by the rule. Added nodes may be assigned any unused node name, thus the result is not unique. We obtain a mapping from the unchanged nodes of the host graph to the result graph as a byproduct. A graph is directly derived from a host graph according to some rule iff there is any way to apply the rule and obtain this graph as the result.

Definition 7 (Rule application, direct derivation). *Let $r = (L, h, p, R)$ be a rule, G, H graphs, $m : V_L \to V_G$ an injective graph morphism and $D := m(V_L \setminus \text{def}(h))$ the set of deleted nodes. Then H is a result of the* application *of r to G with respect to m, written $G \overset{r,m}{\rightsquigarrow} H$, iff there is an injective mapping $m' : V_R \setminus h(V_L \setminus \text{def}(m)) \to V_H$ such that $m = h \circ m'$, $V_H \cap D = \emptyset$ and*

$$\ell_H = (\ell_G \setminus (D \times \mathcal{N}) \cup (m'^{-1} \circ \ell_R)$$
$$V_H = (V_G \setminus D) \cup m'(V_R)$$
$$E_H^\beta = ((E_G^\beta \setminus m(E_L^\beta)) \cap (V_H \times V_H)) \cup m'(E_R^\beta)$$

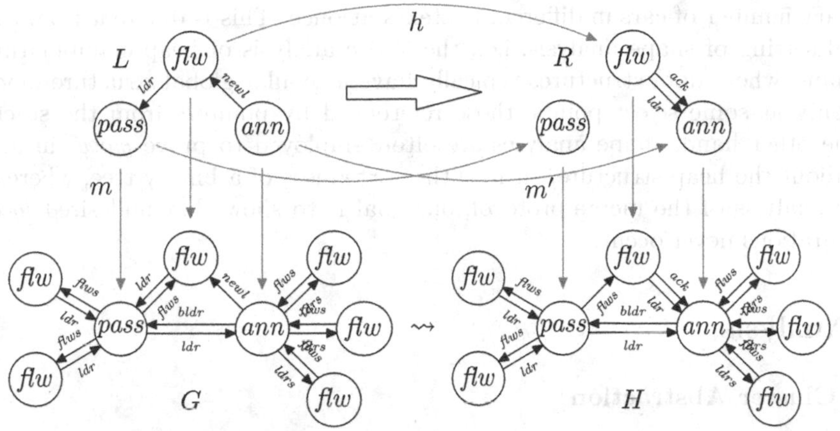

Fig. 1. An example of rule application: A rule $(L, h, \emptyset, R)$ transforming graph G into graph H, as it occurs in the merge protocol [1]

The direct derivation relation $\overset{r}{\rightsquigarrow}$ *is a relation over* $\mathcal{G} \times \mathcal{G}$ *where* $G \overset{r}{\rightsquigarrow} H$ *iff there is a match* m *such that* $G \overset{r,m}{\rightsquigarrow} H$.

In this paper, we are interested in reachability properties, i.e., is a graph with a particular property reachable or not? Therefore, we define the semantics of the graph transformation system simply as the set of reachable graphs.

Definition 8 (Graph transformation system semantics). *The* semantics of a graph transformation system $\mathcal{S}$ *is the smallest set such that* $I \in [\![\mathcal{S}]\!]$ *and, if there are graphs* $G \in [\![\mathcal{S}]\!]$ *and* H *and a rule* $r \in \mathcal{R}$ *such that* $G \overset{r}{\rightsquigarrow} H$, *then* $H \in [\![\mathcal{S}]\!]$.

2.3 The Merge Protocol

Our main benchmark is a graph transformation system modeling the *merge protocol* [2,1]. This protocol is used in car platooning, where autonomous cars on highways form platoons driving at constant speed and distance to save fuel. Its purpose is to allow (1) two cars to form a platoon with the car in front becoming the platoon leader and the other becoming its follower, (2) a car joining an existing platoon as a new follower and (3) merging of two platoons, with the leader on the back handing over all its followers to the leader in front, eventually itself becoming one of the followers.

What makes the merge protocol so difficult to analyze is the vast range of topological configurations all present and evolving at the same time, caused by the protocol's massively distributed nature. For example, a car may receive at any time a request to form a platoon, at the same time receive a request to merge with another platoon, all while being in the middle of any intermediate step of a merge operation, or sending such a request itself—and this happening with an arbitrary number of cars in different contexts at once. This is different from the typical setting of shape analysis, i.e., the static analysis of heap-manipulating programs, where data structures typically have a regular global structure modified only at some select points, those referenced by pointers from the stack. On the other hand, shape analyses are often employed to prove *global* invariants about the heap structure, such as the sortedness of a binary tree, whereas in the analysis of the merge protocol, our goal is to show that undesired *local* configurations never occur.

3 Analysis

3.1 Cluster Abstraction

In the graph transformation systems we consider, unbounded numbers of nodes may be created dynamically. Thus, the state space of such systems is infinite in size, making exact analysis by concrete state-space exploration impossible. To overcome this challenge, we employ a bounded abstraction: each concrete graph of arbitrary size is represented by an abstract graph of bounded size, reducing the infinite state space to a finite one.

We apply *local abstraction* to each node of a given graph, obtaining a bounded set of *clusters*. Local abstraction focusses on one specific node in the graph, henceforth called the *focal node*. It abstracts from all nodes in the graph except for the focal node and its immediate neighborhood, referred to as the *periphery* in the abstraction. The neighborhood consists of the incident edges and the adjacent nodes of the focal node. In addition, neighborhood nodes are merged into summary nodes if they are connected to the focal node by the same spoke (see Definition 3). Further, edges among neighborhood nodes are abstracted into three-valued *constraints*. This yields a *cluster*, which consists of the core node and its periphery. The core node shall have the unique name $core \in \mathcal{V}$. Figure 2 illustrates local abstraction, which is formally defined later.

Local abstraction asymmetrically preserves information about one specific node and some information about its neighborhood only, none about the rest of the graph. To capture the structure of the entire graph, we apply local abstraction to all of its nodes. As the neighborhoods of nodes are overlapping, this preserves some information about the global graph structure.

While a concrete graph may contain an arbitrary number of nodes, the set of distinct clusters is bounded. Thus the abstraction is bounded.

The process described above yields a set of clusters that may contain clusters that differ only with respect to constraints between peripheral nodes. To reduce analysis complexity, such clusters are merged by loosening the constraints.

Definition 9 (Cluster). *A* cluster P *is a tuple* $(G_P, S_P, C_P^{\beta_1}, \ldots, C_P^{\beta_{|\mathcal{E}|}})$ *where* $G_P = (V_P, E_P^{\beta_1}, \ldots, E_P^{\beta_{|\mathcal{E}|}}, \ell_P)$ *is a graph,* $\{core\} \subseteq V_P \subseteq \{core\} \cup \mathcal{SP} \times \mathcal{N}$ *are the node names,* $S_P \subseteq D_P = V_P \setminus \{core\}$ *is a set of* summary nodes, *with* D_P *the set of* peripheral nodes, $C_P^{\beta} : ((D_P \times D_P) \setminus \{(v, v) \mid v \in D_P \setminus S_P\}) \to \{0, 1, \frac{1}{2}\}$

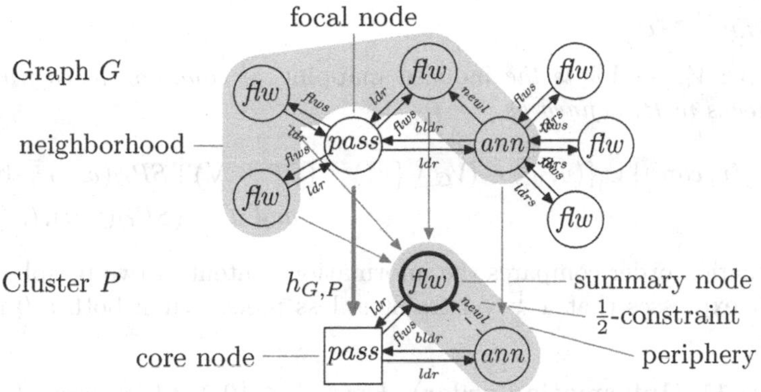

Fig. 2. An example of local abstraction: Graph G with the *pass*-labeled node as focal node is abstracted into cluster P. The periphery of P is an abstraction of the neighborhood of the focal node in G.

are the peripheral constraints, $E_P^\beta \subseteq (\{core\} \times V_P) \cup (V_P \times \{core\})$ *for any* $\beta \in \mathcal{E}$ *and* $SP_P(core, v) \neq \emptyset$ *for all* $v \in D_P$. *We denote the set of all clusters by* $\mathcal{P}$.

Given a graph G and one of its nodes v, local abstraction yields a cluster P with a core node that corresponds to the focal node v. P has one peripheral node per uniquely connected neighborhood node of v, that is, with a unique configuration of neighborhood node label plus non-empty spoke.

The edges connecting the neighborhood nodes are abstracted as follows: If, in G, there are β-labeled edges from all source nodes V_1 to all target nodes V_2, both sets each corresponding to a (possibly summary) node in P, then there is a peripheral 1-constraint in P that involves two nodes corresponding to V_1 and V_2. If there are some, but not all such β-labeled edges, we use a $\frac{1}{2}$-constraint instead. And if there are no such β-labeled edges at all, a 0-constraint. Note that peripheral constraints do not contain information about self-loops of the corresponding concrete nodes.

The byproduct of local abstraction is a mapping $h_{G,P}$. It maps nodes of G to corresponding nodes in P, if any. $h_{G,P}$ is not necessarily injective: If the abstraction contains a summary node, then all corresponding concrete nodes will be mapped to it.

Definition 10 (Local abstraction, induced mapping). *The* local abstraction *of a graph G with respect to a* focal node $v \in V_G$, *denoted by* $\alpha(G, v)$, *is the cluster P that satisfies the following conditions:*

- $V_P = h_{G,P}(V_G)$
- $E_P^\beta = h_{G,P}(E_G^\beta \cap ((\{v\} \times V_G) \cup (V_G \times \{v\})))$
- $S_P = \{u \in D_P \mid |h_{G,P}{}^{-1}(\{u\})| \geq 2\}$
- $C_P^\beta(u_1, u_2) = \begin{cases} 0 & : \forall v_1 \neq v_2 : (h_{G,P}(v_1), h_{G,P}(v_2)) = (u_1, u_2) \Rightarrow (v_1, v_2) \notin E_G^\beta \\ 1 & : \forall v_1 \neq v_2 : (h_{G,P}(v_1), h_{G,P}(v_2)) = (u_1, u_2) \Rightarrow (v_1, v_2) \in E_G^\beta \\ \frac{1}{2} & : else \end{cases}$

– $\ell_P = {h_{G,P}}^{-1} \circ \ell_G$

where $h_{G,P} : V_G \rightharpoonup V_P$ *is the* induced mapping *of concrete nodes from* G *to abstract nodes in* P*, defined as*

$$h_{G,P} = \{(v, core)\} \cup \{(u, u') \in (V_G \setminus \{v\}) \times (\mathcal{SP} \times \mathcal{N}) \mid SP_G(v, u) \neq \emptyset \text{ and } u' = (SP_G(v, u), \ell_G(u))\},$$

The information order compares the information content of two peripheral constraints. It expresses that a $\frac{1}{2}$-constraint is less precise than both a 0 and a 1 constraint.

Definition 11 (Information order). *For* $l_1, l_2 \in \{0, 1, \frac{1}{2}\}$*, we write* $l_1 \sqsubseteq l_2$ *iff* $l_1 = l_2$ *or* $l_2 = \frac{1}{2}$.

Using information order, we define a partial order on clusters P and P' that considers P to be less than or equal to P' if P and P' are equal except for peripheral constraints, and each constraint of P is less than or equal (with respect to the information order) to the corresponding constraint of P'.

Definition 12 (Cluster order). *Let* P *and* P' *be clusters. We write* $P \sqsubseteq P'$ *iff* $G_P = G_{P'}$, $S_P = S_{P'}$ *and* $C^\beta_P(v, v') \sqsubseteq C^\beta_{P'}(v, v')$ *for any* $\beta \in \mathcal{E}$ *and* $v, v' \in V_P$. *We say that* P' *is an upper bound of* P.

Note that both information order and cluster order are partial orders, so the notion of least upper bounds is applicable to them. A least upper bound exists for clusters as long as they differ in peripheral constraints only. It yields a cluster with peripheral constraints that are just weak enough to be consistent with both clusters. In effect, a constraint becomes $\frac{1}{2}$ whenever it differs in the two clusters (or is already $\frac{1}{2}$).

Our abstract domain consists of sets of clusters, such that no pair of clusters is comparable according to the cluster order:

Definition 13 (Abstract topology). *An* abstract topology *is a set* $S \subseteq \mathcal{P}$*, where for no pair* $P_1 \neq P_2 \in S$ *there is a mutual upper bound* $P' \in \mathcal{P}$.

To obtain such an abstract topology from the clusters produced by local abstraction, we impose an order on sets of clusters, with an induced least upper bound. Cluster set S is less than or equal to cluster set S' according to this induced order iff for each cluster P in S, S' contains a cluster P', such that $P \sqsubseteq P'$ according to the cluster order.

Definition 14 (Cluster set order). *Let* S, S' *be sets of clusters. We write* $S \sqsubseteq S'$ *iff for each* $P \in S$*, there is a* $P' \in S'$ *such that* $P \sqsubseteq P'$.

We split the set of clusters into singleton sets, each containing one of the clusters. Then we consider the least upper bound over all of those singleton sets. This means joining any clusters that can be joined and taking the union for those that cannot. At the end, this yields the abstract topology we were looking for. We call this abstract topology the topologization of the cluster set under consideration.

Definition 15 (Topologization). *The* topologization *of a set of clusters $S \subseteq \mathcal{P}$ is the abstract topology $\bigsqcup S = \bigsqcup\{\{P\} \mid P \in S\})$.*

For each equivalence class of clusters from S identical except for peripheral constraints, topologization yields a single, joined, less precise cluster in the resulting topology. Note that we overload the $\bigsqcup$ operator, denoting topologization if applied to a set of clusters, and denoting the least upper bound on cluster sets if applied to sets of sets of clusters. Note further that, given $S \sqsubseteq S'$, we have $\bigsqcup S \sqsubseteq \bigsqcup S'$ and $S \sqsubseteq \bigsqcup S'$, but not necessarily $\bigsqcup S \sqsubseteq S'$.

The full abstraction of a graph is the topologization of the set of clusters obtained by local abstraction of each node of the graph. Each of these nodes corresponds to the core node of one of the clusters in the resulting abstract topology. Conversely, we define topology concretization.

Definition 16 (Cluster abstraction and concretization). *Let $\mathfrak{G} \subseteq \mathcal{G}$. Then the* cluster abstraction *of $\mathfrak{G}$ is the abstract topology $\alpha(\mathfrak{G}) = \bigsqcup\{\alpha(G, v) \mid v \in V_G \wedge G \in \mathfrak{G}\}$. An abstract topology S represents the set of concrete graphs $\gamma(S) = \{G \in \mathcal{G} \mid \alpha(\{G\}) \sqsubseteq S\}$.*

3.2 Abstract Transformer

Thus far, we considered how to apply rules on concrete graphs and how to abstract a graph into an abstract topology. Now, we discuss the application of rules on abstract topologies instead of concrete graphs. We obtain an abstract topology capturing the graphs we would obtain in the concrete. We sacrifice some precision in the abstract transformation to allow for a tractable and efficient implementation.

Rule application to all graphs from the cluster concretization induces an abstract derivation relation between clusters for a given rule and abstract topology. The relation holds if the core nodes of source and target cluster relate to corresponding nodes in the respective host and result graph.

Definition 17 (Induced abstract derivation). *The* induced abstract derivation *is a relation $\overset{r,S}{\Rightarrow} \subseteq \mathcal{P} \times \mathcal{P}$ where $P' \overset{r,S}{\Rightarrow} Q$ iff there are graphs G, H, a match $m : V_L \to V_G$ from r to G and a node $v \in V_G$, such that G is in the cluster concretization of S, $P \sqsubseteq P'$, $G \overset{r,m}{\rightsquigarrow} H$ and $\alpha(H, v) = Q$, where $r = (L, h, p, R)$, $P = \alpha(G, v)$ with induced mapping $h_{G,P} : V_G \to V_P$ and $m \circ h_{G,P} \neq \emptyset$.*

The induced abstract topology is the topology we obtain if we apply full abstraction to the initial graph and then iteratively compute abstract topologies until we reach a fixpoint: We apply any rule in any possible way to any graph from the cluster concretization of the abstract topology from the previous iteration, add the resulting clusters to those that already existed, and take the least upper bound on the cluster set thus obtained.

Definition 18 (Induced abstract topology). *The* induced abstract topology *is the set $[\![\mathcal{S}]\!]^\sharp = [\![\mathcal{S}]\!]^\sharp_n$ where $n = \min\{i \in \mathbb{N} \mid [\![\mathcal{S}]\!]^\sharp_i = [\![\mathcal{S}]\!]^\sharp_{i+1}\}$ and $[\![\mathcal{S}]\!]^\sharp_i$ defined recursively as follows:*

- $[\![\mathcal{S}]\!]_0^\sharp = \alpha(\{I\})$
- $[\![\mathcal{S}]\!]_i^\sharp = \bigsqcup([\![\mathcal{S}]\!]_{i-1}^\sharp \cup \{Q \in \mathcal{P} \mid \exists P \in \mathcal{P}, r \in \mathcal{R} : P \overset{r,[\![\mathcal{S}]\!]_{i-1}^\sharp}{\Rightarrow} Q\})$

Note that the existence of the induced abstract topology follows from the fact that $[\![\mathcal{S}]\!]_i^\sharp \sqsubseteq [\![\mathcal{S}]\!]_{i+1}^\sharp$ and the finiteness of the domain.

Proposition 1. *The induced abstract topology overapproximates the graph transformation system semantics, i.e.,* $[\![\mathcal{S}]\!] \subseteq \gamma([\![\mathcal{S}]\!]^\sharp)$.

Induced abstract derivation, and, consequently, the induced abstract topology involves rule application to an infinite number of graphs. For an implementation, we need to reduce this to a finite number. That this is possible follows from the fact that our domain is finite.

We capture the characteristics of a sufficient, yet finite subset using the notion of abstract matches. While a concrete match relates a left hand side L of a rule to the nodes of a host graph G, the abstract match relates it to a cluster P. The core node of P has a corresponding node in a host graph G. This node has a corresponding focal node in the result graph H. (Recall that we do not permit node deletion.) Local abstraction on the result graph will yield the relevant cluster Q. Q primarily depends on P and the node and edge modifications as stipulated by the rule. Thus, the main components of an abstract match are P and the relation $h_{L,P}$ between the left hand side and the matched nodes of P.

However, indirectly, and perhaps contrary to intuition, Q also depends on some nodes and edges of the host graph G that are *neither* matched *nor* determined by P:

- For each match to a summary node, only one concrete instance will be matched. Thus, Q may depend on the number of additional unmatched instances (captured by *mater* in the following definition). We need to distinguish only the cases of zero, one, and more than one instances, since the latter will always become a summary node after abstraction.
- A $\frac{1}{2}$-constraint in P may become a 0 and 1 constraint in Q, and sometimes remain as is: (a) If two matched peripheral nodes have an unmatched $\frac{1}{2}$-constraint in between, the corresponding concrete edge will be either present or absent in G, captured by *cc*. (b) The concrete edge corresponding to a $\frac{1}{2}$-constraint between a pair of unmatched peripheral nodes will be either present or absent in G. Concrete edges incident to residual materializations of a summary node v with $mater(v) \geq 1$ may be present for all, none or some of the corresponding concrete node pairs. Both cases are captured by *dd*. (c) The same possibilities exist for edges between an unmatched peripheral node and a matched node. The mapping *dc* specifies these edges. In this case, the matched node does not even have to be in P, since it might just be about to become connected to the focal node through application of the rule.

In addition, the match requires that a closure exists, that is, we have a graph G from the cluster concretization for which the match holds.

Definition 19 (Abstract match). *Let $r = (L, h, p, R)$ be a rule and S be an abstract topology. An abstract match from r to S is a tuple $(P, h_{L,P}, mater, dc, cd, dd)$ where*

- *$P \in \mathcal{P}$ is the matched cluster,*
- *$h_{L,P} : V_L \rightharpoonup V_P$ maps the left hand side to the nodes of P,*
- *$mater : D_P \to \{0, 1, 2\}$ specifies the residual materialization count of summary nodes in P,*
- *$dc : (V_L \times D_P \times \{-1, 1\} \times \mathcal{E}) \to \{0, 1, \frac{1}{2}\}$ specifies the materialization of edges from peripheral to matched nodes and vice versa,*
- *$dd : (D_P \times D_P \times \mathcal{E}) \to \{0, 1, \frac{1}{2}\}$ specifies the peripheral edge materialization*
- *$cc : V_L \times V_L \to 2^{\mathcal{E}}$ specifies the materialization of edges among matched nodes*

and the following conditions are satisfied:

- *$P \sqsubseteq P'$ for some $P' \in S$*
- *$h_{L,P}(V_L) \neq \emptyset$*
- *$|h_{L,P}{}^{-1}(core)| < 2$*
- *the following conditions hold for $matched : D_P \to \mathbb{N}$, the induced number of matches, defined as $matched(u) := |h_{L,P}{}^{-1}(\{u\})|$:*

$$matched(u) = 0 \Rightarrow mater(u) = \begin{cases} 2 & \text{if } u \in S_P \\ 1 & \text{otherwise} \end{cases}$$

$$matched(u) = 1 \Rightarrow mater(u) \in \begin{cases} \{1, 2\} & \text{if } u \in S_P \\ \{0\} & \text{otherwise} \end{cases}$$

$$matched(u) > 1 \Rightarrow u \in S_{P_v}$$

- *there is a graph G, a match $m : V_L \to V_G$ from r to G and a node $v \in V_G$ such that $\alpha(G, v) = P$ with induced mapping $h_{G,P} : V_G \rightharpoonup V_P$ and*
  - *$m \circ h_{G,P} = h_{L,P}$,*
  - *$mater(u) = \min\{|h_{G,P}{}^{-1}(\{u\}) \setminus m(V_L)|, 2\}$,*
  - *for all $u \in V_L \setminus m^{-1}(\{v\})$, $u' \in D_P$, $\beta \in \mathcal{E}$, and $d \in \{-1, 1\}$,*

$$dc(u, u', d, \beta) = \begin{cases} 0 & : \forall v' \notin m(V_L) : h_{G,P}(v') = u' \Rightarrow (m(u), v') \in (E_G^\beta)^d \\ 1 & : \forall v' \notin m(V_L) : h_{G,P}(v') = u' \Rightarrow (m(u), v') \notin (E_G^\beta)^d \\ \frac{1}{2} & \text{otherwise,} \end{cases}$$

  - *for all $u, u' \in D_P$, for all $\beta \in \mathcal{E}$,*

$$dd(u, u', \beta) = \begin{cases} 0 & : \forall v_1 \neq v_2 \notin m(V_L) : (h_{G,P}(v_1), h_{G,P}(v_2)) = (u, u') \\ & \qquad \Rightarrow (v_1, v_2) \in E_G^\beta \\ 1 & : \forall v_1 \neq v_2 \notin m(V_L) : (h_{G,P}(v_1), h_{G,P}(v_2)) = (u, u') \\ & \qquad \Rightarrow (v_1, v_2) \notin E_G^\beta \\ \frac{1}{2} & \text{otherwise,} \end{cases}$$

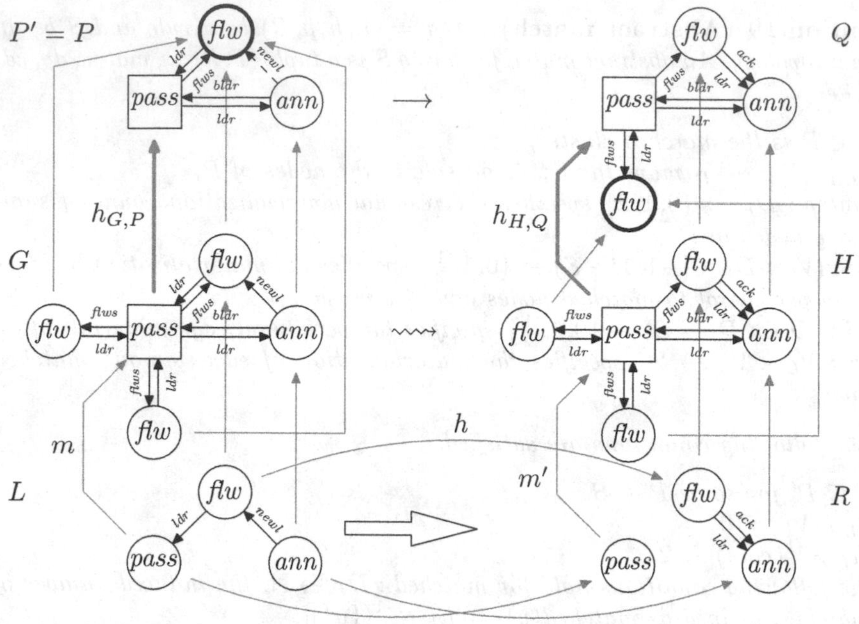

Fig. 3. An example of the abstract transformer

- *for all* $u, u' \in V_L$*,* $(cc(u,u'), cc(u',u)) = SP_G(m(u), m(u'))$*,*
- $G \in \gamma(S)$*, and*
- *the partner constraints* p *are satisfied.*

Since the number of abstract matches is finite, the definition is constructive and a computation method directly follows from it, except for the non-trivial closure check. However, the fact that we are looking for an overapproximation allows us to weaken this check, including the option to ignore it completely. This includes the check that partner constraints are satisfied. Note that at least the partner constraints for ${h_{G,P}}^{-1}(core)$ can be checked without knowledge of the entire graph G.

From the abstract matches, we generate partial concretizations. These are graphs with focal node and neighborhood, just sufficient to capture all potential changes to the cluster caused by rule application and local abstraction of the result. We do not need to consider the full graph, since this is taken care of by symmetry: The additional nodes it contains will be covered by other abstract matches with those nodes as the core node of a cluster. Those, in turn, have their own partial concretizations to account for the impact of the rule application.

Note that edges specified by *dd* and *dc* will never be modified by a rule, for that would require its adjacent nodes both to be matched, which is, by definition, not the case. The set A, in the following definition, splits the unmatched peripheral nodes into two subsets such that those in the set will have respective edges for the $\frac{1}{2}$ case and the complementary nodes will not.

Definition 20 (Partial concretization). *The* partial concretization *function* γ *maps abstract matches* $(P, h_{L,P}, mater, dc, dd, cc)$ *to tuples* $(G, m, h_{G,P})$ *where* G *is a graph,* $m : V_L \rightharpoonup V_G$ *is an injective partial graph morphism from the left hand side to this graph and* $h_{G,P} : V_G \rightharpoonup V_P$ *is a mapping to the abstraction* P*, all defined as follows:*

- $V_G = \{core\} \cup (V_L \setminus {h_{L,P}}^{-1}(\{core\})) \cup \{(u,n) \in D_P \times \mathbb{N} \mid 1 \leq n \leq mater(u)\}$
- $h_{G,P}(u) = \begin{cases} core & \text{if } u = core \\ v & \text{if } u = (v,n) \\ h_{L,P}(u) & \text{if } u \in V_L \setminus {h_{L,P}}^{-1}(\{core\}) \end{cases}$
- $m = \{({h_{L,P}}^{-1}(core), core)\} \cup \{(u,u) \mid u \in (V_L \setminus {h_{L,P}}^{-1}(\{core\}))\}$
- $E_G^\beta = \{(u,u') \in A \times A \mid dd(h_{G,P}(u), h_{G,P}(u'), \beta) \geq \frac{1}{2}\}$
  $\cup \{(u,u') \in V_G \times V_G \mid dd(h_{G,P}(u), h_{G,P}(u'), \beta) = 1\}$
  $\cup \{(u,u') \in m(V_L) \times m(V_L) \mid \beta \in cc(m^{-1}(u), m^{-1}(u'))\}$
  $\cup \{(u,u') \in m(V_L) \times A \mid dc(m^{-1}(u), h_{G,P}(u'), 1, \beta) = \frac{1}{2}\}$
  $\cup \{(u,u') \in m(V_L) \times V_G \mid dc(m^{-1}(u), h_{G,P}(u'), 1, \beta) = 1\}$
  $\cup \{(u,u') \in A \times m(V_L) \mid dc(m^{-1}(u'), h_{G,P}(u), -1, \beta) = \frac{1}{2}\}$
  $\cup \{(u,u') \in V_G \times m(V_L) \mid dc(m^{-1}(u'), h_{G,P}(u), -1, \beta) = 1\}$
  $\cup {h_{G,P}}^{-1}(E_P^\beta)$
  where $A = (D_P \times \{1\}) \cap V_G$
- $\ell_G = (m^{-1} \circ \ell_L) \cup (h_{G,P} \circ \ell_P)$

The abstract transformer describes how clusters are affected by rule application. It presupposes the existence of an abstract match, constructs the corresponding partial concretization, applies the rule, and constructs the modified cluster by local abstraction of the focal node. See Figure 3.2 for an example.

Definition 21 (Abstract transformer). *Let* $r = (L, h, p, R)$ *be a rule and* S *be an abstract topology. The* abstract transformer *(or* direct derivation*) is a relation* $\overset{r,S}{\rightarrow} \subseteq \mathcal{P} \times \mathcal{P}$ *where* $P' \overset{r,S}{\rightarrow} Q$ *iff there is a graph* H *and an abstract match* $\hat{m} = (P, h_{L,P}, mater, dc, dd, cc)$ *from* r *to* S *such that* $P \sqsubseteq P'$*,* $\gamma(\hat{m}) = (G, m, h_{G,P})$*,* $G \overset{r,m}{\rightsquigarrow} H$ *and* $Q = \alpha(H, core)$

The graph morphism m may be partial, i.e., some nodes of the left hand side may map to none of the nodes in G. Not even the focal node needs to be covered. In those cases, we waive the totality requirement that rule application puts on m, thereby modifying only those parts of the partial concretization that are matched. We obtain an abstract topology that overapproximates the system by abstracting the start graph and applying the abstract transformer in a fixpoint iteration.

Definition 22 (Derived abstract topology). *The* derived abstract topology *is the set* $[\mathcal{S}]^\sharp = [\mathcal{S}]^\sharp_n$*, where* $n = \min\{i \in \mathbb{N} \mid [\mathcal{S}]^\sharp_i = [\mathcal{S}]^\sharp_{i+1}\}$ *and* $[\mathcal{S}]^\sharp_i$ *is defined recursively as follows:*

– $[\mathcal{S}]_0^\sharp = \alpha(\{I\})$
– $[\mathcal{S}]_i^\sharp = \bigsqcup([\mathcal{S}]_{i-1}^\sharp \cup \{Q \in \mathcal{P} \mid \exists P \in [\mathcal{S}]_{i-1}^\sharp, r \in \mathcal{R} : P \overset{r,[\mathcal{S}]_{i-1}^\sharp}{\rightarrow} Q\}$
$\cup \{\alpha(\{R\}) \mid (\emptyset, \emptyset, \emptyset, R) \in \mathcal{R}\})$

Note that we assumed the absence of rules with non-empty left hand side that create new nodes. Because of this, we do not need to take care of new clusters that occur as a byproduct of the modification of an existing cluster. Instead, for each rule with empty left hand side, we add the clusters obtained by local abstraction for each right hand side node. This takes place unconditionally, pointing towards the equivalence of node creation and initial graphs in our domain.

Theorem 1. *The derived abstract topology overapproximates the induced abstract topology, i.e.,* $[\![\mathcal{S}]\!]^\sharp \sqsubseteq [\mathcal{S}]^\sharp$.

Corollary 1 (Soundness). *The derived abstract topology overapproximates the graph transformation system semantics, i.e.,* $[\![\mathcal{S}]\!] \subseteq \gamma([\mathcal{S}]^\sharp)$.

Proof. This follows immediately from Proposition 1, Theorem 1, and the monotonicity of cluster concretization.

4 Experimental Evaluation

4.1 Implementation

We implemented cluster abstraction in our tool `astra` 2.0. The implementation differs from theory in minor respects: (a) Partial concretization materializes clusters over the entire left hand side of a rule at once, exploiting symmetry and allowing us to properly check all partner constraints. (b) We do a rudimentary check for the existence of a closure, by checking whether peripheral constraints of unmatched nodes are satisfiable. (c) To cover cases with unmatched core nodes, for each match, we iterate over all possibilities in which one additional cluster can be attached in the periphery. (d) After each iteration, we apply a reduction step, eliminating any cluster whose existence can be ruled out easily, and concretizing $\frac{1}{2}$-constraints if more precise information is available. (e) In various places, we use overapproximation ad hoc in order to improve analysis time.

4.2 Selection of Benchmarks

With `astra` 1.0, we already succeeded to analyze a part of the *merge protocol* [1] with star abstraction [3], a precursor to the method described in this paper. (In a nutshell, cluster abstraction with all peripheral constraints being $\frac{1}{2}$.) It was sufficient to analyze platoon formation and car joining, but not platoon merging, for which state space explosion occurred: Follower handover requires ternary predicates, while star abstraction only preserves binary predicates. This causes a cascade of spurious abstract states, with the analysis eventually spending its time enumerating an intractable number of combinatorial possibilities. The main goal of `astra` 2.0 was to analyze the full protocol. We did this for two

Table 1. Benchmark analysis statistics. cl. = clusters, a.r. = active rules, i.e., applied at least once, m. = abstract matches, rule app. = rule applications, it. = iterations, vfy. = safety property verified. *safety property not expressible as forbidden subgraphs

Benchmark	# cl.	# a.r.	# m.	# rule app.	# it.	time	vfy.
Synchronous merge	873	34	9674	349774	17	0m 14.057s	yes
Asynchronous merge	3069	36	44553	36114603	21	14m 27.977s	yes
AVL trees	1876	302	114284	2221151967	38	757m 9.273s	yes
Firewall	31	4	139	1371	5	0m 0.012s	yes
Firewall 2	96	9	786	45525	7	0m 0.330s	no
Public/private servers 2	239	26	1633	102250	10	0m 1.030s	yes
Dining philosophers	41	8	40	179	7	0m 0.006s	no*
Resources	32	7	100	207	4	0m 0.007s	yes
Mutual exclusion	308	9	2419	1237361	17	0m 56.060s	yes
Red-black trees	263	38	8769	24855500	11	10m 3.145s	yes
Singly-linked lists	7	2	15	13	3	0m 0.000s	yes
Circular buffers	152	2	798	241234	17	2m 43.441s	no*
Euler walks	18	6	47	134	3	0m 0.008s	no*

versions. In addition, we analyzed the *AVL tree* benchmark from [4] and various other benchmarks from the related work: *Firewall, public/private servers, dining philosophers, resources, mutual exclusion*, and *red-black trees* are benchmarks from the AUGUR package [5]; *singly-linked lists, circular buffers* and *Euler walks* for GROOVE are from [6].

The AUGUR package comes with additional benchmarks that we did not analyze: *connections, leader election protocol* and the *Needham–Schroeder protocol* all make use of numerical attributes, which are not yet supported by our tool. *External-internal processes* is merely a stripped-down version of *public and private server 2. Public and private server* contains a subset of the rules from *public and private server 2.* The same holds for the finite-state version of *dining philosophers* versus the infinite-state version, which we analyze. *Red-black trees converted* is a tweaked version of *red-black trees* to ease analysis with AUGUR.

We could analyze the GROOVE benchmarks without modifications. The AUGUR benchmarks, on the other hand, had to be translated from the tool's hyperedge-based approach to one based on nodes and edges. In addition, we had to make a structure-preserving change to the *public/private server* grammar (replacing a specific edge with two edges connected by a node) in order to prevent combinatorial explosion that would otherwise have defied analysis. For *red-black* and *AVL trees*, we manually added invariants about the uniqueness of some labels over the entire graph. These invariants trivially follow from the respective graph transformation systems and it would in principle be easy to find them automatically. However, uniqueness is not expressible in our abstraction, because clusters always represent an arbitrary number of concrete instances.

We checked the safety properties by adding rules specifying respective forbidden subgraphs, producing a node with an error label if found. This approach could not be taken for *dining philosophers, circular buffers* and *Euler walks*, since the respective safety properties quantify over an unbounded number of nodes and hence cannot be formulated as forbidden subgraphs.

4.3 Analysis Results

`astra` was able to analyze all benchmarks. See Table 1 for the number of iterations required for reaching the fixed point, the number of clusters in the final result and the processor time taken. We ran all analyses on an Intel Core 2 Quad CPU Q9550 (2.83GHz) with 4 GB of memory under Linux 3.15, though only 9 MB were used at the peak for the largest benchmark, *asynchronous merge*. Execution time given is the time in user mode as reported by `time`(1).

In all but one of the cases with safety properties expressible as forbidden subgraphs, verification succeeded. Verification failed for *firewall 2* because the abstraction was unable to distinguish locations in front of and behind the firewall.

5 Related Work

Petri graphs are unfoldings of graph transformation systems, abstracted by a cutoff after a defined depth [7]. Reachability can be checked with existing techniques for Petri nets. As we have seen, we were able to analyze a subset of their benchmarks. Once they support negative application conditions (which they currently list as future work), it will be interesting to investigate whether their tool AUGUR [8] can analyze our main target, the merge protocol.

Bauer et al.'s partner abstraction [9] considers connected components instead of overlapping clusters and folds nodes according to neighborhood node and edge labels. In practice, it requires the system to obey friendliness properties that hold only for a simplified merge protocol where processes know each other's state [4]. Rensink and Distefano [10] consider an abstraction similar in design and limitations. Ideas from both approaches were combined and extended in neighborhood abstraction [11]. No friendliness restriction applies, but lacking Bauer's decomposition into components, the GROOVE implementation runs out of memory even on Bauer's simplified merge protocol [6].

Environment abstraction [12] abstracts a system into one process and its environment, i.e., the set of states of all the other processes plus relations to them. Cherem and Rugina [13] propose a local abstraction for shape analysis that tracks individual heap cells and their immediate neighborhood. Bauer et al.'s daisy patterns [14] and our star abstraction [3] are graph abstractions based on the same idea, the former abstracting the transformation rules in addition to the graph. All these abstractions are less precise than cluster abstraction, since none of them tracks peripheral node relationships.

Saksena et al. [15] verify graph transformation systems by symbolic backward reachability analysis. Starting with the undesirable configurations, they compute, by backward rule application in a fixed point iteration, an overapproximation of the set of reachable predecessor configurations, checking whether an initial configuration is among them. While not guaranteed to terminate, their method succeeds in proving loop freedom of an ad hoc routing protocol.

Berdine et al. [16] show that shape analysis of concurrent programs via canonical abstraction [17] leads to state-space explosion even for a toy example. The complexity of expressing cluster abstraction via canonical abstraction confirms this: at least, one abstraction predicate would be needed for each spoke, which is exponential in the number of edge labels. Berdine et al.'s own solution allows efficient analysis of an unbounded number of threads manipulating an unbounded shared heap. However, their abstraction is unable to express direct relations between the state of the threads. Manevich et al. [18] decompose the heap into a bounded number of overlapping components as specified by user-defined location selection predicates. In contrast, our method decomposes the graph by local abstraction of each of the unbounded number of nodes.

Zufferey et al. [19] provide an abstraction for depth-bounded systems (systems with a bound on the longest acyclic path), an expressive class of well-structured transition systems. Unfortunately, the merge protocol does not belong to this class unless one uses a simplified version similar to Bauer's.

6 Conclusions and Future Work

We have seen an abstraction for the analysis of the set of reachable graphs generated by infinite-state graph transformation systems. Using `astra`, our implementation of *cluster abstraction*, we were for the first time able to analyze the full merge protocol. In addition, our method has proven robust and precise enough to allow for the analysis of various benchmarks from the literature.

Future work: (1) We are going to check safety properties that cannot be expressed as forbidden subgraphs, such as quantification over an unbounded number of nodes. (2) We shall explore suitable approximations for the closure check, to preserve more of the global graph structure during rule application. (3) We are going to investigate opportunities to adjust the precision of our analysis. Especially, structure-preserving changes to the graph transformation system before the analysis seem to be an interesting way to give direction to the abstraction. For example, adding edges to the right hand side of rules with a new label that never occurs on a left hand side can keep nodes in the periphery of some clusters, thereby increasing precision. (4) If some cluster may occur at most once, we would like to retain this information. (5) We would like to allow integer values as node and edge attributes, in addition to regular labels. Lifted to the abstraction, it extends clusters by overapproximated values for those attributes, based on abstract domains on integers. (6) Based on a suitable fragment of μ-calculus, we plan to support abstract model checking on an abstract labeled transition systems of clusters, preserving some non-trivial relationships for the transitions, such as size invariants on summary nodes. We plan to extend this to model checking over an abstract labeled transition system, based on a suitable fragment of μ-calculus.

Acknowledgments. We thank Reinhard Wilhelm for many valuable discussions about this work and the anonymous referees for their useful comments.

References

1. Backes, P., Reineke, J.: A graph transformation case study for the topology analysis of dynamic communication systems. In: TTC 2010. CTIT Workshop Proceedings, vol. WP10-03, pp. 107–118. University of Twente, Enschede (2010)
2. Hsu, A., Eskafi, F., Sachs, S., Varaiya, P.: Design of platoon maneuver protocols for IVHS. Technical report, Institute of Transportation Studies, UC Berkeley (1991)
3. Backes, P., Reineke, J.: Abstract topology analysis of the join phase of the merge protocol [using astra]. In: TTC 2010. CTIT Workshop Proceedings, vol. WP10-03, pp. 127–133. University of Twente, Enschede (2010)
4. Backes, P.: Topology analysis of dynamic communication systems. Diploma thesis, Saarland University (March 2008)
5. Kozyura, V., König, B.: Augur 2—A tool for the analysis of (attributed) graph transformation systems using approximative unfolding techniques (April 2008)
6. Zambon, E.: Abstract graph transformation: Theory and practice. PhD thesis, University of Twente (2013)
7. Baldan, P., König, B.: Approximating the behaviour of graph transformation systems. In: Corradini, A., Ehrig, H., Kreowski, H.-J., Rozenberg, G. (eds.) ICGT 2002. LNCS, vol. 2505, pp. 14–29. Springer, Heidelberg (2002)
8. König, B., Kozioura, V.: Augur 2—a new version of a tool for the analysis of graph transformation systems. In: Bruni, R., Varró, D. (eds.) GT-VMT 2006. ENTCS, vol. 2011, pp. 201–210 (2008)
9. Bauer, J., Wilhelm, R.: Static analysis of dynamic communication systems by partner abstraction. In: Riis Nielson, H., Filé, G. (eds.) SAS 2007. LNCS, vol. 4634, pp. 249–264. Springer, Heidelberg (2007)
10. Rensink, A., Distefano, D.: Abstract graph transformation. In: SVV 2005. ENTCS, vol. 157, pp. 39–59 (May 2006)
11. Boneva, I., Kreiker, J., Kurbán, M., Rensink, A., Zambon, E.: Graph abstraction and abstract graph transformations (amended version). Technical Report TR-CTIT-12-26, University of Twente, Enschede, The Netherlands (October 2012)
12. Clarke, E., Talupur, M., Veith, H.: Environment abstraction for parameterized verification. In: Emerson, E.A., Namjoshi, K.S. (eds.) VMCAI 2006. LNCS, vol. 3855, pp. 126–141. Springer, Heidelberg (2006)
13. Cherem, S., Rugina, R.: Maintaining doubly-linked list invariants in shape analysis with local reasoning. In: Cook, B., Podelski, A. (eds.) VMCAI 2007. LNCS, vol. 4349, pp. 234–250. Springer, Heidelberg (2007)
14. Bauer, J., Boneva, I., Rensink, A.: Graph abstraction by daisy patterns. Privately circulated (May 2009)
15. Saksena, M., Wibling, O., Jonsson, B.: Graph grammar modeling and verification of ad hoc routing protocols. In: Ramakrishnan, C.R., Rehof, J. (eds.) TACAS 2008. LNCS, vol. 4963, pp. 18–32. Springer, Heidelberg (2008)
16. Berdine, J., Lev-Ami, T., Manevich, R., Ramalingam, G., Sagiv, M.: Thread quantification for concurrent shape analysis. In: Gupta, A., Malik, S. (eds.) CAV 2008. LNCS, vol. 5123, pp. 399–413. Springer, Heidelberg (2008)
17. Sagiv, M., Reps, T., Wilhelm, R.: Parametric shape analysis via 3-valued logic. ACM Trans. Program. Lang. Syst. 24(3), 217–298 (2002)
18. Manevich, R., Lev-Ami, T., Sagiv, M., Ramalingam, G., Berdine, J.: Heap decomposition for concurrent shape analysis. In: Alpuente, M., Vidal, G. (eds.) SAS 2008. LNCS, vol. 5079, pp. 363–377. Springer, Heidelberg (2008)
19. Zufferey, D., Wies, T., Henzinger, T.A.: Ideal abstractions for well-structured transition systems. In: Kuncak, V., Rybalchenko, A. (eds.) VMCAI 2012. LNCS, vol. 7148, pp. 445–460. Springer, Heidelberg (2012)

A Model for Industrial Real-Time Systems

Md Tawhid Bin Waez[1], Andrzej Wąsowski[2], Juergen Dingel[1], and Karen Rudie[1]

[1] Queen's University, Canada
{waez,dingel}@cs.queensu.ca, karen.rudie@queensu.ca
[2] IT University of Copenhagen, Denmark
wasowski@itu.dk

Abstract. Introducing automated formal methods for large industrial real-time systems is an important research challenge. We propose timed process automata (TPA) for modeling and analysis of time-critical systems which can be open, hierarchical, and dynamic. The model offers two essential features for large industrial systems: (i) compositional modeling with reusable designs for different contexts, and (ii) an automated state-space reduction technique. Timed process automata model dynamic networks of continuous-time communicating control processes which can activate other processes. We show how to automatically establish safety and reachability properties of TPA by reduction to solving timed games. To mitigate the state-space explosion problem, an automated state-space reduction technique using compositional reasoning and aggressive abstractions is also proposed.

1 Introduction

This paper develops a model for the *automated analysis* of *safety* and *reachability* properties in large industrial *time-critical systems*. To fulfill industrial requirements, we consider time-critical systems that are open (communicate with external components), hierarchical (can be decomposed and recomposed into smaller control systems), and dynamic (the decomposition can change over time). In the paper, we use *real-time systems*, meaning time-critical systems that fulfill all these features. The model also facilitates compositional modeling and reusable designs for different contexts.

An *open system* continuously interacts with an unpredictable environment. A good example of time-critical open systems is a pacemaker, which continuously interacts with a heart, an uncontrolled environment. The pacemaker's performance crucially depends on the exact timing of an action performed either by the system or by the environment. The *theory of timed games* [1,2,3,4] is well-known in the research community for the analysis of time-critical open systems.

A *hierarchical system* is a hierarchical composition of smaller systems. An automotive system, developed by an *original equipment manufacturer (OEM)*, may be used in different models of cars. In this case, the system has a *controller* which helps the system adapt to different *environments* and cars. In other words, the system is an open system, which has two distinguished interacting

D. D'Souza et al. (Eds.): VMCAI 2015, LNCS 8931, pp. 153–171, 2015.

segments: the controller and the environment. Typically, these systems consist of other smaller systems in a *hierarchical* structure. For instance, a system Actuator can be a component of a larger system Position, while Position can be a component of another system Brake-by-Wire, and so on. Every component of a system has a specific set of tasks; for example, system Brake-by-Wire may use its component Position to perform some desired tasks in interaction with the environment, and Brake-by-Wire may also indirectly—through using Position—use its sub-component Actuator to perform some desired tasks in interaction with the environment.

A *dynamic system* is a hierarchical system whose components may change over time. Many hierarchical systems have dynamic characteristics, which are activating components only when needed. Dynamic behaviors are an important feature when resource constraints (such as limited memory) do not allow one to keep all the components active at the same time. Sometimes dynamic behaviors are inherent to the system. For example, we applied timed game theory in an industrial project to construct a fault-tolerant framework for a hierarchical open system that has a scheduler, a set of tasks, and a set of subtasks; only the scheduler is active in the initial system-state; subtasks are activated by their parent tasks, and the top level tasks are activated by their scheduler; thus the scheduler controls tasks, and a task controls its subtasks; due to the termination or the initialization of tasks (or subtasks) the structures of the processes may change; thus the system is a dynamic open system [5].

Timed automata (TA) [6,7] are desirable for the development of real-time systems because TA can model and analyze both discrete-time controllable behaviors of the system and continuous-time uncontrollable behaviors of the environment. Timed automata and their more than 80 variants [8] are mostly studied for the development of embedded systems, where behaviors of the components are known and the number of the components is static. As a result, modeling techniques, automated analyses, and other key issues of TA are typically addressed for *static closed systems*. The application domain of TA is growing [8]. In our two projects with General Motors (GM), we used different TA-based analyses to investigate the fault-tolerance of real-time systems, which are part of many large-scale safety-critical systems. During our industrial projects, we observed that continuous-time formal methods of TA may provide the most accurate analysis; however, TA are not suited for industrial real-time systems mainly because of poor *scalability*. Moreover, we found that TA have no structured support for modeling real-time systems, which may lead to cumbersome design details in a large-scale real-time system having several control hierarchies. The paper extends TA to achieve better modeling support and scalability for automated analysis of real-time systems.

We propose *timed process automata (TPA)*, a variant of TA, for the development of industrial real-time systems. The proposed variant provides compositional modeling (with reusable designs for different contexts) and automated analysis—a system needs to be modeled and analyzed using TPA only once when copies of it are used as independent systems or multiple components of a larger system or components of different larger systems or a combination of all previous scenarios. The contributions of this paper include:

1. Timed process automata, the first model that provides compositional modeling with reusable designs for dynamic hierarchical open time-critical systems.
2. Definition of a formal semantics for TPA.
3. An automated analysis for safety and reachability properties of TPA.
4. The first automated state-space reduction technique for time-critical systems, which can be dynamic, hierarchical, and open.

The rest of the paper can be divided into seven sections:

Section 2. Describes the motivation for the work. The motivation is based on the experience achieved from a couple of automotive industrial projects.
Section 3. Provides the required background to understand the paper.
Section 4. Presents the syntax (Sect. 4.1) and the semantics (Sect. 4.2) of TPA, which use start actions, finish actions, final locations, and channels to facilitate compositional modeling to reuse designs without manual alterations.
Section 5. Presents an automated analysis technique—based on timed games—for TPA. The analysis model of a timed process automaton T is constructed by composing a finite number of *timed I/O automata* (TIOA) [9,2,4], a variant of TA, to mimic the execution of T. The analysis model is constructed using an automated technique that allows the designer to avoid manual alteration techniques for different compositions. Other than the automated construction, the constructed analysis models essentially are TIOA models, whose state spaces are too large to analyze industrial real-time systems.
Section 6. Develops an automated state-space reduction technique that converts each callee process into a small automaton having only two locations and two edges, irrespective of the size of the callee. The technique uses structured construction of TPA, compositional reasoning, aggressive abstractions, and fewer synchronizations to ensure smaller state space.
Section 7. Discusses related work. It also classifies TPA depending on the classification of TA variants presented in a previous work [8].
Section 8. Concludes the paper.

2 Motivation

The first goal of the paper is to develop a real-time model, where a designer will not need to readjust a design for different compositions. The second and main goal is to allow automated analysis of the model for industrial systems.

Figure 1 presents an abstract Brake-by-Wire system modeled using TIOA, and the system is developed by an OEM. The model has seven automata representing

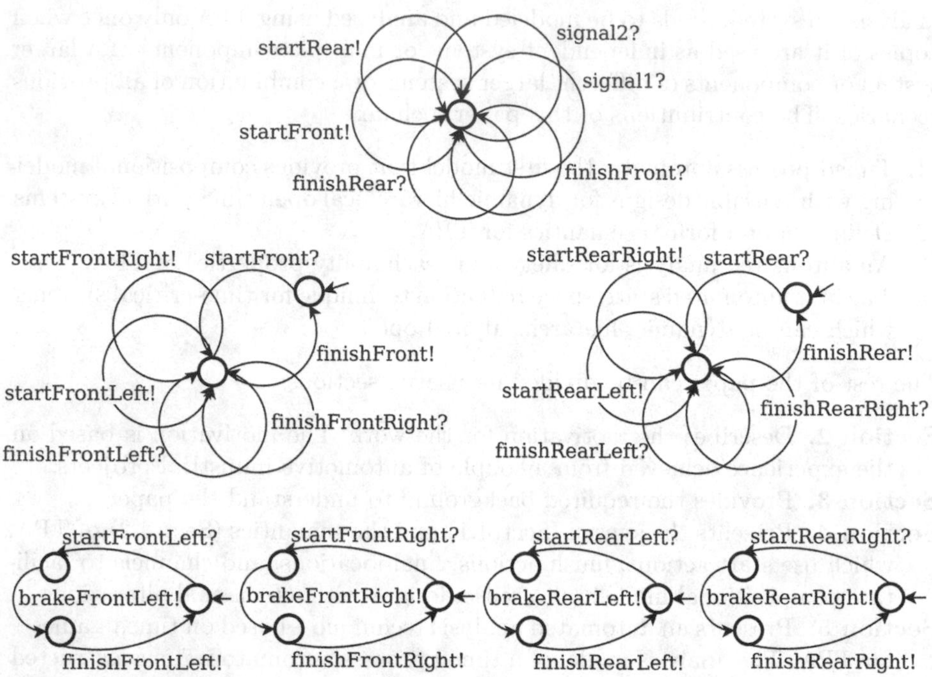

Fig. 1. An abstract Brake-by-Wire system modeled using standard TIOA

different copies of only three elements: one copy of the *main thread* of Brake-by-Wire (the top automaton), two copies of the main thread of Position (the two automata in the middle), and four copies of Actuator system (the four automata in the bottom). Each Position system contains two *children* (Actuator systems) and its main thread that schedules the children, communicates with its parent (the main thread of Brake-by-Wire), and performs some other functions, which cannot be performed by the children. Similarly, the Brake-by-Wire system contains two children (Position systems) and its main thread that schedules the children and performs some other functions, which cannot be performed by the children. In this model, the main thread of Brake-by-Wire is the *root*, which does not have a parent. However, in the future a car manufacturer may include this Brake-by-Wire system in a car and then the main thread of Brake-by-Wire will no longer be the root. Then a central control system may be able to start the main thread of Brake-by-Wire. To analyze the new complex system, a designer will need to manually alter the model again by including *start* and *finish* actions (in the top automaton of Fig. 1). Let us assume a complex system contains N Break-by-Wire systems; to analyze this complex system, a designer will need to manually construct at least $N \times 7$ automata with a proportionally growing alphabet! Existing TA-based modeling techniques do not support compositional modeling with reusable designs for different contexts; that is, a design may need to be altered manually in every composition. All these ad hoc alterations may

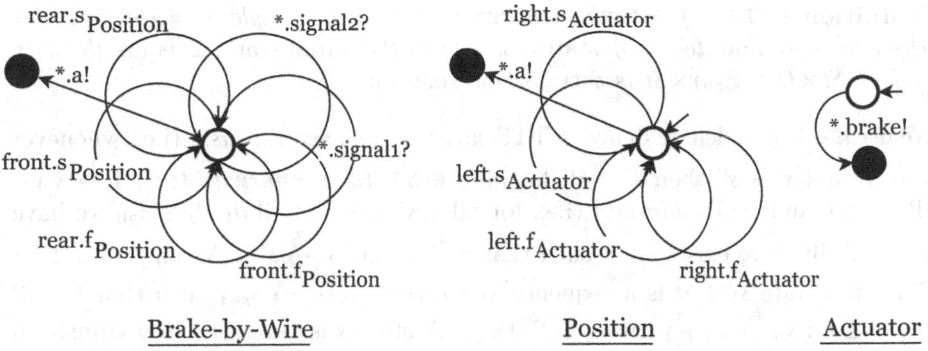

Fig. 2. The same Brake-by-Wire system of Fig. 1 is modeled using TPA

make a large industrial design incomprehensible and error-prone. Figure 2 contains the same Brake-by-Wire system of Fig. 1 modeled by using TPA. Timed process automata always model a system only once. For example, Fig. 2 presents only three TPA, which are equivalent to the seven automata of Fig. 1. Moreover, the number of copies and the root status of Break-by-Wire system has no impact on the new design.

To the best of our knowledge, no automated state-space reduction technique has been developed for the analysis of real-time systems. During our two projects with GM, we noticed that even a (practically) very small real-time system may have a state space too large for automated formal analysis because of hierarchy, dynamic behaviors, and time calculations. We overcame the scalability problem in one of the projects—construction of a fault-tolerance framework [5]—by developing a manual state-space reduction technique that applies aggressive abstractions and uses fewer synchronizations. Applying this manual technique to a design of an industrial system is a challenging task. Moreover, the technique may not work for every real-time systems. A generalized automated reduction technique, therefore, is needed for analysis of large real-time systems, which is provided in this paper by presenting an automated reduction technique for TPA.

3 Background

The semantic construction of TA is expressed using semantics objects called *timed transition systems (TTS)* [10,4,7]. A *timed I/O automaton* [9,2,4] is a timed automaton which has an input alphabet along with a regular output alphabet. The controller plays controllable output transitions and the environment plays uncontrollable input transitions; thus TIOA are a natural model for timed games. Two TIOA are *composable* with each other if they don't have a common output action. The *composition of two well-formed TIOA* forms a larger timed I/O automaton [2,4]. The section defines TTS, TIOA, composition of TIOA, and all other terms required to understand the remaining paper.

Definition 1 *[10,4,7] A* timed transition system *is a tuple* $\mathcal{T} = (St, s_0, \Sigma, \dashrightarrow)$, *where St is an infinite set of* states, $s_0 \in St$ *is the* initial state, Σ *is an alphabet, and* $\dashrightarrow: St \times (\Sigma \cup \mathbb{R}_{\geq 0}) \times St$ *is a* transition relation.

We use $d \in \mathbb{R}_{\geq 0}$ to denote delay. A TTS satisfies *time determinism* (i.e., whenever $s \overset{d}{\dashrightarrow} s'$ and $s \overset{d}{\dashrightarrow} s''$ then $s' = s''$ for all $s \in S$), *time reflexivity* (i.e., $s \overset{0}{\dashrightarrow} s$ for all $s \in S$), and *time additivity* (i.e., for all $s, s'' \in S$ and all $d_1, d_2 \in \mathbb{R}_{\geq 0}$ we have $s \overset{d_1+d_2}{\dashrightarrow} s''$ iff there exists an s' such that $s \overset{d_1}{\dashrightarrow} s'$ and $s' \overset{d_2}{\dashrightarrow} s''$). A *run* ρ of a TTS $\mathcal{T}$ from a state $s_1 \in St$ is a sequence $s_1 \overset{a_1}{\dashrightarrow} s_2 \overset{a_2}{\dashrightarrow} s_3 \cdots \overset{a_n}{\dashrightarrow} s_{n+1}$ such that for all $1 \leq m \leq n : s_m \overset{a_m}{\dashrightarrow} s_{m+1}$ with $a_m \in \Sigma \cup \mathbb{R}_{\geq 0}$. A state s is *reachable* in a transition system $\mathcal{T}$ if and only if there is a run $s_0 \overset{a_0}{\dashrightarrow} s_1 \overset{a_1}{\dashrightarrow} s_2 \cdots \overset{a_{n-1}}{\dashrightarrow} s_n$, where $s = s_n$. *Timed I/O transition systems (TIOTS)* are TTS with input and output modalities on transitions. Timed I/O transition systems are used to define semantics of TIOA.

A *clock* is a non-negative real variable. A *constraint* $\delta \in C(X, V)$ over a set of clocks X and over a set of non-negative finitely bounded integer variables V is generated by the grammar $\delta ::= x_m \prec q \mid k \prec \alpha \mid x_m - x_n \prec q \mid true \mid \Phi \wedge \Phi$, where $q \in \mathbb{Q}_{\geq 0}$, $\alpha \in \mathbb{Z}_{\geq 0}$, $\{x_m, x_n\} \subseteq X$, $k \in V$ and $\prec \in \{<, \leq, >, \geq\}$. Consequently, the set of *clock constraints* $C(X)$ is the set of constraints $C(X, V)$, where $V = \emptyset$. Let $\Psi(V)$ be the set of assignments over the set of variables V.

Definition 2 *[9,2,4,7] A* timed I/O automaton *is a tuple* $\mathcal{A} = (L, l_0, X, V, A, E, I)$, *where L is a finite set of locations, $l_0 \in L$ is the initial location, X is a finite set of clocks, V is a finite set of non-negative finitely bounded integer variables, $A = A_i \oplus A_o$ is a finite set of actions, partitioned into input actions A_i and output actions A_o, $E \subseteq L \times A \times \Phi(X, V) \times \Psi(V) \times 2^X \times L$ is a set of edges, and $I : L \rightarrow C(X)$ is a total mapping from locations to invariants.*

A *clock valuation* over X is a mapping $\mathbb{R}^X_{\geq 0} : X \rightarrow \mathbb{R}_{\geq 0}$. Given a clock valuation v and $d \in \mathbb{R}_{\geq 0}$, we write $v + d$ for the clock valuation in which for each clock $x \in X$ we have $(v+d)(x) = v(x) + d$. For $\lambda \subseteq X$, we write $v[x \mapsto 0]_{x \in \lambda}$ for a clock valuation agreeing with v on clocks in $X \setminus \lambda$, and giving 0 for clocks in λ. For $\phi \in \Phi(X, N)$ and $v \in \mathbb{R}^X_{\geq 0}$, we write $v, N \models \phi$ if v and N satisfy ϕ. Let $e = (l, a, \phi, \theta, \lambda, l')$ be an edge, then l is the source location, a is the action label, and l' is the target location of e; the constraint ϕ has to be satisfied during the traversal of e; the set of clocks $\lambda \in 2^X$ are reset to 0 and the set of non-negative finitely bounded integer variables are updated to θ whenever e is traversed.

Definition 3 *[2,4] Two timed I/O automata $\mathcal{A}^m = (L^m, l_0^m, X^m, N^m, A^m, E^m, I^m)$ and $\mathcal{A}^n = (L^n, l_0^n, X^n, N^n, A^n, E^n, I^n)$ are* composable *with each other when $A_o^m \cap A_o^n = \emptyset$, $X^m \cap X^n = \emptyset$, and $N^m \cap N^n = \emptyset$; when composable, their* composition *is a timed I/O automaton $\mathcal{A} = \mathcal{A}^m || \mathcal{A}^n = (L^m \times L^n, (l_0^m, l_0^n), X^m \cup X^n, N^m \cup N^n, A, E, I)$, where $A = A_i \cup A_o$ with $A_o = A_o^m \cup A_o^n$ and $A_i = (A_i^m \cup A_i^n) \setminus A_o$. The set of edges E contains:*

- *$((l^m, l^n), a, \phi^m \wedge \phi^n, \lambda^m \cup \lambda^n, \theta^m \cup \theta^n, (l'^m, l'^n)) \in E$ for each $(l^m, a, \phi^m, \theta^m, \lambda^m, l'^m) \in E^m$ and $(l^n, a, \phi^n, \theta^n, \lambda^n, l'^n) \in E^n$ if $a \in \{A_i^m \cap A_o^n\} \cup \{A_o^m \cap A_i^n\}$*

– $((l^m, l^n), a, \phi^m, \lambda^m, \theta^m, (l'^m, l^n)) \in E$ *for each* $(l^m, a, \phi^m, \lambda^m, \theta^m, l'^m) \in E^m$ *if* $a \notin A^n$
– $((l^m, l^n), a, \phi^n, \lambda^n, \theta^n, (l^m, l'^n)) \in E$ *for each* $(l^n, a, \phi^n, \lambda^n, \theta^n, l'^n) \in E^n$ *if* $a \notin A^m$

and the set of invariants I *is constructed as follows:* $I(l^m, l^n) = I^m(l^m) \wedge I^n(l^n)$

4 Processes

Timed process automata model processes, where each process is a real-time system. Every process hierarchically contains its active callee processes. Thus the control of a process is hierarchically shared with its active callee processes. The main thread of a process can activate callee processes via communication channels. An active process can receive any input in any state. An active callee process can deactivate itself in any state of the main thread of its caller process. An activated callee process dies within its worst-case execution time. This section presents the syntax and the semantics of TPA.

4.1 Timed Process Automata

Timed process automata are a variant of TIOA. Unlike a timed I/O automaton, a timed process automaton has a finite set of *start actions* A_s, a finite set of *finish actions* A_f, a final location l_f, and a finite set of *channels* C.

The set of *actions* $A = A_i \oplus A_o \oplus A_s \oplus A_f$ of a timed process automaton is a disjoint union of finite sets of input actions A_i, output actions A_o, start actions A_s, and finish actions A_f. For every set of actions A, there exists a bijective mapping between its start actions A_s and finish actions A_f in such a way that for each start action $s_N \in A_s$ there is exactly one finish action $f_N \in A_f$, and vice versa. These actions can be used for starting and terminating processes associated with N. We use s and f with the name N (of another timed process automaton) as a subscript index (e.g., s_N and f_N) to denote a start action and a finish action, respectively. We use the same subscript to indicate *paired* actions. We write a to denote an action in general. Processes synchronize via instantaneous channels. Each TPA uses the same designated symbols for its *public channel* $(*)$ and *caller channel* $(\triangle)$. We use c to denote a channel in general.

Definition 4 *A* timed process automaton *is a tuple* $T = (L, l_0, X, A, C, E, I, l_f)$, *where* L *is a finite set of locations,* $l_0 \in L$ *is the initial location,* X *is a finite set of clocks,* $A = A_i \oplus A_o \oplus A_s \oplus A_f$ *is a finite set of actions as described above,* C *is a finite set of channels,* $E \subseteq (L \times A \times C \setminus \{\triangle, *\} \times \Phi(X) \times 2^X \times L) \cup (L \times (A_i \cup A_o) \times \{\triangle, *\} \times \Phi(X) \times 2^X \times L)$ *is a set of edges,* $I : L \to \Phi(X)$ *is a total mapping from locations to invariants, and* $l_f \in L$ *is a designated final location which does not have any outgoing edges to other locations and has the invariant* $I(l_f) = true$.

Figure 2 presents TPA Brake-by-Wire, Position, and Actuator. In the figure, each initial location has a dangling incoming edge, final locations are filled with black, and TPA names are underlined. The final location l_f of a TPA may be unreachable from the initial location (and then l_f is not shown in the figure).

4.2 Process Executions

Every instance of a timed process automaton is a *process*. Two processes of the same timed process automaton represent two different copies of the same system. Every process has a unique *process identifier*. A *process* is a tuple $P = (\mathsf{id}(P), \mathsf{tpa}(P), \mathsf{channel}(P))$, where $\mathsf{id}(P)$[1] is the process identifier, timed process automaton $\mathsf{tpa}(P)$ defines the execution logic, and *caller channel* $\mathsf{channel}(P)$ is the private channel to communicate with the caller and the other processes which are started via the same channel. A process Q is a *callee* of P if P is the caller of Q. We use $\perp$ to denote the caller channel of the root process. Every process P of $\mathsf{tpa}(P) = (L, l_0, X, A, C, E, I, l_f)$ has its own copy $P.c$ of channel $c \in C$. We write $P.c.a$ meaning that action a is performed via channel $P.c$.

At the same time, no two processes of the same timed process automaton can have the same caller channel. A process P, therefore, may have at most $|C| \times |A_s|$ active callee processes. For example, an instance of automaton Brake-by-Wire of Fig. 2 can activate at most two instances of automaton Position of Fig. 2 at the same time via two different channels front and rear, where the instance of Brake-by-Wire is the caller process of the two instances of Position, which are the callee processes of the instance of Brake-by-Wire. A *subprocess* is a callee or a callee of a subprocess, recursively. For example, every instance of Brake-by-Wire has six subprocesses: two instances of Position and four instances of automaton Actuator of Fig. 2. Every process hierarchically contains all of its subprocesses. Two processes are *siblings* if they have the same caller channel. The caller can use separate channels to differentiate control over different callees, even if they are processes of the same automaton.

A process P starts a process Q of an automaton $\mathsf{tpa}(Q)$ via channel $P.c$ by traversing an edge $e_1 = (\_, \mathrm{s}_{\mathsf{tpa}(Q)}, c, \_, \_, \_)$ labeled by a start action $\mathrm{s}_{\mathsf{tpa}(Q)}$ if there exists no active process of $\mathsf{tpa}(Q)$ with caller channel $P.c$; dually, P traverses an edge $e_2 = (\_, \mathrm{f}_{\mathsf{tpa}(Q)}, c, \_, \_, \_)$ labeled by the paired finish action $\mathrm{f}_{\mathsf{tpa}(Q)}$ whenever Q reaches its final state. No edge labeled by $\mathrm{f}_{\mathsf{tpa}(Q)}$ will ever be traversed if $\mathsf{tpa}(Q)$ is a *non-terminating timed process automaton.* Correspondingly, note that existing processes may start different processes of $\mathsf{tpa}(Q)$—but always with different process identifiers. However, only P listens to finish action $\mathrm{f}_{\mathsf{tpa}(Q)}$ via channel $\mathsf{channel}(Q)$. Process P traverses an edge $e = (\_, a, c, \_, \_, \_)$ when P receives (respectively, sends) an input (resp., output) a in channel $P.c$. Process P communicates with its callee Q via $\mathsf{channel}(Q)$ and with the environment via channel $P.*$.

We formalize the above mechanics of execution by first giving the semantics of the main thread of the process, ignoring its subprocesses in Def. 5 and then giving the semantics of the entire process in Def. 6. The standalone semantics of a process are essentially the same semantics as a standard timed I/O automaton [7,9,2,4]. The main difference is that states are decorated with process identifiers and edges with channel names to distinguish different instances of the same timed process automaton in Def. 6. Also the caller channel $\triangle$ is instantiated for an actual parent process. The technical reason for this will become apparent in Def. 6.

[1] To avoid clutter, we abuse notation by writing P instead of $\mathsf{id}(P)$.

Definition 5 *The* standalone semantics $\mathcal{S}[\![P]\!]$ *of a process* $P = (P, \mathsf{tpa}(P), \mathsf{channel}(P))$ *are a TIOTS* $\mathcal{S}[\![P]\!] = (L \times \mathbb{R}^X_{\geq 0} \times P, (l_0, \mathbf{0}, P), A^P, \twoheadrightarrow)$[2], *where* $\mathsf{tpa}(P) = (L, l_0, X, A, C, E, I, l_\mathrm{f})$, $\mathbf{0}$ *is a function mapping every clock to zero and* $\twoheadrightarrow \subseteq (L \times \mathbb{R}^X_{\geq 0} \times \{P\}) \times (A^P \cup \mathbb{R}_{\geq 0}) \times (L \times \mathbb{R}^X_{\geq 0} \times \{P\})$ *is the transition relation generated by the following rules:*

Action *For each clock valuation* $v \in \mathbb{R}^X_{\geq 0}$ *and each edge* $(l, a, c, \phi, \lambda, l') \in E$ *such that* $v \models \phi$, $v' = v[x \mapsto 0]_{x \in \lambda}$, *and* $v' \models I(l')$ *we have* $(l, v, P) \overset{P.c.a}{\twoheadrightarrow} (l', v', P)$ *if* $c \neq \Delta$, *otherwise* $(l, v, P) \xrightarrow{\mathsf{channel}(P).a} (l', v', P)$

Delay *For each clock valuation* $v \in \mathbb{R}^X_{\geq 0}$ *and for each delay* $d \in \mathbb{R}_{\geq 0}$ *such that* $(v + d) \models I(l)$ *we have* $(l, v, P) \overset{d}{\twoheadrightarrow} (l, v + d, P)$.

The transition system induced by the standalone semantics of a process is time deterministic, time reflexive, and time additive.

Ground timed process automata are TPA that cannot perform a start or finish action ($A_\mathrm{s} \cup A_\mathrm{f} = \emptyset$). Automaton Actuator in Fig. 2, for instance, is a ground timed process automaton. *Compound timed process automata* are TPA that can perform a start or finish action ($A_\mathrm{s} \cup A_\mathrm{f} \neq \emptyset$). For example, Brake-by-Wire and Position in Fig. 2 are compound TPA. A *well-formed channel* cannot be used by two processes sharing an output action. Processes of a *well-formed timed process automaton* have only well-formed channels. Non-recursive TPA are defined inductively using the following rules: (i) every ground timed process automaton is a non-recursive timed process automaton, and (ii) a compound timed process automaton which performs only those start and finish actions whose subscripts are the names of some other existing non-recursive TPA is a non-recursive timed process automaton. All three TPA in Fig. 2, for example, are non-recursive TPA. A process of a non-recursive timed process automaton hierarchically contains only a finite number of subprocesses. The caller may activate an idle process, iteratively. Thus a process may activate a subprocess an arbitrary number of times. In this paper, we are only concerned with non-recursive well-formed TPA.

A *standalone final state* of a process P is (l_f, v, P), where v is any clock valuation. We use st^P, st^P_0, c^P, and st^P_f to denote a standalone state, the standalone initial state, the set of channels, and a standalone final state of process P, respectively. We say that a process P is A'-enabled for a channel $P.c$ if for every reachable standalone state st^P we have $st^P \overset{P.c.a}{\twoheadrightarrow} st'^P$ for some standalone state st'^P for each action $a \in A'$. We require that each process P is A_i-enabled (input enabled) for all channels of P, and A_f-enabled (finish enabled) for all channels of P other than channels $P.\Delta$ and $P.*$ to reflect the phenomenon that inputs from the environment and the deaths of callees are independent events, beyond the control of a process. We present the semantics of a process in the following:

Definition 6 *The* global operational semantics $\mathcal{G}[\![P]\!]$ *(semantics* $[\![P]\!]$ *for short) of a process* $P = (P, \mathsf{tpa}(P), \perp)$ *are a TIOTS* $\mathcal{G}[\![P]\!] = (2^S, s_0, \mathbb{P} \times \mathbb{C} \times \mathbb{A}, \rightarrow)$, *where*

[2] A^P is the set of actions where action names are constructed using regular expression $(P$"."$C \mid \mathsf{channel}(P))$"."$A$.

S is the set of all the standalone states of all the processes in the universe, $\mathsf{tpa}(P) = (L, l_0, X, A, E, I, l_f)$*,* $s_0 = \{st_0^P\}$ *is the initial state,* $\mathbb{P}$ *is the set of all the processes in the universe,* $\mathbb{C}$ *is the set of all the channels in the universe,* $\mathbb{A}$ *is the set of all the actions in the universe, and* $\rightarrow \subseteq 2^S \times (\mathbb{P} \times \mathbb{C} \times \mathbb{A} \cup \mathbb{R}_{\geq 0}) \times 2^S$ *is the transition relation generated by the following rules:*

$$\frac{st^Q \xrightarrow{Q.c.s_T}\!\!\!\!\rightarrow st'^Q \text{ and } c \notin \{\Delta, *\} \qquad \{st^W \in s \mid \mathsf{channel}(W) = Q.c \text{ and } \mathsf{tpa}(W) = T\} = \emptyset \qquad st^Q \in s \qquad (R, T, Q.c) \text{ is a freshly started process}}{s \xrightarrow{Q.c.s_T} s \setminus \{st^Q\} \cup \{st_0^R, st'^Q\}} \ \textsc{Start}$$

$$\frac{st_f^R, st^Q \in s \text{ and } \mathsf{channel}(R) = Q.c \qquad \{st^U \in s \mid \mathsf{channel}(U) \in C^R\} = \emptyset \qquad st^Q \xrightarrow{Q.c.f_{\mathsf{tpa}(R)}}\!\!\!\!\rightarrow st'^Q}{s \xrightarrow{Q.c.f_{\mathsf{tpa}(R)}} s \setminus \{st_f^R, st^Q\} \cup \{st'^Q\}} \ \textsc{Finish}$$

$$\frac{s' = \{st'^Q \mid st^Q \xrightarrow{d}\!\!\!\!\rightarrow st'^Q \text{ and } st^Q \in s \text{ and } (st^Q \neq st_f^Q \text{ or } |s| = 1)\} \qquad |s| = |s'|}{s \xrightarrow{d} s'} \ \textsc{Delay}$$

$$\frac{a \notin \bigcup_{st^Q \in s} A_o^{\mathsf{tpa}(Q)} \qquad s' = \{st^Q \in s \mid st^Q \xrightarrow{Q.*.a}\!\!\!\!\rightarrow st'^Q\}}{s \xrightarrow{a} s \setminus s' \cup \{st'^Q \mid st^Q \xrightarrow{Q.*.a}\!\!\!\!\rightarrow st'^Q \text{ and } st^Q \in s\}} \ \textsc{Input}$$

$$\frac{st^Q \xrightarrow{W.c.a}\!\!\!\!\rightarrow st'^Q \text{ and } a \in A_o^Q \text{ and } st^Q \in s \qquad s' = \{st^R \in s \mid st^R \xrightarrow{W.c.a}\!\!\!\!\rightarrow st'^R \text{ and } W.c \text{ is a channel}\}}{s \xrightarrow{Q.c.a} s \setminus s' \cup \{st'^R \mid st^R \xrightarrow{W.c.a}\!\!\!\!\rightarrow st'^R \text{ and } st^R \in s\}} \ \textsc{Output}$$

A *global state* is a set which holds standalone states of all active processes. The START rule states that the initial standalone state of a freshly started callee is added to the global state whenever the corresponding start action is performed by its caller. The rule also states that no two active processes can have the same timed process automaton and the same caller channel. The FINISH rule prescribes that the standalone-final state of a callee is removed from the global state and the caller executes the corresponding finish action whenever that callee is in the standalone-final state and no standalone state of its subprocesses is in global state. Thus the rule defines *global-final state* (*final state* for short) of a process: a process is in its the final state when the process is in its final location and the process has no active subprocess. The DELAY rule declares that globally a process can delay if that process and all of its active subprocesses can delay in their respective standalone semantics. Every subprocess is a part of the root process and thus if a subprocess is performing an action (or not idle) then the root process is also not idle. The rule also says that a process cannot delay if that process or any of its subprocess is in its global final state. That means a process finishes as soon as it reaches its final state. The INPUT rule states that a process receives an input from the environment via channel *id.∗*. Rule OUTPUT declares a process send an output via channel *id.c* to others who share *id.c*. It follows from the properties of the standalone semantics that the transition system induced by Def. 6 is time deterministic, time reflexive, and time additive. The process semantics, therefore, defines a well-formed TIOTS. This allows us to use TA as a basis for analyzing TPA. A *local run* of the main thread of a process P is a standalone run of P for which there exists a global run of P such that every transition of that standalone run occurs in that global run. The *local behavior* of the main thread of P consists of all of its local runs.

5 Analysis

We are interested in *safety* and *reachability* properties of real-time systems. This section explains how such analyses can be performed using the theory of timed games. A standard timed I/O automaton can be viewed as a concurrent two-player timed game, in which the players decide both which action to play, and when to play it. The input player represents the environment, and the output player represents the system itself. Similarly, the main thread of a process acts as a concurrent two-player timed game: the environment plays input transitions and finish transitions, and the main thread of the process plays output transitions and start transitions. Let's consider interactions of a process defined in the previous section. A process controls its output and start transitions. After starting a callee, the main thread of the caller knows that the paired finish action will arrive within the worst-case execution time of the associated callee. However, the main thread does not have any control on the exact arrival time of a finish action. Finish transitions along with input transitions are uncontrollable. The environment of the main thread of a process consists of all the connected processes (such as caller, siblings, and subprocesses) and all unconnected entities.

A global state of a process is safe if and only if all of the standalone states which it contains are safe locations. A *safety property* asserts that the system remains inside a set of global-safe states regardless of what the environment does. We are interested in *Safety Property I: Given a process P and a set of unsafe locations L_U of P, can the controller avoid L_U in P regardless of what the environment does?* A global state of a process is a target state if and only if at least one of its standalone states contains a target location. A *reachability property* asserts that the system reaches any of the global-target states regardless of what the environment does. We are interested in *Reachability Property I: Given a process P and a set of target locations L_T of P, can the controller reach a location of L_T in P regardless of what the environment does?*

The monolithic analysis constructs a static network of automata to represent all possible global executions by mimicking the hierarchical call tree of the analyzed process. It simulates a process execution by changing states of pre-allocated TIOA which fall into two groups: a *root automaton* to simulate the local behaviors of the main thread of the root process and a finite set of *standalone automata* to simulate the local behaviors of the main threads of the subprocesses.

Standalone Automata. We construct a standalone automaton for each subprocess to simulate the main thread of that process. To construct a standalone

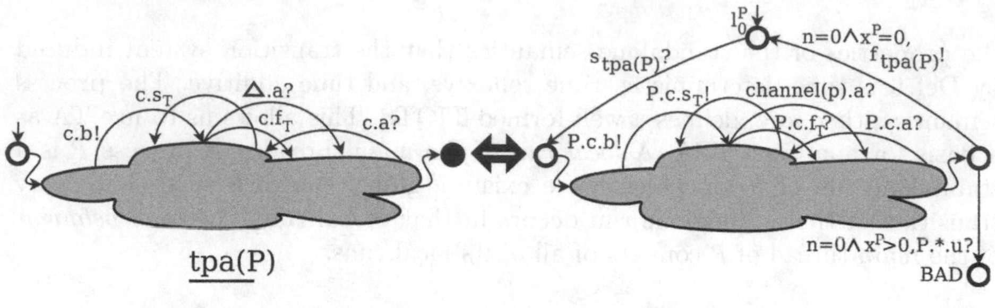

Fig. 3. A generalized view of standalone automata construction

automaton, we prefix the timed process automaton with a simulated start action and suffix it with a simulated finish action. We use non-negative finitely bounded integer variables[3] in standalone automata to count the number of active callees, in order to detect termination. We rename actions (e.g., a) of processes uniformly to encode channel names (e.g., $P.c$) in action names (e.g., $P.c.a$) of standalone automata; because standard TIOA do not support private channels. A standalone automaton includes all the locations and slightly altered edges of the corresponding timed process automaton. Moreover, each standalone automaton has two additional locations: a new initial location l_0^{id} to receive (resp., send) a start (resp., finish) message from (resp., to) the caller, and a new unsafe location BAD to prevent the automaton from waiting in final states instead of finishing. Every start (resp., finish) increments (resp., decrements) a counter variable n. The automaton represents finishing of the process in the final location when $n = 0$. Formally, the standalone automaton of process P is $\mathsf{standalone}(P) = (L \cup \{l_0^{\mathrm{P}}, BAD\}, l_0^{\mathrm{P}}, X \cup \{x^{\mathrm{P}}\}, \{n\}, A^{\mathrm{P}}, E^{\mathrm{P}}, I^{\mathrm{P}})$, where $\mathsf{tpa}(P) = (L, l_0, X, A, C, E, I, l_{\mathrm{f}})$, l_0^{P} and BAD are two newly added locations, x^{P} is a newly added clock, n is a non-negative finitely bounded integer variable with the initial value 0, $A_{\mathrm{o}}^{\mathrm{P}} = A'_{\mathrm{o}} \cup A'_{\mathrm{s}} \cup \{\mathsf{channel}(P).\mathrm{f}_{\mathsf{tpa}(P)}\}$ and $A_{\mathrm{i}}^{\mathrm{P}} = A'_{\mathrm{i}} \cup A'_{\mathrm{f}} \cup \{\mathsf{channel}(P).\,\mathrm{s}_{\mathsf{tpa}(P)}, P{*}u\}$ such that $A'_m = \{\mathsf{channel}(P).a \mid a \in A_m\} \cup \{P.c.a \mid a \in A_m \text{ and } c \in C \setminus \{\triangle\}\}$ where $m \in \{\mathrm{o, s, i, f}\}$ and newly added actions are $\mathsf{channel}(P).\mathrm{s}_{\mathsf{tpa}(P)}$, $\mathsf{channel}(P).\mathrm{f}_{\mathsf{tpa}(P)}$, and $P.*.u$. The set of edges E^{P} contains

- Converted edges that do not communicate via caller channel $\triangle$:
  - An edge $(l, P.c.a, \phi, \xi, \lambda \cup \lambda', l') \in E^{\mathrm{P}}$ for each edge $(l, a, c, \phi, \lambda, l') \in E$, where $c \in C \setminus \{\triangle\}$, the integer assignment is empty $\xi = \emptyset$ when $a \in A_{\mathrm{o}} \cup A_{\mathrm{i}}$, $\xi = \{n--\}$ when $a \in A_{\mathrm{f}}$, and $\xi = \{n++\}$ when $a \in A_{\mathrm{s}}$
- Converted edges that communicate via caller channel $\triangle$:
  - An edge $(l, \mathsf{channel}(P).a, \phi, \emptyset, \lambda \cup \lambda', l') \in E^{\mathrm{P}}$ for each edge $(l, a, \triangle, \phi, \lambda, l') \in E$
- Additional new edges that simulate activation and deactivation:
  - Three more edges $(l_0^{\mathrm{P}}, \mathsf{channel}(P).\mathrm{s}_{\mathsf{tpa}(P)}, \emptyset, \emptyset, X, l_0)$, $(l_{\mathrm{f}}, \mathsf{channel}(P).\mathrm{f}_{\mathsf{tpa}(P)}, n = 0 \wedge x^P = 0, \emptyset, \emptyset, l_0^{\mathrm{P}})$, $(l_{\mathrm{f}}, P.*.u, n = 0 \wedge x^P > 0, \emptyset, \emptyset, BAD)$ are in E^{P}

[3] The use of non-negative finitely bounded integer variables can be avoided if a more cumbersome encoding is used.

$\lambda' = \emptyset$ when $l' \neq l_f$, otherwise $\lambda' = \{x^P\}$. The invariant function I^P maps each location $l \in L$ to $I(l)$ and maps each location $l \in \{l_0^P, BAD\}$ to *true*. The standalone semantics of automaton tpa(P) and the semantics of standalone automaton standalone(P) are essentially the same.

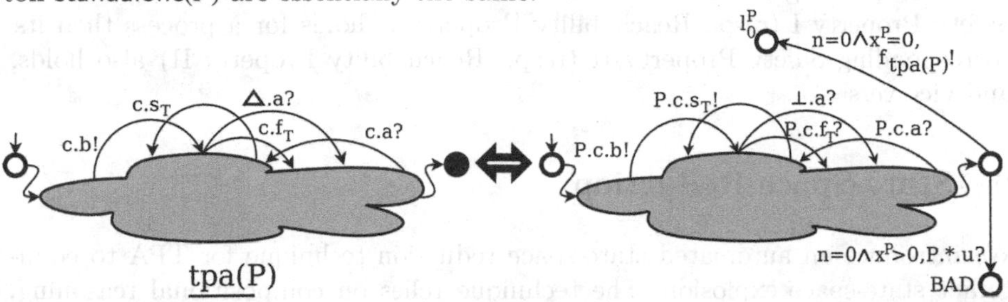

Fig. 4. A generalized view of root automata construction

Root Automata. To analyze a timed process automaton tpa(P) = $(L, l_0, X, A, C, E, I, l_f)$, we construct the root automaton root(P) of process P. Standalone automaton standalone(P) is slightly different from root(P). The differences are: (i) the caller channel is always $\perp$, (ii) the initial location of root automaton root(P) is the location l_0, which is also the initial location of tpa(P), and (iii) root automaton does not have edge $(l_0^P, \perp.s_{\mathsf{tpa}(P)}, \emptyset, \emptyset, X, l_0)$, which simulates activation of P.

Monolithic Analysis Model. The monolithic analysis model of a ground timed processes automaton (such as Actuator) is its root automaton. We construct the monolithic analysis model of automaton tpa(P) in the following iterative manner:

First Step: We construct the root automaton root(P).
Iterative Step: We construct a standalone automaton for each triple (Q, s_T, c), where Q is process for which we have constructed a standalone automaton or the root automaton, tpa(Q) = $(L, l_0, X, A, C, E, I, l_f)$, $c \in C \setminus \{\Delta, *\}$, $s_T \in A_s$, and $(\_, s_T, c, \_, \_, \_) \in E$.

Figures 3–4 present a generalized view of the standalone and root automata constructions (a technical report [11] presents monolithic analysis models of processes of TPA Actuator, Position, and Brake-by-Wire). The monolithic analysis model constructs a parallel composition of all the TIOA constructed above. The construction is finite, and the composition is a timed I/O automaton, because we consider only non-recursive well-formed TPA. The created composition is timed-bisimilar to the global semantics (modulo hiding the special actions and renaming the others). Executions of this composition, when projected on the original alphabet, are identical to the executions of the global semantics. Thus the composition has the same properties. We convert Safety Property I to *Safety Property II: Given a process P and a set of unsafe locations L_U of P, can the controller avoid L_U and all the BAD locations in the analysis model regardless of what the environment does?* We also convert Reachability Property I to *Reachability Property II: Given a process P and a set of target locations L_T of P, can* *the controller reach a location of L_T in the analysis model avoiding all the BAD locations regardless of what the environment does?* Avoiding all the newly added *BAD* locations in the analysis model ensures that each caller process performs the corresponding finish action as soon as the callee finishes. Therefore, if a Safety Property I (resp., Reachability Property I) holds for a process then its corresponding Safety Property II (resp., Reachability Property II) also holds, and vice versa.

6 State-Space Reduction

We introduce an automated state-space reduction technique for TPA to counteract state-space explosion. The technique relies on compositional reasoning, aggressive abstractions, and reducing process synchronizations. In the monolithic analysis of Sect. 5, a callee can be represented by an arbitrary number of standalone automata and each of these automata can be arbitrarily large. The compositional reasoning replaces hierarchical trees of standalone automata representing subprocesses with simple abstractions (Fig. 5)—so called *duration automata*.

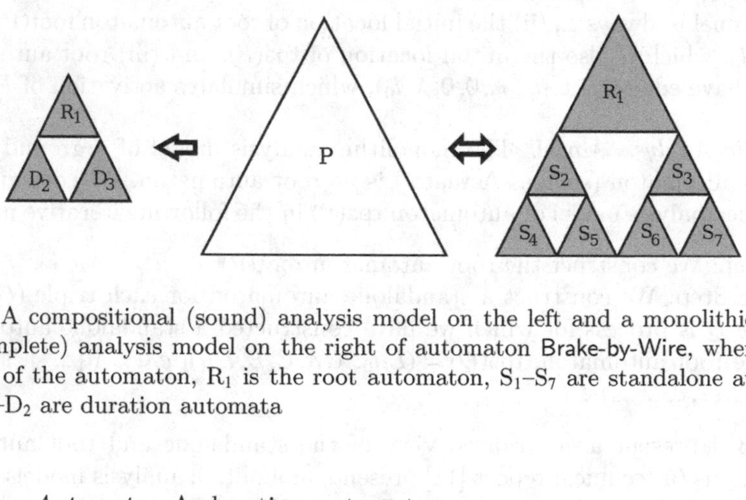

Fig. 5. A compositional (sound) analysis model on the left and a monolithic (sound and complete) analysis model on the right of automaton Brake-by-Wire, where P is a process of the automaton, R_1 is the root automaton, S_1–S_7 are standalone automata, and D_1–D_2 are duration automata

Duration Automata. A duration automaton (Fig. 6) is timed I/O automaton with only two locations: the initial location (l_0^P) and the active location (l_1^P). A duration automaton of an analyzed process abstracts all the information of global executions of the process other than its *worst-case execution time (WCET)*. It can capture safety and reachability properties of interest. The *minimal-time safe reachability* of a target location is the *minimal-time reachability* [12,13] for which the controller has a winning strategy to reach that target location by avoiding unsafe states. We assume that

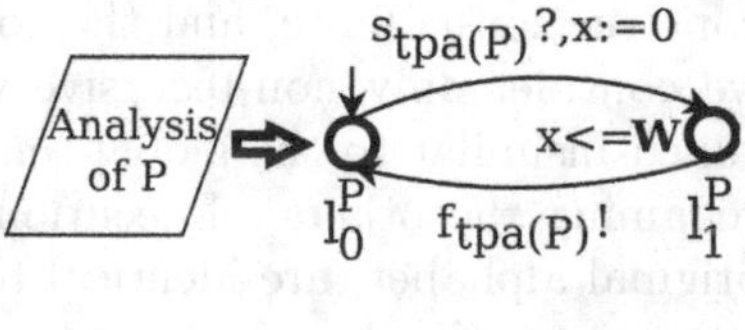

Fig. 6. A generalized view of duration automata construction

the WCET $\mathbf{W}$ of a process P is the minimal-time safe reachability time to reach location l_0^{P} of automaton $\mathsf{root}(P)$ in the analysis model of P. This is a known technique to limit the WCET of a controller [14,15]. The WCET of P is unknown ($\mathbf{W} = \infty$) when there is no winning strategy for the minimal-time safe reachability to reach location l_0^{P} of $\mathsf{root}(P)$. The duration automaton of process P is $\mathsf{duration}(P) = (\{l_0^{\mathrm{P}}, l_1^{\mathrm{P}}\}, l_0^{\mathrm{P}}, \{x^{\mathrm{P}}\}, \emptyset, A^{\mathrm{P}}, E^{\mathrm{P}}, I^{\mathrm{P}})$, where $\mathsf{tpa}(P) = (L, l_0, X, A, C, E, I, l_{\mathrm{f}})$, $A_{\mathrm{i}}^{\mathrm{P}} = \{\mathsf{channel}(P).\mathsf{s}_{\mathsf{tpa}(P)}\}$, $A_{\mathrm{o}}^{\mathrm{P}} = \{\mathsf{channel}(P).\mathsf{f}_{\mathsf{tpa}(P)}\}$, the set of edges $E^{\mathrm{P}} = \{(l_0^{\mathrm{P}}, \mathsf{channel}(P).\mathsf{s}_{\mathsf{tpa}(P)}, \emptyset, \emptyset, \{x^{\mathrm{P}}\}, l_1^{\mathrm{P}}), (l_1^{\mathrm{P}}, \mathsf{channel}(P).\mathsf{f}_{\mathsf{tpa}(P)}, \emptyset, \emptyset, \emptyset, l_0^{\mathrm{P}})\}$, invariant I^{P} maps location l_0^{P} to *true*, and I^{P} maps location l_1^{P} to $x^{\mathrm{P}} \leq \mathbf{W}$.

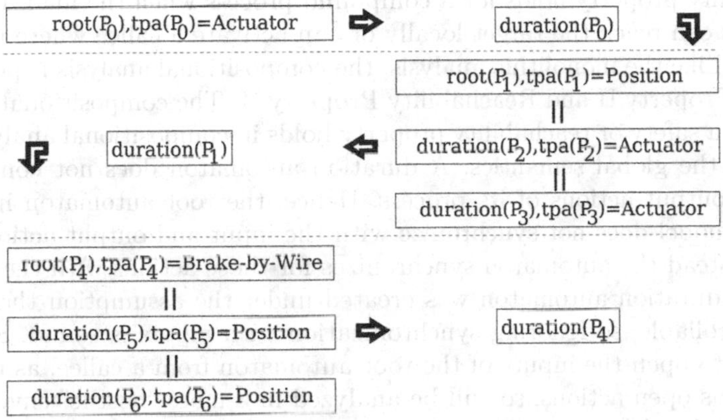

Fig. 7. Steps of the compositional analysis of automaton Brake-by-Wire

Compositional Analysis Model. We construct the compositional analysis model in a bottom-up manner: analysis of a compound process is performed only after analyzing all its callees. Like the monolithic analysis, the compositional analysis model of a ground timed process automaton $\mathsf{tpa}(Q)$ (such as Actuator) is a root automaton of process Q. That timed I/O automaton is analyzed to construct a duration automaton of Q. For a compound process P, we analyze automaton $\mathsf{root}(P)$ in the context of the duration automata of its callees (instead of the entire hierarchical structure of subprocesses). We construct the compositional analysis model of a timed process automaton $\mathsf{tpa}(P)$ in the following manner:

First Step: We construct the root automaton root(P).
Second Step: We construct a duration automaton for each triple (P, s_T, c), where $\mathsf{tpa}(P) = (L, l_0, X, A, C, E, I, l_{\mathrm{f}})$, $c \in C \setminus \{\Delta, *\}$, $\mathsf{s}_T \in A_{\mathrm{s}}$, and $(\_, \mathsf{s}_T, c, \_, \_, \_) \in E$.

Figure 7 presents the compositional analysis procedure of Brake-by-Wire (the detailed models are presented in [11]). The compositional model construction procedure terminates, and the composition of all the above TIOA is a timed I/O automaton, because we consider only non-recursive well-formed TPA. The duration automaton of a process can capture safety properties: if a process has a winning strategy for a safety game, then all locations of its duration automaton are considered safe; otherwise, the active location (l_1^{id}) of the duration automaton is added to the set of unsafe locations L_U. Now this duration automaton can be used as a sound context to analyze the caller automaton for safety. A safety property holds for a compound process when the main thread of the process preserves the property locally and allows the activation of a callee only if that callee also preserves the property. Duration automata can also capture reachability properties: if a process has a winning strategy for a reachability game then the active location (l_1^{id}) of the duration automaton is added to the set of target locations L_T; otherwise, no target location is specified for this callee. This duration automaton can be used as a sound context to analyze the caller automaton for reachability. A reachability property holds for a compound process when the main thread of the process can reach the target locally or can activate a callee where the property holds. Like the monolithic analysis, the compositional analysis is performed for Safety Property II and Reachability Property II. The compositional analysis is sound: if a safety or reachability property holds in compositional analysis then it holds in the global semantics. A duration automaton does not contain any input and output actions of its process. Hence, the root automaton in a compositional model does not synchronize with the input and output actions of its callees—instead the automaton synchronizes for those actions with the environment. The duration automaton was created under the assumption that inputs are uncontrollable, so ignoring synchronization with inputs is sound. Similarly, it is sound to open the inputs of the root automaton from a callee, as they will be treated as open actions, so will be analyzed in a more "hostile" environment than before the abstraction. Therefore, if a property holds in the compositional analysis then it also holds for the monolithic analysis.

Scalability. In all the steps of Fig. 7, the largest composition contains only three automata, and except for the root automaton all are tiny duration automata. Monolithic analysis model of Brake-by-Wire is a composition of seven automata (see [11]). A duration automaton always has a small constant size (modulo the size of the WCET constant), and so its state space is very simple (actually the discrete state space is independent of the input model). We applied our approach to examples like the one presented in our previous work [5]. First, we modeled that problem with standard TIOA using shared variables. The timed games solver Uppaal Tiga [16] produced a large winning strategy (290 MB) for a safety objective for a configuration (C1 of [5])—a combination of different system parameters—in the TIOA model within 94 seconds[4]. After that, we modeled the same system with TPA, and applied the state-space reduction technique. The same solver for the same configuration produced a much smaller winning strategy (100 KB) for the same objective in our compositional model within 0.3 seconds. Experiments for different configurations for the same system (of [5]) revealed that speed up of two orders of magnitude is possible with the compositional technique, while maintaining enough precision to obtain useful strategies for realistic

[4] All the analyses were performed by Uppaal Tiga-0.17 on a PC with an Intel Core i3 CPU at 2.4 GHz, 4 GB of RAM, and running 64-bit Windows 7.

scheduling problems. The size of composition in the monolithic analysis is exponential in the depth of the hierarchy, due to a product construction (it is also linear in the multiplication of sizes of all included standalone automata). In the compositional analysis, the depth of the hierarchy is constant (only two layers) and we only take a product of one root automaton with several constant size duration automata; this explains why the practically obtained speed ups are so dramatic. The efficiency gains are primarily due to the coarse abstraction of safety and reachability properties of an arbitrarily large callee into a tiny duration automaton. Abstraction and compositional reasoning together might provide similar speed ups for TIOA [5]; however, the restrictions that TPA impose on models allow one to automate the procedure.

7 Related Work

Classical TA [6,7] and timed I/O automata [2,4] have explicit modeling support only for static non-hierarchical structures. In 2011, we identified and classified eighty variants of TA into eleven classes in a survey [8] and there may be many more. Timed process automata fall in the class of *TA with resources* [8] because of their ability to model dynamic behaviors, which is required when resource constraints do not permit one to activate all the components at the same time. More precisely, the model is a direct generalization of *task automata* [17], *dynamic networks of TA* [18], and *callable timed automata* [19]. These three variants model only closed systems, while TPA can model both closed and open systems. Task automata model only two layers (a scheduler and its tasks) of hierarchy, while TPA, dynamic networks of TA [18], and callable timed automata are able to model any numbers of hierarchies. Unlike TPA, none of them supports private communication, provides compositional modeling with reusable designs for different contexts, or supports automated state-space reduction technique.

Dynamic networks of continuous-time automata have also been studied in the context of hybrid automata [20,21]. These works model physical environments using differential equations, which restrict the kinds of environments that can be described. In practice, large differential equations make analyses unmanageable, or can only give statistical guarantees [21]. These works focus on system dynamics, and do not support private communication. Timed process automata can be considered as a member of the class of *TA with succinctness* [8] because they hide many design details from the designers to achieve succinctness (like *TA variants with urgency* [22,23,8]). Timed process automata are also timed game automata [1,3,2,4] because the new variant uses timed games for analysis.

8 Conclusion

We have presented timed process automata that captures dynamic activation and deactivation of continuous-time control processes and private communication among the active processes. We have provided a safety and reachability analysis technique for non-recursive well-formed timed process automata. We have also designed an abstraction- and compositional reasoning-based state-space reduction technique for automated analysis of large industrial systems. Our analysis techniques can be applied in practice using any standard timed games solver such as Uppaal Tiga [16] and Synthia [24].

To the best of our knowledge, no prior work on dynamic network of timed automata considered private communication or open systems. This is also the first work that provides two important features for industrial time-critical dynamic open systems development: (i) compositional modeling with reusable designs for different contexts and (ii) automated state-space reduction technique.

It would be interesting to consider a model transformation from subset of *real-time π-calculus* [25,26] to TPA. This transformation might enable controllability analysis of π-calculus for open systems. The converse reduction from TPA to real-time π-calculus could also give several advantages: understanding TPA semantics in terms of the well-established π-calculus formalism, access to tools developed for real-time π-calculus [25], which might permit the analysis of recursive processes; it would also give a familiar automata-like syntax to π-calculus formalisms. It would also be relevant to minimize the number of subprocesses in controller synthesis. One may consider synthesis under this objective in the future, possibly by reduction to *priced/weighted timed automata* [27,28].

References

1. Maler, O., Pnueli, A., Sifakis, J.: On the synthesis of discrete controllers for timed systems. In: Mayr, E.W., Puech, C. (eds.) STACS 1995. LNCS, vol. 900, pp. 229–242. Springer, Heidelberg (1995)
2. de Alfaro, L., Henzinger, T.A., Stoelinga, M.: Timed interfaces. In: Sangiovanni-Vincentelli, A., Sifakis, J. (eds.) EMSOFT 2002. LNCS, vol. 2491, pp. 108–122. Springer, Heidelberg (2002)
3. de Alfaro, L., Faella, M., Henzinger, T.A., Majumdar, R., Stoelinga, M.: The element of surprise in timed games. In: Amadio, R., Lugiez, D. (eds.) CONCUR 2003. LNCS, vol. 2761, pp. 144–158. Springer, Heidelberg (2003)
4. David, A., Larsen, K.G., Legay, A., Nyman, U., Wąsowski, A.: Timed I/O automata: A complete specification theory for real-time systems. In: HSCC (2010)
5. Waez, M.T.B., Wąsowski, A., Dingel, J., Rudie, K.: Synthesis of a reconfiguration service for mixed-criticality multi-core system: An experience report. In: FACS (to appear, 2014)
6. Alur, R., Dill, D.L.: Automata for modeling real-time systems. In: Paterson, M. S. (ed.) ICALP 1990. LNCS, vol. 443, pp. 322–335. Springer, Heidelberg (1990)
7. Alur, R., Dill, D.L.: A theory of timed automata. TCS 126 (1994)
8. Waez, M.T.B., Dingel, J., Rudie, K.: A survey of timed automata for the development of real-time systems. In: CSR (2013)
9. Kaynar, D.K., Lynch, N.A., Segala, R., Vaandrager, F.W.: The Theory of Timed I/O Automata (2006)
10. Henzinger, T.A., Manna, Z., Pnueli, A.: Timed transition systems. In: REX Workshop (1992)
11. Waez, M.T.B., Wąsowski, A., Dingel, J., Rudie, K.: A model for industrial real-time systems. Technical Report 2014-622, Queen's University, ON (2014)

12. Brihaye, T., Henzinger, T.A., Prabhu, V.S., Raskin, J.-F.: Minimum-time reachability in timed games. In: Arge, L., Cachin, C., Jurdziński, T., Tarlecki, A. (eds.) ICALP 2007. LNCS, vol. 4596, pp. 825–837. Springer, Heidelberg (2007)
13. Jurdziński, M., Trivedi, A.: Reachability-time games on timed automata. In: Arge, L., Cachin, C., Jurdziński, T., Tarlecki, A. (eds.) ICALP 2007. LNCS, vol. 4596, pp. 838–849. Springer, Heidelberg (2007)
14. Cassez, F.: Timed games for computing WCET for pipelined processors with caches. In: ACSD (2011)
15. Gustavsson, A., Ermedahl, A., Lisper, B., Pettersson, P.: Towards WCET analysis of multicore architectures using UPPAAL. In: WCET (2010)
16. Behrmann, G., Cougnard, A., David, A., Fleury, E., Larsen, K.G., Lime, D.: UPPAAL-Tiga: Time for playing games! In: Damm, W., Hermanns, H. (eds.) CAV 2007. LNCS, vol. 4590, pp. 121–125. Springer, Heidelberg (2007)
17. Fersman, E., Krčál, P., Pettersson, P., Yi, W.: Task automata: Schedulability, decidability and undecidability. Information and Computation (2007)
18. Campana, S., Spalazzi, L., Spegni, F.: Dynamic networks of timed automata for collaborative systems: A network monitoring case study. In: ISCTS (2010)
19. Boudjadar, A., Vaandrager, F., Bodeveix, J.P., Filali, M.: Extending UPPAAL for the modeling and verification of dynamic real-time systems. In: FSE (2013)
20. Göllü, A., Varaiya, P.: A dynamic network of hybrid automata. In: AIS (1994)
21. David, A., Larsen, K.G., Legay, A., Poulsen, D.B.: Statistical model checking of dynamic networks of stochastic hybrid automata. In: AVoCS (2013)
22. Bornot, S., Sifakis, J., Tripakis, S.: Modeling urgency in timed systems. In: de Roever, W.-P., Langmaack, H., Pnueli, A. (eds.) COMPOS 1997. LNCS, vol. 1536, pp. 103–129. Springer, Heidelberg (1998)
23. Barbuti, R., Tesei, L.: Timed automata with urgent transitions. Acta Informatica (2004)
24. Peter, H.-J., Ehlers, R., Mattmüller, R.: Synthia: Verification and synthesis for timed automata. In: Gopalakrishnan, G., Qadeer, S. (eds.) CAV 2011. LNCS, vol. 6806, pp. 649–655. Springer, Heidelberg (2011)
25. Posse, E., Dingel, J.: Theory and implementation of a real-time extension to the π-calculus. In: Hatcliff, J., Zucca, E. (eds.) FMOODS/FORTE 2010, Part II. LNCS, vol. 6117, pp. 125–139. Springer, Heidelberg (2010)
26. Barakat, K., Kowalewski, S., Noll, T.: A native approach to modeling timed behavior in the pi-calculus. In: Margaria, T., Qiu, Z., Yang, H. (eds.) TASE (2012)
27. Alur, R., La Torre, S., Pappas, G.J.: Optimal paths in weighted timed automata. In: Di Benedetto, M.D., Sangiovanni-Vincentelli, A. (eds.) HSCC 2001. LNCS, vol. 2034, pp. 49–62. Springer, Heidelberg (2001)
28. Behrmann, G., Fehnker, A., Hune, T., Larsen, K., Pettersson, P., Romijn, J., Vaandrager, F.: Minimum-cost reachability for priced timed automata. In: Di Benedetto, M.D., Sangiovanni-Vincentelli, A. (eds.) HSCC 2001. LNCS, vol. 2034, pp. 147–161. Springer, Heidelberg (2001)

Abstraction-Based Computation of Reward Measures for Markov Automata*

Bettina Braitling[1], Luis María Ferrer Fioriti[2], Hassan Hatefi[2], Ralf Wimmer[1], Bernd Becker[1], and Holger Hermanns[2]

[1] Albert-Ludwigs-Universität Freiburg, Germany
{braitlin,wimmer,becker}@informatik.uni-freiburg.de
[2] Saarland University, Saarbrücken, Germany
{ferrer,hhatefi,hermanns}@cs.uni-saarland.de

Abstract. Markov automata allow us to model a wide range of complex real-life systems by combining continuous stochastic timing with probabilistic transitions and nondeterministic choices. By adding a reward function it is possible to model costs like the energy consumption of a system as well.

However, models of real-life systems tend to be large, and the analysis methods for such powerful models like Markov (reward) automata do not scale well, which limits their applicability. To solve this problem we present an abstraction technique for Markov reward automata, based on stochastic games, together with automatic refinement methods for the computation of time-bounded accumulated reward properties. Experiments show a significant speed-up and reduction in system size compared to direct analysis methods.

1 Introduction

During the last few years Markov automata (MA) [1] have become a popular formalism for modelling stochastic systems. Markov automata are compositional, allowing us to model large systems component-wise and to obtain a model for the whole system by combining the models of the components according to fixed composition rules. Markov automata combine nondeterminism with probabilistic behaviour and continuous stochastic timing. Thus they are a generalisation of discrete-time Markov chains (DTMCs), Markov decision processes (MDPs), probabilistic automata (PA), continuous-time Markov chains (CTMCs), and interactive Markov chains (IMCs [2]). Markov automata form the semantic foundation of generalised stochastic Petri nets (GSPNs) [3] and stochastic activity networks (SANs) [4]. For modelling systems as MA, the Markov automata process algebra (MAPA) [5] has been devised. It is accompanied with tool support:

* This work was partly supported by the German Research Council (DFG) as part of the Transregional Collaborative Research Center AVACS (SFB/TR 14), by the EU 7th Framework Programme under grant agreement no. 295261 (MEALS) and 318490 (SENSATION), and by the CAS/SAFEA International Partnership Program for Creative Research Teams.

D. D'Souza et al. (Eds.): VMCAI 2015, LNCS 8931, pp. 172–189, 2015.

SCOOP [5] transforms descriptions in MAPA into the underlying MA and is able to apply reduction techniques to reduce the MA's size.

Such a powerful modelling formalism is, however, only useful in practice if it is accompanied by efficient analysis algorithms. Model checking of MA against continuous stochastic logic (CSL) has been discussed in [6]. Algorithms for a wide range of properties for MA have been developed: long-run average, expected reachability time, and time-bounded reachability probabilities have been considered in [7,8]. Markov reward automata (MRA), which is the extension of MA by rewards, have recently been studied in [9]. The analysis algorithms for MA and MRA are implemented in the tool IMCA[1].

Model checking algorithms for many kinds of properties like time-unbounded reachability, expected reachability costs, and long-run averages can be transferred to MA from simpler models like PA and are similarly efficient. In contrast, checking time-bounded properties is much more expensive. The reason is that the methods based on uniformisation, which make checking time-bounded properties on CTMCs efficient, cannot be applied to MA due to the nondeterminism present there. Instead (like for IMCs [10]) one has to resort to discretisation [7,8,9]: the time until the time bound is split into small intervals such that one can assume that with high probability either none or exactly one step occurs within one interval. For each of these intervals, an unbounded reachability analysis for PA has to be performed. Therefore the analysis of such properties scales badly to large state spaces and is limited to a few thousand states, depending on the structure of the state space and the time bound.

Contributions. To tackle this problem for MRA we present an *abstraction and refinement framework*, the first of its kind. We target *time-bounded accumulated rewards* like "What is the maximal expected cost the system causes within 10 hours of operation?" The MRA at hand is abstracted into a two-player stochastic reward game, which keeps the nondeterminism present in the concrete system separate from the nondeterminism introduced by abstraction. This allows us to compute safe upper and lower bounds on the minimal and maximal reward value of the original system. These bounds are an in-built quality measure for the abstraction, allowing us to refine it. To compute the bounds, we give a fixed point characterisation of time-bounded accumulated rewards on stochastic games, show how to discretise it, and give an estimation of the error caused by the discretisation. Experimental results confirm that our abstraction method yields substantial reductions in system size and reduces the computation times compared to competing tools which work on the concrete state space.

Related Work. This paper continues a series of successful works on abstraction frameworks for simpler probabilistic models, foremost rooted in game-based abstraction for PA [11]. In a preliminary paper [12] we have presented an abstraction framework for time-bounded reachability probabilities for MA, which was

[1] The official homepage available at `http://www-i2.informatik.rwth-aachen.de/imca`.

the first attempt to apply abstraction to MA. Other abstraction methods are restricted to unbounded and step-bounded reachability probabilities in PA: PA-based abstraction [13] abstracts a PA again into a PA whose behaviour is an over-approximation of the behaviour of the original model. It therefore only allows to compute lower bounds on minimal probabilities and upper bounds on maximal probabilities. This is improved by game-based abstraction [11], which yields a probabilistic game. Its advantage is that it yields both upper and lower bounds for minimal and maximal reachability probabilities. Wachter and Zhang [14,15] have proposed menu-based abstraction for PA, which has the same advantage as game-based abstraction, but yields in many practical cases significantly smaller abstractions.

Structure of the paper. In the next section we briefly review the foundations of MA and stochastic games. In Sec. 3 we present our abstraction and refinement method for MA and show how to compute reward measures for stochastic games. The experimental evaluation follows in Sec. 4. We finally summarise the paper with an outlook to future work in Sec. 5. An extended version of this paper with proofs of the main propositions is available at [16].

2 Preliminaries

We first introduce the necessary foundations on stochastic games (SGs), extended by reward functions, which form the basic formalism used in our abstraction framework. We define the properties we consider and give a fixed point characterisation of them for SGs. Finally we define MA as a special case of SGs with a single player.

We denote the set of real numbers by $\mathbb{R}$, the non-negative real numbers by $\mathbb{R}^{\geq 0}$, and by $\mathbb{R}^{\geq 0}_{\infty}$ the set $\mathbb{R}^{\geq 0} \mathbin{\dot\cup} \{\infty\}$. For a finite or countable set S let $\mathrm{Distr}(S)$ denote the set of probability distributions on S, i. e. of all functions $\mu : S \to [0,1]$ with $\sum_{s \in S} \mu(s) = 1$. The support of a distribution μ is given by $\mathrm{Supp}(\mu) = \{s \in S \mid \mu(s) > 0\}$; μ is called Dirac if there is $s \in S$ with $\mu(s) = 1$. It is denoted by ξ_s. Given a set $S' \subseteq S$ we write $\mu(S')$ for $\sum_{s \in S'} \mu(s)$.

2.1 Stochastic Reward Games

Stochastic games are a behavioural model that combines stochastic timing, non-determinism and probabilistic choices. An SG consists of one or more players who can choose between one or more transitions to change the current state. Each choice may influence the behaviour of the other players. A transition consists of a real-valued or infinite rate $\lambda \in \mathbb{R}^{\geq 0}_{\infty}$ and a probability distribution over the successor states. For our work we need the definition of stochastic two-player games:

Definition 1 (Stochastic game). *A* stochastic (continuous-time two-player) game *(SG) is a tuple* $\mathcal{G} = (V, (V_1, V_2), v_{\mathrm{init}}, \mathbf{T})$ *such that* $V = V_1 \mathbin{\dot\cup} V_2$ *is a set of states,* $v_{\mathrm{init}} \in V$ *is the initial state, and* $\mathbf{T} \subseteq V \times \mathbb{R}^{\geq 0}_{\infty} \times \mathrm{Distr}(V)$ *is a transition relation.*

V_1 and V_2 are the states of player 1 and player 2, respectively; we also denote them as V_1- and V_2-states. Transitions $(v, \lambda, \mu) \in \mathbf{T}$ with rate $\lambda < \infty$ are called *Markovian*, transitions with infinite rate *probabilistic*. We denote the set of Markovian and probabilistic transitions by $\mathbf{T}_M$ and $\mathbf{T}_P$, respectively; it holds that $\mathbf{T} = \mathbf{T}_M \dot{\cup} \mathbf{T}_P$. $\mathbf{T}_M(v)$ and $\mathbf{T}_P(v)$ denote the set of Markovian and probabilistic transitions available at state v, respectively. We use $\mathbf{T}(v) = \mathbf{T}_M(v) \dot{\cup} \mathbf{T}_P(v)$ as the set of all transitions available at state v.

The game starts in state v_{init}. If the current state is $v \in V_1$, then it is player 1's turn, otherwise player 2's. The current player chooses a transition $(v, \lambda, \mu) \in \mathbf{T}(v)$ for leaving state v. The rate $\theta_r((v, \lambda, \mu)) = \lambda \in \mathbb{R}^{\geq 0}_{\infty}$ determines how long we stay at v, whereas $\theta_p((v, \lambda, \mu)) = \mu \in \text{Distr}(V)$ gives us the distribution which leads to the successor states. If $\lambda = \infty$, the transition is taken instantaneously. Otherwise, λ is taken as the parameter of an exponential distribution. In this case, the probability that a transition to state $v' \in V$ happens within $t \geq 0$ time units, is given by $\mu(v') \cdot (1 - \mathrm{e}^{-\lambda \cdot t})$. For conciseness, we write λ_{tr} instead of $\theta_r(tr)$ and μ_{tr} instead of $\theta_p(tr)$ for $tr \in \mathbf{T}$.

Paths. The dynamics of SGs is specified by paths. An infinite path $\pi \in (V \times \mathbb{R}^{\geq 0} \times \mathbf{T})^{\omega}$ is an infinite sequence of states, sojourn times, and transitions. A finite path is such a sequence which is finite and ending in a state, i. e. $\pi \in (V \times \mathbb{R}^{\geq 0} \times \mathbf{T})^{\star} \times V$. We usually write $v \xrightarrow{t,tr}$ instead of $(v, t, tr) \in (V \times \mathbb{R}^{\geq 0} \times \mathbf{T})$. We use *Paths** and *Paths*$^{\omega}$ to denote the set of finite and infinite paths, respectively. Given a finite path $\pi = v_0 \xrightarrow{t_0,tr_0} v_1 \xrightarrow{t_1,tr_1} \cdots v_n$, v_i is the $(i+1)$-th state of π, denoted by $\text{St}(\pi, i)$, t_i is the time of staying at v_i, denoted by $\text{Ti}(\pi, i)$, and $\text{Tr}(\pi, i) = tr_i$ is the executed transition for $i \in \{0, \ldots, n-1\}$. Note that v_i is left instantaneously, i. e. $\text{Ti}(\pi, i) = 0$, if $\text{Tr}(\pi, i)$ has an infinite rate. Moreover, $|\pi|$ refers to n, the length of π, and $\text{last}(\pi)$ to v_n, its last state.

Strategies. The nondeterminism which may occur at a state is resolved by a function, which is called a *strategy* (or policy or scheduler). Each player follows its own strategy in order to accomplish its goal. A strategy of player i ($i = 1, 2$) is a partial function $\sigma_i : \mathit{Paths}^{\star} \nrightarrow \text{Distr}(\mathbf{T})$ such that $\sigma_i(\pi) = \eta$ only if $\text{last}(\pi) \in V_i$ and $\text{Supp}(\eta) \subseteq \mathbf{T}(\text{last}(\pi))$. This strategy class is called *generic*, since it uses the complete path history to resolve the nondeterminism.[2] We denote the set of all strategies for player i by Strat_i.

Probability measure. Given strategies σ_1, σ_2 for both players and a state $v \in V$, a probability space on the set of infinite paths starting in v can be constructed. The set of measurable events is thereby a σ-algebra that is induced by a standard cylinder set construction [18] together with a unique probability measure

[2] This class is also known as the class of *early schedulers* [17] because the scheduler makes its choice when entering a state and—in contrast to a late scheduler—may not change its choice while residing in a state. This is the most general scheduler class for MA, since they do not exhibit nondeterminism between Markovian transitions (see Sec. 2.3).

$\Pr_{v,\sigma_1,\sigma_2}$ on the events. $\Pr_{v,\sigma_1,\sigma_2}(\Pi)$ is the probability of the set of paths Π, starting from state v, given that player 1 and player 2 play with strategies σ_1 and σ_2, respectively. Both the σ-algebra and the probability measure are constructed by extending the existing techniques used for MA and IMCs. We omit the details here; for more information see, e. g. [6,19,20].

Zenoness. It may happen that an SG contains an end component consisting of probabilistic transitions only. Such an end component leads to the existence of infinite paths π with finite sojourn times, i. e. $\lim_{n\to\infty}\sum_{i=0}^{n}\mathrm{Ti}(\pi,i) < \infty$. This phenomenon is called *Zenoness.* Since such behaviour has to be considered unrealistic, we assume that the SGs under consideration are non-Zeno, i. e. that they do not contain such end components. Formally, an SG is non-Zeno iff $\forall v \in V : \forall \sigma_1 \in \mathrm{Strat}_1 \wedge \forall \sigma_2 \in \mathrm{Strat}_2 : \Pr_{v,\sigma_1,\sigma_2}\big(\{\pi \mid \lim_{n\to\infty}\sum_{i=0}^{n}\mathrm{Ti}(\pi,i) < \infty\}\big) = 0$.

For more on strategies and on SGs in general we refer to [21,22].

Now we extend SGs by rewards (or costs). We consider two kinds of rewards: *transient rewards* for staying in a certain state and *instantaneous rewards* for taking a transition.

Definition 2 (Stochastic reward game). *A* stochastic reward game *(SRG) is a tuple $\mathcal{G}_{rew} = (\mathcal{G}, \rho_t, \rho_i)$ such that $\mathcal{G}$ is an SG, $\rho_t : \mathbf{T} \to \mathbb{R}^{\geq 0}$ the transient reward function, and $\rho_i : \mathbf{T} \to \mathbb{R}^{\geq 0}$ the instantaneous reward function.*

The transient reward $\rho_t(tr)$ of a transition $tr = (v, \lambda, \mu)$ is the cost of staying in v for one time unit before taking transition tr, i. e. residing in state v for Δ time units yields a transient reward of $\Delta \cdot \rho_t(tr)$. Since a state is immediately left if a transition with infinite rate is chosen, we can assume that the transient reward of such transitions is zero.

The instantaneous reward $\rho_i(tr)$ is the cost of the state change using transition $tr \in \mathbf{T}$. The accumulated reward along a path π is the sum of the costs for the transitions and the costs for staying in the states of the path. We are interested in time-bounded rewards, i.e. the costs accumulated until a time bound T is reached. It is denoted by Rew_T.

$$\begin{aligned} Rew_T(\pi) = &\sum_{i=0}^{n_T-1}\Big(\rho_t\big(\mathrm{Tr}(\pi,i)\big)\cdot \mathrm{Ti}(\pi,i) + \rho_i\big(\mathrm{Tr}(\pi,i)\big)\Big) \\ &+ \rho_t\big(\mathrm{Tr}(\pi,n_T)\big)\cdot\big(T - \sum_{i=0}^{n_T-1}\mathrm{Ti}(\pi,i)\big), \end{aligned} \tag{1}$$

where n_T is the largest number such that $\sum_{i=0}^{n_T-1}\mathrm{Ti}(\pi,i) \leq T$. Each player can independently of the other try to maximise or minimise the expectation of this reward by choosing an appropriate scheduler.

$$\mathcal{R}^{\mathrm{opt}_1}_{\mathrm{opt}_2}(v,T) = \underset{\sigma_1\in\mathrm{Strat}_1}{\mathrm{opt}_1}\ \underset{\sigma_2\in\mathrm{Strat}_2}{\mathrm{opt}_2}\int_{\pi\in Paths^{\omega}} Rew_T(\pi)\,\mathrm{d}\Pr_{v,\sigma_1,\sigma_2}(\pi) \tag{2}$$

is the opt_1-opt_2 expected time-bounded reward (ETR) when player i tries to optimise according to $\text{opt}_i \in \{\inf, \sup\}$ for $i = 1, 2$ and the game starts in state $v \in V$.

2.2 Time-Bounded Reward as a Fixed Point

In this section we provide a fixed point characterisation of the ETR for an SG. In the following we restrict the presentation to the case where player 1 maximises the expected reward, i. e. setting opt_1 to sup in (2). We denote the case by $\mathcal{R}^{\sup}_{\text{opt}}$, where player 2 still has the choice to either minimise or maximise the ETR.

Lemma 1 (Fixed point characterisation). *Given an SRG* $\mathcal{G}_{rew} = (\mathcal{G}, \rho_t, \rho_i)$, *a time bound* $T \geq 0$, $\text{opt} \in \{\inf, \sup\}$, $\text{opt}_v = \sup$ *if* $v \in V_1$ *and* $\text{opt}_v = \text{opt}$ *otherwise.* $\mathcal{R}^{\sup}_{\text{opt}}(\cdot, T)$ *is the least fixed point of the higher order operator* $\Omega_{\text{opt}} : (V \times \mathbb{R}^{\geq 0} \mapsto \mathbb{R}^{\geq 0}) \mapsto (V \times \mathbb{R}^{\geq 0} \mapsto \mathbb{R}^{\geq 0})$, $\text{opt} \in \{\inf, \sup\}$, *such that*

$$\Omega_{\text{opt}}(F)(v,T) = \underset{tr \in \mathbf{T}(v)}{\text{opt}_v} \begin{cases} \left(\rho_i(tr) + \frac{\rho_t(tr)}{\lambda_{tr}}\right)\left(1 - \mathrm{e}^{-\lambda_{tr} T}\right) \\ + \displaystyle\int_0^T \lambda_{tr} \mathrm{e}^{-\lambda_{tr} t} \sum_{v' \in V} \mu_{tr}(v') F(v', T-t) \, \mathrm{d}t, & \text{if } tr \in \mathbf{T}_M(v), \\ \rho_i(tr) + \displaystyle\sum_{v' \in V} \mu_{tr}(v') F(v', T), & \text{if } tr \in \mathbf{T}_P(v). \end{cases} \tag{3}$$

A similar fixed point characterisation can be attained for the case that player 1 minimises the ETR. Both characterisations, however, yield Volterra integral equation systems which are not directly tractable [23]. We demonstrate in Sec. 3.2 how to approximate $\mathcal{R}^{\sup}_{\text{opt}}$ by applying a discretisation technique. Moreover, the characterisation provides a sound theory for the abstraction of MA subject to time-bounded reward analysis (see Sec. 3).

2.3 Markov Automata

For consistency reasons we present MA [1,24,25] as a special case of SGs. This is possible under two conditions: First, we consider only *closed* MA, i. e. we assume that the model to be analysed is not subject to further composition operations. Then the actions with which transitions are labelled do not carry any information and can be omitted. Second, we make the *maximal progress assumption* [25], which is typically made for closed MA before analysis. It says that probabilistic transitions (which are carried out immediately without progress of time) have precedence over Markovian transitions, which are delayed by an exponentially distributed amount of time. Together with the restriction that there is no nondeterminism between Markovian transitions in MA, we obtain the following definition:

Definition 3 (Markov (reward) automaton). *An SG* $\mathcal{M} = (V, (V_1, V_2), v_{\text{init}}, \mathbf{T})$ *is a* Markov automaton *(MA) if* $V_2 = \emptyset$ *and each state* $v \in V$ *contains either only probabilistic transitions* $(v, \infty, \mu) \in \mathbf{T}(v)$ *or a single Markovian transition* $(v, \lambda, \mu) \in \mathbf{T}(v)$ *with* $\lambda < \infty$.

A Markov reward automaton *(MRA) is an SRG* $\mathcal{M}_{rew} = (\mathcal{M}, \rho_t, \rho_i)$ *where* $\mathcal{M}$ *is an MA.*

The fixed point characterisation of the ETR for SRGs is valid for MRA as well. Since the set V_2 is empty for MRA, we can omit the opt subscript from Ω_{opt} as defined in Eq. (3) and simply write it as Ω in this case.

Like SGs can be seen as a generalisation of MA, MA can be seen as the generalisation of some other common models: A (closed) probabilistic automaton (PA) is an MA where all transitions are probabilistic. A PA with $\left|\{\mu \mid (v, \infty, \mu) \in \mathbf{T}(v)\}\right| = 1$ for all $v \in V$ is a discrete-time Markov chain (DTMC). An interactive Markov chain (IMC) is an MA where all distributions occurring in probabilistic transitions are Dirac. A continuous-time Markov chain (CTMC) is an MA with only Markovian transitions.

We partition the state space V of an MA based on the rate of outgoing transitions of the states. A state is called *probabilistic* (*Markovian*) if its outgoing transitions are all probabilistic (Markovian). We assume that there are no *deadlock* states, which have no outgoing transitions. They can be turned into Markovian states by adding a Markovian transition (v, λ, ξ_v) with arbitrary rate $\lambda < \infty$. Then we have $V = \mathit{MS} \,\dot\cup\, \mathit{PS}$ with MS being the Markovian states and PS the probabilistic states.

3 Abstraction and Refinement of MRA

In this section we first describe our abstraction of an MA, then how safe bounds on the maximal (minimal) ETR can be computed on SGs (and therefore also on our abstraction). Finally we will show how an abstraction can be refined in case that it is too coarse, i. e. if it yields bounds that are too far apart.

3.1 Abstraction

The abstraction of an MA $\mathcal{M} = (V, (V, \emptyset), v_{\text{init}}, \mathbf{T})$ is based on a partition of V, which is a set $\mathcal{P} \subseteq 2^V \setminus \{\emptyset\}$ with $\bigcup_{B \in \mathcal{P}} B = V$ and $B \cap B' = \emptyset$ for all $B, B' \in \mathcal{P}$ with $B \neq B'$. For $v \in V$ we denote the unique block B of $\mathcal{P}$ with $v \in B$ by $[v]_{\mathcal{P}}$.

Definition 4 (Lifted distribution). *Let* $\mu \in \text{Distr}(V)$ *be a probability distribution over* V *and* $\mathcal{P}$ *a partition of* V*. The* lifted distribution $\overline{\mu} \in \text{Distr}(\mathcal{P})$ *is given by* $\overline{\mu}(B) = \sum_{v \in B} \mu(v)$ *for* $B \in \mathcal{P}$.

Definition 5 (Labelling function). *Let Lab be a finite set of labels and* $\mathcal{M}$ *an MA. A* labelling function *is a function* $lab : \mathbf{T} \to Lab$ *which is injective at each state, i. e. for all* $v \in V$ *and all* $\text{tr}, \text{tr}' \in \mathbf{T}(v)$ *we have either* $\text{tr} = \text{tr}'$ *or* $lab(\text{tr}) \neq lab(\text{tr}')$*. Additionally we require* $lab(\text{tr}) = \perp$ *iff* tr *is Markovian.*

For a set $B \subseteq V$ of states, we define $Lab(B) = \{lab(tr) \mid \exists v \in B : tr \in \mathbf{T}(v)\}$ as the set of actions which are enabled in B. We also write $Lab(v)$ instead of $Lab(\{v\})$.

A simple, basic way to abstract an MA $\mathcal{M}$ is to use the blocks of a partition $\mathcal{P}$ as abstract states and create the abstract transitions by lifting the distributions as in Def. 4. If two transitions coincide after lifting, they are combined into one abstract transition.

Such an abstraction introduces additional nondeterminism into the system: There is now a nondeterministic choice between transitions which belong to different concrete states, but to the same state in the abstraction. In a basic abstraction, this new, abstract nondeterminism cannot be distinguished from the original, concrete nondeterminism. This makes it impossible to obtain both lower and upper bounds on the actual reward value.

To avoid this effect, we introduced a game abstraction for MA in [12], which we now extend to MRA.

Definition 6 (Game abstraction of MA). *Given an MA $\mathcal{M} = (V, (V, \emptyset), v_{\text{init}}, \mathbf{T})$, a labelling function $lab : \mathbf{T} \to Lab$, and a partition $\mathcal{P} = \{B_1, \ldots B_n\}$ of V such that for all $B \in \mathcal{P}$ either $B \subseteq MS$ or $B \subseteq PS$. We construct the* game abstraction $\overline{\mathcal{M}}^{\mathcal{P},lab} = (\overline{V}, (\overline{V_1}, \overline{V_2}), \overline{v_{\text{init}}}, \overline{\mathbf{T}})$ *with:*

- $\overline{V} = \overline{V_1} \,\dot\cup\, \overline{V_2}$,
- $\overline{V_1} = \mathcal{P}$,
- $\overline{V_2} = \{(B, \alpha) \in \mathcal{P} \times Lab \mid \alpha \in Lab(B)\} \,\dot\cup\, \{*\}$,
- $\overline{v_{\text{init}}} = [v_{\text{init}}]_{\mathcal{P}}$, *and*
- $\overline{\mathbf{T}} = \overline{\mathbf{T}_P} \,\dot\cup\, \overline{\mathbf{T}_M}$ *with*

$$\begin{aligned}
\overline{\mathbf{T}_P} = &\left\{\left([v]_{\mathcal{P}}, \infty, \xi_{([v]_{\mathcal{P}},\alpha)}\right) \mid v \in V \wedge \alpha \in Lab([v]_{\mathcal{P}})\right\} \\
&\dot\cup \left\{\left(([v]_{\mathcal{P}}, \alpha), \infty, \overline{\mu}\right) \mid v \in PS \wedge \alpha \in Lab(v) \wedge (v, \infty, \mu) \in \mathbf{T}_P\right\} \\
&\dot\cup \left\{\left(([v]_{\mathcal{P}}, \alpha), \infty, \xi_*\right) \mid v \in PS \wedge \alpha \in Lab([v]_{\mathcal{P}}) \setminus Lab(v)\right\}, \\
\overline{\mathbf{T}_M} = &\left\{\left(([v]_{\mathcal{P}}, \bot), \lambda, \overline{\mu}\right) \mid v \in MS \wedge (v, \lambda, \mu) \in \mathbf{T}_M\right\} \\
&\dot\cup \left\{(*, 1, \xi_*)\right\}.
\end{aligned}$$

We call $\overline{V_2}$-states of the form $(B, \bot)$ with $B \subseteq MS$ *Markovian* and $\overline{V_2}$-states of the form (B, α) with $\alpha \neq \bot$ and $B \subseteq PS$ *probabilistic*. The $\overline{V_1}$- and $\overline{V_2}$-states strictly alternate.

Player 1 resolves the nondeterminism already present in the concrete MA when it selects at state B a label α present in one of the concrete states of B. Player 2 resolves the nondeterminism introduced by the abstraction by selecting at abstract state (B, α) a concrete state $v \in B$ and firing the lifted transition of state v that has the label α. In case there is no transition with label α in state v, the abstraction goes to a special state $*$ that represents the worst outcome for the property under consideration. This is similar to the menu-based abstraction in [14,15].

In order to abstract an MRA $\mathcal{M}_{rew} = (\mathcal{M}, \rho_t, \rho_i)$ we have to add *abstract reward functions* to the abstraction. For this we need an additional function

$\nu : \overline{\mathbf{T}} \to 2^{\mathbf{T}}$, which maps the abstract transitions back to the corresponding concrete transitions in $\mathcal{M}_{rew}$. For a transition $\overline{tr} = (\overline{v}, \lambda, \overline{\mu}) \in \overline{\mathbf{T}}$ we get:

$$\nu(\overline{tr}) = \begin{cases} \{(v', \infty, \mu) \in \mathbf{T} \mid v' \in B\}, & \text{if } \overline{v} = (B, \alpha) \wedge \alpha \neq \bot \wedge B \subseteq PS, \\ \{(v', \lambda, \mu) \in \mathbf{T} \mid v' \in B\}, & \text{if } \overline{v} = (B, \bot) \wedge B \subseteq MS, \\ \emptyset, & \text{otherwise.} \end{cases}$$

The choice of the reward function depends on whether we want to compute a lower or an upper bound on the (minimal or maximal) ETR. In case of a lower bound, player 2 chooses the smallest possible reward among all transitions which were mapped onto the same abstract transition. The case of an upper bound is analogous.

We give the definition of the reward structures for the case that player 1 maximises the ETR. If player 1 minimises the ETR, the only change is that $\rho_t((*, 1, \xi_*))$ is set to ∞ instead of 0.

Definition 7 (opt-Abstraction-induced SRG). *Given an MRA* $\mathcal{M}_{rew} = (\mathcal{M}, \rho_t, \rho_i)$*, a partition* $\mathcal{P}$ *of the state space, a labelling function lab for the transitions, and* opt $\in \{\inf, \sup\}$*. Then the* opt-Abstraction-induced SRG *(or for short* opt-*AISRG) with respect to* $\mathcal{P}$ *and lab is a tuple* opt-$\overline{\mathcal{M}}_{rew}^{\mathcal{P},lab} = (\overline{\mathcal{M}}^{\mathcal{P},lab}, \overline{\rho_t}^{\text{opt}}, \overline{\rho_i}^{\text{opt}})$*, where* $\overline{\mathcal{M}}^{\mathcal{P},lab}$ *is the game abstraction of* $\mathcal{M}$ *obtained from Def. 6 and* $\overline{\rho_t}^{\text{opt}}$ *and* $\overline{\rho_i}^{\text{opt}}$ *are* abstract transient and instantaneous reward functions *defined as:*

$$\overline{\rho_t}^{\text{opt}}(\overline{tr}) = \begin{cases} \underset{tr \in \nu(\overline{tr})}{\text{opt}} \ \rho_t(tr), & \textit{if } \nu(\overline{tr}) \neq \emptyset, \\ 0, & \textit{otherwise.} \end{cases}$$

and

$$\overline{\rho_i}^{\text{opt}}(\overline{tr}) = \begin{cases} \underset{tr \in \nu(\overline{tr})}{\text{opt}} \ \rho_i(tr), & \textit{if } \nu(\overline{tr}) \neq \emptyset, \\ 0, & \textit{otherwise.} \end{cases}$$

respectively, where $\overline{tr} \in \overline{\mathbf{T}}$ *is an abstract transition.*

We illustrate the abstraction of an MRA in Example 1.

Example 1. Figure 1(a) shows an MRA $\mathcal{M}_{rew}$ together with a partition $\mathcal{P} = \{B_0, B_1\}$. We assume that all probabilistic transitions are labelled with $lab(tr) = \alpha$ and all Markovian transitions with $lab(tr) = \bot$. It holds $PS = \{v_0, v_1, v_2\} = B_0$ and $MS = \{v_3, v_4, v_5\} = B_1$. For each transition tr the rewards are given in the form "$(\rho_i(tr)|\rho_t(tr))$" next to the transition in red colour.

Figure 1(b) shows the resulting game abstraction. The blocks B_0 and B_1 have become $\overline{V_1}$-states, whereas all other states are $\overline{V_2}$-states. We show both reward structures: the values in red colour next to each abstract transition are the minimal rewards in the form "$(\overline{\rho_i}^{\inf}(tr)|\overline{\rho_t}^{\inf}(tr))$"; the blue figures below are the maximal rewards, shown as "$(\overline{\rho_i}^{\sup}(tr)|\overline{\rho_t}^{\sup}(tr))$".

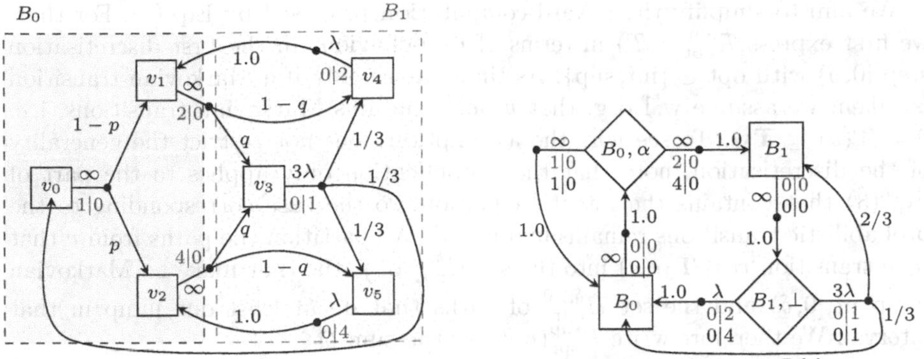

(a) Original MRA $\mathcal{M}_{rew}$ (b) Abstraction $\overline{\mathcal{M}}^{\mathcal{P},lab}_{rew}$

Fig. 1. An example for the game abstraction of an MRA $\mathcal{M}_{rew}$

The soundness of our framework follows from the fact that the least fixed points of the abstract semantics are over- and underapproaximations of the least fixed point in the concrete semantics.

Theorem 1 (Soundness). *Let $\mathcal{M}_{rew} = (\mathcal{M}, \rho_t, \rho_i)$ be an MRA, its high-order operator for the maximal ETR Ω, and $\text{opt-}\overline{\mathcal{M}}^{\mathcal{P},lab}_{rew} = (\overline{\mathcal{M}}^{\mathcal{P},lab}, \overline{\rho_t}^{\text{opt}}, \overline{\rho_i}^{\text{opt}})$, $\text{opt} \in \{\inf, \sup\}$, be a game abstraction with rewards, its high-order operators $\Omega_{\inf}$, $\Omega_{\sup}$. Then:*

$$\text{lfp}(\Omega_{\inf})([v]_{\mathcal{P}}, T) \leq \text{lfp}(\Omega)(v, T) \leq \text{lfp}(\Omega_{\sup})([v]_{\mathcal{P}}, T)$$

for all $v \in V$, and $T \in \mathbb{R}^{\geq 0}$.

3.2 Reward Computation

In this section we describe how to compute optimal ETRs for the general class of SRGs. For this purpose a discretisation technique is employed, which is then applied to the fixed point characterisation given in Lemma 1. The technique yields a discretised fixed point characterisation accompanied by a stable numerical algorithm with strict error bound for computing the optimal ETRs in SRGs.

Discretisation. As stated before, it is not generally feasible to directly solve the fixed point characterisation in Lemma 1 due to the complex integrals occurring in Eq. (3). Instead the SRG subject to analysis needs to be *discretised*. For this, the interval $[0, T]$ is first split into k time steps of size $\delta = \frac{T}{k}$. The discretisation then simplifies the computation of $\mathcal{R}^{\sup}_{\text{opt}}$ by assuming that with high probability at most one Markovian transition fires within each time step. Finally, we provide lower and upper bounds for the error created by the discretisation.

We aim to simplify the reward computation proposed by Eq. (3). For that, we first express $\mathcal{R}^{\sup}_{\text{opt}}(v,T)$ in terms of its behaviour in the first discretisation step $[0,\delta)$ with $\text{opt} \in \{\inf, \sup\}$. As time passes only if a Markovian transition is taken, we assume w.l.o.g. that v only contains Markovian transitions, i.e. $\emptyset \neq \mathbf{T}(v) \subseteq \mathbf{T}_M$. To see why the assumption does not restrict the generality of the discretisation, note that the simplification only applies to the part of Eq. (3) that contains the integral equation, so the case corresponding to the probabilistic transitions remains untouched. We partition the paths from v that take transition $tr \in \mathbf{T}_M(v)$ into the set $\Pi^{\delta,0}_{v,tr}$ of paths that make no Markovian jump in $[0,\delta)$ and the set $\Pi^{\delta,>0}_{v,tr}$ of paths that do at least one jump in that interval. We therefore write $\mathcal{R}^{\sup}_{\text{opt}}(v,T)$ as the sum of

1. The optimal expected reward attained in $[0,\delta)$ by paths from $\Pi^{\delta,>0}_{v,tr}$
2. The optimal expected reward attained in $[\delta,T]$ by paths from $\Pi^{\delta,>0}_{v,tr}$
3. The optimal expected reward attained in $[0,\delta)$ by paths from $\Pi^{\delta,0}_{v,tr}$
4. The optimal expected reward attained in $[\delta,T]$ by paths from $\Pi^{\delta,0}_{v,tr}$

It is not hard to express the last item in terms of $\mathcal{R}^{\sup}_{\text{opt}}(v,T-\delta)$. We further combine the first three items, denoted by $Acc_{tr}(v,T)$, and finally have:

$$\mathcal{R}^{\sup}_{\text{opt}}(v,T) = \operatorname*{opt}_{tr\in\mathbf{T}(v)}{}_{v} \left(Acc_{tr}(v,T) + \mathrm{e}^{-\lambda_{tr}\cdot\delta}\mathcal{R}^{\sup}_{\text{opt}}(v,T-\delta)\right) \tag{4}$$

We can show (see [16]) that $Acc_{tr}(v,T)$ is obtained by:

$$\begin{aligned} Acc_{tr}(v,T) = {} & \left(\rho_i(tr) + \tfrac{\rho_t(tr)}{\lambda_{tr}}\right)\left(1-\mathrm{e}^{-\lambda_{tr}\cdot\delta}\right) \\ & + \int_0^{\delta} \lambda_{tr}\mathrm{e}^{-\lambda_{tr}\cdot t} \sum_{v'\in V} \mu_{tr}(v')\mathcal{R}^{\sup}_{\text{opt}}(v',T-t)\,\mathrm{d}t \end{aligned} \tag{5}$$

As for the fixed point characterisation in Lemma 1, the exact computation of $Acc_{tr}(v,T)$, $\text{opt} \in \{\inf,\sup\}$ is in general intractable. However, if the discretisation constant δ is very small, then, with high probability, at most one Markovian jump happens in each discretisation step. Hence the reward gained by paths carrying multiple Markovian jumps within at least one such interval is negligible and can be omitted from the computation. In other words, the reward gained after the first Markovian jump in each discretisation constant is ignored by this approximation. It naturally induces some error and thereby approximates $Acc_{tr}(v,T)$, denoted by $\widetilde{Acc}_{\delta,tr}(v,k)$ and $\mathcal{R}^{\sup}_{\text{opt}}(v,T)$, denoted by $\tilde{\mathcal{R}}^{\sup}_{\delta,\text{opt}}(v,k)$. As a result we have:

$$\tilde{\mathcal{R}}^{\sup}_{\delta,\text{opt}}(v,k) = \operatorname*{opt}_{tr\in\mathbf{T}(v)}{}_{v} \left(\widetilde{Acc}_{\delta,tr}(v,k) + \mathrm{e}^{-\lambda_{tr}\cdot\delta}\tilde{\mathcal{R}}^{\sup}_{\delta,\text{opt}}(v,k-1)\right) \tag{6}$$

$\widetilde{Acc}_{\delta,tr}$ and $\tilde{\mathcal{R}}^{\sup}_{\delta,\text{opt}}$ both count the number of discretisation steps instead of real time. This makes their computation tractable.

$$\begin{aligned}\widetilde{Acc}_{\delta,\text{opt}}(v,k) &= \left(\rho_i(tr) + \tfrac{\rho_t(tr)}{\lambda_{tr}}\right)\left(1 - \mathrm{e}^{-\lambda_{tr}\cdot\delta}\right)\\ &\quad + \int_0^{\delta} \lambda_{tr}\mathrm{e}^{-\lambda_{tr}\cdot t} \sum_{v'\in V} \mu_{tr}(v')\tilde{\mathcal{R}}^{\sup}_{\text{opt}}(v',k-1)\,\mathrm{d}t \\ &= \Big(\rho_i(tr) + \tfrac{\rho_t(tr)}{\lambda_{tr}} + \sum_{v'\in V}\mu_{tr}(v')\tilde{\mathcal{R}}^{\sup}_{\text{opt}}(v',k-1)\Big)\left(1-\mathrm{e}^{-\lambda_{tr}\cdot\delta}\right)\end{aligned} \tag{7}$$

By using Eq. (6) instead of the Markovian part in Eq. (3) of the fixed point characterisation in Lemma 1, we get a discretised fixed point characterisation which is directly computable.

Definition 8 (Discretised maximum time-bounded reward). *Given an SRG $(\mathcal{G}, \rho_t, \rho_i)$, a time bound $T \geq 0$, and a step size $\delta > 0$ such that $T = k \cdot \delta$ for $k \in \mathbb{N}$. Let* $\text{opt} \in \{\inf, \sup\}$, $\text{opt}_v = \sup$ *if $v \in V_1$ and* $\text{opt}_v = \text{opt}$ *otherwise.* $\mathcal{R}^{\sup}_{\text{opt}}(\cdot, T)$ *is the least fixed point of the higher order operator* $\Omega^{\delta}_{\text{opt}} : (V \times \mathbb{N} \mapsto \mathbb{R}^{\geq 0}) \mapsto (V \times \mathbb{N} \mapsto \mathbb{R}^{\geq 0})$ *such that*

$$\Omega^{\delta}_{\text{opt}}(F)(v,k) = \underset{tr\in\mathbf{T}(v)}{\text{opt}_v} \begin{cases} \Big(\rho_i(tr) + \frac{\rho_t(tr)}{\lambda_{tr}} + \sum_{v'\in V}\mu_{tr}(v')F(v',k-1)\Big)\cdot\left(1-\mathrm{e}^{-\lambda_{tr}\delta}\right) & \\ +\mathrm{e}^{-\lambda_{tr}\delta}F(v,k-1), & \text{if } v \in \mathbf{T}_M(v), \\ \rho_i(tr) + \sum_{v'\in V}\mu_{tr}(v')F(v',k), & \text{if } v \in \mathbf{T}_P(v). \end{cases} \tag{8}$$

Discretisation Error. This section evaluates the precision of the discretisation technique described above. The discretisation technique can be applied to any kind of SRG respecting Def. 2. Its precision can be accordingly assessed for the general class of SRGs. However, opt-AISRGs obtained from MA abstraction have a special structure, namely all their Markovian transitions are controlled by player 2. For this specific structure it is usually possible to find a tighter error bound for time-bounded analysis (see for example [26]). Hence we restrict ourselves to a subclass of SRGs whose Markovian transitions (if there are any) are controlled by one player. In other words, the discretisation of models in this subclass in general introduces a smaller error compared to the general class of SRGs. The subclass is formally defined as:

Definition 9 (Single Markovian Controller SRG). *$\mathcal{G}_{rew} = (\mathcal{G}, \rho_t, \rho_i)$ is called a single Markovian controller SRG (1MC-SRG) iff either $\forall tr \in \mathbf{T}_M : tr \in \mathbf{T}_M(v) \Rightarrow v \in V_1$ or $\forall tr \in \mathbf{T}_M : tr \in \mathbf{T}_M(v) \Rightarrow v \in V_2$.*

The accuracy of $\tilde{\mathcal{R}}^{\sup}_{\text{opt}}$ depends on some parameters including the step size δ. The smaller δ is, the better is the quality of the discretisation. In order to assess the accuracy of the discretisation we first need to define some parameters of SRGs.

Definition 10. *Given an SRG $\mathcal{G}_{rew} = (\mathcal{G}, \rho_t, \rho_i)$, we define the maximum (finite) exit rate existing in $\mathcal{G}$ as $\bar{\mathsf{e}} = \max_{tr \in \mathbf{T}_M} \lambda_{tr}$, and the maximum transient reward existing in ρ_t as $\bar{\mathsf{r}}_t = \max_{tr \in \mathbf{T}} \rho_t(tr)$. Moreover, let $\bar{\mathsf{r}}_i$ be the maximum instantaneous reward that can be earned between two consecutive Markovian jumps. This value can be efficiently computed via the Bellman equation given in [9, Theorem 1] after assigning zero value to all transient rewards.*

The following theorem quantifies the quality of the discretisation.

Theorem 2. *Given an 1MC-SRG $\mathcal{G}_{rew} = (\mathcal{G}, \rho_t, \rho_i)$, time bound $T > 0$ and discretisation step $\delta > 0$ such that $T = k\delta$ for some $k \in \mathbb{N}$. Then for all $v \in V$ we have:*

$$\tilde{\mathcal{R}}^{\sup}_{\delta,\mathrm{opt}}(v,k) \leq \mathcal{R}^{\sup}_{\mathrm{opt}}(v,T) \leq \tilde{\mathcal{R}}^{\sup}_{\delta,\mathrm{opt}}(v,k) + \tfrac{\bar{\mathsf{e}}T}{2}(\bar{\mathsf{r}}_t + \bar{\mathsf{e}}\bar{\mathsf{r}}_i)(1 + \tfrac{\bar{\mathsf{e}}T}{2})\delta$$

Using Theorem 2 it is possible to find a step size that respects a given predefined accuracy level. The proposed error bound is a linear approximation of the original bound (see [16]), which is a more complicated function with the same set of parameters. Since the original bound is tighter, in practice it is used for finding an appropriate step size by applying Newton's method.

3.3 Initial Abstraction and Labelling Function

An important part of the abstraction and later the refinement process is starting with a suitable initial partition $\mathcal{P}$ and labelling function *lab*. On the one hand, if $\mathcal{P}$ is too coarse the resulting game abstraction requires many refinement steps until the desired accuracy is reached. On the other hand, if $\mathcal{P}$ is unnecessarily fine the resulting abstraction will not be able to reduce the size of the state space sufficiently.

A simple way to obtain a partition [12] is by exploiting the actions of the probabilistic transitions in an MA. They are used for synchronisation of different MA. The partition contains one block with all Markovian states and groups the probabilistic states according to the action labels available in a state. The labelling function is given by the action labels of the transitions.

However, experiments have shown that in such a partition transitions in the same block that are labelled with the same action may exhibit very different behaviour. Therefore they trigger refinement steps which can be avoided by a labelling function that takes the similarities of transitions into account. To achieve this, we first define a new initial partition: The Markovian states form one block of $\mathcal{P}$; the probabilistic states are grouped according to the number of outgoing transitions:

$$\mathcal{P} = \{MS\} \,\dot{\cup}\, \{\{v \in PS \mid |\mathbf{T}(v)| = |\mathbf{T}(v')|\} \mid v' \in PS\}.$$

Based on this partition we compute the labelling function *lab*, using a greedy strategy as follows: All Markovian transitions are labelled with $\perp$ as required by

Def. 4. For the transitions of a probabilistic block $B \subseteq PS$ we proceed as follows: We take an arbitrary state $v \in B$ (actually the first one in our list of states) and assign each transition $tr \in \mathbf{T}(v)$ a unique label $lab(tr) := \alpha_{tr}$. Running over the transitions $tr \in \mathbf{T}(v)$, we choose from each state $v' \in B$ with $v' \neq v$ a transition $tr' \in \mathbf{T}(v')$ which is not labelled yet and minimises $m_{\mathcal{P}}(\mu_{tr}, \mu_{tr'})$ defined as follows:

$$m_{\mathcal{P}} : \mathrm{Distr}(V) \times \mathrm{Distr}(V) \to [0,2] \text{ with } m_{\mathcal{P}}(\mu, \mu') = \sum_{B' \in \mathcal{P}} \left|\mu(B') - \mu'(B')\right|.$$

The function $m_{\mathcal{P}}$ is a *pseudo-metric*[3] that measures the similarity of probability distributions with respect to a partition $\mathcal{P}$. Formally we take for each state $v' \in B$ with $v' \neq v$ an arbitrary

$$tr' \in \operatorname*{arg\,min}_{\substack{tr'' \in \mathbf{T}(v') \\ lab(tr'') \text{ is undefined}}} m_{\mathcal{P}}(\mu_{tr}, \mu_{tr''})$$

and set $lab(tr') := \alpha_{tr}$.

By labelling the transitions in this way we ensure that more similar probabilistic transitions belong to the same probabilistic $\overline{V_2}$-state, which prevents unnecessary splitting operations during refinement. Since all states within one probabilistic block B get the same set of labels with this labelling function, we do not need to introduce the $*$-state.

3.4 Refinement

We approximate the maximal ETR $\mathcal{R}^{\sup}$ of an MRA $\mathcal{M}_{rew}$ by computing a lower and an upper bound $\tilde{\mathcal{R}}^{\sup}_{\delta,\inf}$ and $\tilde{\mathcal{R}}^{\sup}_{\delta,\sup}$ with a game abstraction $\overline{\mathcal{M}}^{\mathcal{P},lab}$ and the abstract reward functions $\overline{\rho_t}^{\text{opt}}$ and $\overline{\rho_i}^{\text{opt}}$. If these bounds are too far apart, i. e. $\tilde{\mathcal{R}}^{\sup}_{\delta,\sup} - \tilde{\mathcal{R}}^{\sup}_{\delta,\inf} > \varepsilon$, with ε being a precision threshold, our abstraction is too coarse and needs to be refined. The result of the refinement is a new partition, which in turn leads to a new game abstraction. This refinement-loop is repeated until the intended precision threshold ε is reached.

The reason behind the difference of the bounds can be two different situations: (1) The difference occurs due to different choices in the player 2 strategies $\sigma_2^{\inf}$ and $\sigma_2^{\sup}$. (2) The difference is a result of the different reward structures. In case (1) we can use a strategy-based refinement strategy like in [12]. In case (2) we have to use a refinement strategy based on the reward values.

For this *value-based* refinement strategy we first have to search for a $\overline{V_2}$-state $\overline{v}$ where the values for $\tilde{\mathcal{R}}^{\sup}_{\delta,\inf}$ and $\tilde{\mathcal{R}}^{\sup}_{\delta,\sup}$ differ and the reward functions give different values. More precisely, this means that we have to search for an abstract transition $\overline{tr} \in \overline{\mathbf{T}}$ which was chosen by $\sigma_2^{\inf}$ and $\sigma_2^{\sup}$ and where $\left[\overline{\rho_i}^{\text{opt}}(\overline{tr}) + \frac{\overline{\rho_t}^{\text{opt}}(\overline{tr})}{\lambda_{\overline{tr}}}\right] = r_{\text{opt}}$, $\text{opt} \in \{\inf, \sup\}$, and $r_{\inf} \neq r_{\sup}$.

[3] The function $m_{\mathcal{P}}$ has the following properties: $m_{\mathcal{P}}(\mu, \mu') = m_{\mathcal{P}}(\mu', \mu)$, $m_{\mathcal{P}}(\mu, \mu'') \leq m_{\mathcal{P}}(\mu, \mu') + m_{\mathcal{P}}(\mu', \mu'')$, and $m_{\mathcal{P}}(\mu, \mu) = 0$ for all distributions μ, μ', μ''. However, it is not a metric because $m_{\mathcal{P}}(\mu, \mu') = 0$ does not imply that $\mu = \mu'$ holds.

If we have found such an abstract transition $\overline{tr}$, we split the preceding block B. For this we compute two sets of concrete states, one ($B_{r_{\inf}}$) containing the states with reward $r_{\inf}$, the other ($B_{r_{\sup}}$) containing the states with reward $r_{\sup}$: $B_{r_{\text{opt}}} = \left\{ v \mid v \in B \wedge (v, \lambda, \mu) = tr \in \nu(\overline{tr}) \wedge \left[\rho_i(tr) + \frac{\rho_t(tr)}{\lambda_{tr}}\right] = r_{\text{opt}} \right\}$ with $\text{opt} \in \{\inf, \sup\}$.

In case of an abstract Markovian transition $\overline{tr}$ it may occur that $B_{r_{\text{opt}}} = \emptyset$ since it is possible that no concrete transition $tr \in \nu(\overline{tr})$ matches the constraints. Should this happen for both $B_{r_{\text{opt}}}$ we use the concrete transitions tr which optimise $\left[\rho_i(tr) + \frac{\rho_t(tr)}{\lambda_{tr}}\right]$ instead.

After we have generated the concrete state sets for the minimal and maximal reward, we replace B with $B_{r_{\inf}}$, $B_{r_{\sup}}$ and $B \setminus \left(B_{r_{\inf}} \dot\cup B_{r_{\sup}}\right)$.

Block B is replaced by at least two and at most three new blocks, which leads to a new, strictly finer partition and thus to a new game abstraction of $\mathcal{M}_{rew}$, which in turn can be analysed and refined. This refinement-loop is repeated until the precision threshold ε is reached.

Similar to [12] we apply a "precision trick", i. e. we start with a coarse, temporary precision threshold $\hat{\varepsilon}$ for the refinement-loop. If precision $\hat{\varepsilon}$ is reached, we switch to a higher precision, i. e. we lower $\hat{\varepsilon}$ and continue the refinement-loop. This process is repeated until the final precision ε is reached.

Zenoness. Although we assume the considered MRA $\mathcal{M}_{rew}$ is non-Zeno, i. e. it does not contain probabilistic end components, it may happen that Zenoness is introduced into the abstraction $\overline{\mathcal{M}}_{rew}^{\mathcal{P},lab}$. This occurs, e. g. if a non-cyclic sequence of probabilistic states is partitioned into the same block $B \in \mathcal{P}$. If the instantaneous reward function ρ_i is non-zero within the end component, the value iteration will not terminate since the accumulated reward does not converge.

We avoid this effect with the following method: Before applying value iteration to solve the discretised fixed point characterisation, we employ a standard graph algorithm [27] to search for end components in $\overline{\mathcal{M}}_{rew}^{\mathcal{P},lab}$. If a probabilistic end component is found, we refine the corresponding blocks B into smaller blocks and recompute the abstraction. This process is repeated until all probabilistic end components have been removed. Since there are no probabilistic end components present in $\mathcal{M}_{rew}$, our method will always terminate.

4 Experimental Results

We implemented the described abstraction and refinement framework in C++ in a prototype tool called MeGARA. As mentioned earlier, we are currently concentrating on the maximal ETR only, using discretisation (see Sec. 3.2). We compare our experimental results with those of IMCA [10,7,9], an analyser for MA and IMCs. For our experiments we used the following case studies:

The **Polling System** (PoS) [7,28] consists of two stations and one server. Incoming requests are stored within two queues until they are delivered by the server to their station. With a probability of $p = 0.1$ a request erroneously stays in the queue after if it was delivered to a station. In our experiments we varied

Table 1. Results for the polling system and the queueing system

Name	IMCA			MeGARA				
	#states	r	time	#states	r_{lb}	r_{ub}	#iter.	time
PoS-3-2	1,547	0.830	0:04	657	0.828	0.830	17	0:02
PoS-3-3	14,322	0.922	1:06	5,011	0.920	0.921	19	1:16
PoS-3-4	79,307	0.985	10:59	11,527	0.982	0.985	20	7:02
PoS-4-2	6,667	0.832	0:20	1,513	0.829	0.831	18	0:12
PoS-4-3	131,529	0.924	13:46	**31,992**	0.922	0.923	22	8:55
PoS-5-2	27,659	0.833	1:47	**2,006**	0.830	0.832	18	0:23
QS-2	103	1.768	0:04	76	1.768	1.768	9	0:01
QS-3	163	2.307	0:10	118	2.306	2.306	10	0:02
QS-4	237	2.679	0:19	167	2.678	2.680	13	0:07
QS-8	673	3.351	1:47	455	3.351	3.351	17	0:33
QS-16	2,217	3.530	12:07	1,039	3.530	3.530	24	**2:33**
QS-32	7,993	TO		3,286	3.532	3.532	40	**57:43**

the queue size Q and the number of different request types J. The rewards in this case study represent costs for processing requests and consuming server memory. The model instances are denoted as "PoS-Q-J".

The **Queueing System** (QS) [6] stores requests within two queues of size K, each belonging to a server. Server S_1 handles requests and eliminates them from its queue. Requests processed by server S_2 are either nondeterministically submitted to the queue of S_1, or with probability $q = 0.3$ re-submitted to the queue of S_2, or with probability $(1-q)$ eliminated from the queue. With the help of rewards we explore the average number of jobs in the queues. For our experiments we varied the queue size K. The model instances are denoted as "QS-K".

We created the model files with SCOOP [5], a modelling tool for MA. All experiments were done on a Dual Core AMD Opteron processor with 2.4 GHz per core and 64 GB of memory. Computations which took longer than one hour were aborted and are marked with "TO". Each computation needed less than 4 GB memory, we therefore do not present measurements of the memory consumption.

For all experiments we used time bound $T = 1$ and precision $\varepsilon = 0.01$ in order to compute the maximal ETR.

Table 1 shows the experimental results. The first column contains the name of the respective benchmark instance, the blocks titled "IMCA" and "MeGARA" present the results from IMCA and our abstraction refinement tool, respectively. The columns headed with "#states" give the number of states of the concrete system (in case of IMCA) and the final abstraction (in case of MeGARA). The benchmarks instances are relatively small since the solving of discretised systems is rather expensive [29].

Column "r" contains the maximal ETR computed by IMCA, whereas the columns "r_{lb}" and "r_{ub}" denote the lower and the upper bounds for the abstraction. The columns titled "time" present the total computation time (in format min:s) needed by IMCA and MeGARA, respectively. For our abstraction refinement tool we do not give more detailed time measurements since the better part of the computation time is needed for the repeated analysis of the abstraction, whereas the time needed for the refinement and re-computation of the abstraction is often negligible. For example, for QS-32 we need 57 min and 43 s, of which 57 min and 41 s are spent on the analysis, whereas the time spent on re-computing and refining the abstraction is less than 2 s.

For the instances of PoS our tool needs about the same amount of time as IMCA or is even faster, for the instances of QS we are always faster. As can be seen from the columns "r_{lb}" and "r_{ub}" the quality of our abstraction is always very good. In some cases the value "r" computed by IMCA is slightly higher than r_{ub}, however this deviation is always well within our precision threshold of $\varepsilon = 0.01$. We always achieve a notable compaction of the state space, even for the smallest instances with only a few hundred states. For the bigger instances we can report on compaction rates up to 92 %, e. g. for PoS-5-J we can reduce the system from 27,659 to 2,006 states.

5 Conclusion

We have presented a new abstraction technique for MRA, based on SRGs. We are able to analyse our abstraction regarding ETR properties. Should the quality of the abstraction be too low, we can apply scheduler- and value-based refinement methods. Our experiments show a significant compaction of the state space and a reduction of computation times.

In the future we plan to explore the possibilities of different initial partitions, labelling functions, and refinement techniques. We also plan to work on additional types of properties, e. g. bounded rewards or long-run average.

References

1. Eisentraut, C., Hermanns, H., Zhang, L.: On probabilistic automata in continuous time. In: Proc. of LICS, pp. 342–351. IEEE CS (2010)
2. Hermanns, H. (ed.): Interactive Markov Chains. LNCS, vol. 2428. Springer, Heidelberg (2002)
3. Eisentraut, C., Hermanns, H., Katoen, J.-P., Zhang, L.: A semantics for every GSPN. In: Colom, J.-M., Desel, J. (eds.) PETRI NETS 2013. LNCS, vol. 7927, pp. 90–109. Springer, Heidelberg (2013)
4. Meyer, J.F., Movaghar, A., Sanders, W.H.: Stochastic activity networks: Structure, behavior, and application. In: Proc. of PNPM, pp. 106–115. IEEE CS (1985)
5. Timmer, M., Katoen, J.-P., van de Pol, J., Stoelinga, M.I.A.: Efficient modelling and generation of markov automata. In: Koutny, M., Ulidowski, I. (eds.) CONCUR 2012. LNCS, vol. 7454, pp. 364–379. Springer, Heidelberg (2012)
6. Hatefi, H., Hermanns, H.: Model checking algorithms for Markov automata. ECEASST 53 (2012)
7. Guck, D., Hatefi, H., Hermanns, H., Katoen, J.-P., Timmer, M.: Modelling, reduction and analysis of Markov automata. In: Joshi, K., Siegle, M., Stoelinga, M., D'Argenio, P.R. (eds.) QEST 2013. LNCS, vol. 8054, pp. 55–71. Springer, Heidelberg (2013)
8. Guck, D., Hatefi, H., Hermanns, H., Katoen, J., Timmer, M.: Analysis of timed and long-run objectives for markov automata. Logical Methods in Computer Science 10(3) (2014)
9. Guck, D., Timmer, M., Hatefi, H., Ruijters, E., Stoelinga, M.: Modelling and analysis of Markov reward automata. In: Cassez, F., Raskin, J.-F. (eds.) ATVA 2014. LNCS, vol. 8837, pp. 168–184. Springer, Heidelberg (2014)
10. Guck, D., Han, T., Katoen, J.-P., Neuhäußer, M.R.: Quantitative timed analysis of interactive Markov chains. In: Goodloe, A.E., Person, S. (eds.) NFM 2012. LNCS, vol. 7226, pp. 8–23. Springer, Heidelberg (2012)

11. Kattenbelt, M., Kwiatkowska, M.Z., Norman, G., Parker, D.: A game-based abstraction-refinement framework for Markov decision processes. Formal Methods in System Design 36(3), 246–280 (2010)
12. Braitling, B., Ferrer Fioriti, L.M., Hatefi, H., Wimmer, R., Becker, B., Hermanns, H.: MeGARA: Menu-based game abstraction and abstraction refinement of Markov automata. In: Proc. of QAPL. EPTCS, vol. 154, pp. 48–63 (2014)
13. D'Argenio, P.R., Jeannet, B., Jensen, H.E., Larsen, K.G.: Reduction and refinement strategies for probabilistic analysis. In: Hermanns, H., Segala, R. (eds.) PAPM-PROBMIV 2002. LNCS, vol. 2399, pp. 57–76. Springer, Heidelberg (2002)
14. Wachter, B., Zhang, L.: Best probabilistic transformers. In: Barthe, G., Hermenegildo, M. (eds.) VMCAI 2010. LNCS, vol. 5944, pp. 362–379. Springer, Heidelberg (2010)
15. Wachter, B.: Refined probabilistic abstraction. PhD thesis, Saarland University (2011)
16. Braitling, B., Ferrer Fioriti, L.M., Hatefi, H., Wimmer, R., Hermanns, H., Becker, B.: Abstraction-based computation of reward measures for Markov automata (extended version). Reports of SFB/TR 14 AVACS 106, SFB/TR 14 AVACS (2014), `http://www.avacs.org`
17. Neuhäußer, M.R., Zhang, L.: Time-bounded reachability probabilities in continuous-time Markov decision processes. In: Proc. of QEST, pp. 209–218. IEEE CS (2010)
18. Ash, R.B., Doléans-Dade, C.A.: Probability & Measure Theory, 2nd edn. Academic Press (1999)
19. Neuhäußer, M.R.: Model checking nondeterministic and randomly timed systems. PhD thesis, RWTH Aachen University and University of Twente (2010)
20. Johr, S.: Model checking compositional Markov systems. PhD thesis, Saarland University, Germany (2008)
21. Shapley, L.S.: Stochastic games. Proceedings of the National Academy of Sciences of the United States of America 39(10), 1095 (1953)
22. Brázdil, T., Forejt, V., Krcál, J., Kretínský, J., Kucera, A.: Continuous-time stochastic games with time-bounded reachability. Information and Computation 224, 46–70 (2013)
23. Baier, C., Haverkort, B.R., Hermanns, H., Katoen, J.P.: Model-checking algorithms for continuous-time markov chains. IEEE Trans. Software Eng. 29(6), 524–541 (2003)
24. Eisentraut, C., Hermanns, H., Zhang, L.: Concurrency and composition in a stochastic world. In: Gastin, P., Laroussinie, F. (eds.) CONCUR 2010. LNCS, vol. 6269, pp. 21–39. Springer, Heidelberg (2010)
25. Deng, Y., Hennessy, M.: On the semantics of Markov automata. Information and Computation 222, 139–168 (2013)
26. Fearnley, J., Rabe, M.N., Schewe, S., Zhang, L.: Efficient approximation of optimal control for continuous-time markov games. In: Proc. of FSTTCS. LIPIcs, vol. 13, pp. 399–410. Schloss Dagstuhl - Leibniz-Zentrum fuer Informatik (2011)
27. Chatterjee, K., Henzinger, M.: Faster and dynamic algorithms for maximal end-component decomposition and related graph problems in probabilistic verification. In: Proc. of SODA, pp. 1318–1336. SIAM (2011)
28. Timmer, M., van de Pol, J., Stoelinga, M.I.A.: Confluence reduction for Markov automata. In: Braberman, V., Fribourg, L. (eds.) FORMATS 2013. LNCS, vol. 8053, pp. 243–257. Springer, Heidelberg (2013)
29. Zhang, L., Neuhäußer, M.R.: Model checking interactive Markov chains. In: Esparza, J., Majumdar, R. (eds.) TACAS 2010. LNCS, vol. 6015, pp. 53–68. Springer, Heidelberg (2010)

Proving Guarantee and Recurrence Temporal Properties by Abstract Interpretation*

Caterina Urban and Antoine Miné

ÉNS & CNRS & INRIA, France
{urban,mine}@di.ens.fr

Dedicated to the memory of Radhia Cousot

Abstract. We present new static analysis methods for proving *liveness properties* of programs. In particular, with reference to the hierarchy of temporal properties proposed by Manna and Pnueli, we focus on guarantee (i.e., "something good occurs *at least once*") and recurrence (i.e., "something good occurs *infinitely often*") temporal properties.

We generalize the abstract interpretation framework for termination presented by Cousot and Cousot. Specifically, static analyses of guarantee and recurrence temporal properties are systematically derived by abstraction of the program operational trace semantics.

These methods automatically infer *sufficient preconditions* for the temporal properties by reusing existing numerical abstract domains based on piecewise-defined ranking functions. We augment these abstract domains with new abstract operators, including a *dual widening*.

To illustrate the potential of the proposed methods, we have implemented a research prototype static analyzer, for programs written in a C-like syntax, that yielded interesting preliminary results.

1 Introduction

Temporal properties play a major role in the specification and verification of programs. The hierarchy of temporal properties proposed by Manna and Pnueli [15] distinguishes four basic classes:

- *safety* properties: "something good *always* happens", i.e., the program never reaches an unacceptable state (e.g., partial correctness, mutual exclusion);
- *guarantee* properties: "something good happens *at least once*", i.e., the program *eventually* reaches a desirable state (e.g., termination);
- *recurrence* properties: "something good happens *infinitely often*", i.e., the program reaches a desirable state *infinitely often* (e.g., starvation freedom);
- *persistence* properties: "something good *eventually* happens *continuously*".

* The research leading to these results has received funding from the ARTEMIS Joint Undertaking under grant agreement no. 269335 (ARTEMIS project MBAT) (see Article II.9. of the JU Grant Agreement).

D. D'Souza et al. (Eds.): VMCAI 2015, LNCS 8931, pp. 190–208, 2015.

$$\text{while }^1(\ x\ \geq\ 0\ )\text{ do }^2x\ :=\ x\ +\ 1;$$
$$\text{while }^3(\ true\ )\text{ do}$$
$$\text{if }^4(\ x\leq\ 10\ )\text{ then }^5x\ :=\ x\ +\ 1;\ \text{ else }^6x\ :=\ -\ x;\ \text{ fi}$$

Fig. 1. Program SIMPLE

This paper concerns the verification of programs by static analysis. We set our work in the framework of Abstract Interpretation [9], a general theory of semantic approximation that provides a basis for various successful industrial-scale tools (e.g., Astrée [1]). Abstract Interpretation has to a large extent concerned safety properties and has only recently been extended to program termination [11], which is just a particular guarantee property.

In this paper, we generalize the framework proposed by Cousot and Cousot for termination [11] and we propose an abstract interpretation framework for proving *guarantee* and *recurrence* temporal properties of programs. Moreover, we present new static analysis methods for inferring *sufficient preconditions* for these temporal properties. Let us consider the program SIMPLE in Figure 1, where the program variables are interpreted in the set of mathematical integers[1]. The first while loop is an infinite loop for the values of x greater than or equal to zero: at each iteration the value of x is increased by one. The second while loop is an infinite loop: at each iteration, the value of x is increased by one or negated when it becomes greater than ten. Given the guarantee property "$x = 3$ at least once", where $x = 3$ is the desirable state, our approach is able to automatically infer that the property is true if the initial value of x is smaller than or equal to three. Given the recurrence property "$x = 3$ infinitely often", our approach is able to automatically infer that the property is true if the initial value of x is strictly negative (i.e., if the first while loop is never entered).

Our approach follows the traditional methods for proving liveness properties by means of a well-founded argument (i.e., a function from the states of a program to a well-ordered set whose value decreases during program execution). More precisely, we build a well-founded argument for guarantee and recurrence properties in an incremental way: we start from the desirable program states, where the function has value zero (and is undefined elsewhere); then, we add states to the domain of the function, retracing the program backwards and counting the maximum number of performed program steps as value of the function. Additionally, for recurrence properties, this process is iteratively repeated in order to construct an argument that is also invariant with respect to program execution steps so that even after reaching a desirable state we know that the execution will reach a desirable state again. We formalize these intuitions into *sound* and *complete* guarantee and recurrence semantics that are systematically derived by abstract interpretation of the program operational trace semantics.

In order to achieve effective static analyses, we further abstract these semantics. Specifically, we leverage existing numerical abstract domains based on

[1] For simplicity, this assumption remains valid throughout the rest of the paper.

piecewise-defined ranking functions [21,22,23] by introducing new abstract operators, including a *dual widening*. The piecewise-defined ranking functions are attached to the program control points and represent an *upper bound* on the number of program execution steps before the program reaches a desirable state. They are automatically inferred through backward analysis and yield *sufficient preconditions* for the guarantee and recurrence temporal properties. We prove the soundness of the analysis, meaning that all program executions respecting these preconditions indeed satisfy the temporal properties, while a program execution that does not respect these preconditions might or might not satisfy the temporal properties.

To illustrate the potential of our approach, let us consider again the program SIMPLE in Figure 1. Given the guarantee property "$x = 3$ at least once", the piecewise-defined ranking function inferred at program control point 1 is:

$$f_1^g(x) = \begin{cases} -3x + 10 & x < 0 \\ -2x + 6 & x \geq 0 \wedge x \leq 3 \\ \text{undefined} & \text{otherwise} \end{cases}$$

which bounds the wait (from the control point 1) for the desirable state $x = 3$ by $-3x + 10$ program execution steps if $x < 0$, and by $-2x + 6$ execution steps if $x \geq 0 \ \wedge \ x \leq 3$. In case $x > 3$, the analysis is inconclusive. In fact, if $x > 3$ the guarantee property is never true so the precondition $x \leq 3$ for the guarantee property is the weakest precondition. Given the recurrence property "$x = 3$ infinitely often", the piecewise-defined ranking function at program point 1 bounds the wait for the *next* occurrence of the desirable state $x = 3$ by $-3x+10$ program execution steps:

$$f_1^r(x) = \begin{cases} -3x + 10 & x < 0 \\ \text{undefined} & \text{otherwise} \end{cases}$$

Note that, if $x \geq 0 \wedge x \leq 3$, $x = 3$ occurs once but not infinitely often: f_1^g is defined for $x \geq 0 \wedge x \leq 3$ but not f_1^r. Again, the sufficient precondition $x < 0$ is also a necessary precondition. At program point 3 (i.e., at the beginning of the second while loop), we get the following piecewise-defined ranking function:

$$f_3^g(x) = f_3^r(x) = \begin{cases} -3x + 9 & x \leq 3 \\ -3x + 72 & x > 3 \end{cases}$$

which bounds the wait (from the control point 3) for the next occurrence of $x = 3$ by $-3x + 9$ execution steps if $x \leq 3$, and by $-3x + 72$ execution steps if $x > 3$.

Our Contribution. In summary, this paper makes the following contributions. First, we present an abstract interpretation framework for proving *guarantee* and *recurrence* temporal properties of programs. In particular, we generalize the framework proposed by Cousot and Cousot for termination [11]. Moreover, by means of piecewise-defined ranking function abstract domains [21,22,23], we design new static analysis methods to effectively infer *sufficient preconditions* for these temporal properties, and provide *upper bounds* in terms of program execution steps on the wait before a program reaches a desirable state. Finally, we provide a research prototype static analyzer for programs written in a C-like syntax.

Limitations. In general, liveness properties are used to specify the behavior of *concurrent* programs and are satisfied only under *fairness* hypotheses. In this paper, we model concurrent programs as non-deterministic sequential programs and we assume that the fair scheduler is explicitly represented within the program (e.g., see [13] and Example 6 in Section 8). We plan, as part of our future work, to extend our framework in order to explicitly express and handle fairness properties.

Outline of the Paper. Section 2 introduces the preliminary notions used in the paper. In Section 3, we give a brief overview of Cousot and Cousot's abstract interpretation framework for termination. In Section 4, we define a small specification language to describe guarantee and recurrence properties. The next two sections are devoted to the main contribution of the paper: we formalize our framework for guarantee and recurrence properties in Section 5 and in Section 6, respectively. In Section 7, we present decidable guarantee and recurrence abstractions based on piecewise-defined ranking functions. We describe our prototype static analyzer in Section 8. Finally, Section 9 discusses related work and Section 10 concludes.

2 Trace Semantics

Following [8,11], as a model of the operational semantics of a program, we use a *transition system* $\langle \Sigma, \tau \rangle$, where Σ is the (possibly infinite) set of program states and the program transition relation $\tau \subseteq \Sigma \times \Sigma$ describes the possible transitions between states during program execution. Note that this model allows representing programs with (possibly unbounded) non-determinism.

Let Σ^n be the set of all finite program state sequences of length $n \in \mathbb{N}$. We use ε to denote the empty sequence, i.e., $\Sigma^0 \triangleq \{\varepsilon\}$. The set of final states $\Omega \triangleq \{s \in \Sigma \mid \forall s' \in \Sigma : \langle s, s' \rangle \notin \tau\}$ can be understood as a set of sequences of length one and the program transition relation τ can be understood as a set of sequences of length two. Let $\Sigma^+ \triangleq \bigcup_{n \in \mathbb{N}^+} \Sigma^n$ be the set of all non-empty finite sequences, $\Sigma^* \triangleq \Sigma^0 \cup \Sigma^+$ be the set of all finite sequences, Σ^ω be the set of all infinite sequences, $\Sigma^{+\infty} \triangleq \Sigma^+ \cup \Sigma^\omega$ be the set of all non-empty finite or infinite sequences and $\Sigma^{*\infty} \triangleq \Sigma^* \cup \Sigma^\omega$ be the set of all finite or infinite sequences. We write $\sigma\sigma'$ for the concatenation of sequences $\sigma, \sigma' \in \Sigma^{+\infty}$ (with $\sigma\epsilon = \epsilon\sigma = \sigma$ and $\sigma\sigma' = \sigma$ when $\sigma \in \Sigma^\omega$), $T^+ \triangleq T \cap \Sigma^+$ for the selection of the non-empty finite sequences of $T \subseteq \Sigma^{+\infty}$, $T^\omega \triangleq T \cap \Sigma^\omega$ for the selection of the infinite sequences of $T \subseteq \Sigma^{+\infty}$ and $T \,;\, T' \triangleq \{\sigma s \sigma' \mid s \in \Sigma \wedge \sigma s \in T \wedge s\sigma' \in T'\}$ for the merging of sets of sequences $T, T' \subseteq \Sigma^{+\infty}$.

The *maximal trace semantics* $\tau^{+\infty} \subseteq \Sigma^{+\infty}$ generated by a transition system $\langle \Sigma, \tau \rangle$ is the union of the set of all non-empty finite program execution traces that are terminating with a final state, and the set of all infinite execution traces. It can be expressed as a least fixpoint in the complete lattice $\langle \Sigma^{+\infty}, \sqsubseteq, \sqcup, \sqcap, \Sigma^{\omega}, \Sigma^{+} \rangle$ [8]:

$$\begin{aligned} \tau^{+\infty} &\triangleq \mathrm{lfp}^{\sqsubseteq}\, \phi^{+\infty} \\ \phi^{+\infty}(T) &\triangleq \Omega \sqcup (\tau \,;\, T) \end{aligned} \tag{1}$$

where $T_1 \sqsubseteq T_2 \triangleq T_1^{+} \subseteq T_2^{+} \wedge T_1^{\omega} \supseteq T_2^{\omega}$ and $T_1 \sqcup T_2 \triangleq (T_1^{+} \cup T_2^{+}) \cup (T_1^{\omega} \cap T_2^{\omega})$.

3 Termination Semantics

The Floyd/Turing traditional method for proving program termination [12] consists in inferring ranking functions, namely mappings from program states to elements of a well-ordered set (e.g., $\langle \mathbb{O}, < \rangle$, the well-ordered set of ordinals) whose value decreases during program execution.

In [11], Cousot and Cousot prove the existence of a *most precise program ranking function*[2] $\tau^{\mathrm{t}} \in \Sigma \rightharpoonup \mathbb{O}$ that can be expressed in fixpoint form as follows:

$$\begin{aligned} \tau^{\mathrm{t}} &\triangleq \mathrm{lfp}^{\preccurlyeq}_{\dot{\emptyset}}\, \phi^{\mathrm{t}} \\ \phi^{\mathrm{t}}(v) &\triangleq \lambda s. \begin{cases} 0 & s \in \Omega \\ \sup\{v(s') + 1 \mid \langle s, s' \rangle \in \tau\} & s \in \widetilde{\mathrm{pre}}(\mathrm{dom}(v)) \\ \text{undefined} & \text{otherwise} \end{cases} \end{aligned} \tag{2}$$

where $\dot{\emptyset}$ is the totally undefined function, $v_1 \preccurlyeq v_2 \triangleq \mathrm{dom}(v_1) \subseteq \mathrm{dom}(v_2) \wedge \forall x \in \mathrm{dom}(v_1) : v_1(x) \leq v_2(x)$ and $\widetilde{\mathrm{pre}}(X) \triangleq \{s \in \Sigma \mid \forall s' \in \Sigma : \langle s, s' \rangle \in \tau \Rightarrow s' \in X\}$.

The most precise ranking function τ^{t} extracts the well-founded part of the transition relation τ: starting from the final states in Ω, where the function has value zero, and retracing the program backwards while mapping each program state in Σ definitely leading to a final state (i.e., a program state such that all the traces to which it belongs are terminating) to an ordinal in $\mathbb{O}$ representing an upper bound on the number of program execution steps remaining to termination. The domain $\mathrm{dom}(\tau^{\mathrm{t}})$ of τ^{t} is the set of states definitely leading to program termination; any trace starting in a state $s \in \mathrm{dom}(\tau^{\mathrm{t}})$ must terminate in at most $\tau^{\mathrm{t}}(s)$ execution steps, while at least one trace starting in a state $s \notin \mathrm{dom}(\tau^{\mathrm{t}})$ does not terminate:

Theorem 1. *A program terminates for all execution traces starting from an initial state $s \in \Sigma$ if and only if $s \in \mathrm{dom}(\tau^{\mathrm{t}})$.*

We would like to emphasize the elegance of the abstract interpretation theory which allows to tie together seemingly unrelated semantics by *different* abstractions of the *same* operational trace semantics, i.e., the maximal trace semantics

[2] $A \rightharpoonup B$ is the set of partial maps from a set A to a set B.

(1) [8]. The semantics, rather than being first derived by intuition and then proved correct, are systematically derived by abstract interpretation. Specifically, in [11], in order to derive the most precise ranking function (2), Cousot and Cousot define the following abstraction functions:

- The *prefix abstractions* $\text{pf} \in \Sigma^{+\infty} \to \mathcal{P}(\Sigma^{+\infty})$ and $\text{pf} \in \mathcal{P}(\Sigma^{+\infty}) \to \mathcal{P}(\Sigma^{+\infty})$ yield respectively the set of prefixes of a sequence $\sigma \in \Sigma^{+\infty}$ and the set of prefixes of a set of sequences $T \subseteq \Sigma^{+\infty}$:

$$\begin{aligned} \text{pf}(\sigma) &\triangleq \{\sigma' \in \Sigma^{+\infty} \mid \exists \sigma'' \in \Sigma^{*\infty} : \sigma = \sigma'\sigma''\} \\ \text{pf}(T) &\triangleq \bigcup\{\text{pf}(\sigma) \mid \sigma \in T\} \end{aligned} \tag{3}$$

  The *neighborhood* of a sequence $\sigma \in \Sigma^{+\infty}$ in a set of sequences $T \subseteq \Sigma^{+\infty}$ is the set of sequences $\sigma' \in T$ with a common prefix with σ: $\{\sigma' \in T \mid \text{pf}(\sigma) \cap \text{pf}(\sigma') \neq \emptyset\}$.
- The *termination abstraction* $\alpha^{\text{t}} \in \mathcal{P}(\Sigma^{+\infty}) \to \mathcal{P}(\Sigma^{+})$ selects from a set of sequences $T \subseteq \Sigma^{+\infty}$ the sequences that are finite and whose neighborhood in T consists only of finite traces:

$$\alpha^{\text{t}}(T) \triangleq \{\sigma \in T^{+} \mid \text{pf}(\sigma) \cap \text{pf}(T^{\omega}) = \emptyset\} \tag{4}$$

  Example 1. Let $T = \{ab, aba, ba, bb, ba^{\omega}\}$, then $\alpha^{\text{t}}(T) = \{ab, aba\}$. In fact, $\text{pf}(ab) \cap \text{pf}(ba^{\omega}) = \emptyset$ and $\text{pf}(aba) \cap \text{pf}(ba^{\omega}) = \emptyset$, while $\text{pf}(ba) \cap \text{pf}(ba^{\omega}) = \{b, ba\}$ and $\text{pf}(bb) \cap \text{pf}(ba^{\omega}) = \{b\}$. □
- The *transition abstraction* $\vec{\alpha} \in \mathcal{P}(\Sigma^{+\infty}) \to \mathcal{P}(\Sigma \times \Sigma)$ extracts from a set of sequences $T \subseteq \Sigma^{+\infty}$ the smallest transition relation $r \subseteq \Sigma \times \Sigma$ that generates T:

$$\vec{\alpha}\,(T) \triangleq \{\langle s, s'\rangle \mid \exists \sigma, \sigma' \in \Sigma^{*\infty} : \sigma s s' \sigma' \in T\}$$
- The *ranking abstraction* $\alpha^{\text{rk}} \in \mathcal{P}(\Sigma \times \Sigma) \to (\Sigma \rightharpoonup \mathbb{O})$ provides the rank of the elements in the domain of a relation $r \subseteq \Sigma \times \Sigma$:

$$\alpha^{\text{rk}}(r)s \triangleq \begin{cases} 0 & \forall s' \in \Sigma : \langle s, s'\rangle \notin r \\ \sup\left\{ \alpha^{\text{rk}}(r)s' + 1 \;\middle|\; \begin{array}{c} s' \in \text{dom}(\alpha^{\text{rk}}(r)) \\ \wedge \langle s, s'\rangle \in r \end{array} \right\} & \text{otherwise} \end{cases}$$
- The *variant abstraction* $\alpha^{\text{v}} \in \mathcal{P}(\Sigma^{+}) \to (\Sigma \rightharpoonup \mathbb{O})$ provides the rank of the elements in the domain of the smallest transition relation that generates a set of sequences $T \subseteq \Sigma^{+}$:

$$\alpha^{\text{v}}(T) \triangleq \alpha^{\text{rk}}(\vec{\alpha}\,(T)) \tag{5}$$

The most precise ranking function (2) can now be explicitly defined as abstract interpretation of the program maximal trace semantics (1) [11]:

$$\tau^{\text{t}} \triangleq \alpha^{\text{v}}(\alpha^{\text{t}}(\tau^{+\infty}))$$

In Section 5 and Section 6, we will follow the same abstract interpretation approach in order to systematically derive sound and complete semantics for proving guarantee and recurrence temporal properties of programs.

$$\delta ::= X \mid n \mid -\delta \mid \delta_1 \diamond \delta_2 \qquad X \in \mathcal{X},\ n \in \mathbb{Z},\ \diamond \in \{+,-,*,/\}$$
$$\beta ::= \text{true} \mid \text{false} \mid !\beta \mid \beta_1 \vee \beta_2 \mid \beta_1 \wedge \beta_2 \mid \delta_1 \bowtie \delta_2 \qquad \bowtie \in \{<,\leq,=,\neq,>,\geq\}$$
$$\varphi ::= \beta \mid l : \beta \mid \varphi_1 \vee \varphi_2 \mid \varphi_1 \wedge \varphi_2 \qquad l \in \mathcal{L}$$

Fig. 2. Syntax of State Properties

4 Specification Language

In general, we define a program *property* as a set of sequences. A program has a certain property if all the program execution traces belong to the property. In this paper, with respect to the hierarchy of temporal properties proposed in [15], we focus on guarantee ("something good happens *at least once*") and recurrence ("something good happens *infinitely often*") properties. In particular, we consider guarantee and recurrence properties that are expressible by temporal logic.

We define a small specification language, which will be used to describe properties of program states. Let $\mathcal{X}$ be a finite set of program variables. We split the program state space Σ into program control points $\mathcal{L}$ and environments $\mathcal{E} \triangleq \mathcal{X} \to \mathbb{Z}$, which map each program variable to an integer value. In Figure 2 we define inductively the syntax of the state properties. The predicate $l : \beta$ allows specifying a state property at a particular control point $l \in \mathcal{L}$. We write $s \models \varphi$ when the state $s \in \Sigma$ has the property φ, and $\Sigma_\varphi \triangleq \{s \in \Sigma \mid s \models \varphi\}$ for the set of states $\Sigma_\varphi \subseteq \Sigma$ that have the property φ.

In the following, we define the program properties of interest by means of the temporal operators *always* $\Box$ and *eventually* $\Diamond$.

The *guarantee properties* are expressible by a temporal formula of the form $\Diamond\varphi$, for some state property φ. The formula expresses that at least one state in every program execution trace has the property φ, but it does not promise any repetition. In general, the guarantee properties are used to ensure that some event happens once during a program execution, such as program termination or eventual consistency. Indeed, program termination can be expressed as the guarantee property $\Diamond l_e : \text{true}$, where $l_e \in \mathcal{L}$ is the program final control point.

The *recurrence properties* are expressible by a temporal formula of the form $\Box\Diamond\varphi$, for some state property φ. The formula expresses that infinitely many states in every program execution trace have the property φ. In general, the recurrence properties are used to ensure that some event happens infinitely many times during a program execution (e.g., a request is always eventually answered).

5 Guarantee Temporal Properties

In the following, we generalize Section 3 from termination to guarantee properties. We define a sound and complete semantics for proving guarantee temporal properties by abstract interpretation of the program maximal trace semantics.

Let $S \subseteq \Sigma$ be a set of states and let $S^{+\infty} \subseteq \Sigma^{+\infty}$ be the set of non-empty finite or infinite sequences of states in $S \subseteq \Sigma$. In the following, we write $\bar{S} \triangleq \Sigma \setminus S$ for the set of states that are not in S and $T^S \triangleq T \cap S^{+\infty}$ for the selection of the sequences of T that are non-empty sequences of states in S.

In order to define our semantics we need the following abstraction functions:

- The *subsequence abstraction* $\alpha^{s} \in \mathcal{P}(\Sigma^{+\infty}) \rightarrow \mathcal{P}(\Sigma^{+\infty})$ extracts from a set of sequences $T \subseteq \Sigma^{+\infty}$ the subsequences of sequences in T:

$$\alpha^{s}(T) \triangleq \{\sigma \in \Sigma^{+\infty} \mid \exists \sigma' \in \Sigma^{*}, \sigma'' \in \Sigma^{*\infty} : \sigma'\sigma\sigma'' \in T\}$$

- The *guarantee abstraction* $\alpha^{g} \in \mathcal{P}(\Sigma) \rightarrow \mathcal{P}(\Sigma^{+\infty}) \rightarrow \mathcal{P}(\Sigma^{+})$, given a set of states $S \subseteq \Sigma$ and a set of sequences $T \subseteq \Sigma^{+\infty}$, extracts from $T \subseteq \Sigma^{+\infty}$ the subsequences of sequences of T whose neighborhood in $\alpha^{s}(T)$ consists only of sequences of states in $\bar{S}$ that are terminating with a state $s \in S$:

$$\alpha^{g}(S)T \triangleq \left\{\sigma s \in \alpha^{s}(T) \cap \Sigma^{+} \;\middle|\; \begin{array}{l} s \in S \wedge \sigma \in \bar{S}^{*} \wedge \\ \forall \sigma' \in \mathrm{pf}(\sigma) : T^{\sigma'} \cap \bar{S}^{+\infty} = \emptyset \end{array}\right\} \quad (6)$$

where $\mathrm{pf} \in \Sigma^{+\infty} \rightarrow \mathcal{P}(\Sigma^{+\infty})$ is the prefix abstraction (3) of Section 3 and $T^{\sigma} \triangleq \{\sigma\sigma'' \in \Sigma^{+\infty} \mid \sigma'' \in \Sigma^{*\infty} \wedge \exists \sigma' \in \Sigma^{*\infty} : \sigma'\sigma\sigma'' \in T\}$ is the set of suffixes of sequences of $T \subseteq \Sigma^{+\infty}$ with prefix $\sigma \in \Sigma^{+\infty}$.

Example 2. Let $T = \{cd^{\omega}, (cd)^{\omega}\}$, then $T^{d} = \{d^{\omega}, (dc)^{\omega}\}$. □

Example 3. Let $T = \{(abcd)^{\omega}, (cd)^{\omega}, a^{\omega}, cd^{\omega}\}$ and $S = \{c\}$, then $\alpha^{g}(S)T = \{c, bc\}$. Let us consider the trace $(abcd)^{\omega}$: the subsequences of $(abcd)^{\omega}$ that are terminating with c (and never encounter c before) are $\{c, bc, abc, dabc\}$. Let us consider the subsequence abc: $T^{ab} \cap \bar{S}^{+\infty} = \emptyset$ but $T^{a} \cap \bar{S}^{+\infty} = \{a^{\omega}\}$. Now let us consider $dabc$: $T^{dab} \cap \bar{S}^{+\infty} = \emptyset$ and $T^{da} \cap \bar{S}^{+\infty} = \emptyset$ but $T^{d} \cap \bar{S}^{+\infty} = \{d^{\omega}\}$. □

The *guarantee semantics* $\tau^{g} \in \mathcal{P}(\Sigma) \rightarrow (\Sigma \rightharpoonup \mathbb{O})$ of a program can now be defined by abstract interpretation of the program maximal trace semantics (1):

$$\tau^{g}(S) \triangleq \alpha^{v}(\alpha^{g}(S)\tau^{+\infty}) = \mathrm{lfp}^{\preccurlyeq}_{\dot{\emptyset}}\, \phi^{g}(S)$$

$$\phi^{g}(S)v \triangleq \lambda s. \begin{cases} 0 & s \in S \\ \sup\{v(s') + 1 \mid \langle s, s'\rangle \in \tau\} & s \in \widetilde{\mathrm{pre}}(\mathrm{dom}(v)) \wedge s \notin S \\ \text{undefined} & \text{otherwise} \end{cases} \quad (7)$$

where $\alpha^{v} \in \mathcal{P}(\Sigma^{+}) \rightarrow (\Sigma \rightharpoonup \mathbb{O})$ is the variant abstraction (5) presented in Section 3.

Intuitively, given a set of states $S \subseteq \Sigma$, the guarantee semantics $\tau^{g}(S)$ is defined starting from the states in S and retracing the program backwards while mapping each program state definitely leading to S (i.e., a program state such that all the traces to which it belongs eventually reach a state in S) to an ordinal in $\mathbb{O}$ representing an upper bound on the number of program execution steps remaining to S. The domain $\text{dom}(\tau^{g}(S))$ of $\tau^{g}(S)$ is the set of states definitely leading to a state in S: any trace starting in a state $s \in \text{dom}(\tau^{g}(S))$ must reach a state in S in at most $\tau^{g}(S)s$ execution steps, while at least one trace starting in a state $s \notin \text{dom}(\tau^{g}(S))$ does not reach S.

Note that, when S is the set of final states Ω, $\phi^{g}(\Omega) = \phi^{t}$ and we rediscover precisely Cousot and Cousot's termination semantics [11] presented in Section 3.

Let φ be a state property. We define the *φ-guarantee semantics* $\tau^{g}_{\varphi} \in \Sigma \rightharpoonup \mathbb{O}$:

$$\tau^{g}_{\varphi} \triangleq \tau^{g}(\Sigma_{\varphi}) \tag{8}$$

The semantics τ^{g}_{φ} is sound and complete for proving a guarantee property $\Diamond\varphi$:

Theorem 2. *A program satisfies a guarantee property $\Diamond\varphi$ for all execution traces starting from an initial state $s \in \Sigma$ if and only if $s \in \text{dom}(\tau^{g}_{\varphi})$.*

6 Recurrence Temporal Properties

In the following, we define a sound and complete semantics for proving recurrence temporal properties by abstract interpretation of the program maximal trace semantics, following the same approach used in Section 5 for guarantee temporal properties. In particular, the recurrence semantics that we are going to define reuses the guarantee semantics of Section 5 as starting point: from the guarantee that some event happens once during a program execution, the recurrence semantics ensures that the event happens infinitely many times.

In order to define our semantics we need the following abstraction function:

– The *recurrence abstraction* $\alpha^{r} \in \mathcal{P}(\Sigma) \to \mathcal{P}(\Sigma^{+\infty}) \to \mathcal{P}(\Sigma^{+})$, given a set of states $S \subseteq \Sigma$ and a set of sequences $T \subseteq \Sigma^{+\infty}$, extracts from T the subsequences of sequences of T whose neighborhood in $\alpha^{s}(T)$ consists only of sequences of states in $\bar{S}$ that are terminating with a state in S, and that are prefixes of sequences of T that reach infinitely often a state in S:

$$\begin{aligned} \alpha^{r}(S)T &\triangleq \text{gfp}^{\subseteq}_{\alpha^{g}(S)T}\ \phi^{\alpha^{r}}(T, S) \\ \phi^{\alpha^{r}}(T, S)T' &\triangleq \alpha^{g}(\widetilde{\text{pre}}(T)T' \cap S)T \end{aligned} \tag{9}$$

where $\widetilde{\text{pre}}(T)T' \triangleq \{s \in \Sigma \mid \forall\sigma \in \Sigma^{*}, \sigma' \in \Sigma^{*\infty} : \sigma s \sigma' \in T \Rightarrow \text{pf}(\sigma') \cap T' \neq \emptyset\}$ and $\alpha^{g} \in \mathcal{P}(\Sigma) \to \mathcal{P}(\Sigma^{+\infty}) \to \mathcal{P}(\Sigma^{+})$ is the guarantee abstraction (6) of Section 5.

To explain intuitively (9), we use the Kleene dual fixpoint theorem [8] to rephrase $\alpha^{r}(S)T$ as follows:

$$\alpha^{r}(S)T = \bigcap_{i \in \mathbb{N}} T_{i+1} \quad \text{where } T_{i+1} \triangleq \left[\phi^{\alpha^{r}}(T, S)\right]^{i} (\alpha^{g}(S)T)$$

Then, for $i = 0$, we get the set $T_1 = \alpha^{g}(S)T$ of subsequences of sequences of T that guarantee S at least *once*. For $i = 1$, starting from T_1, we derive the set of states $S_1 = \widetilde{\text{pre}}(T)T_1 \cap S$ (i.e., $S_1 \subseteq S$) whose successors all belong to the subsequences in T_1, and we get the set $T_2 = \alpha^{\text{g}}(S_1)T$ of subsequences of sequences of T that guarantee S_1 at least once and thus guarantee S at least *twice*. Note that all the subsequences in T_2 terminate with a state $s' \in S_1$ and therefore are *prefixes* of subsequence of T that reach S at least twice. More generally, for each $i \in \mathbb{N}$, we get the set T_{i+1} of subsequences which are *prefixes* of subsequences of T that reach S at least $i+1$ times, i.e., the subsequences that guarantee S at least $i+1$ times. The greatest fixpoint thus guarantees S *infinitely often*.

Example 4. Let $T = \{(cd)^\omega, ca^\omega, d(be)^\omega\}$ and let $S = \{b, c, d\}$. For $i = 0$, we have $T_1 = \alpha^{\text{g}}(S)T = \{b, eb, c, d\}$. For $i = 1$, we derive $S_1 = \{b, d\}$, since $c(dc)^\omega \in T$ and $\text{pf}((dc)^\omega) \cap T_1 = \{d\} \neq \emptyset$ but $ca^\omega \in T$ and $\text{pf}(a^\omega) \cap T_1 = \emptyset$. We get $T_2 = \alpha^{\text{g}}(S_1)T = \{b, eb, d\}$. For $i = 2$, we derive $S_2 = \{b\}$, since $d(be)^\omega \in T$ and $\text{pf}((be)^\omega) \cap T_1 = \{b\} \neq \emptyset$ but $d(cd)^\omega \in T$ and $\text{pf}((cd)^\omega) \cap T_2 = \emptyset$. We get $T_3 = \alpha^{\text{g}}(S_2)T = \{b, eb\}$ which is the greatest fixpoint: the only subsequences of sequences in T that guarantee S infinitely often start with b or eb. □

The *recurrence semantics* $\tau^{\text{r}} \in \mathcal{P}(\Sigma) \to (\Sigma \rightharpoonup \mathbb{O})$ of a program can now be defined by abstract interpretation of the program maximal trace semantics (1):

$$\tau^{\text{r}}(S) \triangleq \alpha^{\text{v}}(\alpha^{\text{r}}(S)\tau^{+\infty}) = \text{gfp}^{\preccurlyeq}_{\tau^{\text{g}}(S)} \phi^{\text{r}}(S)$$

$$\phi^{\text{r}}(S)v \triangleq \lambda s. \begin{cases} v(s) & s \in \text{dom}(\tau^{\text{g}}(\widetilde{\text{pre}}(\text{dom}(v)) \cap S)) \\ \text{undefined} & \text{otherwise} \end{cases} \tag{10}$$

where $\alpha^{\text{v}} \in \mathcal{P}(\Sigma^+) \to (\Sigma \rightharpoonup \mathbb{O})$ is the variant abstraction (5) presented in Section 3 and $\tau^{\text{g}} \in \mathcal{P}(\Sigma) \to (\Sigma \rightharpoonup \mathbb{O})$ is the guarantee semantics (7) defined in Section 5. Note that, given the definition of (7), (10) contains a nested fixpoint.

Given a set of states $S \subseteq \Sigma$, the recurrence semantics $\tau^{\text{r}}(S)$ maps each program state definitely leading infinitely many times to S to an ordinal in $\mathbb{O}$ representing an upper bound on the number of execution steps remaining to the *next occurrence* of a state in S: any trace starting in a state $s \in \text{dom}(\tau^{\text{r}}(S))$ must reach the next occurrence of a state in S in at most $\tau^{\text{r}}(S)s$ execution steps, while at least one trace starting in a state $s \notin \text{dom}(\tau^{\text{r}}(S))$ reaches a state in S at most finitely many times.

Let φ be a state property. We the define *φ-recurrence semantics* $\tau^{\text{r}}_{\varphi} \in \Sigma \rightharpoonup \mathbb{O}$:

$$\tau^{\text{r}}_{\varphi} \triangleq \tau^{\text{r}}(\Sigma_{\varphi}) \tag{11}$$

The semantics $\tau^{\text{r}}_{\varphi}$ is sound and complete for proving a recurrence property $\Box\Diamond\varphi$:

Theorem 3. *A program satisfies a recurrence property $\Box\Diamond\varphi$ for all execution traces starting from an initial state $s \in \Sigma$ if and only if $s \in \text{dom}(\tau^{\text{r}}_{\varphi})$.*

7 Piecewise-Defined Ranking Functions

The termination semantics τ^{t} of Section 3, the φ-guarantee semantics $\tau_{\varphi}^{\mathrm{g}}$ of Section 5 and the φ-recurrence semantics $\tau_{\varphi}^{\mathrm{r}}$ of Section 6 are usually *not computable* (i.e., when the program state space is infinite).

In [21,22,23], we present decidable abstractions of τ^{t} by means of piecewise-defined ranking functions over natural numbers [21], over ordinals [22] and with relational partitioning [23]. In the following, we will briefly recall the main characteristics of these abstractions and we will show how to modify the abstract domains in order to obtain decidable abstractions of $\tau_{\varphi}^{\mathrm{g}}$ and $\tau_{\varphi}^{\mathrm{r}}$ as well.

7.1 Abstract Termination Semantics

The formal treatment given in the previous sections is defined over general transition systems. In practice, it is sufficient to provide a transfer function for each atomic instruction of a programming language to define a semantics for all the programs in the language and obtain an effective static analysis after opportune abstraction.

In [21], we provide an isomorphic definition of the termination semantics $\tau^{\mathrm{t}} \in \Sigma \rightharpoonup \mathbb{O}$ for a C-like programming language by partitioning with respect to the set of program control points $\mathcal{L}$: $\tau^{\mathrm{t}} \in \mathcal{L} \to (\mathcal{E} \rightharpoonup \mathbb{O})$. In this way, to each control point $l \in \mathcal{L}$ corresponds a function $v \in \mathcal{E} \rightharpoonup \mathbb{O}$ and to each program statement i corresponds a transfer function $[\![i]\!]^{\mathrm{t}} \in (\mathcal{E} \rightharpoonup \mathbb{O}) \to (\mathcal{E} \rightharpoonup \mathbb{O})$. As an example, given an assignment $x := e$ of the expression e to the variable $x \in \mathcal{X}$, the transfer function is defined as follows:

$$[\![x := e]\!]^{\mathrm{t}} v \triangleq \lambda\rho. \begin{cases} \sup\{v(\rho[x \mapsto z]) + 1 \mid z \in [\![e]\!]\rho\} & \forall z \in [\![e]\!]\rho : \rho[x \mapsto z] \in \mathrm{dom}(v) \\ \text{undefined} & \text{otherwise} \end{cases}$$

where $[\![e]\!] \in \mathcal{E} \to \wp(\mathbb{Z})$ maps an environment $\rho \in \mathcal{E}$ to the set of all possible values for the expression e in the given environment. In case of a loop statement the transfer function involves a least fixpoint. More details can be found in [21].

Subsequently, in [21,22,23] we present an abstract termination semantics $\tau^{\alpha^{\mathrm{t}}} \in \mathcal{L} \to \mathcal{V}$: to each program control point $l \in \mathcal{L}$ corresponds an element $v \in \mathcal{V}$ of an abstract domain $\mathcal{V}$, equipped with a concretization function $\gamma \in \mathcal{V} \to (\mathcal{E} \rightharpoonup \mathbb{O})$ and a sound abstract transfer function $[\![i]\!]^{\alpha^{\mathrm{t}}} \in \mathcal{V} \to \mathcal{V}$ for each program statement i. In particular, the elements of the abstract domain $\mathcal{V}$ are piecewise-defined ranking functions represented by means of two parameter abstract domains: an abstract domain whose elements establish the shape of the pieces of the ranking functions, and an abstract domain whose elements represent the value of the ranking functions within their pieces. As an example, in [21] we consider piecewise-defined ranking functions whose pieces have the shape of intervals and whose value is represented by an affine function.

The abstract transfer functions are combined together to compute an abstract ranking function for a program through backward analysis. The starting point is the constant function equal to zero at the program final control point. This function is then propagated backwards towards the program initial control point taking assignments and tests into account and, in case of loops, solving least fixpoints by iteration with a widening operator. We give an intuition for how the abstract assignment transfer function works by means of the following example:

Example 5. Let us consider the piecewise-defined ranking function with value $2x+1$ for $x \in [-\infty, 3]$ and undefined elsewhere, and the assignment $x := x+1$. The abstract assignment transfer function substitutes the variable x with the expression $x+1$ and increases the value of the function by one (to take into account that one more program step is needed before termination). The result is the piecewise-defined ranking function with value $2(x+1)+1+1 = 2x+4$ for $x+1 \in [-\infty, 3]$ (i.e., $x \in [-\infty, 2]$) and undefined elsewhere. □

We refer to [21,22,23] for more details.

The abstract transfer functions are *sound* with respect to the approximation order $v_1 \sqsubseteq v_2 \triangleq \mathrm{dom}(v_1) \supseteq \mathrm{dom}(v_2) \wedge \forall x \in \mathrm{dom}(v_2) : v_1(x) \leq v_2(x)$ (see [10] for further discussion on approximation and computational order of an abstract domain):

Theorem 4. $[\![i]\!]^{\mathrm{t}}\gamma(v) \sqsubseteq \gamma([\![i]\!]^{\alpha^{\mathrm{t}}} v)$

The backward analysis computes an over-approximation of the value of the most precise ranking function τ^{t} and an *under-approximation* of its domain of definition $\mathrm{dom}(\tau^{\mathrm{t}})$. In this way, an abstraction provides *sufficient preconditions* for program termination: if the abstraction is defined on a program state, then all the program execution traces branching from that state are terminating.

7.2 Abstract Guarantee Semantics

In the following, we describe how to reuse the piecewise-defined ranking function abstract domains introduced in [21,22,23] and what changes are required in order to obtain decidable abstractions of the φ-guarantee semantics $\tau_\varphi^{\mathrm{g}}$ (8).

First, as before, we partition the φ-guarantee semantics $\tau_\varphi^{\mathrm{g}} \in \Sigma \rightharpoonup \mathbb{O}$ with respect to the set of program control points $\mathcal{L}$: $\tau_\varphi^{\mathrm{g}} \in \mathcal{L} \to (\mathcal{E} \rightharpoonup \mathbb{O})$. The transfer functions $[\![i]\!]_\varphi^{\mathrm{g}} \in (\mathcal{E} \rightharpoonup \mathbb{O}) \to (\mathcal{E} \rightharpoonup \mathbb{O})$ behave as the transfer functions for the termination semantics but in addition they *reset* the value of the ranking function for the environments that have the property φ. As an example, the transfer function for an assignment $x := e$ is now defined as follows:

$$[\![x := e]\!]^{\mathrm{g}} v \triangleq \lambda\rho. \begin{cases} 0 & \rho \models \varphi \\ \sup\{v(\rho[x \mapsto z]) + 1 \mid z \in [\![e]\!]\rho\} & \rho \not\models \varphi \wedge \forall z \in [\![e]\!]\rho : \rho[x \mapsto z] \in \mathrm{dom}(v) \\ \text{undefined} & \text{otherwise} \end{cases}$$

where $\rho \models \varphi$ means that the environment $\rho \in \mathcal{E}$ has the property φ (cf. Section 4).

Then, we define the abstract φ-guarantee semantics $\tau_\varphi^{\alpha^{\mathrm{g}}} \in \mathcal{L} \to \mathcal{V}$: to each program control point $l \in \mathcal{L}$ corresponds a piecewise-defined ranking function

$v \in \mathcal{V}$. To each program statement i corresponds a *sound* (with respect to the approximation order $\sqsubseteq$) abstract transfer function $[\![i]\!]^{\alpha^{\mathrm{g}}}_{\varphi} \in \mathcal{V} \to \mathcal{V}$:

Theorem 5. $[\![i]\!]^{\mathrm{g}}_{\varphi}\gamma(v) \sqsubseteq \gamma([\![i]\!]^{\alpha^{\mathrm{g}}}_{\varphi} v)$

We give an intuition for how the abstract assignment transfer function now works by means of the following example:

Example 6. Let us consider the guarantee property $\Diamond(x = 3)$ and let us consider again, as in Example 5, the piecewise-defined ranking function with value $2x+1$ for $x \in [-\infty, 3]$ and undefined elsewhere, and the assignment $x := x + 1$. As in Example 5, the abstract assignment transfer function substitutes the variable x with the expression $x + 1$ and increases the value of the function by one. Unlike Example 5, it also resets the value of the function for $x \in [3, 3]$. The result is the piecewise-defined ranking function with value $2x + 4$ for $x \in [-\infty, 2]$, 0 for $x \in [3, 3]$ and undefined elsewhere. □

As before, the abstract transfer functions are combined together through backward analysis. The starting point is now the constant function equal to zero only for the environments that have the property φ, and undefined elsewhere, at the program final control point. The backward analysis computes an over-approximation of the value of the function $\tau^{\mathrm{g}}_{\varphi}$ and an *under-approximation* of its domain of definition $\mathrm{dom}(\tau^{\mathrm{g}}_{\varphi})$. In this way, an abstraction provides *sufficient preconditions* for the guarantee property $\Diamond\varphi$: if the abstraction is defined on a program state, then all the program execution traces branching from that state *eventually* reach a state with the property φ. Note that, when the property φ is l_e : true, where $l_e \in \mathcal{L}$ is the program final control point, we rediscover the backward termination analysis from Section 7.1.

7.3 Abstract Recurrence Semantics

In the following, we describe how to reuse the piecewise-defined ranking function abstract domains introduced in [21,22,23] and what changes are required in order to obtain decidable abstractions of the φ-recurrence semantics $\tau^{\mathrm{r}}_{\varphi}$ (11).

As before, we associate each program control point $l \in \mathcal{L}$ with a different ranking function $v \in \mathcal{V}$: $\tau^{\mathrm{r}}_{\varphi} \in \mathcal{L} \to (\mathcal{E} \rightharpoonup \mathbb{O})$. The transfer functions $[\![i]\!]^{\mathrm{r}}_{\varphi} \in (\mathcal{E} \rightharpoonup \mathbb{O}) \to (\mathcal{E} \rightharpoonup \mathbb{O})$ behave as the transfer functions for the guarantee semantics with the only difference that they *reset* the value of the ranking function for the environments that have the property φ *only if* all successors of the environments (by means of the program statement i) belong to the domain of the ranking function; hence, they ensure that each time φ is satisfied, it will be satisfied again in the future. As an example, the transfer function for an assignment $x := e$ is defined as follows:

$$[\![x := e]\!]^{\mathrm{r}} v \triangleq \lambda\rho. \begin{cases} 0 & \rho \models \varphi \ \wedge\ \forall z \in [\![e]\!]\rho :\ \rho[x \mapsto z] \in \mathrm{dom}(v) \\ \sup\{v(\rho[x \mapsto z]) + 1 \mid z \in [\![e]\!]\rho\} & \rho \not\models \varphi \ \wedge\ \forall z \in [\![e]\!]\rho :\ \rho[x \mapsto z] \in \mathrm{dom}(v) \\ \text{undefined} & \text{otherwise} \end{cases}$$

Then, we define the abstract φ-recurrence semantics $\tau_\varphi^{\alpha^r} \in \mathcal{L} \to \mathcal{V}$ by means of *sound* (with respect to $\sqsubseteq$) abstract transfer functions $[\![i]\!]_\varphi^{\alpha^r} \in \mathcal{V} \to \mathcal{V}$:

Theorem 6. $[\![i]\!]_\varphi^{r}\gamma(v) \sqsubseteq \gamma([\![i]\!]_\varphi^{\alpha^r} v)$

We give an intuition for how the abstract assignment transfer function now works by means of the following example:

Example 7. Let us consider the guarantee property $\Box\Diamond(x = 3)$ and let us consider again, as in Example 6, the piecewise-defined ranking function with value $2x+1$ for $x \in [-\infty, 3]$ and undefined elsewhere, and the assignment $x := x + 1$. Unlike Example 6, the abstract assignment transfer function does not reset the value of the function for $x \in [3, 3]$ because the ranking function is undefined for $x \in [4, 4]$ (i.e., the successor of the environment $x \in [3, 3]$ by means of the assignment $x := x + 1$). The result is the piecewise-defined ranking function with value $2x + 4$ for $x \in [-\infty, 2]$, and undefined elsewhere.

Let us consider instead the piecewise-defined ranking function with value $2x + 1$ for $x \in [-\infty, 4]$ and undefined elsewhere. The result of the assignment $x := x + 1$ is now the piecewise-defined ranking function with value $2x + 4$ for $x \in [-\infty, 2]$, 0 for $x \in [3, 3]$ and undefined elsewhere. □

Since the program final states cannot satisfy a recurrence property, the starting point of the recurrence backward analysis is now the totally undefined function at the program final control point. This function is then propagated backwards towards the program initial control point.

Note that, in case of a loop statement, according to the definition (10) of τ_φ^r from Section 5, the transfer function involves a least fixpoint *nested* into a greatest fixpoint. Nested fixpoints are solved by iteration with the same widening operator used for termination [23] for the least fixpoint, and a new *dual widening* operator $\bar{\nabla}$ for the greatest fixpoint. The dual widening $\bar{\nabla}$ obeys (*i*) $\gamma(A) \sqcap \gamma(B) \sqsubseteq \gamma(A \mathbin{\bar{\nabla}} B)$, and (*ii*) for any sequence $(X_n)_{n\in\mathbb{N}}$, the sequence $Y_0 = X_0$, $Y_{n+1} = Y_n \mathbin{\bar{\nabla}} X_{n+1}$ stabilizes (i.e., $\exists i: Y_{i+1} = Y_i$). Dual widenings are rather unknown and, up to our knowledge, only few practical instance has been proposed (e.g., [5,18]). In our case, the dual widening $\bar{\nabla}$ enforces the termination of the analysis by preventing the set of pieces of a piecewise-defined ranking function from growing indefinitely: given two piecewise-defined ranking functions $v_1 \in \mathcal{V}$ and $v_2 \in \mathcal{V}$, it enforces the piecewise-definition of the first function v_1 on the second function v_2. Then, for each piece of the ranking functions, it maintains the value of the function only if both v_1 and v_2 are defined on that piece (cf. Figure 3).

The backward analysis computes an over-approximation of the value of the function τ_φ^r and an *under-approximation* of its domain $\text{dom}(\tau_\varphi^r)$. In this way, an abstraction provides *sufficient preconditions* for the recurrence property $\Box\Diamond\varphi$: if the abstraction is defined on a program state, then all the program execution traces branching from that state *always eventually* reach a state with the property φ.

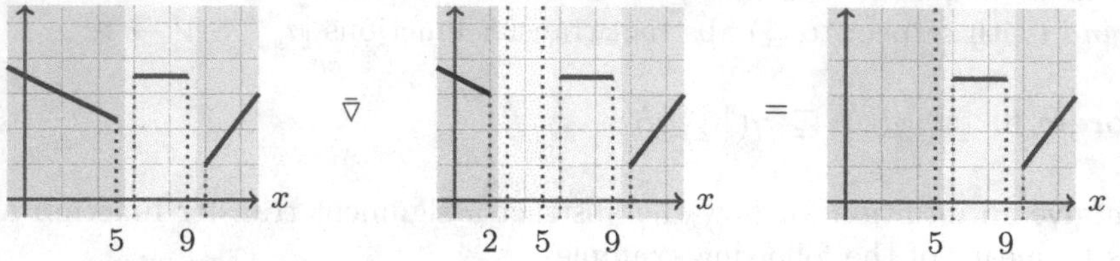

Fig. 3. Example of Dual Widening

$^1c := 1;$
while $^2($ *true* $)$ do
$\quad ^3x := c;$
$\quad$ while $^4(\ x > 0\ )$ do $^5x := x - 1;\ ^6c := c + 1;$

Fig. 4. Program COUNT-DOWN

8 Implementation

We have incorporated the static analysis methods for guarantee and recurrence temporal properties that we have presented into our prototype static analyzer FuncTion based on piecewise-defined ranking functions. It is available online[3].

The prototype accepts (non-deterministic) programs written in a C-like syntax and, when the guarantee or recurrence analysis methods are selected, it accepts state properties written as C-like pure expressions. It is written in OCaml and, at the time of writing, the available abstract domains to control the pieces of the ranking functions are based on intervals, octagons and convex polyhedra, and the available abstract domain to represent the value of the ranking functions is based on affine functions. The operators for the intervals, octagons and convex polyhedra abstract domains are provided by the APRON library [14]. It is also possible to activate the extension to ordinal-valued ranking functions [22] and tune the precision of the analysis by adjusting the widening delay.

The analysis proceeds by structural induction on the program syntax, iterating loops with widening (and, for recurrence properties, both widening and dual widening) until stabilization. In case of nested loops, the analysis stabilizes the inner loop for each iteration of the outer loop.

To illustrate the effectiveness of our new static analysis methods, we consider more examples besides the program SIMPLE of Section 1.

Example 8. Let us consider the program COUNT-DOWN in Figure 4 and the recurrence property $\Box\Diamond x = 0$. At each iteration of the outer loop, the variable x takes the value of some counter c (which initially has value one); then, the inner loop decreases the value of x and increases the value of the counter c until x becomes less than or equal to zero. The recurrence property is clearly satisfied

[3] `http://www.di.ens.fr/~urban/FuncTion.html`

```
while ¹( true ) do
    ²x := ?;
    while ³( x ≠ 0 ) do
        if ⁴( x > 0 ) then ⁵x := x − 1; else ⁶x := x + 1; fi
```

Fig. 5. Program SINK

and indeed our prototype (parameterized by intervals and affine functions) is able to prove it: the piecewise-defined ranking function inferred at program control point 1 bounds the wait for the *next* occurrence of the desirable state $x = 0$ by five program execution steps (i.e., executing the assignment $c := 1$, testing the outer loop condition, executing the assignment $x := c$, testing the inner loop condition and executing the assignment $x := x - 1$). The analysis infers a more interesting raking function associated to program control point 4:

$$f_4^r(x,c) = \begin{cases} 3c+2 & x < 0 \wedge c > 0 \\ 3 & x < 0 \wedge c = 0 \\ 1 & x = 0 \wedge c \geq 0 \\ 3x-1 & (x = 1 \wedge c \geq -1) \vee (x \geq 2 \wedge c \geq -2) \\ \text{undefined} & \text{otherwise} \end{cases}$$

The function bounds the wait for the next occurrence of $x = 0$ by $3c+2$ execution steps if $x < 0 \wedge c > 0$, by 3 execution steps if $x < 0 \wedge c = 0$ (i.e., testing the inner loop condition, testing the outer loop condition and executing the assignment $x := c$), by 1 execution step if $x = 0 \wedge c \geq 0$ (i.e., testing the inner loop condition) and by $3x-1$ execution steps if $(x = 1 \wedge c \geq -1) \vee (x \geq 2 \wedge c \geq -2)$. In the last case there is a precision loss due to a lack of expressiveness of the intervals abstract domain: if x is strictly positive at program control point 4, the weakest precondition ensuring infinitely many occurrences of the desirable state $x = 0$ is $c \geq -x$ (which is not representable in the intervals abstract domain). □

Example 9. Let us consider the program SINK in Figure 5 and the recurrence property $\Box\Diamond x = 0$. At each iteration of the outer loop, the value of the variable x is reset by the non-deterministic assignment $x := ?$; then, the inner loop decreases or increases the value of x until it becomes equal to zero. Note that the program features *unbounded non-determinism* due to the assignment $x := ?$. The recurrence property is clearly satisfied, however the number of execution steps between two occurrences of the desirable state $x = 0$ is unbounded. Our prototype (parameterized by intervals and *ordinal-valued* ranking functions) is able to prove it as, at program control point 1, it finds a ranking function defined everywhere; its value is $\omega + 8$, meaning that the number of execution steps between two occurrences of the desirable state $x = 0$ is unbounded but *finite*. □

```
flag1 := 0; flag2 := 0;

[ while 1( true ) do                           ]    [ while 1( true ) do                           ]
[    2flag1 := 1                               ]    [    2flag2 := 1                               ]
[    3turn := 2                                ] || [    3turn := 1                                ]
[    while 4( flag2 ≠ 0 ∧ turn ≠ 1 ) do        ]    [    while 4( flag1 ≠ 0 ∧ turn ≠ 2 ) do        ]
[        BUSY_WAIT                             ]    [        BUSY_WAIT                             ]
[    5CRITICAL_SECTION                         ]    [    5CRITICAL_SECTION                         ]
[    6flag1 := 0                               ]    [    6flag2 := 0                               ]
```

Fig. 6. Program PETERSON (Peterson's Algorithm)

Example 10. Let us consider the program PETERSON, Peterson's algorithm for mutual exclusion, in Figure 6. Note that *weak fairness* assumptions are required in order to guarantee bounded bypass (i.e., a process cannot be bypassed by any other process in entering the critical section for more than a finite number of times). Since at the moment our prototype is not able to directly analyze concurrent programs, we have modeled the algorithm as a fair non-deterministic sequential program which interleaves execution steps from both processes while enforcing 1-bounded bypass (i.e., a process cannot be bypassed by any other process in entering the critical section for more than once). Our prototype is able to prove that both processes are allowed to enter their critical section infinitely often. □

These and additional examples are available from FuncTion web interface.

9 Related Work

In the recent past, a large body of work has been devoted to proving liveness properties of (concurrent) programs.

A successful approach for proving liveness properties is based on a transformation from model checking of liveness properties to model checking of *safety* properties [3]. The approach looks for and exploits lasso-shaped counterexamples. A similar search for lasso-shaped counterexamples has been used to generalize the model checking algorithm IC3 to deal with liveness properties [4]. However, in general, counterexamples to liveness properties in infinite-state systems are not necessarily lasso-shaped. Our approach is not counterexample-based and is meant for proving liveness properties directly, without reduction to safety properties.

In [20], Podelski and Rybalchenko present a method for the verification of liveness properties based on transition invariants [19]. The approach, as in [24], reduces the proof of a liveness properties to the proof of *fair termination* by means of a program transformation. It is at the basis of the industrial-scale tool Terminator [6]. By contrast, our method is meant for proving liveness properties directly, without reduction to termination. Moreover, it avoids the cost of explicit checking for the well-foundedness of the transition invariants.

A distinguishing aspect of our work is the use of infinite height abstract domains, equipped with (dual) widening. We are aware of only one other such work: in [16], Massé proposes a method for proving arbitrary temporal properties based on abstract domains for lower closure operators. A small analyzer is presented in [17] but the approach remains mainly theoretical. We believe that our framework, albeit less general, is more straightforward and of practical use.

An emerging trend focuses on proving *existential* temporal properties (e.g., proving that there exists a particular execution trace). The most recent approaches [2,7] are based on counterexample-guided abstraction refinement. Our work is designed for proving universal temporal properties (i.e., valid for all program execution traces). We leave proving existential temporal properties as part of our future work.

Finally, to our knowledge, the inference of sufficient preconditions for guarantee and recurrence program properties, and the ability to provide upper bounds on the wait before a program reaches a desirable state, is unique to our work.

10 Conclusion and Future Work

In this paper, we have presented an abstract interpretation framework for proving *guarantee* and *recurrence* temporal properties of programs. We have systematically derived by abstract interpretation new sound static analysis methods to effectively infer *sufficient preconditions* for these temporal properties, and to provide *upper bounds* on the wait before a program reaches a desirable state.

It remains for future work to express and handle fairness properties. We also plan to extend the present framework to the full hierarchy of temporal properties [15] and more generally to *arbitrary* (universal and existential) liveness properties.

References

1. Bertrane, J., Cousot, P., Cousot, R., Feret, J., Mauborgne, L., Miné, A., Rival, X.: Static Analysis and Verification of Aerospace Software by Abstract Interpretation. In: AIAA (2010)
2. Beyene, T.A., Popeea, C., Rybalchenko, A.: Solving Existentially Quantified Horn Clauses. In: Sharygina, N., Veith, H. (eds.) CAV 2013. LNCS, vol. 8044, pp. 869–882. Springer, Heidelberg (2013)
3. Biere, A., Artho, C., Schuppan, V.: Liveness Checking as Safety Checking. Electronic Notes in Theoretical Computer Science 66(2), 160–177 (2002)
4. Bradley, A.R., Somenzi, F., Hassan, Z., Zhang, Y.: An Incremental Approach to Model Checking Progress Properties. In: FMCAD, pp. 144–153 (2011)
5. Chakarov, A., Sankaranarayanan, S.: Expectation Invariants for Probabilistic Program Loops as Fixed Points. In: Müller-Olm, M., Seidl, H. (eds.) SAS 2014. LNCS, vol. 8723, pp. 85–100. Springer, Heidelberg (2014)

6. Cook, B., Gotsman, A., Podelski, A., Rybalchenko, A., Vardi, M.Y.: Proving that Programs Eventually do Something Good. In: POPL, pp. 265–276 (2007)
7. Cook, B., Koskinen, E.: Reasoning About Nondeterminism in Programs. In: PLDI, pp. 219–230 (2013)
8. Cousot, P.: Constructive Design of a Hierarchy of Semantics of a Transition System by Abstract Interpretation. ENTCS 6, 77–102 (1997)
9. Cousot, P., Cousot, R.: Abstract Interpretation: A Unified Lattice Model for Static Analysis of Programs by Construction or Approximation of Fixpoints. In: POPL, pp. 238–252 (1977)
10. Cousot, P., Cousot, R.: Higher Order Abstract Interpretation and Application to Comportment Analysis Generalizing Strictness, Termination, Projection, and PER Analysis. In: ICCL, pp. 95–112 (1994)
11. Cousot, P., Cousot, R.: An Abstract Interpretation Framework for Termination. In: POPL, pp. 245–258 (2012)
12. Floyd, R.W.: Assigning Meanings to Programs. In: Proceedings of Symposium on Applied Mathematics, vol. 19, pp. 19–32 (1967)
13. Francez, N.: Fairness. Springer (1986)
14. Jeannet, B., Miné, A.: APRON: A Library of Numerical Abstract Domains for Static Analysis. In: Bouajjani, A., Maler, O. (eds.) CAV 2009. LNCS, vol. 5643, pp. 661–667. Springer, Heidelberg (2009)
15. Manna, Z., Pnueli, A.: A Hierarchy of Temporal Properties. In: PODC, pp. 377–410 (1990)
16. Massé, D.: Property Checking Driven Abstract Interpretation-Based Static Analysis. In: Zuck, L.D., Attie, P.C., Cortesi, A., Mukhopadhyay, S. (eds.) VMCAI 2003. LNCS, vol. 2575, pp. 56–69. Springer, Heidelberg (2002)
17. Massé, D.: Abstract Domains for Property Checking Driven Analysis of Temporal Properties. In: Rattray, C., Maharaj, S., Shankland, C. (eds.) AMAST 2004. LNCS, vol. 3116, pp. 349–363. Springer, Heidelberg (2004)
18. Miné, A.: Inferring Sufficient Conditions with Backward Polyhedral Under-Approximations. In: NSAD. ENTCS, vol. 287, pp. 89–100 (2012)
19. Podelski, A., Rybalchenko, A.: Transition Invariants. In: LICS, pp. 32–41 (2004)
20. Podelski, A., Rybalchenko, A.: Transition Predicate Abstraction and Fair Termination. In: POPL, pp. 132–144 (2005)
21. Urban, C.: The Abstract Domain of Segmented Ranking Functions. In: Logozzo, F., Fähndrich, M. (eds.) Static Analysis. LNCS, vol. 7935, pp. 43–62. Springer, Heidelberg (2013)
22. Urban, C., Miné, A.: An Abstract Domain to Infer Ordinal-Valued Ranking Functions. In: Shao, Z. (ed.) ESOP 2014. LNCS, vol. 8410, pp. 412–431. Springer, Heidelberg (2014)
23. Urban, C., Miné, A.: A Decision Tree Abstract Domain for Proving Conditional Termination. In: Müller-Olm, M., Seidl, H. (eds.) SAS 2014. LNCS, vol. 8723, pp. 302–318. Springer, Heidelberg (2014)
24. Vardi, M.Y.: Verification of Concurrent Programs: The Automata-Theoretic Framework. Annals of Pure and Applied Logic 51(1-2), 79–98 (1991)

Tree Automata-Based Refinement with Application to Horn Clause Verification

Bishoksan Kafle[1,*] and John P. Gallagher[1,2,**]

[1] Roskilde University, Denmark
[2] IMDEA Software Institute, Madrid, Spain

Abstract. In this paper we apply tree-automata techniques to refinement of abstract interpretation in Horn clause verification. We go beyond previous work on refining trace abstractions; firstly we handle tree automata rather than string automata and thereby can capture traces in any Horn clause derivations rather than just transition systems; secondly, we show how algorithms manipulating tree automata interact with abstract interpretations, establishing progress in refinement and generating refined clauses that eliminate causes of imprecision. We show how to derive a refined set of Horn clauses in which given infeasible traces have been eliminated, using a recent optimised algorithm for tree automata determinisation. We also show how we can introduce disjunctive abstractions selectively by splitting states in the tree automaton. The approach is independent of the abstract domain and constraint theory underlying the Horn clauses. Experiments using linear constraint problems and the abstract domain of convex polyhedra show that the refinement technique is practical and that iteration of abstract interpretation with tree automata-based refinement solves many challenging Horn clause verification problems. We compare the results with other state of the art Horn clause verification tools.

1 Introduction

In this paper we apply tree-automata techniques to refinement of abstract interpretation in Horn clause verification. We go beyond previous work on refining trace abstractions [23]; firstly, we handle tree automata rather than word automata and thereby can capture traces in any Horn clause derivations rather than just transition systems; secondly, we show how algorithms manipulating tree automata interact with abstract interpretations, establishing progress in refinement and generating refined clauses that eliminate causes of imprecision.

More specifically, we show how to construct tree automata capturing both the traces (derivations) of a given set of Horn clauses and also one or more infeasible traces discovered after abstract interpretation of the clauses. From these we construct a refined automaton in which the infeasible trace(s) have been eliminated and a new set of clauses is constructed from the refined automaton.

* Supported by EU FP7 project ENTRA (Project 318337).
** Supported by Danish Research Council grant FNU 10-084290.

D. D'Souza et al. (Eds.): VMCAI 2015, LNCS 8931, pp. 209–226, 2015.

This guarantees progress in that the same infeasible trace cannot be generated (in *any* abstract interpretation). In addition, the clauses are restructured during the elimination of the trace, leading to more precise abstractions which can lead to better invariant generation in subsequent iterations. The refinement is manifested in the refined clauses, rather than in an accumulated set of properties as in the counterexample-guided abstraction refinement (CEGAR) [8] approach. We rely on the abstract interpretation of the clauses to generate useful properties, rather than hoping to find them during the refinement itself.

We also show how we can introduce disjunctive abstractions selectively by splitting states in the tree automaton. The approach is independent of the abstract domain and constraint theory underlying the Horn clauses. Experiments using linear constraint problems and the abstract domain of convex polyhedra show that the refinement technique is practical and that iteration of abstract interpretation with tree automata-based refinement solves many challenging Horn clause verification problems. We compare the results with other state of the art Horn clause verification tools.

The main contributions of this paper are the following; (1) We construct a correspondence between computations using Horn clauses and finite tree automata (FTA) (Section 3). (2) We construct a refined set of clauses directly from a tree automaton representation of the clauses and an infeasible trace; the trace is eliminated from the refined clauses (Section 3.5) (3) We propose a "splitting" operator on FTAs (Section 2) and describe its role in Horn clause verification (Section 4.1). (4) We demonstrate the feasibility of our approach in practice applying it to Horn clause verification problems (Section 5).

2 Finite Tree Automata

Finite tree automata (FTAs) are mathematical machines that define so-called recognisable tree languages, which are possibly infinite sets of terms that have desirable properties such as closure under Boolean set operations and decidability of membership and emptiness.

Definition 1 (Finite tree automaton). *An FTA $\mathcal{A}$ is a tuple (Q, Q_f, Σ, Δ), where Q is a finite set of states, $Q \subseteq Q_f$ is a set of final states, Σ is a set of function symbols, and Δ is a set of transitions. We assume that Q and Σ are disjoint.*

Each function symbol $f \in \Sigma$ has an arity $n \geq 0$, written as $\mathsf{ar}(f) = n$. The function symbols with arity 0 are called constants. $\mathsf{Term}(\Sigma)$ is the set of ground terms or trees constructed from Σ where $t \in \mathsf{Term}(\Sigma)$ iff $t \in \Sigma$ is a constant or $t = f(t_1, t_2, ..., t_n)$ where $\mathsf{ar}(f) = n$ and $t_1, t_2, ..., t_n \in \mathsf{Term}(\Sigma)$. Similarly $\mathsf{Term}(\Sigma \cup Q)$ is the set of terms/trees constructed from Σ and Q, treating the elements of Q as constants.

Each transition in Δ is of the form $f(q_1, q_2, ..., q_n) \to q$ where $\mathsf{ar}(f) = n$. Given $\delta \in \Delta$ we refer to its left- and right-hand-sides as $\mathsf{lhs}(\delta)$ and $\mathsf{rhs}(\delta)$ respectively. Let $\Rightarrow$ be a one-step rewrite in which $t_1 \Rightarrow t_2$ iff t_2 is the result of replacing one subterm of t_1 equal to $\mathsf{lhs}(\delta)$ by $\mathsf{rhs}(\delta)$, from some $\delta \in \Delta$. The reflexive, transitive closure of $\Rightarrow$ is $\Rightarrow^*$. We say there is a run (resp. successful run) for $t \in \mathsf{Term}(\Sigma)$ if $t \Rightarrow^* q$ where $q \in Q$ (resp. $q \in Q_f$), and we say that t is *accepted* if t has a successful run. An FTA $\mathcal{A}$ defines a set of terms, that is, a tree language, denoted by $\mathcal{L}(\mathcal{A})$, as the set of all terms accepted by $\mathcal{A}$.

Definition 2 (Deterministic FTA (DFTA)). *An FTA* (Q, Q_f, Σ, Δ) *is called bottom-up deterministic iff* Δ *has no two transitions with the same left hand side.*

We omit the adjective "bottom-up" in this paper and just refer to deterministic FTAs. Runs of a DFTA are deterministic in the sense that for every $t \in \mathsf{Term}(\Sigma)$ there is at most one $q \in Q$ such that $t \Rightarrow^* q$.

2.1 Operations on FTAs

FTAs are closed under Boolean set operations, but for our purposes we mention only union and difference of automata, where in addition we assume that the signature Σ is fixed and that the states of FTAs are disjoint from each other when applying operations (the states can be renamed apart).

Definition 3 (Union of FTAs). *Let* $\mathcal{A}^1, \mathcal{A}^2$ *be FTAs* $(Q^1, Q^1_f, \Sigma, \Delta^1)$ *and* $(Q^2, Q^2_f, \Sigma, \Delta^2)$ *respectively. Then* $\mathcal{A}^1 \cup \mathcal{A}^2 = (Q^1 \cup Q^2, Q^1_f \cup Q^2_f, \Sigma, \Delta^1 \cup \Delta^2)$, *and we have* $\mathcal{L}(\mathcal{A}^1 \cup \mathcal{A}^2) = \mathcal{L}(\mathcal{A}^1) \cup \mathcal{L}(\mathcal{A}^2)$.

Determinisation plays a key role in the theory of FTAs. As far as expressiveness is concerned, we can limit our attention to DFTAs since for every FTA $\mathcal{A}$ there exists a DFTA $\mathcal{A}^d$ such that $\mathcal{L}(\mathcal{A}) = \mathcal{L}(\mathcal{A}^d)$ [9]. The standard construction builds a DFTA $\mathcal{A}^d$ whose states are elements of the powerset of the states of $\mathcal{A}$. The textbook procedure for constructing $\mathcal{A}^d$ from $\mathcal{A}$ [9] is not viewed as a practical procedure for manipulating tree automata, even fairly small ones. In a recent work Gallagher *et al.* [14] developed an optimised algorithm for determinisation, whose worst-case complexity remains unchanged, but which performs dramatically better than existing algorithms in practice. A critical aspect of the algorithm is that the transitions of the determinised automaton are generated in a potentially very compact form called *product form*, which can often be used directly when manipulating the determinised automaton.

Definition 4 (Product Transition). *A* product transition *is of the form* $f(Q_1, \ldots, Q_n) \to q$ *where* Q_i *are sets of states and* q *is a state. The product transition represents a set of transitions* $\{f(q_1, \ldots, q_n) \to q \mid q_i \in Q_i, i = 1..n\}$. *Thus* $\Pi_{i=1}^n |Q_i|$ *transitions are represented by a single product transition.*

Alternatively, we can regard a product transition as introducing ϵ-transitions. An ϵ-transition has the form $q_1 \to q_2$ where q_1, q_2 are states. ϵ-transitions can be eliminated, if desired. Given a product transition $f(Q_1, \ldots, Q_n) \to q$, introduce n new non-final states $s_1, \ldots, s_n$ corresponding to $Q_1, \ldots, Q_n$ respectively and replace the product transition by the set of transitions $\{f(s_1, \ldots, s_n) \to q\} \cup$

$\{q' \to s_i \mid q' \in Q_i, 1 = 1..n\}$. It can be shown that this transformation preserves the language of the FTA.

Given FTAs $\mathcal{A}^1$ and $\mathcal{A}^2$ there exists an FTA $\mathcal{A}^1 \setminus \mathcal{A}^2$ such that $\mathcal{L}(\mathcal{A}^1 \setminus \mathcal{A}^2) = \mathcal{L}(\mathcal{A}_1) \setminus \mathcal{L}(\mathcal{A}^2)$. To construct the difference FTA we use union and determinisation and exploit the following property of determinised states [14].

Property 1. Let $\mathcal{A}^d$ be the DFTA constructed from $\mathcal{A}$. Let Q be the states of $\mathcal{A}$. Then there is a run $t \Rightarrow^* q$ in $\mathcal{A}$ if and only if there is a run $t \Rightarrow^* Q'$ in $\mathcal{A}^d$ where $Q' \in 2^Q$, such that $q \in Q'$.

Furthermore recall that a term is accepted by at most one state in a DFTA. This gives rise to the following construction of the difference FTA $\mathcal{A}^1 \setminus \mathcal{A}^2$. We first form the DFTA for the union of the two FTAs and then remove those of its final states containing the final states of $\mathcal{A}^2$. In this way we remove the terms, and only the terms (by Property 1), accepted by $\mathcal{A}^2$. The availability of a practical algorithm for determinisation is what makes this construction of the difference FTA feasible.

Definition 5 (Construction of difference of FTAs). *Let $\mathcal{A}^1, \mathcal{A}^2$ be FTAs $(Q^1, Q^1_f, \Sigma, \Delta^1)$ and $(Q^2, Q^2_f, \Sigma, \Delta^2)$ respectively. Let $(\mathcal{Q}', \mathcal{Q}'_f, \Sigma, \Delta')$ be the determinisation of $\mathcal{A}^1 \cup \mathcal{A}^2$. Let $\mathcal{Q}^2 = \{Q' \in \mathcal{Q}' \mid Q' \cap Q^2_f \neq \emptyset\}$. Then $\mathcal{A}^1 \setminus \mathcal{A}^2 = (\mathcal{Q}', \mathcal{Q}'_f \setminus \mathcal{Q}^2, \Sigma, \Delta')$.*

Next we introduce a new operation over FTA called *state splitting.* which consists of splitting a state q into a number of states, based on a partition of the set of transitions whose rhs is q. We define this splitting as follows:

Definition 6 (Splitting a state in an FTA). *Let $\mathcal{A} = (Q, Q_f, \Sigma, \Delta)$ be an FTA. Let $q \in Q$ and $\Delta_q = \{t \in \Delta \mid \mathsf{rhs}(t) = q\}$. Let $\Phi = \{\Delta^1_q, \ldots, \Delta^k_q\}$ $(k > 1)$ be some partition of Δ_q. Introduce k new states $q_1, \ldots, q_k$. Then the FTA $\mathsf{split}_\Phi(\mathcal{A})$ is $(Q^s, Q^s_f, \Sigma, \Delta^s)$ where:*

- *$Q^s = Q \setminus \{q\} \cup \{q_1, \ldots, q_k\}$;*
- *$Q^s_f = Q_f \setminus \{q\} \cup \{q_1, \ldots, q_k\}$ if $q \in Q_f$, otherwise $Q^s_f = Q_f$;*
- *$\Delta^s = \mathsf{unfold}_q(\Delta \setminus \Delta_q \cup \{\mathsf{lhs}(t) \to q_i \mid t \in \Delta^i_q, i = 1..k\})$, where $\mathsf{unfold}_q(\Delta')$ is the result of repeatedly replacing a transition $f(\ldots, q, \ldots) \to s \in \Delta'$ by the set of k transitions $\{f(\ldots, q_1, \ldots) \to s, \ldots, f(\ldots, q_k, \ldots) \to s\}$ until no more such replacements can be made.*

We have $\mathcal{L}(\mathcal{A}) = \mathcal{L}(\mathsf{split}_\Phi(\mathcal{A}))$.

3 Horn Clauses and Their Trace Automata

A constrained Horn clause (CHC) is a first order predicate logic formula of the form $\forall(\phi \wedge p_1(X_1) \wedge \ldots \wedge p_k(X_k) \to p(X))$ $(k \geq 0)$, where ϕ is a conjunction of constraints with respect to some background theory, X_i, X are (possibly empty) vectors of distinct variables, $p_1, \ldots, p_k, p$ are predicate symbols, $p(X)$ is the head of the clause and $\phi \wedge p_1(X_1) \wedge \ldots \wedge p_k(X_k)$ is the body.

There is a distinguished predicate symbol false which is interpreted as false. In practice the predicate false only occurs in the head of clauses; we call clauses whose head is false *integrity constraints*, following the terminology of deductive databases. They are also sometimes referred to as negative clauses. We follow the syntactic conventions of constraint logic programs and write a clause as $p(X) \leftarrow \phi, p_1(X_1), \ldots, p_k(X_k)$.

3.1 Interpretations and Models

An interpretation of a set of CHCs is represented as a set of *constrained facts* of the form $A \leftarrow \phi$ where A is an atomic formula $p(Z_1, \ldots, Z_n)$ where $Z_1, \ldots, Z_n$ are distinct variables and ϕ is a constraint over $Z_1, \ldots, Z_n$. The constrained fact $A \leftarrow \phi$ is shorthand for the set of variable-free facts $A\theta$ such that $\phi\theta$ holds in the constraint theory, and an interpretation M denotes the set of all facts denoted by its elements; M assigns true to exactly those facts. $M_1 \subseteq M_2$ if the set of denoted facts of M_1 is contained in the set of denoted facts of M_2.

Minimal models. A model of a set of CHCs is an interpretation that satisfies each clause. There exists a minimal model with respect to the subset ordering, denoted $M[\![P]\!]$ where P is the set of CHCs. $M[\![P]\!]$ can be computed as the least fixed point (lfp) of an immediate consequences operator (called S_P^D in [25, Section 4]), which is an extension of the standard T_P operator from logic programming, extended to handle the constraint domain D. Furthermore $\mathsf{lfp}(S_P^D)$ can be computed as the limit of the ascending sequence of interpretations $\emptyset, S_P^D(\emptyset), S_P^D(S_P^D(\emptyset)), \ldots$. This sequence provides a basis for abstract interpretation of CHC clauses. The minimal model of P is equivalent to the set of atomic logic consequences of P.

3.2 The Constrained Horn Clause Verification Problem.

Given a set of CHCs P, the CHC verification problem is to check whether there exists a model of P. Obviously any model of P assigns false to the bodies of integrity constraints. We restate this property in terms of the derivability of the predicate false. Let $P \models F$ mean that F is a logical consequence of P, that is, that every interpretation satisifying P also satisfies F.

Lemma 1. *P has a model if and only if* $P \not\models \mathsf{false}$.

This lemma holds for arbitrary interpretations (only assuming that the predicate false is interpreted as false), uses only the textbook definitions of "interpretation" and "model" and does not depend on the constraint theory. Due to the equivalence of the minimal model of P with the set of atomic logical consequences of P, we have yet another equivalent formulation of the CHC verification problem.

Lemma 2. *P has a model if and only if* $\mathsf{false} \notin M[\![P]\!]$.

```
c1. mc91(A,B) :- A > 100, B = A-10.
c2. mc91(A,B) :- A =< 100, C = A+11, mc91(C,D), mc91(D,B).
c3. false :- A =< 100,  B > 91, mc91(A,B).
c4. false :- A =< 100, B =< 90, mc91(A,B).
```

Fig. 1. Example CHCs. The McCarthy 91-function.

It is this formulation that is most relevant to our method, since we compute over-approximations of $M[\![P]\!]$ by abstract interpretation. That is, if $\mathsf{false} \notin M'$ where $M[\![P]\!] \subseteq M'$ then we have shown that P has a model.

3.3 Trace Automata for CHCs

Before constructing the trace automaton we introduce identifiers for each clause. An identifier is a function symbol whose arity is the same as the number of atoms in the clause body. For instance a clause $p(X) \leftarrow \phi, p_1(X_1), \ldots, p_k(X_k)$ is assigned a function symbol with arity k. More than one clause can be assigned the same function symbol, but all the clauses with the same identifier have the same structure, including their constraints; that is, they differ only in one or more predicate names. Given a set of CHCs and a set Σ of ranked function symbols, let $\mathsf{id}_P : P \rightarrow \Sigma$ be the assignment of function symbols to clauses.

Definition 7 (Trace FTA for a set of CHCs). *Let P be a set of CHCs. Define the trace FTA for P as $\mathcal{A}_P = (Q, Q_f, \Sigma, \Delta)$ where*

- *Q is the set of predicate symbols of P;*
- *$Q_f \subseteq Q$ is the set of predicate symbols occurring in the heads of clauses of P;*
- *Σ is a set of function symbols;*
- *$\Delta = \{c(p_1, \ldots, p_k) \rightarrow p \mid$ where $c \in \Sigma,\ c = \mathsf{id}_P(cl)$, where $cl = p(X) \leftarrow \phi, p_1(X_1), \ldots, p_k(X_k)\}$.*

The elements of $\mathcal{L}(\mathcal{A}_P)$ are called trace terms for P. In Section 4 we will see that several clauses differing only in their predicate names are assigned the same function symbol.

To motivate readers, we present an example set of CHCs P in Figure 1 which will be used throughout this paper. This is an interesting problem in which the computations are trees rather than linear sequences.

Example 1. Let P be the set of CHCs in Figure 1. Let id_P map the clauses to $c_1, \ldots, c_4$ respectively. Then $\mathcal{A}_P = (Q, Q_f, \Sigma, \Delta)$ where:

$$\begin{array}{lll} Q &= \{\mathtt{mc91}, \mathtt{false}\} & \Delta = \{c_1 \rightarrow \mathtt{mc91}, \\ Q_f &= \{\mathtt{mc91}, \mathtt{false}\} & \quad c_2(\mathtt{mc91}, \mathtt{mc91}) \rightarrow \mathtt{mc91}, \\ \Sigma &= \{c_1, c_2, c_3, c_4\} & \quad c_3(\mathtt{mc91}) \rightarrow \mathtt{false},\ c_4(\mathtt{mc91}) \rightarrow \mathtt{false}\} \end{array}$$

For each trace term there exists a corresponding derivation tree called an AND-tree, which is unique up to variable renaming. The concept of an AND-tree is derived from [33] and [16].

Definition 8 (AND-tree for a trace term). *Let P be a set of CHCs and let $t \in \mathcal{L}(\mathcal{A}_P)$. Denote by $\mathsf{AND}(t)$ the following labelled tree, where each node of $\mathsf{AND}(t)$ is labelled by a clause and an atomic formula.*

1. *For each subterm $c_j(t_1, \ldots, t_k)$ of t there is a corresponding node in $\mathsf{AND}(t)$ labelled by an atom $p(X)$ and (a renamed variant of) some clause $p(X) \leftarrow \phi, p_1(X_1), \ldots, p_k(X_k)$ such that $c_j = \mathsf{id}_P(p(X) \leftarrow \phi, p_1(X_1), \ldots, p_k(X_k))$; the node's children (if $k > 0$) are the nodes corresponding to $t_1, \ldots, t_k$ and are labelled by $p_1(X_1), \ldots, p_k(X_k)$.*
2. *The variables in the labels are chosen such that if a node n is labelled by a clause, the local variables in the clause body do not occur outside the subtree rooted at n.*

Definition 9 (Trace constraints). *Let P be a set of CHCs. The set of constraints of a trace $t \in \mathcal{L}(\mathcal{A}_P)$, represented as $\mathsf{constr}(t)$ is the set of all constraints in the clause labels of $\mathsf{AND}(t)$.*

Definition 10 (Feasible trace). *We say that a trace term t is feasible if $\mathsf{constr}(t)$ is satisfiable.*

Definition 11 (FTA for a trace term). *Let P be a set of CHCs and $t \in \mathcal{L}(\mathcal{A}_P)$. The FTA $\mathcal{A}_t$ (whose construction is trivial) such that $\mathcal{L}(\mathcal{A}_t) = \{t\}$ is called* the FTA for t. *The states of $\mathcal{A}_t$ are chosen to be disjoint from those of $\mathcal{A}_P$.*

Example 2 (Trace FTA). Consider the FTA in Example 1. Let $t = c_3(c_2(c_1, c_1))$. Each $\mathtt{node_i}$ represents a label in the trace. Then $\mathcal{A}_t = (Q, Q_f, \Sigma, \Delta)$ is defined as:

$$\begin{aligned} Q &= \{\mathtt{node_1}, \mathtt{node_2}, \mathtt{node_3}, \mathtt{node_4}\} \\ Q_f &= \{\mathtt{node_1}\} \\ \Sigma &= \{c_1, c_2, c_3, c_4\} \\ \Delta &= \{c_1 \rightarrow \mathtt{node_3},\ c_1 \rightarrow \mathtt{node_4},\ c_2(\mathtt{node_3}, \mathtt{node_4}) \rightarrow \mathtt{node_2}, \\ &\quad\ c_3(\mathtt{node_2}) \rightarrow \mathtt{node_1}\} \end{aligned}$$

and Σ is the same as in $\mathcal{A}_P$. The trace t is not feasible since $\mathsf{constr}(t) = \{\mathtt{A} \leq 100, \mathtt{B} > 91, \mathtt{A} \leq 100, \mathtt{C} = \mathtt{A} + 11, \mathtt{C} > 100, \mathtt{D} = \mathtt{C} - 10, \mathtt{D} > 100, \mathtt{B} = \mathtt{D} - 10\}$ and this is not satisfiable.

Definition 12 (Constrained trace atom). *Let P be a set of CHCs and $t \in \mathcal{L}(\mathcal{A}_P)$. Let $p(X)$ be the atom labelling the root of $\mathsf{AND}(t)$. Then the constrained trace atom of t is $\forall X.(\exists \bar{Z}.\mathsf{constr}(t) \rightarrow p(X))$, where $\bar{Z} = \mathsf{vars}(\mathsf{constr}(t)) \setminus X$.*

We now restate a standard result from constraint logic programming [25] in terms of the concepts defined above.

Proposition 1. *Let P be a set of CHCs.*

1. *Then for all $t \in \mathcal{L}(\mathcal{A}_P)$ the constrained trace atom for t is a logical consequence of P. (Note that if t is not feasible this is trivially true).*

2. *If $p(a)$ is in the minimal model of P, there exists a feasible trace $t \in \mathcal{L}(\mathcal{A}_P)$ whose constrained trace atom is of the form $\forall X.\phi \rightarrow p(X)$ where the constraint $\phi[X/a]$ is true.*

Assuming that the constraint theory has a complete satisfiability procedure, part 1 of Proposition 1 corresponds to the standard soundness result for resolution-based proof systems, and part 2 corresponds to completeness.

3.4 Model-Preserving Transformation of Trace Automata

Proposition 1 implies that the constrained trace atoms for the feasible traces describe exactly the elements of the minimal model, which is equivalent to the set of atomic logical consequences of P. As a consequence the set of feasible traces in $\mathcal{L}(\mathcal{A}_P)$ can be regarded as a representation of the minimal model of P.

If we transform $\mathcal{A}_P$ to another FTA while preserving the set of traces, we also preserve the feasible traces. More generally, we can transform $\mathcal{A}_P$ to another FTA $\mathcal{A}'$ so long as $\mathcal{L}(\mathcal{A}') \subseteq \mathcal{L}(\mathcal{A}_P)$ and the elements of $\mathcal{L}(\mathcal{A}_P) \setminus \mathcal{L}(\mathcal{A}')$ are all infeasible. In this case the feasible traces of $\mathcal{L}(\mathcal{A}')$ are still a representation of the minimal model of P. We will exploit this in our refinement procedure (see Section 4).

3.5 Generation of CHCs from a Trace FTA

Now we describe a procedure (Algorithm 1) for generating a set of clauses P' from an FTA $\mathcal{A} = (Q, Q_f, \Sigma, \Delta)$ and a set of clauses P. We assume that Σ is the same as that of $\mathcal{A}_P$; so Σ is the range of the function id_P mapping clauses of P to function symbols. The transitions Δ are not in product form; a modification of the algorithm and its correctness proposition is possible for product form but we omit that here. We first introduce an injective function for renaming the states of $\mathcal{A}$ since we need predicate names for the generated clauses.

$$\rho : Q \rightarrow \mathsf{Predicates}$$

The function ρ maps each FTA state to a distinct predicate name. The algorithm simply generates a clause for each transition, applying the renaming function from states to predicates, and introducing variables arguments according to the pattern obtained from any clause with the corresponding identifier (all clauses with the same identifier having the same variable pattern).

Apart from generating a set of clauses P', Algorithm 1 also generates the clause identification mapping $\mathsf{id}_{P'}$, preserving the function symbols from the FTA. In this way the set of traces is preserved from P to P'. The correctness of Algorithm 1 is expressed by the following proposition.

Proposition 2. *Let P be a set of CHCs and let $\mathcal{A}$ be an FTA whose signature is the same as that of $\mathcal{A}_P$. Let P' be the set of clauses generated from $\mathcal{A}$ and P by Algorithm 1. Then $\mathcal{L}(\mathcal{A}_{P'}) = \mathcal{L}(\mathcal{A})$. Furthermore if $\mathcal{L}(\mathcal{A}_{P'})$ includes all the feasible traces of $\mathcal{L}(\mathcal{A}_P)$ then the minimal model of P' is the same as the minimal model of P, modulo predicate renaming.*

Input: An FTA $\mathcal{A} = (Q, Q_f, \Sigma, \Delta)$ and a set of Horn clauses P
Output: A set of Horn clauses P'
$P' \leftarrow \emptyset$;
for *each* $c_i(q_1, \ldots, q_n) \to q$ *(where* $n \geq 0$*)* $\in \Delta$ **do**
  let $c = p(X) \leftarrow \phi, p_1(X_1), \ldots, p_n(X_n)$ be any clause in P where $\mathsf{id}_P(c) = c_i$;
  $c_{new} = \rho(q)(X) \leftarrow \phi, \rho(q_1)(X_1), \ldots, \rho(q_n)(X_n)$;
  $\mathsf{id}_{P'}(c_{new}) = c_i$;
  $P' \leftarrow P' \cup \{c_{new}\}$;
end
return P';

Algorithm 1. ALGORITHM for generating a set of clauses from an FTA

Example 3 (Generation of clauses from an FTA). Consider the following transitions, relating to the signature for the program in Figure 1. The set of states is {`[false]`, `[mc91]`, `[e,false]`, `[mc91,e1]`}. (These are elements of the powerset of the set of states {`false`,`mc91`,`e`,`e1`}, which were generated by the determinisation algorithm).

```
c1 -> [mc91, e1].
c2([mc91, e1],[mc91, e1]) -> [mc91].
c2([mc91],[mc91]) -> [mc91].
c2([mc91, e1],[mc91]) -> [mc91].
c2([mc91],[mc91, e1]) -> [mc91].
c3([mc91]) -> [false].
c4([mc91, e1]) -> [false].
c4([mc91]) -> [false].
c3([mc91, e1]) -> [e, false].
```

The clauses generated by Algorithm 1 are the following, with the renaming function $\rho = \{[\texttt{false}] \mapsto \texttt{false}, [\texttt{mc91}] \mapsto \texttt{mc91}, [\texttt{e}, \texttt{false}] \mapsto \texttt{false\_1}, [\texttt{mc91}, \texttt{e1}] \mapsto \texttt{mc91\_1}\}$. Below we also show the clause identifiers (the id function for the generated clauses) showing that several clauses can have the same identifier, thus preserving traces.

```
c1: mc91_1(A,B) :-  A>100, B=A-10.
c2: mc91(A,B) :-  A=<100,  C=A+11, mc91_1(C,D),  mc91_1(D,B).
c2: mc91(A,B) :-  A=<100,  C=A+11, mc91(C,D),  mc91(D,B).
c2: mc91(A,B) :-  A=<100,  C=A+11, mc91_1(C,D),  mc91(D,B).
c2: mc91(A,B) :-  A=<100,  C=A+11, mc91(C,D), mc91_1(D,B).
c3: false :- A =< 100, B > 91, mc91(A,B).
c4: false :- A =< 100, B =< 90, mc91(A,B).
c4: false :- A =< 100, B =< 90, mc91_1(A,B).
c3: false_1 :- A =< 100, B > 91, mc91_1(A,B).
```

3.6 Abstract Interpretation of Constrained Horn Clauses

Abstract interpretation [10] is a static program analysis techniques which derives sound over-approximations by computing abstract fixed points. Convex polyhedron analysis (CPA) [11] is a program analysis technique based on abstract interpretation [10]. When applied to a set of CHCs P it constructs an over-approximation M' of the minimal model of P, where M' contains at most one constrained fact $p(X) \leftarrow \phi$ for each predicate p. The constraint ϕ is a conjunction of linear inequalities, representing a convex polyhedron. The first application of convex polyhedron analysis to CHCs was by Benoy and King [4].

We summarise briefly the elements of convex polyhedron analysis for CHC; further details (with application to CHC) can be found in [11,4]. The abstract interpretation consists of the computation of an increasing sequence of elements of the abstract domain of tuples of convex polyhedra (one for each predicate) $\mathcal{D}^n$. We construct a monotonic *abstract semantic function* $F_P : \mathcal{D}^n \rightarrow \mathcal{D}^n$ for the set of Horn clauses P, approximating the concrete semantic "immediate consequences" operator. Since $\mathcal{D}^n$ contains infinite increasing chains, a *widening* operator for convex polyhedra [11] is needed to ensure convergence of the sequence. The sequence computed is $Z_0 = \bot^n$, $Z_{n+1} = Z_n \nabla F_P(Z_n)$ where ∇ is a widening operator for convex polyhedra and the empty polyhedron is denoted $\bot$. The conditions on ∇ ensure that the sequence stabilises; thus for some finite j, $Z_i = Z_j$ for all $i > j$ and furthermore the value Z_j represents an over-approximation of the least model of P. Much research has been done on improving the precision of widening operators. One technique is known as widening-upto, or widening with thresholds [22]. A threshold is an assertion that is combined with a widening operator to improve its precision.

Our tool for convex polyhedral abstract interpretation, called CPA in the rest of this paper, uses the Parma Polyhedra Library [2] to implement the operations on convex polyhedra, and incorporates a threshold generation phase based on the method described by Lakhdar-Chaouch *et al.* [27], as well as a constraint strengthening pre-processing which propagates constraints both forwards and backwards in the clauses of P. Space does not permit a detailed explanation.

4 Refinement of Horn Clauses Using Trace Automata

If an over-approximation of the clauses derived by polyhedral abstraction does not contain false, the clauses are safe. However if false is contained in the approximation, we do not know whether the clauses are unsafe or whether the approximation was too imprecise. In such cases we can produce a trace term using the clauses in P which justifies the abstract derivation of false. The feasibility of this trace can be checked by a constraint satisfiability check. If the trace is feasible, then it corresponds to a proof of unsafety. Otherwise, refinement is considered based on this trace. In some approaches, a more precise abstract domain is derived from the trace. In our refinement approach, which is described next, we aim to generate a modified set of clauses that could yield a better approximation. This is achieved through the steps shown in Algorithm 2.

Input: A set of Horn clauses P and an infeasible trace t
Output: A set of Horn clauses P'

1. construct the trace FTA $\mathcal{A}_P$ (Definition 7);
2. construct an FTA $\mathcal{A}_t$ such that $\mathcal{L}(\mathcal{A}_t) = \{t\}$ (Definition 11);
3. compute the difference FTA $\mathcal{A}_P \setminus \mathcal{A}_t$ (Definition 5);
4. generate P' from $\mathcal{A}_P \setminus \mathcal{A}_t$ and P (Algorithm 1) ;

return P';

Algorithm 2. Algorithm for clause refinement

Both $\mathcal{A}_P$ and $\mathcal{A}_t$ in Algorithm 2 are deterministic by construction, however their union is not. Determinisation is used to generate the difference FTA (step 3) and its result is in product form. The program P' has the same model (modulo predicate renaming) as P, since the steps result in the removal of an infeasible trace but all other traces are preserved.

Removal of one trace from the clauses might not seem much of a refinement. However, the restructuring of the clauses required to remove a trace can split the predicates. This restructuring is the effect of determinisation, which isolates the infeasible trace. This in turn can induce a more precise abstract interpretation, with less precision loss due to convex hull operations and widening.

The correctness of this refinement follows from Proposition 2. In particular $\mathsf{false} \in M[\![P]\!]$ if and only if $\mathsf{false} \in M[\![P']\!]$ (assuming that the predicate renaming at least preserves the predicate name false).

Example 4. Consider again the FTA shown in Example 3. This is in fact the determinisation of $\mathcal{A}_P \cup \mathcal{A}_t$ where P is the set of clauses in Figure 1 and $\mathcal{A}_t$ where t is the infeasible trace `c3(c1)`. The only accepting state of $\mathcal{A}_t$ is `e`; thus to construct the difference $\mathcal{A}_P \setminus \mathcal{A}_t$ we need only to remove from the automaton the states containing `e`, namely `[mc91,e]`. We can also remove any transitions containing this state in the right hand side. This leaves the following FTA and refined program, using the same renaming function as in Example 3. In this program, the infeasible trace corresponding to `c3(c1)` cannot be constructed.

```
c1 -> [mc91, e1].
c2([mc91, e1],[mc91, e1]) -> [mc91].
c2([mc91],[mc91]) -> [mc91].
c2([mc91, e1],[mc91]) -> [mc91].
c2([mc91],[mc91, e1]) -> [mc91].
c3([mc91]) -> [false].
c4([mc91]) -> [false].
c4([mc91, e1]) -> [false].

c1: mc91_1(A,B) :-  A>100, B=A-10.
c2: mc91(A,B) :-  A=<100,  C=A+11, mc91_1(C,D),  mc91_1(D,B).
c2: mc91(A,B) :-  A=<100,  C=A+11, mc91(C,D),  mc91(D,B).
c2: mc91(A,B) :-  A=<100,  C=A+11, mc91_1(C,D),  mc91(D,B).
c2: mc91(A,B) :-  A=<100,  C=A+11, mc91(C,D),  mc91_1(D,B).
```

```
c3: false :- A =< 100, B > 91, mc91(A,B).
c4: false :- A =< 100, B =< 90, mc91(A,B).
c4: false :- A =< 100, B =< 90, mc91_1(A,B).
```

It can be seen that although the infeasible trace was very simple, its removal led to a considerably restructured set of clauses. We have not shown the product form here, which is in fact somewhat more compact.

The refinement process guarantees progress; that is, the infeasible computation once eliminated never arises again. Due to the construction of the id mapping for P' the traces in the languages of the FTAs of P and P' are preserved, apart from the eliminated trace.

Proposition 3 (Progress). *Let P be a set of CHCs, and t be a trace in P. Let P' be a refined set of CHCs obtained from P after the removal of t. Then t cannot be generated in any approximation of P'.*

After the removal of the trace t (step 3 of Algorithm 2) the language of $\mathcal{A}_P \setminus \mathcal{A}_t$ does not contain t. Then using Algorithm 1 to generate P', t will not be a possible trace in P'. It is physically impossible to construct t, in any abstract domain.

4.1 Further Refinement: Splitting a State in the Trace FTA

We also apply a tree-automata-based transformation to split states representing predicates where convex hull operations have lost precision. A typical case is where a number of clauses with the same head predicate contain disjoint constraints, such as a predicate representing an if-then-else statement in an imperative program. The clauses defining the statement will have a clause for the *then* branch and a clause for the *else* branch. The respective constraints in these clauses are disjoint since one is the negation of the other. The convex hull will thus contain the whole space for the variables involved in these constraints.

As defined in Definition 6, the FTA state corresponding to such a predicate can be split. We partition the transitions corresponding to the clauses according to the disjoint groups of constraints and apply the procedure in Definition 6, preserving the set of traces. Thus the feasible traces and the model of the resulting clauses is preserved. This enhances precision of polyhedral analysis [15].

Splitting has to be carried out in a controlled manner to prevent blow up in the size of FTA and hence on the size of the clauses generated. With this in mind we split only those states appearing in a counterexample trace.

5 Experiments on CHC Benchmark Problems

Our tool consists of an implementation of a *convex polyhedra analyser* for CLP written in Ciao Prolog[1] interfaced to the Parma Polyhedra Library [2] as well as an implementation of an FTA determiniser written in Java. It takes as input a

[1] `http://ciao-lang.org/`

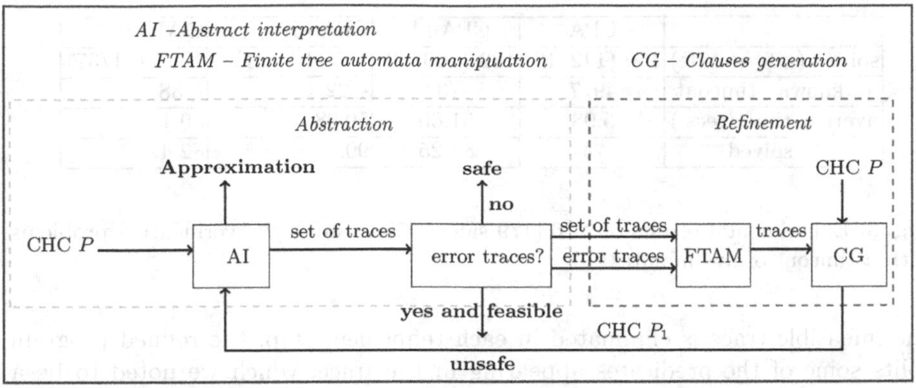

Fig. 2. *Abstraction-refinement scheme in Horn clause verification*

CLP program and returns "safe", "unsafe" or "unknown" (after timeout). The benchmark set contains 216 CHCs verification problems (179 safe and 37 unsafe problems), taken mainly from the repositories of several state-of-the-art software verification tools such as DAGGER [19] (21 problems), TRACER [26] (66 problems), InvGen [21] (68 problems), and also from the TACAS 2013 Software Verification Competition [5] (52 problems). Most of these problems are available in C and they were first translated to CLP form[2]. The chosen problems are representatives of different categories of the Software Verification Competition (loops, control flow and integer, SystemC etc.) as well as specific problems used to demonstrate the strength of different verification tools. The benchmarks are available from `http://akira.ruc.dk/~kafle/VMCAI15-Benchmarks.zip`. The experiments were carried out on an Intel(R) quad-core computer with a 2.66GHz processor running Debian 5 in 6 GB memory.

5.1 Summary of Results

The results of our experiments are summarised in Table 3. Column CPA summarises the results using our own *convex polyhedra analyser* (Section 3.6) with no refinement step. Column CPA+R shows the results obtained by iterating the CPA algorithm with the refinement step described in Section 4, Algorithm 2. Column CPA+R+Split incorporates the FTA-based state splitting into the refinement step (Section 4.1). Column QARMC shows the results obtained on the same problems using the QARMC tool [31].

5.2 Discussion of Results

The results show that CPA is reasonably effective on its own, solving 74% (160/216) of the problems, though it times out for seven problems. When combined with a refinement phase we can solve 22 further problems. Although only

[2] Thanks to Emanuele De Angelis for the translation.

	CPA	CPA+R	CPA+R+Split	QARMC
solved (safe/unsafe)	160 (142/18)	182 (160/22)	195 (164/31)	178 (141/37)
unknown/ timeout	49/7	-/34	-/22	-/38
average time (secs.)	5.98	51.66	50.08	59.1
% solved	74	84.25	90.27	82.4

Fig. 3. Experimental results on 216 (179 safe / 37 unsafe) CHC verification problems with a timeout of five minutes

one infeasible trace is eliminated in each refinement step, the refined program splits some of the predicates appearing in the trace, which we noted to be a crucial point of precision for polyhedral analysis [15]. When adding the state splitting refinement we solve an additional 13 problems. Further splitting would solve more problems but we are unwilling to introduce uncontrolled splitting due to the blow up in program size that could result. The maximum number of iterations required to solve a problem was 8. Although the timeout limit was five minutes, only 5% of the solved problems required more than one minute. QARMC tends to perform more (but faster) iterations.

Our implementation uses the product form for DFTAs produced by the determinisation algorithm, although the formalisation of refinement in Section 4 uses only standard FTA transitions. Although the traces for clauses with predicates produced from product states differ from the original clauses, they can be regarded as representing the original traces, by unfolding the clauses resulting from ϵ-transitions. Product form adds to the scalability of the approach, especially for Horn clauses with more than one body atom.

5.3 Comparison with Other Tools

Our results improve on QARMC both in average time and the number of instances solved. Out of 216 problems QARMC solves 178 problems with an average time of 59 seconds whereas we can solve 195 problems with an average time of 50 seconds. However, all unsafe programs in the benchmark set are solved by QARMC in contrast to ours. Convex polyhedral analysis is good at finding the required invariants to prove a program safe and due to this we solved more safe problems than QARMC. QARMC seems to be more effective at finding bugs. Most of the problems challenging to us come from particular categories e.g. SystemC (modelled over fixed size integers) and Control Flow and Integer Variables of [5] which requires some specific techniques to solve. Safe problems challenging to us are also challenging to QARMC though this is not the case for unsafe problems.

6 Related Work

The work by Heizmann et al. [23,24] uses word automata to construct a framework for abstraction refinement. Our work could certainly be regarded as extending that framework to tree-structured computations, using tree automata instead of (nested) word automata. However our aim is rather different. We use automata techniques to *perform* the refinement whereas in [23] automata notation is only used to re-express the verification problem, shifting the verification problem to the construction of "interpolant automata", without providing any automata-based algorithms to do this. On the other hand we discuss the practicality of the automata-based approach on a set of challenging problems.

While we eliminate only one trace at a time in the described procedure, the FTA difference algorithm extends naturally to eliminating (infinite) sets of traces. However in our setting that does not seem a useful goal – to find an automaton describing an infinite set of infeasible traces often amounts to solving the original problem.

Verification of CLP programs using abstract interpretation and specialisation has been studied for some time. The use of an over-approximation of the semantics of a program can be used to establish safety properties – if a state or property does not appear in an over-approximation, it certainly does not appear in the actual program behaviour. A general framework for logic program verification through abstraction was described by Levi [29]. Peralta *et al.* [30] introduced the idea of using a Horn clause representation of imperative languages and a convex polyhedral analyser to discover invariants of a program. Another approach is taken in the work of De Angelis *et al.* [12,13] on applying program specialisation to achieve verification. Unfolding and folding operations play a vital role in that approach, and hence the program structure is changed much more fundamentally than in our approach.

CEGAR [8] has been successfully used in verification to automatically refine (predicate) abstractions [7,28] to reduce false alarms but not much has been explored in refining abstractions in the convex polyhedral domain. Some work on this (with progress guarantee) has been done in [1] and [19]. [1] uses the powerset domain, while [19] uses a Hint DAG to gain precision lost during the convex hull operation. Both make use of interpolation. The use of interpolation in refinement in verification of Horn clauses is explored in [6,20]. In our approach we guarantee elimination of only one trace and elimination of others depends on properties of the abstract interpretation techniques. By contrast in interpolation-based techniques the refinement introduces new properties which guarantee progress and the elimination of all counterexamples covered by those properties. However the effectiveness of interpolation-based refinement depends on the generation of "good" interpolants, which is a matter of continuing research, for example by Rümmer *et al.* [32]. A number of tools implementing predicate abstraction and refinement are available, such as HSF [18] and BLAST [3]. TRACER [17] is a verification tool based on CLP that uses symbolic execution.

A point of contrast is that in our approach, the refinements are embedded in the clauses whereas in CEGAR they are accumulated in the set of properties used for property-based abstraction. Also we rely on the abstraction using convex polyhedral analysis to discover invariants whereas CEGAR-based approaches rely on interpolation in the refinement stage to discover relevant properties. Polyhedral analysis is more expensive, yet seems (along with the threshold assertions, see Section 3.6) to be very effective at finding invariants even on the first iteration. A weakness of invariant generation using interpolation is that the interpolants must share variables with the unsatisfiable part of the constraints, typically those in the integrity constraints, which can be insufficient for finding invariants of inner recursive predicates. Informally one can say that approaches differ in where the "hard work" is performed. In the CEGAR approaches and in [23] the refinement step is crucial, and interpolation plays a central role. In our approach, by contrast, most of the hard work is done by the abstract interpretation, which finds useful invariants. Finding the most effective balance between abstraction and refinement techniques is a matter of ongoing research.

7 Conclusion and Future work

In this paper we presented a procedure for abstraction refinement in Horn clause verification based on tree automata. This was achieved through a combination of abstraction (using abstraction interpretation) followed by a trace refinement (using finite tree automata). The refinement is independent of the abstract domain used. The practicality of our approach was demonstrated on a set of Horn clause verification problems.

In the future, we will investigate the elimination of a larger set of infeasible traces in each refinement step, possibly by generalising a trace using interpolation or by discovering a set of infeasible traces. The optimisation of our tool chain is also an important topic for future work as it is clear that our prototype, built by chaining together tools using shell scripts, contains much redundancy.

Acknowledgements. We thank the anonymous referees for useful comments.

References

1. Albarghouthi, A., Gurfinkel, A., Chechik, M.: Craig interpretation. In: Miné, A., Schmidt, D. (eds.) SAS 2012. LNCS, vol. 7460, pp. 300–316. Springer, Heidelberg (2012)
2. Bagnara, R., Hill, P.M., Zaffanella, E.: The Parma Polyhedra Library: Toward a complete set of numerical abstractions for the analysis and verification of hardware and software systems. Science of Computer Programming 72(1–2), 3–21 (2008)
3. Ball, T., Levin, V., Rajamani, S.K.: A decade of software model checking with SLAM. Commun. ACM 54(7), 68–76 (2011)
4. Benoy, F., King, A.: Inferring argument size relationships with CLP($\mathcal{R}$). In: Gallagher, J. (ed.) LOPSTR 1996. LNCS, vol. 1207, pp. 204–223. Springer, Heidelberg (1997)
5. Beyer, D.: Second competition on software verification - (summary of SV-COMP 2013). In: Piterman, N., Smolka, S.A. (eds.) TACAS 2013. LNCS, vol. 7795, pp. 594–609. Springer, Heidelberg (2013)

6. Bjørner, N., McMillan, K., Rybalchenko, A.: On solving universally quantified Horn clauses. In: Logozzo, F., Fähndrich, M. (eds.) SAS 2013. LNCS, vol. 7935, pp. 105–125. Springer, Heidelberg (2013)
7. Burke, M., Soffa, M.L. (eds.): Proceedings of the 2001 ACM SIGPLAN Conference on Programming Language Design and Implementation (PLDI), Snowbird, Utah, USA, June 20-22. ACM (2001)
8. Clarke, E.M., Grumberg, O., Jha, S., Lu, Y., Veith, H.: Counterexample-guided abstraction refinement for symbolic model checking. J. ACM 50(5), 752–794 (2003)
9. Comon, H., Dauchet, M., Gilleron, R., Löding, C., Jacquemard, F., Lugiez, D., Tison, S., Tommasi, M.: Tree automata techniques and applications (2007), `http://www.grappa.univ-lille3.fr/tata` (release October 12, 2007)
10. Cousot, P., Cousot, R.: Abstract interpretation: A unified lattice model for static analysis of programs by construction or approximation of fixpoints. In: Graham, R.M., Harrison, M.A., Sethi, R. (eds.) POPL, pp. 238–252. ACM (1977)
11. Cousot, P., Halbwachs, N.: Automatic discovery of linear restraints among variables of a program. In: Proceedings of the 5th Annual ACM Symposium on Principles of Programming Languages, pp. 84–96 (1978)
12. De Angelis, E., Fioravanti, F., Pettorossi, A., Proietti, M.: Verifying programs via iterated specialization. In: Albert, E., Mu, S.-C. (eds.) PEPM, pp. 43–52. ACM (2013)
13. De Angelis, E., Fioravanti, F., Pettorossi, A., Proietti, M.: VeriMAP: A tool for verifying programs through transformations. In: Ábrahám, E., Havelund, K. (eds.) TACAS 2014 (ETAPS). LNCS, vol. 8413, pp. 568–574. Springer, Heidelberg (2014)
14. Gallagher, J.P., Ajspur, M., Kafle, B.: An Optimised Algorithm for Determinisation and Completion of Finite Tree Automata. Technical Report 145, Roskilde University, Denmark, (September 2014), `http://akira.ruc.dk/~jpg/dfta.pdf`
15. Gallagher, J.P., Kafle, B.: Analysis and transformation tools for constrained Horn clause verification. TPLP, 14(4-5) (additional materials in online edition), 90–101 (2014)
16. Gallagher, J.P., Lafave, L.: Regular approximation of computation paths in logic and functional languages. In: Danvy, O., Thiemann, P., Glück, R. (eds.) Dagstuhl Seminar 1996. LNCS, vol. 1110, pp. 115–136. Springer, Heidelberg (1996)
17. Gange, G., Navas, J.A., Schachte, P., Søndergaard, H., Stuckey, P.J.: Failure tabled constraint logic programming by interpolation. TPLP 13(4-5), 593–607 (2013)
18. Grebenshchikov, S., Gupta, A., Lopes, N.P., Popeea, C., Rybalchenko, A.: HSF(C): A software verifier based on Horn clauses - (competition contribution). In: Flanagan, C., König, B. (eds.) TACAS 2012. LNCS, vol. 7214, pp. 549–551. Springer, Heidelberg (2012)
19. Gulavani, B.S., Chakraborty, S., Nori, A.V., Rajamani, S.K.: Automatically refining abstract interpretations. In: Ramakrishnan, C.R., Rehof, J. (eds.) TACAS 2008. LNCS, vol. 4963, pp. 443–458. Springer, Heidelberg (2008)
20. Gupta, A., Popeea, C., Rybalchenko, A.: Solving recursion-free horn clauses over LI+UIF. In: Yang, H. (ed.) APLAS 2011. LNCS, vol. 7078, pp. 188–203. Springer, Heidelberg (2011)
21. Gupta, A., Rybalchenko, A.: InvGen: An efficient invariant generator. In: Bouajjani, A., Maler, O. (eds.) CAV 2009. LNCS, vol. 5643, pp. 634–640. Springer, Heidelberg (2009)
22. Halbwachs, N., Proy, Y.E., Raymound, P.: Verification of linear hybrid systems by means of convex approximations. In: LeCharlier, B. (ed.) SAS 1994. LNCS, vol. 864, pp. 223–237. Springer, Heidelberg (1994)

23. Heizmann, M., Hoenicke, J., Podelski, A.: Refinement of trace abstraction. In: Palsberg, J., Su, Z. (eds.) SAS 2009. LNCS, vol. 5673, pp. 69–85. Springer, Heidelberg (2009)
24. Heizmann, M., Hoenicke, J., Podelski, A.: Nested interpolants. In: Hermenegildo, M.V., Palsberg, J. (eds.) Proceedings of POPL 2010, pp. 471–482. ACM (2010)
25. Jaffar, J., Maher, M.: Constraint Logic Programming: A Survey. Journal of Logic Programming 19/20, 503–581 (1994)
26. Jaffar, J., Murali, V., Navas, J.A., Santosa, A.E.: TRACER: A symbolic execution tool for verification. In: Madhusudan, P., Seshia, S.A. (eds.) CAV 2012. LNCS, vol. 7358, pp. 758–766. Springer, Heidelberg (2012)
27. Lakhdar-Chaouch, L., Jeannet, B., Girault, A.: Widening with thresholds for programs with complex control graphs. In: Bultan, T., Hsiung, P.-A. (eds.) ATVA 2011. LNCS, vol. 6996, pp. 492–502. Springer, Heidelberg (2011)
28. Launchbury, J., Mitchell, J.C. (eds.): Conference Record of POPL 2002: The 29th SIGPLAN-SIGACT Symposium on Principles of Programming Languages, Portland, OR, USA, January 16-18. ACM (2002)
29. Levi, G.: Abstract interpretation based verification of logic programs. Electr. Notes Theor. Comput. Sci. 40, 243 (2000)
30. Peralta, J.C., Gallagher, J.P., Saglam, H.: Analysis of imperative programs through analysis of constraint logic programs. In: Levi, G. (ed.) SAS 1998. LNCS, vol. 1503, pp. 246–261. Springer, Heidelberg (1998)
31. Podelski, A., Rybalchenko, A.: ARMC: The logical choice for software model checking with abstraction refinement. In: Hanus, M. (ed.) PADL 2007. LNCS, vol. 4354, pp. 245–259. Springer, Heidelberg (2007)
32. Rümmer, P., Hojjat, H., Kuncak, V.: Disjunctive interpolants for horn-clause verification. In: Sharygina, N., Veith, H. (eds.) CAV 2013. LNCS, vol. 8044, pp. 347–363. Springer, Heidelberg (2013)
33. Stärk, R.F.: A direct proof for the completeness of SLD-resolution. In: Börger, E., Kleine Büning, H., Richter, M.M. (eds.) CSL 1989. LNCS, vol. 440, pp. 382–383. Springer, Heidelberg (1990)

Abstracting and Counting Synchronizing Processes

Zeinab Ganjei, Ahmed Rezine*, Petru Eles, and Zebo Peng

Linköping University, Sweden

Abstract. We address the problem of automatically establishing synchronization dependent correctness (e.g. due to using barriers or ensuring absence of deadlocks) of programs generating an arbitrary number of concurrent processes and manipulating variables ranging over an infinite domain. Automatically checking such properties for these programs is beyond the capabilities of current verification techniques. For this purpose, we describe an original logic that mixes two sorts of variables: those shared and manipulated by the concurrent processes, and ghost variables referring to the number of processes satisfying predicates on shared and local program variables. We then combine existing works on counter, predicate, and constrained monotonic abstraction and nest two cooperating counter example based refinement loops for establishing correctness (safety expressed as non reachability of configurations satisfying formulas in our logic). We have implemented a tool (PACMAN, for predicated constrained monotonic abstraction) and used it to perform parameterized verification for several programs whose correctness crucially depends on precisely capturing the number of synchronizing processes.

Keywords: parameterized verification, counting logic, barrier synchronization, deadlock freedom, multithreaded programs, counter abstraction, predicate abstraction, constrained monotonic abstraction.

1 Introduction

We address the problem of automatic and parameterized verification for concurrent multithreaded programs. We focus on synchronization related correctness as in the usage by programs of barriers or integer shared variables for counting the number of processes at different stages of the computation. Such synchronizations orchestrate the different phases of the executions of possibly arbitrary many processes spawned during runs of multithreaded programs. Correctness is stated in terms of a new counting logic that we introduce. The counting logic makes it possible to express statements about program variables and variables counting the number of processes satisfying some properties on the program variables. Such statements can capture both individual properties, such as assertion violations, and global properties such as deadlocks or relations between

---

* In part supported by the 12.04 CENIIT project.

D. D'Souza et al. (Eds.): VMCAI 2015, LNCS 8931, pp. 227–244, 2015.

the numbers of processes (e.g., the total number of spawner processes is smaller or equal to the number of spawned processes).

Synchronization among concurrent processes is central to the correctness of many shared memory based concurrent programs. This is particularly true in certain applications such as scientific computing where a number of processes, parameterized by the size of the problem or the number of cores, is spawned in order to perform heavy computations in phases. For this reason, when not implemented individually using shared variables, constructs such as (dynamic) barriers are made available in mainstream libraries and programming languages such as Pthreads, java.util.concurrent or OpenMP.

Automatically taking into account the different phases by which arbitrary many processes can pass is already tricky for concurrent boolean programs with barriers. It is now folklore that concurrent boolean programs can be encoded using counter machines where counters track the number of processes at each program location. In case the concurrent processes can only read, test and write shared boolean variables, or spawn and join other processes, the obtained counter machine is essentially a Vector Addition System (VAS) for which state reachability is decidable [3,10]. For instance, works such as [6,7] build on this idea. Such translations cannot exclude behaviors forbidden by the barriers, e.g., there is no process still in the reading phase when some process crossed the barrier to the writing phase. The reason is that VASs are inherently monotonic (more processes can do more things). However, a counter machine transition that models a barrier will need to test that all processes are finished with the current phase and are waiting to cross the barrier. In other words, that the number of processes not waiting for the barrier is zero. This makes it possible to encode counter machines for which reachability is undecidable.

To make the problem more difficult, barriers may be implicitly implemented using integer program variables that count the number of processes at certain locations. Still, program correctness might depend on the fact that these program variables do implement a barrier. Existing techniques, such as symmetric predicate abstraction [7], generate (broadcast) concurrent boolean programs for integer manipulating concurrent programs. The obtained transition systems are monotonic and cannot exclude behaviors forbidden by the implicit barriers. In this work, we build on such methods and strengthen the obtained transition systems using automatically generated invariants in order to obtain counter machines that over-approximate the concurrent program behavior and still enforce barriers semantics. We then build on our work on constrained monotonic abstraction [4] in order to decide state reachability by automatically generating and refining monotonic over-approximations for such systems.

Our approach consists in nesting two counter example guided abstraction refinement loops. We summarize our contributions in the following points.

1. We define a *counting logic* that allows us to express statements about program variables and about the number of processes satisfying certain predicates on the program variables.

2. We implement the outer loop by leveraging on existing symmetric predicate abstraction techniques [7]. We encode resulting boolean programs in terms of a counter machine where reachability of the concurrent program configurations satisfying a *counting property* from our logic is captured as a reachability problem for a target state of the counter machine.
3. We explain how to strengthen the counter machine using *counting invariants*, i.e. properties from our logic that hold on all runs. We generate these invariants using classical thread modular analysis techniques [11].
4. We leverage on existing constrained monotonic abstraction techniques [15,4] to implement the inner loop and to address the state reachability problem.
5. We have implemented both loops, together with automatic counting invariants generation, in a prototype (PACMAN) that automatically establishes or refutes counting properties such as deadlock freedom and assertions.

Related work. Several works consider automatic parameterized verification for concurrent programs. The works in [13,1] automatically check for cutoff conditions. Except for checking larger instances, it is unclear how to refine entailed abstractions. Similar to [2], we combine auxiliary invariants obtained on certain variables in order to strengthen a reachability analysis. In [9], the authors propose an approach that synthesizes counters and uses them to build correctness proofs. The proofs are then checked against programs given as control flow nets. We instead discover the counters, including counters tracking local and mixed thread predicates, and build sound over-approximations that have to be checked. In [6], the authors present a highly optimized coverability checking approach for VASs with broadcasts. We need more than coverability of monotonic systems. In [14], the authors adopt symbolic representations that can track inter-thread predicates. This yields a non monotonic system and the authors force monotonicity as in [15,4]. They however do not explain how to refine the obtained decidable monotonic abstraction for an undecidable problem. In [5], the authors prove termination for depth-bounded systems by instrumenting a given over-approximation with counters and sending the numerical abstraction to existing termination provers. We automatically generate the abstractions on which we establish safety properties. In addition, and as stated earlier, over-approximating the concurrent programs we target with (monotonic) well structured transition systems would result in spurious runs. The works that seem most closely related to our work are [4,8]. We introduced (constrained) monotonic abstraction in [15,4]. Monotonic abstraction was not combined with predicate abstraction, nor did it explicitly target counting properties or dynamic barrier based synchronization. In [8], the authors propose a predicate abstraction framework for concurrent multithreaded programs. As explained earlier such abstractions cannot exclude runs forbidden by synchronization mechanisms such as barriers. In our work, we build on [8] in order to handle shared and local integer variables.

Outline. We start by illustrating our approach using an example in Sec. 2 and introduce some preliminaries in Sec. 3. We then define concurrent programs and describe our counting logic in Sec. 4. Next, we explain the different phases of our nested loops in Sec. 5 and report on our experimental results in Sec. 6. We finally conclude in Sec. 7. Proofs and examples are available in [12].

2 A Motivating Example

Consider the concurrent program described in Fig. 1. In this example, a *main* process spawns (transition t_1) an arbitrary number (*count*) of *proc* processes (at location lc_{ent} in *proc*). All processes share four integer variables (namely *max*, *prev*, *wait* and *count*) and a single boolean variable *proceed*. Initially, the variables *wait* and *count* are 0 while *proceed* is false. The other variables may assume non-deterministic values. Each *proc* process possesses a local integer variable *val* that can only be read or written by its owner. Each *proc* process assigns to *max* the value of its local variable *val* in case the later is larger than the former. Transitions t_6 and t_7 essentially implement a barrier in the sense that all *proc* processes must have reached lc_3 in *proc* in order for any of them to move to location lc_4. After the barrier, the *max* value should be larger or equal to any previous local *val* value stored in the shared *prev* (i.e., $prev \leq max$ should hold). Observe that *prev* is essentially a ghost variable we add to check that *max* is indeed larger than any initial value of the local, and possibly modified, *val*. Violation of this assertion can be captured with the *counting predicate* (introduced in Sec. 4) $(proc@lc_4 \wedge \neg(prev \leq max))^{\#} \geq 1$ stating that the number of processes at location lc_4 in *proc* and witnessing that $prev > max$ is larger or equal than 1. Observe that we could have used an error state to capture assertion violations. However, our counting logic (see Sec. 4) also allows us to express global properties (e.g., there are more processes with $flag = \mathtt{tt}$ than those with $flag = \mathtt{ff}$). We use counting properties to capture such global configurations. These properties can already capture assertion violations.

```
int   max, prev, wait, count := *, *, 0, 0
bool  proceed := ff
main :
  t1 : lc_ent ▶ lc_ent :  count := count + 1;
                          spawn(proc)
  t2 : lc_ent ▶ lc1    :  proceed := tt
  ...

proc :
  int val := *
  t3 : lc_ent ▶ lc1 :  prev := val
  t4 : lc1    ▶ lc2 :  max ≥ val
  t5 : lc1    ▶ lc2 :  max < val; max := val
  t5 : lc2    ▶ lc3 :  val := *
  t6 : lc3    ▶ lc4 :  wait := wait + 1
  t7 : lc4    ▶ lc5 :  proceed ∧ (wait = count)
  t8 : lc5    ▶ ...
```

```
(3, 7, 0, 0, ff) {(main@lc_ent)}
   ↓ t1
(3, 7, 0, 1, ff) {(main@lc_ent)(proc@lc_ent, 9)}
   ↓ t1
(3, 7, 0, 2, ff) {(main@lc_ent)(proc@lc_ent, 9)^2}
   ↓ t3
(3, 9, 0, 2, ff) {(main@lc1)(proc@lc_ent, 9)(proc@lc1, 9)}
   ↓ t2
(3, 9, 0, 2, tt) {(main@lc1)(proc@lc_ent, 9)(proc@lc1, 9)}
   ↓ ...
  ...
   ↓ t7
(9, 9, 2, 2, tt) {(main@lc1)(proc@lc5, 9)(proc@lc5, 9)}
   ↓ ...
  ...
```

Fig. 1. The max example (left) and a possible run (right). The run starts with the *main* process being at location lc_{ent} where $(max, prev, wait, count, proceed) = (3, 7, 0, 0, \mathtt{ff})$.

The assertion $(proc@lc_5 \wedge \neg(prev \leq max))^{\#} \geq 1$ is never violated when starting from a single main process. In order to establish this fact, any verification procedure needs to take into account the barrier in t_7 in addition to the two sources of infinitness; namely, the infinite domain of the variables and the number of *procs* that may participate in the run. Any sound analysis that does not take into account that the *count* variable holds the number of spawned *proc* processes and that *wait* represents the number of *proc* processes at locations lc_3 or later will not be able to discard scenarios were a *proc* process executes $prev := val$ (possibly violating the assertion) although one of them is at lc_5 in *proc*.

Our nested CEGAR, called **P**redica**t**ed **C**onstrained **M**onotonic **A**bstraction and depicted in Fig. 2, systematically leverages on simple facts that relate numbers of processes to the variables manipulated in the program. This allows us to verify or refute safety properties (e.g., assertions, deadlock freedom) depending on complex behaviors induced by constructs such as dynamic barriers. We illustrate our approach on the max example of Fig. 1.

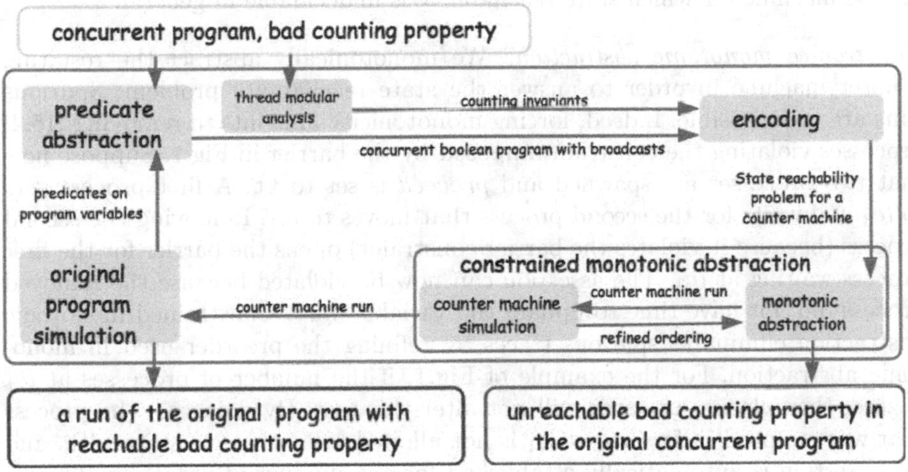

Fig. 2. Predicated Constrained Monotonic Abstraction

From concurrent programs to boolean concurrent programs. We build on recent predicate abstraction techniques for concurrent programs [8]. Such techniques would initially discard all variables and predicates and only keep the control flow together with the *spawn* and *join* statements. This leads to a number of counter example guided abstraction refinement steps (the outer CEGAR loop in Fig. 2) that require the addition of new predicates. Our implementation adds the predicates *proceed*, $prev \leq val$, $prev \leq max$, $wait \leq count$, $count \leq wait$. It is worth noticing that all variables of the obtained concurrent program are booleans. Hence, one would need a finite number of counters in order to faithfully capture the behavior of the abstracted program using counter abstraction.

From concurrent boolean programs to counter machines. Given a concurrent boolean program, we generate a monotonic counter machine for which reachability of a final state is equivalent to the violation of the assertion by the boolean program. Each counter in the machine counts the number of processes at some location with a given valuation of the local variables. One state in the counter machine represents reaching a configuration violating the assertion. State reachability is here decidable [3,10]. Such a machine cannot relate the number of processes in certain locations (e.g., the number of spawned processes *proc* so far) to the shared predicates that hold at a machine state (e.g., that $count = wait$). For this reason, we make use of the auxiliary invariants [2]:

$$count = \sum_{lc \text{ } proc \text{ location}} (proc@lc)^{\#} \qquad wait = \sum_{lc_i \text{ } proc \text{ location}, i \geq 3} (proc@lc_i)^{\#}$$

We automatically generate such invariants using a simple thread modular analysis [11] that tracks the number of processes at each location. We then strengthen the counter machine using such invariants. This results in a more precise machine for which state reachability is undecidable in general.

Constrained monotonic abstraction. We monotonically abstract the resulting counter machine in order to answer the state reachability problem. Spurious runs are now possible. Indeed, forcing monotonicity amounts to removing [15,4] processes violating the constraint imposed by the barrier in Fig.1. Suppose now that two processes are spawned and *proceed* is set to `tt`. A first process gets to lc_3 and waits for the second process that moves to lc_1. Removing the second process (because it violates the barrier constraint) opens the barrier for the first process waiting at lc_3. The assertion can now be violated because the removed process did not have time to update the variable *max*. Constrained monotonic abstraction eliminates spurious traces by refining the preorder used in monotonic abstraction. For the example of Fig.1, if the number of processes at lc_1 is zero, then closing upwards will not alter this fact. By doing so, the process that was removed in forward at lc_1 is not allowed to be there to start with, and the assertion is automatically established for any number of processes. The inner loop of our approach (i.e., the constrained monotonic abstraction loop) can automatically add more elaborate refinements such as comparing the number of processes at different locations. Unreachability of the control location establishes safety of the concurrent program.

Trace Simulation. Counter examples obtained in the counter machine correspond to feasible runs as far as the concurrent boolean program is concerned. Such runs can be simulated on the original program to find new predicates (e.g., using Craig interpolation) and use them in the next iteration of the outer loop.

3 Preliminaries

We use $\mathbb{N}$ and $\mathbb{Z}$ to mean the sets of natural and integer numbers respectively. We let k denote a constant in $\mathbb{Z}$. Unless otherwise stated, we use lower case letters such as v, s, l to mean integer variables and $\tilde{v}, \tilde{s}, \tilde{l}$ to mean boolean variables with values in $\mathbb{B}$. We use upper case letters such as V, S, L (resp. $\tilde{V}, \tilde{S}$ and $\tilde{L}$) to mean sets of integer (resp. boolean) variables. We let $\sim$ be an element in $\{<, \leq, =, \geq, >\}$. An arithmetic expression e (resp. boolean expression π) belonging to the set $\mathtt{exprs}(V)$ (resp. $\mathtt{preds}(\tilde{V}, E)$) of arithmetic expressions (resp. boolean predicates) over integer variables V (resp. boolean variables $\tilde{V}$ and arithmetic expressions E) is defined as follows.

$$e ::= k \,\big|\, v \,\big|\, (e + e) \,\big|\, (e - e) \,\big|\, k\, e \qquad\qquad v \in V$$
$$\pi ::= b \,\big|\, \tilde{v} \,\big|\, (e \sim e) \,\big|\, \neg\pi \,\big|\, \pi \wedge \pi \,\big|\, \pi \vee \pi \qquad\qquad \tilde{v} \in \tilde{V}, e \in E$$

We write $vars(e)$ to mean all variables v appearing in e, and $vars(\pi)$ to mean all variables $\tilde{v}$ and v appearing in π or in e in π. We also write $atoms(\pi)$ (the set of atomic predicates) to mean all comparisons $(e \sim e)$ appearing in π. We use greek lower case letters such as σ, η, ν (resp. $\tilde{\sigma}, \tilde{\eta}, \tilde{\nu}$) to mean mappings from variables to $\mathbb{Z}$ (resp. $\mathbb{B}$). Given n mappings $\nu_i : V_i \to \mathbb{Z}$ such that $V_i \cap V_j = \emptyset$ for each $i, j : 1 \leq i \neq j \leq n$, and an expression $e \in \mathtt{exprs}(V)$, we write $val_{\nu_1,\ldots,\nu_n}(e)$ to mean the expression obtained by replacing each occurrence of a variable v appearing in some V_i by the corresponding $\nu_i(v)$. In a similar manner, we write $val_{\nu,\tilde{\nu},\ldots}(\pi)$ to mean the predicate obtained by replacing the occurrence of integer and boolean variables as stated by the mappings $\nu, \tilde{\nu}, etc.$ Given a mapping $\nu : V \to \mathbb{Z}$ and a set $subst = \{v_i \leftarrow k_i | 1 \leq i \leq n\}$ where variables $v_1, \ldots v_n$ are pairwise different, we write $\nu\,[subst]$ to mean the mapping ν' such that $\nu'(v_i) = k_i$ for each $1 \leq i \leq n$ and $\nu'(v) = \nu(v)$ otherwise. We abuse notation and write $\nu\,[\{v_i \leftarrow v_i' | 1 \leq i \leq n\}]$, for $\nu : V \to \mathbb{Z}$ where variables $v_1, \ldots v_n$ are in V and pairwise different and variables $v_1', \ldots v_n'$ are pairwise different and not in V, to mean the mapping $\nu' : (V \setminus \{v_i | 1 \leq i \leq n\}) \cup \{v_i' | 1 \leq i \leq n\} \to \mathbb{Z}$ and such that $\nu'(v_i') = \nu(v_i)$ for each $i : 1 \leq i \leq n$, and $\nu'(v) = \nu(v)$ otherwise. We define $\tilde{\nu}\,[\{\tilde{v}_i \leftarrow b_i | 1 \leq i \leq n\}]$ and $\tilde{\nu}\,[\{\tilde{v}_i \leftarrow \tilde{v}_i' | 1 \leq i \leq n\}]$ in a similar manner.

A multiset m over a set X is a mapping $X \to \mathbb{N}$. We write $x \in m$ to mean $m(x) \geq 1$. The size $|m|$ of a multiset m is $\sum_{x \in X} m(x)$. We sometimes view a multiset m as a sequence $x_1, x_2, \ldots, x_{|m|}$ where each element x appears $m(x)$ times. We write $x \oplus m$ to mean the multiset m' such that $m'(y)$ equals $m(y) + 1$ if $x = y$ and $m(y)$ otherwise.

4 Concurrent Programs and Counting Logic

To simplify the presentation, we assume a concurrent program (or program for short) to consist in a single non-recursive procedure manipulating integer variables. Arguments and return values are passed using shared variables. Programs where arbitrary many processes run a finite number of procedures can be encoded by having the processes choose a procedure at the beginning.

Syntax. A procedure in a program (S, L, T) is given in terms of a set T of transitions $(lc_1 \blacktriangleright lc_1' : stmt_1), (lc_2 \blacktriangleright lc_2' : stmt_2), \ldots$ operating on two finite sets of integer variables, namely a set $S = \{s_1, s_2, \ldots\}$ of shared variables and a set $L = \{l_1, l_2 \ldots\}$ of local variables. Each transition $(lc \blacktriangleright lc' : stmt)$ involves two locations lc and lc' and a statement $stmt$. We let Loc mean the set of all locations appearing in T. We always distinguish two locations, namely an entry location lc_{ent} and an exit location lc_{ext}. Program syntax is given in terms of pairwise different variables $v_1, \ldots v_n$ in $S \cup L$, expressions $e_1, \ldots e_n$ in $\mathtt{exprs}(S \cup L)$ and predicate π in $\mathtt{preds}(\mathtt{exprs}(S \cup L))$.

$$\text{prog} ::= (s := (k \mid *))^* \quad \underline{proc:} \quad (l := (k \mid *))^* \quad (lc \blacktriangleright lc : stmt)^+$$
$$stmt ::= spawn \mid join \mid \pi \mid v_1, \ldots, v_n := e_1, \ldots, e_n \mid stmt; stmt$$

Semantics. Initially, a single process starts executing the procedure with both local and shared variables initialized as stated in their definitions. Executions might involve an arbitrary number of spawned processes. The execution of any process (whether initial or spawned with the statement *spawn*) starts at the entry location lc_{ent}. Any process at an exit point lc_{ext} can be eliminated by a process executing a *join* statement. An assume π statement blocks if the predicate π over local and shared variables does not evaluate to true. Each transition is executed atomically without interruption from other processes.

More formally, a *configuration* is given in terms of a pair (σ, m) where the *shared state* $\sigma : S \to \mathbb{Z}$ is a mapping that associates an integer value to each variable in S. An *initial shared state* (written σ_{init}) is a mapping that complies with the initial constraints for the shared variables. The multiset m contains *process configurations*, i.e., pairs (lc, η) where the location lc belongs to Loc and the *process state* $\eta : L \to \mathbb{Z}$ maps each local variable to an integer value. We also write η_{init} to mean an *initial process state*. An *initial multiset* (written m_{init}) maps all (lc, η) to 0 except for a single (lc_{ent}, η_{init}) mapped to 1. We introduce a relation $\overset{stmt}{\underset{P}{\rightarrowtail}}$ in order to define statements semantics (Fig. 3). We write $(\sigma, \eta, m) \overset{stmt}{\underset{P}{\rightarrowtail}} (\sigma', \eta', m')$, where σ, σ' are shared states, η, η' are process states, and m, m' are multisets of process configurations, in order to mean that a process at process state η when the shared state is σ and the other process configurations are represented by m, can execute the statement $stmt$ and take the program to a configuration where the process is at state η', the shared state is σ' and the configurations of the other processes are captured by m'. For instance, a process can always execute a join if there is another process at location lc_{ext} (rule *join*). A process executing a multiple assignment atomically updates shared and local variables values according to the values taken by the expressions of the assignment before the execution (rule *assign*).

A P *run* ρ is a sequence $(\sigma_0, m_0), t_1, ..., t_n, (\sigma_n, m_n)$. The run is P *feasible* if $(\sigma_i, m_i) \xrightarrow[P]{t_{i+1}} (\sigma_{i+1}, m_{i+1})$ for each $i\ :\ 0 \leq i < n$ and σ_0 and m_0 are initial. Each of the configurations (σ_i, m_i), for $i\ :\ 0 \leq i \leq n$, is then said to be *reachable*.

$$\frac{(\sigma,\eta,m) \xrightarrow[P]{stmt} (\sigma',\eta',m')}{(\sigma,(lc,\eta)\oplus m) \xrightarrow[P]{(lc \blacktriangleright lc':stmt)} (\sigma',(lc',\eta')\oplus m')} : trans \qquad \frac{val_{\sigma,\eta}(\pi)}{(\sigma,\eta,m) \xrightarrow[P]{\pi} (\sigma,\eta,m)} : assume$$

$$\frac{(\sigma,\eta,m) \xrightarrow[P]{stmt} (\sigma',\eta',m') \quad (\sigma',\eta',m') \xrightarrow[P]{stmt'} (\sigma'',\eta'',m'')}{(\sigma,\eta,m) \xrightarrow[P]{stmt;stmt'} (\sigma'',\eta'',m'')} : seq \qquad \frac{m = ((lc_{ext},\eta')\oplus m')}{(\sigma,\eta,m) \xrightarrow[P]{join} (\sigma,\eta,m')} : join$$

$$\frac{subst_A = \{v_i \leftarrow val_{\sigma,\eta}(e_i) \mid v_i \in A\}}{(\sigma,\eta,m) \xrightarrow[P]{v_1,\ldots v_n,:=e_1,\ldots e_n} (\sigma[subst_S],\eta[subst_L],m)} : assign \qquad \frac{m' = (lc_{ent},\eta_{init})\oplus m}{(\sigma,\eta,m) \xrightarrow[P]{spawn} (\sigma,\eta,m')} : spawn$$

Fig. 3. Semantics of concurrent programs

Counting Logic. We use $@Loc$ to mean the set $\{@lc \mid lc \in Loc\}$ of boolean variables. Intuitively, $@lc$ evaluates to `tt` exactly when the process evaluating it is at location lc. We associate a *counting variable* $(\pi)^{\#}$ to each predicate π in $\mathtt{preds}(@Loc, \mathtt{exprs}(S \cup L))$. Intuitively, in a given program configuration, the variable $(\pi)^{\#}$ counts the number of processes for which the predicate π holds. We let $\Omega_{Loc,S,L}$ be the set $\{(\pi)^{\#} \mid \pi \in \mathtt{preds}(@Loc, \mathtt{exprs}(S \cup L))\}$. A *counting predicate* is any predicate in $\mathtt{preds}(\mathtt{exprs}(S \cup \Omega_{Loc,S,L}))$. Elements in $\mathtt{exprs}(S \cup L)$ and $\mathtt{preds}(@Loc, \mathtt{exprs}(S \cup L))$ are evaluated wrt. a shared configuration σ and a process configuration (lc, η). For instance, $val_{\sigma,(lc,\eta)}(v)$ is $\sigma(v)$ if $v \in S$ and $\eta(v)$ if $v \in L$ and $val_{\sigma,(lc,\eta)}(@lc') = (lc = lc')$. We abuse notation and write $val_{\sigma,m}(\omega)$ to mean the evaluation of the counting predicate ω wrt. a configuration (σ, m). More precisely, $val_{\sigma,m}((\pi)^{\#}) = \sum_{(lc,\eta)\text{ s.t. } val_{\sigma,(lc,\eta)}(\pi)} m((lc,\eta))$ and the valuation $val_{\sigma,m}(v) = \sigma(v)$ for $v \in S$. Our counting logic is quite expressive. For instance, we can capture assertion violations, deadlocks or program invariants. For location lc, we let $En(lc)$ in $\mathtt{preds}(\mathtt{exprs}(\Omega_{Loc,S,L}))$ define when a process can fire some transition from lc. The following counting predicates capture sets of configurations from Fig. 1.

$$\omega_{assert} = (proc@lc_5 \wedge \neg(prev \leq max))^{\#} \geq 1 \quad \omega_{inv} = (count = \sum_{lc\ proc\ \text{location}} (proc@lc)^{\#})$$

$$\omega_{deadlock} = \bigwedge_{lc\ proc\ \text{location}} \neg En(lc) \wedge \bigwedge_{lc\ main\ \text{location}} \neg En(lc)$$

5 Relating Layers of Abstractions

We formally describe in the following the four steps involved in our predicated constrained monotonic abstraction approach (see Fig. 2).

5.1 Predicate Abstraction

Given a program $P = (S, L, T)$ and a number of predicates Π on the variables $S \cup L$, we leverage on existing techniques (such as [7]) in order to generate an abstraction in the form of a boolean program $\texttt{abstOf}_{\Pi}(P) = \left(\tilde{S}, \tilde{L}, \tilde{T}\right)$ where all shared and local variables take boolean values. To achieve this, Π is partitioned into three sets Π_{shr}, Π_{loc} and Π_{mix}. Predicates in Π_{shr} only mention variables in S and those in Π_{loc} only mention variables in L. Predicates in Π_{mix} mention both shared and local variables of P. A bijection associates a predicate $\texttt{predOf}(\tilde{v})$ in Π_{shr} (resp. $\Pi_{mix} \cup \Pi_{loc}$) to each $\tilde{v}$ in $\tilde{S}$ (resp. $\tilde{L}$).

In addition, there are as many transitions in T as in $\tilde{T}$. For each $(lc \blacktriangleright lc' : stmt)$ in T there is a corresponding $(lc \blacktriangleright lc' : \texttt{abstOf}_{\Pi}(stmt))$ with the same source and destination locations lc, lc', but with an abstracted statement $\texttt{abstOf}_{\Pi}(stmt)$ that may operate on the variables $\tilde{S} \cup \tilde{L}$. For instance, statement $(count := count + 1)$ in Fig. 1 is abstracted with the multiple assignment:

$$\begin{pmatrix} wait\_leq\_count, \\ count\_leq\_wait \end{pmatrix} := \begin{pmatrix} choose\,(wait\_leq\_count, \texttt{ff}), \\ choose\,(\neg wait\_leq\_count \wedge count\_leq\_wait, wait\_leq\_count) \end{pmatrix} \quad (1)$$

The value of the variable $count\_leq\_wait$ after execution of the multiple assignment (1) is $\texttt{tt}$ if $\neg wait\_leq\_count \wedge count\_leq\_wait$ holds, $\texttt{ff}$ if $wait\_leq\_count$ holds, and is equal to a non deterministically chosen boolean value otherwise. In addition, abstracted statements can mention the local variables of passive processes, i.e., processes other than the one executing the transition. For this, we make use of the variables $\tilde{L}_p = \left\{\tilde{l}_p | \tilde{l} \text{ in } \tilde{L}\right\}$ where each $\tilde{l}_p$ denotes the local variable $\tilde{l}$ of passive processes. For instance, the statement $prev := val$ in Fig. 1 is abstracted with the multiple assignment (2). Here, the local variable $prev\_leq\_val$ of each process other than the one executing the statement (written $prev\_leq\_val_p$) is separately updated. This corresponds to a broadcast where the local variables of all passive processes need to be updated.

$$\begin{pmatrix} prev\_leq\_val, \\ prev\_leq\_max, \\ prev\_leq\_val_p \end{pmatrix} := \begin{pmatrix} \texttt{tt}, \\ choose \begin{pmatrix} \neg prev\_leq\_val & prev\_leq\_val \\ \wedge\ prev\_leq\_max \text{ '} & \wedge\ \neg prev\_leq\_max \end{pmatrix}, \\ choose \begin{pmatrix} \neg prev\_leq\_val & prev\_leq\_val \\ \wedge\ prev\_leq\_val_p \text{ '} & \wedge\ \neg prev\_leq\_val_p \end{pmatrix} \end{pmatrix} \quad (2)$$

Syntax and semantics of boolean programs. We describe the syntax of boolean programs. Variables $\tilde{v}_1, \ldots, \tilde{v}_n$ are in $\tilde{S} \cup \tilde{L} \cup \tilde{L}_p$. Predicate π is in $\texttt{preds}(\tilde{S} \cup \tilde{L})$, and predicates $\pi_1, \ldots, \pi_n$ are in $\texttt{preds}(\tilde{S} \cup \tilde{L} \cup \tilde{L}_p)$. We further require for the multiple assignment that if $\tilde{v}_i \in \tilde{S} \cup \tilde{L}$ then $vars(\pi_i) \subseteq \tilde{S} \cup \tilde{L}$.

$$\begin{aligned} \mathrm{prog} &::= (\tilde{s} := (\texttt{tt} \mid \texttt{ff} \mid *))^* \ proc: \ (\tilde{l} := (\texttt{tt} \mid \texttt{ff} \mid *))^* \ (lc \blacktriangleright lc : stmt)^+ \\ stmt &::= spawn \mid join \mid \pi \mid \tilde{v}_1, \ldots, \tilde{v}_n := \pi_1, \ldots, \pi_n \mid stmt; stmt \end{aligned}$$

Apart from the variables being now boolean, the main difference between Fig. 4 and Fig. 3 is the *assign* statement. For this, we write $(\tilde{\sigma}, \tilde{\eta}, \tilde{\eta}_p) \xrightarrow[\texttt{abstOf}_{\Pi}(P)]{\tilde{v}_1, \ldots \tilde{v}_n := \pi_1, \ldots \pi_n} (\tilde{\sigma}', \tilde{\eta}', \tilde{\eta}_p')$ and mean that $\tilde{\eta}_p'$ is obtained in the following way. First, we change the domain of $\tilde{\eta}_p$ from $\tilde{L}$ to $\tilde{L}_p$ and obtain $\tilde{\eta}_{p,1} = \tilde{\eta}_p \left[\left\{\tilde{l} \leftarrow \tilde{l}_p | \tilde{l} \in \tilde{L}\right\}\right]$, then we let $\tilde{\eta}_{p,2} = \tilde{\eta}_{p,1}\left[\left\{\tilde{v}_i \leftarrow val_{\tilde{\sigma},\tilde{\eta},\tilde{\eta}_{p,1}}(\pi_i) | \tilde{v}_i \in \tilde{L}_p \text{ in lhs of the assignment}\right\}\right]$. Finally, we obtain $\tilde{\eta}'_p = \tilde{\eta}_{p,2}\left[\left\{\tilde{l}_p \leftarrow \tilde{l} | \tilde{l} \in \tilde{L}\right\}\right]$. This step corresponds to a broadcast. An $\mathtt{abstOf}_{\Pi}(P)$ run is a sequence $(\tilde{\sigma}_0, \tilde{m}_0), \tilde{t}_1, ..., \tilde{t}_n, (\tilde{\sigma}_n, \tilde{m}_n)$. It is *feasible* if $(\tilde{\sigma}_i, \tilde{m}_i) \xrightarrow[\mathtt{abstOf}_{\Pi}(P)]{\tilde{t}_{i+1}} (\tilde{\sigma}_{i+1}, \tilde{m}_{i+1})$ for each $i : 0 \leq i < n$ and $\tilde{\sigma}_0$, $\tilde{m}_0$ are initial. Configurations $(\tilde{\sigma}_i, \tilde{m}_i)$, for $i : 0 \leq i \leq n$, are then said to be reachable.

$$\frac{(\tilde{\sigma}, \tilde{\eta}, \tilde{m}) \xrightarrow[\mathtt{abstOf}_{\Pi}(P)]{stmt} (\tilde{\sigma}', \tilde{\eta}', \tilde{m}')}{(\tilde{\sigma}, (lc, \tilde{\eta}) \oplus \tilde{m}) \xrightarrow[\mathtt{abstOf}_{\Pi}(P)]{(lc \blacktriangleright lc' : stmt)} (\tilde{\sigma}', (lc', \tilde{\eta}') \oplus \tilde{m}')} : trans \qquad \frac{val_{\tilde{\sigma},\tilde{\eta}}(\pi)}{(\tilde{\sigma}, \tilde{\eta}, \tilde{m}) \xrightarrow[\mathtt{abstOf}_{\Pi}(P)]{\pi} (\tilde{\sigma}, \tilde{\eta}, \tilde{m})} : assume$$

$$\frac{(\tilde{\sigma}, \tilde{\eta}, \tilde{m}) \xrightarrow[\mathtt{abstOf}_{\Pi}(P)]{stmt} (\tilde{\sigma}', \tilde{\eta}', \tilde{m}') \text{ and } (\tilde{\sigma}', \tilde{\eta}', \tilde{m}') \xrightarrow[\mathtt{abstOf}_{\Pi}(P)]{stmt'} (\tilde{\sigma}'', \tilde{\eta}'', \tilde{m}'')}{(\tilde{\sigma}, \tilde{\eta}, \tilde{m}) \xrightarrow[\mathtt{abstOf}_{\Pi}(P)]{stmt;stmt'} (\tilde{\sigma}'', \tilde{\eta}'', \tilde{m}'')} : sequence$$

$$\frac{\tilde{m}' = (lc_{ent}, \tilde{\eta}_{init}) \oplus \tilde{m}}{(\tilde{\sigma}, \tilde{\eta}, \tilde{m}) \xrightarrow[\mathtt{abstOf}_{\Pi}(P)]{spawn} (\tilde{\sigma}, \tilde{\eta}, \tilde{m}')} : spawn \qquad \frac{\tilde{m} = ((lc_{ext}, \tilde{\eta}') \oplus \tilde{m}')}{(\tilde{\sigma}, \tilde{\eta}, \tilde{m}) \xrightarrow[\mathtt{abstOf}_{\Pi}(P)]{join} (\tilde{\sigma}, \tilde{\eta}, \tilde{m}')} : join$$

$$\frac{\begin{array}{c} \tilde{\sigma}' = \tilde{\sigma}[\{\tilde{v}_i \leftarrow val_{\tilde{\sigma},\tilde{\eta}}(\pi_i) | \tilde{v}_i \in \tilde{S}\}] \\ \tilde{\eta}' = \tilde{\eta}[\{\tilde{v}_i \leftarrow val_{\tilde{\sigma},\tilde{\eta}}(\pi_i) | \tilde{v}_i \in \tilde{L}\}] \\ h : \{1, ...|\tilde{m}|\} \rightarrow \{1, ...|\tilde{m}'|\} \text{ some bijection associating each } (lc_p, \tilde{\eta}_p)_i \in \tilde{m} \\ \text{to some } (lc_p, \tilde{\eta}'_p)_{h(i)} \in \tilde{m}' \text{ s.t. } (\tilde{\sigma}, \tilde{\eta}, \tilde{\eta}_p) \xrightarrow[\mathtt{abstOf}_{\Pi}(P)]{\tilde{v}_1, ... \tilde{v}_n := \pi_1, ... \pi_n} (\tilde{\sigma}', \tilde{\eta}', \tilde{\eta}'_p) \end{array}}{(\tilde{\sigma}, \tilde{\eta}, \tilde{m}) \xrightarrow[\mathtt{abstOf}_{\Pi}(P)]{\tilde{v}_1, ... \tilde{v}_n := \pi_1, ... \pi_n} (\tilde{\sigma}', \tilde{\eta}', \tilde{m}')} : assign$$

Fig. 4. Semantics of boolean concurrent programs

Relation between P and $\mathtt{abstOf}_{\Pi}(P)$. Given a shared state $\tilde{\sigma}$, we let $\mathtt{predOf}(\tilde{\sigma})$ denote the predicate $\bigwedge_{\tilde{s} \in \tilde{S}}(\tilde{\sigma}(\tilde{s}) \Leftrightarrow \mathtt{predOf}(\tilde{s}))$. In a similar manner, we let $\mathtt{predOf}(\tilde{\eta})$ denote $\bigwedge_{\tilde{l} \in \tilde{L}}(\tilde{\eta}(\tilde{l}) \Leftrightarrow \mathtt{predOf}(\tilde{l}))$. Notice that $vars(\mathtt{predOf}(\tilde{\sigma})) \subseteq S$ and $vars(\mathtt{predOf}(\tilde{\eta})) \subseteq S \cup L$. We abuse notation and use $val_{\sigma}(\tilde{\sigma})$ (resp. $val_{\sigma,\eta}(\tilde{\eta})$) to mean that $val_{\sigma}(\mathtt{predOf}(\tilde{\sigma}))$ (resp. $val_{\sigma,\eta}(\mathtt{predOf}(\tilde{\eta}))$) holds. We also use $val_{\tilde{\sigma},\tilde{\eta}}(\pi)$, for a boolean combination π of predicates in Π, to mean the predicate obtained by replacing each π' in $\Pi_{mix} \cup \Pi_{loc}$ (resp. Π_{shr}) with $\tilde{\eta}(\tilde{v})$ (resp. $\tilde{\sigma}(\tilde{v})$) where $\mathtt{predOf}(\tilde{v}) = \pi'$. We let $val_{\sigma,m}(\tilde{m})$ mean there is a bijection $h : \{1, ...|\tilde{m}|\} \rightarrow \{1, ...|\tilde{m}'|\}$ s.t. we can associate to each $(lc, \eta)_i$ in m an $(lc, \tilde{\eta})_{h(i)}$ in $\tilde{m}$ such that $val_{\sigma,\eta}(\tilde{\eta})$ for each $i : 1 \leq i \leq |m|$. The *concretization* of an $\mathtt{abstOf}_{\Pi}(P)$ configuration $(\tilde{\sigma}, \tilde{m})$ is $\gamma((\tilde{\sigma}, \tilde{m})) = \{(\sigma, m) | val_{\sigma}(\tilde{\sigma}) \wedge val_{\sigma,m}(\tilde{m})\}$. The *abstraction* of (σ, m) is $\alpha((\sigma, m)) = \{(\tilde{\sigma}, \tilde{m}) | val_{\sigma}(\tilde{\sigma}) \wedge val_{\sigma,m}(\tilde{m})\}$. We initialize the $\mathtt{abstOf}_{\Pi}(P)$ variables such that for each initial σ_{init}, m_{init} of P, there are $\tilde{\sigma}_{init}, \tilde{m}_{init}$ with $\alpha((\sigma_{init}, m_{init})) = \{(\tilde{\sigma}_{init}, \tilde{m}_{init})\}$. The abstraction $\alpha(\rho)$ of a P run $\rho = (\sigma_0, m_0), t_1, ...t_n, (\sigma_n, m_n)$ is the singleton set of P runs $\{(\tilde{\sigma}_0, \tilde{m}_0), \tilde{t}_1, ...\tilde{t}_n, (\tilde{\sigma}_n, \tilde{m}_n) | \alpha((\sigma_i, m_i)) = \{(\tilde{\sigma}_i, \tilde{m}_i)\} \text{ and } \tilde{t}_i = \mathtt{abstOf}_{\Pi}(t_i)\}$.

Definition 1 (predicate abstraction). *Let $P = (S, L, T)$ be a program and $\texttt{abstOf}_{\Pi}(P) = \left(\tilde{S}, \tilde{L}, \tilde{T}\right)$ be its abstraction wrt. Π. The abstraction is said to be effective and sound if $\texttt{abstOf}_{\Pi}(P)$ can be effectively computed and to each feasible P run ρ corresponds a non empty set $\alpha(\rho)$ of feasible $\texttt{abstOf}_{\Pi}(P)$ runs.*

5.2 Encoding into a Counter Machine

Assume a program $P = (S, L, T)$, a set $\Pi_0 \subseteq \mathtt{preds}(\mathtt{exprs}(S \cup L))$ of predicates and two counting predicates, an invariant ω_{inv} in $\mathtt{preds}(\mathtt{exprs}(S \cup \Omega_{Loc,S,L}))$ and a target ω_{trgt} in $\mathtt{preds}(\mathtt{exprs}(\Omega_{Loc,S,L}))$. We write $\mathtt{abstOf}_{\Pi}(P) = \left(\tilde{S}, \tilde{L}, \tilde{T}\right)$ to mean the abstraction of P wrt. $\Pi = \cup_{(\pi)\# \in vars(\omega_{inv}) \cup vars(\omega_{trgt})} atoms(\pi) \cup \Pi_0$. Intuitively, this step results in the formulation of a state reachability problem of a counter machine $enc\,(\mathtt{abstOf}_{\Pi}(P))$ that captures reachability of abstractions of ω_{trgt} configurations with $\mathtt{abstOf}_{\Pi}(P)$ runs that are strengthened wrt. ω_{inv}.

$$\frac{\delta = [q : op : q'] \text{ and } \theta \overset{op}{\underset{M}{\rightarrowtail}} \theta'}{(q, \theta) \xrightarrow[M]{\delta} (q', \theta')} : transition$$

$$\frac{}{\theta \overset{nop}{\underset{M}{\rightarrowtail}} \theta} : nop \qquad \frac{\theta \overset{op}{\underset{M}{\rightarrowtail}} \theta' \text{ and } \theta' \overset{op'}{\underset{M}{\rightarrowtail}} \theta''}{\theta \overset{op;op'}{\underset{M}{\rightarrowtail}} \theta''} : seq$$

$$\frac{\exists A.val_{\theta}(\pi) \wedge \theta' = \theta\left[\{c_i \leftarrow val_{\theta}(e_i) \,|\, i : 1 \leq i \leq n\}\right]}{\theta \overset{grd \Rightarrow (c_1 \ldots c_n := e_1 \ldots e_n)}{\underset{M}{\rightarrowtail}} \theta'} : gcmd$$

Fig. 5. Semantics of a counter machine

A counter machine M is a tuple $(Q, C, \Delta, Q_{Init}, \Theta_{Init}, q_{trgt})$ where Q is a finite set of states, C is a finite set of counters (i.e., variables ranging over $\mathbb{N}$), Δ is a finite set of transitions, $Q_{Init} \subseteq Q$ is a set of initial states, Θ_{Init} is a set of initial counters valuations (i.e., mappings from C to $\mathbb{N}$) and q_{trgt} is a state in Q. A transition δ in Δ is of the form $[q : op : q']$ where the operation op is either the identity operation *nop*, a guarded command $grd \Rightarrow cmd$, or a sequential composition of operations. We use a set A of auxiliary variables ranging over $\mathbb{N}$. These are meant to be existentially quantified when firing the transitions as explained in Fig. 5. A guard grd is a predicate in $\mathtt{preds}(\mathtt{exprs}(A \cup C))$ and a command cmd is a multiple assignment $c_1, \ldots, c_n := e_1, \ldots, e_n$ that involves $e_1, \ldots e_n$ in $\mathtt{exprs}(A \cup C)$ and pairwise different $c_1, \ldots c_n$ in C. We only write grd (resp. cmd) in case cmd is empty (resp. grd is $\mathtt{tt}$) in $grd \Rightarrow cmd$.

A *machine configuration* is a pair (q, θ) where q is a state in Q and θ is a mapping $C \to \mathbb{N}$. Semantics are given in Fig. 5. A configuration (q, θ) is *initial* if $q \in Q_{Init}$ and $\theta \in \Theta_{Init}$. An M run ρ_M is a sequence $(q_0, \theta_0), \delta_1, \ldots (q_n, \theta_n)$.

It is *feasible* if (q_0, θ_0) is initial and $(q_i, \theta_i) \xrightarrow[M]{\delta_{i+1}} (q_{i+1}, \theta_{i+1})$ for $i : 0 \leq i < n$. The machine state reachability problem is to decide whether there is an M feasible run $(q_0, \theta_0), \delta_1, \ldots (q_n, \theta_n)$ s.t. $q_n = q_{trgt}$.

Encoding. We describe in the following a counter machine $enc(\mathtt{abstOf}_{\Pi}(P))$ obtained as an encoding of the boolean program $\mathtt{abstOf}_{\Pi}(P)$. Recall $\mathtt{abstOf}_{\Pi}(P)$ results from an abstraction (Def. 1) wrt. $\cup_{(\pi)^\# \in vars(\omega_{inv}) \cup vars(\omega_{trgt})} atoms(\pi) \cup \Pi_0$ of the concurrent program P. The machine $enc(\mathtt{abstOf}_{\Pi}(P))$ is a tuple $(Q, C, \Delta, Q_{Init}, \Theta_{Init}, q_{trgt})$. Each state in Q is either the target state q_{trgt} or is associated to a shared state $\tilde{\sigma}$ of $\mathtt{abstOf}_{\Pi}(P)$. We write $q_{\tilde{\sigma}}$ to make the association explicit. There is a bijection that associates a process configuration $(lc, \tilde{\eta})$ to each counter $c_{(lc,\tilde{\eta})}$ in C. Transitions Δ coincide with $\cup_{t \in \tilde{T}} \Delta_t \cup \Delta_{trgt}$ as described in Fig. 6. We abuse notation and associate to each statement *stmt* appearing in $\mathtt{abstOf}_{\Pi}(P)$ the set $enc(stmt)$ of tuples $[(\tilde{\sigma}, \tilde{\eta}) : op : (\tilde{\sigma}', \tilde{\eta}')]_{stmt}$ generated in Fig. 6. Given a multiset $\tilde{m}$ of program configurations, we write $\theta_{\tilde{m}}$ to mean the mapping associating $\tilde{m}((lc, \tilde{\eta}))$ to each counter $c_{(lc,\tilde{\eta})}$ in C. We let Q_{Init} be the set $\{q_{\tilde{\sigma}} | \tilde{\sigma}$ is an initial shared state of $\mathtt{abstOf}_{\Pi}(P)\}$, and Θ_{Init} be the set $\{\theta_{\tilde{m}} | \tilde{m}((lc_{ent}, \tilde{\eta})) = 1$ for an $\tilde{\eta}$ initial in $\mathtt{abstOf}_{\Pi}(P)$ and 0 otherwise$\}$. We associate a program configuration $(\tilde{\sigma}, \tilde{m})$ to each machine configuration $(q_{\tilde{\sigma}}, \theta_{\tilde{m}})$. The machine encodes $\mathtt{abstOf}_{\Pi}(P)$ in the following sense:

Lemma 1. *q_{trgt} is $enc(\mathtt{abstOf}_{\Pi}(P))$ reachable iff a configuration $(\tilde{\sigma}, \tilde{m})$ s.t. $\omega_{trgt}\left[\left\{(\pi)^\# \leftarrow \sum_{\{(lc,\tilde{\eta}) | val_{\tilde{\sigma},(lc,\tilde{\eta})}(\pi)\}} \tilde{m}(lc, \tilde{\eta}) | (\pi)^\# \in vars(\omega_{trgt})\right\}\right]$ is reachable in $\mathtt{abstOf}_{\Pi}(P)$.*

Observe that all transitions of a boolean program $\mathtt{abstOf}_{\Pi}(P)$ are monotonic, i.e., if a configuration $(\tilde{\sigma}', \tilde{m}')$ is obtained from $(\tilde{\sigma}, \tilde{m})$ using a transition, then the same transition can obtain a configuration larger (i.e., has the same and possibly more processes) than $(\tilde{\sigma}', \tilde{m}')$ from any configuration larger than $(\tilde{\sigma}, \tilde{m})$. This reflects in the monotonicity of all transitions in Fig. 6 (except for rule *target*). Rule *target* results in monotonic machine transitions for all counting predicates ω_{trgt} that denote upward closed sets of processes. This is for instance the case of predicates capturing assertion violation but not of those capturing deadlocks (see Sec. 4). An encoding $enc(\mathtt{abstOf}_{\Pi}(P))$ is said to be monotonic if all its transitions are monotonic. Checking program assertion violations always results in monotonic encodings.

Lemma 2. *State reachability of all monotonic encodings is decidable.*

However, monotonic encodings correspond to coarse over-approximations. Intuitively, bad configurations (such as those where a deadlock occurs, or those obtained in a backward exploration for a barrier based program as described in the running example) are no more guaranteed to be upward closed. This loss of precision is irrevocable for techniques solely based on monotonic encodings. To regain some of the lost precision, we constrain the runs using counting invariants.

$$\frac{(lc \blacktriangleright lc' : stmt) \text{ and } [(\tilde{\sigma}, \tilde{\eta}) : op : (\tilde{\sigma}', \tilde{\eta}')]_{stmt}}{(q_{\tilde{\sigma}} : c_{(lc,\tilde{\eta})} \geq 1 \Rightarrow (c_{(lc,\tilde{\eta})})^{--}; op; (c_{(lc',\tilde{\eta}')})^{++} : q_{\tilde{\sigma}'}) \in \Delta_{(lc \blacktriangleright lc' : stmt)}} : transition$$

$$\frac{}{(q_{\tilde{\sigma}} : \omega_{trgt} \left[\left\{(\pi)^{\#} \leftarrow \sum_{\{(lc,\tilde{\eta}) | val_{\tilde{\sigma},(lc,\tilde{\eta})}(\pi)\}} c_{((lc,\tilde{\eta}))} | (\pi)^{\#} \in vars(\omega_{trgt})\right\}\right] : q_{trgt}) \in \Delta_{trgt}} : target$$

$$\frac{[(\tilde{\sigma}, \tilde{\eta}) : op : (\tilde{\sigma}', \tilde{\eta}')]_{stmt} \text{ and } [(\tilde{\sigma}', \tilde{\eta}') : op' : (\tilde{\sigma}'', \tilde{\eta}'')]_{stmt'}}{[(\tilde{\sigma}, \tilde{\eta}) : op; op' : (\tilde{\sigma}'', \tilde{\eta}'')]_{stmt;stmt'}} : sequence$$

$$\frac{val_{\tilde{\sigma},\tilde{\eta}}(\pi)}{[(\tilde{\sigma}, \tilde{\eta}) : nop : (\tilde{\sigma}, \tilde{\eta})]_{\pi}} : assume \quad \frac{}{\left[(\tilde{\sigma}, \tilde{\eta}) : (c_{(lc_{ent}, \tilde{\eta}_{init})})^{++} : (\tilde{\sigma}, \tilde{\eta})\right]_{spawn}} : spawn$$

$$\frac{}{\left[(\tilde{\sigma}, \tilde{\eta}) : c_{(lc_{ext}, \tilde{\eta}')} \geq 1 \Rightarrow (c_{(lc_{ext}, \tilde{\eta}')})^{--} : (\tilde{\sigma}, \tilde{\eta})\right]_{join}} : join$$

$$\frac{\begin{array}{c}\tilde{\sigma}' = \tilde{\sigma}[\{\tilde{v}_i \leftarrow val_{\tilde{\sigma},\tilde{\eta}}(\pi_i) | \tilde{v}_i \in \tilde{S}\}] \qquad \tilde{\eta}' = \tilde{\eta}[\{\tilde{v}_i \leftarrow val_{\tilde{\sigma},\tilde{\eta}}(\pi_i) | \tilde{v}_i \in \tilde{L}\}] \\ B = \left\{a_{(lc,\tilde{\eta}_p),(lc,\tilde{\eta}'_p)} | lc \in Loc \text{ and } (\tilde{\sigma}, \tilde{\eta}, \tilde{\eta}_p) \xrightarrow[\texttt{abstOf}_{\Pi}(P)]{\tilde{v}_1,\ldots\tilde{v}_n := \pi_1,\ldots\pi_n} (\tilde{\sigma}', \tilde{\eta}', \tilde{\eta}'_p)\right\}\end{array}}{\left[(\tilde{\sigma}, \tilde{\eta}) : \left(\begin{array}{c}\bigwedge_{(lc,\tilde{\eta}_p)}(c_{(lc,\tilde{\eta}_p)} = \sum_{a_{(lc,\tilde{\eta}_p),(lc,\tilde{\eta}'_p)} \in B} a_{(lc,\tilde{\eta}_p),(lc,\tilde{\eta}'_p)}) \\ \Rightarrow \bigcup_{(lc,\tilde{\eta}'_p)} \left\{c_{(lc,\tilde{\eta}'_p)} := \sum_{a_{(lc,\tilde{\eta}_p),(lc,\tilde{\eta}'_p)} \in B} a_{(lc,\tilde{\eta}_p),(lc,\tilde{\eta}'_p)}\right\}\end{array}\right) : (\tilde{\sigma}', \tilde{\eta}')\right]_{\tilde{v}_1,\ldots\tilde{v}_n := \pi_1,\ldots\pi_n}} : assign$$

Fig. 6. Encoding of the transitions of a boolean program $\left(\tilde{S}, \tilde{L}, \tilde{T}\right)$, given a counting target ω_{trgt}, to the transitions $\Delta = \cup_{t \in \tilde{T}} \Delta_t \cup \Delta_{trgt}$ of a counter machine

$$\frac{[q_{\tilde{\sigma}} : op : q_{\tilde{\sigma}'}] \in \Delta}{[q_{\tilde{\sigma}} : grd_{\tilde{\sigma}}(\omega_{inv}); op; grd_{\tilde{\sigma}'}(\omega_{inv}) : q_{\tilde{\sigma}'}] \in \Delta'} \; strengthen$$

Fig. 7. Strengthening of a machine transition given a counting invariant ω_{inv} and using the predicate $grd_{\tilde{\sigma}}(\omega_{inv})$ in $\mathbf{preds}(\mathbf{exprs}(C))$ and defined as $\exists S.\texttt{predOf}(\tilde{\sigma}) \wedge \omega_{inv}\left[\left\{(\pi)^{\#} \leftarrow \sum_{\{(lc,\tilde{\eta}) | val_{\tilde{\sigma},(lc,\tilde{\eta})}(\pi)\}} c_{((lc,\tilde{\eta}))} | (\pi)^{\#} \in vars(\omega_{inv})\right\}\right]$

Lemma 3. *Any feasible P run has a feasible $\texttt{abstOf}_{\Pi}(P)$ run with a feasible run in any machine obtained as the strengthening of enc$(\texttt{abstOf}_{\Pi}(P))$ wrt. some P invariant $\omega_{inv} \in \mathbf{preds}(\mathbf{exprs}(S \cup \Omega_{Loc,S,L}))$.*

The resulting machine is not monotonic in general and we can encode the state reachability of a two counter machine.

Lemma 4. *State reachability is in general undecidable after strengthening.*

5.3 Constrained Monotonic Abstraction and Preorder Refinement

This step addresses the state reachability problem for a counter machine $M = (Q, C, \Delta, Q_{Init}, \Theta_{Init}, q_{trgt})$. As stated in Lem. 4, this problem is in general undecidable for strengthened encodings. The idea here [15] is to force monotonicity with respect to a well-quasi ordering $\preceq$ on the set of its configurations. A classical backward exploration that systematically closes upwards the obtained configurations $\mathbf{Up}_{\preceq}((q, \theta))$ is then sound and guaranteed to terminate [15]. We start with the natural component wise preorder $\theta \preceq \theta'$ defined as $\wedge_{c \in C} \theta(c) \leq \theta'(c)$. Intuitively, $\theta \preceq \theta'$ holds if θ' can be obtained by "adding more processes to" θ. If no run is found, then `not_reachable` is returned. Otherwise a run is obtained and simulated on M. If the run is possible, it is sent to the fourth step of our approach (described in Sect. 5.4). Otherwise, the upward closure step $\mathbf{Up}_{\preceq}((q,\theta))$ responsible for the spurious run is identified and an interpolant I (with $vars(I) \subseteq C$) is used to refine the preorder as follows: $\preceq_{i+1} := \{(\theta,\theta') | \theta \preceq_i \theta' \wedge (val_\theta(I) \Leftrightarrow val_{\theta'}(I))\}$. Although stronger, the new preorder is again a well quasi ordering and the run is guaranteed to be eliminated in the next round. We refer the reader to [4] for more details.

Lemma 5 (CMA [4]). *Constrained Monotonic Abstraction is sound and effective and each round does terminate given the preorder is a well quasi ordering.*

5.4 Simulation on the Original Concurrent Program

A given run of the counter machine $(Q, C, \Delta, Q_{Init}, \Theta_{Init}, q_{trgt})$ is simulated by this step on the original concurrent program $P = (S, L, T)$. This is possible because to each step of the counter machine run corresponds a unique and concrete transition of P. This step is classical in counter example guided abstraction refinement approaches. In our case, we need to differentiate the variables belonging to different processes during the simulation. As usual in such frameworks, if the run turns out to be possible then we have captured a concrete run of P that violates an assertion and we report it. Otherwise, we deduce predicates that make the run infeasible and send them to step 1 (Sect. 5.1).

Theorem 1 (predicated constrained monotonic abstraction). *Assume an effective and sound predicate abstraction. If the constrained monotonic abstraction step returns* `not_reachable`*, then no configuration satisfying ω_{trgt} is reachable in P. If a P run is returned by the simulation step, then it reaches a configuration where ω_{trgt} holds. Every iteration of the outer loop terminates given the inner loop terminates. Every iteration of the inner loop terminates.*

Notice that there is no general guaranty that we establish or refute the safety property (the problem is undecidable). For instance, it may be the case that one of the two loops does not terminate or that we need to add predicates relating local variables of two different processes.

6 Experimental Results

We report on experiments with our prototype PACMAN(for predicated constrained monotonic abstraction). We have conducted our experiments on an Intel Xeon 2.67GHz processor with 8GB of RAM. To the best of our understanding, the reported examples which require refinements of the natural preorder cannot be verified by techniques such as [6,7]. Indeed, such approaches always adopt monotonic abstractions when the correctness of these examples crucially depends on the fact that non-monotonic behaviors of barriers are taken into account.

Table 1. Checking assertion violation with PACMAN

example	P	$enc(\texttt{abstOf}_{\Pi}(P))$	outer loop		inner loop		results	
			num.	preds.	num.	preds.	time(s)	output
max	5:2:8	18:16:104	4	5	6	2	192	correct
max-bug	5:2:8	18:8:55	3	4	5	2	106	trace
max-nobar	5:2:8	18:4:51	3	3	3	0	24	trace
readers-writers	3:3:10	9:64:121	5	6	5	0	38	correct
readers-writers-bug	3:3:10	9:7:77	3	3	3	0	11	trace
parent-child	2:3:10	9:16:48	3	4	5	2	73	correct
parent-child -nobar	2:3:10	9:1:16	2	1	2	0	3	trace
simp-bar	5:2:9	8:16:123	3	3	5	2	93	correct
simp-nobar	5:2:9	8:7:67	3	2	3	0	13	trace
dynamic-barrier	5:2:8	8:8:44	3	3	3	0	8	correct
dynamic-barrier-bug	5:2:8	8:1:14	2	1	2	0	3	trace
as-many	3:2:6	8:4:33	3	2	6	3	62	correct
as-many-bug	3:2:6	8:1:9	2	1	2	0	2	trace

Table 2. Checking deadlock with PACMAN

example	P	$enc(\texttt{abstOf}_{\Pi}(P))$	outer loop		inner loop		results	
			num.	preds.	num.	preds.	time(s)	output
bar-bug-no.1	4:2:7	7:16:66	4	4	6	2	27	trace
bar-bug-no.2	4:3:8	9:16:95	4	3	4	0	33	trace
bar-bug-no.3	3:2:6	6:16:78	5	4	6	1	21	trace
correct-bar	4:2:7	7:16:62	4	4	6	2	18	correct
ddlck bar-loop	4:2:10	8:8:63	3	2	3	0	16	trace
no-ddlck bar-loop	4:2:9	7:16:78	4	3	4	0	19	correct

All predicate abstraction predicates and counting invariants have been derived automatically. For the counting invariants, we implemented a thread modular analysis operating on the polyhedra numerical domain. This took less than 11 seconds for all the examples we report here. For each example, we report on the number of transitions and variables both in P and in the resulting counter machine. We also state the number of refinement steps and predicates automatically obtained in both refinement loops.

We report on experiments checking assertion violations in Tab.1 and deadlock freedom in Tab.2. For both cases we consider correct and buggy (by removing the barriers for instance) programs. PACMAN establishes correctness and exhibits faulty runs as expected. The tuples under the P column respectively refer to the number of variables, procedures and transitions in the original program. The tuples under the $enc(\texttt{abstOf}_{\Pi}(P))$ column refer to the number of counters, states and transitions in the extended counter machine.

We made use of several optimizations. For instance, we discarded shared and local states corresponding to unsatisfiable combinations of predicates, we used automatically generated invariants (such as $(wait \leq count) \wedge (wait \geq 0)$ for the max example in Fig.1) to filter the state space. Such heuristics dramatically helped our state space exploration algorithms. Still, our prototype did not terminate on several larger examples. We are working on improiving scalability by coming up and combining with more clever optimisations.

7 Conclusions and Future Work

We have presented a technique, predicated constrained monotonic abstraction, for the automated verification of concurrent programs whose correctness depends on synchronization between arbitrary many processes, for example by means of barriers implemented using integer counters and tests. We have introduced a new logic and an iterative method based on combination of predicate, counter and monotonic abstraction. Our prototype implementation gave encouraging results and managed to automatically establish or refute program assertions and deadlock freedom. To the best of our knowledge, this is beyond the capabilities of current automatic verification techniques. Our current priority is to improve scalability by leveraging on techniques such as cartesian and lazy abstraction, partial order reduction, or combining forward and backward explorations. We also aim to generalize to richer variable types.

Acknowledgments. The authors would like to thank the anonymous reviewers for their helpful remarks and relevant references.

References

1. Abdulla, P.A., Haziza, F., Holík, L.: All for the price of few. In: Giacobazzi, R., Berdine, J., Mastroeni, I. (eds.) VMCAI 2013. LNCS, vol. 7737, pp. 476–495. Springer, Heidelberg (2013)
2. Abdulla, P.A., Annichini, A., Bensalem, S., Bouajjani, A., Habermehl, P., Lakhnech, Y.: Verification of infinite-state systems by combining abstraction and reachability analysis. In: Halbwachs, N., Peled, D. (eds.) CAV 1999. LNCS, vol. 1633, pp. 146–159. Springer, Heidelberg (1999)
3. Abdulla, P.A., Čerāns, K., Jonsson, B., Tsay, Y.-K.: General decidability theorems for infinite-state systems. In: Proc. LICS 1996, 11th IEEE Int. Symp. on Logic in Computer Science, pp. 313–321 (1996)
4. Abdulla, P.A., Chen, Y.-F., Delzanno, G., Haziza, F., Hong, C.-D., Rezine, A.: Constrained monotonic abstraction: A CEGAR for parameterized verification. In: Gastin, P., Laroussinie, F. (eds.) CONCUR 2010. LNCS, vol. 6269, pp. 86–101. Springer, Heidelberg (2010)
5. Bansal, K., Koskinen, E., Wies, T., Zufferey, D.: Structural counter abstraction. In: Piterman, N., Smolka, S.A. (eds.) TACAS 2013. LNCS, vol. 7795, pp. 62–77. Springer, Heidelberg (2013)
6. Basler, G., Hague, M., Kroening, D., Ong, C.-H.L., Wahl, T., Zhao, H.: BOOM: Taking boolean program model checking one step further. In: Esparza, J., Majumdar, R. (eds.) TACAS 2010. LNCS, vol. 6015, pp. 145–149. Springer, Heidelberg (2010)

7. Donaldson, A., Kaiser, A., Kroening, D., Wahl, T.: Symmetry-aware predicate abstraction for shared-variable concurrent programs. In: Gopalakrishnan, G., Qadeer, S. (eds.) CAV 2011. LNCS, vol. 6806, pp. 356–371. Springer, Heidelberg (2011)
8. Donaldson, A., Kaiser, A., Kroening, D., Wahl, T.: Symmetry-aware predicate abstraction for shared-variable concurrent programs. In: Gopalakrishnan, G., Qadeer, S. (eds.) CAV 2011. LNCS, vol. 6806, pp. 356–371. Springer, Heidelberg (2011)
9. Farzan, A., Kincaid, Z., Podelski, A.: Proofs that count. In: Proceedings of the 41st ACM SIGPLAN-SIGACT Symposium on Principles of Programming Languages, POPL 2014, pp. 151–164. ACM, New York (2014)
10. Finkel, A., Schnoebelen, P.: Well-structured transition systems everywhere! Theoretical Comput. Sci. 256(1-2), 63–92 (2001)
11. Flanagan, C., Qadeer, S.: Thread-modular model checking. In: Ball, T., Rajamani, S.K. (eds.) SPIN 2003. LNCS, vol. 2648, pp. 213–224. Springer, Heidelberg (2003)
12. Ganjei, Z., Rezine, A., Eles, P., Peng, Z.: Abstracting and counting synchronizing processes. Technical report, Linköping University, Software and Systems (2014)
13. Kaiser, A., Kroening, D., Wahl, T.: Dynamic cutoff detection in parameterized concurrent programs. In: Touili, T., Cook, B., Jackson, P. (eds.) CAV 2010. LNCS, vol. 6174, pp. 645–659. Springer, Heidelberg (2010)
14. Kaiser, A., Kroening, D., Wahl, T.: Lost in abstraction: Monotonicity in multithreaded programs. In: Baldan, P., Gorla, D. (eds.) CONCUR 2014. LNCS, vol. 8704, pp. 141–155. Springer, Heidelberg (2014)
15. Rezine, A.: Parameterized Systems: Generalizing and Simplifying Automatic Verification. PhD thesis, Uppsala University (2008)

Debugging Process Algebra Specifications

Gwen Salaün[1] and Lina Ye[2]

[1] University of Grenoble Alpes, Inria, LIG, CNRS, France
[2] Department of Computer Science, Supélec, France

Abstract. Designing and developing distributed and concurrent applications has always been a tedious and error-prone task. In this context, formal techniques and tools are of great help in order to specify such concurrent systems and detect bugs in the corresponding models. In this paper, we propose a new framework for debugging value-passing process algebra through coverage analysis. We illustrate our approach with LNT, which is a recent specification language designed for formally modelling concurrent systems. We define several coverage notions before showing how to instrument the specification without affecting original behaviors. Our approach helps one to improve the quality of a dataset of examples used for validation purposes, but also to find ill-formed decisions, dead code, and other errors in the specification. We have implemented a tool for automating our debugging approach, and applied it to several real-world case studies in different application areas.

1 Introduction

Recent computing trends promote the development of software applications that are intrinsically parallel, distributed and concurrent. However, designing and developing distributed software has always been a tedious and error-prone task, and the ever increasing software complexity is making matters even worse. Therefore, it is impossible for any human being to foresee all the possible executions of this kind of application, which thus can hardly be free of bugs. In this context, formal techniques and tools are of great help in order to detect bugs in abstract models of concurrent systems. Although we are still far from proposing techniques and tools avoiding the existence of bugs in complex, real-world software systems, we know how to automatically chase and find bugs that would be very difficult, if not impossible, to detect manually.

A variety of formal specification languages has been developed over the last few decades, such as algebraic specifications (CASL), state-based formalisms (VDM, Z, B), automata-based languages (FSM, UML state diagrams, Statecharts), Petri nets or (value-passing) process algebras. Process algebras were designed for modelling concurrent systems and present several advantages compared to similar specification languages (such as automata-based languages or Petri nets): they are equipped with formal semantics, compositional notations, and are expressive enough to provide several levels of abstraction (*e.g.*, data with LOTOS or mobility with π-calculus); real-world systems can be specified

D. D'Souza et al. (Eds.): VMCAI 2015, LNCS 8931, pp. 245–262, 2015.

using textual notations, and there exist several verification toolboxes for them (CADP, mCRL2, LTSA, FDR2, etc.). In contrast, the syntax of process algebras is still hard to understand and use, particularly for non-experts. In order to fill this gap, LNT [7] was proposed a few years ago. LNT is a value-passing process algebra inspired from the E-LOTOS standard [19] and from imperative programming languages. LNT supports both the description of complex data types and of concurrent processes using the same user-friendly syntax. LNT specifications can be analyzed using CADP [13], a toolbox that provides various verification techniques and tools such as model checking, compositional verification, or performance evaluation. LNT is already used by several universities for teaching and research purposes, and by companies (such as STMicroelectronics or Orange labs) for designing and verifying different kinds of systems.

When using model checking techniques as those available in CADP, we usually have an LNT specification of a system, a dataset of validation examples, and a set of temporal properties to be verified on the system being designed. When we apply the LNT specification on a validation example, we obtain a Labelled Transition System (LTS), which corresponds to all the possible executions of the specification for this example. These LTSs are computed automatically using CADP exploration tools (enumerative approach). A validation example defines a set of inputs to the LNT specification and is similar to a test case in the testing domain. The LTS generation without explicit inputs might turn out to be impossible due to the enumeration on possibly infinite data domains. Bounding the exploration is a solution but this often results in huge LTSs (state explosion), which are therefore very long to analyze. This is why, in this setting, we prefer to work with a set of concrete inputs that we call validation examples in this paper.

The aforementioned properties can be verified on the generated LTS using model checking techniques. At this stage, building the set of validation examples and debugging the system is a real burden, in particular for non-experts. Counterexamples (sequences of actions violating the property) provided by model checkers are the only feedback one may have, and analysing such diagnostics may be very complicated, especially when the counterexample consists of hundreds of actions. More precisely here are a couple of issues that may arise during this phase: (i) we do not know whether the set of validation examples covers all the possible execution scenarios described in the LNT specification; (ii) the LNT specification may contain ill-formed decisions, non-synchronizable actions, and dead code, which require to be corrected, and are not necessarily found using model checking techniques.

Structural coverage is considered as one important metric of software quality and is normally used in implementation testing [21]. Coverage criteria can guide the selection of test cases as well as software reliability estimation. One common approach is to use coverage analysis for measuring the quality of the suite of test cases, which is often evaluated by its ability to detect mutants, *i.e.*, potential faults that are artificially inserted [16]. Several coverage criteria are well established, such as instruction coverage, decision coverage, data-flow coverage, and path coverage. In this paper, we explore a different angle of the same question that relates to specification coverage. We demonstrate how to improve the quality of validation examples, and more importantly to debug specifications through coverage analysis. Formal specification languages have already benefited from tool-supported coverage metrics, such as SDL with Telelogic's Tau that measures the coverage of states and transitions, and VDM with IFAD's VDMTools [2].

In this paper, we are interested in debugging value-passing process algebra through coverage analysis, and we applied it to LNT specifications. We first define block, decision, and action coverage for specifications before showing how to insert probes to collect coverage information. Then we present how to analyze coverage based on the collected information in two steps. In the first step, we simultaneously analyze block and decision coverage to locate uncovered areas. We define a relationship between blocks and decisions, which is used to detect ill-formed decisions as well as to choose the uncovered parts that may contain non-synchronizable actions. In the second step, we perform action coverage analysis in these selected uncovered parts to find out the non-synchronizable actions. We implemented a tool to automate our approach, and we applied it to more than one hundred LNT specifications including six real-world case studies. It is worth emphasizing that we found several important issues for these specifications (*e.g.,* incomplete dataset of validation examples, ill-formed decisions, non-synchronizable actions, and dead code).

The main contributions of this paper are as follows:

- We developed new techniques to debug formal specifications, illustrated by LNT.
- We proved that applying our techniques has no impact on the original behaviors of the system by proving branching equivalence preservation.
- We implemented these techniques as a tool, CAL, built on top of the publicly available and widely-used CADP verification toolbox.
- We applied CAL to more than one hundred LNT specifications including six real-world systems.

The rest of this paper is organized as follows. In Section 2, we briefly introduce LNT. In Section 3, our solution for LNT coverage analysis is presented, including how to insert probes without impact on the original system behaviors as well as how to compute coverage in two steps. Section 4 describes our implementation and experimental results. Sections 5 and 6 present related work and concluding remarks, respectively.

2 Overview of LNT

The LNT specification language is an improved variant of the E-LOTOS standard [19]. LNT combines the best features of imperative and functional programming languages on the one hand, and value-passing process algebras on the other. Therefore, LNT supports both the description of complex data types and of concurrent processes using the same user-friendly syntax. LNT formal operational semantics is defined in terms of LTSs. For the sake of brievity, we show in Table 1 the syntax and semantics of a fragment of LNT, where x_i and T_i represent a variable and its type respectively, E denotes a logical expression, V is either a variable or an expression with type coercion, and V_i are its possible values [7].

Table 1. Syntax and operational semantics of LNT fragment

$\mathbb{B} ::= \textbf{stop} \mid \mathbb{B}_1;\ \mathbb{B}_2 \mid \textbf{select}\ \mathbb{B}_1[]...[]\mathbb{B}_n\ \textbf{end select} \mid \textbf{par}\ G\ in\ \mathbb{B}_1\|\|...\|\|\mathbb{B}_n\ \textbf{end par} \mid \textbf{if}\ E\ \textbf{then}\ \mathbb{B}\ \textbf{end if} \mid \textbf{case}\ V\ \textbf{in}\ V_1 \rightarrow \mathbb{B}_1 \mid ... \mid V_m \rightarrow \mathbb{B}_m\ \textbf{end case} \mid \textbf{while}\ E\ \textbf{loop}\ \mathbb{B}\ \textbf{end loop}$
$(SEQ1)\dfrac{\mathbb{B}_1 \xrightarrow{\beta} \mathbb{B}_1'}{\mathbb{B}_1; \mathbb{B}_2 \xrightarrow{\beta} \mathbb{B}_1'; \mathbb{B}_2}$ $\quad (SEQ2)\dfrac{\mathbb{B}_1 \xrightarrow{\delta} \mathbb{B}_1' \quad \mathbb{B}_2 \xrightarrow{\beta} \mathbb{B}_2'}{\mathbb{B}_1; \mathbb{B}_2 \xrightarrow{\beta} \mathbb{B}_2'}$
$(SEL)\dfrac{k \in [1,n] \quad \mathbb{B}_k \xrightarrow{\beta} \mathbb{B}_k'}{\textbf{select}\ \mathbb{B}_1[]...[]\mathbb{B}_n\ \textbf{end select} \xrightarrow{\beta} \mathbb{B}_k'}$
$(PAR)\dfrac{k \in [1,n] \quad \mathbb{B}_k \xrightarrow{\beta} \mathbb{B}_k' \quad gate(\beta) \neq G}{\textbf{par}\ G\ \textbf{in}\ \mathbb{B}_1\|\|...\|\|\mathbb{B}_n\ \textbf{end par} \xrightarrow{\beta} \textbf{par}\ G\ \textbf{in}\ \mathbb{B}_1\|\|...\|\|\mathbb{B}_k'\|\|...\|\|\mathbb{B}_n\ \textbf{end par}}$
$(COM)\dfrac{I \subseteq [1,n] \quad \forall k \in I. \mathbb{B}_k \xrightarrow{\beta} \mathbb{B}_k' \quad gate(\beta) = G \quad j \in I}{\textbf{par}\ G\ \textbf{in}\ \mathbb{B}_1\|\|...\|\|\mathbb{B}_n\ \textbf{end par} \xrightarrow{\beta} \textbf{par}\ G\ \textbf{in}\ \mathbb{B}_1\|\|...\|\|\mathbb{B}_j'\|\|...\|\|\mathbb{B}_n\ \textbf{end par}}$
$(IF1)\dfrac{[\![E]\!] = true \quad \mathbb{B} \xrightarrow{\beta} \mathbb{B}'}{\textbf{if}\ E\ \textbf{then}\ \mathbb{B}\ \textbf{end if} \xrightarrow{\beta} \mathbb{B}'}$ $\quad (IF2)\dfrac{[\![E]\!] = false}{\textbf{if}\ E\ \textbf{then}\ \mathbb{B}\ \textbf{end if} \xrightarrow{\delta} stop}$
$(WHILE1)\dfrac{[\![E]\!] = true \quad \mathbb{B} \xrightarrow{\pi} \mathbb{B}' \quad \mathbb{B}' \xrightarrow{\delta} \mathbb{B}}{\textbf{while}\ E\ \textbf{loop}\ \mathbb{B}\ \textbf{end loop} \xrightarrow{\pi} \textbf{while}\ E\ \textbf{loop}\ \mathbb{B}\ \textbf{end loop}}$
$(WHILE2)\dfrac{[\![E]\!] = false}{\textbf{while}\ E\ \textbf{loop}\ \mathbb{B}\ \textbf{end loop} \xrightarrow{\delta} stop}$
$(CASE)\dfrac{j \in 1,...m\ (\forall k \in 1,...,j-1)[\![V == V_k]\!] = false, [\![V == V_j]\!] = true \quad \mathbb{B}_j \xrightarrow{\beta} \mathbb{B}'}{\textbf{case}\ V\ \textbf{in}\ V_1 \rightarrow \mathbb{B}_1 \mid ... \mid V_m \rightarrow \mathbb{B}_m\ \textbf{end case} \xrightarrow{\beta} \mathbb{B}'}$

LNT processes are built from action, sequential composition (;), choice (**select**), parallel composition (**par**), condition (**if, case, while**), and termination (**stop**). Communication is carried out by rendezvous on gates G (multiple synchronization points) with bidirectional transmission of multiple values. For simplicity, in Table 2, we consider actions with only two values being sent in both directions. The gate on which an action β takes place is denoted by $gate(\beta)$, and we use π to denote a sequence of actions. Particularly, an action can be an emission (!) or a reception (?). The special action δ is used for successful termination. The internal action is denoted by the special gate i, which cannot be used for synchronization. Processes are parameterized by sets of actions (alphabets) and input/output data variables.

LNT specifications can be analyzed using CADP [13], a verification toolbox dedicated to the design, analysis, and verification of asynchronous systems consisting of concurrent processes interacting via message passing.

3 Coverage Analysis

In this section, we show how to analyze structural coverage for LNT specifications, which helps one to improve the quality of the dataset of validation examples as well as to detect several issues in the specification, *i.e.*, ill-formed or unnecessary decisions, non-synchronizable actions, and dead code.

3.1 Terminology

One well-known coverage criteria is the instruction coverage, *i.e.*, the number of executed instructions out of the total number of instructions. It is used for measuring code quality, *i.e.*, checking the existence of non-executed code. However, this coverage requires checking each instruction separately, which is not efficient for large programs. Since several instructions can be in the same block, for efficiency reasons it makes more sense to keep track of blocks rather than individual instructions. Note that 100% block coverage implies 100% instruction coverage. This is why we choose *block coverage* as the first criterion. However, from block coverage, we cannot deduce outcomes of decisions, *e.g.*, whether a loop reaches its termination condition or whether the false outcome of a decision is evaluated. To solve this, we consider *decision coverage* as the second criterion, which takes a more in-depth view of the program. Furthermore, note that for LNT, synchronization points between processes are modelled by rendezvous on synchronized actions. To check whether all actions are well designed to be synchronizable, we choose *action coverage* as a third criterion. It is a special metric for concurrent languages.

Let us define the notion of blocks for LNT. We first define control instructions in LNT that will be used to determine blocks.

Definition 1 *(LNT Control Instruction). The Control Instructions (CIs) of an LNT specification include conditional instructions (**if, case, while**), parallel and choice ones (**par, select**), and termination (**stop**).*

Definition 2 *(LNT Block). Given an LNT specification, an LNT block is the largest sequence of instructions free of CIs. Particularly, we call a block without action a silent block.*

Now we formally define the notion of coverage for blocks, actions, and decisions. In the following, we simply call LNT block as block if there is no ambiguity. In LNT, a decision is a Boolean expression composed of conditions and zero or more Boolean operators. Particularly, for case statements, each branch is considered as one decision. For example, given the following case statement:

$$\textbf{case } V \textbf{ in } \;\; V_0 \rightarrow I_0 \;\mid V_1 \rightarrow I_1 \;\mid V_2 \rightarrow I_2 \;\; \textbf{end case}$$

we have the following three decisions, one per branch:

- $V == V_0$;
- $V == V_1$;
- $V == V_2$.

Definition 3 *(Covered block, action, and decision). Let s be an LNT specification and ds be a dataset of validation examples. We have the following notions:*

- *a block b (an action a, resp.) in s is said to be covered w.r.t. ds if b (a, resp.) is executed by at least one example $e \in ds$, denoted by $C^{s:B}_{ds}(b)$ ($C^{s:A}_{ds}(a)$, resp.), simply $C^B(b)$ ($C^A(a)$, resp.) if there is no ambiguity;*
- *a decision d in s is said to be covered w.r.t ds if $\exists e_1, e_2 \in ds$, such that the true outcome of d is evaluated by e_1 and the false outcome is evaluated by e_2, denoted by $C^{s:D}_{ds}(d)$, simply $C^D(d)$. Specially, if only true (false, resp.) outcome of d is evaluated, we denote this by $C^{D:t}(d)$ ($C^{D:f}(d)$, resp.).*

Definition 4 *(Block (Decision, Action, resp.) coverage). Let s be an LNT specification and ds be a dataset of validation examples. Block (Decision, Action, resp.) coverage w.r.t. s and ds, denoted by BC^s_{ds} (DC^s_{ds}, AC^s_{ds}, resp.), is the percentage of the number of covered blocks (decisions, actions, resp.) out of their total number. Formally, $BC^s_{ds} = \|B_c\|/\|B\|$ ($DC^s_{ds} = \|D_c\|/\|D\|$, $AC^s_{ds} = \|A_c\|/\|A\|$, resp.), where $B_c = \{b \in B \mid C^B(b)\}$ ($D_c = \{d \in D \mid C^D(d)\}$, $A_c = \{a \in A \mid C^A(a)\}$, resp.) and B (D, A, resp.) is the set of all blocks (decisions, actions, resp.) in the given specification. If there is no ambiguity, we simply denote the three coverage as BC, DC, and AC.*

3.2 Probe Insertion

To measure structural coverage of LNT, we instrument the code with probes in order to collect coverage information. Before showing how to do this, we first define LTS, which will be used to explicitly capture such coverage information.

Definition 5 *(LTS) An LTS is a tuple $L = (S_L, s^0_L, \Sigma_L, T_L)$ where S_L is a finite set of states; $s^0_L \in S_L$ is the initial state; Σ_L is a finite set of actions; $T_L \subseteq S_L \times \Sigma_L \times S_L$ is a finite set of transitions.*

Given an LTS obtained from applying an LNT specification on one validation example, the only elements of the specification contained in this LTS are actions. Hence, to analyze the structural coverage, we propose to insert probes as new actions, whose presence in the LTS explicitly shows their coverage information. When inserting such probes, it is important to preserve the original system behaviors when all probes are hidden as internal actions. It is reasonable to consider probes as internal actions because they are represented by fresh and non-synchronized actions, which do not interfere with the existing instructions. In the following, we denote the set of LTSs corresponding to the dataset of validation examples by Δ.

Block. To measure the block coverage, we insert a probe P at the end of each block. The presence of P in Δ implies that its associated block is covered, *i.e.*, $\exists L \in \Delta$, such that $P \in \Sigma_L$.

Decision. Table 2 illustrates how probes are inserted for decisions in LNT. For decision coverage, to obtain the evaluated outcome(s) of a given decision E, we equip the corresponding probe with this decision as its parameter, *i.e.*, $P\ (!E)$. The parameter $!E$ displays the outcome of the decision E. Precisely, if the decision E is evaluated to both true and false for a validation example, then in its corresponding LTS, we have the action $P\ !TRUE$ as well as $P\ !FALSE$. Otherwise, if it is evaluated to only true (false, resp.), what we obtain in the LTS is $P\ !TRUE$ ($P\ !FALSE$, resp.). The decision E is covered if $\exists L_1, L_2 \in \Delta$, such that $P\ !TRUE \in \Sigma_{L_1}, P\ !FALSE \in \Sigma_{L_2}$.

In Table 2, for the **if** construct, we add the corresponding probe just before it to catch its outcome. For the **case** construct, its operational semantics is to sequentially pick the first condition that holds true. To capture such semantics, we first represent a decision for each branch by a different probe, *i.e.*, P_1 for $V = V_1$ and P_2 for $V = V_2$. At the beginning of each corresponding branch, we add its probe with parameter $TRUE$ and the probes representing all its precedent branches with parameter $FALSE$. In this way, only probes with evaluated decisions appear in the corresponding LTSs. For the loop construct (**while**), probes should be inserted both before and after the corresponding construct to guarantee that both outcomes of the decision are obtained if it is covered. Otherwise, with the probe only before the construct, we will never capture the false outcome if the value of decision is first true and then becomes false. With the probe only after the construct, the true outcome cannot be caught in the same situation.

Table 2. Probe insertion for decisions

Types	Before Insertion	After Insertion
If	**if** E **then** B_1 **end if**	$P(!E)$; **if** E **then** B_1 **end if**
Case	**case** V **in** $V_1 \rightarrow B_1$ $\vert V_2 \rightarrow B_2$ **end case**	**case** V **in** $V_1 \rightarrow$ $\underline{P_1(!TRUE)}$;B_1 $\vert V_2 \rightarrow$ $\underline{P_1(!FALSE); P_2(!TRUE)}$;$B_2$ **end case**
While	**while** E **loop** B_1 **end loop**	$\underline{P(!E)}$; **while** E **loop** B_1 **end loop**; $\underline{P(!E)}$

Action. For action coverage, we insert a probe just after the target action, whose presence in an LTS indicates that this action is covered. Even though actions can be manifested by themselves in LTSs, probes are still necessary. The reason is that in an LNT specification, one action may be used several times at different places. Each appearance of an action is called its instance. The presence of an action in Δ does not mean that all its instances are covered. To determine which exact instance of an action is not yet covered if there is any, we use different probes to distinguish all action instances.

Critical Block and Decision. Now we define critical blocks and decisions that are located at the beginning of a choice branch, whose corresponding probes should be inserted in a different way to preserve system behaviors.

Definition 6 *(Critical block (decision)). Given a silent block (decision), if it is a subpart of a select construct such that there is no action before it in the corresponding choice branch, then it is called a critical block (decision).*

Intuitively, given a critical block or decision, if we insert its probe as described before, this probe becomes the first action in the corresponding choice branch. In this case, the branching structure will be altered ($\tau.a+b$ and $a+b$, in a CCS-like notation [20], are not branching equivalent). To solve this problem, Table 3 shows how to insert probes for critical blocks and decisions in a different way to keep the original behaviors, where B_i^s denotes a silent block. For a critical block, an additional variable, initialized as 0, is used to indicate whether this block is completely executed. This variable is then used as the parameter of the corresponding probe inserted after the choice construct. If the value is 1 (0, resp.), then this block is covered (not covered, resp.), represented by $P(!1)$ ($P(!0)$, resp.) in the corresponding LTS. For a critical decision, an extra variable, initialized as 2, is used as the parameter of the corresponding probe inserted after the choice construct. The value being 1 (0, resp.) represents true (false, resp.) outcome of the decision. Particularly, if the value is 2, then the decision is not even evaluated.

Table 3. Probe insertion for critical blocks and critical decisions

Criterion	Types	Before Insertion	After Insertion
Block		**select** B_1^s [] B_2 **end select**	tag:=0; **select** B_1^s; tag:=1 [] B_2 **end select** $P(!tag)$
Decision	If	**select** B_1^s; **if** E **then** B_2 **end if**; B_3 [] B_4 **end select**	tag:=2; **select** B_1^s; **if** E **then** tag:=1 **else** tag:=0 **end if**; **if** E **then** B_2 **end if**; B_3 [] B_4 **end select** $P(!tag)$
	Case	**select** B_1^s; **case** V **in** $V_1 \rightarrow B_2$ $\|V_2 \rightarrow B_3$ **end case**; B_4 [] B_5 **end select**	tag1:=2; tag2:=2; **select** B_1^s; **case** V **in** $V_1 \rightarrow tag1 := 1; B_2$ $\|V_2 \rightarrow tag1 := 0; tag2 := 1; B_3$ **end case**; ...**end select**; $P_1(!tag1)$; $P_2(!tag2)$
	While	**select** B_1^s; **while** E **loop** B_2 **end loop**; B_3[]B_4 **end select**	tag1:=2; tag2:=2; **select** B_1^s; **if** E **then** tag1:=1 **else** tag1:=0 **end if**; **while** ... **end loop**; **if** E **then** tag2:=1 **else** tag2:=0 **end if**; B_3[]B_4 **end select**; $P(!tag1)$; $P(!tag2)$

3.3 Behavior Preservation

In this section, we prove the behavioral equivalence between the original LNT specification and the one with inserted probes hidden as internal actions, which is called an extended specification in the following. We consider here branching bisimulation, which is one of the finest behavioral equivalences studied in process theory [22]. This equivalence preserves the branching structure of systems by considering all intermediate states including those with internal transitions. We prove the branching equivalence directly on LNT specification, which is actually a process algebra. The underlying model of process algebra is its corresponding LTS, where each process represents a state in its LTS.

Definition 7 *(Branching bisimulation). A branching bisimulation relation R is a binary relation over a process algebra such that it is symmetric and satisfies the following transfer property: if pRq and $p \xrightarrow{a} p'$, then one of the two following conditions should be satisfied:*

– *$a = \tau$ and $p'Rq$;*

– *there is a sequence of transitions $q \xrightarrow{\tau^*} q'' \xrightarrow{a} q'$, pRq'' and $p'Rq'$.*

If there is a branching bisimulation relation R between p and q, then p and q are branching bisimilar, denoted by $p \approx_b q$.

Theorem 1 *Let s be an LNT specification, s' be its corresponding extended specification (both s and s' are processes), then s and s' are branching bisimilar, i.e., $s \approx_b s'$.*

Proof. From Definition 7 and the fact that the only difference between s and s' is the set of inserted probes that are considered as internal actions, it follows that to prove this theorem, we have to show that $\forall \tau_P \in s'$, where τ_P represents a probe considered as an internal action, for a binary relation R, the condition Υ is satisfied, where Υ: $\forall \tau_P \in s', p \xrightarrow{\tau_P} p' \Rightarrow pRp'$. This means that any inserted probe has no impact on the original behaviors in terms of branching structures. Next we demonstrate, without loss of generality, that this is true for each probe.

1. For an action a in any composition or construct, it can be directly deduced that its corresponding probe satisfies the condition Υ, from the silent step law in process algebra, denoted by L_τ: $a.\tau_P \approx_b a$ (CCS-like notation, which will be used in the following for the sake of brievity).
2. For a block B, we analyze its corresponding probe in three different constructs separately, *i.e.*, sequential, parallel and choice.
   - For B in a sequential composition that is not inside any parallel and choice construct, its probe satisfies the condition Υ since it is not possible for this probe to change the branching structure.
   - For B in a parallel composition that is not inside any choice construct, there are two possible situations. One is that the corresponding probe τ_P inserted for B is the first action in the corresponding parallel branch, where B must be a silent block. Another one is that τ_P is not the first action in this branch. For the latter one, τ_P satisfies Υ from L_τ. Now we analyze the first situation in the following way.
     Base case: consider $(\tau_P.a)||b$, for which we have $\tau_P.a||b = \tau_P.(a||b) + b.\tau_P.a$. From this, the τ_P in $b.\tau_P.a$ satisfies Υ. Moreover, from L_τ, we further get $\tau_P.(a||b) + b.\tau_P.a = \tau_P.(a||b) + b.a$. Now we show that this τ_P also satisfies Υ because $b.a$ is included in $a||b$ since $a||b = a.b + b.a$.
     Induction: now consider $(\tau_P.a)||(b_1.\dots.b_n) = \tau_P.(a||(b_1.\dots.b_n)) + b_1.((\tau_P.$

$a))||(b_2.....b_n))$. Now we suppose that τ_P in $(\tau_P.a)||(b_2.....b_n)$ satisfies Υ and thus can be reduced to $a||(b_2.....b_n)$. This follows that the first τ_P also satisfies Υ since $b_1.(a||(b_2.....b_n))$ is included in $(a||(b_1.....b_n))$. In the same way, the induction is applied to structures with more than two parallel branches.
  - For B in a parallel composition that itself is inside a choice construct, suppose that there is no action before B in the corresponding branch and B is a silent block. Then B is a critical block and its corresponding probe is inserted after the choice construct, which satisfies Υ.
  - For B in a choice construct, either B is a critical block, or there is an action before B. For the former case, the corresponding probe is inserted after the choice construct and thus satisfies Υ. The probe of the latter case also satisfies Υ from L_τ.

3. For a decision E, if it is not critical, the probe satisfy Υ from L_τ. If it is critical, we avoid $\tau_P.a + b \not\approx_b a + b$ by inserting the corresponding probe in the sequential composition after the choice construct, which then satisfies Υ. Actually the demonstration follows the exact same line as described above for blocks.

Now we have shown that each probe inserted as described in Section 3.2 does not alter the original behaviors of the system in terms of branching structure and this proves this theorem. ■

3.4 Coverage Computing

If we simultaneously insert probes for all three criteria to compute their coverage, the corresponding LTSs would suffer from the state explosion problem. To solve this, we separate the coverage analysis into two steps. In a first step, we insert probes for blocks and decisions to reveal those uncovered. The entry of a block may be controlled by the outcome of a decision, *e.g.*, the true outcome of an **if** instruction allows the execution to enter its associated block. For such a block, its coverage may be prevented by two possible reasons: the outcome of its controlling decision prohibits the execution from entering it, or only a part of the block is executed due to non-synchronizable actions. In a second step, we are more interested in those partially covered blocks whose entry is allowed by a decision to discover non-synchronizable actions.

Definition 8 *(Dependency of block on decision).*
- *Given a block b and a decision d, if the execution of b is dependent of the true (false, resp.) outcome of d, this dependency is denoted by* $b \Rightarrow_{pd} d$ *(*$b \Rightarrow_{nd} d$*, resp.).*
- *If* $b \Rightarrow_{pd} d$ *or* $b \Rightarrow_{nd} d$*, we denote it* $b \Rightarrow_d d$*.*

A block whose entry is allowed is an executable block. Such a block either has no dependent decision or is permitted to be entered by its associated decision. In other words, if an executable block is dependent of the true (false, resp.) outcome of a decision d, then this outcome of d is covered.

Definition 9 *(Executable block). A block b is executable if one of the following conditions is satisfied:*
- $\nexists d$ *such that* $b \Rightarrow_d d$;
- *if* $b \Rightarrow_d d$, *then either* $b \Rightarrow_{pd} d$ *and* $C^{D:t}(d)$, *or* $b \Rightarrow_{nd} d$ *and* $C^{D:f}(d)$.

Definition 10 *(Partially covered block). A block is a partially covered block if it is executable but not covered.*

Figure 1 overviews our coverage analysis in two steps. In the first step, we repeatedly apply the specification with probes for both blocks and decisions on each validation example to obtain the corresponding LTS. Block and decision coverages are simultaneously analyzed on these LTSs to obtain their coverage results, denoted by R_{BC} and R_{DC}, respectively. We have $R_{BC} = \{BC, \Gamma_{UB}\}$ and $R_{DC} = \{DC, \Gamma_{C^{D:t}}, \Gamma_{C^{D:f}}\}$, where BC (DC, resp.) is the percentage of block (decision, resp.) coverage, Γ_{UB} is the set of uncovered blocks, and $\Gamma_{C^{D:t}}$ ($\Gamma_{C^{D:f}}$, resp.) is the set of decisions whose true (false, resp.) outcome is covered. We can deduce whether an uncovered block is executable and thus calculate the set of partially covered blocks with R_{BC} and R_{DC}. In the second step, we insert probes for actions in this set of blocks before obtaining the corresponding LTSs and then perform action coverage analysis. The result of action coverage is $R_{AC} = \{AC, \Gamma_{PA}\}$, where AC is the percentage of action coverage, and Γ_{PA} is the set of non-synchronizable actions.

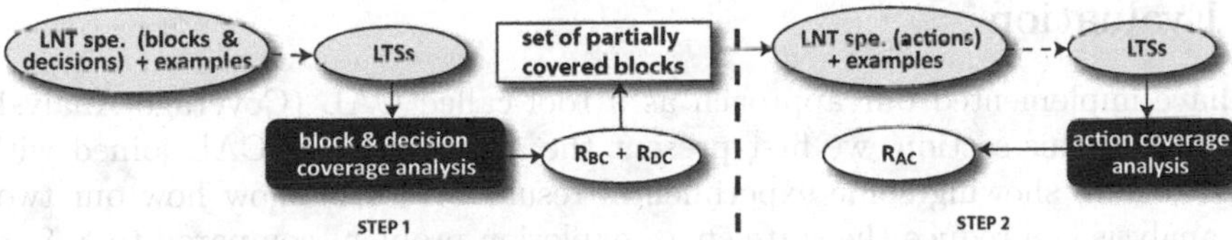

Fig. 1. Overview of coverage analysis in two steps

3.5 Results Analysis

Given the coverage results described in the precedent section, two reasons can explain why the coverage percentages are lower than 100%:

1. lack of validation examples;
2. defects contained in the corresponding LNT specification.

For the first reason, the solution is to add examples that can explore those missing execution scenarios. For instance, suppose that the false outcome of a decision is never covered by the current dataset, we should add examples where the value of this decision can be evaluated to false. If there is no such examples, then we should consider the second reason. For example, if we define one specification with two input parameters and both have two possible values, then we have in total four validation examples. In this case, if a coverage percentage cannot achieve 100%, then there must be some errors in the specification since there is no other possible examples (for illustration see the case study named AgtReconfig in Section 4). We list in the following the different types of errors that may be the source of the uncovered parts, which can be deduced thanks to the results obtained in the precedent section, *e.g.*, $\Gamma_{C^{D:f}}, \Gamma_{C^{D:t}}, \Gamma_{PA}$, etc.:

- **Ill-formed decision:** given a decision d such that $d \in \Gamma_{C^{D:f}}$ and $d \notin \Gamma_{C^{D:t}}$ ($d \in \Gamma_{C^{D:t}}$ and $d \notin \Gamma_{C^{D:f}}$, resp.), if $\exists b$, such that $b \Rightarrow_{pd} d$ ($b \Rightarrow_{nd} d$, resp.), this means that the uncovered outcome of a decision controls at least one block. Such situation is probably due to an ill-formed decision. For example, if a block is within an **if** conditional construct that always has false outcome, then this block is never covered.
- **Unnecessary decision:** given a decision d such that $d \in \Gamma_{C^{D:f}}$ and $d \notin \Gamma_{C^{D:t}}$ ($d \in \Gamma_{C^{D:t}}$ and $d \notin \Gamma_{C^{D:f}}$, resp.), if $\nexists b$, such that $b \Rightarrow_{pd} d$ ($b \Rightarrow_{nd} d$, resp.), this means that the uncovered outcome of a decision controls no block. Such decisions can be safely removed, *e.g.*, the false outcome of an **if** conditional construct is never achieved.
- **Non-synchronizable actions:** for an action a, if $a \in \Gamma_{PA}$, then its corresponding synchronization is ill-designed, *i.e.*, there is bad match between the received and the sent parameter types of the corresponding actions.
- **Dead code:** a piece of unreachable code in an uncovered block $b \in \Gamma_{UB}$ is called dead code if it is not due to the errors described above. This may be caused for example by wrong location of **stop**.

4 Evaluation

We have implemented our approach as a tool called CAL (Coverage Analysis of LNT). In this section, we first present the architecture of CAL joined with CADP before showing some experimental results. We also show how our two-step analysis can reduce the state space explosion problem compared to a more naive approach, where the three coverage criteria are simultaneously computed.

4.1 Implementation

The architecture of CAL with the cooperation of CADP is shown in Figure 2. The input of CAL is an LNT specification with a dataset of validation examples. The LNT specification is instrumented with probes for different criteria as described in Section 3.2. Then CAL calls CADP compilers to repeatedly apply the instrumented LNT specification on each validation example to obtain its corresponding explicit LTS. In this way, we can obtain a set of LTSs associated to the dataset of examples. Afterwards, the ANALYSER tool of CAL measures the coverage percentage and provides other results as described in Section 3.4. All experiments were conducted on a server machine that has six 3.07 GHz processors and 11.7 GB of RAM. Considering that CADP has interfaces for reading LTSs that can be used by an application program written in C or C++, CAL is implemented in C, using gcc with version 3.4.3. The version of CADP used in our evaluation is BETA-VERSION 2014-c "Amsterdam".

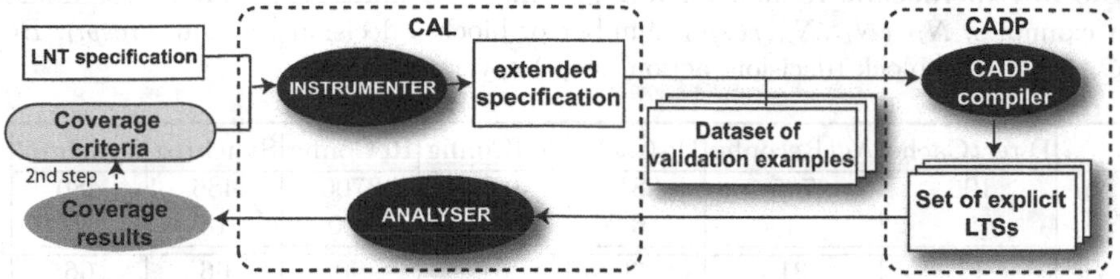

Fig. 2. Implementation architecture of CAL with CADP

4.2 Experimental Results

To evaluate our approach, we have applied our tool to more than one hundred LNT specifications, including six real-world case studies in different application areas (hardware, cloud computing, multi-agent systems, and synchronization protocols). Table 4 lists the six case studies with their designer and a short description.

Table 4. Details of six real-world case studies

Case Study	Designer	Description
DirectCache	STMicroelectronics	deals with cache coherence in multiprocessor systems by using a common directory.
AgtReconfig	Inria	provides an agent-based mechanism allowing distributed applications to be reconfigured at run-time [8].
DisCache	STMicroelectronics	ensures data consistency in multiprocessor shared memory systems that allow multiple copies of a datum [1].
SelfConfig	Inria, Orange labs	automates the configuration of a cloud application that is distributed on more than one virtual machine without requiring any centralized server [9,24,10].
ReConfig	Inria, Orange labs	reconfigures a running system composed of a set of interconnected components, where multiple failures occurring at reconfiguration time are tolerated [5].
Synchro	Inria	realizes the multiway rendezvous of LNT, where all parallel processes are organized in a hierarchical structure [11].

Table 5 lists both the size of the six case studies, *i.e.*, number of lines and validation examples, and their coverage results. Their size varies from 196 to 3700 lines. The number of validation examples differs from several to 200, which depends on the available input domain. For example, in the specification of AgtReconfig, the major process is defined with only two parameters that has two possible values. In this case, we can have four validation examples in total.

Table 5. Experimental results, where N_L: number of lines, N_{VE}: number of validation examples, N_B ($N_D, N_A, resp.$): number of blocks (decisions, actions, *resp.*), BC ($DC, AC, resp.$): block (decision, action, resp.) coverage

	DirectCache	AgtReconfig	DisCache	SelfConfig	ReConfig	Synchro1	Synchro2
N_L	196	785	981	1635	3700	486	480
N_{VE}	5	4	6	60	200	18	30
N_B	12	31	33	31	90	66	66
BC	83.3%	67.7%	93.9%	83.8%	97.8%	62.1%	100%
N_D	12	27	23	23	89	50	50
DC	83.3%	74.1%	91.3%	73.9%	92.1%	60%	100%
N_A	9	50	33	32	53	72	72
AC	100%	64%	100%	93.8%	96.2%	68.1%	100%

In this table, we show two versions for the Synchro case study, the first version is called Synchro1 and the second one Synchro2. The second version was obtained using our coverage results on the first version, as described in Section 3.4 and Section 3.5. Particularly, the block coverage was improved from 62.1% to 100%. This demonstrates the interest of the subsequent utilization of the measured coverage information computed by our approach. Precisely, to achieve 100% for this case study, the authors have not only added 12 complementary validation examples but have also corrected several non-synchronizable actions.

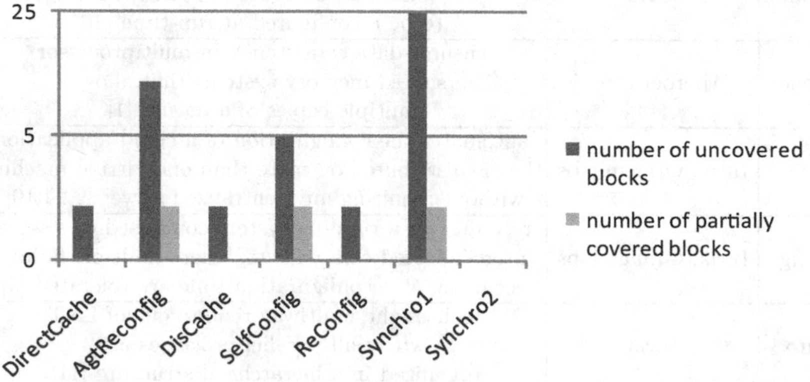

Fig. 3. Executability of uncovered blocks

Another point is that for several case studies (DirectCache, DisCache, and ReConfig), all uncovered blocks were not executable, which is shown in Figure 3. In this case, the first step of coverage analysis is sufficient. For other case studies, the majority of uncovered blocks were not executable. This means that we consider very few blocks in the action analysis.

Besides improving the quality of validation examples, our coverage analysis also identified all types of errors described in Section 3.5. For example, several crucial ill-formed decisions affecting the whole system behaviors were detected and corrected for ReConfig, which were not discovered by model checking. Another point that we want to emphasize is that the analysis results can help in correcting the corresponding bugs in the implementation. In ReConfig for instance, the ill-formed decisions in the LNT specification, detected in the LTS models, helped the developers of the corresponding Java implementation (Orange labs) to locate and correct them immediately.

To show the efficiency of our approach, we compare it with a more naive approach, where three criteria are simultaneously analyzed. We greatly reduce the number of probes for all case studies that we tested when adopting our approach in two steps. Take AgtReconfig as example, the total number of probes is 108 with the naive approach and is only 60 with ours. In our experiments, the reduced number of states and transitions for all case studies are between 30% and 60% thanks to the reduced number of probes. Furthermore, for some validation examples of Synchro2, we could not even construct the corresponding LTSs using the naive approach within a reasonable time (a few hours) but succeeded using ours within one hour.

5 Related Work

Step-by-step execution for LOTOS is proposed in [17], which is also called interactive simulation. The authors take the role of the environment by providing events to the specification and then by observing the results. Although useful for debugging, step-by-step execution is probably the simplest and weakest validation technique available for LOTOS. In [4], the authors propose to measure the completeness of an example suite in terms of the structural coverage described in LOTOS, where a probe is inserted after every action to check its achievement. However, they do not consider the decisions, whose coverage may have an important impact on the action coverage. The authors of [12] consider action, decision, and condition coverage for LOTOS. These criteria are measured totally separately. Furthermore, both works do not check behavioral equivalence between the original specification and the extended one. By using new actions as probes, their insertion techniques imply that only weak trace equivalence is preserved. This is the weakest equivalence and thus not suitable for safety-critical systems, where altering branching structure could have serious consequences since an internal transition may alter the desired behavior of the system. Furthermore, compared to keeping weak trace equivalence, we guarantee the finest branching equivalence with probes considered as internal action, which however does not degrade the performance. The reason is that to preserve branching equivalence, as described in Section 3.2, for each critical block and critical decision, we only move their corresponding probe from inside the corresponding choice construct to after it. In other words, the number of probes required is not increased.

In [18], the authors propose an approach to test specifications by first formulating properties that should hold in the specification and then applying model checking or theorem proving to find violations. However, it is very difficult to select the set of properties such that they can evaluate all behaviors in the specification. This is also the case for LNT specification, where some faults detected by our coverage analysis cannot be identified by model checking. Model checking techniques are also used to automatically generate test cases that satisfy coverage criteria [15]. Similarly, in [14], a suite of test sequences are generated from SCR requirements specification by using a model checker's ability to construct counterexamples. Differently, our approach does not only improve the quality of validation examples, but more importantly detect faults in the specification through coverage analysis.

Coverage based testing is a widely used technique in software engineering and different coverage criteria are described in classical books on software testing, *e.g.*, [21]. Test coverage is considered as an essential factor to enhance new proposed models for software reliability estimation. For example, Piwowarsky *et al.* [23] predict software reliability based on the fact that the fault removal rate is a linear function of the code coverage. Cai and Lyu [6] propose to incorporate testing time and test coverage together into one single mathematical form to estimate the software reliability. However, in this paper, our goal is not to discover the quantitative relation between coverage analysis and fault detection rate but to directly debug formal specification by using coverage techniques.

6 Conclusion

In this paper, we have proposed a new approach to debug process algebra specifications, illustrated by LNT. First, we have introduced several coverage notions before showing how to insert probes to measure them by keeping the same behaviors. Second, we have proposed the coverage analysis in two steps such that we are able to find out uncovered parts keeping the number of probes as small as possible. The obtained results can be considered as efficient guides to either complete validation examples or correct errors in the given specification. Third, we have applied our implemented tool, CAL, to six real-world case studies. It is worth pointing out that our approach can also be applied to other value-passing process algebra such as CSP with FDR2 or Promela with SPIN.

So far we have defined an elementary set of coverage criteria, therefore one perspective of our work is to extend to other criteria for coverage analysis, such as multiple condition coverage, modified condition/decision coverage variants, or some criteria based on data flow [3].

Acknowledgements. This work has been supported by the OpenCloudware project (2012-2015), which is funded by the French *Fonds national pour la Société Numérique* (FSN), and is supported by *Pôles* Minalogic, Systematic, and SCS. We would like to thank Radu Mateescu for his valuable suggestions to improve the paper.

References

1. Afek, Y., Brown, G., Meritt, M.: Lazy Caching. ACM Transactions on Programming Languages and Systems 15(1), 182–205 (1993)
2. Agerholm, S., Larsen, P.G.: The IFAD VDM Tools: Lightweight Formal Methods. In: Hutter, D., Traverso, P. (eds.) FM-Trends 1998. LNCS, vol. 1641, pp. 326–329. Springer, Heidelberg (1999)
3. Ammann, P., Offutt, J., Xu, W.: Coverage Criteria for State Based Specifications. In: Hierons, R.M., Bowen, J.P., Harman, M. (eds.) Formal Methods and Testing. LNCS, vol. 4949, pp. 118–156. Springer, Heidelberg (2008)
4. Amyot, D., Logrippo, L.: Structural Coverage for LOTOS - a Probe Insertion Technique. In: Proc. of TestCom 2000, pp. 19–34. Kluwer, B. V. (2000)
5. Boyer, F., Gruber, O., Salaün, G.: Specifying and Verifying the SYNERGY Reconfiguration Protocol with LOTOS NT and CADP. In: Butler, M., Schulte, W. (eds.) FM 2011. LNCS, vol. 6664, pp. 103–117. Springer, Heidelberg (2011)
6. Cai, X., Lyu, M.R.: Software Reliability Modeling with Test Coverage: Experimentation and Measurement with a Fault-Tolerant Software Project. In: Proc. of ISSRE 2007, pp. 17–26. IEEE (2007)
7. Champelovier, D., Clerc, X., Garavel, H., Guerte, Y., McKinty, C., Powazny, V., Lang, F., Serwe, W., Smeding, G.: Reference Manual of the LOTOS NT to LOTOS Translator, Version 5.4. INRIA/VASY (2011)
8. Cornejo, M.A., Garavel, H., Mateescu, R., Palma, N.D.: Specification and Verification of a Dynamic Reconfiguration Protocol for Agent-Based Applications. In: Zieliński, K., Geihs, K., Laurentowski, A. (eds.) Proc. of DAIS 2002. IFIP AICT, vol. 70, pp. 229–242. Springer, Heidelberg (2002)
9. Etchevers, X., Coupaye, T., Boyer, F., De Palma, N., Salaün, G.: Automated Configuration of Legacy Applications in the Cloud. In: Proc. of UCC 2011, pp. 170–177. IEEE Computer Society (2011)
10. Etchevers, X., Salaün, G., Boyer, F., Coupaye, T., De Palma, N.: Reliable Self-deployment of Cloud Applications. In: Proc. of SAC 2014, pp. 1331–1338. ACM (2014)
11. Evrard, H., Lang, F.: Formal Verification of Distributed Branching Multiway Synchronization Protocols. In: Beyer, D., Boreale, M. (eds.) FMOODS FORTE 2013. LNCS, vol. 7892, pp. 146–160. Springer, Heidelberg (2013)
12. Fraser, G., Weiglhofer, M., Wotawa, F.: Coverage Based Testing with Test Purposes. In: Proc. of QSIC 2008, pp. 199–208. IEEE (2008)
13. Garavel, H., Lang, F., Mateescu, R., Serwe, W.: CADP 2010: A Toolbox for the Construction and Analysis of Distributed Processes. In: Abdulla, P.A., Leino, K.R.M. (eds.) TACAS 2011. LNCS, vol. 6605, pp. 372–387. Springer, Heidelberg (2011)
14. Gargantini, A., Heitmeyer, C.: Using Model Checking to Generate Tests from Requirements Specifications. In: Proc. of ESEC/FSE 1999, vol. 24, pp. 146–162. ACM (1999)
15. Gargantini, A., Riccobene, E.: ASM-Based Testing: Coverage Criteria and Automatic Test Sequence. Journal of Universal Computer Science 7(11), 1050–1067 (2001)
16. Gopinath, R., Jensen, C., Groce, A.: Code Coverage for Suite Evaluation by Developers. In: Proc. of ICSE 2014. ACM (2014)
17. Guillemot, R., Logrippo, L.: Derivation of Useful Execution Trees from LOTOS Specifications by using an Interpreter. In: Proc. of FORTE 1988, pp. 311–325. North-Holland Publishing Co. (1988)

18. Heitmeyer, C.L., Kirby, J., Labaw, B.G., Archer, M., Bharadwaj, R.: Using Abstraction and Model Checking to Detect Safety Violations in Requirements Specifications. IEEE Trans. Software Eng. 24(11), 927–948 (1998)
19. ISO/IEC. Enhancements to LOTOS (E-LOTOS). International Standard 15437: International Organization for Standardization — Information Technology (2001)
20. Milner, R.: Communication and Concurrency. Prentice Hall (1989)
21. Myers, G.J.: The Art of Software Testing, Second Edition. John Wiley & Sons, Inc. (2004)
22. De Nicola, R., Vaandrager, F.: Three Logics for Branching Bisimulation. J. ACM 42(2), 458–487 (1995)
23. Piwowarski, P., Ohba, M., Caruso, J.: Coverage Measurement Experience during Function Test. In: Proc. of ICSE 1993, pp. 287–301. IEEE (1993)
24. Salaün, G., Etchevers, X., Palma, N., Boyer, F., Coupaye, T.: Verification of a Self-configuration Protocol for Distributed Applications in the Cloud. In: Proc. of SAC 2012, pp. 1278–1283. ACM (2012)

Property Directed Polyhedral Abstraction*

Nikolaj Bjørner[1] and Arie Gurfinkel[2]

[1] Microsoft Research
[2] SEI/CMU

Abstract. This paper combines the benefits of Polyhedral Abstract Interpretation (poly-AI) with the flexibility of Property Directed Reachability (PDR) algorithms for computing safe inductive convex polyhedral invariants. We develop two algorithms that integrate Poly-AI with PDR and show their benefits on a prototype in Z3 using a preliminary evaluation. The algorithms mimic traditional forward Kleene and a chaotic backward iterations, respectively. Our main contribution is showing how to replace expensive convex hull and quantifier elimination computations, a major bottleneck in poly-AI, with demand-driven property-directed algorithms based on interpolation and model-based projection. Our approach integrates seamlessly within the framework of PDR adapted to Linear Real Arithmetic, and allows to dynamically decide between computing convex and non-convex invariants as directed by the property.

1 Introduction

Linear Real Arithmetic (LRA) enjoys a prominent rôle in symbolic model checking. Semantics of many program statements and properties can be expressed using LRA. In practice, it is often sufficient to limit the verification of such programs to a search for linear arithmetic invariants [20,19,15,9,22,26,10,24,7]. These methods, however, cover only a tiny fraction of the search space of LRA invariants, and even worse, miss simple invariants.

$x \leftarrow y \leftarrow z \leftarrow 0$
ℓ_0: **while** $*$ **do**
| $x \leftarrow x+1;\ y \leftarrow y+1;\ z \leftarrow z-2$
end
ℓ_1: **while** $*$ **do**
| $x \leftarrow x-1;\ y \leftarrow y-3;\ z \leftarrow z+2$
end
ℓ_2: **assert** $x \leq 0 \rightarrow z \geq 0 \wedge y \leq 0$

Fig. 1. Program Bouncy

Consider for example the program Bouncy in Fig. 1. It increments and decrements variables x, y, z in tandem. There is a simple proof of the assertion by using convex polyhedra invariant: $\ell_0 \rightarrow 2x = 2y = -z$, $\ell_1 \rightarrow 2x = -z \wedge y \leq x$. On the other hand, an abstraction-refinement proof that starts from either end (the initial state or the assertion) gets stuck in this example deriving specialized assertions about exact values of each variable. Convex polyhedral invariants, however, are often insufficient. For example, they cannot express disequalities

* This material is based upon work funded and supported by the Department of Defense under Contract No. FA8721-05-C-0003 with Carnegie Mellon University for the operation of the Software Engineering Institute, a federally funded research and development center. This material has been approved for public release and unlimited distribution. DM-0001643.

D. D'Souza et al. (Eds.): VMCAI 2015, LNCS 8931, pp. 263–281, 2015.

(e.g., $x \neq y$), and many disjunctive extensions (e.g.,[25,4,17,1]) have been proposed to remedy this.

This paper embarks on the quest of devising practical property directed [8] polyhedral abstraction algorithms [13]. Our grander ambition is to enable practical model checking methods that search effectively the relevant space of all linear invariants. However, the goal of this paper is more modest: import the search for convex linear invariants, as done by abstract interpretation, into a property directed framework, and do so efficiently. The resulting approach should retain the advantages of restricting the search in an abstract space as well as limiting derived invariants to only the ones that are sufficient for establishing a given property. Indeed, we claim that the combination of polyhedral abstraction and property directed model checking allows to simultaneously address limitations of each approach when they are used in isolation.

The first step towards this goal is a modular account of PDR (Section 3), and the first complete description in Section 4 of $\mathcal{A}$PDR: PDR for LRA. We then develop two main ingredients, a *forward* procedure, $\mathcal{F}$PDR in Section 5, that produces convex polyhedra invariants; and a *backward*, $\mathcal{B}$PDR in Section 6, for complements of convex polyhedra. $\mathcal{F}$PDR mimics forward Kleene iteration, and $\mathcal{B}$PDR mimics backward chaotic iteration, respectively. We present the ingredients in isolation and show that they can be combined in Section 7 in a framework we call PolyPDR. A crucial enabler for PolyPDR is the *syntactic convex closure* method from [5] (Section 2). It allows us to avoid maintaining polyhedra explicitly, in contrast to main tools [3] for polyhedral abstraction that rely on computationally expensive steps that amount to quantifier elimination. To use syntactic convex closure effectively, we integrate a novel algorithm, CCSAT, that finds polyhedra invariants incrementally as *half-space interpolants* [2]. The resulting method inherits several features from polyhedral abstract interpretation and allows to refine the abstraction lazily based on a proof search. The $\mathcal{B}$PDR method dually computes co-convex polyhedra invariants. Section 8 reports on a preliminary evaluation on selected examples that are known to be difficult to $\mathcal{A}$PDR, yet are easy for $\mathcal{F}$PDR or $\mathcal{B}$PDR.

Verification with Interpolation-based MC versus Polyhedral AI. We believe that this work also sheds light on the relationship between abstract interpretation-based and interpolation-based approaches for discovering convex arithmetic invariants. Recall that a *Craig Interpolant* of two inconsistent formulas A and B is a formula I such that $A \to I$, $I \to \neg B$, and the free variables of I are common to A and B. Interpolation-based model checkers use interpolants as oracles to extract constraints relevant for verifying a given property. Table 1 summarizes interpolation procedures for LRA. In the table, *Bool*, *Mono*, *DNF*, and *HalfSpace* stand for Boolean combinations of linear inequalities, monomials (i.e., conjunctions of literals), disjunction of monomials, and a single linear inequality, respectively. Note that the procedures are partial — they are only defined when an interpolant of the particular kind exists. For example, a half-space interpolant might not exists even when A and B are inconsistent.

Table 1. Interpolation algorithms for Linear Real Arithmetic (LRA)

Name	Domain	Algorithm
SmtItp	*Bool* × *Bool* → *Bool*	MathSAT5 [11]
Itp	*Mono* × *Bool* → *Mono*	GPDR [19]
HalfItp	*DNF* × *DNF* → *HalfSpace*	[2]
HalfItp	*Bool* × *Mono* → *HalfSpace*	CCSAT (Sec. 5.2)
PolyItp	*Mono* × *Bool* → *Mono*	—

The general interpolation procedure SmtItp does not guarantee that the interpolant is convex (or a monomial), even if the inputs are. This makes it difficult to compare it to AI. For other procedures, the key difference is that in AI all operations are typically restricted to the faces of the input polyhedra, whereas interpolation operates over linear combinations (so called Farkas consequences) of the input constraints. We show in Section 5.3 that this leads to a significant difference in the two approaches. To unify MC and polyhedral AI, we suggest it is necessary to restrict interpolants to a subset of faces of A that suffice to separate B. Such an interpolant, we call it PolyItp, can be implemented using Fourier-Motzkin-based decision procedures for LRA (e.g., [14,23]), but we are not aware of any interpolation or verification procedures based on it.

2 Preliminaries: Closures and Polyhedral Abstraction

In this section we recall some main notions from Polyhedral Abstraction. The construction for *syntactic convex closures* [5] is central to our quest: it lets us write down the convex closure of two convex polyhedra as the solutions to a linear arithmetic formula. We also recall basic notions from polyhedral abstraction to set the stage for our property directed approach.

2.1 Convex Hulls and Syntactic Convex Closures

Let X be a subset of $\mathbb{Q}^n$. We write $\overline{X}$ for the topological closure of X. X is called *closed* if it is invariant under topological closure, i.e., $\overline{X} = X$. We write $CH(X)$ for the *convex hull* of X defined as the set of all affine combinations of points in X:

$$CH(X) \equiv \{\lambda \boldsymbol{x} + (1 - \lambda \boldsymbol{y}) \mid \boldsymbol{x}, \boldsymbol{y} \in X, 0 \leq \lambda \leq 1\}.$$

X is called *convex* if it is invariant under the convex hull. A convex hull of a closed set is not necessarily closed. In particular, a convex hull of a closed set and a point is not closed. For example,

$$CH(x = 0 \wedge y = 1 \ \vee \ x \geq 0 \wedge x = y) \ \equiv \ 0 \leq x \leq y < x + 1.$$

We write $CC(X) \equiv \overline{CH(X)}$ for the convex closure of X. Of course:

$$CC(x = 0 \wedge y = 1 \ \vee \ x \geq 0 \wedge x = y) \ \equiv \ 0 \leq x \leq y \leq x + 1.$$

A *closed polyhedron* $P(\boldsymbol{x}) \subseteq \mathbb{Q}^n$ is a set of solutions to a conjunction of linear non-strict inequalities, of the form $A\boldsymbol{x} \leq a$. P is closed and convex. In the rest of the paper, unless noted otherwise, we do not distinguish between the syntactic and semantic representation of P. We also restrict our attention to closed polyhedra, i.e., systems with non-strict inequalities only. While this is a significant limitation, in practice, we use systems over $\mathbb{Q}$ to approximate systems over $\mathbb{N}$. Hence, the restriction can be enforced before the relaxation.

A very useful property of convex closure is that it can be computed by Linear Programming, using, what we call, a *syntactic convex closure.*

Definition 1 (Syntactic Convex Closure). *[5] Let $\{P_i(\boldsymbol{x}) = A_i\boldsymbol{x} \leq \boldsymbol{a}_i\}$ be a set of polyhedra. The* syntactic convex closure *$cc(\{P_i\})$ is defined as follows:*

$$cc(\{P_i\}) \equiv \left(\boldsymbol{x} = \sum_i \boldsymbol{z}_i\right) \wedge \left(1 = \sum_i \sigma_i\right) \wedge \bigwedge_i (A_i \boldsymbol{z}_i \leq \sigma_i \boldsymbol{a}_i \wedge \sigma_i \geq 0)$$

where $\{\boldsymbol{z}_i\}$ and $\{\sigma_i\}$ are fresh variables different from $\boldsymbol{x}$.

Convex closure can be computed by existentially quantifying all variables introduced by the syntactic convex closure transformation.

Theorem 1. *[5] Let $\{P_i(\boldsymbol{x}) = A_i\boldsymbol{x} \leq \boldsymbol{a}_i\}$ be a set of polyhedra. Then,*

$$CC(\{P_i\}) \equiv \exists V \cdot cc(\{P_i\})$$

where $V = \{\boldsymbol{z}_i\} \cup \{\sigma_i\}$.

This syntactic form is the basis of our approach.

2.2 Polyhedral Abstract Interpretation

We give a brief overview of polyhedral abstract domain that is necessary to understand our results. The reader is referred to [12,13] for more details. The polyhedral abstract domain over $\mathbb{Q}^n$ is a tuple $\langle \mathcal{P}, \alpha, \gamma, \top, \bot, \sqcap, \sqcup, \nabla \rangle$, where $\mathcal{P}$ is the set of all polyhedra over $\mathbb{Q}^n$, and for $X \subseteq \mathbb{Q}^n$ and $P_1, P_2 \in \mathcal{P}$,

$$\alpha(X) = CC(X) \quad \gamma(P_1) = P_1 \quad P_1 \sqcup P_2 = CC(\{P_1, P_2\}) \quad P_1 \sqcap P_2 = P_1 \cap P_2$$

and ∇ is a operator satisfying extrapolation ($P_1 \sqcup P_2 \subseteq P_1 \nabla P_2$), and convergence: for any increasing sub-sequence of $\mathbb{Q}^n$, $X_0 \subseteq X_1 \subseteq \cdots$, the sequence Y_i, defined as follows,

$$Y_0 = X_0 \qquad\qquad Y_n = Y_{n-1} \nabla (Y_{n-1} \sqcup X_n)$$

is ultimately convergent, (i.e., there is an $N \in \mathbb{N}$ s.t. $Y_N = Y_{N+1}$). The standard polyhedra widening [13] ∇_s is defined as follows:

$$P_1 \nabla_s P_2 = \{H \text{ is a half-space of } P_1 \mid P_2 \to H\}$$

and is often extended to also keep the constraints of P_2 that are mutually redundant with those in P_1 [18]. Note that for simplicity, we assume that an abstract domain is a subset of a concrete one, making γ an identity.

Given post- and pre-transformers we can define abstract versions using convex closures as follows:

$$post_\alpha(X) = CC(post(X)) \qquad pre_\alpha(X) = CC(pre(X))$$

Forward abstract interpretation computes an over-approximation of the transitive closure of *post* by iterating the Kleene iteration sequence $\{Y_i\}$ until convergence, where

$$Y_0 = \alpha(X) \qquad Y_n = \begin{cases} Y_{n-1} \sqcup post_\alpha(Y_{n-1}) & \text{if } n \notin W \\ Y_{n-1} \nabla (Y_{n-1} \sqcup post_\alpha(Y_{n-1})) & \text{if } n \in W \end{cases} \tag{1}$$

and W is an infinite subset of $\mathbb{N}$ that determines the widening strategy. Note that each Y_i over-approximates the set of states reachable in i steps or less. Alternatively, abstract interpretation can be done using chaotic iteration strategy by computing the sequence $\{Z_i\}$:

$$Z_0 = \alpha(X) \quad s_n \in post(\gamma(Z_{n-1})) \quad Z_n = \begin{cases} Z_{n-1} \sqcup \alpha(s_{n-1}) & \text{if } n \notin W \\ Z_{n-1} \nabla (Z_{n-1} \sqcup \alpha(s_{n-1})) & \text{if } n \in W \end{cases} \tag{2}$$

Intuitively, the sequence $\{Z_i\}$ over-approximates the sequence $\{s_i\}$ of states reachable by iterative application of best abstract transformer $post_\alpha$ and concretization γ. Backward abstract interpretation is defined similarly to over-approximate transitive closure of *pre*.

3 Property Directed Reachability

This section introduces a modular, rule-based, description of property directed reachability. It simplifies the presentation of our refinements to PDR throughout the paper.

3.1 Symbolic Reachability

A symbolic reachability problem is given by a tuple:

$$\langle \boldsymbol{v}, Init, \rho, Bad \rangle \tag{3}$$

where $\boldsymbol{v}$ is a set of state variables. *Init* and *Bad* are formulae with free variables in $\boldsymbol{v}$ representing the initial and bad states, respectively, and $\rho(\boldsymbol{v}, \boldsymbol{v}')$ is a transition relation. The problem is to decide whether there is a state in *Init* that can reach a state in *Bad*. Formally, a bad state is reachable, if there is an N, such that the following formula is satisfiable:

$$Init(\boldsymbol{v}_0) \wedge \bigwedge_{i=0}^{N-1} \rho(\boldsymbol{v}_i, \boldsymbol{v}_{i+1}) \wedge Bad(\boldsymbol{v}_N) \tag{4}$$

The bad states are unreachable if there exists a formula I over $\boldsymbol{v}$, called an inductive invariant, such that

$$\big((I \wedge \rho) \vee Init'\big) \rightarrow I' \qquad\qquad I \rightarrow \neg Bad \tag{5}$$

We have used $Init'$ and I' for formulas where the variables $\boldsymbol{v}$ are replaced by primed versions $\boldsymbol{v}'$.

Example 1. The transition system for program Bouncy (Fig. 1) is given by $\boldsymbol{v} = x, y, z, \pi$, where π is a program counter, and *Init*, *Bad*, and ρ are defined as follows:

$$Init \equiv x = y = z = \pi = 0 \quad Bad \equiv x \leq 0 \wedge (z < 0 \vee y \geq 0) \tag{6}$$

$$\begin{aligned}\rho \equiv\ & (\pi = 0 \wedge \pi' = 0 \wedge x' = x + 1 \wedge y' = y + 1 \wedge z' = z - 2) \vee \\ & (\pi = 0 \wedge \pi' = 1 \wedge x' = x \wedge y' = y \wedge z' = z) \vee \\ & (\pi = 1 \wedge \pi' = 1 \wedge x' = x - 1 \wedge y' = y - 3 \wedge z' = z + 2) \vee \\ & (\pi = 1 \wedge \pi' = 2 \wedge x' = x \wedge y' = y \wedge z' = z)\end{aligned} \tag{7}$$

Bad is unreachable, and a certificate is

$$(\pi = 0 \rightarrow 2x = 2y = -z) \wedge ((\pi = 1 \vee \pi = 2) \rightarrow 2x = -z \wedge y \leq x) \tag{8}$$

3.2 A Rule Based Algorithm Description

The finite state model checking algorithm IC3 was introduced in [8]. It maintains sets of clauses $R_0, \ldots, R_i, \ldots, R_N$, called a *trace*, that are properties of states reachable in i steps from the initial states *Init*. Elements of R_i are called *lemmas*. In the following, we assume that R_0 is initialized to *Init*. After establishing that $Init \rightarrow \neg Bad$, the algorithm maintains the following invariants (for $0 \leq i < N$):

Invariant 1

$$R_i \rightarrow \neg Bad \qquad\qquad R_i \rightarrow R_{i+1} \qquad\qquad R_i \wedge \rho \rightarrow R'_{i+1}$$

That is, each R_i is safe, the trace is monotone, and R_{i+1} is inductive relative to R_i. In practice, the algorithm enforces monotonicity by maintaining $R_{i+1} \subseteq R_i$.

We introduce the following shorthand for convenience

$$\mathcal{F}(R) \equiv (R \wedge \rho) \vee Init' \tag{9}$$

Data: Q a queue of counter-examples. Initially, $Q = \emptyset$.
Data: N a level indication. Initially, $N = 0$.
Data: $R_0, R_1, \dots, R_N$ is a trace. Initially, $R_0 = Init$.
repeat

- **Unreachable** If there is an $i < N$ s.t. $R_{i+1} \to R_i$, return *Unreachable*.
- **Reachable** If there is an m s.t. $\langle m, 0\rangle \in Q$ return *Reachable*.
- **Unfold** If $R_N \to \neg Bad$, then set $N \leftarrow N + 1$, $R_N \leftarrow \top$.
- **Candidate** If for some m, $m \to R_N \wedge Bad$, then add $\langle m, N\rangle$ to Q.
- **Decide** If $\langle m, i+1\rangle \in Q$ and there are m_0 and m_1 s.t. $m_1 \to m$, $m_0 \wedge m_1'$ is satisfiable, and $m_0 \wedge m_1' \to \mathcal{F}(R_i) \wedge m'$, then add $\langle m_0, i\rangle$ to Q.
- **Conflict** For $0 \leq i < N$: given a candidate model $\langle m, i+1\rangle \in Q$ and clause φ, such that $\neg\varphi \subseteq m$, if $\mathcal{F}(R_i \wedge \varphi) \to \varphi$, then add φ to R_j, for $j \leq i+1$.
- **Leaf** If $\langle m, i\rangle \in Q$, $0 < i < N$ and $\mathcal{F}(R_{i-1}) \wedge m'$ is unsatisfiable, then add $\langle m, i+1\rangle$ to Q.
- **Induction** For $0 \leq i < N$, a clause $(\varphi \vee \psi) \in R_i$, $\varphi \notin R_{i+1}$, if $\mathcal{F}(R_i \wedge \varphi) \to \varphi$, then add φ to R_j, for each $j \leq i+1$.

until ∞;

Algorithm 1. IC3/PDR

Alg. 1 summarizes, in a simplified form, a variant of the IC3 algorithm. The algorithm maintains a queue of counter-examples Q. Each element of Q is a tuple $\langle m, i\rangle$ where m is a monomial over $\boldsymbol{v}$ and $0 \leq i \leq N$. Intuitively, $\langle m, i\rangle$ means that a state m can reach a state in *Bad* in $N - i$ steps. Initially, Q is empty, $N = 0$ and $R_0 = Init$. Then, the rules are applied (possibly in a non-deterministic order) until either **Unreachable** or **Reachable** rule is applicable. **Unfold** rules extends the current trace and increases the level at which counterexample is searched. **Candidate** picks a set of bad states. **Decide** extends a counter-example from the queue by one step. **Conflict** blocks a counterexample and adds a new lemma. **Leaf** moves the counterexample to the next level. Finally, **Induction** generalizes a lemma inductively. A typical schedule of the rules is to first apply all applicable rules except for **Induction** and **Unfold**, followed by **Induction** at all levels, then **Unfold**, and then repeating the cycle.

Define *post* and *post** as follows:

$$post(R) = \exists \boldsymbol{v}_0 \cdot R(\boldsymbol{v}_0) \wedge \rho(\boldsymbol{v}_0, \boldsymbol{v}) \qquad post^*(R) = \bigvee_{0 \leq i < \omega} post^i(R) \tag{10}$$

The dual operators *pre* and *pre** are defined similarly. A direct consequence of Invariant 1 is that R_i over-approximates i applications of the forward image, e.g., R_i is an over-approximation of states reachable in at most i steps:

Proposition 1. $\bigvee_{j \leq i} post^j(Init) \ \to\ R_i$

Theorem 2. *If PDR (Alg. 1) returns from* **Reachable** *then property (4) holds. If PDR returns from* **Unreachable** *with $R_{i+1} \to R_i$, then R_i satisfies* (5).

We have omitted many important optimizations and generalizations instrumental for the efficiency of PDR. For example, when propagating the monomial m in the **Decide** rule, it is useful to keep m_0 as general (i.e., weak) as possible to minimize backtracking during model search. Similarly, **Induction** can be applied to each new lemma created by the **Conflict** rule. These and other important insights are described in depth by others (e.g., [8,19]).

4 $\mathcal{A}$PDR: PDR for Linear Real Arithmetic

In this section, we describe $\mathcal{A}$PDR, a generalization of PDR to Linear Real Arithmetic (LRA). The presentation is based on GPDR [19] and SPACER [21]. To our knowledge, this is the first complete description of $\mathcal{A}$PDR[1].

The input to $\mathcal{A}$PDR is a transition system $\langle \boldsymbol{v}, \mathit{Init}, \rho, \mathit{Bad}\rangle$, as in PDR, except that the variables $\boldsymbol{v}$ are rational and *Init*, *Bad*, and ρ are formulas in LRA. Naturally, the lemmas and the trace maintained by $\mathcal{A}$PDR are in LRA as well.

In principle, PDR as presented in Alg. 1 is applicable to LRA directly. However, **Decide** and **Conflict** rules are quite weak for LRA. In particular, they do not guarantee even a bounded progress of the algorithm – in LRA, PDR might diverge within a fixed level [21].

$\mathcal{A}$PDR extends PDR with two new rules, **Decide**$^{\mathcal{A}}$ and **Conflict**$^{\mathcal{A}}$ that replace **Decide** and **Conflict** rules, respectively. The new rules are shown in Algorithm 2. In the rules, we use P and $P_{\downarrow}$ to indicate a conjunction and $P^{\uparrow}$ a disjunction of linear inequalities, respectively. The **Decide**$^{\mathcal{A}}$ is based on *Model Based Projection* (MBP) that under-approximates existential quantification. MBP was introduced in [21] and is defined as follows. Let φ be a formula, $U \subseteq \mathit{Vars}(\varphi)$ a subset of variables of φ, and P a model of φ. Then, $\psi \in \textsc{Mbp}(U, P, \varphi)$ is a model based projection if (a) ψ is a monomial, (b) $\mathit{Vars}(\psi) \subseteq \mathit{Vars}(\varphi) \setminus U$, (c) $P \models \psi$, (d) $\psi \rightarrow \exists V \cdot \varphi$. Furthermore, for a fixed U and a fixed φ, MBP is finite. In [21], an MBP function is defined for LRA based on Loos-Weispfenning quantifier elimination. Note that finiteness of MBP ensures that **Decide**$^{\mathcal{A}}$ can only be applied finitely many times for a fixed set of lemmas R_i.

The **Conflict**$^{\mathcal{A}}$ rule is based on *Craig interpolation* (ITP). Given two formulas $A[\boldsymbol{x}, \boldsymbol{z}]$ and $B[\boldsymbol{y}, \boldsymbol{z}]$ such that $A \wedge B$ is unsatisfiable, a Craig interpolant $I[\boldsymbol{z}] = \textsc{Itp}(A[\boldsymbol{x}, \boldsymbol{z}], B[\boldsymbol{y}, \boldsymbol{z}])$, is a formula such that $A[\boldsymbol{x}, \boldsymbol{z}] \rightarrow I[\boldsymbol{z}]$ and $I[\boldsymbol{z}] \rightarrow \neg B[\boldsymbol{y}, \boldsymbol{z}]$. Note that in the context of **Conflict**$^{\mathcal{A}}$, B is always a monomial. In this case, we further require that the interpolant is a clause (i.e., a negation of a monomial). An algorithm for extracting LRA clause interpolants from the theory lemmas produced during DPLL(T) proof is given in [19]. There is an important difference between **Conflict** and **Conflict**$^{\mathcal{A}}$ rules. While by the definition of ITP, in **Conflict**$^{\mathcal{A}}$ $\mathcal{F}(R_i) \rightarrow P^{\uparrow}$, the corresponding requirement of **Conflict** is weaker: $\mathcal{F}(R_i \wedge P^{\uparrow}) \rightarrow P^{\uparrow}$. It is not clear how to extend this to LRA.

[1] Previous versions omit important aspects of IC3, such as priority queues, inductive blocking. The addition of model based projection helps ensuring termination at fixed levels.

Decide$^{\mathcal{A}}$ If $\langle P, i+1\rangle \in Q$ and there is a model $m(\boldsymbol{v}, \boldsymbol{v}')$ s.t. $m \models \mathcal{F}(R_i) \wedge P'$, add $\langle P_\downarrow, i\rangle$ to Q, where $P_\downarrow \in \textsc{Mbp}(\boldsymbol{v}', m, \mathcal{F}(R_i) \wedge P')$.

Conflict$^{\mathcal{A}}$ For $0 \leq i < N$, given a counterexample $\langle P, i+1\rangle \in Q$ s.t. $\mathcal{F}(R_i) \wedge P'$ is unsatisfiable, add $P^\uparrow = \textsc{Itp}(\mathcal{F}(R_i)(\boldsymbol{v}_0, \boldsymbol{v}), P)$ to R_j for $j \leq i+1$.

Algorithm 2. $\mathcal{A}$PDR.

An appealing feature of PDR is that it generates separate lemmas to block spurious counter-examples. These lemmas can be strengthened and leverage mutual induction. In propositional PDR, the space of lemmas is bounded by the number of propositional variables. This guarantees convergence. Clearly, this is not the case for arithmetic. However, we can show that $\mathcal{A}$PDR guarantees to explore increasingly longer execution paths.

Theorem 3. *In any infinite execution of $\mathcal{A}$PDR, the rule **Unfold** is enabled infinitely often.*

Several other approaches have been suggested to lift IC3 to arithmetic. [9] extracts lemmas as a side-effect of an incremental quantifier-elimination procedure that enumerates satisfiable cubes, then eliminates variables from the cubes; [20] develops IC3 for timed automata. More recent attention has been focused on combination with predicate abstraction and arithmetic [10,7]. The abstraction is refined (using interpolants) if the concrete interpretation is able to strengthen inductive lemmas or block abstract counter-examples, otherwise preference is given to a search over existing abstract predicates. In this setting, the interpolation queries also include formulas from the abstract domain.

5 $\mathcal{F}$PDR: Deriving Convex Invariants

In this section, we present our first major contribution – an algorithm, called $\mathcal{F}$PDR, to compute convex invariants. The algorithm terminates when it either finds a convex polyhedral invariant, or an abstract counter-example that cannot be refuted by the best polyhedral abstract transformer $post_\alpha$. Conceptually, the main difference between $\mathcal{F}$PDR and $\mathcal{A}$PDR is that $\mathcal{F}$PDR uses an abstract post-image $post_\alpha$ instead of the concrete *post* of $\mathcal{A}$PDR. Furthermore, $\mathcal{F}$PDR restricts $R_0, \ldots, R_N$ to be convex polyhedra, i.e., conjunctions of linear inequalites. $\mathcal{F}$PDR uses the same data structures as $\mathcal{A}$PDR but maintains a stronger invariant:

Invariant 2 ($\mathcal{F}$PDR) *$\neg Bad \leftarrow R_i \rightarrow R_{i+1} \leftarrow post_\alpha(R_i)$ and for $0 \leq i \leq N$, R_i are convex polyhedra.*

To realize $\mathcal{F}$PDR, we extend $\mathcal{A}$PDR with two new rules, **Conflict**$^{\mathcal{F}}$ and **Decide**$^{\mathcal{F}}$ shown in Alg. 3. The new rules create abstract counter-example traces that may not correspond to concrete traces. We differentiate abstract states by inserting them into AQ instead of Q, which is not used in $\mathcal{F}$PDR.

Data: AQ a queue of abstract counter-examples. Initially, $AQ = \emptyset$.
Reachable$^{\mathcal{F}}$ If there is an m s.t. $\langle m, 0\rangle \in AQ$ return *AbstractReachable*.
Decide$^{\mathcal{F}}$ If $\langle P, i+1\rangle \in AQ$ and there is a model $m(\boldsymbol{v}, \boldsymbol{v}')$ s.t. $m \models CC(\mathcal{F}(R_i)) \wedge P'$, add $\langle P_\downarrow, i\rangle$ to AQ, where $P_\downarrow = \textsc{Mbp}(\boldsymbol{v}', m, CC(\mathcal{F}(R_i)) \wedge P')$.
Conflict$^{\mathcal{F}}$ For $0 \le i < N$, given a counterexample $\langle P, i+1\rangle \in AQ$ s.t. $CC(\mathcal{F}(R_i)) \wedge P'$ is unsatisfiable, add $P^\uparrow = \textsc{HalfItp}(CC(\mathcal{F}(R_i))(\boldsymbol{v}_0, \boldsymbol{v}), P)$ to R_j for $j \le i+1$.

Algorithm 3. $\mathcal{F}$PDR.

To understand the rules, recall that the best abstract transformer for polyhedra is defined as $post_\alpha(R_i)[\boldsymbol{v}] = CC(\exists \boldsymbol{v}_0 \cdot \mathcal{F}(R_i)(\boldsymbol{v}_0, \boldsymbol{v}))$. The only difference between $\mathcal{F}$PDR and $\mathcal{A}$PDR rules is that $\mathcal{F}$PDR uses convex closure of the formulas representing the post-image. Furthermore, the **Conflict**$^{\mathcal{F}}$ rule uses half-space interpolant $\textsc{HalfItp}(A, B)$ of [2] that restricts interpolants to a single inequality (i.e., a half-space). **Conflict**$^{\mathcal{F}}$ is well defined because both A and B are convex. Hence, by Farkas lemma, there exists a half-space separating them. Invariant 2 follows immediately from the rules.

In the rest of this section, we establish the main properties of $\mathcal{F}$PDR show how to implement the rules in Alg. 3 efficiently, and, discuss the relationship between $\mathcal{F}$PDR and polyhedral Abstract Interpretation.

5.1 Properties

$\mathcal{F}$PDR over-approximates the abstract iteration sequence (1).

Proposition 2. *Let $R_0, \ldots, R_N$ be a trace of $\mathcal{F}$PDR and $0 \le i \le N$. Then,* $\left(\bigsqcup_{j \le i} post^j_\alpha(Init)\right) \rightarrow R_i$.

Proposition 2 is an immediate consequence of **Conflict**$^{\mathcal{F}}$ rule. Note the analogy with Proposition 1.

Since the abstract post-image over-approximates the concrete post-image, whenever $\mathcal{F}$PDR returns from **Unreachable**, it has found a concrete inductive invariant that certifies that *Bad* is unreachable from *Init*.

Proposition 3. *Let $R_0, \ldots, R_N$ be a trace of $\mathcal{F}$PDR and $0 < i \le N$ be such that $R_i \rightarrow R_{i-1}$, then $post^*(Init) \cap Bad = \emptyset$*

Finally, $\mathcal{F}$PDR returns from **Reachable**$^{\mathcal{F}}$ only if there does not exist an unreachability certificate that can be established using the best abstract post-image That is, every abstract iteration sequence (1), independently of the widening operator or other strategy heuristics, reaches a bad state.

Proposition 4. *Traces found by $\mathcal{F}$PDR are contained in the abstraction:*

$$\langle P, 0\rangle \in AQ \quad \textit{implies } post^N_\alpha(Init) \cap Bad \neq \emptyset.$$

Proof. By construction, $\langle P, N\rangle \cap Bad \neq \emptyset$. Then, by induction on the size of N that $\langle P, i\rangle \in AQ$ implies that $post_{\alpha}^{N-i}(P) \cap Bad \neq \emptyset$. □

Propositions 2 and 3 establish soundness of $\mathcal{F}$PDR. Proposition 4 provides an interesting form of completeness: $\mathcal{F}$PDR is guaranteed to terminate when the polyhedral abstract domain is too weak to refute a counterexample (i.e., a false alarm). However, $\mathcal{F}$PDR might still diverge when *Bad* is unreachable even if the abstract domain is strong enough to refute every finite counterexample.

5.2 Implementation

The main bottleneck in implementing the $\mathcal{F}$PDR rules in Alg. 3 is deciding satisfiability $CC(\varphi) \wedge P$ of a convex closure $CC(\varphi)$ of an arbitrary formula φ and a monomial P, where both φ and P are over LRA. A naïve algorithm is to (a) compute a DNF of φ, (b) compute the convex closure $\psi = CC(\varphi)$ of the disjuncts, and (c) check satisfiability of $\psi \wedge P$. This however, is not efficient: both the explicit computation of the DNF and the convex closure are exponential in the size of φ. Instead, we propose a novel algorithm CCSAT that avoids an explicit convex closure computation by a combination of the syntactic convex closure construction and interpolation.

The pseudo-code for algorithm CCSAT(φ, P) is shown in Alg. 4. The inputs to CCSAT are a formula $\varphi[\boldsymbol{v}, \boldsymbol{v}']$ and a monomial $P[\boldsymbol{v}]$. The output is either UNSAT and an interpolant between $CC(\varphi)$ and P, or SAT and a model-based projection of $\boldsymbol{v}$ from $CC(\varphi) \wedge P$. CCSAT replaces an expensive up-front convex closure computation with an iterative approximation using syntactic convex closure cc (see Def. 1). The algorithm maintains the set M of implicants of φ such that $CC(M)$ under-approximates $CC(\varphi)$. In each iteration, checking whether $CC(M)$ and φ are consistent is reduced to an SMT-check using the syntactic representation $cc(M)$ of the convex closure $CC(M)$. Note that $cc(M)$ is an SMT-formula that is linear in $|M|$ and is easy to compute. If $cc(M)$ and P are consistent, their model is used to derive the model-based projection. Otherwise, interpolation is used to construct an over-approximation $P^{\uparrow}$ of $cc(M)$. Crucially, since both $cc(M)$ and P are monomials, even a general interpolation procedure ITP of [19] guarantees that $P^{\uparrow}$ is a half-space. Thus, no special HALFITP procedure is needed. If $P^{\uparrow}$ contains φ, then $P^{\uparrow}$ is an interpolant between $CC(\varphi)$ and P', and CCSAT terminates. Otherwise, CCSAT picks another implicant m of φ that contains at least one point outside of $P^{\uparrow}$, adds it to M, and repeats the loop.

Example 2. We illustrate a run of CCSAT(φ, P), where $\varphi[x, y]$ and $P[x, y]$ are defined as follows:

$$\varphi \equiv ((0 \leq y \leq 1) \wedge (0 \leq x \leq 4) \wedge (x \leq 1 \vee x \geq 2)) \vee ((2 \leq y \leq 3) \wedge (2 \leq x \leq 3))$$
$$P \equiv x = 5 \wedge y = 4$$

First, an implicant $m_1 = (0 \leq y \leq 1) \wedge (0 \leq x \leq 1)$ is chosen and blocked by $P_1^{\uparrow} = (y \leq 3)$. Second, $m_2 = (2 \leq x \leq 3) \wedge (2 \leq y \leq 3)$ is chosen and blocked by $P_2^{\uparrow} = (x \leq 4)$. Since $\varphi \rightarrow P_2^{\uparrow}$, the algorithm terminates with (UNSAT, $P_2^{\uparrow}$).

Input: $\varphi[\boldsymbol{v}, \boldsymbol{v}'], P[\boldsymbol{v}]$
$M \leftarrow \emptyset$
while $cc(M) \wedge P' \models \bot$ **do**
  $P^{\uparrow}[\boldsymbol{v}'] \leftarrow \textsc{Itp}(cc(M), P')$
  if $\varphi \wedge \neg P^{\uparrow}[\boldsymbol{v}'] \models \bot$ **then**
    return UNSAT, $P^{\uparrow}[\boldsymbol{v}]$
  else
    $m \leftarrow implicant(\varphi)$ such that $m \wedge \neg P^{\uparrow}[\boldsymbol{v}'] \not\models \bot$
    $M \leftarrow M \cup \{m\}$
  end
end
let m be s.t. $m \models cc(M) \wedge P'$
$P_{\downarrow} \leftarrow \textsc{Mbp}(\boldsymbol{v}', m, cc(M) \wedge P')$
return SAT, $P_{\downarrow}$

Algorithm 4. CCSAT: Decides satisfiability of $CC(\varphi) \wedge P'$. It produces either a half-interpolant or a model-based projection.

The soundness of CCSAT follows immediately from the exit condition of the while loop. Running time is bounded by the number of distinct propositional implicants of φ.

Proposition 5. CCSAT *terminates.*

Proof. For all $m_i, m_j \in M$, by construction, there exists a polyhedron $P^{\uparrow}$ such that $m_i \to P^{\uparrow}$ and $m_j \to \neg P^{\uparrow}$. Thus, all elements of M are distinct. Furthermore, φ has only finitely many distinct propositional implicants. □

The rules in Alg 3 are implemented by first using CCSAT to decide whether $CC(\mathcal{F}(R_i)) \wedge P$ is satisfiable, and then applying either the **Decide**$^{\mathcal{F}}$ or the **Conflict**$^{\mathcal{F}}$ rule, as applicable.

In conclusion, we remark that CCSAT is interesting in its own right as an alternative algorithm for computing half-space (or *beautiful*) interpolants of [2]. In particular, let φ be a formula and $P_0, \ldots, P_k$ be monomials over LRA. Then, $\text{CCSAT}(\varphi, cc(\{P_0, \ldots, P_k\}))$ is a half-space interpolant of φ and $\bigvee_{i=0}^{k} P_i$, if such an interpolant exists.

5.3 Discussion

What is the relationship between $\mathcal{F}$PDR and the traditional Kleene iteration sequence (1)? Both compute convex invariants, but can one simulate the other? Let K be a natural number. For simplicity, consider a convergent Kleene sequence $Y_0, \ldots, Y_K$ in which widening is only applied at the last step. That is, $\forall i \geq k \cdot Y_i = Y_K$, and $W = \{K\}$. Similarly, take an N-step execution of $\mathcal{F}$PDR with $N \geq K$, so that R_K is well defined. Let $Inv(R_K)$ stand for an inductive subset of R_K, i.e., a subset that satisfies the first equation of (5). We are interested in two questions: (Q1) given K and a run of $\mathcal{F}$PDR, is there a Kleene sequence such that $Y_K = Inv(R_K)$; and (Q2) given K and a convergent Kleene sequence, is there a run of PDR such that $Y_K = Inv(R_K)$. While we do not give complete answers, in the rest of the section we explore some special cases.

We use the following transition system as a running example:

$$Init(x, y, z) \equiv x - y \leq 0 \wedge x + y \leq 0 \wedge z = 1/2 \quad Bad(x, y, z) \equiv x \geq 2 \tag{11}$$

$$\begin{aligned}\rho(x, y, z, x', y', z') \equiv y' = y \wedge (x \leq 1 \rightarrow x' = x + z \wedge z' = 1/2 \times z) \wedge \\ (x > 1 \rightarrow x' = x \wedge z' = z)\end{aligned} \tag{12}$$

Note that the set of reachable states is $(x - y < 1) \wedge (x + y < 1)$.

First, consider an execution of $\mathcal{F}$PDR that converges with an inductive invariant $x \leq 3/2 \wedge z \leq 1/2$. A Kleene sequence with standard widening cannot converge on this invariant for any value of K. In particular, the strongest Y_i is of the form $x - y \leq s(i) \wedge x + y \leq s(i)$, where $s(i) = \sum_{j=1}^{j \leq i} 2^{-j}$. Since the standard widening only drops constraints, any Kleene sequence converges to $\top$. The key difference here is that the Kleene iteration with standard widening is restricted to the faces of the polyhedra appearing in the sequence Y_i, while $\mathcal{F}$PDR is limited only by interpolation (i.e., any linear combinations of constraints appearing in R_{K-1} and in the transition relation ρ). In this particular example, other choices for widening can easily simulate $\mathcal{F}$PDR. Moreover, with a suitable (but not necessarily efficiently computable) widening operator, a Kleene sequence can simulate any other method for discovering convex invariants.

Second, consider a variant of the example above, where z is not changed: i.e, replace $z' = 1/2 \times z$ by $z' = z$ in (12). In this example, Kleene iteration converges to the exact set of reachable states in 2 steps. No widening is required. On the other hand, $\mathcal{F}$PDR, as presented, does not simulate the Kleene iteration. Once again, the issue is that $\mathcal{F}$PDR is not restricted to the faces of the polyhedra involved. In fact, our formulation of the **Conflict**$^{\mathcal{F}}$ rule further restricts the set of lemmas to half-spaces of the form $P^{\uparrow} = \textsc{HalfItp}(\varphi, P)$. Alternatively, we can redefine **Conflict**$^{\mathcal{F}}$ to use $P^{\uparrow} = \textsc{PolyItp}(\varphi, P)$, where $\textsc{PolyItp}(A, B)$ is a polyhedral interpolant consisting of some faces of A (we assume that A is convex). Note that $\textsc{PolyItp}$ can be implemented, for example, by quantifying out local variables from the subset of A inconsistent with B. We believe that with this redefinition of **Conflict**$^{\mathcal{F}}$, $\mathcal{F}$PDR can simulate the Kleene iteration. However, an efficient implementation of $\textsc{PolyItp}$ that avoids explicit quantifier elimination remains open. In summary, $\mathcal{F}$PDR and Kleene iteration are quite distinct algorithms for computing convex inductive invariants. Their existing implementation are unlikely to simulate one another. We leave further theoretical and practical exploration of this question to future work.

We conclude this section with an interesting connection between $\mathcal{F}$PDR and widening refinement for AI (e.g., [16,1]). While there is no explicit widening in $\mathcal{F}$PDR, it is implicit in the choice of half-spaces added by **Conflict**$^{\mathcal{F}}$. Whenever some half-spaces are not added in a given iteration (i.e., too much widening), further iterations refine the trace, until all imprecisions introduced by a sub-optimal choices in all previous applications of the **Conflict**$^{\mathcal{F}}$ rule are removed. This mimics the more elaborate algorithms of [16,1].

6 $\mathcal{B}$PDR: Co-convex Invariants

Not all necessary invariants can be expressed as convex polyhedra. Take for example,

$$Init \equiv x = y = 0 \quad Bad \equiv x > 1000 \ \wedge \ y > 1000$$
$$\rho \equiv (x < 100 \vee y < 100) \wedge x' \leq x + 1 \wedge y' \leq y + 1$$

The inductive invariant $x \leq 100 \vee y \leq 100$ is not convex, but its complement is. We call such invariants *co-convex*. In this section, we devise a property directed algorithm $\mathcal{B}$PDR, that finds co-convex invariants. Dually to $\mathcal{F}$PDR, $\mathcal{B}$PDR mimics chaotic iteration (2) with the best abstract pre-image.

The rules for $\mathcal{B}$PDR, are shown in Alg. 5. As before, the algorithm maintains a trace $R_0, \ldots, R_N$, but each R_i is restricted to a *single clause* (disjunction of inequalities). We assume that *Bad* is convex, otherwise, take $CC(Bad)$ as the new set of bad states. Thus, $\neg Bad$ is co-convex. $\mathcal{B}$PDR maintains the following invariant:

Invariant 3 $\neg Bad \leftarrow \neg CC(S) \leftarrow R_i \rightarrow R_{i+1} \leftarrow \mathcal{F}(R_i)$. $\forall 0 \leq i \leq N \cdot R_i$ *is co-convex.*

$\mathcal{B}$PDR is based on the observation that the transitive closure $pre^*_\alpha(Bad)$ of the abstract pre-image is convex. Thus, instead of maintaining a *queue* Q of counterexamples, $\mathcal{B}$PDR maintains a *set* S s.t. the convex closure $CC(S)$ of S under-approximates $pre^*_\alpha(Bad)$, i.e., $CC(S) \subseteq pre^*_\alpha(Bad)$. In each iteration, $\mathcal{B}$PDR either extends S by adding a state that reaches the convex closure of S in 1 or 0 steps (**Decide**$^\mathcal{B}$ and **Candidate**$^\mathcal{B}$ rules), or strengthen some R_i (**Conflict**$^\mathcal{B}$ rule). Since there is no queue, **Reachable**$^\mathcal{B}$ checks whether there are states in the intersection of *Init* and convex closure $CC(S)$ of bad-reaching states. Furthermore, **Leaf** is unnecessary and **Induction** is disabled. **Decide**$^\mathcal{B}$ is very similar to **Decide**$^\mathcal{F}$ of $\mathcal{F}$PDR. The only difference is that convex closure is applied to the bad states. **Conflict**$^\mathcal{B}$ is more complex. First, since there is no queue of counterexamples, we must find the smallest i at which the rule is applicable. Second, since the trace R_i of $\mathcal{B}$PDR is restricted to single clauses, the rule can only change the content of R_i. To guarantee monotonicity of the trace, we stutter the transition relation, i.e., we use $R'_{i-1} \vee \mathcal{F}(R_{i-1})$ as the transformer instead of $\mathcal{F}(R_{i-1})$. Finally, we compute lemmas by *backward* interpolation. We let the bad states be the A-part of the interpolant, and use the backward interpolation property: $I = \textsc{Itp}(A, B)$ iff $\neg I = \textsc{Itp}(B, A)$. Note that since $CC(S)$ is convex, the interpolant $P^\uparrow$ is convex, and the backward interpolant $\neg P^\uparrow$ is co-convex.

Unlike $\mathcal{F}$PDR, implementing $\mathcal{B}$PDR rules is straightforward. Since in Alg. 5 CC is only applied to the set S of convex polyhedra, all applications of CC are simply replaced by its syntactic version *cc*.

$\mathcal{B}$PDR satisfies similar properties to $\mathcal{F}$PDR, but relative to the pre-image. In particular, whenever $\mathcal{B}$PDR returns from **Unreachable**, it has found a concrete inductive invariant:

Reachable$^{\mathcal{B}}$ If $Init \wedge CC(S)$ is satisfiable, return *AbstractReachable*
Candidate$^{\mathcal{B}}$ If for some P, $P \to R_N \wedge Bad$, then $S \leftarrow S \cup \{P\}$.
Decide$^{\mathcal{B}}$ If there is an $0 < i \leq N$ and a model $m(\boldsymbol{v}, \boldsymbol{v}')$ s.t.
$m \models \mathcal{F}(R_i) \wedge CC(S)'$, then $S \leftarrow S \cup \{P_{\downarrow}\}$, where
$P_{\downarrow} = \textsc{Mbp}(\boldsymbol{v}', m, \mathcal{F}(R_i) \wedge CC(S)')$.
Conflict$^{\mathcal{B}}$ If there exists a minimal $0 < i \leq N$ s.t.
$(R'_{i-1} \vee \mathcal{F}(R_{i-1})) \wedge CC(S)' \models \bot$. Then, $R_i \leftarrow \neg P^{\uparrow}[\boldsymbol{v}]$, $N \leftarrow i+1$, and
$R_N \leftarrow \top$, where $P^{\uparrow}[\boldsymbol{v}'] = \textsc{Itp}(CC(S)', R'_{i-1} \vee \mathcal{F}(R_{i-1}))$.

Algorithm 5. $\mathcal{B}$PDR

Proposition 6. *Let $R_0, \ldots, R_N$ be a trace of $\mathcal{B}$PDR and $0 < i \leq N$ be such that $R_i \to R_{i+1}$, then $Init \cap pre^*(Bad) = \emptyset$.*

Similarly, $\mathcal{B}$PDR returns from **Reachable**$^{\mathcal{B}}$ only if there is no invariant that can be established using best abstract pre-image. That is, every backward chaotic iteration sequence (2) started from *Bad* states, reaches a state in *Init*.

Proposition 7. *Traces found by $\mathcal{B}$PDR are contained in the abstraction:*

$$Init \cap CC(Bad) \neq \emptyset \quad implies \quad Init \cap pre^*_{\alpha}(Bad) \neq \emptyset\,.$$

It is also interesting to see whether $\mathcal{B}$PDR simulates backward chaotic iteration. Here, the correspondence is much more direct. The choice of s_i in (2) is in one-to-one correspondence with the choice of $P_{\downarrow}$ in **Decide**$^{\mathcal{B}}$. Widening choices in (2) correspond to constraints dropped by the interpolation during computation of $P^{\uparrow}$ in **Conflict**$^{\mathcal{B}}$. In practice, the key difference is again in the choice of the lemmas found by interpolation. On one hand, the chaotic iteration with standard widening is restricted to the faces of the polyhedra involved. On the other hand, $\mathcal{B}$PDR is restricted to half-spaces found by interpolation.

7 Combinations

In the previous sections, we have presented 3 algorithms, $\mathcal{A}$PDR, $\mathcal{F}$PDR, and $\mathcal{B}$PDR, for computing linear, convex, and co-convex sufficient inductive invariants, respectively. In this section, we present a uniform framework that combines the three algorithms.

First, note that **Conflict**$^{\mathcal{B}}$ rule of $\mathcal{B}$PDR is significantly different from the corresponding rules of $\mathcal{A}$PDR and $\mathcal{F}$PDR. Unlike in $\mathcal{A}$PDR and $\mathcal{F}$PDR, **Conflict**$^{\mathcal{B}}$ only modifies one element R_i of the trace, and ensures that each R_i contains a single clause. This, however, is only necessary to prune the search space to be co-convex invariants. To unify $\mathcal{B}$PDR with the other algorithms, we replace **Conflict**$^{\mathcal{B}}$ with **Conflict**$^{\mathcal{AB}}$ shown in Alg. 6. Note that **Conflict**$^{\mathcal{AB}}$ still uses the convex closure $CC(S)$ of bad-reaching states S, but it adds the new lemma $P^{\uparrow}$ to all levels below i. $\mathcal{B}$PDR remains sound with the new rule. However, it

Conflict$^{\mathcal{AB}}$ If there exists a $0 < i \leq N$ s.t. $\mathcal{F}(R_{i-1}) \wedge CC(S)' \models \bot$.
$R_j \leftarrow R_j \wedge \neg P^{\uparrow}[\boldsymbol{v}]$ for $0 < j \leq i$, where $P^{\uparrow}[\boldsymbol{v}'] = \textsc{Itp}(CC(S)', \mathcal{F}(R_{i-1}))$.

Conflict$^{\mathcal{AFB}}$ If there exists a $0 < i \leq N$ s.t. $CC(\mathcal{F}(R_{i-1})) \wedge CC(S)' \models \bot$.
$R_j \leftarrow R_j \wedge P^{\uparrow}[\boldsymbol{v}]$ for $0 < j \leq i$, where
$P^{\uparrow}[\boldsymbol{v}'] = \textsc{HalfItp}(CC(\mathcal{F}(R_{i-1})), CC(S)')$.

Algorithm 6. Additional conflict rules for $\mathcal{B}$PDR

no longer mimics backward chaotic iteration, and produces more than just co-convex invariants.

Second, we add a new rule **Conflict**$^{\mathcal{AFB}}$, shown in Alg. 6 that combines the corresponding rules of $\mathcal{F}$PDR and $\mathcal{B}$PDR by taking the convex closures of both the post-image and the bad-reaching states. Note that in this case, interpolation guarantees that the corresponding lemma is a single inequality (i.e., a half-space). The rule is implemented efficiently using CCSAT from Section 5.2.

Finally, the combined algorithm, called PolyPDR, is obtained by combining all the rules of PDR (Alg. 1), $\mathcal{A}$PDR (Alg. 2), $\mathcal{F}$PDR (Alg. 3), $\mathcal{B}$PDR (Alg. 5), and the new $\mathcal{B}$PDR rules (Alg. 6), except for **Conflict**$^{\mathcal{B}}$, **Reachable**$^{\mathcal{F}}$, and **Reachable**$^{\mathcal{B}}$. PolyPDR maintains 3 kinds of counterexamples: a queue of concrete counterexamples Q from PDR, a queue of abstract counterexamples AQ from $\mathcal{F}$PDR, and a set of abstract counterexamples S from $\mathcal{B}$PDR. States from Q can reach a state in *Bad*, states in AQ can abstractly reach a state in *Bad* via the abstract post-image, and states in S are reachable from *Bad* via the abstract pre-image. The soundness of PolyPDR follows directly from the soundness of individual algorithms: it either finds a concrete counterexample in Q, or finds a concrete or an abstract sufficient inductive invariant.

We suggest two schemes to apply the rules of PolyPDR to combine the effects of abstract and concrete reasoning: *pre-processing* and *in-processing*. The pre-processing scheme starts with enabling only the rules of $\mathcal{F}$PDR and $\mathcal{B}$PDR, and applying them until either the algorithm terminates, or the pre-conditions of **Reachable**$^{\mathcal{F}}$ or **Reachable**$^{\mathcal{B}}$ become true (i.e., an abstract counterexample is found). Then, the rules of $\mathcal{F}$PDR and $\mathcal{B}$PDR are disabled and the rules of $\mathcal{A}$PDR are enabled. This scheme is similar to first running an abstract interpreter to discover an inductive invariant, and then using $\mathcal{A}$PDR to strengthen it or find a counterexample. The two stages, abstract and concrete, communicate by the lemmas learned in the trace.

The in-processing scheme also starts with enabling only $\mathcal{F}$PDR and $\mathcal{B}$PDR rules. Then, whenever the pre-conditions for **Reachable**$^{\mathcal{F}}$ or **Reachable**$^{\mathcal{B}}$ become true, abstract counterexamples AQ and S are reset. Next, the control is given to $\mathcal{A}$PDR rules, until the **Unfold** rule is applied. At this point, the $\mathcal{A}$PDR rules are disabled, the rules of $\mathcal{F}$PDR and $\mathcal{B}$PDR are enabled, and the cycle repeats. This scheme mimics the abstraction-refinement loop of Vinta [1]. First, an abstract interpreter is used to compute an inductive, but not (necessarily) sufficient invariant. Then, the concrete reasoning is used to refine the invariant and rule out false alarms. Whenever the concrete strengthening is not inductive, the abstract reasoning is repeated starting from it. Again, the communication between the abstract and concrete reasoning is captured by the lemmas computed in the trace.

8 Evaluation

We have implemented variants of $\mathcal{F}$PDR and $\mathcal{B}$PDR algorithms in Z3. For the $\mathcal{F}$PDR variant, we have extended $\mathcal{A}$PDR with the **Decide**$^{\mathcal{F}}$ rule, but not the **Conflict**$^{\mathcal{F}}$ rule. This makes our $\mathcal{F}$PDR algorithm a generalization step for $\mathcal{A}$PDR. Whenever a candidate model is blocked by **Conflict**$^{\mathcal{A}}$, we check whether the learned lemma $P^{\uparrow}$ can be generalized to be convex. For the $\mathcal{B}$PDR variant, we have implemented a hybrid algorithm by adding the rule **Conflict**$^{\mathcal{AB}}$ to $\mathcal{A}$PDR. Furthermore, our $\mathcal{B}$PDR implementation is limited to the incomplete projection-based generalization strategy of [19], instead of the complete MBP-based strategy presented here. Hence, it sometimes diverges without making progress (i.e., gets into an infinite execution in which **Unfold** rule is never applied). Our implementation and benchmarks are available in the `cc` branch of `https://z3.codeplex.com/SourceControl/network/forks/arie/zag`.

To answer the main question posed in the Introduction, we have selected several benchmarks that are easy for polyhedral abstraction, but are hard for PDR-based approaches, from [2] and Z3 regression test suite. While the examples are small, they illustrate well the benefits of the new approach. The results are summarized in Fig. 2. In the figure, ϵ and ∞ mean "solved in under a second" and "did not terminate", respectively. In all cases, except for `ev`-series of examples, Z3 was configured with the default configuration options and restricted to Linear Arithmetic (an optional UTVPI solver was disabled using `fixedpoint.use_utvpi=false` command line option). For `ev`-series, Z3 is further restricted to projection-based generalization strategy of [19] using command line option `fixedpoint.use_model_generalizer=true`. The original Z3 algorithm diverges on all examples except for `d03` and `david`. $\mathcal{F}$PDR performs the best. However, generalizing using convex closures interferes with default algorithm for lemma generation in Z3. This makes `david` hard for $\mathcal{F}$PDR. $\mathcal{B}$PDR often diverges. For some cases (`ev`, `ev1`) this is due to the fact that *Bad* is not convex. For others (`xyz2`, `addadd`) this is a problem with our use of projection-based generalization. Finally, the `gcnr` example, originally from [16], and also used in [22,2], remains unsolved.

Name	Z3	$\mathcal{F}$PDR	$\mathcal{B}$PDR
`addadd`	∞	ϵ	∞
`d03`	ϵ	ϵ	ϵ
`david`	ϵ	∞	ϵ
`ev-down`	∞	ϵ	ϵ
`ev-up`	∞	ϵ	ϵ
`ev`	∞	ϵ	∞
`ev1`	∞	ϵ	∞
`updown`	∞	ϵ	ϵ
`xyz`	∞	ϵ	ϵ
`xyz2`	∞	ϵ	∞
`gcnr`	∞	∞	∞

Fig. 2. Results

We believe that this evaluation, albeit limited and preliminary, demonstrates the advantages of our framework. It shows the clear benefits of integrating polyhedral abstraction as a component within $\mathcal{A}$PDR.

9 Summary

This paper developed property directed model checking procedures using polyhedral abstraction. We showed how to combine syntactic convex closures with interpolation to incrementally compute abstractions, and we correspondences between Kleene, chaotic abstract interpretation and property directed reachability. We evaluated the new approaches on exemplary benchmarks. This work sheds furter light on the synergy of polyhedral abstraction and interpolation-based model checking.

References

1. Albarghouthi, A., Gurfinkel, A., Chechik, M.: Craig Interpretation. In: Miné, A., Schmidt, D. (eds.) SAS 2012. LNCS, vol. 7460, pp. 300–316. Springer, Heidelberg (2012)
2. Albarghouthi, A., McMillan, K.L.: Beautiful interpolants. In: Sharygina, Veith (eds.) [27], pp. 313–329
3. Bagnara, R., Hill, P.M., Zaffanella, E.: The parma polyhedra library: Toward a complete set of numerical abstractions for the analysis and verification of hardware and software systems. CoRR, abs/cs/0612085 (2006)
4. Bagnara, R., Hill, P.M., Zaffanella, E.: Widening operators for powerset domains. STTT 9(3-4), 413–414 (2007)
5. Benoy, F., King, A., Mesnard, F.: Computing Convex Hulls with a Linear Solver. TPLP 5(1-2), 259–271 (2005)
6. Biere, A., Bloem, R. (eds.): CAV 2014. LNCS, vol. 8559. Springer, Heidelberg (2014)
7. Birgmeier, J., Bradley, A.R., Weissenbacher, G.: Counterexample to induction-guided abstraction-refinement (CTIGAR). In: Biere, Bloem (eds.) [6], pp. 831–848
8. Bradley, A.R.: SAT-Based Model Checking without Unrolling. In: Jhala, R., Schmidt, D. (eds.) VMCAI 2011. LNCS, vol. 6538, pp. 70–87. Springer, Heidelberg (2011)
9. Cimatti, A., Griggio, A.: Software Model Checking via IC3. In: Madhusudan, P., Seshia, S.A. (eds.) CAV 2012. LNCS, vol. 7358, pp. 277–293. Springer, Heidelberg (2012)
10. Cimatti, A., Griggio, A., Mover, S., Tonetta, S.: IC3 Modulo Theories via Implicit Predicate Abstraction. In: Ábrahám, E., Havelund, K. (eds.) TACAS 2014. LNCS, vol. 8413, pp. 46–61. Springer, Heidelberg (2014)
11. Cimatti, A., Griggio, A., Sebastiani, R.: Efficient Generation of Craig Interpolants in Satisfiability Modulo Theories. ACM Trans. Comput. Log. 12(1), 7 (2010)
12. Cousot, P., Cousot, R.: Abstract Interpretation Frameworks. J. Log. Comput. 2(4), 511–547 (1992)
13. Cousot, P., Halbwachs, N.: Automatic discovery of linear restraints among variables of a program. In: Aho, A.V., Zilles, S.N., Szymanski, T.G. (eds.) POPL, pp. 84–96. ACM Press (1978)
14. de Moura, L., Jovanović, D.: A Model-Constructing Satisfiability Calculus. In: Giacobazzi, R., Berdine, J., Mastroeni, I. (eds.) VMCAI 2013. LNCS, vol. 7737, pp. 1–12. Springer, Heidelberg (2013)
15. Grebenshchikov, S., Lopes, N.P., Popeea, C., Rybalchenko, A.: Synthesizing software verifiers from proof rules. In: PLDI (2012)

16. Gulavani, B.S., Chakraborty, S., Nori, A.V., Rajamani, S.K.: Refining abstract interpretations. Inf. Process. Lett. 110(16), 666–671 (2010)
17. Gurfinkel, A., Chaki, S.: BOXES: A Symbolic Abstract Domain of Boxes. In: Cousot, R., Martel, M. (eds.) SAS 2010. LNCS, vol. 6337, pp. 287–303. Springer, Heidelberg (2010)
18. Halbwachs, N.: Détermination automatique de relations linéaires vérifiées par les variables d'un programme. PhD thesis, Grenoble (1979)
19. Hoder, K., Bjørner, N.: Generalized Property Directed Reachability. In: Cimatti, A., Sebastiani, R. (eds.) SAT 2012. LNCS, vol. 7317, pp. 157–171. Springer, Heidelberg (2012)
20. Kindermann, R., Junttila, T., Niemelä, I.: SMT-Based Induction Methods for Timed Systems. In: Jurdziński, M., Ničković, D. (eds.) FORMATS 2012. LNCS, vol. 7595, pp. 171–187. Springer, Heidelberg (2012)
21. Komuravelli, A., Gurfinkel, A., Chaki, S.: SMT-Based Model Checking for Recursive Programs. In: Biere, Bloem (eds.) [6], pp. 17–34
22. Komuravelli, A., Gurfinkel, A., Chaki, S., Clarke, E.M.: Automatic Abstraction in SMT-Based Unbounded Software Model Checking. In: Sharygina, Veith (eds.) [27], pp. 846–862
23. Korovin, K., Voronkov, A.: Solving Systems of Linear Inequalities by Bound Propagation. In: Bjørner, N., Sofronie-Stokkermans, V. (eds.) CADE 2011. LNCS(LNAI), vol. 6803, pp. 369–383. Springer, Heidelberg (2011)
24. McMillan, K.L.: Lazy annotation revisited. In: Biere, A., Bloem, R. (eds.) CAV 2014. LNCS, vol. 8559, pp. 243–259. Springer, Heidelberg (2014)
25. Rival, X., Mauborgne, L.: The trace partitioning abstract domain. ACM Trans. Program. Lang. Syst. 29(5) (2007)
26. Rümmer, P., Hojjat, H., Kuncak, V.: Disjunctive interpolants for horn-clause verification. In: Sharygina, N., Veith, H. (eds.) CAV 2013. LNCS, vol. 8044, pp. 347–363. Springer, Heidelberg (2013)
27. Sharygina, N., Veith, H. (eds.): CAV 2013. LNCS, vol. 8044. Springer, Heidelberg (2013)

Abstraction of Arrays Based on Non Contiguous Partitions*

Jiangchao Liu and Xavier Rival

INRIA, ENS, CNRS, Paris, France
{jliu,rival}@di.ens.fr

Abstract. Array partitioning analyses split arrays into contiguous partitions to infer properties of cell sets. Such analyses cannot group together non contiguous cells, even when they have similar properties. In this paper, we propose an abstract domain which utilizes semantic properties to split array cells into groups. Cells with similar properties will be packed into groups and abstracted together. Additionally, groups are not necessarily contiguous. This abstract domain allows to infer complex array invariants in a fully automatic way. Experiments on examples from the Minix 1.1 memory management demonstrate its effectiveness.

1 Introduction

Arrays are ubiquitous, yet their mis-use often causes software defects. Therefore, a large number of works address the automatic verification of array manipulating programs. In particular, partitioning abstractions [5,11,13] split arrays in sets of contiguous groups of cells, in order to, hopefully, infer they enjoy similar properties. A traditional example is that of an initialization loop, with the usual invariant that splits the array in an initialized zone and an uninitialized region.

However, when cells that have similar properties are not contiguous, these approaches cannot infer adequate array partitions. This happens for unsorted arrays of structures, when there is no relation between indexes and cell fields. Then, there are usually relations among cell fields. This phenomenon can be observed in low-level software, such as operating system services and critical embedded systems drivers, which rely on static array zones instead of dynamically allocated blocks [20]. When cells with similar properties are not contiguous, traditional partition based techniques are unlikely to infer relevant partitions / precise array invariants. Figure 1 illustrates the Minix 1.1 Memory Management Process Table (MMPT) main structure. The array of structures `mproc` defined in Figure 1(a) stores the process descriptors. Each descriptor comprises a field `mparent` that stores the index of the parent process in `mproc`, and a field `mpflag` that stores the process status. Figure 1(c) depicts the concrete values stored in `mproc` to describe the process topology shown in Figure 1(b) (we show only 8 processes). An element

* The research leading to these results has received funding from the European Research Council under the FP7 grant agreement 278673, Project MemCAD, and from the ARTEMIS Joint Undertaking no 269335 (see Article II.9 of the JU Grant Agreement).

D. D'Souza et al. (Eds.): VMCAI 2015, LNCS 8931, pp. 282–299, 2015.

```
1 struct mproc {
2         unsigned mpflag;
3         int mparent;
4. } mproc[24];
```

(a) Definition of array `mproc`

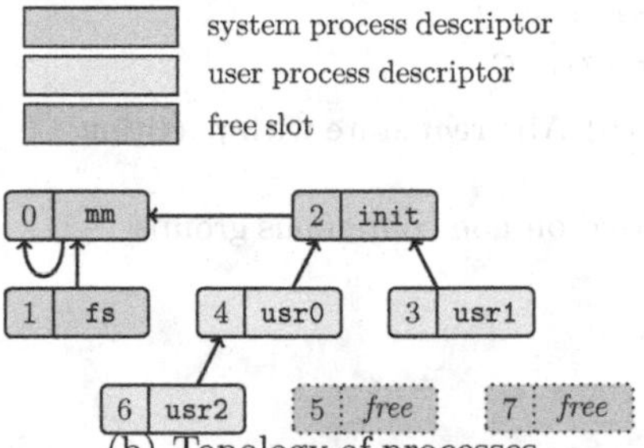

(b) Topology of processes

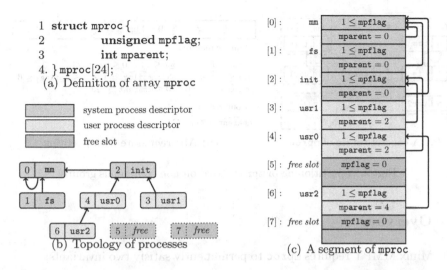

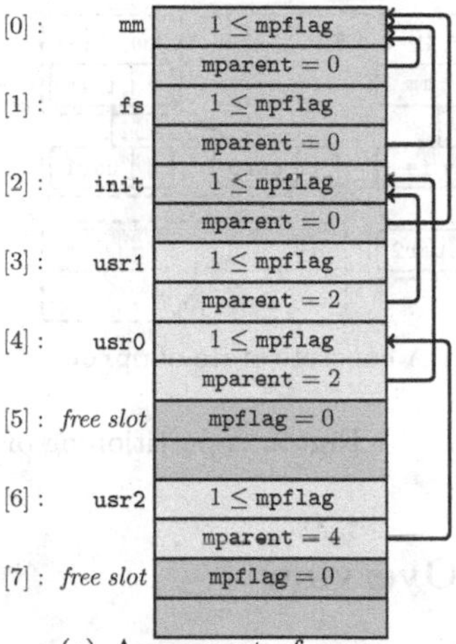

(c) A segment of `mproc`

Fig. 1. Minix 1.1 Memory Management Process Table (MMPT) structure

of `mproc` is a process descriptor when its field `mpflag` is strictly positive and a free slot if it is null. Minix 1.1 uses the three initial elements of `mproc` to store the descriptor of the memory management service, the file system service and the init process. Descriptors of other processes appear in a random order. In the example of Figure 1, `init` has two children whose descriptors are in `mproc`[3] and `mproc`[4]; similarly, the process corresponding to `mproc`[4] has a single child the descriptor of which is in `mproc`[6]. Moreover, Minix assumes a parent-child relation between `mm` and `fs`, as `mm` has index 0 and the parent field of `fs` stores 0. To abstract the process table state, valid process descriptors and free slots should be partitioned into *different groups*.

Traditional, contiguous partitioning cannot achieve this for two reasons: (1) the order of process descriptors in `mproc` cannot be predicted, hence is random in practice, and (2) there is no simple description of the boundaries between these regions (or even their sizes) in the program state. The symbolic abstract domain by Dillig, Dillig and Aiken [8] also fails here as it cannot attach arbitrary abstract properties to summarized cells.

In this paper, we set up an abstract domain to partition the array into non contiguous groups for process descriptors and free slot so as to infer this partitioning and precise invariants (Section 2) automatically. Our contributions are:

1. An abstract domain that partitions array elements according to semantic properties, and can represent non contiguous partitions (Section 3).
2. Static analysis algorithms for the computation of abstract post-conditions (Sections 4 and Section 5), widening and inclusion check (Section 6).
3. The implementation and the evaluation of the analysis on the inference of tricky invariants in an excerpt of the Minix 1.1 Memory Management Process Table (MMPT) and other challenging array examples (Section 7).

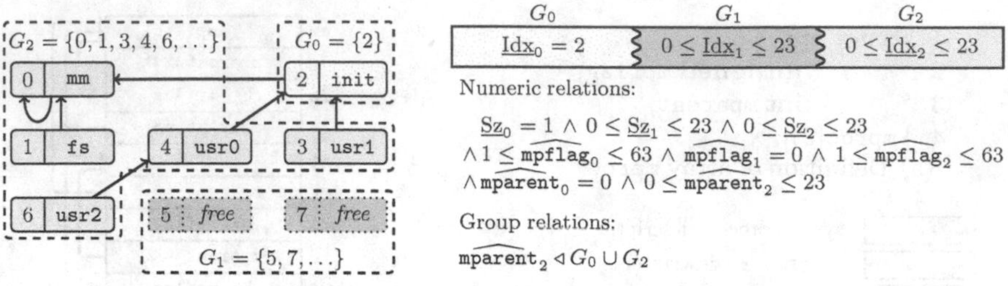

(a) A concrete state of `mproc` (b) Abstract state with partition

Fig. 2. A partitioning of `mproc` based on non contiguous groups

2 Overview

The Minix MMPT requires `mproc` to permanently satisfy two invariants:

1. Each valid process descriptor has a `mparent` field, that should store a value in $[0, 23]$, hence represents a valid index in `mproc`: this entails the absence of out-of-bound accesses in process table management functions.
2. The `mparent` field of any valid process descriptor should be the index of a valid process descriptor: as a process can only complete its exit phase when its parent calls wait, failure to maintain a parent for each process could cause a terminating process to become dangling and never be eliminated.

To verify these invariants, we propose to check that all system calls preserve them. We design an automatic analysis to verify that, if they are called in a state that satisfies these invariants, they return in a state that also satisfies them. A concrete state is displayed in Figure 2(a), and its abstraction is shown in Figure 2(b). Group 0 contains only the process descriptor of `init`. Group 1 collects all free slots. Group 2 consists of all the valid process descriptors except that of `init`. The reason why we split `init` out into a separate group is that it is often treated in a special manner by OS routines. We let G_i denote the set of indexes of all the elements in group i.

The abstract state shown in Figure 2(b) ties each group to properties of its elements. These will be formally defined in Section 3. By the Minix specification, the elements of group 2 satisfy the following correctness conditions $\mathcal{C}$:

- their indexes are in $[0, 23]$, which we note $0 \leq \underline{\text{Idx}}_2 \leq 23$ in Figure 2(b);
- their flags are in $[1, 63]$ (valid process descriptors have a strictly positive flag), which we note $1 \leq \widehat{\texttt{mpflag}_2} \leq 63$;
- their parents are valid indexes, which we note $0 \leq \widehat{\texttt{mparent}_2} \leq 23$;
- their parents are indexes of valid process descriptors, hence are also in group 0 or group 2, which we note $\widehat{\texttt{mparent}_2} \triangleleft G_0 \cup G_2$;
- the size of group 2 is between 0 and 23, which we note $0 \leq \underline{\text{Sz}}_2 \leq 23$.

Our abstraction relies on *disjoint* groups as other array partitioning abstractions [11,13]. However, our abstraction *does not* assume each group consists of a contiguous set of cells. The *non-contiguousness* of groups is represented by

```
    void cleanup(int child){
      ...
⓪     int parent = mproc[child].mparent;
①     if(parent == 2){
②       mproc[parent].mpflag = 1;
③       mproc[child].mpflag = 0;
④       for(i = 0; i < 24; i++){
⑤         if(mproc[i].mpflag > 0)
            if(i != parent)
              if(mproc[i].mparent == child)
                mproc[i].mparent = 2;
        }
⑥     }else{...}...}
```

(a) A simplified excerpt of `cleanup`

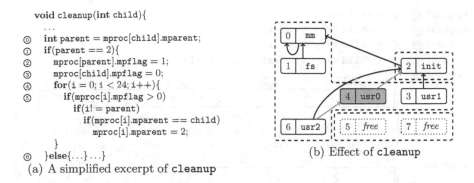

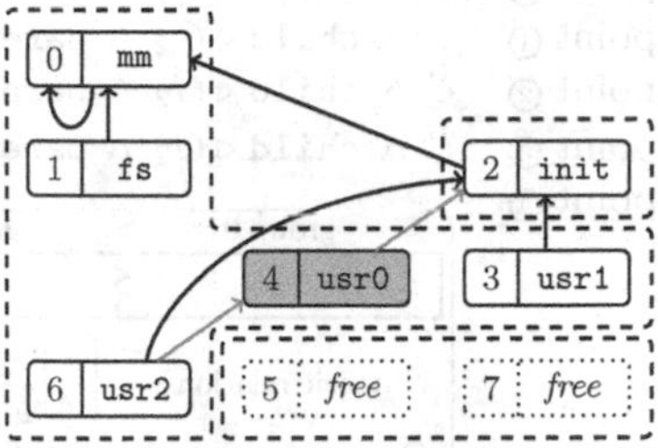

(b) Effect of `cleanup`

Fig. 3. Minix 1.1 process table management, system function `cleanup`

winding separation lines in Figure 2(b). To characterize groups, our abstraction relies not only on constraints on indexes, but also on semantic properties of the cell contents: while groups 1 and 2 correspond to a similar range, the `mpflag` values of their elements are different (0 in group 1 and any value in $[1, 63]$ in group 2). Therefore our abstraction can express both contiguous and non contiguous partitions. In this example, we believe the abstract state of Figure 2(b) is close to the programmer's intent, where the array is a collection of unsorted elements.

We now consider the verification of Minix MMPT management procedures. We focus on `cleanup`, which turns elements of `mproc` that describe hanging processes into free slots. Figure 3(a) displays an excerpt of a simplified, recursion free version of `cleanup`, which is chosen to highlight the analysis difficulties. The call `cleanup`(4) in the state of Figure 2(a) will remove process `usr0` and falls in that case; the result is shown in Figure 3(b): process `usr2` becomes a child of `init`, while the record formerly associated to `usr0` turns into a free slot.

Function `cleanup` should be called in a correct Minix process table state and be applied to a child process in group 2, which we note `child`$\triangleleft G_2$. Figure 4 overviews the steps of the automatic static analysis of the excerpt of `cleanup`. The analysis proceeds by computing abstract post-conditions and loop invariants [3]. In this section, we focus on (1) cell materialization, (2) termination of the loop analysis and (3) removal of unnecessary groups.

From the precondition, fields `mparent` of all elements in group 2 are indexes in groups G_0 or G_2 (abstract state at point ⓪). The test entails `mparent` is 2 at point ② (corresponding to process `init`). Combining this, with the fact that group 0 has exactly one element ($\underline{\mathrm{Sz}}_0 = 1$) at index 2 ($\underline{\mathrm{Idx}}_0 = 2$), the analysis infers that `parent` can only be in group 0 (point ②). Therefore, the update at point ② affects a group with a single element, hence, is a *strong update*, and produces predicate at point ③. However, at that point, the next update is not strong, since `mproc`[`child`] may be any element of group 2, which may have more than one element (it has at least one element since `child` $\triangleleft G_2$, thus $\underline{\mathrm{Sz}}_2 \geq 1$). Therefore, our domain *materializes* the array element being assigned by splitting group 2 into two groups, labeled 2 and 3. Both groups inherit predicates from former group 2.

At point ⓪ $\mathcal{C} \wedge \mathtt{child} \triangleleft G_2$
At point ① $\mathcal{C} \wedge \mathtt{child} \triangleleft G_2 \wedge \mathtt{parent} \triangleleft G_2 \cup G_0$
At point ② $\mathcal{C} \wedge \mathtt{child} \triangleleft G_2 \wedge \mathtt{parent} \triangleleft G_0$
At point ③ $\mathcal{C} \wedge \mathtt{child} \triangleleft G_2 \wedge \mathtt{parent} \triangleleft G_0 \wedge \widehat{\mathtt{mpflag}_0} = 1$
At point ④
At point ⑤
At point ⑥

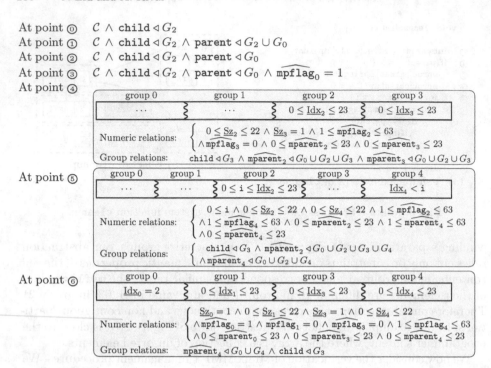

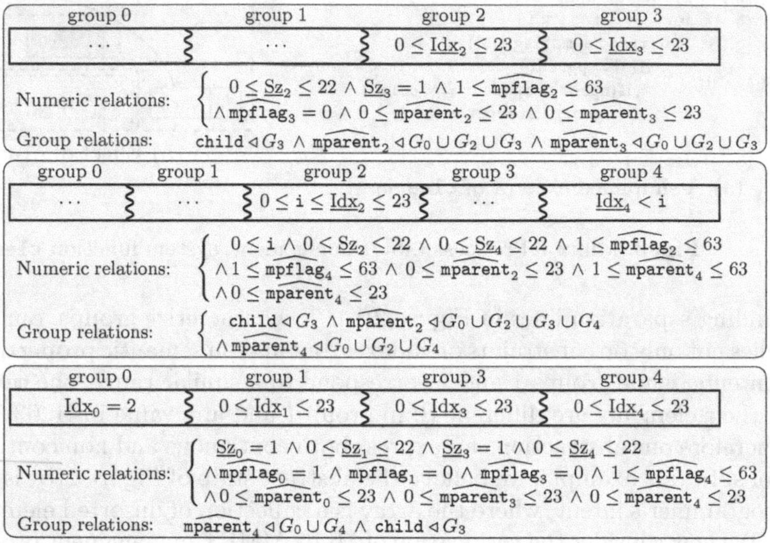

Fig. 4. Overview of the analysis of `cleanup`

Additionally, group 3 has a single element ($\underline{\mathrm{Sz}_3} = 1$), thus the analysis performs a strong update and generates the abstract state of ④.

The analysis of all the statements in the program follows similar principles. We only discuss the termination of the analysis here, as our abstract domain has infinite chains (the number of groups is not bounded), hence the analysis of loops requires a terminating binary widening operator [3]. Widening associates groups of its inputs with groups of its result (ensuring the number of groups can only decrease to guarantee termination), and over-approximates group properties. After two widening iterations, our analysis produces abstract post-fixpoint ⑤, where group 1 describes free slots, group 0 describes `init`, group 3 consists of `child` (just cleaned up) and groups 2 (resp., 4) represent valid process descriptors with indexes greater (resp., lower) than `i`. Our analysis can also decrease the number of groups, when some become redundant, e.g., when the analysis proves a group empty. For instance, the loop fixpoint ⑤ shows that indexes of elements in group 2 are greater than `i`. Thus, after the loop exit, any element of group 2 should have an index greater than 24, which implies this group is empty. Hence, this group is removed, and the analysis produces post-condition ⑥, which entails correctness condition $\mathcal{C}$ (note that group 3, corresponding to `child` now describes a free slot).

3 Abstract Domain and Abstraction Relation

In this section, we formalize abstract elements and their concretization. We describe the abstraction of the contents of arrays, using numeric constraints, in Section 3.1. Then, we extend it with relations between groups in Section 3.2.

3.1 The Non-contiguous Array Partition Domain

Concrete States. Our domain abstracts arrays of complex data structures. To highlight its core principle and simplify the formalization, we make two assumptions on the programs to analyze. First, there is no array access through pointer dereference (handling them would only require a product with a pointer domain), thus all array index expressions are of the form a[ex]. Secondly, all variables are either base type (e.g., scalar) variables (denoted by $\mathbb{X}$) or arrays of structures (denoted by $\mathbb{A}$). Structures are considered arrays of length 1, and arrays of scalars are considered arrays of structures made of a single field. A concrete state σ is a partial function mapping basic cells (base variables and fields of array elements) into values (which are denoted by $\mathbb{V}$). We let $\mathbb{N}$ denote non-negative integers and $\mathbb{F}$ denote the set of fields. Thus, the set $\mathbb{S}$ of concrete states is defined by $\mathbb{S} = (\mathbb{A} \times \mathbb{N} \times \mathbb{F} \cup \mathbb{X}) \rightarrow \mathbb{V}$. More specifically, the set of all fields of elements of array a are denoted by $\mathbb{F}_{\mathsf{a}}$, and the set of valid indexes in a is denoted by $\mathbb{N}_{\mathsf{a}}$.

Non-contiguous array partition. Our analysis partitions each array into one or several *groups* of cells. A group is represented by an abstraction G_i of the set of indexes of its elements, where subscript i identifies the group. We let $\mathbb{G}$ denote the set of group names $\{G_i \mid i \geq 0\}$. An *array partition* is a function $p : \mathbb{A} \rightarrow \mathcal{P}(\mathbb{G})$ which maps each array variable to a set of groups. We always enforce the constraint that groups of distinct arrays should have distinct names, to avoid confusion ($\forall a_1, a_2 \in \mathbb{A}, a_1 \neq a_2 \Rightarrow p(a_1) \cap p(a_2) = \emptyset$). To express properties of group contents, sizes, and indexes, we adjoin numeric abstract values to partition p. This numeric information is split into a conjunction made of two parts.

First, a global component n^{g} constrains base type variables, group sizes and group fields. Group fields are marked as *summary dimensions* [10] in n^{g}, that is as numeric abstract domain dimensions that account for one or more concrete cell(s), whereas base type variables and group sizes are non-summary dimension, i.e., each of them represents exactly one concrete cell.

Second, for each group G_i, the index $\underline{\mathrm{Idx}}_i$ is constrained by a numeric abstract value n^i. This second component is needed because our abstract domain allows empty groups, and when group G_i is empty, $\underline{\mathrm{Idx}}_i$ has no value, which is expressed by $n^i = \bot$. Intuitively, in the concrete level, $\underline{\mathrm{Idx}}_i$ denotes a possibly empty set of values (an empty group example will be provided in Section 7.2).

To sum up, an abstract element is a pair $(p, \overrightarrow{n})$ where $\overrightarrow{n}$ is a tuple $(n^{\mathsf{g}}, n^0, \ldots, n^{k-1})$, and p defines k array partitions. Our abstract domain is parameterized by the choice of a numeric abstract domain $\mathbb{N}^{\sharp}$, so as to tune the analysis precision and cost. In this paper, we use the octagon abstract domain [18].

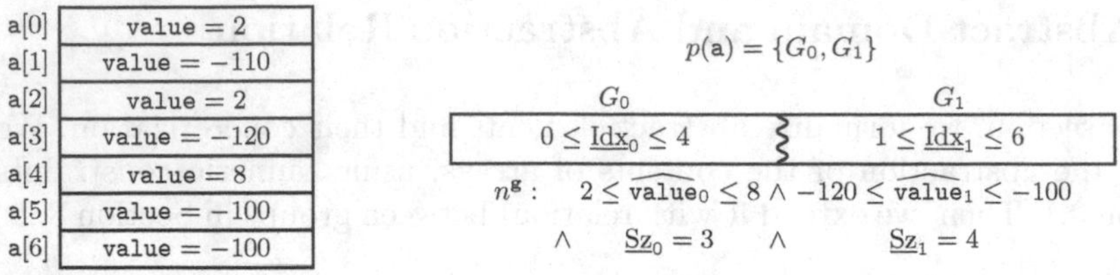

(a) Concrete array $\mathbb{X}$ (b) Abstract state $a^\sharp$

Fig. 5. An abstraction in our domain

Example 1. Figure 5(a) displays a concrete state, with an array of integers a of length 7 (each cell is viewed as a structure with a single field value). Figure 5(b) shows an abstraction $a^\sharp = (p, \overrightarrow{n})$ into two groups G_0, G_1, where G_0 (resp., G_1) contains all cells storing a positive (resp., negative) values. This abstraction reveals the array stores no value in $[-99, 1]$.

Concretization. A *concrete numeric mapping* is a function ν, mapping each base type variable to one value, each structure field to a non empty set of values and each index to a possibly empty set of values. We write $\gamma_{\mathbb{N}^\sharp}$ for the concretization of numeric elements, which maps a set of numeric constraints $\overrightarrow{n}$ into a set of functions ν as defined above. The concretization $\gamma_{\mathbb{N}^\sharp}(n^i)$ of constraints over group G_i is such that, when $n^i = \perp$ and $\nu \in \gamma_{\mathbb{N}^\sharp}(n^i)$, then $\nu(\underline{\mathrm{Idx}}_i) = \emptyset$. Then, $\gamma_{\mathbb{N}^\sharp}(n^{\mathtt{g}}, n^0, \ldots, n^{k-1}) = \gamma_{\mathbb{N}^\sharp}(n^{\mathtt{g}}) \cap \gamma_{\mathbb{N}^\sharp}(n^0) \ldots \gamma_{\mathbb{N}^\sharp}(n^{k-1})$. A *valuation* is a function $\psi \in \Psi = \mathbb{G} \rightarrow \mathcal{P}(\mathbb{Z})$, and interprets each group by the set of indexes it represents in a given concrete state.

Additionally, we use the following four predicates to break up the definition of concretization:

$$\begin{array}{rcl}
\mathrm{P_v}(\psi) & \stackrel{\text{def.}}{\iff} & \forall \mathtt{a} \in \mathbb{A}, \bigcup_{G_i \in p(\mathtt{a})} \psi(G_i) = \mathbb{N}_{\mathtt{a}} \\
& & \quad \wedge (\forall G_i, G_j \in p(\mathtt{a}), i \neq j \Rightarrow \psi(G_i) \cap \psi(G_j) = \emptyset) \\
\mathrm{P_b}(\sigma, \nu) & \stackrel{\text{def.}}{\iff} & \forall \mathtt{v} \in \mathbb{X}, \nu(\mathtt{v}) = \sigma(\mathtt{v}) \\
\mathrm{P_i}(\nu, \psi) & \stackrel{\text{def.}}{\iff} & \forall \mathtt{a} \in \mathbb{A}, G_i \in p(\mathtt{a}), \psi(G_i) = \nu(\underline{\mathrm{Idx}}_i) \wedge |\psi(G_i)| = \nu(\underline{\mathrm{Sz}}_i) \\
\mathrm{P_c}(\sigma, \psi, \nu) & \stackrel{\text{def.}}{\iff} & \forall \mathtt{a} \in \mathbb{A}, \mathtt{f} \in \mathbb{F}_{\mathtt{a}}, G_i \in p(\mathtt{a}), j \in \psi(G_i), \sigma(\mathtt{a}, j, \mathtt{f}) \in \nu(\widehat{\mathtt{f}}_i)
\end{array}$$

Predicate $\mathrm{P_v}(\psi)$ states that each array element belongs to *exactly one group* (equivalently, groups form a partition of the array indexes). Predicate $\mathrm{P_b}(\sigma, \nu)$ expresses that ν and σ consistently abstract base type variables. Predicate $\mathrm{P_i}(\nu, \psi)$ expresses that ν and ψ consistently abstract group indexes. Last, predicate $\mathrm{P_c}(\sigma, \psi, \nu)$ states σ and ν define compatible abstractions of groups contents.

Definition 1 (Concretization). *Concretization $\gamma_{\mathbb{P}}$ is defined by:*

$$\gamma_{\mathbb{P}}(p, \overrightarrow{n}) \stackrel{def.}{::=} \{(\sigma, \psi, \nu) \mid \nu \in \gamma_{\mathbb{N}^\sharp}(\overrightarrow{n}) \wedge \mathrm{P_v}(\psi) \wedge \mathrm{P_b}(\sigma, \nu) \wedge \mathrm{P_i}(\nu, \psi) \wedge \mathrm{P_c}(\sigma, \psi, \nu)\}$$

3.2 Relation Predicates

The abstraction we have defined so far can describe non-contiguous groups of cells, yet lacks important predicates, that are necessary for the analysis. Let us consider assignment `parent` = `mproc[child].mparent` in `cleanup` (Figure 3(a)). Numeric constraints localize `child` in $[0, 23]$, but this information does not determine precisely which group does cell `mproc[child]` belong to. In particular, the analysis will ignore from that point whether `parent` is the index of a valid process descriptor or not. To avoid this imprecision, we extend abstract states with *relation predicates*, that express properties such as the membership of the value of a variable in a group. They are defined by the grammar below:

Definition 2 (Relation predicates).

$$\begin{array}{rlll} r ::= & r \wedge r & & \textit{a conjunction of predicates} \\ | & \mathbf{true} & & \textit{empty} \\ | & \mathtt{v} \lhd G^{\mathtt{a}} & \textit{where } \mathtt{v} \in \mathbb{X} & \textit{var-index predicate} \\ | & \widehat{\mathtt{f}}_i \lhd G^{\mathtt{a}} & \textit{where } \mathtt{f} \in \mathbb{F}_{\mathtt{a}}, G_i \in p(\mathtt{a}) & \textit{content-index predicate} \\ G^{\mathtt{a}} ::= & G^{\mathtt{a}} \cup G_i & \textit{where } G_i \in p(\mathtt{a}) & \textit{a disjunction of groups in } \mathtt{a} \\ | & G_i & \textit{where } G_i \in p(\mathtt{a}) & \end{array}$$

A relation predicate r is a conjunction of atomic predicates. Predicate $\mathtt{v} \lhd G^{\mathtt{a}}$ means the value of variable `v` is an index in G^a, where G^a is a disjunction of a set of groups of array `a`. Similarly, predicate $\widehat{\mathtt{f}}_i \lhd G^a$ means that all fields `f` of cells in group i are indexes of elements of $G^{\mathtt{a}}$. As an example, if $G^{\mathtt{a}} = G_1 \cup G_3$, then $\mathtt{v} \lhd G^{\mathtt{a}}$ expresses that the value of `v` is either the index of a cell in G_1 or the index of a cell in G_3.

Example 2. We consider function `cleanup` of Figure 3(a). The pre-condition for the analysis of Figure 4 is based on correctness property $\mathcal{C}$, hence partitions `mproc` in three groups, thus $p(\mathtt{mproc}) = \{G_0, G_1, G_2\}$. Additionally, `cleanup` should be called on a valid process descriptor different from that of `init`, hence `child` should be in group G_2, which corresponds to predicate $\mathtt{child} \lhd G_2$. Then `parent` is initialized as the parent of `child`. Since $\widehat{\mathtt{mparent}}_2 \lhd G_0 \cup G_2$, `parent` is a valid process descriptor index, and the analysis derives $\mathtt{parent} \lhd G_0 \cup G_2$. Hence, at point ①, the analysis will derive relations $r = \mathtt{child} \lhd G_2 \wedge \mathtt{parent} \lhd G_0 \cup G_2 \wedge \ldots$.

Similarly, in the **else** branch of condition **if**(`parent` == 2), the analysis derives that $\mathtt{parent} \lhd G_2$.

Concretization. We now extend the concretization to account for relations. First, we let ψ be defined on disjunction of groups, and let $\psi(G_0 \cup \ldots \cup G_i) = \psi(G_0) \cup \ldots \cup \psi(G_i)$. We write $\mathbb{D}^\sharp$ for the set of triples $(p, \overrightarrow{n}, r)$.

Definition 3 (Abstract states and their concretization). *An* abstract state *$a^\sharp$ is a triple $(p, \overrightarrow{n}, r) \in \mathbb{D}^\sharp$. The* concretization $\gamma_{\mathbb{D}^\sharp}$ *is defined by:*

$$\begin{array}{rl} \gamma_{\mathbb{D}^\sharp}(p, \overrightarrow{n}, r) ::= & \{\sigma \mid \exists \psi, \nu,\ (\sigma, \psi, \nu) \in \gamma_{\mathrm{aux}}(p, \overrightarrow{n}, r)\} \\ \gamma_{\mathrm{aux}}(p, \overrightarrow{n}, \mathbf{true}) ::= & \gamma_{\mathbb{P}}(p, \overrightarrow{n}) \\ \gamma_{\mathrm{aux}}(p, \overrightarrow{n}, \mathtt{v} \lhd G^{\mathtt{a}}) ::= & \{(\sigma, \psi, \nu) \in \gamma_{\mathbb{P}}(p, \overrightarrow{n}) \mid \sigma(\mathtt{v}) \in \psi(G^{\mathtt{a}})\} \\ \gamma_{\mathrm{aux}}(p, \overrightarrow{n}, \mathtt{f}_i \lhd G^{\mathtt{a}}) ::= & \{(\sigma, \psi, \nu) \in \gamma_{\mathbb{P}}(p, \overrightarrow{n}) \mid \forall k \in \psi(G_i),\ \sigma(\mathtt{a}, k, \mathtt{f}) \in \psi(G^{\mathtt{a}})\} \\ \gamma_{\mathrm{aux}}(p, \overrightarrow{n}, r_0 \wedge r_1) ::= & \gamma_{\mathrm{aux}}(p, \overrightarrow{n}, r_0) \cap \gamma_{\mathrm{aux}}(p, \overrightarrow{n}, r_1) \end{array}$$

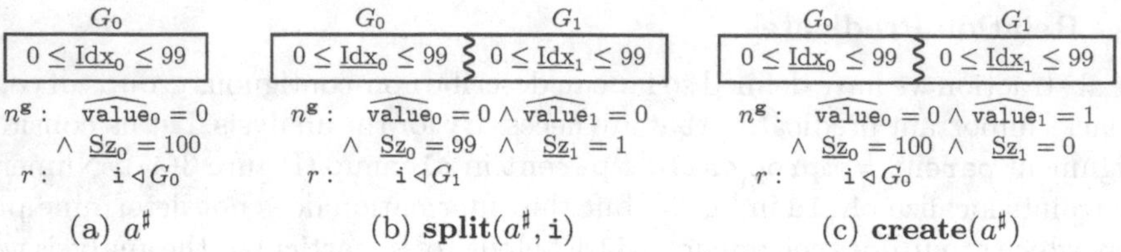

Fig. 6. Partition splitting and creation in array a from abstract state $a^\sharp$

4 Basic Operators on Partitions

In this section, we define basic operations on partitions (such as creation and merge), that abstract transfer functions and operators rely on.

Splitting and creation. Unless specified otherwise, our analysis initially partitions each array into a single group, with no contents constraint. Additional groups get introduced during the analysis, by two basic operations:

1. Operator **split** replaces a group with two groups, that inherit the properties of the group they replace (also, membership in the old group turns into membership in the join of the new groups). It is typically applied to materialize a cell of a given index (in the group bounds) and enable a strong update.
2. Operator **create** introduces an empty group and is used to generalize abstract states in join and widening (note any field property is satisfied by the empty group; the analysis selects properties depending on the context).

Both operators preserve concretization.

Example 3. Figure 6(a) defines an abstract state $(p, \overrightarrow{n}, r)$ with a single array, fully initialized to 0, and represented by a single group. Applying operator **split** to that abstract state and to index $\mathtt{i}$ produces the abstract state of Figure 6(b), where G_1 is a group with exactly one element, with the same constraints $\underline{\mathrm{Idx}}$ and $\widehat{\mathtt{value}}$ as in the previous state. Similarly, Figure 6(c) shows a possible result for **create**.

Merging groups. Fine partitions with many groups can provide great precision but may incur increased analysis cost. Therefore, the analysis can also force the fusion of several groups into one by calling operation **merge** on a set of groups. This is performed either as part of join and widening or when transfer functions detect some groups get assigned similar values.

Example 4. Figure 7(a) defines an abstract state $a^\sharp$ which describes an array with two groups. Applying **merge** to $a^\sharp$ and set $\{0, 1\}$ produces the state shown in Figure 7(b), with a single group and coarser predicates, obtained by joining the constraints over the contents of the initial groups.

Reduction. Our abstract domain can be viewed as a product abstraction and can benefit from *reduction* [4]. In $a^\sharp = (p, \overrightarrow{n}, r)$, components $\overrightarrow{n}$ and r may help refining each other. For instance, in Figure 4, the analysis infers at point ① that

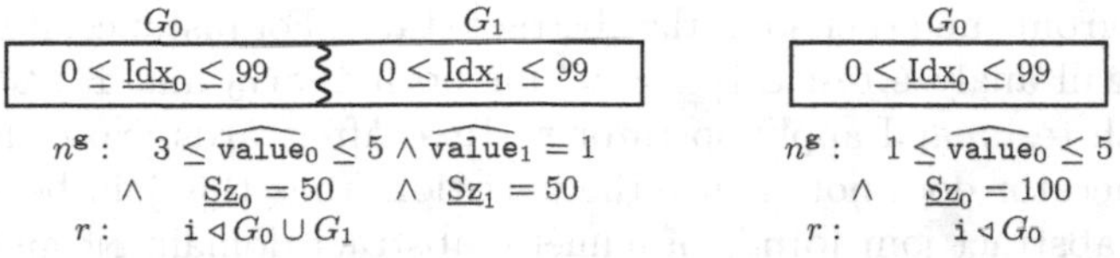

G_0
G_1
$0 \leq \underline{\mathrm{Idx}}_0 \leq 99$
$0 \leq \underline{\mathrm{Idx}}_1 \leq 99$
$n^{\mathrm{g}}: \; 3 \leq \widehat{\mathtt{value}}_0 \leq 5 \wedge \widehat{\mathtt{value}}_1 = 1$
$\wedge \; \underline{\mathrm{Sz}}_0 = 50 \; \wedge \underline{\mathrm{Sz}}_1 = 50$
$r: \; \mathtt{i} \triangleleft G_0 \cup G_1$
G_0
$0 \leq \underline{\mathrm{Idx}}_0 \leq 99$
$n^{\mathrm{g}}: \; 1 \leq \widehat{\mathtt{value}}_0 \leq 5$
$\wedge \; \underline{\mathrm{Sz}}_0 = 100$
$r: \; \mathtt{i} \triangleleft G_0$

(a) $a^\sharp$ (b) **merge**$(a^\sharp, \{0, 1\})$

Fig. 7. Merging in abstract state $a^\sharp$

$\mathtt{parent} \triangleleft G_0 \cup G_2$ and $\underline{\mathrm{Idx}}_0 = 2$. Combining this with the numerical information derived from test $\mathtt{parent} == 2$, the analysis should derive that $\mathtt{parent} \triangleleft G_0$ (i.e., parent is the index of init). Conversely, r may refine the information on $\overrightarrow{n}$: if $\mathtt{child} \triangleleft G_2$, then group G_2 has at least one element, thus $\underline{\mathrm{Sz}}_2 \geq 1$.

Such steps are performed by a *partial reduction* operator **reduce**, which strengthens the numeric and relation predicates, without changing the global concretization [4] (the optimal reduction would be overly costly to compute). This reduction is done lazily: for instance, the analysis will attempt to generate relations between i and $\underline{\mathrm{Idx}}_i$ only when i is used as an index to access the array G_i corresponds to.

Basic operations **split**, **create**, **merge** and **reduce** are sound:

Theorem 1 (Soundness). *If $a^\sharp$ is an abstract state,* t *an array, G_i a group, then $\gamma_{\mathbb{D}^\sharp}(a^\sharp) \subseteq \gamma_{\mathbb{D}^\sharp}(\mathbf{split}(a^\sharp, \mathtt{t}, G_i))$ and $\gamma_{\mathbb{D}^\sharp}(\mathbf{create}(a^\sharp, \mathtt{t})) = \gamma_{\mathbb{D}^\sharp}(a^\sharp)$. Moreover, if S is a set of groups, $\gamma_{\mathbb{D}^\sharp}(a^\sharp) \subseteq \gamma_{\mathbb{D}^\sharp}(\mathbf{merge}(a^\sharp, \mathtt{t}, S))$. Similarly,* **reduce** *does not change concretization.*

5 Transfer Functions

Our analysis of C programs proceeds by forward abstract interpretation [3]. In this section, we study the abstract transfer functions for tests and assignments.

5.1 Analysis of Conditions

In the concrete level, if ex is an expression, test ex? filters out states that do not let ex evaluate into TRUE. Its concrete semantics can thus be defined as a function over sets of states, by $\forall \mathcal{S} \subseteq \mathbb{S}, \; [\![\mathtt{ex}?]\!](\mathcal{S}) = \{\sigma \in \mathcal{S} \mid [\![\mathtt{ex}]\!](\sigma) = \mathtt{TRUE}\}$.

Intuitively, the abstract interpretation of a test from abstract state $a^\sharp = (p, \overrightarrow{n}, r)$ can directly improve the constraints in the numeric component $\overrightarrow{n}$, which can then be propagated into r by **reduce**. The numeric test will derive new constraints only over non summary dimensions, thus tests over fields of groups that contain more than one element will not refine abstract values.

When a test involves an array cell as in $\mathtt{a[i]} == 0?$, and if the group that cell belongs to cannot be known precisely, a more precise post-condition can be derived by performing a *locally disjunctive analysis*, that applies numeric test to each possible group, and then joins the abstract states. For instance, if $\mathtt{i} \lhd G_0 \cup G_1$, the analysis will analyze test $\mathtt{a}[\mathtt{i}] == 0$? for both $\mathtt{i} \lhd G_0$ and $\mathtt{i} \lhd G_1$, join the results of both tests, and apply operator **reduce** afterwards. Note that the abstract test operator does not change the partition, thus this join boils down to applying the abstract join $\mathbf{join}_{\mathbb{N}^\sharp}$ of numeric abstract domain $\mathbb{N}^\sharp$ and set intersection to relations viewed as sets of atomic relations. The resulting join operator, limited to cases where both arguments have the same partitioning is defined by $\mathbf{join}_{\equiv}((p, \overrightarrow{n}_0, r_0), (p, \overrightarrow{n}_1, r_1)) = (p, \mathbf{join}_{\mathbb{N}^\sharp}(\overrightarrow{n}_0, \overrightarrow{n}_1), r_0 \cap r_1)$. It is sound: $\forall i \in \{0, 1\}, \gamma_{\mathbb{D}^\sharp}(p, \overrightarrow{n}_i, r_i) \subseteq \gamma_{\mathbb{D}^\sharp}(\mathbf{join}_{\equiv}((p, \overrightarrow{n}_0, r_0), (p, \overrightarrow{n}_1, r_1)))$.

Abstract transfer function **test** is *sound* in the sense that:

$$\forall \sigma \in \gamma_{\mathbb{D}^\sharp}(a^\sharp),\ [\![\mathtt{ex}]\!] = \mathtt{TRUE} \Longrightarrow \sigma \in \gamma_{\mathbb{D}^\sharp}(\mathbf{test}(\mathtt{ex}, a^\sharp))$$

Example 5. We consider the analysis of the code studied in Section 2. At the beginning of the first iteration of the loop, $\mathtt{i}$ is equal to 0, so $\mathtt{mproc}[\mathtt{i}]$ may be in G_1 or in G_2. Then, the analysis of test $\mathtt{mproc}[\mathtt{i}].\mathtt{mpflag} > 0$ will locally create two disjuncts corresponding to each of these groups. However, in the case of G_1, $\widehat{\mathtt{mpflag}_1} = 0$, thus the numeric test $\widehat{\mathtt{mpflag}_1} > 0$ will produce abstract value $\bot$ denoting the empty set of states. Therefore, only the second disjunct contributes to the abstract post-condition. Thus, the analysis derives $\mathtt{i} \lhd G_2$.

5.2 Assignment

Given l-value $\mathtt{lv}$ and expression $\mathtt{ex}$, the concrete semantics of assignment $\mathtt{lv} = \mathtt{ex}$ writes the value of $\mathtt{ex}$ into the cell $\mathtt{lv}$ evaluates to. It can thus be defined as a function over states, by $[\![\mathtt{lv} = \mathtt{ex}]\!](\sigma) = \sigma[[\![\mathtt{lv}]\!](\sigma) \leftarrow [\![\mathtt{ex}]\!](\sigma)]$.

In the abstract level, given abstract pre-condition $a^\sharp = (p, \overrightarrow{n}, r)$, an abstract post-condition for $\mathtt{lv} = \mathtt{ex}$ can be done in three steps: (1) materialization of the memory cell that gets updated, (2) call to $\mathbf{assign}_{\mathbb{N}^\sharp}$ in $\mathbb{N}^\sharp$ [14], and update of the relations, and (3) reduction of the resulting abstract state.

Materialization. When $\mathtt{lv}$ denotes an array cell, it should get *materialized* into a group consisting of a single cell, before strong updates can be performed on $\overrightarrow{n}$ and r. To achieve this, the analysis computes which group(s) $\mathtt{lv}$ may evaluate into in abstract state $a^\sharp$. If there is a single such group G_i, that contains a single cell (i.e., $\underline{\mathrm{Sz}}_i = 1$), then materialization is already achieved. If there is a single such group G_i, but $\underline{\mathrm{Sz}}_i$ may be greater than 1, then the analysis calls **split** in order to divide G_i into a group of size 1 and a group containing the other elements. Last, when there are several such groups (e.g., when $\mathtt{lv}$ is $\mathtt{a}[\mathtt{i}]$ and $\mathtt{i} \lhd G_0 \cup G_1$), the analysis first calls **merge** to merge all such groups and then falls back to the case where $\mathtt{lv}$ can only evaluate into a single group.

Note that in the last case, the merge of several groups may incur a loss in precision since the properties of several groups get merged before the abstract assignment takes place. We believe this loss in precision is acceptable here. The other option would be to produce a *disjunction* of abstract states, yet it would increase significantly the analysis cost and the gain in precision would be unclear, as programmers typically view those disjunctions of groups of cells as having similar roles. Our experiments (Section 7) did confirm this observation.

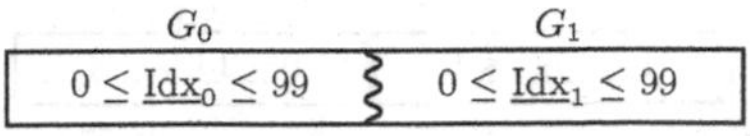

$$\begin{array}{rll} n^{\mathrm{g}}: & \widehat{\mathtt{value}}_0 = 0 \;\wedge & \underline{\mathrm{Sz}}_0 = 99 \\ & \wedge\; \widehat{\mathtt{value}}_1 = 1 \;\wedge & \underline{\mathrm{Sz}}_1 = 1 \\ r: & \mathtt{i} \lhd G_1 & \wedge\; \widehat{\mathtt{value}}_1 \lhd G_0 \cup G_1 \end{array}$$

Fig. 8. Post-condition of assignment $\mathtt{a[i]} = 1$

Constraints. New relations can be inferred after assignment operations in two ways. First, when both sides are base variables, they get propagated: for instance, if $\mathtt{u} \lhd G_i$, then after assignment $\mathtt{v} = \mathtt{u}$, we get $\mathtt{v} \lhd G_i$. Second, when the right hand side is an array cell as in $\mathtt{parent} = \mathtt{mproc[child].mparent}$ in the example of Section 2, the analysis first looks for relations between fields and indexes such as $\widehat{\mathtt{mparent}}_2 \lhd G_0 \cup G_2$, and propagate them to the l-value. In this phase, the numeric assignment relies on local disjuncts that are merged right after the abstract assignment, as we have shown in the case of condition tests (Section 5.1).

The abstract transfer function for assignment is sound in the sense that:

$$\forall \sigma \in \gamma_{\mathbb{D}^\sharp}(a^\sharp),\ \sigma[[\![\mathtt{lv}]\!](\sigma) \leftarrow [\![\mathtt{ex}]\!](\sigma)] \in \gamma_{\mathbb{D}^\sharp}(\mathbf{assign}(a^\sharp, \mathtt{lv}, \mathtt{ex}))$$

Example 6. We consider $\mathtt{a[i]} = 1$ and abstract the pre-condition shown in Figure 6(a). The l-value evaluates into an index in G_0, but this group has several elements, thus it is split, as shown in Figure 6(b). Then, the assignment boils down to a strong update in G_1, and produces the post-condition shown in Figure 8. Note that reduction strengthens relations with $\widehat{\mathtt{value}}_1 \lhd G_0 \cup G_1$.

6 Join, Widening and Inclusion Check

Our analysis proceeds by standard abstract interpretation, and uses widening and inclusion tests to compute abstract post-fixpoints for loops and abstract join for control flow union (e.g., after an **if** statement). All these operators face the same difficulties: when their inputs do not have a similar of clearly "matching" groups they have to re-partition the arrays so that precise information can be computed. We discuss this issue in detail in the case of join.

6.1 Join and the Group Matching Problem

Let us consider two abstract states $a_0^\sharp, a_1^\sharp$ with the same number of groups for each array, that we assume to have the same names. Then, the operator $\mathbf{join}_{\equiv}$ introduced in Section 5.1 computes an over-approximation for $a_0^\sharp, a_1^\sharp$, by joining predicates for each group name, the global numeric invariants and the side relations. However, this straightforward approach may produce very imprecise results if applied directly. As an example, we show two abstract states $a_0^\sharp$ and $a_1^\sharp$ in Figure 9(a) and Figure 9(b), that are similar up to a group name permutation. The direct join is shown in Figure 9(c). We note that the exact size of groups and the tight constraints over $\mathtt{value}$ were lost. Conversely, if the same operation is

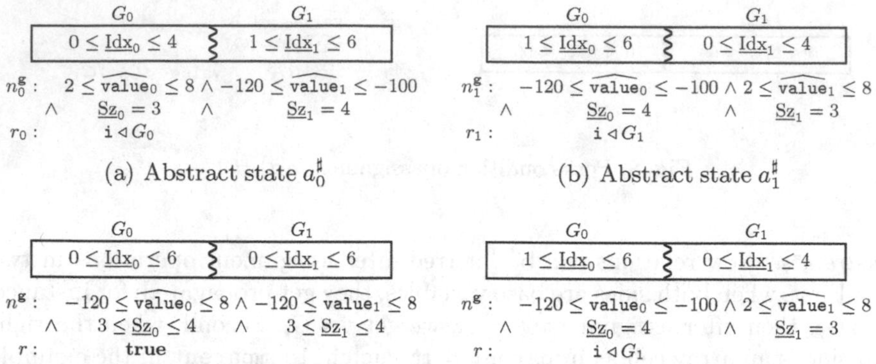

(a) Abstract state $a_0^\sharp$ (b) Abstract state $a_1^\sharp$

(c) Imprecise join result (d) Precise join result

Fig. 9. Impact of the group matching on the abstract join

done after a permutation of group names, an optimal result is found, as shown in Figure 9(d). This *group matching problem* is actually even more complicated in general as $a_0^\sharp, a_1^\sharp$ usually do not have the same number of groups.

To properly associate G_0 in Figure 9(a) with G_1 in Figure 9(b), the analysis should take into account the *group field properties*. This is achieved with the help of a ranking function $\mathbf{rank} : \mathbb{G} \times \mathbb{G} \rightarrow \mathbb{N}$, which computes a distance between groups in different abstract states by comparing their properties: $\mathbf{rank}(G_i, G_j)$ returns a monotone function of the number of common constraints over the fields and indexes of G_i and G_j in $\vec{n}_0$ and $\vec{n}_1$. A high value of $\mathbf{rank}(G_i, G_j)$ indicates G_i of $a_0^\sharp$ and G_j of $a_1^\sharp$ are likely to describe sets of cells with similar properties.

Using the set of $\mathbf{rank}(G_i, G_j)$ values, the analysis computes a *pairing* $\leftrightarrow$, that is a relation between groups of $a_0^\sharp$ and groups of $a_1^\sharp$ (this step relies on heuristics; a non optimal pairing will impact only precision, but not soundness) and then apply a group matching which transforms both arguments into "compatible" abstract states using the following (symmetric) principles:

- if there is no G_j such that $G_i \leftrightarrow G_j$, then an empty such group is created with **create**;
- if $G_i \leftrightarrow G_j$ and $G_i \leftrightarrow G_k$, then G_i is split into two groups, respectively paired with G_j and G_k;
- if G_i is mapped only to G_j, G_j is mapped only to G_i, and $i \neq j$, then one of them is renamed accordingly.

After this process has completed, a pair of abstract states are produced that have the same number of groups, and $\mathbf{join}_\equiv$ can be applied. This defines abstract join operator **join**. The soundness of **join** follows from the soundness of $\mathbf{join}_\equiv$ (trivial), and the soundness of **split** and **create**:

Theorem 2 (Soundness)

$$\forall a_0^\sharp, a_1^\sharp,\ \gamma_{\mathbb{D}^\sharp}(a_0^\sharp) \subseteq \gamma_{\mathbb{D}^\sharp}(\mathbf{join}(a_0^\sharp, a_1^\sharp)) \wedge \gamma_{\mathbb{D}^\sharp}(a_1^\sharp) \subseteq \gamma_{\mathbb{D}^\sharp}(\mathbf{join}(a_0^\sharp, a_1^\sharp))$$

```
0 :  if(random()){
1 :     a[i] = 1;
2 :  }
3 :  ...
```

$$G_0 \qquad\qquad G_1$$
$$\boxed{0 \leq \underline{\text{Idx}}_0 \leq 99} \; \Big\} \; \boxed{0 \leq \underline{\text{Idx}}_1 \leq 99}$$

$n^g :\quad \widehat{\text{value}_0} = 0 \;\wedge\; \widehat{\text{value}_1} = 1 \qquad r : \; \text{i} \lhd G_0 \cup G_1$

$\wedge\; 99 \leq \underline{\text{Sz}}_0 \leq 100 \;\wedge\; 0 \leq \underline{\text{Sz}}_1 \leq 1$

(a) Simple join   (b) Join result

Fig. 10. Join of a one group state with a two groups state

Example 7. We assume a is an integer array of length 100 and i is an integer variable storing a value in $[0, 99]$, and consider the program of Figure 10(a). At the exit of the **if** statement, the analysis needs to join the abstract states shown in Figure 6(a) (that has a single group) and in Figure 8 (that has two groups). We note that G_0 in Figure 6(a) has similar properties as G_0 in Figure 8, thus they get paired. Moreover, G_1 in Figure 8 is paired to no group, so a new group is created (as in Figure 6(c), and paired to it. At that stage $\textbf{join}_=$ applies, and returns the abstract state shown in Figure 10(b).

6.2 Widening

The widening algorithm is similar to that of join. The restriction of widening to *compatible* abstract states is defined by $\textbf{widen}_=((p, \overrightarrow{n}_0, r_0), (p, \overrightarrow{n}_1, r_1)) = (p, \textbf{widen}_{\mathbb{N}^\sharp}(\overrightarrow{n}_0, \overrightarrow{n}_1), r_0 \cap r_1)$ (note that r_0, r_1 are finite sets of relations, and intersections of finite sets of relations naturally terminates).

The group matching algorithm of Section 6.1 does not ensure termination, as it could create more and more groups. Therefore **widen** relies on a slightly modified group matching algorithm, which will never call **split** and **create**. Instead, it will always match each group of an argument to at least one group of the other argument, and call **merge** when two (or more) groups of one argument are paired with a group of the other. This group matching ensures termination. Therefore, the resulting **widen** operator is a sound and terminating widening operator [3]. For better precision, the analysis always uses **join** for the first abstract iteration for a loop, and uses widening afterwards.

6.3 Inclusion Check

To check the termination of sequences of abstract iterates over loops, and the entailment of post-conditions, the analysis uses a sound inclusion check operator **is_le**: when **is_le**$(a_0^\sharp, a_1^\sharp)$ returns TRUE, then $\gamma_{\mathbb{D}^\sharp}(a_0^\sharp) \subseteq \gamma_{\mathbb{D}^\sharp}(a_1^\sharp)$.

Like **join**, such an operator is easy to define on compatible abstract states, using an inclusion check operator **is_le**$_{\mathbb{N}^\sharp}$ for $\mathbb{N}^\sharp$: if **is_le**$_{\mathbb{N}^\sharp}(\overrightarrow{n}_0, \overrightarrow{n}_1) = $ TRUE and r_1 is included in r_0 (as a set of constraints), then $\gamma_{\mathbb{D}^\sharp}(p, \overrightarrow{n}_0, r_0) \subseteq \gamma_{\mathbb{D}^\sharp}(p, \overrightarrow{n}_1, r_1)$, hence we let **is_le**$_=$ return TRUE in that case.

The group matching algorithm for **is_le** is different, although it is based on similar principles. Indeed, it modifies the groups in the left argument so as to construct an abstract state with the same groups as the right argument, using **create**, **split** and **merge**.

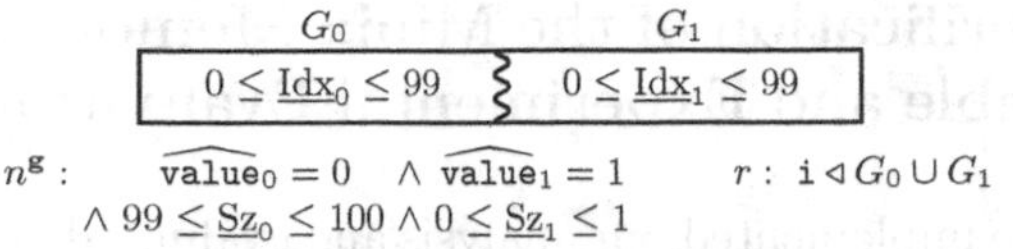

7 Verification of the Minix Memory Management Process Table and Experimental Evaluation

We have implemented our analysis and evaluated how it copes with two classes of programs: (1) the Minix Memory Management Process Table, and (2) academic examples used in related works, where contiguity of groups is sometimes unnecessary for the verification. Our analyzer uses the MemCAD analyzer front-end, and the APRON [14] implementation of octagons [18].

7.1 Verification of Memory Management Part in Minix

The main data-structure of the Memory Management operating system service of Minix 1.1 is the MMPT `mproc`, which contains memory management information for each process. At start up, it is initialized by function `mm_init`, which creates process descriptors for `mm`, `fs` and `init`. After that, `mproc` should satisfy property $\mathcal{C}$ (Section 2). Then, it gets updated by system calls `fork`, `wait` and `exit`, which respectively create a process, wait for terminated children process descriptors be removed, and terminate a process. Each of these functions should be called only in a state that satisfies $\mathcal{C}$, and should return a state that also satisfies $\mathcal{C}$. System calls `wait` and `exit` call the complex utility function `cleanup` discussed in Section 2, to reclaim descriptors of terminated processes.

If property $\mathcal{C}$ was violated, several critical issues could occur. First, system calls could crash due to out-of-bound accesses, e.g., when accessing `mproc` through field `mparent`. Moreover, higher level, hard to debug issues could occur, such as the persistence of dangling processes, that would never be eliminated.

Therefore, we verified (1) that `mm_init` properly establishes $\mathcal{C}$ (with no pre-condition), and (2) that `fork`, `wait` and `exit` preserve $\mathcal{C}$ using our analysis (i.e., the analysis of each of these functions from pre-condition $\mathcal{C}$ returns a post-condition that also satisfies $\mathcal{C}$). Note that function `cleanup` was inlined in `wait` and `fork` in a recursion free form (currently not supported by our analyzer), as well as statements irrelevant to `mproc`.

Our tool achieves the verification of all these four functions. The results are shown in the first four lines of the table in Figure 11, including analysis time and peak number of groups for array `mproc`.

The analysis of `mm_init` and `fork` is very fast. The analysis of `exit` and `wait` also succeeds, although it is more complex due to the intricate structure of `cleanup` (which consists of five loops and many conditions) which requires 194 joins. Despite this, the maximum number of groups remains reasonable (seven in the worst case).

7.2 Application on Other Cases

We now consider a couple of examples from the literature, where arrays are used as containers, i.e., where the relative order of groups does not matter for the program's correctness. The purpose of this study is to examplify other examples of cases our abstract domain is adequate for. Program `int_init` consists of a simple

Program	LOCs	Verified property	Time(s)	Max. groups	Description
`mm_init`	26	establishes C	0.092	4	Minix MMPT: `mproc` init
`fork`	22	preserves C	0.109	3	Minix MMPT sys call
`exit`	68	preserves C	5.41	7	Minix MMPT sys call
`wait`	70	preserves C	5.41	7	Minix MMPT sys call
`complex`	21	$\forall i \in [0, 54], a[i] \geq -1$	0.296	4	Example from [5]
`int_init`	8	$\forall i \in [0, N], a[i] = 0$	0.025	3	Array initialization

Fig. 11. Analysis results (timings measured on Ubuntu 12.04.4, with 16 Gb of RAM, on an Intel Xeon E3 desktop, running at 3.2 GHz)

```
2  int a[56];
3  for(int i = 0; i < 56; i++){
    ①
4      a[i] = 0;
    ②
   }
5  a[55] = random();
6  for(int i = 0; i < 55; i++){
    ③
7      int index = 21 * i%55;
8      int num = random();
9      if(num < 0){num = -1;}
10     a[index] = num;
   }
11 assert(∀i ∈ [0, 54], a[i] > -1);
```

(a) Test case `complex`

state ① G_0 G_1

$\boxed{i \leq \underline{Idx}_0 \leq 55 \quad 0 \leq \underline{Idx}_1 \leq i - 1}$

$n^g: \underline{Sz}_0 = 56 - i \wedge \underline{Sz}_1 = i \wedge \widehat{value}_1 = 0$
$r: i \triangleleft G_0$

state ② G_0 G_1 G_2

$\boxed{i+1 \leq \underline{Idx}_0 \leq 55 \quad 0 \leq \underline{Idx}_1 \leq i - 1 \quad \underline{Idx}_2 - i}$

$n^g: \underline{Sz}_0 = 55 - i \wedge \underline{Sz}_1 = i \wedge \underline{Sz}_2 = 1$
$\widehat{value}_1 = 0 \wedge \widehat{value}_2 = 0$
$r: i \triangleleft G_2$

state ③ G_1 G_2 G_3

$\boxed{0 \leq \underline{Idx}_1 \leq 54 \quad 0 \leq \underline{Idx}_2 \leq 54 \quad \underline{Idx}_3 = 55}$

$n^g: \underline{Sz}_1 = 54 \wedge \underline{Sz}_2 = 1 \wedge \underline{Sz}_3 = 1$
$-1 \leq \widehat{value}_1 \wedge -1 \leq \widehat{value}_2$
$r: i \triangleleft G_1 \cup G_2$

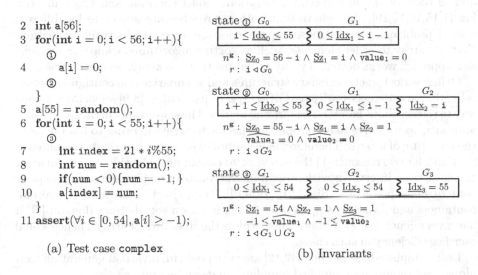

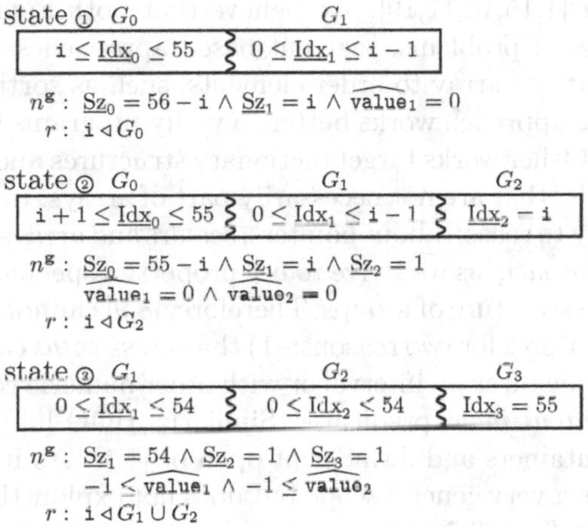

(b) Invariants

Fig. 12. Array random accesses

initialization loop. Our analysis succeeds here, and can handle other cases relying on basic segments, although our algorithms are not specific to segments (and are geared towards the abstraction of non contiguous partitions).

Moreover, Figure 12 shows `complex`, an excerpt of an example from [5]. The second example is challenging for most existing techniques, as observed in [5] since resolving `a[index]` at line 10 is tricky. As shown in Figure 11, our analysis handles these two loops well, with respectively 4 and 3 groups.

The invariant of the first initialization loop in Figure 12 is abstract state ① (at line 4): group G_1 accounts for initialized cells, whereas cells of G_0 remain to be initialized. The analysis of `a[i] = 0`; from ① materializes a single uninitialized cell, so that a strong update produces abstract state ②. At the next iteration, and after increment operation `i++`, widening merges G_2 with G_1, which produces abstract state ① again. At loop exit, the analysis derives G_0 is empty as $56 \leq \underline{Idx}_0 \leq 55$. At this stage, this group is eliminated. The analysis of the second loop converges after two widening iterations, and produces abstract state ③. We note that group

G_3 is kept separate, while groups G_1 and G_2 get merged when the assignment at line 10 is analyzed (Section 5.2). This allows to prove the assertion at line 11.

8 Related Work and Conclusion

In this paper, we have presented a novel abstract domain that is tailored for arrays, and that relies on partitioning, without imposing the constraint that the cells of a given group be contiguous.

Most array analyses require each group be a contiguous array *segment*. This view is used both in abstract interpretation based static analysis tools [5,11,13] and in tools based on invariant generation, model checking and theorem proving [1,15,16,17,19]. We believe that both approaches are adequate for different sets of problems: segment based approaches are adequate to verify algorithms that use array to order elements, such as sorting algorithms, while our segmentless approach works better to verify programs that use arrays as dictionaries.

Other works target dictionary structures and summarize non contiguous sets of cells, that are not necessarily part of arrays. In particular, [8,9] seeks for a unified way to reason about pointers, scalars and arrays. These works are orthogonal to our approach, as we strive to use properties specific to arrays in order to reason about the structure of groups. Therefore, [8,9] cannot express the invariants presented in Section 2 for two reasons: (1) the *access paths* cannot describe the contents of array elements as an interval or with other numeric constraints; (2) they cannot express *content-index* predicates. Similarly, HOO [6] is an effective abstract domain for containers and JavaScript open objects. As it uses a set abstract domain [7], it has a very general scope but does not exploit the structure of arrays, hence would sacrifice efficiency in such cases.

Last, template-base methods [2,12] are very powerful invariant generation techniques, yet require user supplied templates and can be quite costly.

Our approach has several key distinguishing factors. First, it not only relies on index relation, but also exploits semantic properties of array elements, to select groups. Second, relation predicates track lightweight properties, that would not be captured in a numerical domain. Last, it allows empty groups, which eliminated the need for any global disjunction in our examples (a few assignments and tests benefit from cheap, local disjunctions). Finally, experiments show it is effective at inferring non trivial array invariants with non contiguous groups, and verify a challenging operating system data-structure.

References

1. Alberti, F., Ghilardi, S., Sharygina, N.: Decision procedures for flat array properties. In: Ábrahám, E., Havelund, K. (eds.) TACAS 2014. LNCS, vol. 8413, pp. 15–30. Springer, Heidelberg (2014)
2. Beyer, D., Henzinger, T.A., Majumdar, R., Rybalchenko, A.: Invariant synthesis for combined theories. In: Cook, B., Podelski, A. (eds.) VMCAI 2007. LNCS, vol. 4349, pp. 378–394. Springer, Heidelberg (2007)

3. Cousot, P., Cousot, R.: Abstract interpretation: A unified lattice model for static analysis of programs by construction or approximation of fixpoints. In: POPL (1977)
4. Cousot, P., Cousot, R.: Systematic design of program analysis frameworks. In: POPL (1979)
5. Cousot, P., Cousot, R., Logozzo, F.: A parametric segmentation functor for fully automatic and scalable array content analysis. In: POPL (2011)
6. Cox, A., Chang, B.-Y.E., Rival, X.: Automatic analysis of open objects in dynamic language programs. In: Müller-Olm, M., Seidl, H. (eds.) SAS 2014. LNCS, vol. 8723, pp. 134–150. Springer, Heidelberg (2014)
7. Cox, A., Chang, B.-Y.E., Sankaranarayanan, S.: QUIC graphs: Relational invariant generation for containers. In: Castagna, G. (ed.) ECOOP 2013. LNCS, vol. 7920, pp. 401–425. Springer, Heidelberg (2013)
8. Dillig, I., Dillig, T., Aiken, A.: Fluid updates: Beyond strong vs. Weak updates. In: Gordon, A.D. (ed.) ESOP 2010. LNCS, vol. 6012, pp. 246–266. Springer, Heidelberg (2010)
9. Dillig, I., Dillig, T., Aiken, A.: Precise reasoning for programs using containers. In: POPL (2011)
10. Gopan, D., DiMaio, F., Dor, N., Reps, T., Sagiv, M.: Numeric domains with summarized dimensions. In: Jensen, K., Podelski, A. (eds.) TACAS 2004. LNCS, vol. 2988, pp. 512–529. Springer, Heidelberg (2004)
11. Gopan, D., Reps, T., Sagiv, M.: A framework for numeric analysis of array operations. In: POPL (2005)
12. Gulwani, S., McCloskey, B., Tiwari, A.: Lifting abstract interpreters to quantified logical domains. In: POPL (2008)
13. Halbwachs, N., Péron, M.: Discovering properties about arrays in simple programs. In: PLDI (2008)
14. Jeannet, B., Miné, A.: APRON: A library of numerical abstract domains for static analysis. In: Bouajjani, A., Maler, O. (eds.) CAV 2009. LNCS, vol. 5643, pp. 661–667. Springer, Heidelberg (2009)
15. Jhala, R., McMillan, K.L.: Array abstractions from proofs. In: Damm, W., Hermanns, H. (eds.) CAV 2007. LNCS, vol. 4590, pp. 193–206. Springer, Heidelberg (2007)
16. Kovács, L., Voronkov, A.: Finding loop invariants for programs over arrays using a theorem prover. In: Chechik, M., Wirsing, M. (eds.) FASE 2009. LNCS, vol. 5503, pp. 470–485. Springer, Heidelberg (2009)
17. McMillan, K.L.: Quantified invariant generation using an interpolating saturation prover. In: Ramakrishnan, C.R., Rehof, J. (eds.) TACAS 2008. LNCS, vol. 4963, pp. 413–427. Springer, Heidelberg (2008)
18. Miné, A.: The octagon abstract domain. In: HOSC (2006)
19. Seghir, M.N., Podelski, A., Wies, T.: Abstraction refinement for quantified array assertions. In: Palsberg, J., Su, Z. (eds.) SAS 2009. LNCS, vol. 5673, pp. 3–18. Springer, Heidelberg (2009)
20. Sotin, P., Rival, X.: Hierarchical shape abstraction of dynamic structures in static blocks. In: Jhala, R., Igarashi, A. (eds.) APLAS 2012. LNCS, vol. 7705, pp. 131–147. Springer, Heidelberg (2012)

From Verification to Optimizations

Rigel Gjomemo[1], Kedar S. Namjoshi[2], Phu H. Phung[1,3],
V.N. Venkatakrishnan[1], and Lenore D. Zuck[1]

[1] University of Illinois at Chicago
{rgjomemo,phu,venkat,lenore}@cs.uic.edu
[2] Bell Laboratories, Alcatel-Lucent
kedar@research.bell-labs.com
[3] University of Gothenburg, Sweden

Abstract. Compilers perform a static analysis of a program prior to optimization. The precision of this analysis is limited, however, by strict time budgets for compilation. We explore an alternative, new approach, which links *external* sound static analysis tools into compilers. One of the key problems to be solved is that of propagating the source-level information gathered by a static analyzer deeper into the optimization pipeline. We propose a method to achieve this, and demonstrate its feasibility through an implementation using the LLVM compiler infrastructure. We show how assertions obtained from the Frama-C source code analysis platform are propagated through LLVM and are then used to substantially improve the effectiveness of several optimizations.

1 Introduction

An optimizing compiler is commonly structured as a sequence of passes. The input of each pass is a *source* code that is first analyzed and, using the analysis information, transformed to a *target* code, which then becomes the source of the next pass in the sequence. Each pass uses static analysis to guide optimization, but the precision of this analysis is limited due to strict time budgets for compiling (e.g., the GCC wiki has as rule 1: "Do not add algorithms with quadratic or worse behavior, ever.") As a result, end users of compilers such as LLVM do not benefit from advances in algorithms for program analysis and verification. These advanced methods are, however, implemented in static analysis tools, which are now widely used to detect programming errors during software development. Examples such tools for C programs include BLAST [10], Frama-C [5], and F-Soft [11], all of which employ SMT solvers to produce high-quality and precise (inductive) invariants.

Static analysis tools are less time-constrained and are thus able to carry out much deeper analysis of program behavior. In this work we explore how the information gathered by such tools can be used to augment the internal analysis of a compiler, and whether this offers any practical benefit. While the compile-time cost of employing additional tools may be high, it is often the case that runtime improvements in optimization outweigh this additional cost, for

D. D'Souza et al. (Eds.): VMCAI 2015, LNCS 8931, pp. 300–317, 2015.

large frequently used code such as kernels and name servers. One approach is to implement these as optional features inside the compiler. Yet another option, employed here, is that of importing the analysis results computed by *external* static analysis and software verification tools. There is much to be gained from this modular approach, which decouples analysis from transformation. However, there are two key challenges to be overcome: Linking the output of an analysis tool to the C program representation in the compiler front-end, and propagating the assertions through the program transformations performed at the back-end.

Let us consider the problem of propagating information through a series of optimization passes. The static analysis tool produces information about a source program, say S. However, the various passes of a compiler transform S successively into programs $S = S_0, S_1, S_2, \ldots, S_f = T$, where T denotes the final target code. To use information gathered for S_0 at the kth compilation stage ($k > 0$), one must have a way of transforming this information into a form that is meaningful for program S_{k-1}.

A simple example can illustrate this problem. Suppose that the program S has variables x and y, and the static analysis tool concludes that $(x < y)$ is invariant. Now suppose that the first stage of compilation renames x and y to "temporary" variables t_1 and t_2 respectively. The assertion $(x < y)$ is meaningless for the second compilation stage (from S_1 to S_2); to be useful, it must be transformed to $(t_1 < t_2)$.

How can assertions be transformed? It is desirable to avoid manually tailoring the propagation of assertions to each transformation, a laborious and possibly error-prone task. Our approach offers a *uniform* method for assertion propagation, which is based on the notion of refinement "witnesses" [14]. Note that when the refinement relation induced by a transformation is available, it can be used to transform any invariant on the source program to an invariant on the target program [1]. We obtain the refinement relation by instrumenting the optimization to produce a refinement relation as it transforms a program. (The validity of the generated relation can be checked independently, using SMT solvers. A valid relation is a "witness" to the correctness of the optimization, hence the name.)

Many standard optimizations only introduce, remove, or rename variables. Thus, witness relations are often conjunctions of equalities between a pair of corresponding source/target variables at a program point (or of the form $v_t = E(V_s)$ where v_t is a target variable, V_s are a source variables, and E is a simple arithmetic expression.) For example, the witness for a dead-variables elimination transformation states that the values of live variables are preserved. In the common case that the invariant depends on a single variable, its propagation can be carried out by simply keeping track of the action that is applied to the variable, without requiring logical manipulations.

In the implementation described in this paper, we handle this common case. The invariants are obtained from the value-range analysis of the Frama-C source code analysis platform [5,3]. Among other information, Frama-C (via its Value

[1] Precisely, if φ is invariant for program S, and T refines S through relation W, then $\langle W \rangle \varphi$ is invariant for T.

Analysis plug-in) produces invariants which express constant limits on the range of a program variable (e.g., $10 \leq x \leq 20$). Such invariants are propagated through LLVM optimizations using a mechanism we describe in Sec. 3. The propagated invariants are used to augment LLVM's own analysis information for optimizations such as instruction combination and buffer overrun checking[2]. Sec. 5 describes some experimental results showing gains vary depending on the relative accuracy of LLVM vs. Frama-C for each benchmark.

The prototype of our implementation is available at `http://www.cs.uic.edu/phu/projects/aruna/index.html`.

2 Approach by Example

We use LLVM [12] as our target compiler infrastructure due to its widespread use in academic and industrial settings, as well as its ability to handle a wide variety of source languages. Among several tools (e.g., [5,2,18,9,1,13]) that can be used to obtain external assertions to feed into LLVM, we focus our discussion on Frama-C. In particular, we focus on the use of Frama-C to perform *value analysis*, an abstract-interpretation-based analysis, to obtain various domains of integers (sets of values, intervals, periodic intervals), floating points, and addresses for pointers. The value range analysis results obtained from Frama-C are more powerful than those available in most compilers, and, as we demonstrate, in LLVM.

Consider the code in Fig. 1(a). Even when compiled using the most aggressive optimization scheduler (`-O3` option of Clang), LLVM's optimizer does not detect that the `else` branch in location `L6` is dead (and leaves the branch `L6-L7` intact.)

In Fig. 1(b) we show the ACSL ([6], see also `http://frama-c.com/acsl.html`) assertions produced by the Frama-C's Value Analysis as comments. We note that here examples are given at the C-level for readability, rather then the SSA LLVM bitcode. The assumption of SSA form allows to consider each assertion in a basic block (single-entry single-exit straight line code) to be implicitly the conjunction of assertions preceding it.

We thus omit describing how the assertions produced by Frama-C (comments in Fig. 1(b)) are propagated from the Clang input. The first pass that LLVM performs that is relevant to us is to replace weak inequalities by strict inequalities, possibly at the "cost" of introducing new variables, and replacing, signed comparisons between integers with unsigned ones (subscripted by u) whenever the integers are known to be non-negative.

Consider the uncommented lines in Fig. 1(c). There, a new line (L0) is added in which a temporary variable `tmp1` is assigned the value $i - 1$, which, when $i \geq 1$, is non-negative, and hence line L1 does not test it is greater than 0. This allows LLVM to replace the conjunction of the test in L1 by a single unsigned test for `tmp1` $<_u 10$. Following the quest to replace tests of weak inequality to tests for strict inequalities, LLVM replaces that tests in L2 and L3 by their strict equivalents. Finally, the $j + i$ expression that appears in line L4 (Fig. 1(b)) is

[2] The latter inserts checks; the invariants help identify some which as unnecessary.

replaced by two lines, one (L3.1) that assigns a new `tmp2` the value $j+i$, and the other (L4) tests whether $\texttt{tmp2} \geq k$ (this inequality is left in its weak form, since neither of the operands is a constant.)

Since the original program does not have the new temporaries, there is no value-range analysis for them. However, we can propagate the assertion $i \geq 1 \wedge i \leq 10$ to the assertion $\texttt{tmp1}= i-1 \wedge \texttt{tmp1} \geq 0 \wedge \texttt{tmp1} \leq 9$, as appears in L1' of Fig. 1(c). Similarly, using the assertion for i and the assertion $j \geq 5$ (from L2'), we can propagate the assertion $\texttt{tmp2} = i+j \wedge \texttt{tmp2} \geq 6$, which is shown in line L3.1' of Fig. 1(c). Since $k \leq 4$ and $\texttt{tmp2} \geq 6$, the test in L4 can be flagged as trivially true, so that the `else` branch can be eliminated, resulting in the code in Fig. 1(d). (The LLVM passes that accomplish this optimization are instruction combination followed by constant folding followed by jump threading and dead code elimination.)

```
L1: if(i>=1 && i<=10)
L2:     if(j>=5)

L3:         if(k <= 4)


L4:             if(j+i >= k)
L5:                 j++;
L6:             else
L7:                 j-;
L8: return j;
```

(a) source

```
L1: if(i>=1 && i<=10)
L1':  /*@assert i >= 1 && i<=10*/
L2:   if(j>=5 )
L2':    /*@assert j >= 5  */
L3:     if(k <= 4)
L3':      /*@assert k <= 4*/
L4:     if(j+i >= k)
L5:         j++;
L6:       else
L7:         j-;
L8: return j;
```

(b) with value analysis

```
L0: tmp1 = i-1
L1: if(tmp1 <u 10)
L1':/*@assert tmp1>=0 && tmp1 <=9*/
L2:    if(j>4)
L2':   /*@assert j >= 5  */
L3:    if(k < 5)
L3':   /*@assert k <= 4*/
L3.1:     tmp2 = j+i
L3.1':    /*@assert tmp2 >= 6*/
L4:       if(tmp2 >= k)
L5:          j++;
L6:       else
L7:          j-;
L8: return j;
```

(c) before instruction combination.

```
L0: tmp1 = i-1
L1: if(tmp1 <u 10)
L1':/*@assert tmp1>=0 && tmp1 <=9*/
L2:  if(j>4)
L2':    /*@assert j > 4*/
L3:     if(k < 5)
L3':    /*@assert k < 5*/

L5:         j++;



L8: return j;
```

(d) after using assertions.

Fig. 1. Code example illustrating our approach

3 External Invariant Usage in LLVM

In this section, we discuss our approach for propagating and using invariants produced by third party verification tools inside LLVM's code transformation passes. As indicated in the introduction, the general approach is based on constructing a refinement witness for each optimization. We describe the theoretical foundations, practical considerations, and the implementation. [14] has a detailed description of the approach while here we only give an overview of it.

Refinement Relations. Consider an optimization opt. The optimization opt can be viewed as a transformer from the source program S into the target program $T = \mathsf{opt}(S)$. Informally, opt is correct if every behavior of T is a possible behavior of S – i.e., the transformation does not introduce undefined outcomes (such as a divide-by-zero) or non-termination, which do not already exist in S. If S is transition deterministic and S and T have identical initial states, this also implies that every behavior of S has a corresponding one in T. This notion can be formalized in several ways, depending on the notion of behavior that is to be preserved. We choose to apply a refinement relation that maps T-states into S-states. A valid refinement relation for a single procedure must:

- Relate every initial S-state into an initial T-state;
- Relate every initial T-state into an initial S-state;
- Be a simulation relation from T to S. The simulation condition may be single-step simulation or the more relaxed stuttering simulation, and
- Relate every final state T-state into a final S-state with the same return value(s).

(Note that here we are assuming that both S and T have the same observables and that the return values are observables. Extending the definition for the case where the observables are not the same requires adding a mapping between observables.)

These conditions ensure (by induction) that for any terminating T-computation there is a corresponding terminating S-computation with same return value, and that every non-terminating T-computation has a corresponding non-terminating S-computation. With the assumption of transition determinism, this also implies that every terminating S-computation has a corresponding terminating T-computation.

Invariant Propagation. Constructing a refinement relation from T to S ensures the correctness of the transformation $T = \mathsf{opt}(S)$. We call such a relation a *witness.* A witness also provides a means to propagate invariants from S to T through the following theorem.

Theorem 1. *Given a witness W for $T = \mathsf{opt}(S)$, and let V_S (resp. V_T) denote S's (resp. T's) variables. Let $\langle W\rangle(\varphi) = (\exists V_S : W(V_T, V_S) \wedge \varphi(V_S))$ (thus, $\langle W\rangle(\varphi)$ is the pre-image of φ under W). Then for any invariant φ of S, $\langle W\rangle(\varphi)$ is an invariant for T. Moreover, if φ is inductive, so is $\langle W\rangle(\varphi)$.*

Proof. Consider any execution σ of T. By definition of W, there is an execution δ of S such that every state of σ is related by W to a state of δ. As φ is an invariant for S, every state of δ satisfies φ; hence (by definition), every state of σ satisfies $\langle W \rangle(\varphi)$. Inductiveness is preserved since the relation W connects a step of T to a (stuttering) step of S. □

Generating witnesses. The problem of determining whether a program refines another is, in general, undecidable. However, in the cases we study here, it's usually possible to generate a witness relation by augmenting an optimization opt with a *witness generator* – an auxiliary function, wgen, that computes a candidate witness, $W = \mathsf{wgen}(T, S)$, for a source S and a target T. The tuple (T, W, S) can then be passed to a refinement checker, which checks the validity of $W = \mathsf{wgen}(T, S)$ (by checking each refinement condition). Note that generation and propagation are independent steps.

Effective manipulation of witnesses. Obviously, to make the above work in practice it is vital that the generation and propagation of witnesses be carried out effectively. This implies that the witness should be expressed in a logic for which checking is decidable, and for which propagation is computable.

We suppose that witnesses are defined on a basic-block level. Thus, for the check, a program transition is execution of the straight-line (non-looping) code in a basic block. This can usually be expressed as a quantifier-free, array theory formula. (The arrays encode memory.)

What makes this feasible in practice is that the witness relations for standard optimizations can also be expressed in quantifier-free, decidable theories. In fact, they are often simply conjunctions of equalities of the form $v_T = E(u_S)$ where v is either a variable name or memory content and $E(u_S)$ is similar or possibly a simple arithmetic expression over source variable names and constants. For instance, a renaming of variable x to x' has witness $x'_T = x_S$, dead code elimination has a witness which asserts the equality $x_T = x_S$ for all live variables x, and so forth. (More examples are given in [14].)

Propagation is the computation of $\langle W \rangle(\varphi)$. For witnesses and assertions expressed in a logic which supports quantifier elimination, one can compute a "closed form" solution. If not, one can still use witnesses to answer queries, as follows. To check whether an assertion q is true in T given the propagated invariant for φ, one must check the validity of $[\langle W \rangle(\varphi) \Rightarrow q]$. This is equivalent to the validity of $[\varphi(V_S) \wedge W(V_T, V_S) \Rightarrow q(V_T)]$. Note that, when φ is quantifier-free, so is the second formula. Thus, it is not necessary to carry out quantifier elimination in order to use propagated invariants.

For the experimental work described here, the invariants obtained from Frama-C are of the form $\bigwedge_{v \in V} l_v \leq v \leq h_v$ where the l_v and h_v are integer constants. The transformations of of the form $V_T = \mathcal{E}(V_S)$ where $\mathcal{E}$ is a simple arithmetic expression over V_S. Using similarly simple arithmetic manipulations one can compute the pre-image of the invariant. E.g., if $2 \leq x \leq 4$ is φ and $y = 2x + 1$ is W, then the propagated invariant is $5 \leq y \leq 9$.

Formally, for value-range analysis, φ is of the form $\bigwedge_{v \in V_S} l_v \leq v \leq h_v$. We then have:

$$\langle W \rangle(\varphi) \;=\; (\exists V_S : V_T = \mathcal{E}(V_S) \wedge \bigwedge_{v \in V_S} l_v \leq v \leq h_v)$$

which is of the form $\bigwedge_{v \in V_T} l_v \leq v \leq h_v$. To compute the exact bound for each $u \in V_T$ we need only to track the bounds of the S-variables that appear in the r-h-s of u's definition (as per W) and do the obvious arithmetic manipulations to obtain the bounds for u.

4 System Description

4.1 Background on LLVM

LLVM's back-end comprises a set of passes that operate on a single static assignment intermediate (SSA) language referred to as LLVM IR or bitcode, which is produced by the Clang front end. There are two types of these passes. One set of passes, called the *analysis passes* gather different types of information about the program, such as loop, alias, and variable evolution, but do not perform any code transformations. The other set, called the *transformation passes* in turn use the information gathered by the analysis passes to reason about and optimize the code. Taken together, they implement several algorithms for program analysis and transformation, such as alias analysis, scalar evolution, instruction simplification, etc.

As mentioned in Sec. 1, recent advances in analysis and verification techniques are not usually included in production compilers due to performance requirements and the implementation effort needed. Our approach aims to address this problem by facilitating the use of results from external verification tools inside the compiler. Using the witness mechanism described in the previous section, we propagate assertions (for which we also use the term annotations interchangeably) obtained from tools such as Frama-C through the various backend passes of LLVM. By this, we decouple the need for updating the compiler frequently as newer or improved program analysis algorithms become available, as our system is designed to obtain assertions from cutting-edge program analysis tools such as Frama-C. We propagate the assertions to the compiler backend, and employ them in program optimization. However, in realizing this approach, there are a number of practical challenges that must be overcome.

4.2 Practical Challenges

These challenges stem from language heterogeneities among the source and intermediate language as well as the code transformations along the sequence of passes. We describe each of these challenges in more detail.

Source-IR Mapping. The first challenge faced by our approach is that of propagating invariants from the source code through the front-end to the LLVM IR. In fact, due to the LLVM IR's SSA nature, every source variable can be mapped to several SSA versions in the LLVM IR, and consequently invariants about that source variable must also be bound to those SSA versions. In the case of the C language, an additional problem is posed by its scoping rules where same-named local variables can live in different scopes.

For example, Fig. 2(a) containing a snippet of C source code and Fig. 2(b) containing the corresponding LLVM IR code (simplified for space reasons) up to the comparison `i+size<200`. The two variables `i` declared in two different scopes (L3, L8) are both declared in the entry block in the LLVM IR (L15 for the outer scope `i`, and L16 for the inner scope `i`). However, the invariants (L2, L7) are both with respect to the same identifier `i`, and need to be correctly bound to the corresponding IR variables. Furthermore, these variables are used in different basic blocks; Their values are loaded from memory into SSA variables (L20, L21, L28), which are then used in the following instructions.

```
L0: int j = 0;
L1:  int Arr[N];
L2: /*@assert i>=0 &&
    i<=20*/
L3: int i=getArrNo();
L4: /*@assert size>=0 &&
    size<=100*/
L5: int size=getArrSize(i);
L6: while(j<size)
L7:   /*@assert i>=0
      && i<=99*/
L8:   int i = getArrVal();
L9:   if(i+size<200)
L10:     Arr[j] = setVal(i);
L11:  else
L12:     ...
L13:  j++;
```

(a) C source code.

```
L14: entry: //entry basic block
L15:    %i = alloca i32  //allocate outer i
L16:    %i1 = alloca i32 //allocate inner i
L17:    ...
L18:    br BB %5      //jump to basic block 5
L19: BB:5  //basic block 5
L20:    %7 = load %j
L21:    %8 = load %size
L22:    %9 = icmp slt i32 %8, %9 //j<size
L23:    br %9, ifTrue %10, ifFalse %22
                  //conditional jump
L24: BB:10
L25:    %11 = call @getArrVal() //call function
L26:    store %11, %i1    //store result in %i1
L27:    %12 = load %i1
L28:    %13 = load %size
L29:    %14 = add %12, %13 //i+size
L30:    %15 = icmp slt %14, 200 //i+size<200
L31:    br %15, ifTrue %16, ifFalse %19
                          //conditional jump
```

(b) Corresponding LLVM IR.

Fig. 2. Example illustrating propagation challenges from C code to LLVM bitcode

Intermediate Operations. Another problem introduced by LLVM's IR is its three address code nature: Consider the test `i+size < 200` in L9 of Fig. 2(b). It is compiled to two loads (L27, L28) and an addition (L29), followed by the comparison L30, which based on the invariant information will always be true. In order to fold it and set the value of `%15` to `true`, it is necessary to propagate the value-range information on `size` and `i` (therefore on `%12` and `%13`) to the value-range information on `%14`.

Code Transformation. The LLVM IR undergoes transformations along the sequence of passes, and the assertions must be transformed accordingly. Consider, the transformation of `L1` from Fig. 1(b) to Fig. 1(c), where the test $(i \geq 1) \wedge (i \leq 10)$ is replaced by the assignment `tmp1=` $i - 1$ followed by the test `tmp1` $<_u$ 10. This entails computing the bounds on `tmp1` and verifying the correct use of $<_u$. Other passes, such as `mem2reg`, which promotes memory to registers, may make even more drastic changes such as removing `load` and `store` operations or introducing ϕ functions.

4.3 System Architecture

The architecture of our system is depicted in Figure 3. The input to the system is a C source program and a set of invariants generated for that program by verification tools. The C source code is annotated with the invariants and the annotated source code is compiled by the front end into LLVM IR. Before being passed to the standard LLVM backend, the IR program is processed by two LLVM passes that we wrote: *Annotation Mapping* and *Annotation Propagation.* The former binds the assertions contained in the annotations to the SSA versions of the source code variables, while the latter combines the assertions and propagates them to the intermediate operations that use those variables. These two passes are run before any other pass, in order to operate on the IR program version produced by the front end' s code generation step.

We assume that every optimization pass generates a witness of its correctness (see [14]), and, with the assertions produced by the external static analysis tools, the witnesses are propagated to the passes that can utilize them. The experiments described in this paper use per-variable value range assertions, hence the assertions propagated are conjunctions of equalities (as described in Sec. 3) and are easy to implement, without the need for explicit logical manipulation, as explained in Sec. 3.

The value range invariants are currently used in three optimizations, namely *array bounds check* insertion, *integer overflow check removal,* and *instruction combination.* The first is a set of passes that insert run time checks for every array reference in a program to detect out of bounds accesses. The second is an optimization pass that we wrote to safely remove run time checks inserted by LLVM when it is invoked with the bounds-checking option. The third is a modified *instruction combination* pass that operates on comparison simplifications. We describe each component of our system in more detail next.

CIL-based rewriter. Our approach uses a subset of ACSL to express assertions, which are supplied to the framework through an input file (see Figure 1). ACSL allows for a wide variety of first order global and statement assertions. For instance, this includes value-range assertions about variables and ghost variables in each program location of the type $a \geq 0 \ \wedge \ a \leq 10$ and $a = 10$.

One of our goals is to support a wide variety of program analysis tools as sources for assertions. A clean, compiler-independent way to do this is by storing the assertions in 'dummy' string variables before the corresponding instructions

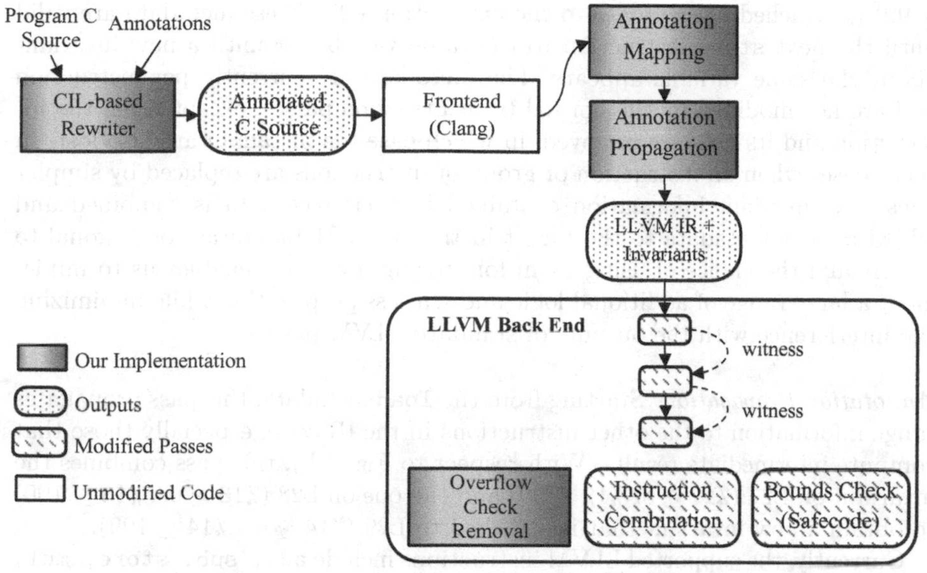

Fig. 3. System Architecture

in the source code. These variables are specially named so that they do not interfere with the existing program variables. As the assertions are encoded as assignments to special variables, these assertions are propagated to the LLVM IR. To do this, we implemented a rewriter based on CIL [16] to inject assertion strings into C source files. The result of this rewriting is shown in Listing 1.2, where statement 1 is the injected one.

Listing 1.1. C Source

```
1 int* a=malloc(X*Y
2          *sizeof(int));
3 *(a+X+Y-1)= Z;
4 m= max(a, X*Y);
```

Listing 1.2. Annotated Code

```
1 char *acsl_b_1="X==2 && Y==4";
2 int* a=malloc(X*Y*sizeof(int));
3 *(a+X+Y-1)= Z;
4 m= max(a, X*Y);
```

Annotation Mapping. The goal of the *Annotation Mapping* pass is to bind every invariant written in terms of source variables to the correct SSA variable versions in the IR code. These variables are typically created by LLVM `load` instructions before being used. To achieve its goal, the *Annotation Mapping* pass consults the debugging information, which contains mappings between `load` instructions and source code variables as well as information about the source scope of the original variable. The scope information is used to disambiguate between the SSA versions of the same-named source code variables.

Our pass binds invariants to `load` instructions by attaching to them LLVM metadata containing the upper and lower bound of the range of the corresponding variable. For instance, with respect to Fig. 2(b), the invariant $(\%12 \geq 0 \wedge \%12$

≤ 99) is attached as metadata to the instruction L27. These metadata are valid until the next `store` instruction to the same variable or until a new invariant about the same variable appears. The metadata are currently per-instruction and are not modified by the normal transformation passes, except when the instruction and its uses are removed, in which case the metadata are also lost. In those cases when an instruction or group of instructions are replaced by simpler ones, the invariant information contained in their metadata is combined and added as new metadata to the target instructions. Metadata are orthogonal to the IR and the choice of using them for storing invariants enables us to implement a large range of additional logic and witness propagation while minimizing the interference with the outputs of standard LLVM passes.

Annotation Propagation. Starting from the `load` metadata, this pass propagates range information to the other instructions in the IR code, especially those that compute intermediate results. With respect to Fig. 2(b), this pass combines the invariant on L27 ($\%12 \geq 0 \wedge \%12 \leq 99$) and the one on L28 ($\%13 \geq 0 \wedge \%13 \leq 100$) to obtain a new invariant that is attached to L29 ($\%14 \geq 0 \wedge \%14 \leq 199$).

Currently, the supported LLVM instructions include `add`, `sub`, `store`, `mul`, `sdiv`, `udiv`, `sext`, `zext`, and `getelementptr`.[3] The binary arithmetic instructions are supported via an LLVM class, `ConstantRange`, which is used to represent constant ranges and provides the capability to perform such arithmetic operations on ranges. The `sext` and `zext` operations on ranges yield the same range. For the `getelementptr` operation, which takes in input an array reference and an index and returns a pointer to the corresponding array element, we use two types of metadata, one contains the index range and the other contains the size of the array, if known at compile time. This latter type of metadata is widely used in the bounds check elimination pass.

4.4 Optimizations

Bounds Check Removal (Safecode). Safecode [7] is a tool composed as a sequence of passes, which insert calls to run time bounds checking procedures before every array access in the LLVM IR. While ensuring safety of memory accesses, however, it introduces substantial overhead at run time. More specifically, these functions are inserted before every `getelementptr` instruction and `store` or `load` instruction that makes use of the value returned by `getelementptr`. For instance, consider Fig. 4, which contains the rest of the LLVM IR code that follows Fig. 2(b) and which contains an array access. In this code, a function call (L38) is inserted after the `getelementptr` instruction (L37) and before the `store` instruction (L39). In addition to bounds checking, these functions perform several pointer arithmetic operations increasing the program's execution costs.

If, however, at compile time, it can be proved that an array access will never be out of bounds during execution, then the bounds checks on that access can be removed. To do so, in our implementation, we modify the Safecode passes

[3] `http://llvm.org/docs/LangRef.html`

to consult the two types of metadata (related to the index range and to the array size) for the getelementptr instructions. If, using this information, it is determined that out of bounds access is not possible, then the calls to the bounds checking functions are removed.

```
L32:  BB:16
L33:    %17 = load %i1
L34:    %18 = call @setVal(%17) //setVal(i)
L35:    %19 = load %j
L36:    %20 = sext %19 to i64
L37:    %21 = getelementptr %array, %20 //Arr[j]
L38:    %el = call @checkGEP(%array, %21, 200)
L39:    call @checkStore(%array, %el, 200)
L40:    store i32 %18, i32* %21 //Arr[j] <- setVal(i)
L41:    br BB %19
L42:  BB:19
L43:    ...//j++
L44:    br %5
```

Fig. 4. An Example (continued)

Integer Overflow Check Removal. Another use of the range information is to remove unnecessary integer overflow checks inserted by some of the -fsanitize family of Clang options. As shown in Fig. 5, these options transform every operation that may result in overflow into a procedure call (L3), which performs the operation and sets an overflow flag. If overflow occurs, the control flow jumps to an error handling procedure (basic block handle_overflow), otherwise execution proceeds normally (basic block cont).

```
L1:    %12 = load %i1
L2:    %13 = load %size
L3:    %14 = call @llvm.sadd.with.overflow(%12, %13)
L4:    %15 = extract overflow flag
L5:    br %15, ifTrue %cont, ifFalse %handle_overflow
L6   handle_overflow:
L7:    call usban_handle_overflow()
L8:    br %cont
L9:  cont:
L10    ...
```

Fig. 5. Integer Overflow Detection Example

The key intuition here is that if range information is available at compile time for the operands, then the possibility of overflow may be checked at compile time and unnecessary checks will be removed. In fact, each check transforms simple (and frequent) operations like additions into procedure calls and comparisons, incurring in high performance costs. Our pass, which at compile time is run after the `-fsanitize` passes, checks the possible value range of the result and removes the integer overflow procedure calls if it determines that overflow is not possible.

Instruction Combination. Instruction combination is a powerful transformation pass in LLVM, which simplifies instructions based on algebraic properties. One instruction on which the pass operates is the *integer comparison* instruction (`icmp`), which performs comparisons between integers. The result of this instruction is placed in a boolean variable, which is usually consulted by branching instructions to issue jumps to the true or false target basic blocks.

The use of range information in this case is fairly straightforward once it is available to the pass. In particular, if the ranges of the two variables being compared at run time are known at compile time and disjoint, then the comparison result is folded to either true or false. With respect to Fig. 2(b), using the range information on the variable `%14`, the comparison is folded and L31 is transformed into (`br TRUE, ifTrue %16, ifFalse %19`). Next, the standard jump-threading pass replaces L31 with an unconditional jump (`br %16`), while the dead code elimination pass removes L30 and L29, which are not used anymore.

5 Evaluation

In this section, we present our experimental results on above mentioned optimization passes in LLVM using our framework. We use a set of small to medium size benchmarks that are listed in Table 1.

Table 1. Benchmarks with brief description and size information

Benchmark	Brief description	LoC	Frama-C (ms)
Susan[7]	Low Level Image Processing	1463	528
NEC Matrix[8]	Matrix operations	113	2
CoreMark[9]	CPU performance with list and matrix operations	1831	251
Linpack[10]	Floating point computing power	579	11044
Dijkstra[7]	Network routing	141	6
Mxm[10]	Matrix-matrix multiplication problem A = B * C	373	9

[7] `http://www.eecs.umich.edu/mibench/source.html`
[8] Part of the NEC Lab benchmarks for F-soft [11]
[9] `http://www.eembc.org/coremark/download_coremark.php`
[10] `http://people.sc.fsu.edu/j̃burkardt/c_src/linpack_bench/linpack_bench.html`

Experimental Methodology. As mentioned earlier, we use the Frama-C tool [5] as our input source for assertions for the benchmarks. Frama-C is based on abstract interpretation and it can be configured with different options that control its running time and accuracy. The running times of Frama-C on the benchmark files, with its default options, are displayed in Table 1. For the Linpack benchmark instead, Frama-C was configured to unroll loops 1000 times. In particular, we extract the value range information from Frama-C's internal state, and its translation to ACSL format. To this end, we have implemented a Frama-C plug-in, which visits the program's AST tree and the value analysis plug-in's state, and writes the value ranges available at each program point in a separate annotation file. Using these assertions, the CIL-based rewriter transforms the C source file by injecting these assertions at the corresponding program locations as described in Section 4.3. After the rewriting step, the annotated sources are passed through the Clang front end of the LLVM compiler.

In our experiments, we report on the optimizations to the benchmarks. Our comparisons are made by running the benchmarks under the unmodified LLVM that does not include our optimizations. We report both the percentage of checks that are removed using our framework (a *static* measure of improvements), and also the percentage savings in running time (a *runtime* measure of improvements). Our runtime tests were performed on a GNU-Linux machine running the Ubuntu distribution 12.04, with Intel Xeon CPU at 2.40GHz.

5.1 Array Bound-Check Optimization

Fig. 6 shows our check elimination and runtime improvement results over the benchmarks. Each benchmark is presented in two bars for check elimination and runtime improvement percentage. The check elimination improvements are observed by counting the number of checks on original code and comparing them with the results on optimized code.

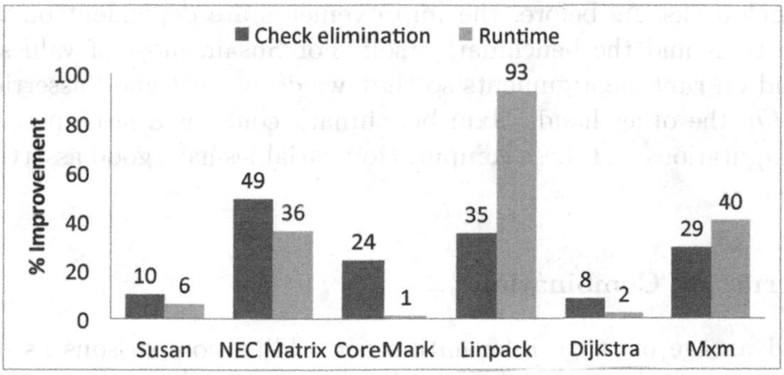

Fig. 6. Percentage check elimination and Runtime Improvement of Boundcheck (Safecode) optimization

As illustrated by Fig. 6, there is a wide variety in our improvement results. This variety is due to several factors. Some of these include the following: (a) Frama-C is not able to produce assertions for every array access as it is not possible to determine the size of those arrays at compile time, or (b) because our prototype does not support certain types of array accesses yet. In particular, we noticed that in some benchmarks, it is not possible for Frama-C to determine the size of the arrays in the case these array initializations depend on some runtime arguments. In these cases, the improvement results are not significant. For example, among the benchmarks, Dijkstra (a network routing algorithm) only obtains 8% of bound check elimination since its computations heavily depend on runtime arguments which are based on the input data. In contrast, with a good quality of assertions, our approach obtains very appealing improvements. For instance, NEC Matrix gains the best improvement of 49% in our experiments. This is due to fact that the benchmark has many array accesses, and most of which have good assertions from Frama-C. In addition, the runtime improvements depend on the location of the eliminated checks. If they are located in portions of code that are not executed very often (e.g., initialization code in CoreMark), then the runtime improvement is not significant. If, however, they are located in a portion of the code that is executed often (e.g., Linpack) the improvements can be significantly better. It is worth noting that our optimizations are done based on Frama-C's sound analysis, and therefore carry the same guarantees of the safety of array accesses under LLVM's Safecode bounds checking.

5.2 Integer Overflow Check

The chart in Fig. 7 illustrates the improvement on the integer overflow check elimination by our framework. Similar to the previous experiment, here too we report on both check elimination and runtime improvements for the benchmarks. The checks are inserted for the LLVM IR's operations of multiplication (`mul`), addition (`add`), and subtraction (`sub`). As shown in the figure, the improvement ranges from 7% (Susan) to 60% (Mxm) of checking code of integer overflow on the benchmarks. As before, the improvements are dependent on the quality of assertions and the benchmark itself. For Susan, most of values of variable depend on runtime arguments so that we do not get good assertions from Frama-C. On the other hand, Mxm benchmark contains a large percentage of integer computations and these computation variables have good assertions from Frama-C.

5.3 Instruction Combination

To take advantage of range information for folding comparisons as described in our examples, we have modified the Instruction Combination pass in LLVM (`-instcombine`). We have tested our implementation with a number of small examples and our implementation is able to perform the optimization successfully. In our experiments with the above benchmarks, the opportunities for applying

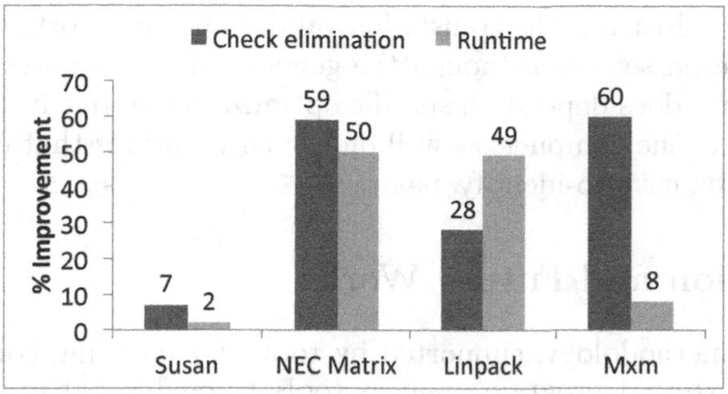

Fig. 7. Percentage check elimination and runtime improvement of Integer Overflow Check Optimization

these optimization does not arise. This is due to the fact that, in these benchmarks, Frama-C does not produce assertions for branch expressions that lead the branch condition to be evaluated to either true or false at compile time. We have noticed that larger benchmarks such as bind and gcc and oggenc provide opportunities for such optimization, but Frama-C does not successfully compile these benchmarks out of the box. We have been working with the Frama-C development team to get assertions on these larger benchmarks.

6 Related Work

To the best of our knowledge, our work is the first that uses analysis information derived by third party tools, which are not as restricted as production compilers, to improve compiler optimizations. The key issue is that of invariant propagation. Our implementation results show that, for the common case of single-variable invariants, we can carry out this propagation quite simply, which results in substantial improvements to compiler optimizations. Propagation lets a compiler use the results of sophisticated program analyses without incurring the cost of the analysis during compilation. We strongly believe that this is a promising approach that will has much potential for improvements.

There are several tools and compiler extensions which combine sophisticated analysis with code transformation. Examples are Klee [4] (for symbolic execution), Polly [9] (for polyhedral optimization), CCured [15] (for bounds checking) and IOC (Integer Overflow Checker) [8]. The key new element introduced by our work is in loosening the coupling between analysis and optimization, i.e., providing a mechanism for introducing the results of *any* sound program analysis into a standard compiler (or, more generally, a program transformation), without requiring that the analysis be built into the compiler.

The idea of propagating assertions through a witness mechanism was first introduced in [14]. Witness generation is itself a variant of the translation validation framework introduced in [17] and developed by several researchers (cf. the citations in [14]). Just like the translation validation framework, it does not depend on specific passes (even though the generation of witnesses, on which we do not focus here, does depend on specific optimizations), but it depends on the ability to "tweak" the compiler, as well on the assumptions that each optimization is a separate, easy-to-identify, pass.

7 Conclusion and Future Work

We describe a methodology, supported by tools, for enabling compilers to use the results of external program analysis tools to enable better optimizations. The assertions produced by the external tools are propagated, through the witness approach, through the LLVM optimizations passes. We demonstrate the methodology by improving three LLVM optimizations using the Frama-C value analysis plugin. We are currently expanding our approach to encompass other static analyses as well as targeting other LLVM passes, such as scalar evolution and loop optimizations.

Acknowledgements. We thank Drew Dean for pointing us to this topic in the context of the DARPA CSFV project. Thanks are due to Ted Ballou and Anokh Kishore for their help with the experiments. We also thank Jens Palsberg for many useful comments on this work. Phu Phung is supported by the Swedish Research Council (VR) under an International Postdoc grant. This material is based on research sponsored by DARPA under agreement number FA8750-12-C-0166. The U.S. Government is authorized to reproduce and distribute reprints for Governmental purposes notwithstanding any copyright notation thereon. The views and conclusions contained herein are those of the authors and should not be interpreted as necessarily representing the official policies or endorsements, either expressed or implied, of DARPA or the U.S. Government.

References

1. Aiken, A., Bugrara, S., Dillig, I., Dillig, T., Hackett, B., Hawkins, P.: An overview of the Saturn project. In: 7th ACM SIGPLAN-SIGSOFT Workshop on Program Analysis for Software Tools and Engineering (PASTE), pp. 43–48 (2007)
2. Albarghouthi, A., Gurfinkel, A., Li, Y., Chaki, S., Chechik, M.: UFO: Verification with interpolants and abstract interpretation. In: Piterman, N., Smolka, S.A. (eds.) TACAS 2013 (ETAPS 2013). LNCS, vol. 7795, pp. 637–640. Springer, Heidelberg (2013)
3. Bonichon, R., Cuoq, P.: A mergeable interval map. Studia Informatica Universalis 9(1), 5–37 (2011)
4. Cadar, C., Dunbar, D., Engler, D.: KLEE: Unassisted and automatic generation of high-coverage tests for complex systems programs. In: 8th USENIX Conference on Operating Systems Design and Implementation, OSDI 2008, pp. 209–224. USENIX Association (2008)
5. Cuoq, P., Kirchner, F., Kosmatov, N., Prevosto, V., Signoles, J., Yakobowski, B.: Frama-C, A software analysis perspective. In: Eleftherakis, G., Hinchey, M., Holcombe, M. (eds.) SEFM 2012. LNCS, vol. 7504, pp. 233–247. Springer, Heidelberg (2012)

6. Delahaye, M., Kosmatov, N., Signoles, J.: Common specification language for static and dynamic analysis of C programs. In: 28th Annual ACM Symposium on Applied Computing, SAC, pp. 1230–1235 (2013)
7. Dhurjati, D., Adve, V.: Backwards-Compatible Array Bounds Checking for C with Very Low Overhead. Technical report, Shanghai, China (May 2006)
8. Dietz, W., Li, P., Regehr, J., Adve, V.: Understanding integer overflow in C/C++. In: 34th International Conference on Software Engineering, ICSE 2012, pp. 760–770. IEEE Press (2012)
9. Grosser, T., Größlinger, A., Lengauer, C.: Polly – performing polyhedral optimizations on a low-level intermediate representation. Parallel Processing Letters 22(4) (2012)
10. Henzinger, T.A., Jhala, R., Majumdar, R., Sutre, G.: Lazy abstraction. In: POPL, pp. 58–70 (2002)
11. Ivančić, F., Yang, Z., Ganai, M.K., Gupta, A., Shlyakhter, I., Ashar, P.: F-SOFT: Software Verification Platform. In: Etessami, K., Rajamani, S.K. (eds.) CAV 2005. LNCS, vol. 3576, pp. 301–306. Springer, Heidelberg (2005)
12. Lattner, C., Adve, V.S.: LLVM: A compilation framework for lifelong program analysis & transformation. In: CGO, pp. 75–88 (2004), `llvm.org`
13. Leino, K.R.M.: Extended Static Checking: A ten-year perspective. In: Informatics – 10 Years Back. 10 Years Ahead, pp. 157–175 (2001)
14. Namjoshi, K.S., Zuck, L.D.: Witnessing program transformations. In: Logozzo, F., Fähndrich, M. (eds.) SAS 2013. LNCS, vol. 7935, pp. 304–323. Springer, Heidelberg (2013)
15. Necula, G.C., Condit, J., Harren, M., McPeak, S., Weimer, W.: CCured: Type-safe retrofitting of legacy software. ACM Trans. Program. Lang. Syst. 27(3), 477–526 (2005)
16. Necula, G.C., McPeak, S., Rahul, S.P., Weimer, W.: CIL: Intermediate language and tools for analysis and transformation of C programs. In: Nigel Horspool, R. (ed.) CC 2002. LNCS, vol. 2304, pp. 213–228. Springer, Heidelberg (2002)
17. Pnueli, A., Strichman, O., Siegel, M.: Translation validation: From DC+ to c*. In: Hutter, D., Traverso, P. (eds.) FM-Trends 1998. LNCS, vol. 1641, pp. 137–150. Springer, Heidelberg (1999)
18. Teitelbaum, T.: Codesurfer. ACM SIGSOFT Software Engineering Notes 25(1) (2000)

Foundations of Quantitative Predicate Abstraction for Stability Analysis of Hybrid Systems

Pavithra Prabhakar and Miriam García Soto

IMDEA Software Institute, Madrid, Spain
{pavithra.prabhakar,miriam.garcia}@imdea.org

Abstract. We investigate the formal connections between "quantitative predicate abstractions" for stability analysis of hybrid systems and "continuous simulation relations". It has been shown recently that stability is not bisimulation invariant, and hence, stronger notions which extend the classical simulation and bisimulation relations with continuity constraints have been proposed, which force preservation of stability. In another direction, a quantitative version of classical predicate abstraction has been proposed for approximation based stability analysis of certain classes of hybrid systems. In this paper, first, we present a general framework for quantitative predicate abstraction for stability analysis. We then show that this technique can be interpreted as constructing a one dimensional system which continuously simulates the original system. This induces an ordering on the class of abstract systems and hence, formalizes the notion of refinement.

Keywords: Stability Analysis, Simulations/Bisimulations, Hybrid Systems, Abstraction-Refinement.

1 Introduction

Hybrid systems refer to systems which consist of mixed discrete continuous behaviors. They manifest in embedded control systems, which typically consist of one or more embedded processors controlling physical entities. Stability is a fundamental property in control system design. Intuitively, stability captures the notion that small perturbations to the initial state or input to a system result in only small variations in the behavior of the system. In this paper, we investigate the formal foundations for an abstraction based analysis approach for stability analysis of hybrid systems.

The classical approach to stability analysis in control theory is based on Lyapunov functions (see, for instance, [10]). Here, stability of a continuous dynamical system is established by exhibiting a Lyapunov function - a continuously differentiable function on the state-space such that its value is zero at the equilibrium point and positive everywhere else, and the value of the function decreases along any execution of the system. A Lyapunov function is analogous to the ranking function for proving termination of discrete programs [5]. The approach has

D. D'Souza et al. (Eds.): VMCAI 2015, LNCS 8931, pp. 318–335, 2015.

been extended to hybrid systems in the form of common and multiple Lyapunov functions [21,6,11]. Automated analysis involves starting with a template which serves as a candidate Lyapunov function, and then using constraint/optimization solvers to deduce the unknown parameters of the template. For instance, for a polynomial template with coefficients as parameters, the requirements of Lyapunov function can be encoded as a sum-of-squares programming problem, which can be efficiently solved using tools such as SOSTOOLS [16,15,14]. One of the major limiting factors of this approach is the ingenuity required in providing the right templates; and automatically learning the templates is a challenge which has not been adequately addressed (except for some recent work [9]). Moreover, if a template fails to satisfy the conditions of Lyapunov function, then it typically does not provide insights into the potential reasons for instability or towards the choice of better templates for succeeding iterations.

To overcome some of the limitations of template based search, an alternate approach based on abstractions has been investigated [19,20]. However, the development of such an approach is not straightforward. Simulations and bisimulations [13] are the foundational basis for abstraction and minimization based analysis. Recent results [17,18] show that stability is not bisimulation invariant, and a simulation relation between two systems does not suffice to preserve stability. A stronger notion that extends stability with continuity constraints is proposed and shown to preserve stability. These negative results suggest that traditional abstraction techniques will need to be modified for stability analysis.

In [19,20], a quantitative version of predicate abstraction was proposed for stability analysis. Recall that predicate abstraction [7] constructs a finite graph which simulates a given system. The finite graph is obtained by partitioning the state-space of the system into a finite number of regions using a finite set of predicates. The regions correspond to the nodes of the graph and an edge between two nodes indicates the possibility of an execution starting from the region corresponding to the source of the edge to the region corresponding to its target. Predicate abstraction has been widely applied for safety verification in the context of both discrete and hybrid systems [4,2,3,22]. However, the finite graph does not provide useful information towards deciding the stability of the system. Hence, in [19,20], a modified abstraction procedure is proposed, which annotates the finite graph with quantitative information for the purpose of stability analysis. The edges of the graph are annotated with a weight which captures the ratio of the distance to the origin of final state to that of the initial state, of the executions corresponding to the edge. Then stability is inferred by analyzing certain structural properties about the graph, such as, the absence of cycles with the product of weights on its edges greater than 1.

In this paper, we investigate the formal foundations for the quantitative predicate abstraction proposed in [19,20]. First, we present a general framework for quantitative predicate abstraction and identify conditions on the hybrid system and the predicates for which the approach is sound. Next, we establish a formal connection between the abstract weighted graph and the concrete hybrid system using the notion of continuous simulations. For this, we interpret a weighted graph as representing a one-dimensional hybrid system whose executions follow the edges in the graph and satisfy the weight constraints on them. We show that the one-dimensional hybrid system representing the weighted graph "continuously simulates" the concrete hybrid system from which the graph is constructed. This establishes a partial ordering on the abstract weighted graphs, and formalizes the notion of refinement.

2 Preliminaries

Sets of numbers. Let $\mathbb{R}$, $\mathbb{R}_{\geq 0}$ and $\mathbb{N}$ denote the set of real numbers, non-negative real numbers and natural numbers, respectively. We use $[n]$ to denote the set $\{0, \cdots, n\}$. We use a superscript ∞ to indicate that ∞ is included in the set. For example, $\mathbb{R}^{\infty}_{\geq 0}$ denotes the set $\mathbb{R}_{\geq 0} \cup \{\infty\}$. Given a subset $I \subseteq \mathbb{R}$, *last*(I) denotes the least upper bound of I in $\mathbb{R}^{\infty}$.

Euclidean space $\mathbb{R}^n$. Given $x \in \mathbb{R}^n$, let $(x)_i$ denote the i-th component of x. Let $\|x\|$ denote the Euclidean norm of x, that is, $[\sum_i (x)_i^2]^{1/2}$. Given $\epsilon \geq 0$ and $x \in \mathbb{R}^n$, $\mathcal{B}_\epsilon(x)$ denotes the open ball of radius ϵ around x, that is, $\mathcal{B}_\epsilon(x) = \{y \mid \|x-y\| < \epsilon\}$. Given a finite set Q, we extend the metric on $\mathbb{R}^n$ to an extended pseudo-metric on $Q \times \mathbb{R}^n$ as follows: The distance between $(q_1, x_2), (q_2, x_2) \in Q \times \mathbb{R}^n$, denoted $\|(q_1, x_1) - (q_2, x_2)\|$, is given by, $\|x_1 - x_2\|$. Further, $\|(q, x)\| = \|x\|$ will denote the norm of (q, x).

Functions. Let $dom(f)$ denote the domain of a function f. Given $A, B \subseteq \mathbb{R}^n$. Given a function $f : A \to B$, and a set $A' \subseteq A$, we use $f(A')$ to denote the set $\{b \mid \exists a \in A', f(a) = b\}$. For an element $b \in B$, the inverse of f at b, denoted $f^{-1}(b)$, is the set $\{a \in A : f(a) = b\}$. Given a function $f : A \to B$, where A is equipped with a total ordering with a least element 0 and a difference operator ($a - b$ when $a > b$), we define f_t and f^t to be the function f restricted to the domain up to t and to the domain starting from t. More precisely, f_t is the function with domain $\{t' \in A \mid t' \leq t\}$ and $f_t(t') = f(t)$ for all $t' \in dom(f_t)$. Similarly, f^t is the function with domain $\{t' \geq 0 \mid \exists t'' \in A, t'' \geq t, t'' - t = t'\}$ and $f^t(t') = f(t'')$, where $t'' - t' = t$, for all $t' \in dom(f^t)$.

Set-valued function. A *set-valued function* $R : A \rightsquigarrow B$ is a function which maps every element of A to a set of elements in B. Given $A' \subseteq A$, $R(A') = \cup_{a \in A'} R(a)$. Every relation $R \subseteq A \times B$ can be interpreted as a set-valued function from A to B, where for any $a \in A$, $R(a) = \{b \mid (a, b) \in R\}$. We interchangeably use R to represent both the relation and the set-valued function it represents. The inverse of R, denoted R^{-1}, is the set $\{(b, a) \mid (a, b) \in R\}$.

A set-valued function $R : A \rightsquigarrow B$ is said to be *continuous* at a point $a \in A$ if

$$\forall \epsilon > 0, \exists \delta > 0 \text{ such that } R(\mathcal{B}_\delta(a)) \subseteq \mathcal{B}_\epsilon(R(a)).$$

Sequences. A sequence over a set A is a function $S : D \to A$, where $D = [n]$ for some n, or $D = \mathbb{N}$. The size of the sequence S, denoted $|S|$, is n if $D = [n]$, in which case S is said to be a finite sequence, and ∞, otherwise. We also represent S by enumerating its elements as in $S(0), S(1), \ldots$.

Graphs. A *graph* G is a triple (V, L, E), where V is a finite set of vertices, L a finite set of labels and $E \subseteq V \times L \times V$ is a finite set of edges. A *path* of a graph is a finite or infinite sequence of vertices and edges $\pi = v_0 e_0 v_1 e_1 \ldots$. A *cycle* is a finite path where the first and the last vertices are the same; and it is *simple* if all the vertices except the last are distinct.

A weighted function is an extension of a graph with a weighting function on the edges. A *weighted graph* $G = (V, L, E, W)$ where (V, L, E) is a graph and $W : E \to \mathbb{R}^{\infty}_{\geq 0}$ is a weighting function. The weight of a finite path π is the product of the weights on the edges. Hence, given $\pi = v_0 e_0 v_1 e_1 \ldots e_n v_n$, $W(\pi) = \Pi_{i=0}^{n} W(e_i)$. The maximum weight value of the graph, denoted $MW(G)$, is $\max_{e \in E} W(e)$.

Linear expressions, homogeneity. A *linear expression* is an expression of the form $a \cdot x + b$, where $a \in \mathbb{R}^n$, x is a tuple of n-variables and $b \in \mathbb{R}$; and it is called *homogeneous* if b is the zero vector. Given a linear expression $\eta := a \cdot x + b$, it defines a function $[\![\eta]\!] : \mathbb{R}^n \to \mathbb{R}$ where given a valuation $v \in \mathbb{R}^n$, $[\![\eta]\!]$ maps it to the value $a \cdot v + b$. A *linear constraint or predicate* c is given by $\eta \sim 0$, where η is a linear expression and $\sim$ is a relational operator in $\{<, \leqslant, =\}$. Let $[\![c]\!]$ denote the set of all $v \in \mathbb{R}^n$ such that $[\![\eta]\!](v) \sim 0$, where c is given by $\eta \sim 0$. Given a set of linear constraints C, it defines the set $P = \cap_{c \in C} [\![c]\!]$ denoted $[\![C]\!]$. A *convex polyhedral* set is a set defined by a finite set of linear constraints C.

Polyhedral partition. A partition $\mathcal{P}$ of $\mathbb{R}^n$ into convex polyhedral sets is a finite set of convex polyhedral sets $\{P_1, \ldots, P_k\}$ such that $\cup_{i=1}^{k} P_i = \mathbb{R}^n$ and for each $i \neq j$, $P_i \cap P_j = \emptyset$.

3 Hybrid Systems

In this section, we present a semantic model for hybrid systems. We then define a concrete class of hybrid system, namely, piecewise linear dynamical systems, which we use in the sequel to illustrate the theoretical concepts.

3.1 A Semantic Definition of Hybrid Systems

Hybrid systems are systems exhibiting mixed discrete and continuous behaviors. We present a semantic model of a hybrid system as consisting of discrete transitions and continuous trajectories. For a concrete specification formalism, see the hybrid automaton model [1,8]. Let us fix a finite set Q and a set $X = \mathbb{R}^n$, for some n. Given an element $(q, x) \in Q \times X$, $[q, x]_D = q$ and $[q, x]_C = x$.

Trajectories. A *trajectory* over (Q, X) is a function $\tau : I \to Q \times X$, where I is either $[0, T]$ for some $T \in \mathbb{R}_{\geq 0}$ or $[0, \infty)$, such that $[\tau]_D$ is finitely varying ($[\tau]_D$ restricted up to time t has finite number of discontinuities for any $t \in [0, T]$) and $[\tau]_C$ is a continuous function. We denote the set of all trajectories over (Q, X) by *Traj*(Q, X).

The last time of a trajectory τ, $ltime(\tau)$, is $last(dom(\tau))$. The first state of the trajectory τ, denote $fstate(\tau)$, is $\tau(0)$, and if $ltime(\tau) < \infty$, then the last state of τ, denoted $lstate(\tau)$, is $\tau(ltime(\tau))$. The set of states of τ, denoted $States(\tau)$, is the set $\{\tau(t) \mid t \in dom(\tau)\}$. Given a time $t \in dom(\tau)$, the prefix of τ up to time t is the trajectory τ_t and the suffix of τ from time t is τ^t.

Transitions. A *transition* over a pair (Q, X) is a pair $\iota = ((q_1, x_1), (q_2, x_2)) \in (Q\times X)\times(Q\times X)$. We denote the set of all transitions over (Q, X) by $Trans(Q, X)$. For a transition $\iota = ((q_1, x_1), (q_2, x_2))$, $ltime(\iota) = 0$, $fstate(\iota) = (q_1, x_1)$, $lstate(\iota) = (q_2, x_2)$ and $States(\iota) = \{(q_1, x_1), (q_2, x_2)\}$.

Hybrid system definition. A *hybrid system* $\mathcal{H}$ is a tuple (Q, X, Σ, Δ), where:

- Q is a finite set of control locations;
- $X = \mathbb{R}^n$, for some n, is the continuous state-space;
- $\Sigma \subseteq Trans(Q, X)$ is a set of transitions; and
- $\Delta \subseteq Traj(Q, X)$ is a set of trajectories.

The dimension of $\mathcal{H}$ is n and the state-space, $States(\mathcal{H})$, is $Q \times X$.

Executions. An execution of a hybrid system is a finite or infinite sequence of transitions and trajectories. An *execution* of a hybrid system $\mathcal{H}$ is a sequence $\sigma : D \to \Sigma \cup \Delta$, such that for all $0 \leqslant i < |\sigma|$, $lstate(\sigma(i)) = fstate(\sigma(i+1))$, and if σ is an infinite sequence then $\sum_{i:\sigma(i)\in\Delta} last(dom(\sigma(i))) = \infty$. Let $Exec(\mathcal{H})$ denote the set of all executions of $\mathcal{H}$.

Let $fstate(\sigma) = fstate(\sigma(0))$ and if $|\sigma| < \infty$ and $last(\sigma(|\sigma|)) < \infty$, then $lstate(\sigma) = lstate(\sigma(|\sigma|))$. Let $States(\sigma) = \cup_{i\in dom(\sigma)} States(\sigma(i))$.

Hybrid time domain. We define a hybrid time domain for an execution, so that we can interpret the execution as a function from this domain to the states of the hybrid system. Given an execution $\sigma : D \to \Sigma \cup \Delta$, the hybrid time domain of σ, denoted $htd(\sigma)$, is the set $\{(i, 0) \mid i \in dom(\sigma), \sigma(i) \in \Sigma\} \cup \{(i, t) \mid i \in dom(\sigma), \sigma(i) \in \Delta, t \in dom(\sigma(i))\}$. The execution σ can be represented as a function f_σ from $htd(\sigma)$ to $States(\mathcal{H})$, where for $(i, t) \in htd(\sigma)$, $f_\sigma(i, t) = fstate(\sigma(i))$ if $\sigma(i) \in \Sigma$, and $\sigma(i)(t)$ otherwise. Note that there is a bijection from the set of executions to the functions they represent. Given two points (i_1, t_1) and (i_2, t_2) in a hybrid time domain, we define an ordering between them as $(i_1, t_1) < (i_1, t_2)$ if $i_1 < i_2$, or $i_1 = i_2$ and $t_1 < t_2$. We then denote by $\sigma_{(i,t)}$ and $\sigma^{(i,t)}$, prefix of σ up to (i, t) and suffix of σ from (i, t), respectively. $\sigma_{(i,t)}$ is given by the function $(f_\sigma)_{(i,t)}$ and $\sigma^{(i,t)}$ is given by the function $(f_\sigma)^{(i,t)}$.

Splitting trajectories and executions. We say that (τ_1, τ_2) is a *splitting* of a *trajectory* τ, denoted $\tau = \tau_1 \circ \tau_2$, if there exists $t \in dom(\tau)$ such that $\tau_1 = \tau_t$ and $\tau_2 = \tau^t$. Similarly, (σ_1, σ_2) is a *splitting* of an *execution* σ, denoted $\sigma = \sigma_1 \circ \sigma_2$, if there exists an $(i, t) \in htd(\sigma)$ such that $\sigma_1 = \sigma_{(i,t)}$ and $\sigma_2 = \sigma^{(i,t)}$. Note that splitting is associative that is $\sigma = (\sigma_1 \circ \sigma_2) \circ \sigma_3$ if and only if $\sigma = \sigma_1 \circ (\sigma_2 \circ \sigma_3)$. Hence, for a splitting of σ or τ into n parts, we do not need to specify the splitting order. Further, we write $\sigma = \sigma_1 \circ \sigma_2 \circ \ldots$ to denote a splitting of σ into infinitely many parts, that is, there exist $\sigma'_1, \sigma'_2, \ldots$, such that $\sigma = \sigma_1 \circ \sigma'_1$ and for $i \geq 1$, $\sigma'_i = \sigma_{i+1} \circ \sigma'_{i+1}$.

3.2 Illustration Using Piecewise Linear Dynamical Systems

Next, we instantiate the semantic model with a concrete class of hybrid systems, namely, piecewise linear dynamical systems. These are systems in which the state-space is partitioned into a finite set of convex polyhedral sets, each of which is associated with a linear dynamical system.

Definition 1. *An n-dimensional* piecewise linear dynamical system *(PLDS) $\mathcal{M}$ is a pair $(\mathcal{P}, F)$, where $\mathcal{P}$ is a finite partition of $\mathbb{R}^n$ into convex polyhedral sets and $F : \mathcal{P} \to \mathbb{R}^{n\times n}$ is a function associating an $n \times n$ matrix with every element of the partition.*

An n-dimensional *PLDS*, $\mathcal{M} = (\mathcal{P}, F)$, is represented as a hybrid system with the tuple (Q, X, Σ, Δ), where

- the control location set Q is equal to the partition $\mathcal{P}$,
- the continuous state-space X is equal to $\mathbb{R}^n$,
- the set of transitions Σ is contained in $\{((P_1, x), (P_2, x)) \in (Q\times X)\times(Q\times X) : P_1 \neq P_2,\ \mathit{Closure}(P_1) \cap \mathit{Closure}(P_2) \neq \emptyset\}$ and
- the set of trajectories Δ includes every $\tau : I \to \mathcal{P} \times \mathbb{R}^n$ such that there exists $P \in \mathcal{P}$ with $[\tau]_D(t) = P$ and $[\dot{\tau}]_C = F(P) \cdot [\tau]_C$ for all $t \in \mathit{dom}(\tau)$.

Example 1. Consider the following linear dynamical systems:

$$\begin{pmatrix}\dot{x}\\ \dot{y}\end{pmatrix} = \begin{pmatrix}0 & 1\\ -0.1 & 0\end{pmatrix}\begin{pmatrix}x\\ y\end{pmatrix} \text{ and } \begin{pmatrix}\dot{x}\\ \dot{y}\end{pmatrix} = \begin{pmatrix}0 & 1\\ -4 & 0\end{pmatrix}\begin{pmatrix}x\\ y\end{pmatrix}$$

where $x = x(t)$ and $y = y(t)$. Let us call the matrices A and B, respectively. The phase portraits for the systems are shown in Figure 1.

Next, we define two piecewise linear dynamical systems $\mathcal{M}_1$ and $\mathcal{M}_2$, where $\mathcal{M}_1$ follows the dynamics associated with B in the positive quadrant and the quadrant diagonally opposite to it, and the dynamics A in the other two quadrants. $\mathcal{M}_2$ follows A in the quadrants in which $\mathcal{M}_1$ follows B, and follows B in the quadrants in which $\mathcal{M}_1$ follows A. A sample of execution for the systems $\mathcal{M}_1$ and $\mathcal{M}_2$ is depicted in Figure 2(a) and 2(b), respectively. Each of the executions consist of four trajectories each of which belongs to a particular location (a quadrant), and discrete transitions which change locations at the boundaries of the quadrants.

4 Lyapunov and Asymptotic Stability

In this section, we define two classical notions of stability in control theory for hybrid systems, namely, Lyapunov and asymptotic stability. We will focus on

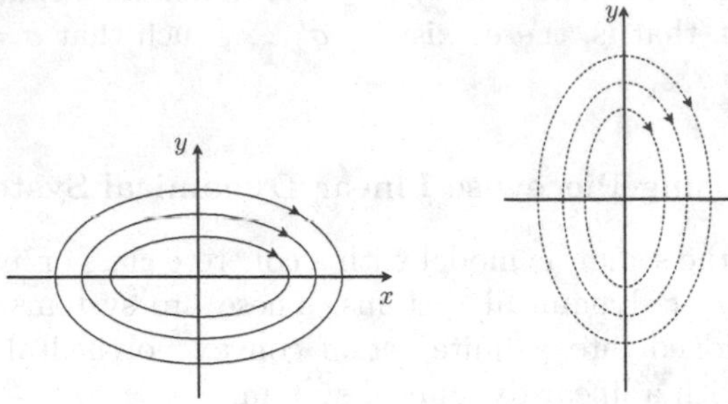

(a) $\dot{x} = Ax$ (b) $\dot{x} = Bx$

Fig. 1. Phase portraits

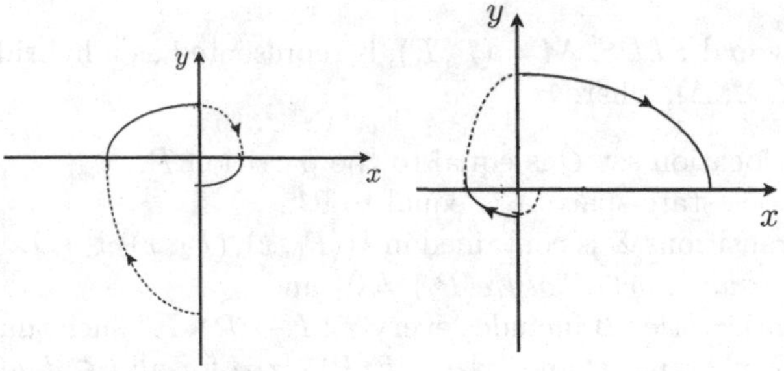

(a) System $\mathcal{M}_1$ (b) System $\mathcal{M}_2$

Fig. 2. Sample executions

stability with respect to an equilibrium point. For simplicity of presentation, we consider the origin in the continuous state-space of the hybrid system to be the equilibrium point. For an n-dimensional hybrid system $\mathcal{H}$, we use $0_{\mathcal{H}}$ to denote the origin $\overline{0} \in \mathbb{R}^n$.

Lyapunov stability captures the notion that small perturbations in the initial state of the system result in only small perturbations of the eventual behaviors.

Definition 2. *A set of executions $S \subseteq Exec(\mathcal{H})$ is said to be* Lyapunov stable *if for every $\epsilon > 0$, there exists a $\delta > 0$ such that for every execution $\sigma \in S$ with $[fstate(\sigma)]_C \in \mathcal{B}_\delta(0_{\mathcal{H}})$, $[States(\sigma)]_C \subseteq \mathcal{B}_\epsilon(0_{\mathcal{H}})$.*

A hybrid system $\mathcal{H}$ is said to be Lyapunov stable, if $Exec(\mathcal{H})$ is Lyapunov stable.

Asymptotic stability requires convergence in addition to Lyapunov stability. An execution σ of $\mathcal{H}$ is said to *converge* to $0_{\mathcal{H}}$, denoted $Conv(\sigma, 0_{\mathcal{H}})$, if for every $\epsilon > 0$, there exists a pair $(i, t) \in htd(\sigma)$ such that $[States(\sigma_{(i,t)})]_C \subseteq \mathcal{B}_\epsilon(0_{\mathcal{H}})$.

Definition 3. *A set of executions* $S \subseteq Exec(\mathcal{H})$ *is said to be* asymptotically stable *if it is Lyapunov stable and there exists a* $\delta > 0$ *such that every* $\sigma \in S$ *with* $[fstate(\sigma)]_C \in \mathcal{B}_\delta(0_\mathcal{H})$, $Conv(\sigma, 0_\mathcal{H})$ *holds.*

A hybrid system $\mathcal{H}$ is said to be asymptotically stable if $Exec(\mathcal{H})$ is asymptotically stable.

In Example 1, the dynamics of the linear systems of Figure 1(a) and 1(b) describe executions moving along an ellipsoid around the origin, the equilibrium point. Both systems are Lyapunov stable, since the executions remain close to the equilibrium point when they start close to the equilibrium point. For *PLDS* $\mathcal{M}_1$ depicted in Figure 2(a), the executions eventually approach the equilibrium point, hence, $\mathcal{M}_1$ is asymptotically stable. On the other hand, the system $\mathcal{M}_2$ exhibits instability, since its executions, represented in Figure 2(b), diverge with respect to the equilibrium point.

5 Quantitative Predicate Abstraction

In this section, we present a quantitative predicate abstraction technique for analyzing stability of hybrid systems, which generalizes the abstraction techniques in [19] and [20] for the class of piecewise constant derivative systems and polyhedral switched systems, respectively. In particular, we identify a condition on the interaction between the hybrid system and the predicates used in the abstraction, which renders the method sound. We illustrate the approach on the class of piecewise linear dynamical systems.

5.1 Weighted Graphs as Quantitative Abstractions

In the context of safety verification, a finite abstraction of a concrete system is constructed from a partition of the state space of the system into a finite number of regions. The nodes in the finite abstraction correspond to the regions and the edges between two nodes capture the existence of an execution in the concrete system starting from a state in the region corresponding to the first node to a state in the region corresponding to the second node. This defines an abstract system, a finite graph, which over-approximates the behaviors of the concrete system, and hence, safety of the abstract system implies the safety of the concrete system.

However, for stability verification, it does not suffice to merely construct a system which over-approximates the behaviors of the concrete system. We need to capture some quantitative information about the evolution of the distance of the states to the origin along an execution. Hence, we annotate the finite graph with weights. More precisely, we interpret the nodes in the abstract graph as regions, an edge in the graph as the existence of a potential execution from one region to other evolving through a third region, and the weights as the scaling in the distance to the origin of the execution as it traverses from the first region to the second one.

We need some auxiliary constructs in the construction of the weighted graph. Let $\mathcal{H} = (Q, X, \Sigma, \Delta)$ be a hybrid system and $P_1, P_2, P \subseteq States(\mathcal{H})$. We define a predicate which represents pairs of states (s_1, s_2) such that there exists a trajectory which enters P through P_1 at s_1, remains in P for sometime and exits P through P_2 at s_2. More precisely,

$$ReachRel^C_{\mathcal{H}}(P_1, P, P_2) := \{(s_1, s_2) \in P_1 \times P_2 \mid \exists \tau \in \Delta : fstate(\tau) = s_1, \\ lstate(\tau) = s_2 \text{ and } \tau(t) \in P \text{ for all } 0 < t < ltime(\tau)\}.$$

Also, we define a predicate containing the pairs of states (s_1, s_2) such that there exists a transition from P_1 to P_2 where s_1 is contained in P_1 and s_2 in P_2, it is

$$ReachRel^D_{\mathcal{H}}(P_1, P_2) := \{(s_1, s_2) \in P_1 \times P_2 \mid \exists \iota = (s_1, s_2) \in \Sigma\}.$$

Definition 4. *A weighted graph $G = (V, V \cup \{\gamma\}, E, W)$ is a* quantitative abstraction *of a hybrid system $\mathcal{H}$ with respect to an abstraction function α : $States(\mathcal{H}) \rightarrow V$ if the following hold. Given $v_1, v_2 \in V$, define*

$$Z^C(v_1, v, v_2) = ReachRel^C_{\mathcal{H}}(\alpha^{-1}(v_1), \alpha^{-1}(v), \alpha^{-1}(v_2)).$$

$$Z^D(v_1, v_2) = ReachRel^D_{\mathcal{H}}(\alpha^{-1}(v_1), \alpha^{-1}(v_2)).$$

– *Edge condition: For every $v_1, v_2 \in V$,*

$$Z^C(v_1, v, v_2) \neq \emptyset \Rightarrow (v_1, v, v_2) \in E, Z^D(v_1, v_2) \neq \emptyset \Rightarrow (v_1, \gamma, v_2) \in E.$$

– *Weight conditions:*
  - *For every edge $e = (v_1, v, v_2)$.*

$$v \neq \gamma \Rightarrow \sup_{(s_1, s_2) \in Z^C(v_1, v, v_2)} \frac{\|s_2\|}{\|s_1\|} \leq W(e).$$

$$v = \gamma \Rightarrow \sup_{(s_1, s_2) \in Z^D(v_1, v_2)} \frac{\|s_2\|}{\|s_1\|} \leq W(e).$$

Note that even when α is fixed, there are several weighted graphs quantitatively abstracting the concrete system. However, there is a minimal graph which quantitatively abstracts the concrete system with respect to a given α.

Definition 5. *A* minimal quantitative abstraction *G of a hybrid system $\mathcal{H}$ with respect to an abstraction function α satisfies the implication on the edge conditions and the inequality in the weight conditions in both directions.*

Next, we identify a condition on the abstraction function α and the hybrid system $\mathcal{H}$ which will ensure that the abstract graph captures all the executions of $\mathcal{H}$.

Definition 6. *A hybrid system $\mathcal{H}$ is well-behaved with respect to an abstraction function α : States($\mathcal{H}$) $\rightarrow V$ if for every continuous trajectory τ of $\mathcal{H}$, the function $\alpha \circ \tau$ is finitely varying on V.*

From now on, we assume that the following assumption holds.

Assumption 1 *The hybrid system is well-behaved with respect to the choice of the quantitative predicate abstraction.*

The following theorem provides efficiently verifiable conditions on the abstract weighted graph which imply stability of the concrete system.

Theorem 1. *Let $G = (V, L, E, W)$ be a quantitative abstraction of a hybrid system $\mathcal{H}$ which satisfies Assumption 1. Consider the following conditions:*

G1 there is no edge e in G with infinite weight, that is, $W(e) < +\infty, \forall e \in E$,
G2 every simple cycle π of G satisfies $W(\pi) \leqslant 1$ and
G3 every simple cycle π of G satisfies $W(\pi) < 1$.

Then:

- *$\mathcal{H}$ is Lyapunov stable if conditions G1 and G2 hold and*
- *$\mathcal{H}$ is asymptotically stable if conditions G1 and G3 hold.*

We defer the proof of Theorem 1 to Section 6.3. Once we establish a connection between quantitative abstractions and continuous simulations, the proof of Theorem 1 is straightforward. We briefly explain the motivation for the conditions *G1* – *G3* in the theorem. For every execution of the hybrid system, there is a path in the graph such that the weights on the path provide an upper bound on how far the execution deviates with respect to the origin. Condition *G1* states that the executions which eventually remain within a particular region do not diverge; while Conditions *G2* (and *G3*) capture the fact that the executions which switch between regions infinitely often do not diverge (do converge).

Remark 1. One of the main highlights of the quantitative abstraction based stability analysis is that the method returns a counter-example in the event of a failure, indicating a potential reason for instability. For instance, a cycle of weight greater than one in the weighted graph expresses the possible existence of an infinite diverging execution.

5.2 Illustration on *PLDS*

In this section, we illustrate the quantitative abstraction based stability analysis on the class of piecewise linear dynamical systems. We use as the abstraction function a polyhedral partition of the state-space, and show that piecewise linear dynamical systems are well-behaved with respect to the polyhedral partition. We then illustrate the abstraction procedure on a simple example.

Let us fix an n-dimensional *PLDS* $\mathcal{M} = (\mathcal{P}, F)$. Recall that for this class of hybrid systems, the control location set is the partition $\mathcal{P}$ and the continuous state-space is $\mathbb{R}^n$. A state is represented as $(P, x) \in \mathcal{P} \times \mathbb{R}^n$. Fix a set of predicates on $\mathbb{R}^n$, which results in a partition $\mathcal{P}'$. The abstraction function is then given by $\alpha_{\mathcal{P},\mathcal{P}'}((P, x)) = (P, P')$, where $x \in P'$ and $P' \in \mathcal{P}'$. Next, we observe that a *PLDS* is well-behaved with respect to the abstraction function defined above, hence Assumption 1 holds.

Proposition 1. *Given a square matrix $A \in \mathbb{R}^n$ and a variable $t \in \mathbb{R}$, the exponential matrix e^{At} is a square matrix whose elements are linear combinations of terms of the form $ct^k e^{at} \cos(bt + d)$, where $a, b, c, d \in \mathbb{R}$ and $0 \leqslant k \leqslant n - 1$ is an integer.*

Proposition 2. *Given an n-dimensional PLDS $\mathcal{M} = (\mathcal{P}, F)$ and a partition $\mathcal{P}'$ of $\mathbb{R}^n$, $\mathcal{M}$ is well-behaved with respect to $\alpha_{\mathcal{P},\mathcal{P}'}$.*

Proof. Consider a trajectory $\tau : [0, T] \to \mathcal{P} \times \mathbb{R}^n$ in $\mathcal{M}$ such that for all t, $[\tau(t)]_D = P$, and $[\tau(t)]_C = e^{F(P)t}x_0$, where $P \in \mathcal{P}$ and x_0 is the initial continuous state of the trajectory. Define B to be the maximum of $bT + d$, where $\cos(bt + d)$ appears in the exponential matrix $e^{F(P)t}$ as given by Proposition 1. It is shown in [12], that the first order theory of reals with addition, multiplication, exponentiation and restricted cos and sin functions is o-minimal. This implies that the subset of reals defined by any formula with one free variable in the logic can be expressed as a finite union of intervals. Restricted cos and sin functions are those which are identical to cos and sin in a finite interval, and 0 everywhere else. Hence, we have that $\langle \mathbb{R}, \leqslant, +, \cdot, e, \sin|_{[0,B]}, \cos|_{[0,B]} \rangle$ is an o-minimal structure.

Next, we show that the trajectory enters and leaves a region of $\mathcal{P}'$ only finitely many times. Since, the number of regions is finite, this establishes that τ is finitely varying. Fix a polyhedron $P' \in \mathcal{P}'$. The following first-order logic formula $\varphi(t)$ over $\langle \mathbb{R}, \leqslant, +, \cdot, e, \sin|_{[0,B]}, \cos|_{[0,B]} \rangle$ defines the set of all times at which the trajectory τ is in P'.

$$\varphi(t) = \exists x (x \in P' \wedge 0 \leqslant t \leqslant T \wedge x = e^{F(P)t} x_0)$$

The last conjunct is expressible in the language due to Proposition 1. Further, though the sin and cos are restricted, they only take arguments in the range $[0, B]$, due to t being restricted to the interval $0 \leq t \leq T$ and the way B is computed. Hence, due to o-minimality, the times at which τ is in P' is a finite union of intervals, and we obtain that τ exits P' only finitely many times in the interval $[0, T]$.

The hybrid system $\mathcal{M}$ is well-behaved with respect to $\alpha_{\mathcal{P},\mathcal{P}'}$, since, any finite restriction of a trajectory (with a possibly infinite domain) has finite number of discontinuities with respect to $\mathcal{P}'$. □

Remark 2. Note that the above proof extends to any partition which is definable in the theory with addition, multiplication and exponentiation.

Next, we illustrate the quantitative abstraction construction and analysis on the systems $\mathcal{M}_1$ and $\mathcal{M}_2$ in Example 1. The graphs G_1 and G_2 in Figure 3

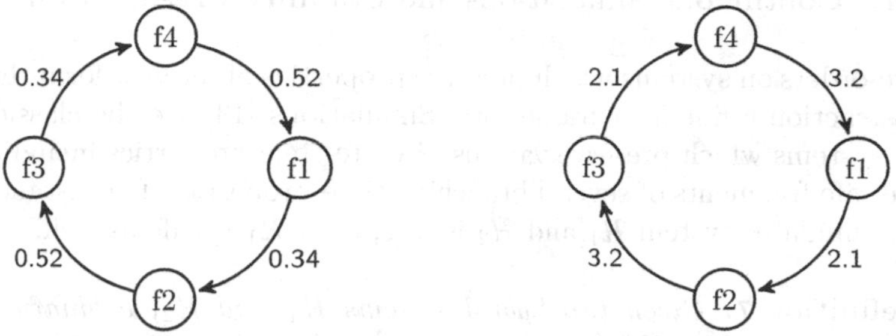

(a) Weighted graph G_1 (b) Weighted graph G_2

Fig. 3. Quantitative Abstractions

are quantitative predicate abstractions of $\mathcal{M}_1$ and $\mathcal{M}_2$ respectively. The state-space is partitioned by using the linear inequalities $\{x = 0, x > 0, x < 0, y = 0, y > 0, y < 0\}$. This partition generates 9 different regions, the four quadrants, the four positive and negative axes, which correspond to the boundary of the quadrants, and the origin. In this example, a simple construction of the weighted graph is presented, where the nodes corresponding to the quadrants and origin are eliminated because of redundancy. In practice, we may need to prune the graph to obtain useful results. The nodes $f1$ and $f3$ correspond to the positive and negative x axes, respectively, and the nodes $f2$ and $f4$ to the positive and negative y axes, respectively. There are several methods to compute weights based on reachable set computation for linear dynamics.

Note that G_1 satisfies conditions *G1* and *G2* which implies Lyapunov stability of $\mathcal{M}_1$. On the other hand, G_2 does not satisfy conditions *G2* or *G3*. Though we cannot conclude instability of $\mathcal{M}_2$, G_2 returns a counterexample, namely, the cycle $f1f2f3f4f1$ with weight > 1, explaining a potential reason for instability. The counterexample suggests that an infinite diverging execution is feasible by following the cycle infinitely many times. Such an execution exists in this case, for instance, repeating a scaled version of the execution shown in Figure 2(b) infinitely. However, in general, a diverging execution might not exist, as the counter-example could be due to the conservativeness of the abstraction.

6 Foundations of Quantitative Abstraction

In this section, we present the connection between quantitative abstractions and continuous simulations. First, we present an overview of continuous simulations between hybrid systems and show that they preserve stability. Next, we interpret a quantitative abstraction as a one dimensional hybrid system, which continuously simulates the original one, and hence, preserves stability. We use these results to provide a proof of Theorem 1. The connection between quantitative abstraction and continuous simulations also enables us to define a partial ordering on the abstract weighted graphs, thus, formalizing the notion of refinement.

6.1 Continuous Simulations and Stability Preservation

Pre-orders on systems which preserve properties of interest form the basis of any abstraction refinement framework. Simulations [13] are the classical pre-orders on systems which preserve various discrete-time properties including safety and the safe fragments of several branching time properties. For instance, if a system $\mathcal{H}_2$ simulates system $\mathcal{H}_1$ and $\mathcal{H}_2$ is safe, then $\mathcal{H}_1$ is safe as well.

Definition 7. *Given two hybrid systems $\mathcal{H}_1$ and $\mathcal{H}_2$, a binary relation $R \subseteq (Q_1 \times X_1) \times (Q_2 \times X_2)$ is said to be a* simulation *from $\mathcal{H}_1$ to $\mathcal{H}_2$, denoted $\mathcal{H}_1 \preceq^R \mathcal{H}_2$, if the following hold for every $(s_1, s_2) \in R$:*

- *for every transition $(s_1, s_1') \in \Sigma_1$, there exists a transition $(s_2, s_2') \in \Sigma_2$ such that $(s_1', s_2') \in R$; and*
- *for every trajectory $\tau_1 \in \Delta_1$ with $fstate(\tau_1) = s_1$, there exists a trajectory $\tau_2 \in \Delta_2$ with $fstate(\tau_2) = s_2$ such that $dom(\tau_1) = dom(\tau_2)$ and for all $t \in dom(\tau_1)$, $(\tau_1(t), \tau_2(t)) \in R$.*

However, it was observed in [17] that simulations do not suffice to preserve stability. Instead, a stronger notion which extends simulations with continuity constraints was proposed and shown to preserve stability. Below we present a simplified version of the definition of the relation and the stability preservation theorem in [17], as required for our setting.

Definition 8. *A binary relation R is a* continuous simulation *from $\mathcal{H}_1$ to $\mathcal{H}_2$, denoted $\mathcal{H}_1 \preceq_c^R \mathcal{H}_2$ if*

A1 R a simulation from $\mathcal{H}_1$ to $\mathcal{H}_2$;
A2 R and R^{-1} are continuous at $0_{\mathcal{H}_1}$ and $0_{\mathcal{H}_2}$, respectively;
A3 if $R((q_1, x_1), (q_2, x_2))$, then $x_1 = 0_{\mathcal{H}_1}$ if and only if $x_2 = 0_{\mathcal{H}_2}$; and
A4 $\exists \gamma > 0, \forall (q, x), [(q, x)]_C \in \mathcal{B}_\gamma(0_{\mathcal{H}_1}) \Rightarrow R(q, x) \neq \emptyset$.

Condition *A3* states that the states corresponding to the origin in one system are mapped to the states corresponding to the origin in the other. Condition *A4* states that the image of the relation R is not empty in a small neighborhood around the origin.

Theorem 2 ([17]). *Let R be a continuous simulation from $\mathcal{H}_1$ to $\mathcal{H}_2$. Then:*

- *$\mathcal{H}_2$ is Lyapunov stable implies $\mathcal{H}_1$ is Lyapunov stable.*
- *$\mathcal{H}_2$ is asymptotically stable implies $\mathcal{H}_1$ is asymptotically stable.*

This result shows that continuous simulations preserve both Lyapunov stability and asymptotic stability. The proof of the theorem is similar to that of the proof in [17].

6.2 Quantitative Predicate Abstraction as a One-Dimensional Hybrid System

A predicate abstraction procedure constructs a simpler system which simulates the original system. Hence, it preserves all properties preserved by simulations. In order to deduce a similar result for stability analysis, we need to formally relate the hybrid system with a quantitative abstraction of the system. Hence, we interpret the weighted graph as representing a simple one dimensional hybrid system, and show that this one dimensional system continuously simulates the original system. First, we define the one-dimensional system from the graph and specify conditions which characterize their stability properties.

Given a weighted graph G, we construct a one-dimensional hybrid system $\mathcal{H}_G$. The discrete locations of $\mathcal{H}_G$ correspond to the nodes of G. Transitions correspond to pair of states such that scaling associated with continuous states is bounded by the weight of the edge corresponding to the discrete states. Similarly, a trajectory of $\mathcal{H}_G$ corresponds to following a finite or infinite path in G such that the scaling of any prefix of the trajectory corresponding to a prefix of the path is bounded by the weight associated with the prefix of the path. Furthermore, the scalings associated with any prefix of the trajectory is bounded by the maximum weight of an edge in the graph.

Definition 9. *Given an edge $e = (v_1, v, v_2)$ of a weighted graph $G = (V, V \cup \{\gamma\}, E, W)$, we define the set of trajectories corresponding to it, denoted Traj(e), as the set of all finite trajectories τ over $(V, \mathbb{R})$ satisfying:*

- $[\tau(0)]_D = v_1$;
- $\exists v, \forall 0 < t < last(dom(\tau)), [\tau(t)]_D = v$ *and* $\|\tau(t)\|/\|\tau(0)\| \leq MW(G)$; *and*
- $[\tau(ltime(\tau))]_D = v_2$ *and* $0 \leq \|\tau(ltime(\tau))\|/\|\tau(0)\| \leq W(e)$.

A weight on an edge in a quantitative abstraction is an upper bound on the scaling associated with the last time of an execution; however, the scalings associated with all the intermediate time points are bounded by the weight of the edge corresponding to the prefixes of the execution. Hence, in *Traj*(e) we only allow trajectories such that the scalings associated with the intermediate points is bounded by the maximum weight of an edge in the graph.

We will also define a set of infinite trajectories which is allowed by the graph.

$$InfTraj(G) = \{\tau \in Traj(V, \mathbb{R}) \mid ltime(\tau) = +\infty, \exists v \in V,$$

$$\forall t \in dom(\tau), [\tau(t)]_D = v, 0 \leq \|\tau(t)\|/\|\tau(0)\| \leq MW(G)\}$$

Definition 10. *Given a weighted graph $G = (V, V \cup \{\gamma\}, E, W)$, we define a hybrid system $\mathcal{H}_G = (V, \mathbb{R}_{\geq 0}, \Sigma, \Delta)$, where:*
$\Sigma = \{((v_1, r_1), (v_2, r_2)) \mid (v_1, \gamma, v_2) \in E, r_2/r_1 \leq W(v_1, \gamma, v_2)\}$.
$\Delta = \{\tau \mid \exists$ *finite or infinite splitting* $\tau = \tau_1 \circ \tau_2 \circ \ldots$, *such that* $\forall i$, *either* $\exists e = (v_1, v, v_2) \in E, \tau_i \in Traj(e)$ *or* $\tau_i \in InfTraj(G)\}$.

The next theorem characterizes when $\mathcal{H}_G$ is Lyapunov stable.

Theorem 3. *Given a weighted graph G, $\mathcal{H}_G$ is Lyapunov stable if and only if*

C1 G does not contain any edges with infinite weights, that is, $W(e) < +\infty$ for every edge e of G.
C2 G does not contain simple cycles whose weight is strictly greater than 1, that is, $W(\pi) \leq 1$ for every simple cycle π of G.

Note that $\mathcal{H}_G$ constructed above is in general not asymptotically stable, since *InfTraj*(G) consists of infinite trajectories which do not converge. Hence we interpret G as another one-dimensional hybrid system $\mathcal{H}_G^{Conv}$ which consists of infinite trajectories remaining within a single region and converging if there are no infinite weight edges.

$$\mathit{InfTrajConv}(G) = \{\tau \in \mathit{Traj}(V, \mathbb{R}) \mid \mathit{Conv}(\tau, 0)\} \cap \mathit{InfTraj}(G)$$

$\mathcal{H}_G^{Conv}$ is same as $\mathcal{H}_G$ except that *InfTraj*(G) in the definition of Δ is replaced by *InfTrajConv*(G) if G has no edges with infinite weight.

Theorem 4. *Given a weighted graph G, $\mathcal{H}_G^{Conv}$ is asymptotically stable if and only if Condition C1 holds and*

C3 G does not contain simple cycles whose weight is greater than or equal to 1, that is, $W(\pi) < 1$ for every simple cycle π of G.

6.3 Quantitative Predicate Abstraction as Continuous Simulation

Next, we show that there exists a simulation between $\mathcal{H}$ and the one-dimensional systems $\mathcal{H}_G$ and $\mathcal{H}_G^{Conv}$.

Theorem 5. *Let G be a quantitative abstraction of $\mathcal{H}$ with respect to α. Then $R = \{((q, x), (\alpha((q, x)), \|x\|)) \mid (q, x) \in \mathit{States}(\mathcal{H})\}$ is a continuous simulation from $\mathcal{H}$ to $\mathcal{H}_G$ and from $\mathcal{H}$ to $\mathcal{H}_G^{Conv}$.*

Now we are ready to provide a proof of Theorem 1.

Proof of theorem 1. Let us consider a hybrid system $\mathcal{H}$ and a quantitative abstraction G of $\mathcal{H}$ with respect to α. Suppose conditions *G1* and *G2* hold for G. We want to prove Lyapunov stability for $\mathcal{H}$. Due to conditions *G1* and *G2*, Theorem 3 states that $\mathcal{H}_G$ is Lyapunov stable. By Theorem 5, we know there exists a continuous simulation R, defined as in the theorem, from $\mathcal{H}$ to $\mathcal{H}_G$. Then, by Theorem 2, we obtain $\mathcal{H}$ is Lyapunov stable.

Next, we prove the second part of Theorem 1. Suppose conditions *G1* and *G3* hold for G. We want to show asymptotic stability for the hybrid system $\mathcal{H}$. Since, Conditions *G1* and *G3* hold, we obtain from Theorem 4 that $\mathcal{H}_G^{Conv}$ is asymptotically stable. Then, from Theorem 5, we know that there is a continuous simulation R from $\mathcal{H}$ to $\mathcal{H}_G^{Conv}$. Finally, from Theorem 2, we obtain $\mathcal{H}$ is asymptotically stable. □

6.4 Refinements

The interpretation of the weighted graph as a one-dimensional system also provides a natural notion of refinements on the graphs.

Definition 11. *Let $\mathcal{H}_1$ and $\mathcal{H}_2$ be hybrid systems and R a binary relation such that $\mathcal{H}_1 \preceq_c^R \mathcal{H}_2$. A hybrid system $\mathcal{H}_3$ is a* refinement *of $\mathcal{H}_2$ with respect to $\mathcal{H}_1$, if there exist binary relations R_1 and R_2 such that $\mathcal{H}_1 \preceq_c^{R_1} \mathcal{H}_3 \preceq_c^{R_2} \mathcal{H}_2$.*

Theorem 6. *Let $\mathcal{H}$ be a hybrid system, and α_1 : States($\mathcal{H}$) $\to V_1$ and α_2 : States($\mathcal{H}$) $\to V_2$ be two abstraction functions such that for every $v_2 \in V_2$ there exists $v_1 \in V_1$ with $\alpha_2^{-1}(v_2) \subseteq \alpha_1^{-1}(v_1)$. Let G_1 and G_2 be the minimal quantitative abstractions of $\mathcal{H}$ with respect to α_1 and α_2, respectively. Then:*

1. *$\mathcal{H}_{G_1}$ simulates $\mathcal{H}_{G_2}$.*
2. *$\mathcal{H}_{G_1}^{Conv}$ simulates $\mathcal{H}_{G_2}^{Conv}$.*

In particular, $\mathcal{H}_{G_2}$ is a refinement of $\mathcal{H}_{G_1}$ with respect to $\mathcal{H}$ and $\mathcal{H}_{G_2}^{Conv}$ is a refinement of $\mathcal{H}_{G_1}^{Conv}$ with respect to $\mathcal{H}$.

Remark 3. Note that Theorem 6 will not be true for arbitrary abstractions $\mathcal{H}_{G_1}$ and $\mathcal{H}_{G_2}$. Hence, we enforce minimality, however, this can be relaxed to any abstraction construction procedure which is monotonic with respect to the abstraction functions. A consequence of the theorem is that, it establishes a partial ordering on the abstract graphs based on a partial ordering on the abstraction functions. Hence, the ordering on the abstraction functions can be used to obtain refinements of the graphs. For instance, adding more predicates yields a refinement.

7 Conclusion

In this paper, we presented the formal foundations for the quantitative predicate abstraction based stability analysis by establishing connections with continuous simulation relations. Here, we have ignored the computational issues related to the computation of abstractions and refinements. These have been explored to some extent in [19,20] for the class of piecewise constant derivative systems and polyhedral switched systems. Future work will focus on extending this approach to hybrid systems with richer dynamics. Further, since, a failure to prove stability returns a potential counter-example, one can build a framework of counter-example guided abstraction refinement for stability analysis, which will be explored in the future.

Acknowledgement. The research leading to the results in the paper has received funding from the People Programme (Marie Curie Actions) of the European Union's Seventh Framework Programme (FP7/2007-2013) under REA grant agreement no. 631622.

References

1. Alur, R., Courcoubetis, C., Henzinger, T.A., Ho, P.-H.: Hybrid automata: An algorithmic approach to the specification and verification of hybrid systems. In: Grossman, R.L., Nerode, A., Ravn, A.P., Rischel, H. (eds.) HS 1991 and HS 1992. LNCS, vol. 736, pp. 209–229. Springer, Heidelberg (1993)
2. Alur, R., Dang, T., Ivančić, F.: Counter-example guided predicate abstraction of hybrid systems. In: Garavel, H., Hatcliff, J. (eds.) TACAS 2003. LNCS, vol. 2619, pp. 208–223. Springer, Heidelberg (2003)
3. Alur, R., Dang, T., Ivancic, F.: Predicate abstraction for reachability analysis of hybrid systems. ACM Transactions on Embedded Computing Systems 5(1), 152–199 (2006)
4. Ball, T., Majumdar, R., Millstein, T., Rajamani, S.K.: Automatic predicate abstraction of C programs. In: Proceedings of the ACM SIGPLAN 2001 Conference on Programming Language Design and Implementation, PLDI 2001, pp. 203–213. ACM, New York (2001)
5. Cook, B., Podelski, A., Rybalchenko, A.: Proving program termination. Commun. ACM 54(5), 88–98 (2011)
6. Goebel, R., Sanfelice, R., Teel, A.: Hybrid dynamical systems. IEEE Control Systems, Control Systems Magazine 29, 28–93 (2009)
7. Graf, S., Saidi, H.: Construction of abstact state graphs with PVS. In: Proceedings of the International Conference on Computer Aided Verification, pp. 72–83 (1997)
8. Henzinger, T.A.: The Theory of Hybrid Automata. In: Proceedings of the IEEE Symposium on Logic in Computer Science, pp. 278–292 (1996)
9. Kapinski, J., Deshmukh, J.V., Sankaranarayanan, S., Arechiga, N.: Simulation-guided lyapunov analysis for hybrid dynamical systems. In: 17th International Conference on Hybrid Systems: Computation and Control (part of CPS Week), HSCC 2014, Berlin, Germany, April 15-17, pp. 133–142 (2014)
10. Khalil, H.K.: Nonlinear Systems. Prentice-Hall, Saddle River (1996)
11. Lin, H., Antsaklis, P.J.: Stability and stabilizability of switched linear systems: A survey of recent results. IEEE Transactions on Automatic Control 54(2), 308–322 (2009)
12. Lou van den Dries, A.M., Marker, D.: The elementary theory of restricted analytic fields with exponentiation. Annals of Mathematics, Second Series 140(1), 183–205 (1994)
13. Milner, R.: Communication and Concurrency. Prentice-Hall, Inc. (1989)
14. Möhlmann, E., Theel, O.: Stabhyli: A tool for automatic stability verification of non-linear hybrid systems. In: Proceedings of the International Conference on Hybrid Systems: Computation and Control, pp. 107–112. ACM, New York (2013)
15. Papachristodoulou, A., Prajna, S.: On the construction of Lyapunov functions using the sum of squares decomposition. In: Conference on Decision and Control (2002)
16. Parrilo, P.A.: Structure Semidefinite Programs and Semialgebraic Geometry Methods in Robustness and Optimization. PhD thesis, California Institute of Technology, Pasadena, CA (May 2000)
17. Prabhakar, P., Dullerud, G.E., Viswanathan, M.: Pre-orders for reasoning about stability. In: Proceedings of the International Conference on Hybrid Systems: Computation and Control, pp. 197–206 (2012)

18. Prabhakar, P., Liu, J., Murray, R.M.: Pre-orders for reasoning about stability properties with respect to input of hybrid systems. In: Proceedings of the International Conference on Embedded Software, EMSOFT 2013, Montreal, QC, Canada, September 29-October 4, pp. 1–10 (2013)
19. Prabhakar, P., Garcia Soto, M.: Abstraction based model-checking of stability of hybrid systems. In: Sharygina, N., Veith, H. (eds.) CAV 2013. LNCS, vol. 8044, pp. 280–295. Springer, Heidelberg (2013)
20. Prabhakar, P., Soto, M.G.: An algorithmic approach to stability verification of polyhedral switched systems. In: American Control Conference (2014)
21. Sontag, E.D.: Input to state stability: Basic concepts and results. In: Nonlinear and Optimal Control Theory, pp. 163–220. Springer (2006)
22. Tiwari, A.: Abstractions for hybrid systems. Formal Methods in System Design 32(1), 57–83 (2008)

An Experimental Evaluation of Deliberate Unsoundness in a Static Program Analyzer

Maria Christakis, Peter Müller, and Valentin Wüstholz

Department of Computer Science
ETH Zurich, Switzerland
{maria.christakis,peter.mueller,valentin.wuestholz}@inf.ethz.ch

Abstract. Many practical static analyzers are not completely sound by design. Their designers trade soundness to increase automation, improve performance, and reduce the number of false positives or the annotation overhead. However, the impact of such design decisions on the effectiveness of an analyzer is not well understood. This paper reports on the first systematic effort to document and evaluate the sources of unsoundness in a static analyzer. We developed a code instrumentation that reflects the sources of deliberate unsoundness in the .NET static analyzer Clousot and applied it to code from six open-source projects. We found that 33% of the instrumented methods were analyzed soundly. In the remaining methods, Clousot made unsound assumptions, which were violated in 2–26% of the methods during concrete executions. Manual inspection of these methods showed that no errors were missed due to an unsound assumption, which suggests that Clousot's unsoundness does not compromise its effectiveness. Our findings can guide users of static analyzers in using them fruitfully, and designers in finding good trade-offs.

1 Introduction

Many practical static analyzers are not completely sound by design. Their designers often trade soundness in order to increase automation, improve performance, reduce the number of false positives or the annotation overhead, and achieve a modular analysis. As a result, such static analyzers become precise and efficient in detecting software bugs, but at the cost of making implicit, unsound assumptions about certain program properties. For example, ESC/Java uses bounded loop unrolling to reduce the overhead of writing loop invariants, and Spec# ignores exceptional control flow to speed up verification.

Despite how common such design decisions are, their practical impact on the effectiveness of static analyzers is not well understood. There are various approaches in the literature that study the efficiency and precision of static analyzers by measuring, for instance, their performance and the number of false positives [2]. In this paper, we focus on a different perspective: we report on the first systematic effort to document and evaluate the sources of deliberate unsoundness in a static analyzer. We present a code instrumentation that reflects the sources of unsoundness in the static analyzer Clousot [10], an abstract interpretation tool for .NET and Code Contracts [9]. This instrumentation adapts

D. D'Souza et al. (Eds.): VMCAI 2015, LNCS 8931, pp. 336–354, 2015.

our earlier technique to make the unsound assumptions of a static analyzer explicit where they occur by automatically inserting annotations into the analyzed code [6]. Most of these assumptions are motivated by Clousot's design goal to analyze programs modularly without imposing an excessive annotation overhead. To evaluate the impact of Clousot's unsound assumptions, we instrumented code from six open-source projects, measured how often the unsound assumptions were violated during executions of the projects' test suites, and determined whether Clousot missed bugs due to unsound assumptions.

The contributions of this paper are the following:

- We report on the first systematic effort to document all sources of unsoundness in an industrial-strength static analyzer. We focus on Clousot, a widely used, commercial static analyzer.
- We present a code instrumentation that reflects the unsoundness in Clousot. Most sources of unsoundness in Clousot are precisely captured by our encoding.
- We perform an experimental evaluation that, for the first time, sheds light on how often the unsound assumptions of a static analyzer are violated in practice and whether they cause the analyzer to miss bugs.

In our experiments, 33% of the instrumented methods were analyzed soundly. In the remaining methods, Clousot made unsound assumptions, which were violated in 2–26% of the methods during concrete executions. Manual inspection of these methods showed that no errors were missed due to an unsound assumption, which suggests that Clousot's unsoundness does not compromise its effectiveness. We expect these results to guide users of static analyzers in using them fruitfully, for instance, in deciding how to complement static analysis with testing, and to assist designers of static analyzers in finding good trade-offs.

Outline. Sect. 2 explains all sources of unsoundness in Clousot and how we instrument most of them. Sect. 3 gives an overview of our implementation. In Sect. 4, we present and discuss our experimental results. We review related work in Sect. 5 and conclude in Sect. 6.

2 Unsoundness in Clousot

In this section, we present a complete list of Clousot's sources of deliberate unsoundness and demonstrate how most of these can be expressed through simple annotations. We have elicited Clousot's unsound assumptions during the last two years by studying publications, extensively testing the tool, and having numerous discussions with its designers. Note that a formal proof that Clousot is sound modulo the issues we document here is beyond the scope of our paper.

We make the unsoundness of a static analyzer explicit by automatically annotating the analyzed code with `assumed` statements, also called *explicit assumptions*. An `assumed` statement is of the form `assumed` P, where P is a boolean expression, and denotes that a static analyzer *unsoundly* assumed property P at this point in the code; that is, the analyzer assumed P without checking that it actually holds. Note that `assumed` statements are different from the classical `assume` statements, which express properties that the user *intends* the static analyzer to take for granted.

Each unsound assumption in Clousot applies to a specific syntactic category such as a kind of statement or expression (for instance, because Clousot's abstract transformer does not soundly reflect the semantics of that syntactic category). We say that an explicit assumption *precisely* captures the unsound assumption for a syntactic category if for all elements e of that category and all executions τ of e, Clousot's analysis is sound iff the execution τ does not violate e's explicit assumption. Here, *sound* means that the concrete states of τ lie within the concretization of the corresponding abstract states. We say that an explicit assumption *over-approximates* the unsound assumption if there is an element e and an execution τ of e such that Clousot's analysis is sound, but the execution τ violates e's explicit assumption. Conversely, an explicit assumption *under-approximates* the unsound assumption if there is an element e and an execution τ of e such that Clousot's analysis is *not* sound, but the execution τ *does not* violate e's explicit assumption.

2.1 Heap Properties

Clousot treats the following aspects of the heap unsoundly: object invariants, aliasing, write effects, and method purity.

Object Invariants. Code Contracts provide object (or class) invariants to express which objects are considered valid. Clousot checks the invariant of the receiver at the end of a method or constructor, and assumes it in the pre-state of a method execution and after a call. However, the checks are insufficient to justify these assumptions [8]. That is, Clousot makes the following unsound assumptions to facilitate modular checking: *Clousot assumes the invariant of the receiver object in the pre-state of instance methods, without checking it at call sites*; moreover *Clousot assumes the invariant of the receiver after a call to an inherited method on* `this`, *without fully checking it.*

```
class C {
  bool b;

  invariant !b;

  void M() {
    assumed invariant(this, typeof(C));
    b = true;
    N();
    assert !b;
  }

  void N() {
    assumed invariant(this, typeof(C));
    assert !b;
  }
}
```

The C# code on the right illustrates the first unsoundness. Method `M` violates the invariant of its receiver before calling `N`. (We use the keywords `invariant` and `assert` to denote Code Contracts' object invariants and assertions.) The gray boxes in the code are discussed later. Clousot assumes the invariant of the receiver in the pre-state of method `N`, which is unsound since it does not check this invariant at call sites of `N`, in particular, before the call to `N` in `M`. So Clousot emits no warning for the assertion in `N`, although it will not hold when `N` is called from `M`. The fact that there is no warning for the assertion in `M` is a consequence of the same unsoundness. Clousot checks the receiver's invariant in the post-state of method N; this check succeeds because of the same unsound assumption in N's pre-state. The check in the post-state justifies assuming the invariant after the call.

We capture this unsoundness by introducing an **assumed** statement at the beginning of each instance method in classes that declare or inherit object invariants. As shown in the gray boxes in the code, these explicit assumptions use a predicate invariant(o, t), which holds iff object o satisfies the object invariants defined in class t in conjunction with all invariants inherited from t's super-classes. Here, type t is the type of the class in which the method is defined; the corresponding type object is retrieved with the typeof expression in C#. We label this kind of explicit assumption as "invariants at method entries" (**IE**). We will refer to such labels in our experimental evaluation.

This explicit assumption captures the first unsoundness precisely because any method execution in which the explicit assumption is violated (that is, where the receiver's invariant does not hold in the pre-state), will be analyzed with an unsound abstraction of the initial state (unless Clousot's abstract domains do not reflect the invariant anyway, which we ignore here). This does not necessarily mean that Clousot misses errors because the unsoundness might be irrelevant for the checks performed on the method body. Conversely, if the abstraction of the initial state is unsound because the receiver's invariant is violated, the explicit assumption will be false. Note that there are programs for which this will never happen; some explicit assumptions may always hold in these programs (and still be precise according to our definition).

The code on the right illustrates the second unsoundness. Method M of the sub-class calls the inherited method N of the super-class on the current receiver, and N violates the invariant declared in the sub-class. However, since Clousot's analysis is modular, Sub's invariant is not considered when analyzing Super and, therefore, Clousot does not detect this invariant violation. Nevertheless, Clousot assumes the invariant of this after the call to N in M, which is unsound. As a result, no warnings are emitted.

```
class Super {
  bool b;

  void N() { b = true; }
}

class Sub : Super {
  invariant !b;

  Sub() { b = false; }

  void M() {
    N();
    assumed invariant(this, typeof(Sub));
    assert !b;
  }
}
```

We precisely capture this unsoundness by introducing an **assumed** statement after each call to an inherited method on the current receiver in classes that declare or inherit object invariants. The explicit assumption states that the object invariant of this holds for the enclosing class (here, Sub) and its super-classes. We label this kind of explicit assumption as "invariants at call sites" (**IC**).

Aliasing. To avoid the overhead of a precise heap analysis, *Clousot ignores certain side-effects due to aliasing.* For operations with side-effects, such as field updates, Clousot unsoundly assumes that heap locations not explicitly aliased in the code are non-aliasing and, thus, not affected.

As an example of this unsoundness, consider method `M` below. (We use the keyword `requires` to denote preconditions.) Clousot assumes that array `a` is not modified by the update to array `b`, although `a` and `b` might point to the same array in some calls to `M`. As a result, no warning is emitted.

```
void M(int[] a, int[] b) {
  requires a != null && b != null;
  requires 0 < a.Length && 0 < b.Length;
  assumed a == null || !object.ReferenceEquals(a, b);
  a[0] = 0;
  assumed b == null || !object.ReferenceEquals(b, a);
  b[0] = 1;
  assert a[0] == 0;
}
```

Clousot abstracts the heap by a *heap-graph*, which maintains equalities about access paths. The nodes of the heap-graph denote symbolic values, which represent concrete values, such as object references and primitive values. An edge of the heap-graph denotes how the symbolic value of the target node is retrieved from the symbolic value of the source node, for instance, by dereferencing a field or calling a pure method. (Programmers may declare a method as pure to indicate that it makes no visible state changes.) All access paths in the heap-graph are rooted in a local variable or a method parameter. When two access paths lead to the same symbolic value, they represent the same concrete value, that is, must be aliases. However, when two access paths lead to distinct symbolic values, they may represent the same or different concrete values, that is, may or may not be aliases. Nevertheless, Clousot unsoundly assumes in this case that updating the heap through one path will not affect values read through the other.

We precisely capture this unsoundness by introducing an `assumed` statement before every side-effecting operation that unsoundly affects the values in the heap-graph, that is, when the side effect is reflected only on some symbolic values, although other symbolic values may represent the same heap locations. Specifically, for each field, property, or array update (side effects via calls are discussed below), we determine the set of symbolic values that are distinct from the symbolic value for the receiver r of the update, but may be aliases of r. This set is computed based on the heap-graph in the pre-state of the update and on type information. For each element s of this set, our explicit assumption has a conjunct expressing that the concrete values represented by r and s (and given by the access paths leading to the symbolic values) are non-aliasing.

In our example, Clousot's heap abstraction uses distinct symbolic values for the arrays `a` and `b` in the initial heap-graph. Thus, for the first array update, r represents `a` and the set of possible aliases consists of `b`. Hence, the explicit assumption expresses that `a` and `b` are not aliases. The explicit assumption for the second array update is analogous. Note that we call `ReferenceEquals` since the `==` operator may be overloaded in C#. We label this kind of explicit assumption as "aliasing" (**A**).

Write Effects. To avoid a non-modular, inter-procedural analysis or having to provide explicit write effect specifications, *Clousot uses unsound heuristics to determine the set of heap locations that are modified by a method call.* Clousot then assumes that all other heap locations are not modified. This assumption is unsound since the heuristics in general may not include all heap locations that are modified by a call.

The code on the right illustrates this unsoundness. Clousot assumes that the call to method N in M modifies only the fields of the receiver object, and leaves the elements of the array unchanged. As a result, it does not emit a warning for the assertion. Note that this unsoundness is caused by Clousot's heuristics for write effects, regardless of whether a and b are aliases.

```
class C {
  int[] a;

  void M() {
    var b = new int[1];
    a = b;
    N();
    assumed b == null || !writtenObjects().Contains(b));
    assert b[0] == 0;
  }

  void N() {
    if (a != null && 0 < a.Length) { a[0] = 1; }
  }
}
```

We capture this unsoundness by introducing an assumed statement after each call, stating that all heap locations in the heap-graph that Clousot assumes to remain unmodified by the call are indeed not modified. This is achieved by comparing all symbolic values in the heap-graph before and after the call and using their access paths to retrieve the concrete values they represent. The explicit assumption has a conjunct for each unmodified concrete object reference stating that it is not contained in the actual write effect of the method for the last call. To obtain the actual write effect, we instrument the program to provide the function writtenObjects, which returns the set of objects that were modified by the most recently executed call (including any objects that were modified indirectly through method calls). We label this kind of explicit assumption as "write effects" (**W**). Note that this explicit assumption subsumes the aliasing unsoundness for calls because it covers all objects Clousot assumes to be left unchanged by a call, no matter whether this assumption is caused by ignoring certain aliasing situations or by the unsound heuristics for write effects. In method M above, writtenObjects returns the set consisting of array a and, since a and b refer to the same array, the explicit assumption is violated at runtime.

How precisely we capture this unsoundness depends on the definition of function writtenObjects. If the function returns an over- or under-approximation of the set of heap locations modified by the most recently executed call then our assumptions over- or under-approximate Clousot's unsoundness, respectively. In our implementation, writtenObjects is precise for methods that we instrument, but under-approximates the write effects of library methods (see Sect. 3).

Purity. Users may explicitly annotate a method with the Code Contracts attribute Pure to express that the method makes no visible state changes. To avoid the overhead of a purity analysis, *Clousot assumes that all methods annotated with the* Pure *attribute as well as all property getters indeed make no visible state changes.* (We will refer to property getters and methods annotated with Pure as "pure methods".) Moreover, Clousot uses unsound heuristics to determine which heap locations affect the result of a pure method, that is, the method's *read effect. Clousot then assumes that all pure methods deterministically return the same value when called in states that are equivalent with respect to their assumed read effects.*

We capture the first unsoundness with the explicit assumptions about write effects described above. After each call to a pure method, we introduce an **assumed** statement stating that all heap locations in the heap-graph remained unmodified.

Method `M` on the right illustrates the second unsoundness. Clousot assumes that both calls to the pure method `Random` in `M` deterministically return the same value, and no warning is emitted.

Method `N` on the right illustrates another aspect of this unsoundness. Clousot assumes that the result of the pure method `First` depends only on the state of its receiver, but not on the state of array `a`. Therefore, no warning is emitted about the assertion in `N` even though `a[0]` is modified after the first call to `First`.

```
class C {
  void M() {
    var r = Random();
    assumed r == Random();
    assert r == Random();
    assumed r == Random();
  }

  [Pure] int Random() {
    return (new object()).GetHashCode();
  }
}

class D {
  int[] a;

  void N() {
    requires a != null && 0 < a.Length;
    var v = First();
    assumed v == First();
    a[0] = v + 1;
    assumed v == First();
    assert v == First();
    assumed v == First();
  }

  [Pure] int First() {
    requires a != null && 0 < a.Length;
    return a[0];
  }
}
```

Clousot's heap-graph maintains information about which values may be retrieved by calling a pure method. For instance, after the first call to `Random` in `M`, the heap-graph maintains an equality of `r` and a call to `Random`. This information becomes unsound if (1) the pure method is not deterministic, (2) an object is modified, but Clousot unsoundly assumes that the pure method does not depend on that object, or (3) an object is modified, but Clousot does not reflect the modification correctly in the heap-graph. The latter case is covered by the explicit assumptions for aliasing and write effects. We capture the former two cases as follows: (1) We generate an explicit assumption after each call to a pure method stating that the method still yields the value stored in the heap-graph. This assumption under-approximates Clousot's unsoundness due to non-determinism since even a non-deterministic method might return the same result several times in a row. (2) Whenever the heap-graph retains a value for a pure method call across a statement that may modify the heap, we generate an explicit assumption stating that the method still yields the value stored in the heap-graph. This assumption precisely captures the case that Clousot may assume a too small read effect, as for method `First`. We label these explicit assumptions as "purity" (**P**).

2.2 Method-Local Properties

We now present the sources of unsoundness in Clousot that are related to properties local to a method. We divide them into two categories, integral-type arithmetic and exceptional control flow.

Integral-Type Arithmetic. To reduce the number of false positives, *Clousot ignores overflow in integral-type arithmetic operations and conversions.* That is, Clousot treats bounded integral-type expressions as unbounded (except for `checked` expressions, which raise an exception when an overflow occurs).

The code on the right illustrates the unsoundness for operations. Although the assertion fails when an overflow occurs, no warning is emitted.

```
int a = ...;
assumed (long)(a + 1) == (long)a + (long)1;
a = a + 1;
assert int.MinValue < a;
```

We precisely capture this unsoundness by introducing an `assumed` statement before each bounded arithmetic operation that might overflow (and is not `checked`) stating that the operation returns the same value as its unbounded counterpart. We encode this unbounded counterpart by performing the operation on operands with types for which no overflow will occur, for instance, `long` instead of `int` as in the example above, or arbitrarily large integers (`BigInteger`) instead of `long`. We label this kind of explicit assumption as "overflows" (**O**).

The code on the right illustrates the unsoundness for conversions. Even though the assertion fails due to an overflow that occurs when converting `a` to a `short` integer, Clousot does not emit any warnings.

```
int a = int.MaxValue;
assumed a == (short)a;
short b = (short)a;
assert (int)b == int.MaxValue;
```

We precisely capture this unsoundness by introducing an `assumed` statement for each integral-type conversion to a type with smaller value range stating that the value before the conversion is equal to the value after the conversion, as shown above. We label this kind of explicit assumption as "conversions" (**CO**).

Exceptional Control Flow. Exceptions add a large number of control-flow transitions and, thus, complicate static analysis. To avoid losing efficiency and precision, many static analyzers ignore exceptional control flow. *Clousot ignores* `catch` *blocks and assumes that the code in a* `finally` *block is executed only after a non-exceptional exit point of the corresponding* `try` *block has been reached.*

```
try {
  throw new Exception();
} catch (Exception) {
  assumed false;
  assert false;
}
```

The code on the right illustrates the unsoundness for `catch` blocks. Since Clousot ignores the `catch` block, no warning is emitted about the assertion.

We precisely capture this unsoundness by introducing an `assumed` statement at the beginning of each `catch` block stating that the block is unreachable, as shown in the code above. We label this kind of explicit assumption as "catch blocks" (**C**).

The code on the right illustrates the unsoundness for `finally` blocks. Since Clousot assumes that the `finally` block is entered only when the `try` block executes normally, no warning is emitted about the assertion. (We use * to denote an arbitrary boolean condition.)

```
bool b = false;
bool $noException$ = false;
try {
  if (*)
    throw new Exception();
  b = true;
  $noException$ = true;
} finally {
  assumed $noException$;
  assert b;
}
```

We precisely capture this unsoundness by introducing an `assumed` statement at the beginning of each `finally` block stating that the block is entered only when the `try` block terminates normally. This is expressed by introducing a fresh boolean variable for each `try` block, which is initially false and set to true at all non-exceptional exit points of the `try` block, as shown in the code. The `assumed` statement then states that this variable is true. We label this kind of explicit assumption as "finally blocks" (**F**).

2.3 Static Class Members

Here, we describe the sources of unsoundness for static fields and main methods.

Static Fields. To avoid the complications of class initialization [5] and to reduce the annotation overhead and the number of false positives, *Clousot assumes that static fields of reference types contain non-null values.*

As an example of this unsoundness, consider the code on the right, for which no warnings are emitted.

```
static int[] a;

void M() {
  assumed a != null;
  assert a != null;
}
```

We precisely capture this unsoundness by introducing an `assumed` statement for each read access to a static field of reference type stating that the field is non-null, as shown in the code. We label this kind of explicit assumption as "static fields" (**S**).

Main Methods. When a main method is invoked by the runtime system, the array of strings that is passed to the method and the array elements are never null. To relieve its users from providing preconditions for main methods, *Clousot assumes that the string array passed to a main method and its elements are non-null for all invocations of the method.*

As an example, consider the code on the right. Although method `M` calls `Main` with a null argument, no warning is emitted about the assertions in `Main`.

```
void M() {
  Main(null);
}

public static void Main(string[] args) {
  assumed args != null && forall arg in args | arg != null;
  assert args != null;
  assert args.Length == 0 || args[0] != null;
}
```

We precisely capture this unsoundness by introducing an `assumed` statement at the beginning of each main method stating that the parameter array and its elements are non-null, as shown in the code above. (We use the `forall` keyword to denote Code Contracts' universal quantifiers.) We label this kind of explicit assumption as "main methods" (**M**).

2.4 Uninstrumented Unsoundness

In the rest of this section, we give an overview of the remaining sources of unsoundness in Clousot, which we do not instrument:

- *Concurrency*: Clousot does not reason about concurrency and assumes that the analyzed code runs without interference from other threads.
- *Reflection*: Clousot assumes that the analyzed method does not use reflection.
- *Unmanaged code*: Clousot checks memory safety for unmanaged code, but does not consider its effects on the analyzed method.
- *Static initialization*: Clousot assumes that the analyzed code runs without interference from a static initializer.
- *Iterators*: Clousot does not analyze iterator methods (C#'s `yield` statements).
- *Library contracts*: Clousot assumes that the contracts provided for libraries such as the .NET API are correct.
- *Floating-point numbers*: Under certain circumstances, Clousot assumes that operations on floating-point numbers are commutative.

A very coarse way of capturing the first five sources of unsoundness would be to introduce an `assumed false` statement at each program point that starts a thread, invokes reflection, or contains unmanaged code, as well as in each static initializer and for each `yield` statement. Such an instrumentation would grossly over-approximate Clousot's unsound assumptions (for instance, many static initializers do not interfere with the execution of the analyzed method). However, a more precise instrumentation is complicated and would require explicit assumptions for most statements, for instance, to detect data races. Incorrect library contracts could be detected by introducing an explicit assumption for the postcondition of each call into the library. We omit these assumptions because they are orthogonal to the design of the static analyzer. Finally, we do not instrument the unsoundness about floating-point numbers because we were not able to precisely determine where the assumptions occur.

Note that we do not consider Clousot's inference of method contracts and object invariants in this paper. In the presence of inference, an unsound assumption in a method m might affect not only the analysis of m but also of methods whose analysis assumes properties inferred from m, in particular, m's postcondition and the object invariant of the class containing m. One solution is to introduce an explicit assumption whenever Clousot assumes a postcondition or invariant that was inferred unsoundly; one can then determine easily which methods have been analyzed soundly by inspecting the instrumented method body. Another solution is to rely on the existing instrumentation, which is sufficient to reveal unsound inference during the execution of the program. If the postcondition of a method or constructor m was inferred unsoundly, we detect an assumption violation when executing a call to m, and analogously if m violates an inferred invariant.

3 Implementation

To evaluate whether Clousot's sources of unsoundness are violated in practice, we have implemented a tool chain that instruments code with explicit assumptions and checks them at runtime.

Instrumentation. The instrumentation stage runs Clousot on a given .NET program, which contains code and optionally specifications expressed in Code Contracts, and instruments the sources of unsoundness of the tool as described in the previous section. For this purpose, we have implemented *Inspector-Clousot*, a wrapper around Clousot that uses the debug output emitted during the analysis to instrument the program (at the binary level).

Runtime Checking. In the runtime checking stage, we first run the existing Code Contracts binary rewriter to transform Code Contracts specifications into runtime checks. We subsequently run a second rewriter, called *Explicit-Assumption-Rewriter*, that transforms all `assumed` statements of the instrumented program into logging operations. More specifically, this rewriter replaces each explicit assumption `assumed` P by an operation that logs the program point of the `assumed` statement, which kind of unsoundness it expresses, and whether the assumed property P is violated. If P contains method calls, we do not further log assumed properties in the callees.

The Explicit-Assumption-Rewriter also instruments each method to compute its set of written objects by keeping track of all object allocations and updates to instance fields and array elements. The set of written objects of a method consists of the objects that have been modified but are not newly allocated by the method. The set of written objects for a call to an uninstrumented (library) method is always empty, that is, our instrumentation under-approximates the objects actually modified by such a method.

4 Experimental Evaluation

In this section, we present our experiments for evaluating whether Clousot's unsound assumptions are violated in practice and whether these violations cause Clousot to miss errors.

For our experiments, we used code from six open-source C# projects (see Tab. 1) from different application domains. We selected only applications that come with a test suite so that the experiments achieve good code coverage. We chose three applications to contain Code Contracts specifications to evaluate the explicit assumptions about object invariants. We ran our tool chain on at least

Table 1. Applications selected for our experiments. The first two columns describe the C# applications. The third column indicates whether the applications contain Code Contracts. The fourth column shows the number of analyzed methods per project. The fifth column shows how many of the methods with explicit assumptions that were hit at runtime contained assumption violations.

Application	Description	CC	Analyzed methods	Methods with violations
BCrypt.Net[1]	Password-hashing library	no	21	1 / 12 (8.3%)
Boogie[2]	Verification language and engine	yes	299	2 / 119 (1.7%)
ClueBuddy[3]	GUI application for board game	yes	139	16 / 67 (23.9%)
Codekicker.BBCode[4]	BBCode-to-HTML translator	no	179	2 / 58 (3.4%)
DSA[5]	Data structures and algorithms library	no	213	26 / 99 (26.3%)
Scrabble (for WPF)[6]	GUI application for Scrabble	yes	127	8 / 41 (19.5%)

one substantial DLL from these applications to perform the instrumentation described in the previous sections. For invoking Clousot, we enabled all checks, set the warning level to the maximum, and disabled all inference options. We subsequently ran tests from the test suite of each application and logged which explicit assumptions were hit at runtime and which of those were violated. Finally, we manually inspected a large number of methods to determine whether Clousot misses any errors because of its unsound assumptions.

4.1 Experimental Results: Instrumentation

Fig. 1 presents the percentage of analyzed methods from each project versus the number of `assumed` statements in the methods. An *analyzed* method is checked by Clousot but not necessarily hit at runtime by the test suite of a project. We analyzed a total of 978 methods with Clousot. As shown in the figure, the majority of these methods (860) contain less than 5 `assumed` statements, and a large number of those (326) are soundly checked, that is, do not contain any explicit assumptions. There are only 20 methods with more than 10 `assumed` statements. In these methods, the prevailing sources of unsoundness are "invariants at call sites" (**IC**), "write effects" (**W**), "purity" (**P**), and "overflows" (**O**).

Fig. 2 shows the average number of bytecode instructions in the analyzed methods versus the number of `assumed` statements in the methods. Notice that most methods that are soundly checked contain only a small number of bytecode instructions. A manual inspection of these methods showed that many of them are setters, getters, or (default) constructors. Our results indicate that methods with more instructions contain a larger number of `assumed` statements.

1 `http://bcrypt.codeplex.com`, rev: `d05159e21ce0`
2 `http://boogie.codeplex.com`, rev: `8da19707fbf9`
3 `https://github.com/AArnott/ClueBuddy`, rev: `c1b64ae97c01fec249b2212018f589c2d8119b59`
4 `http://bbcode.codeplex.com`, rev: `80132`
5 `http://dsa.codeplex.com`, rev: `96133`
6 `http://wpfscrabble.codeplex.com`, rev: `20226`

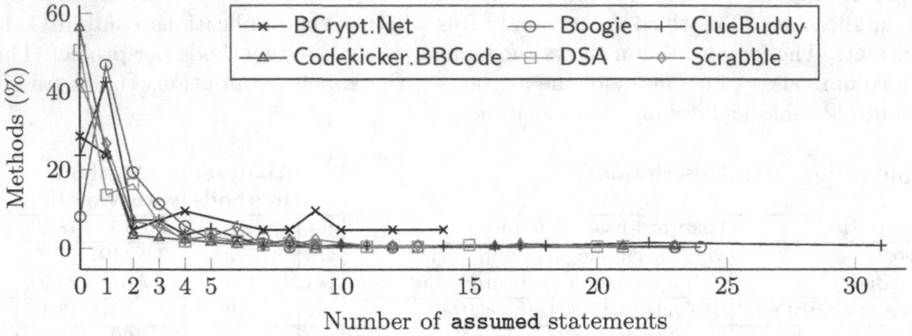

Fig. 1. The percentage of analyzed methods from each project versus the number of assumed statements in the methods.

Fig. 3 shows Clousot's sources of unsoundness versus the number of assumed statements that are introduced in the analyzed methods of each project. The results are dominated by the assumptions that are introduced for each method (**IE**) or for common statements (**IC**, **W**, **P**). The unsound treatment of aliasing (**A**) affects relatively few methods, even though it could be introduced for each field, property, or array update. Assumptions about "main methods" (**M**) were not introduced because there are either no main methods at all (for instance, in libraries) or not in the portions of the code that we analyzed and instrumented.

4.2 Experimental Results: Runtime Checking

The experimental results for the instrumentation alone provide very limited insight into the impact of Clousot's unsoundness. For instance, while some explicit assumptions reflect details of the analysis (such as **A** and **W**, which are based on Clousot's heap-graph), others merely indicate the existence of a syntactic element (for instance, we generate one assumption of kind **C** per catch-block). Moreover, some explicit assumptions are not violated in any concrete program execution; for instance, the assumptions of kind **M** always hold if a program does not call a main method. To better understand the impact of Clousot's un-

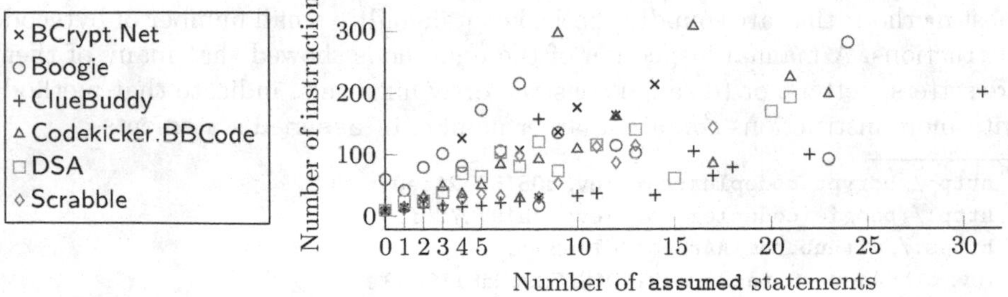

Fig. 2. The average number of bytecode instructions in the analyzed methods from each project versus the number of assumed statements in the methods

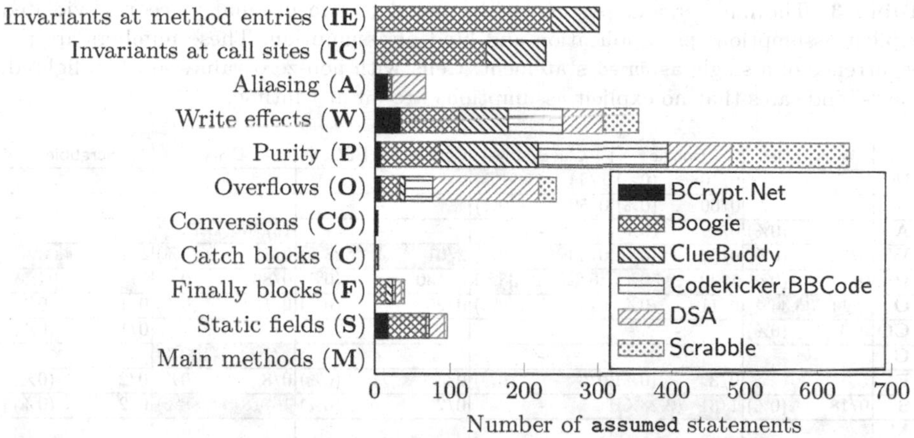

Fig. 3. Clousot's sources of unsoundness versus the number of **assumed** statements that are introduced in the analyzed methods of each project

Table 2. The number and percentage (rounded to two decimal places) of violated explicit assumptions per application and kind of assumption. These numbers include all executions of a single **assumed** statement. Cells with non-zero values are highlighted; the "-" indicates that no explicit assumptions are hit at runtime.

	BCrypt.Net	Boogie	ClueBuddy	Codekicker.BBCode	DSA	Scrabble
IE	-	0/1694124 (0%)	275/27318 (1.01%)	-	-	-
IC	-	0/628440 (0%)	0/9759 (0%)	-	-	-
A	0/25844436 (0%)	0/24771 (0%)	-	-	131/992 (13.21%)	-
W	0/6419169 (0%)	0/372851 (0%)	0/3589 (0%)	82/11577 (0.71%)	0/613 (0%)	25/5011 (0.50%)
P	0/6405279 (0%)	27/108506 (0.02%)	12198/241385 (5.05%)	0/10311 (0%)	0/1008 (0%)	425/21580 (1.97%)
O	102488804/326722626 (31.37%)	0/569258 (0%)	0/547 (0%)	0/1196 (0%)	0/6053 (0%)	0/909 (0%)
CO	0/6633876 (0%)	-	-	-	-	0/2 (0%)
C	-	-	-	-	1/1 (100%)	-
F	-	0/53246 (0%)	0/325 (0%)	0/114 (0%)	0/43 (0%)	0/65 (0%)
S	0/708 (0%)	1/155080 (0%)	-	0/7 (0%)	129/640 (20.16%)	0/15 (0%)
M	-	-	-	-	-	-

IE : invariants at method entries
IC : invariants at call sites
A : aliasing
W : write effects
P : purity
O : overflows
CO : conversions
C : catch blocks
F : finally blocks
S : static fields
M : main methods

sound assumptions, we measure how often the generated explicit assumptions are violated during concrete program executions.

Tab. 2 shows the number and percentage of violated explicit assumptions per application and kind of assumption. These numbers include *all executions* of a single **assumed** statement. That is, different executions of the same **assumed** statement in different method invocations or loop iterations are counted separately. Tab. 3 shows the corresponding numbers when counting only per *occurrence* of an **assumed** statement rather than per execution. For example, in BCrypt.Net, the assumption violations shown in Tab. 2 occur in only 4 **assumed** statements (see Tab. 3), which are all in the body of the same loop.

Table 3. The number and percentage (rounded to two decimal places) of violated explicit assumptions per application and kind of assumption. These numbers are per occurrence of a single `assumed` statement. Cells with non-zero values are highlighted; the "-" indicates that no explicit assumptions are hit at runtime.

	BCrypt.Net	Boogie	ClueBuddy	Codekicker.BBCode	DSA	Scrabble
IE	-	0/108 (0%)	7/44 (15.91%)	-	-	-
IC	-	0/60 (0%)	0/59 (0%)	-	-	-
A	0/16 (0%)	0/1 (0%)	-	-	16/46 (34.78%)	-
W	0/30 (0%)	0/32 (0%)	0/43 (0%)	2/61 (3.28%)	0/51 (0%)	1/25 (4.00%)
P	0/7 (0%)	1/40 (2.50%)	10/81 (12.35%)	0/130 (0%)	0/86 (0%)	11/85 (12.94%)
O	4/11 (36.36%)	0/11 (0%)	0/5 (0%)	0/25 (0%)	0/134 (0%)	0/13 (0%)
CO	0/3 (0%)	-	-	-	-	0/1 (0%)
C	-	-	-	-	1/1 (100%)	-
F	-	0/3 (0%)	0/5 (0%)	0/3 (0%)	0/8 (0%)	0/2 (0%)
S	0/18 (0%)	1/31 (3.23%)	-	0/2 (0%)	16/18 (88.88%)	0/2 (0%)
M	-	-	-	-	-	-

IE : invariants at method entries
IC : invariants at call sites
A : aliasing
W : write effects
P : purity
O : overflows
CO : conversions
C : catch blocks
F : finally blocks
S : static fields
M : main methods

4.3 Manual Inspection

We manually inspected a large number of explicit assumptions, including all violated assumptions, and made the following observations.

- "Invariants at method entries" (**IE**): Only Boogie and ClueBuddy contain invariant specifications, and all violations are found in ClueBuddy. These violations are all caused by constructors that call property setters in their body. The object invariants are, therefore, violated on entry to the setters since the constructors have not yet established the invariants. Objects that escape from their constructors are a well-known problem; a possible solution is to annotate methods that may operate on partially-initialized objects and, thus, must not assume their invariants [16].
- "Invariants at call sites" (**IC**): These assumptions are never violated because in all of our applications, sub-classes do not strengthen the object invariants of their super-classes such that calls to inherited methods could violate them.
- "Aliasing" (**A**): These assumptions are violated only in DSA. All violations occur in nine methods of two classes implementing singly and doubly-linked lists. For example, one violation occurs in method `AddAfter` when expressions `this.Tail`, `this.Head`, and the node to be added are aliased. The small number of these violations suggests that there is only a limited practical need for performing a sound, but expensive heap analysis. However, an analyzer could optionally allow users to run a sound heap analysis, for instance, for methods with violations of "aliasing" assumptions.
- "Write effects" (**W**): Tab. 3 shows that these assumptions are hardly ever violated. By inspecting assumptions of this kind that are not violated, we confirmed that the write effects assumed by Clousot are usually conservative.

- "Purity" (**P**): Most of these assumptions are violated for pure methods that return newly-allocated objects, that is, for non-deterministic methods. In applications without Code Contracts, these assumptions are introduced only in property getters, but are never violated.
- "Overflows" (**O**): These assumptions are violated only in BCrypt.Net. All violations occur in an `unchecked` block, which suppresses overflow exceptions. This indicates that, in this application, overflows are actually expected to occur or even intended.
- "Conversions" (**CO**): These assumptions are never violated. Our manual inspection showed that the value ranges of the converted expressions are sufficiently small such that no overflow may occur.
- "Catch blocks" (**C**): Only one assumption of this kind was introduced in a method that removes a value from an AVL tree in application DSA. An auxiliary method throws an exception when the AVL tree is empty. Catching this exception violates the assumption. This violation could be avoided by using an out-parameter instead of an exception to signal that the tree was empty.
- "Finally blocks" (**F**): Our instrumentation introduced only 39 assumptions about "finally blocks". The majority of these `finally` blocks are added by the compiler to desugar `foreach` statements. If the body of the `foreach` statement does not throw an exception, these assumptions are not violated.
- "Static fields" (**S**): The violations of these assumptions are, in some cases, due to static fields being lazily initialized, that is, being assigned non-null values after having first been read. Supporting lazy initialization via a language construct, such as Scala's "lazy val" declarations, could help avoid such violations. In other cases, the values of static fields are passed as arguments to library methods, which are designed to handle null arguments.

Missed Errors. The violation of an explicit assumption does not necessarily mean that Clousot misses errors since the resulting unsoundness may be irrelevant for the subsequent checks. To determine whether the assumption violations detected in our experiments might lead to missed errors, we manually inspected the containing methods of all 70 violations (computed from Tab. 3). We did not find any runtime errors or assertion violations that Clousot missed due to its unsound assumptions. With the exception of a few cases, it was fairly straightforward to determine whether an assumption violation could conceal an error. For instance, violations of explicit assumptions about "purity" (**P**) are harmless when there is only a single call to the pure method. The same holds for explicit assumptions about "aliasing" (**A**) when the updated field, property, or array element is not accessed after the update.

The fact that we did not find any missed errors due to assumption violations possibly indicates that providing slightly weaker soundness guarantees in certain situations in favor of performance, precision, and low annotation overhead does not compromise Clousot's effectiveness; its unsound assumptions are not problematic in the code and executions we investigated.

4.4 Threats to Validity

We identified the following threats to the validity of our experiments:

- *Instrumentation*: It is possible that we missed some of Clousot's unsound assumptions. Since we elicited the assumptions very diligently, it seems unlikely that we overlooked any major sources of unsoundness. There are several sources of unsoundness that we identified, but do not capture (see Sect. 2.4). For most of these sources, a syntactic check suffices to determine whether a program might be affected. Moreover, even though our instrumentation captures most of Clousot's unsound assumptions precisely, it under-approximates the unsound treatment of write effects for calls to uninstrumented (library) methods and of non-deterministic pure methods. As a result, it is possible that Clousot's analysis of a method is unsound even though all runtime checks for explicit assumptions pass (this is very unlikely for non-deterministic pure methods).
- *Runtime checking*: We measured assumption violations in executions of the projects' test suites. There were no failing tests, that is, any errors detected by the test suites have been fixed. This explains in part why we did not find any errors missed by Clousot. However, in our manual inspection of the violated assumptions, we checked the entire method, that is, all execution paths of the method for all its input states, not just the code covered by the test suite. Thus, we could have detected errors that the tests missed.
- *Project selection and sample size*: The projects in our experiments were chosen from different application domains. All projects were required to include a test suite. We selected projects with and without Code Contracts. Since Clousot analyzes each method modularly, we were able to pick those DLLs that have the most comprehensive test suites. We ran Clousot on 978 methods; `assumed` statements were added in 652 methods, 396 out of which were hit during the execution of the projects' test suites. Therefore, we believe that our projects are representative for a large class of C# code bases.

5 Related Work

To the best of our knowledge, there is no existing work on experimentally evaluating sources of deliberate unsoundness in static analyzers.

There are, however, several approaches for ensuring soundness of static analyzers and checkers, ranging from manual proofs [14], over interactive and automatic proofs [3,4], to less formal techniques, such as "smoke checking" [1].

Many static analyzers compromise soundness to improve on other qualities such as precision or efficiency (see Cousot and Cousot [7] for an overview), and there is existing work on evaluating these other qualities of analyzers in practice. For instance, Sridharan and Fink [15] evaluate the efficiency of Andersen's pointer analysis, and Liang et al. [11] evaluate the precision of different heap abstractions. We show that such evaluations are also possible for the unsoundness in static analyzers, and propose a practical approach for doing so.

Our explicit assumptions could be used to express semantic environment conditions inferred from a base program, as in VMV [13]; a new version of the program could then be instrumented with these inferred conditions (in the form of assumptions) to reduce the number of warnings reported by Clousot. Moreover, our technique could be applied in "probabilistic static analyzers" [12] to determine the probabilities of their judgments about analyzed code. Specifically, one could estimate the probability that an unsound assumption holds (or is violated) based on its value along a number of concrete executions.

Finally, we refer the reader to `http://soundiness.org` for the "soundiness" movement in static program analysis, which brings forward the ubiquity of unsoundness in static analyzers, draws a distinction between analyzers with specific, well-defined soundness trade-offs and tools that are not concerned with soundness at all, and issues a call to the research community to clearly identify the nature and extent of unsoundness in static analyzers.

6 Conclusion

In this paper, we report on the first systematic effort to document and evaluate the sources of deliberate unsoundness in a widely used, commercial static analyzer. Our technique is general and applicable to any analyzer whose unsoundness is expressible using a code instrumentation. In particular, we have explained how to derive the instrumentation by concretizing relevant portions of the abstract state (in our case, the heap-graph). We believe that this approach generalizes to a large class of assumptions made by static analyzers.

Our work can help designers of static analyzers in finding good trade-offs. We encourage them to document all compromises of soundness and to motivate them empirically. Such a documentation facilitates tool integration since other static analyzers or test case generators could be applied to compensate for the explicit assumptions. Information about violated assumptions (for instance, collected during testing) could also be valuable in identifying methods that require special attention during testing and code reviews. Finally, our results could be used to derive programming guidelines and language designs that mitigate the unsoundness of a static analyzer.

Acknowledgments. We are especially grateful to Francesco Logozzo for numerous discussions and his active support; this work would not have been possible without his help. We also thank Mike Barnett, Manuel Fähndrich, and Herman Venter for their valuable help and feedback, and the reviewers for their constructive comments.

References

1. Barnett, M., Chang, B.-Y.E., DeLine, R., Jacobs, B., Leino, K.R.M.: Boogie: A modular reusable verifier for object-oriented programs. In: de Boer, F.S., Bonsangue, M.M., Graf, S., de Roever, W.-P. (eds.) FMCO 2005. LNCS, vol. 4111, pp. 364–387. Springer, Heidelberg (2006)

2. Bessey, A., Block, K., Chelf, B., Chou, A., Fulton, B., Hallem, S., Gros, C.-H., Kamsky, A., McPeak, S., Engler, D.R.: A few billion lines of code later: Using static analysis to find bugs in the real world. CACM 53, 66–75 (2010)
3. Besson, F., Cornilleau, P.-E., Jensen, T.: Result certification of static program analysers with automated theorem provers. In: Cohen, E., Rybalchenko, A. (eds.) VSTTE 2013. LNCS, vol. 8164, pp. 304–325. Springer, Heidelberg (2014)
4. Blazy, S., Laporte, V., Maroneze, A., Pichardie, D.: Formal verification of a C value analysis based on abstract interpretation. In: Logozzo, F., Fähndrich, M. (eds.) SAS 2013. LNCS, vol. 7935, pp. 324–344. Springer, Heidelberg (2013)
5. Christakis, M., Emmisberger, P., Müller, P.: Dynamic test generation with static fields and initializers. In: Bonakdarpour, B., Smolka, S.A. (eds.) RV 2014. LNCS, vol. 8734, pp. 269–284. Springer, Heidelberg (2014)
6. Christakis, M., Müller, P., Wüstholz, V.: Collaborative verification and testing with explicit assumptions. In: Giannakopoulou, D., Méry, D. (eds.) FM 2012. LNCS, vol. 7436, pp. 132–146. Springer, Heidelberg (2012)
7. Cousot, P., Cousot, R., Feret, J., Miné, A., Mauborgne, L., Monniaux, D., Rival, X.: Varieties of static analyzers: A comparison with ASTRÉE. In: TASE, pp. 3–20. IEEE Computer Society (2007)
8. Drossopoulou, S., Francalanza, A., Müller, P., Summers, A.J.: A unified framework for verification techniques for object invariants. In: Vitek, J. (ed.) ECOOP 2008. LNCS, vol. 5142, pp. 412–437. Springer, Heidelberg (2008)
9. Fähndrich, M., Barnett, M., Logozzo, F.: Embedded contract languages. In: SAC, pp. 2103–2110. ACM (2010)
10. Fähndrich, M., Logozzo, F.: Static contract checking with abstract interpretation. In: Beckert, B., Marché, C. (eds.) FoVeOOS 2010. LNCS, vol. 6528, pp. 10–30. Springer, Heidelberg (2011)
11. Liang, P., Tripp, O., Naik, M., Sagiv, M.: A dynamic evaluation of the precision of static heap abstractions. In: OOPSLA, pp. 411–427. ACM (2010)
12. Livshits, B., Lahiri, S.K. In: defense of probabilistic static analysis. In: APPROX (2014)
13. Logozzo, F., Lahiri, S.K., Fähndrich, M., Blackshear, S.: Verification modulo versions: Towards usable verification. In: PLDI, pp. 294–304. ACM (2014)
14. Midtgaard, J., Adams, M.D., Might, M.: A structural soundness proof for Shivers's escape technique: A case for Galois connections. In: Miné, A., Schmidt, D. (eds.) SAS 2012. LNCS, vol. 7460, pp. 352–369. Springer, Heidelberg (2012)
15. Sridharan, M., Fink, S.J.: The complexity of Andersen's analysis in practice. In: Palsberg, J., Su, Z. (eds.) SAS 2009. LNCS, vol. 5673, pp. 205–221. Springer, Heidelberg (2009)
16. Summers, A.J., Müller, P.: Freedom before commitment: A lightweight type system for object initialisation. In: OOPSLA, pp. 1013–1032. ACM (2011)

Bounded Implementations of Replicated Data Types

Madhavan Mukund*, Gautham Shenoy R.**, and S.P. Suresh***

Chennai Mathematical Institute, India
{madhavan,gautshen,spsuresh}@cmi.ac.in

Abstract. Replicated data types store copies of identical data across multiple servers in a distributed system. For the replicas to satisfy eventual consistency, these data types should be designed to guarantee conflict free convergence of all copies in the presence of concurrent updates. This requires maintaining history related metadata that, in principle, is unbounded.

Burkhardt et al have proposed a declarative framework to specify eventually consistent replicated data types (ECRDTs). Using this, they introduce replication-aware simulations for verifying the correctness of ECRDT implementations. Unfortunately, this approach does not yield an effective strategy for formal verification.

By imposing reasonable restrictions on the underlying network, we recast their declarative framework in terms of standard labelled partial orders. For well-behaved ECRDT specifications, we are able to construct canonical finite-state reference implementations with bounded metadata, which can be used for formal verification of ECRDT implementations via CEGAR. We can also use our reference implementations to design more effective test suites for ECRDT implementations.

1 Introduction

Replicated data types are used by web services that need to maintain multiple copies of the same data across different servers to provide better availability and fault tolerance. Clients can access and update data at any copy. Replicated data types cover a wide class of data stores that include distributed databases and DNS servers, as well as NoSQL stores such as Redis and memcached. The CAP theorem [1] shows that it is impossible for replicated data types to provide both strong consistency and high availability in the presence of network and node failures. Hence, web services that aim to be highly available in the presence of faults opt for a weaker notion of consistency known as *eventual consistency*. Eventual consistency allows copies to be inconsistent for a finite period of time. However, the web service must ensure that conflicts arising due to concurrent

* Partially supported by Indo-French CNRS LIA Informel and a grant from Infosys Foundation.
** Supported by TCS Research Fellowship.
*** Partially supported by a grant from Infosys Foundation.

D. D'Souza et al. (Eds.): VMCAI 2015, LNCS 8931, pp. 355–372, 2015.

updates across the multiple copies are resolved to guarantee that all the copies eventually agree. *Conflict-free Replicated Data Types (CRDTs)*, introduced in [2,3], are a sub class of replicated data types that are eventually consistent and conflict free.

An abstract specification of a data type describes its properties independent of any implementation. Such a specification plays a crucial role in formal verification of the correctness of any implementation of the data type. Most of the early work on CRDTs described these data types through implementations [2–5]. Recently, a comprehensive framework has been proposed in [6] to provide declarative specifications for a wide variety of replicated data types, along with a methodology to prove the correctness of an implementation via replication aware simulations. Unfortunately this strategy does not lend itself to effective formal verification of the implementations.

Finite state abstractions have been widely studied in the context of formal verification. Model checking, for instance, uses techniques such as state space enumeration, abstract interpretation and symbolic execution to algorthmically verify if an abstract finite state system satisfies its specification. Finite state models such as automata over distributed words, communicating finite state machines and Petri nets have been successfully used to model and verify concurrent and distributed systems.

In this paper, we focus on a class of CRDTs known as the *Commutative Replicated Data Types (CmRDTs)* whose replicas broadcast every update they receive from a client. The key contributions of our work are as follows

- Demonstrating the use of labelled partial orders as a framework for providing declarative specifications of CmRDTs.
- Generalizing the *gossip problem* introduced in [7] and providing a bounded solution to this problem assuming bounded concurrency.
- Using the bounded solution of the gossip problem to obtain finite state implementations of CmRDTs whose specifications satisfy certain properties.

The paper is organized as follows. In Section 2 we introduce replicated data types. Following this, we show how to use standard labelled partial orders as a framework for declarative specification for CmRDTs. After defining bounded CmRDTs, we generalize the gossip problem and provide a bounded solution in Section 5. We then show how this bounded solution can be used to derive a bounded implementation of CmRDTs. In the next section we show how bounded implementations can be used in the formal verification of CmRDTs. In the final section we summarize our work and discuss interesting challenges.

2 Replicated Data Types

We consider distributed systems consisting of a set $\mathcal{R}$ of N replicas, denoted $[0..N-1]$. We use p, q, r, s and their primed variants to range over $\mathcal{R}$. These replicas are interconnected through an asynchronous network. We assume that replicas can crash and recover infinitely often. However, when a replica recovers from a crash it is expected to resume operation from some safe state that it was in before the crash. We are interested in replicated data types that are implemented on top of such distributed systems.

A replicated data type exposes a set of side-effect-free operations known as *queries* for clients to obtain information contained in the data type. It makes available a set of state-modifying operations known as *updates* to allow clients to update the contents of the data type. For example in a replicated set, *contains* is a query method, while *add* and *delete* are update methods.

At any point, a client can interact with any one of the N replicas. The replica that services a query (respectively, update) request from the client is said to be the *source replica* for that query (respectively, update). The source replica uses its local information to process the query. Similarly, it updates its local state on receiving an update request from the client.

In this paper, we restrict our attention to a class of replicated data types called *Commutative Replicated Data Types (CmRDTs)*, introduced in [2]. In these data types, each time a replica receives an update request from a client, it applies the update locally and broadcasts to all the other replicas a message containing the data that they require to apply this update. On receiving this broadcast, each replica performs a local update using the data sent by the source replica. We assume that the updates are delivered in causal order—that is, if update u_1 at replica r_1 is initiated before update u_2 at replica r_2, then every replica receives information about u_1 before information about u_2. We shall define this notion formally in the next section. Under this assumption, we note that when a replica receives and applies an update operation, its state would contain the effect of all operations that causally precede the current update. We now define some terminology introduced in [2,3] to reason about these data types.

A CmRDT $\mathcal{D}$ is a tuple $(\mathcal{V}, \mathcal{Q}, \mathcal{U})$ where:

- $\mathcal{V}$ is the underlying set of values stored in the datatype and is called the *universe* of a replicated datatype. For instance, the universe of a replicated read-write register is the set of integers that the register can hold.
- $\mathcal{Q}$ denotes the set of query methods exposed by the replicated data type.
- $\mathcal{U}$ denotes the set of update methods.

The send and receive components of a broadcast that follows an update operation are denoted by **send** and **receive**, respectively. We denote by $\mathcal{M}$ the set $\{\textbf{send}, \textbf{receive}\}$.

For an instance of an operation $o \in \mathcal{Q} \cup \mathcal{U} \cup \mathcal{M}$, we use *Rep*$(o)$, *Op*$(o)$ and *Args*(o) to denote the source replica, operation name and arguments, respectively, of the operation.

Definition 1 (Run). *A* run *of a replicated data type is a pair* (α, φ) *where*

- α *is a sequence of operations* $I o_1 o_2 \dots o_n$*, where* I *is a special operation that initializes the states of all the* N *replicas, and each* $o_i \in \mathcal{Q} \cup \mathcal{U} \cup \mathcal{M}$.
- φ *is a partial function from* $[0..n]$ *to* $2^{[0..n]}$ *such that*
  - $dom(\varphi) = \{i \leq n \mid o_i \text{ is a } \textbf{send} \text{ operation}\}$.

- *$\forall j \in \varphi(i) : j > i$ and o_j is a* **matching receive** *operation. In particular, the matching receive operation at replica r is denoted by $\varphi_r(i)$.*

Note that every update operation in a run $Io_1o_2 \ldots o_n$ will be followed by a send operation where the source replica broadcasts details of this update to all other replicas. Without loss of generality, we assume that this send event is the next event in the run: in other words, if o_i is an update event, then the send event that broadcasts details of o_i to all other replicas is the event o_{i+1}.

For $\alpha = Io_1o_2 \ldots o_n$, we let $\alpha[j]$ denote the operation o_j and $\alpha[:j]$ denote the prefix $Io_1o_2 \ldots o_j$. Note that $\alpha[0]$ (and hence $\alpha[:0]$) is always I. The subsequence of α consisting of all operations with source replica r is denoted α^r. (By convention, every replica r is a source replica for I.)

The state of replica r at the end of the run α is denoted by $S^r(\alpha)$.

Definition 2 (History). *Let (α, φ) be a run and r be a replica. The* history *of r with respect α, denoted by $\mathcal{H}^r(\alpha)$ is the set of all update operations whose effects are applied at r, either directly or indirectly, to arrive at the state $S^r(\alpha)$. Formally, $\mathcal{H}^r(\alpha)$ is inductively defined as follows:*

– *For $\alpha = I$, $\forall r \in \mathcal{R} : \mathcal{H}^r(\alpha) = \emptyset$*

– *For $i > 0$,*
$$\mathcal{H}^r(\alpha[:i]) = \begin{cases} \mathcal{H}^r(\alpha[:i{-}1]) & \text{if } Rep(\alpha[i]) \neq r \text{ or } \\ & \quad Op(\alpha[i]) \in \mathcal{Q} \cup \{\mathbf{send}\} \\ \mathcal{H}^r(\alpha[:i{-}1]) \cup \{\alpha[i]\} & \text{if } Rep(\alpha[i]) = r \text{ and } \\ & \quad Op(\alpha[i]) \in \mathcal{U} \\ \mathcal{H}^r(\alpha[:i{-}1]) \cup \mathcal{H}^s(\alpha[:j]) & \text{if } Rep(\alpha[i]) = r, \\ & \quad Op(\alpha[i]) = \mathbf{receive}, \\ & \quad Rep(\alpha[j]) = s, \\ & \quad \text{and } \varphi_r(j) = i \end{cases}$$

We define causality and concurrency for pairs of update operations as follows.

Definition 3 (Happened-Before and Concurrency). *Let $u = \alpha[i]$ and $u' = \alpha[j]$ be update operations at source replicas r and r', respectively, in a run (α, φ). We say that u has* happened before *u', denoted $u \xrightarrow{\text{hb}} u'$, if $u \in \mathcal{H}^{r'}(\alpha[:j{-}1])$.*

If neither $u \xrightarrow{\text{hb}} u'$ nor $u' \xrightarrow{\text{hb}} u$, we say that u and u' are concurrent. *This is denoted by $u \parallel u'$.*

Strong eventual consistency (SEC) [3] is a stronger variant of *eventual consistency* [8] that is useful for reasoning about the correctness of replicated systems.

Definition 4 (Strong Eventual Consistency). *Let (α, φ) be a run and let r, r' be a pair of replicas. We say that the replicated data type satisfies strong eventual consistency if r and r' are query equivalent whenever $\mathcal{H}^r(\alpha) = \mathcal{H}^{r'}(\alpha)$— that is, for any query after α, r and r' return the same values.*

Note that strong eventual consistency does not refer to the order in which updates are applied at a particular replica. As long as the sets of updates applied at two replicas are the same, the observable behaviour of the replicas is identical. *Commutative replicated data types (CmRDTs)* [2,3] are a class of replicated data types that satisfy strong eventual consistency by construction. The definition of CmRDTs ensures that replicas do not need to detect or resolve conflicts. The following characterization of CmRDTs is from [3].

Definition 5 (CmRDT). *A replicated data type is said to be a commutative replicated data type (CmRDT) iff for any pair of update operations u, u' if $u \parallel u'$ then u and u' are commutative. If $u \xrightarrow{hb} u'$ then at every replica, the effect of u is applied before applying the effect of u'.*

The recent paper [6] provides a comprehensive declarative framework for specification of a large class of replicated data types. The framework is very general and accommodates a wide variety of data stores. For instance, it allows reasoning about data stores with multiple replicated objects, with arbitrary delivery patterns for messages. The variety of features permitted in the declarative framework render it impractical for effective verification of CmRDTs. Retaining the core idea from [6], we provide the specifications of CmRDTs in terms of standard labelled partial orders [9,10] in the next section.

3 Labelled Partial Orders Models for Replicated Data Types

Let (α, φ) be a run of a replicated data type. We define $\mathcal{E}_\alpha$ to be the set of *events* associated with **send** and **receive** operations in α.

$\mathcal{E}_\alpha = \{e_i \mid 0 \leq i < |\alpha|, Op(\alpha[i]) \in \mathcal{U} \cup \{\textbf{receive}\}\}$. Each $e_i \in \mathcal{E}_\alpha$ corresponds to some operation $\alpha[i]$ in α. We define $Rep(e_i)$, $Op(e_i)$ and $Args(e_i)$ to be $Rep(\alpha[i])$, $Rep(\alpha[i])$ and $Args(\alpha[i])$.

We extend φ to $\mathcal{E}_\alpha$ as follows. For $e_i \in \mathcal{E}_\alpha$, let $\alpha[i]$ be the corresponding event in α. If $\alpha[i] \in \mathcal{U}$, recall that $\alpha[i+1]$ is assumed to be the send event where the effect of this update is broadcast to all other replicas. We define $\varphi_\alpha(e_i) = \{e_j \mid j \in \varphi(i+1)\}$. Further, we define $\varphi_{r,\alpha}(e_i) = e_j$ if $e_j \in \varphi_\alpha(e_i) \wedge Rep(e_j) = r$.

For a replica r, let $\mathcal{E}^r_\alpha = \{e \in \mathcal{E}_\alpha \mid Rep(e) = r\}$. Since each replica is sequential, all events in $\mathcal{E}^r_\alpha$ are totally ordered. Let $\leq^r_\alpha$ denote this total order on $\mathcal{E}^r_\alpha$. We define $\preceq_\alpha$ to be the smallest partial order on $\mathcal{E}_\alpha$ such that:

- For any replica r, and any pair of events $e, e' \in \mathcal{E}^r_\alpha$, $e \leq^r_\alpha e' \implies e \preceq_\alpha e'$.
- For any event $e \in \mathcal{E}_\alpha$ with $Op(e) = \textbf{receive}$, $\varphi^{-1}_\alpha(e) \preceq_\alpha e$.

We say that a pair of events $e, e' \in \mathcal{E}$ are *concurrent* (denoted by $e \parallel e'$) when neither $e \preceq e'$ nor $e' \preceq e$.

Definition 6 (Trace). *A run (α, φ) gives rise to an associated* labelled partial order $(\mathcal{E}_\alpha, \varphi_\alpha, \preceq_\alpha)$. *We shall use the term* trace *(borrowed from the theory of Mazurkiewicz traces [9]) to refer to this labelled partial order.*

We usually drop the subscript α and assume that the trace that we refer to has an associated run α. Recall that we have assumed that messages are delivered in causal order. This can be formalized in the trace framework as follows:

$$\forall e_i, e_j \in \mathcal{E} : (\, Op(e_i) = Op(e_j) = \textbf{receive} \wedge \\ Rep(e_i) = Rep(e_j) \wedge \varphi^{-1}(e_i) \preceq \varphi^{-1}(e_j)\,) \implies e_i \preceq e_j.$$

Definition 7 (Subtrace). *Let $t = (\mathcal{E}, \varphi, \preceq)$ be a trace. Each subset $\mathcal{E}' \subseteq \mathcal{E}$ defines a* subtrace *$t^{\mathcal{E}'} = (\mathcal{E}', \varphi', \preceq')$ where $\varphi' = \varphi|_{\mathcal{E}'}$ and $\preceq' = \preceq|_{\mathcal{E}'}$.*

Note that a subtrace can have "holes"—we could have three events $e \preceq e' \preceq e''$ in t and a subtrace t' containing $\{e, e''\}$ but not e'.

If X is a predicate that defines the subset $\mathcal{E}' \subseteq \mathcal{E}$ then t^X denotes the subtrace $t^{\mathcal{E}'}$. As special cases, $t^{\mathcal{U}}$ and $t^{\mathbf{receive}}$ respectively denote the subtraces consisting of only the update events and **receive** events in t, respectively. We shall denote by $\mathcal{E}^{\mathcal{U}}$ and $\mathcal{E}^{\mathbf{receive}}$ their respective event sets. For a pair of traces t and t', the notions $t \subseteq t', t \cup t'$ and $t \cap t'$, are defined in the standard manner. For $t = (\mathcal{E}, \varphi, \preceq)$, we write $e \in t$ to mean that $e \in \mathcal{E}$.

Definition 8 (Downward Closure). *Let $t = (\mathcal{E}, \varphi, \preceq)$ be a trace. A subset $\mathcal{E}' \subseteq \mathcal{E}$ is said to be* downward closed *if $\forall e, e' \in \mathcal{E} : (e \preceq e' \wedge e' \in \mathcal{E}' \implies e \in \mathcal{E}')$*

In particular, for an event e, the downward closure of e is defined to be the set $\downarrow e = \{e' \in \mathcal{E} \mid e' \preceq e\}$.

Clearly, the entire set of events $\mathcal{E}$ is downward closed. Also, if $\mathcal{E}'$ and $\mathcal{E}''$ are downward closed subsets of $\mathcal{E}$, then so are $\mathcal{E}' \cup \mathcal{E}''$ and $\mathcal{E}' \cap \mathcal{E}''$. If $\mathcal{E}'$ is a downward closed set and $\mathcal{E}''$ is the set of maximal events in $\mathcal{E}'$, then $\mathcal{E}' = \bigcup_{e \in \mathcal{E}''} \downarrow e$.

Definition 9 (Ideal). *Let $t = (\mathcal{E}, \varphi, \preceq)$ and $\mathcal{E}' \subseteq \mathcal{E}$. The subtrace $t^{\mathcal{E}'}$ is said to be an* ideal *if $\mathcal{E}'$ is downward closed.*

In particular, if $\mathcal{E}' = \downarrow e$ for some $e \in \mathcal{E}$, then we refer to the ideal $t^{\mathcal{E}'}$ as the prime trace *generated by e and denote it by t_e.*

Definition 10. *Let $t = (\mathcal{E}, \varphi, \preceq)$ be an ideal. Then,*

- *$Events(t)$ denotes $\mathcal{E}$, the set of events in t.*
- *$Count(t) = |Events(t)|$ denotes the number of events in $\mathcal{E}$.*
- *$maxSet(t)$ denotes the set $\{e \in \mathcal{E} \mid \nexists e' \in \mathcal{E} : e \preceq e'\}$ of* maximal events *in t.*
- *For a replica r, the* maximal r event *in t, denoted by $max_r(t)$, is an event e such that $Rep(e) = r$ and $\forall e' \in \mathcal{E} : Rep(e') = r \implies e' \preceq e$. (Note that $max_r(t)$ is always defined since the event corresponding to the initialization operation I is an r event for every replica r.)*
- *The* r-view *of t is the ideal generated by $max_r(t)$ and is denoted by $\partial_r(t)$.*
- *The* latest r' event *that r is aware of in the ideal t, denoted by $latest_{r \to r'}(t)$ is defined to be $max_{r'}(\partial_r(t))$.*

The behaviour of a replicated data type is the set of traces that it generates. Note that this set is downward closed—if a trace t is present in the set then all ideals in t are also present in the set. We shall denote this set by $\mathcal{T}$. We let $\mathcal{T}_p$ denote the set of all prime traces in $\mathcal{T}$. In the trace framework, the definitions of happened-before and concurrency are straightforward.

Definition 11 (Happened Before and Concurrency). *Let* $t = (\mathcal{E}, \varphi, \preceq)$ *be a trace with events* e *and* e' *that are associated with update operations* u *and* u'*, respectively. Then* u *is said to have* happened before u'*, denoted* $u \xrightarrow{\text{hb}} u'$*, if* $e \preceq e'$*, and* u *and* u' *are said to be* concurrent *if neither* $e \preceq e'$ *nor* $e' \preceq e$*.*

We can now reformulate *strong eventual consistency (SEC)* as follows.

Definition 12 (Strong Eventual Consistency(SEC)). *Let* t *be a trace and let* r, r' *be a pair of replicas. We say that the replicated data type satisfies strong eventual consistency if the replicas* r *and* r' *are query equivalent whenever* $Events(\partial_r(t)^{\mathcal{U}}) = Events(\partial_{r'}(t)^{\mathcal{U}})$*.*

Note that strong eventual consistency refers only to the subtraces $\partial_r(t)^{\mathcal{U}}$ and $\partial_{r'}(t)^{\mathcal{U}}$ defined by the updates events in the r and r' views of t. These views may have different sets of **receive** events.

We now show how we can specify CmRDTs in the framework of traces.

3.1 Specifications of CmRDTs

The internal state of a replicated data type is exposed to the client via queries. Hence, a specification framework for a CmRDT should provide mechanisms for uniformly defining the behaviour of any query operation that is applied at replica at any stage of the computation, based on the update operations in the history of the replica at that stage. Note that in the framework of traces, the history of a replica corresponds to the update events in view of the replica, which is a prime trace. Hence, we define the specification of a CmRDT with respect to prime traces.

Definition 13 (Declarative Specification). *Let* $\mathcal{D} = (\mathcal{V}, \mathcal{Q}, \mathcal{U})$ *be a CmRDT. Let* $\mathcal{A} = \bigcup_{q \in \mathcal{Q}} Args(q)$*. The specification of* $\mathcal{D}$*, is a function* $Spec_{\mathcal{D}} : \mathcal{Q} \times \mathcal{A} \times \mathcal{T}_p \rightarrow \mathcal{V}$ *which determines the return value of any query* $q \in \mathcal{Q}$ *in any prime trace* $t \in \mathcal{T}_p$*.*

We highlight the key differences between our declarative specification and the one proposed in [6]. Since messages in CmRDTs are causally delivered, the $\preceq$ relation in the trace framework captures both the visibility relation *vis* and the replica order relation *ro* from [6]. However, while $\preceq$ is a partial order, *vis* is only defined to be an acyclic relation over the events, while *ro* is the union of total orders that is recovered by restricting $\preceq$ to events of the same replica. In [6], the *execution context* of an event is defined to be the set of all events that are visible to the event. The specification defines the return value of each query in every execution context. In the trace framework, the execution context for an event is the ideal generated by that event.

We now provide declarative specifications for a few CmRDTs in the framework of traces.

PN Counters. A PN counter maintains a counter by keeping track of the number of increments and decrements it receives. A query should return the latest count that a replica is aware of.

- $\mathcal{U} = \{Inc, Dec\}$
- $\mathcal{Q} = \{Fetch\}$ and $arity(Fetch) = 0$
- **Specification:** Let t be a trace. Let $I = \{e \in t \mid Op(e) = Inc\}$ and $D = \{e \in t \mid Op(e) = Dec\}$. In any prime trace t,

$$Spec_{Counter}(Fetch, \bot, t) = Count(t^I) - Count(t^D)$$

MV registers An MV register is a read-write register that on a read, returns the values of the latest (possibly concurrent) writes.

- $\mathcal{U} = \{Write\}$
- $\mathcal{Q} = \{Read\}$ and $arity(Read) = 0$
- **Specification:** Let $W = \{e \in t \mid Op(e) = Write\}$. In any prime trace t,

$$Spec_{MVReg}(Read, \bot, t) = \bigcup Args(maxSet(t^W))$$

OR sets An OR set is a distributed set that follows the "add-wins" semantics for concurrent adds and deletes of the same element.

- $\mathcal{U} = \{Add, Delete\}$
- $\mathcal{Q} = \{Contains\}$ and $arity(Contains) = 1$
- **Specification:** For an element $x \in \mathcal{V}$, define a predicate $U_x = \{e \in t \mid x \in Args(e)\}$. In any prime trace t,

$$Spec_{ORSet}(Contains, (x), t) = True \iff \exists e \in maxSet(t^{U_x}) : Op(e) = Add$$

In the next section, we discuss how declarative specifications in terms of labelled partial orders can be used to obtain bounded implementations for a class of *well-behaved* CmRDTs.

4 Bounded CmRDTs

In this section we discuss sufficient conditions for replicated data types to have a bounded implementation.

Definition 14. *We say that an implementation of a CmRDT is bounded if the information maintained by every replica and the contents of each message propagating an update are bounded, regardless of the length of the computation.*

Finite state implementations have played an important role in formal verification of reactive systems. We shall see later that they can be used for verification of replicated data types as well. We use the example of OR-Sets to discuss the challenges involved in arriving at a bounded implementation.

Observe that if the universe $\mathcal{V}$ of an OR-Set is unbounded, we cannot hope to achieve a bounded implementation since we need labels of unbounded size to name the elements in $\mathcal{V}$, even if the size of the actual set is bounded. Hence, we assume that $\mathcal{V}$ is bounded, in order to achieve a bounded implementation.

If the size of $\mathcal{V}$ is bounded by K, then the number of unique queries is also bounded by K. In the OR-Set specification, for an element $x \in \mathcal{V}$, the query **contains**(x) requires only the maximal x-events present in the view of the replica. The number of such maximal x-events is bounded by N. This implies that the number of events required to answer a query at any point in time is bounded by KN. Thus, in a reference implementation, it suffices to keep track of only this finite fragment of the partial order at any replica. Replicas can purge from their view events that are no longer relevant for answering any queries.

However, this requires the causal order between the relevant events to be correctly maintained by the replicas. Typically, vector clocks have been used to track causality among the events of a distributed system. However, vector clocks grow monotonically as the computation progresses. Hence, any implementation that uses vector clocks cannot be bounded.

Earlier work such as [7, 11] has implemented bounded timestamping in distributed systems by solving what is known as the *gossip problem*. In the next section, we present a generalized version of the gossip problem and provide a bounded solution to it. We then use the bounded solution to arrive at a bounded implementation for a class of well behaved replicated data types.

5 Generalized Gossip Problem

Consider a distributed system with N replicas. Whenever a replica interacts with a client, it does some local processing and broadcasts a message to all the other replicas. This is similar to the behaviour of CmRDTs described earlier. Suppose now that every replica keeps track of the latest event it knows about every other replica in the system. During a broadcast, along with the message, each replica r also sends across its knowledge about the latest event of every other replica r' in the system. A recipient r'' needs to correctly compute for every replica r' whether its knowledge of the latest r' event is more up to date than the knowledge of r' that it has received from r. This is known as the *gossip problem*, and has been studied in [7, 11].

In the generalized gossip problem, instead of maintaining just the latest events, we assume that every replica keeps track of a bounded subtrace of its view which we refer to as the primary information.

Definition 15 (Information graphs). *An information graph G of a trace $t = (\mathcal{E}, \preceq, \varphi)$ is a subtrace t^E where $E \subseteq_{\text{fin}} \mathcal{E}^{\mathcal{U}}$. We denote the set of all information graphs of t by $\mathcal{G}(t)$. Let $\mathcal{G} = \bigcup_{t \in \mathcal{T}} \mathcal{G}(t)$.*

Definition 16 (Primary information). *A* primary information function *is a function $f : \mathcal{T}_p \rightarrow \mathcal{G}$ that assigns an information graph to each prime trace so that the following conditions are satisfied.*

– $f(t) \in \mathcal{G}(t)$.
– *For any trace* $t = \downarrow e$ *and* $e' \in maxSet(t \setminus \{e\})$, $f(t) \cap \downarrow e' \subseteq f(\downarrow e')$.

A primary information function f is said to be bounded *if* $\exists M\ \forall t : |f(t)| \leq M$.

Our goal is to ensure that $f(\downarrow e)$ can be computed from $f(\downarrow e_1), \ldots, f(\downarrow e_n)$ and e, where $\{e_1, \ldots, e_n\} = maxSet(\downarrow e \setminus \{e\})$. We refer to this as the **(generalized) gossip problem** for a primary information function f. Observe that even if $f(t)$ is a bounded set for every t, we still need an unbounded set of labels to unambiguously identify the events.

We say that the gossip problem for f has a bounded solution if we can update f using a bounded set of labels to identify the events. Clearly we must ensure that no two distinct events in the primary information have the same labels. Hence, each replica needs to identify which of its events are in the primary information of other replicas. To capture this, we define secondary information.

Definition 17 (Secondary information). *A function* $F : \mathcal{R} \times \mathcal{T}_p \to 2^{(\mathcal{E}^0)}$ $(\mathcal{E}^0 = \bigcup_{t \in \mathcal{T}_p} Events(t))$ *is a* secondary information function *for a primary information function f if, for each prime trace* $t = \downarrow e$*:*

1. $Events(f(\partial_r(t))) \cap \mathcal{E}^{\mathcal{U}} \subseteq F(r,t) \subseteq Events(t) \cap \mathcal{E}^r$.
2. $F(r,t) = F(r, \downarrow max_r(t))$ *if e is not an r-event.*
3. $F(r,t)$ *is computable from e,* $\bigcup_{e' \in maxSet(\downarrow e \setminus \{e\})} F(Rep(e'), \downarrow e')$ *and* $f(t)$*, if e is an r-event.*
4. *If e and e′ are r-events such that* $e' \in \downarrow e \setminus F(r, \downarrow e)$*, then for any r′ and t′,* $e \in \partial_{r'}(t') \implies e' \notin f(\partial_{r'}(t'))$.
5. *For an r-event* $e' \in t \setminus F(r,t)$*, if* $e' \in f(\downarrow e'')$*, then* $\varphi_{r''}(e'') \in \partial_r(t)$ *for all r″.*

A secondary information function F is said to be bounded *if* $\exists M\ \forall r\ \forall t : |F(r,t)| \leq M$.

The first three conditions are straightforward: they say that F is locally updatable and that it subsumes f. The fourth condition states, in essence, that r can reuse the label of an event e' that has left $F(r,t)$ for a new event e, since at the point when another replica r' receives e, e' would have moved out of its primary information, so there is no ambiguity in the labelling. The last condition is subtle and crucial for the next proof. It states that if r has generated a label for an event e' and potentially reused it for a later event after e' leaves $F(r,t)$, then there is no update event e'' by another replica r' that could potentially send this reused label later to an agent. In other words, such sends have been delivered to all replicas before r reuses the label.

Theorem 18 (Bounded solution for gossip). *Let f be a primary information function such that the gossip problem for f has a solution. It has a bounded solution if there is a bounded secondary information function F for f.*

Proof. Let the gossip problem for f have a solution, and let the bound on F be M. Clearly $M + 1$ labels suffice to label each event in $F(r,t)$ uniquely, for any

t. We fix a label set $\mathcal{L}$ of size $M+1$. For any t, we label events in $F(r,t)$ with pairs (r,ℓ), such that $\ell \in \mathcal{L}$. We also maintain a marking function that identifies events in $f(t)$, and the ordering $\prec$ restricted to $f(t)$. As a trace progresses, we can reassign an unused label (there is at least one) to each new event in the set F. Since both f and F after each event e are computable from the values of f and F at the maximal r events in t, the marking and ordering can also be updated.

Finally, replica r can reuse labels for events in $F(r,t)$ without fear of confusion because of condition 4 in the definition of secondary information. If e' and e are two r update events with $e' \prec e$ that are assigned the same label (r,ℓ), then clearly $e' \in t \setminus F(r,t)$. When r' receives the event e (let us say this receive event is e_1 and $t' = \downarrow e_1$), $e' \notin f(\partial_{r'}(t')) = f(t')$. Thus r' can decide if the received event is new or old by referring to the f at the receive event.

Let e' and e be r-update events such that $t = \downarrow e$ and $e' \in t \setminus F(r,t)$. Suppose r uses the same label (r,ℓ) for e and e'. A replica r'' can receive an event with label (r,ℓ) from a replica $r' \neq r$. This means that there is an r'-event e'' such that $e' \in f(\downarrow e'')$. (Note that replicas communicate their primary information to others.) But condition 5 ensures that $\varphi_{r''}(e'') \in \partial_r(t)$, so this send happens before the label (r,ℓ) is reused.

Thus there is no ambiguity caused either by sends by the same replica or by sends by different replicas. This shows that a bounded secondary information function implies a bounded labelling solution. □

5.1 Bounded Solution

In the gossip problem considered in [7,11], the primary information f at t is the set $\{max_{r'}(\partial_r(t)) \mid r, r' \in \mathcal{R}\}$ along with some more information that ensures that the gossip problem for f is solvable. A bounded solution for f is provided in [11] when f itself is bounded, but under additional restrictions on the traces of the system. A notion of acknowledgements is introduced, and all traces of the system are required to have at most B unacknowledged messages.

In [11], replicas piggyback acknowledgements to previously received messages in their subsequent broadcasts. Hence, the bound on unacknowledged messages requires that replicas communicate with each other at regular intervals. Such a solution would not work in CmRDTs, because replicas broadcast messages only when they interact with a client. Hence, we need a stronger guarantee from the underlying messaging system. One such condition is defined below.

Definition 19 (B-concurrency). *A trace t is B-concurrent if for every $e \in t$, $|\{e' \in t \mid e' \parallel e\}| \leq B$. A system is B-concurrent if all its traces are B-concurrent.*

The following theorem is the main result in this section. It implies (in conjunction with Theorem 18) that for a B-concurrent system and a bounded primary information function f, if the gossip problem for f has a solution, then it has a bounded solution.

Theorem 20. *If f is a bounded primary function defined on a B-concurrent system, there is a bounded secondary information function for f.*

Proof. Let the bound on f be M. To define the function F, we need the notion of *recent updates.* An r-update event e is recent (in a trace t) if $e \in f(\partial_r(t))$ or there are at most B r-updates after e in $\partial_r(t)$. We define the function F as follows: $F(r,t) = \{e \in \partial_r(t) \mid e \text{ is a recent } r\text{-update event}\}$.

Clearly $|F(r,t)| \leq M + B + 1$ for any r and t, and conditions 1, 2 and 3 in the definition of secondary information function easily hold.

Condition 4 is relatively simple. $e' \in (\downarrow e \setminus F(r, \partial_r(\downarrow e)))$ implies that $e' \notin f(\partial_r(\downarrow e))$. Hence for any t' such that $e \in \partial_{r'}(t')$, by definition of a primary information function, it is the case that $e' \notin f(\partial_{r'}(t'))$.

Condition 5 is proved as follows. If $e' \in t \setminus F(r,t)$, then there are $B+1$ r-update events after e'. Suppose there is e'' with $e' \in f(\downarrow e'')$ such that $\varphi_{r''}(e'') \notin \partial_r(t)$, for some replica r''. Then there are more than B events concurrent with e'', which contradicts B-concurrency.

Thus whenever f is a primary information function with a bound M in a B-concurrent system, there is a secondary information function F for f with bound $M + B + 1$. □

5.2 Bounding CmRDTs Using Generalized Gossip Problem

Definition 21. *Let $\mathcal{D} = (\mathcal{V}, \mathcal{Q}, \mathcal{U})$ be a CmRDT. We say that a function $f_\mathcal{D} : \mathcal{T}_p \to \mathcal{T}$ is a* specification-subtrace function *iff:*

$$\forall q \in \mathcal{Q}\ \forall t \in \mathcal{T}_p\ \forall args \in \mathcal{V}^{arity(q)} : \ Spec_\mathcal{D}(q, args, t) = Spec_\mathcal{D}(q, args, f_\mathcal{D}(t))$$

Thus, a specification-subtrace function picks for every prime trace a subtrace that is sufficient to answer every query of the CmRDT, as per its specification. The identity map is a trivial specification-subtrace function for any CmRDT.

We now provide a sufficient condition for a CmRDT to have a bounded implementation.

Theorem 22. *A CmRDT $\mathcal{D} = (\mathcal{V}, \mathcal{Q}, \mathcal{U})$ has a bounded implementation in a distributed system whose underlying network guarantees B-concurrent traces if there exists a locally computable specification-subtrace function $f_\mathcal{D}$ that is a bounded primary information function*

Proof. From Theorem 20, we know that the generalized gossip problem has a bounded solution in a distributed system whose traces are B-concurrent. The bounded solution for the gossip problem with primary information function $f_\mathcal{D}$ maintains at every replica r in any trace t, $f_\mathcal{D}(\partial_r(t))$. Since $f_\mathcal{D}$ is also a specification-subtrace function for $\mathcal{D}$, by definition, the information maintained is sufficient to answer every query correctly as per the specification of $\mathcal{D}$.

Thus, whenever a replica gets an update request $u(args)$ from the client, it is sufficient if it annotates the new event e with $u(args)$ and invokes the bounded solution to the generalized gossip problem. Also, it is sufficient to implement each query operation $q \in \mathcal{Q}$ as per the specification of $Spec_\mathcal{D}(q, args, f_\mathcal{D}(\partial_r(t)))$. This provides a bounded implementation for $\mathcal{D}$. □

Let us revisit the case of OR-Sets for which $|\mathcal{V}| \leq K$.

Definition 23. *Let $t \in \mathcal{T}_p$ be any prime-ideal of an OR-Set. Let $\mathcal{E}(x,t) = \{e \in t \mid Args(e) = x \wedge Op(e) \in \mathcal{U}\}$. Let*

$$\mathcal{E}(t) = \{\bigcup_{r\in\mathcal{R}} max_r(t^{\mathcal{U}})\} \cup \bigcup_{x\in\mathcal{V}} maxSet(\partial_r(t)^{\mathcal{E}(x,t)}).$$

We define $f_{ORSet}(t) = t^{\mathcal{E}(t)}$.

From the definition of f_{ORSet} and the specification of OR-Sets presented earlier in Section 3, the following result is evident:

Lemma 24. *f_{ORSet} is a specification-subtrace function for OR-Sets.*

We show that f_{ORSet} is a bounded primary information function.

Lemma 25. *f_{ORSet} is a computable bounded primary information function.*

Proof. In the following proof, we drop the subscript *ORSet* from f_{ORSet} and use f, for ease of presentation.

Let $t \in \mathcal{T}_p$ be any prime ideal.

From the definition, $f(t)$ is a subtrace of t consisting of only the maximal $\mathcal{U}$ events corresponding to each element $x \in \mathcal{V}$ along with the maximal r-update events for each replica r. Thus, $f(t) \in \mathcal{G}(t)$.

Let $t = \downarrow e$ and $e' \in maxSet(t \setminus \{e\})$. Let $t' = \downarrow e'$. Now, an event $e'' \in f(t)$ iff $\exists r \in \mathcal{R}$ such that e'' is an r-maximal update event in t or $\exists x \in \mathcal{V}$ such that e'' is a maximal x-event in t. For an $e'' \in t'$, since $t' \subseteq t$, it is clear that if e'' is a maximal x-event in t then, e'' is also a maximal x-event in t'. Similarly if $e'' \in t'$ and e'' is an r-maximal update event in t then e'' is an r-maximal update event in t'. Thus, $e'' \in f(t')$. Hence, $f(t) \cap t' \subseteq f(t')$.

Thus we have shown that f is a primary information function.

For each replica r, there is one maximal r-update event in any trace t. For each element x, there can be at most N maximal x-events in any prime ideal t. Since $|\mathcal{V}| \leq K$, there can be at most KN events corresponding to the maximal update events. Thus, in any prime ideal t, $|f(t)| \leq KN$, so f is bounded.

Finally to show that f admits a solution to the generalized gossip problem, we establish that $f(t)$ can be locally computed from e, and $\bigcup_{e'\in maxSet(t\setminus\{e\})} f(\downarrow e')$.

We introduce the following notation which will be used below: For any prime trace t'', we write $f(t'') = (E'', \rightarrow'')$ to denote that the set of events in $f(t'')$ is E'' and the trace order restricted to E'' in $f(t'')$ is $\rightarrow''$.

Now, let $Rep(e) = r$. We consider the following cases:

Case e is an x-update event: Let $\{e'\} = maxSet(t \setminus \{e\})$. Let $t' = \downarrow e'$, with $f(t') = (E', \rightarrow')$. Let $E_m = \{e\} \cup E'$ and $\rightarrow_m = \rightarrow' \cup \{(e'', e) \mid e'' \in E'\}$, with $t_m = (E_m, \rightarrow_m)$. It is easy to see that if $e'' \in f(t)$ then $e'' \in E_m$. Moreover, since $f(t') \in \mathcal{G}(t')$ and $t' \subseteq t$, the ordering on events of $f(t')$ is given by $\rightarrow'$ which is consistent with their ordering in t. Finally e is a maximal event in

t and hence is above other event in E_m. Both these are captured in $\rightarrow_m$. Hence we can compute $f(t)$ by picking the subtrace of t_m containing the maximal r' events for every $r' \in \mathcal{R}$ and maximal y events for every $y \in \mathcal{V}$. Thus $f(t)$ can be computed from $f(t')$ and e.

Case e is a receive event: Let $\{e', e''\} = maxSet(t \setminus \{e\})$. Let $Rep(e') = r$ and $Rep(e'') = r'$ Let $t = \downarrow e$, $t' = \downarrow e'$ and $t'' = \downarrow e''$. We let $f(t') = (E', \rightarrow')$ and $f(t'') = (E'', \rightarrow'')$.

By causal delivery, every event $e''' \in t'' \setminus \{e''\}$ is already in t'. So if such an $e''' \notin f(t')$ then $e''' \notin f(t)$. Also, any event $e''' \in (f(t') \cap t'') \setminus f(t'')$ is not going to feature in $f(t)$, from the definition of primary information. Such an event can be identified correctly in $f(t')$ since it will be the case that $(e''', max_{r'}(t')) \in \rightarrow'$. Thus, the events required to compute $f(t)$ are $E_m = \{e''\} \cup E' \setminus \{e''' \mid e''' = max_{r'}(t') \vee e''' \rightarrow' max_{r'}(t')\}$. Let $\rightarrow_m = (E_m \times E_m) \cap (\rightarrow' \cup \rightarrow'')$. Then, $f(t)$ can be computed from $t_m = (E_m, \rightarrow_m)$ by picking the subtrace from t_m consisting of the maximal r'' events from every replica r'' and maximal x-events for every element $x \in \mathcal{V}$. Thus $f(t)$ can be computed from $f(t')$, $f(t'')$ and e. $\square$

Hence, from Lemmas 24 and 25 we can conclude that an OR Set with a bounded universe has a bounded implementation in a distributed system whose underlying network guarantees B-concurrent traces.

We present the bounded implementation for OR-Sets via a bounded solution for the generalized gossip problem in Algorithm 1 (page 370). The algorithm stores the relevant information view of a replica in (V, P). It uses a free set of labels F which can be used to label a new update event at the replica and a retired set of labels R (line 4) which keeps track of the labels that are no longer relevant but might still be active in the system.

Lines 9–19 describe the GENERATENODE() method that generates a new node corresponding to the latest update event (Line 38). This method picks an unused label from F (line 12) and increments the retired-duration of the labels in R (line 13). The labels which have been in the retired set for a duration of B-sends can be recycled (Lines 15, 16). The node consists of the replica id, the label and the private information that the client would have passed on to the replica (Line 18). We shall later see that this private information will be the name of the update function as well as the argument to it.

Helpers GETREP() and GETLABEL() return the replica id and the label associated with a node, respectively (Lines 21–29). Helper GETMAXIMAL() returns the maximal events in the partial order (V', P') (Lines 31–35).

The SEND() method (Lines 37–41) creates a new node and computes the new partial order with this new node as the maximal node (Lines 38–40). It locally recomputes the value of the primary information (Line 41) and then broadcasts the updated partial order to all the other replicas (Line 42). The RECEIVE() method recomputes the relevant information based on the new information that the replica has received.

RECOMPUTERELEVANT() method merges the relevant information at the replica along with the updated partial order that it has received and recomputes the relevant information from this new subtrace (Line 49). It then records the nodes that were present in the relevant information prior to recomputing but are no longer present (Line 53 and 54). It retires the labels corresponding to these nodes (Line 55). Finally it updates its primary information with the one that was computed in Line 50 (Line 56).

The second part of the algorithm describes how OR Sets can be implemented using the bounded solution to the gossip problem. Whenever a replica receives an update request from the client, it invokes the SEND() method with the update name and the argument as the private information (Lines 18–22). Lines 9–20 implement the specification-subtrace function for OR-Set that retains only the maximal events corresponding to each element of the universe along with the maximal events corresponding to each replica in the system. Lines 28–34 implement the EXISTS query method that returns True if there is at least one maximal node corresponding to the x that was added due to an ADD update operation.

6 Applications to Verification

A bounded reference implementation can be used for verification. We outline two scenarios in which such an implementation is useful.

CEGAR. Counterexample Guided Abstraction Refinement, or CEGAR, is an iterative technique to verify reachability properties of software systems [12]. In the CEGAR approach, one uses abstraction techniques from program analysis and other domains to build a finite-state abstraction of a given implementation. This abstraction is designed to over-approximate the behaviour of the original system.

The finite-state approximation is run through a model-checker to verify if the safety property is met. If no unsafe state is reachable, it means that the original system is safe since the abstracted system over-approximates the actual behaviour. On the other hand, if the model-checker asserts that an unsafe state is reachable, the counterexample generated by the model-checker is executed on the original system. If the counterexample is valid, a bug has been found. If the counterexample is infeasible, the abstraction was too coarse and a refinement of the abstraction is calculated. This process is iterated until a safe abstraction is reached or a valid bug is detected.

As we have noted, implementations of replicated data types need to keep track of metadata about past operations in order to reconcile conflicts. These are typically done using unbounded objects such as counters or vector clocks. To apply CEGAR to such an implementation, we can derive a finite state abstraction and run it synchronously with our bounded reference implementation. We can characterize each reachable state of the abstraction as legal or illegal depending on whether or not it is query equivalent to the reference implementation. We can then follow the usual CEGAR methodology outlined above.

Algorithm 1. Bounded Reference Implementation

```
Bounded Reference Implementation
V: Set of nodes
P: Partial order on V
F: Set of available labels.
R: Set of pair of retired labels and
a modulo B+1 counter.
// E captures the relation ≺
// Each replica stores a copy of
V, E, F and R
    initially ∅, ∅, 𝓛, ∅

helper GENERATENODE(priv):
Returns v ∈ 𝒩
    Let l ∈ F
    Let F := F \ {l}
    Let R' := {(l', c' + 1) | (l', c') ∈ R}
    Let F' := {(l', c') ∈ R' | c' = B}
    R := R' \ F'
    F := F ∪ {l' | (l', c') ∈ F'}
    Let rep := myID()
    Let v' := (l, rep, priv)
    return v'

helper GETREP(v):
Returns the replica associated with a Node.
    Let v = (l, r, p)
    return r

helper GETLABEL(v):
Returns the replica associated with a Node.
    Let v = (l, r, p)
    return l

helper GETMAXIMAL(V', P'):
Returns the set of maximal nodes in the
partial order
    Let V^max := {v ∈ V' |
    ¬∃v' ∈ V' : (v, v') ∈ P'}
    return V^max

generic SEND(priv):
    Let v' := GENERATENODE(priv)
    Let V' := V ∪ {v'}
    Let P' := P ∪ {(v, v') | v ∈ V}
    RECOMPUTERELEVANT(V', P')
    Broadcast (V', P') to all other replicas

generic RECEIVE(V', P'):
    RECOMPUTERELEVANT(V', P')
helper RECOMPUTERELEVANT(V', P'):
// Recomputes the relevant information
// in the partial order (V ∪ V', E ∪ P')
// and retires the irrelevant labels.
    Let (V'', P'') := f(V ∪ V', P ∪ P')
    Let {v'} := GETMAXIMAL(V', P')
    Let rep := myId()
    Let L := {GETLABEL(v) |
    v ∈ V ∪ {v'} \ V'', GETREP(v) = rep}.
    Let R := R ∪ {(l, 0) | l ∈ L}
    (V, P) := (V'', P'')
```

```
OR Set
helper GETOP(v):
    Let v = (l, r, (opname, x))
    return opname

helper GETARGS(v):
    Let v = (l, r, (opname, x))
    return x

helper f_ORSet(V', P'):
  For x ∈ 𝒱:
    Let V_x := {v ∈ V' | GETARGS(v) = x}
    Let P_x := P'' ∩ (V_x × V_x)
    Let V_x^max := GETMAXIMAL(V_x, P_x)
  For r ∈ ℛ:
    Let V_r := {v ∈ V' | GETREP(v) = r}
    Let P_r := P'' ∩ (V_r × V_r)
    Let V_r^max := GETMAXIMAL(V_r, P_r)
Let V'' := ⋃_{x∈𝒱} V_x^max ∪ ⋃_{r∈ℛ} V_r^max
Let P'' := P' ∩ (V'' × V'')
return (V'', P'')

update ADD(x):
    SEND((ADD, x))

update DELETE(x):
    SEND((DELETE, x))

query EXISTS(x):
    Let V_x^add := {v ∈ V |
        GETARGS(v) = x ∧ GETOPv = ADD}
    If V_x^add ≠ ∅:
    Then
        return True
    Else:
        return False
```

Testing of Distributed Systems. While verification approaches such as CEGAR can be used in a white box setting where we have access to internal details of the implemenation under test, in a black box scenario we have to rely on testing.

Effective testing of distributed systems is a challenging task. The first problem is that we cannot typically test the system globally, so we have to apply tests locally using notations such as TTCN [13]. Even when such a methodology is available, there are two criteria that are difficult to establish for test suites:

coverage and redundancy. In both cases, the main source of complexity is the presence of concurrency. In a concurrent system, it is very difficult to estimate if a test suite covers a reasonable set of reachable global states because of many different linearizations possible. Secondly, it is not obvious to what extent tests are overlapping, again because of reordering of independent events.

For the coverage problem, we can construct test suites that cover different portions of the state space of the reference implementation. If this coverage is widespread, we can have more confidence in the coverage of the implementation under test. For redundancy, once again we can use the underlying independence relation to identify when two tests overlap by checking how much the corresponding traces overlap as partial orders. In the replicated data type scenario, we may in fact want to generate redundant test cases that differ only in the order of concurrent events in order to validate eventual consistency.

7 Conclusion and Summary

The theory of replicated data types is still at a formative stage. In early work [2,3] eventually consistent replicated data types have been specified operationally, in terms of a proposed implementation. This often leaves the actual behaviour of the data type unclear under different combinations of concurrent updates.

This deficiency has been addressed in [6], which introduces a theory of declarative specifications for replicated data types. However, the model proposed in [6] is very general and hence ineffective for actual verification.

Most practical distributed systems provide strong guarantees on the underlying message subsystem, such as causal delivery. In fact, causal delivery is assumed to hold for the implementations described in [2, 3]. If we assume causal delivery, we have shown that we can drastically simplify the declarative framework proposed in [6] and work with standard labelled partial orders.

Borrowing ideas from Mazurkiewicz trace theory, we have formulated a generalization of the gossip problem and shown that this can be used to derive bounded implementations for replicated data types, provided we have an additional guarantee of bounded concurrency. Though bounded concurrency seems like a very strong property, it is automatically achieved if we combine causal message delivery with bounded message delays. The only complication that can arise is from a replica crashing. However, if we assume that when a replica wakes up from a crash, it first processes all pending receive actions before initiating any sends, we retain bounded concurrency. Note that causal delivery is also infeasible if we do not make similar assumptions about how a crashed process recovers.

Our main contribution is a systematic approach to construct bounded reference implementations for replicated data types. We have argued that this kind of implementation is useful for both verification and testing.

In future work, we would like to explore further benefits of declarative specifications for replicated data types. In particular, one challenging problem is to develop a theory in which we can compose such specifications to derive complex replicated data types by combining simpler ones.

References

1. Gilbert, S., Lynch, N.A.: Brewer's conjecture and the feasibility of consistent, available, partition-tolerant web services. SIGACT News 33(2), 51–59 (2002)
2. Shapiro, M.: Preguiça, N., Baquero, C., Zawirski, M.: A comprehensive study of Convergent and Commutative Replicated Data Types. Rapport de recherche RR-7506, INRIA (January 2011), `http://hal.inria.fr/inria-00555588/PDF/techreport.pdf`
3. Shapiro, M., Preguiça, N.M., Baquero, C., Zawirski, M.: Conflict-free replicated data types. In: SSS, pp. 386–400 (2011)
4. Bieniusa, A., Zawirski, M., Preguiça, N.M., Shapiro, M., Baquero, C., Balegas, V., Duarte, S.: An optimized conflict-free replicated set. CoRR abs/1210.3368 (2012)
5. Mukund, M., Shenoy R., G., Suresh, S.P.: Optimized OR-sets without ordering constraints. In: Chatterjee, M., Cao, J.-n., Kothapalli, K., Rajsbaum, S. (eds.) ICDCN 2014. LNCS, vol. 8314, pp. 227–241. Springer, Heidelberg (2014)
6. Burkhardt, S., Gotsman, A., Yang, H., Zawirski, M.: Replicated data types: specification, verification, optimality. In: The 41st Annual ACM SIGPLAN-SIGACT Symposium on Principles of Programming Languages, POPL 2014, San Diego, CA, USA, January 20-21, pp. 271–284 (2014)
7. Mukund, M., Sohoni, M.A.: Keeping track of the latest gossip in a distributed system. Distributed Computing 10(3), 137–148 (1997)
8. Vogels, W.: Eventually consistent. ACM Queue 6(6), 14–19 (2008)
9. Mazurkiewicz, A.: Trace theory. In: Brauer, W., Reisig, W., Rozenberg, G. (eds.) APN 1986. LNCS, vol. 255, pp. 278–324. Springer, Heidelberg (1987)
10. Pratt, V.: Modeling concurrency with partial orders. International Journal of Parallel Programming 15(1), 33–71 (1986)
11. Mukund, M., Narayan Kumar, K., Sohoni, M.A.: Bounded time-stamping in message-passing systems. Theor. Comput. Sci. 290(1), 221–239 (2003)
12. Clarke, E.M., Grumberg, O., Jha, S., Lu, Y., Veith, H.: Counterexample-guided abstraction refinement for symbolic model checking. J. ACM 50(5), 752–794 (2003)
13. Willcock, C., Deiß, T., Tobies, S., Keil, S., Engler, F., Schulz, S.: An Introduction to TTCN-3. Wiley (2005)

Proving Memory Safety of the ANI Windows Image Parser Using Compositional Exhaustive Testing

Maria Christakis[1,*] and Patrice Godefroid[2]

[1] Department of Computer Science
ETH Zurich, Switzerland
maria.christakis@inf.ethz.ch
[2] Microsoft Research
Redmond, USA
pg@microsoft.com

Abstract. We report in this paper how we proved memory safety of a complex Windows image parser written in low-level C in only three months of work and using only three core techniques, namely (1) symbolic execution at the x86 binary level, (2) exhaustive program path enumeration and testing, and (3) user-guided program decomposition and summarization. We also used a new tool, named MicroX, for executing code fragments in isolation using a custom virtual machine designed for testing purposes. As a result of this work, we are able to prove, for the first time, that a Windows image parser is *memory safe*, i.e., free of any buffer-overflow security vulnerabilities, *modulo* the soundness of our tools and several additional assumptions regarding bounding input-dependent loops, fixing a few buffer-overflow bugs, and excluding some code parts that are not memory safe by design. In the process, we also discovered and fixed several limitations in our tools, and narrowed the gap between systematic testing and verification.

1 Introduction

Systematic dynamic test generation [18,9] consists of repeatedly running a program both concretely and symbolically. The goal is to collect symbolic constraints on inputs from predicates in branch statements along the execution, and then to infer variants of the previous inputs, using a constraint solver, in order to steer the next execution of the program toward an alternative program path. By systematically repeating this process, the entire set of execution paths of a program can, in principle, be explored. This approach to automatic test generation has become popular over the last several years, and has been implemented in many tools such as EXE [10], jCUTE [33], SAGE [21], Pex [36], KLEE [8], BitBlaze [34], and Apollo [2] to name a few. These tools vary by the programming languages, properties, and application domains they target, but

[*] The work of this author was mostly done while visiting Microsoft Research.

D. D'Souza et al. (Eds.): VMCAI 2015, LNCS 8931, pp. 373–392, 2015.

they have all been successful in discovering new bugs missed by more conventional techniques. Notably, SAGE is credited to have found roughly one third of all the security bugs discovered by file fuzzing during the development of Microsoft's Windows 7 [6]. Despite their success and popularity, the tools above have never been used so far for program *verification* of a non-trivial application, i.e., for proving the absence of specific classes of bugs.

In this paper, we show how we used and enhanced these techniques to prove memory safety of the ANI Windows image parser. This parser is responsible for processing structured graphics files to display "ANImated" cursors and icons on more than a billion PCs. Such animated icons are ubiquitous in practice (like the spinning ring or hourglass on Windows), and their domain of use ranges from web pages and blogs, instant messaging and e-mails, to presentations and video clips. The ANI parser consists of thousands of lines of low-level C code spread across hundreds of functions. Yet, this parser is sequential (no concurrency or real-time constraints). It is also of security interest: in 2007, a critical out-of-band security patch was released for code in this parser (MS07-017) costing Microsoft and its users millions of dollars [35,24]. A motivation for this work was to determine whether the ANI parser is now free of security-critical buffer overflows.

We show how systematic dynamic test generation can be applied and extended to program verification. To achieve this, we address the two main limitations of dynamic test generation, namely imperfect symbolic execution and path explosion. For the former, we extended the tool SAGE to improve its symbolic execution engine so that it could handle all the x86 instructions of that specific ANI parser. To deal with path explosion, we used a combination of function inlining, restricting the bounds of input-dependent loops, and function summarization. We also used a new tool, named MicroX, for executing code fragments in isolation using a custom virtual machine designed for testing purposes. We emphasize that the focus of our work is restricted to proving the absence of attacker-controllable memory-safety violations (as precisely defined in Sect. 3).

At a high-level, the main contributions of this paper are: (1) We report on the first application of systematic dynamic test generation for *verifying* a real, complex, security-critical, entire program. Our work sheds light on the shrinking gap between systematic testing and verification in a model-checking style. (2) To our knowledge, this is the first time that an operating-system (Windows or other) *image parser* has been *proven free of security-critical buffer overflows.* (3) We are also not aware of any past attempts at program verification *without using any static program analysis*; all the techniques and tools used in this work are exclusively dynamic.

This paper is organized as follows. In Sect. 2, we recall basic principles of systematic dynamic test generation and compositional symbolic execution, and briefly present the SAGE and MicroX tools used in this work. In Sect. 3, we precisely define memory safety, show how to verify it compositionally, and discuss how we used and extended SAGE and MicroX for verification. Sect. 4 presents an overview of the ANI Windows image parser. In Sect. 5, we present our verification results in detail. During the course of this work, we discovered several memory-safety violations in the ANI parser code, which are discussed in Sect. 6. We review related work in Sect. 7 and conclude in Sect. 8.

2 Background

2.1 Systematic Dynamic Test Generation

Systematic dynamic test generation [18,9] consists of repeatedly running a program both concretely and symbolically. The goal is to collect symbolic constraints on inputs from predicates in branch statements along the execution, and then to infer variants of the previous inputs, using a constraint solver, in order to steer the next execution of the program toward an alternative path.

Symbolic execution means executing a program with symbolic rather than concrete values. Assignment statements are represented as functions of their (symbolic) arguments, while conditional statements are expressed as constraints on symbolic values. Side-by-side concrete and symbolic executions are performed using a concrete store M and a symbolic store S, which are mappings from memory addresses (where program variables are stored) to concrete and symbolic values, respectively. For a program path w, a *path constraint* ϕ_w is a logic formula that characterizes the input values for which the program executes along w. Each symbolic variable appearing in ϕ_w is, thus, a program input. Each constraint is expressed in some theory[1] T decided by a constraint solver, i.e., an automated theorem prover that can return a satisfying assignment for all variables appearing in constraints it proves satisfiable.

All program paths can be enumerated by a search algorithm that explores all possible branches at conditional statements. The paths w for which ϕ_w is satisfiable are feasible, and are the only ones that can be executed by the actual program provided the solutions to ϕ_w characterize exactly the inputs that drive the program through w. Assuming that the constraint solver used to check the satisfiability of all formulas ϕ_w is sound and complete, this use of symbolic execution for programs with finitely many paths amounts to program verification.

2.2 Compositional Symbolic Execution

Systematically testing and symbolically executing all feasible program paths does not scale to large programs. Indeed, the number of feasible paths can be exponential in the program size, or even infinite in the presence of loops with an unbounded number of iterations. This *path explosion* can be alleviated by performing symbolic execution *compositionally* [15,1].

In compositional symbolic execution, a summary ϕ_f for a function (or any program sub-computation) f is defined as a logic formula over constraints expressed in theory T. Summary ϕ_f can be generated by symbolically executing each path of function f, then generating an input precondition and output postcondition

[1] A theory is a set of logic formulas.

for each path, and bundling together all path summaries in a disjunction. Precisely, ϕ_f is defined as a disjunction of formulas ϕ_{w_f} of the form

$$\phi_{w_f} = pre_{w_f} \wedge post_{w_f}$$

where w_f denotes an intraprocedural path in f, pre_{w_f} is a conjunction of constraints on the inputs of f, and $post_{w_f}$ a conjunction of constraints on the outputs of f. An input to a function f is any value that can be read by f, while an output of f is any value written by f. Therefore, ϕ_{w_f} can be computed automatically when symbolically executing the intraprocedural path w_f: pre_{w_f} is the path constraint along path w_f but expressed in terms of the function inputs, while $post_{w_f}$ is a conjunction of constraints, each of the form $v' = S(v)$, where v' is a fresh symbolic variable created for each program variable v modified during the execution of w_f (including the return value), and where $S(v)$ denotes the symbolic value associated with v in the program state reached at the end of w_f. At the end of the execution of w_f, the symbolic store is updated so that each such value $S(v)$ is replaced by v'. When symbolic execution continues after the function returns, such symbolic values v' are treated as inputs to the calling context. Summaries can be re-used across different calling contexts.

For instance, given the function `is_positive` below,

```
int is_positive(int x) {
  if (x > 0) return 1;
  return 0;
}
```

a summary ϕ_f for this function can be

$$\phi_f = (x > 0 \wedge ret = 1) \vee (x \leq 0 \wedge ret = 0)$$

where ret denotes the value returned by the function.

Symbolic variables are associated with function inputs (like x in the example) and function outputs (like ret in the example) in addition to whole-program inputs. In order to generate a new test to cover a new branch b in some function, all the previously known summaries can be used to generate a formula ϕ_P symbolically representing all the paths discovered so far during the search. By construction [15], symbolic variables corresponding to function inputs and outputs are all bound in ϕ_P, and the remaining free variables correspond exclusively to whole-program inputs (since only those can be controlled for test generation).

For instance, for the program `P` below,

```
#define N 100
void P(int s[N]) { // N inputs
  int i, cnt = 0;
  for (i = 0; i < N; i++) cnt = cnt + is_positive(s[i]);
  if (cnt == 3) error(); // (*)
}
```

a formula ϕ_P to generate a test covering the `then` branch `(*)` given the above summary ϕ_f for function `is_positive` can be

$$(ret_0 + ret_1 + \ldots + ret_{N-1} = 3) \wedge$$

$$\bigwedge_{0 \leq i < N} ((s[i] > 0 \wedge ret_i = 1) \vee (s[i] \leq 0 \wedge ret_i = 0))$$

where ret_i denotes the return value of the ith call to function `is_positive`. Even though program P has 2^N feasible whole-program paths, compositional test generation can cover symbolically all those paths with at most 4 test inputs: 2 tests to cover both branches in function `is_positive` plus 2 tests to cover both branches of the `if` statement `(*)`. In this example, compositionality avoids an exponential number of tests and calls to the constraint solver at the cost of using more complex formulas with more disjunctions.

When, where, and how compositionality is worth using in practice is still an open question (e.g., [15,1,5,26]), which we discuss later in this paper.

2.3 SAGE and MicroX

Our ANI verification work was carried out using extensions of two existing tools: SAGE [21] and MicroX [16]. SAGE is a whitebox fuzzer for security testing, which implements systematic dynamic test generation and performs dynamic symbolic execution at the x86 binary level. It is optimized to scale to very large execution traces (billions of x86 instructions) and programs (like Excel). SAGE also implements a limited form of summaries [19] as well as specialized forms of summaries for dealing with floating-point computations [17] and input-dependent loops [22]. The feature for floating-point computations was not used in this work as the ANI parser considered here does not include floating point instructions, while the latter feature is too limited to deal with all the ANI input-dependent loops—we handled those differently as explained in Sect. 5.2.

MicroX is a newer tool [16] for executing code fragments in isolation, without user-provided test drivers or input data, using a custom virtual machine (VM) designed for testing purposes. Given any user-specified code location in an x86 binary, the MicroX VM starts executing the code at that location, intercepts all memory operations before they occur, allocates memory on-the-fly in order to perform those read/write memory operations, and provides input values according to a customizable *memory policy*, which defines what read memory accesses should be treated as inputs. By default, an input is defined as any value read from an uninitialized function argument, or through a dereference of a previous input (recursively) that is used as an address. This memory policy is typically adequate for testing C functions. No test driver/harness is required: MicroX discovers automatically and dynamically the input/output signature of the code being run. Input values are provided as needed along the execution and can be generated in various ways, e.g., randomly or using some other test-generation tool like SAGE. When used with SAGE, the very first test inputs are generated randomly; then, SAGE symbolically executes the code path taken by the given execution, generates a path constraint for that (concrete) execution, and solves new alternate path constraints that, when satisfiable, generate new input values guiding future executions along new paths.

3 Proving Memory Safety

3.1 Defining Memory Safety

To prove memory safety during systematic dynamic test generation, all memory accesses need to be checked for possible violations. Whenever a memory address a stored in a program variable v (i.e., $a = M(v)$) is accessed during execution, the concrete value a of the address is first checked "passively" to make sure it points to a valid memory region mr_a (as done in standard tools like Purify, Valgrind and AppVerifier); then, if this address a was obtained by computing an expression e that depends on an input (i.e., $e = S(v)$), the symbolic expression e is also checked "actively" by injecting a new *bounds-checking* constraint

$$0 \leq (e - mr_a.base) < mr_a.size$$

in the path constraint to make sure other input values cannot trigger a buffer overflow or underflow at this point of the program execution [10,20]. How to keep track of the base address $mr_a.base$ and size $mr_a.size$ of each valid memory region mr_a during the program execution is discussed in work on precise symbolic pointer reasoning [14].

As an example, consider the following function:

```
void buggy(int x) {
  char* buf[10];
  buf[x] = 1;
}
```

If this function is run with `x=1` as input, the concrete execution is memory safe as the memory access `buf[1]` is in bounds. In order to force systematic dynamic test generation to discover that this program is not memory safe, it is mandatory to inject the constraint $0 \leq x < 10$ in the current path constraint when the statement `buf[x]=1` is executed. This constraint is later negated and solved leading to other input values for `x`, such as -1 or 10, with which the function will be re-tested and caught violating memory safety.

A program execution w is called *attacker memory safe* [17] if every memory access during w in program P, which is extended with bound checks for all memory accesses, is either within bounds, i.e., memory safe, or input independent, i.e., its address has no input-dependent symbolic value, and hence, is not controllable by an attacker through the untrusted input interface. A program is called attacker memory safe if all its executions are attacker memory safe.

Thus, the notion of attacker memory safety is weaker than traditional memory safety: a memory-safe program execution is always attacker memory safe, while the converse does not necessarily hold. For instance, an attacker-memory-safe program might perform a flawless and complete validation of all its untrusted inputs, but might still crash (for instance, by accessing the address `NULL`) in error-handling code that is executed exclusively after a trusted system call fails.

Security testing is primarily aimed at checking attacker memory safety since buffer overflows that cannot be controlled by the attacker are not security critical. In the rest of this paper, we focus on attacker memory safety, but we will often refer to it simply as memory safety for convenience.

3.2 Proving Attacker Memory Safety Compositionally

In order to prove memory safety compositionally, bounds-checking constraints need to be recorded inside summaries and evaluated for each calling context.

Consider the following function bar:

```
void bar(char* buf, int x) {
  if ((0 <= x) && (x < 10)) buf[x] = 1;
}
```

If we analyze bar in isolation without knowing the size of the input buffer buf, we cannot determine whether the buffer access buf[x] is memory safe. When we summarize function bar, we include in the precondition of the function that bar accesses the address buf+x when the condition $(0 \leq x) \wedge (x < 10)$ holds. A summary for this function executed with, say, x=3 can then be:

$$(0 \leq x) \wedge (x < 10) \wedge (0 \leq x < mr_{\texttt{buf}}.size) \wedge (\texttt{buf[x]} = 1)$$

Later, when analyzing higher-level functions calling bar, these bounds-checking constraints can be checked because the buffer bounds will then be known. For instance, consider the following function foo that calls bar:

```
void foo(int x) {
  char *buf = malloc(5);
  bar(buf, x);
}
```

If foo calls bar with x=3, the precondition of the above path summary for bar is satisfied. The bounds-checking constraint can be simplified with $mr_{\texttt{buf}}.size = 5$ in this calling context and negated to obtain the new path constraint,

$$(0 \leq x) \wedge (x < 10) \wedge \neg(0 \leq x < 5)$$

which after simplification is

$$(0 \leq x) \wedge (x < 10) \wedge ((x < 0) \vee (x \geq 5))$$

This constraint is satisfiable with, say, $x = 7$, and running foo and bar with that new input value will then detect a memory-safety violation in bar.

To sum up, the procedure we use for proving memory safety compositionally is as follows. We record bounds-checking constraints in the preconditions of intraprocedural path-constraint summaries. Whenever a path summary is used in a specific calling context, we check whether its precondition contains any bounds-checking constraint. If so, we check whether the size of the memory region appearing in the bounds-checking constraint is known. If this is the case, we generate a new alternate path constraint defined as the conjunction of the current path constraint and the negation of the bounds-checking constraint, where the size of the memory region is replaced by the current size. We then attempt to solve this alternate path constraint with the constraint solver, which then generates a new test if the constraint is satisfiable.

For real C functions, the logic representations of their pre- and postconditions can quickly become very complex and large. We show later in this paper that, by using summarization sparingly and at well-behaved function interfaces, these representations remain tractable.

We have implemented in SAGE the compositional procedure for proving memory safety described in this section.

3.3 Verification with SAGE and MicroX

In order to use SAGE for *verification*, we *turned on maximum precision* for symbolic execution: all runtime checkers (for buffer overflows and underflows, division by zero, etc.) were turned on as well as precise symbolic pointer reasoning [14], any x86 instruction unhandled by symbolic execution was reported, every path constraint was checked to be satisfiable before negating constraints, we checked that our constraint solver, the Z3 automated theorem prover [13], never timed out on any constraint, and we also checked the absence of any *divergence*, which occurs whenever a new test generated by SAGE does not follow the expected program path. When all these options are turned on and all the above checks are satisfied, symbolic execution of an individual path has *perfect precision*: path constraint generation and solving is *sound and complete* (Sect. 2.1).

Moreover, we *turned off* all the *unsound state-space pruning* techniques and heuristics implemented in SAGE to limit path explosion, such as limiting the number of constraints generated for each program branch and constraint subsumption, which eliminates constraints logically implied by other constraints injected at the same program branch (most likely due to successive iterations of an input-dependent loop) using a cheap syntactic check [21]. How we dealt with path explosion in this work is discussed in Sect. 5.2 and 5.3.

As we describe in Sect. 5, we also used MicroX in conjunction with SAGE in order to prove memory safety of individual ANI functions in isolation. Memory safety of a function is *proven for any calling context* (soundly and completely) by MicroX and SAGE if all possible function input values are considered, symbolic execution of every function path is sound and complete, all function paths can be enumerated and tested in a finite (and small enough) amount of time, and all the checks defined above are satisfied for all executions. Instead of manually writing a unit test driver that explicitly identifies all input parameters (and their types) for each function, MicroX provided this functionality automatically [16].

During this work, many functions were not verified at first for various reasons: we discovered and fixed several x86 instructions unhandled by SAGE's symbolic execution engine, we also fixed several root causes of divergences (by providing custom summaries for nondeterministic-looking functions, like `malloc` and `memcpy`, whose execution paths depend on memory alignment), and we fixed a few imprecision bugs in SAGE's code. These SAGE limitations were much more easily identified when verifying small functions in isolation with MicroX rather than during whole-application fuzzing. After removing those limitations, we were able to verify that many individual ANI functions are memory safe (Sect. 5.1). The remaining functions could not be verified so easily mostly because of path explosion due to input-dependent loops (Sect. 5.2) or due to too many paths in functions lower in the callgraph (Sect. 5.3).

4 The ANI Windows Parser

The ANI Windows parser is written mostly in C, while the remaining code is written in x86 assembly. The implementation involves at least 350 functions defined in 5 Windows DLLs. The parsing of input bytes from an ANI file takes place in at least 110 functions defined in 2 DLLs, namely in `user32.dll`, which is responsible for 80% of the parsing code, and in `gdi32.dll`, which is responsible for the remaining 20%[2]. `user32.dll` creates and manages the Windows user interface, such as windows, mouse events and menus. Many functions defined in `user32.dll` call into `gdi32.dll`, which is the graphics device interface associated with drawing and handling two-dimensional objects as well as managing fonts. There are 47 functions defined in `user32.dll` that implement functionality of the ANI parser. These functions alone compile to approximately 3,050 x86 instructions.

5 Verification Results

We proved memory safety of the ANI Windows image parser by targeting the 47 functions that are defined in `user32.dll` and are responsible for 80% of the parsing code (Sect. 4). The remaining 20% refers to at least 63 `gdi32.dll` functions that are called (directly or indirectly) by the 47 `user32.dll` functions. In addition to those `user32.dll` and `gdi32.dll` functions, the parser also exercises code in at least 240 other functions (for a total of at least 350 functions). As shown by sound and complete symbolic execution, all these other functions do not (directly or indirectly) parse any input bytes from an ANI file and are by definition attacker memory safe. For the purpose of this work, the `gdi32.dll` and all these other functions can be viewed as *inlined* to the `user32.dll` functions, which are the top-level functions of the parser. Verifying those 47 `user32.dll` functions while inlining all remaining sub-functions is, thus, equivalent to proving attacker memory safety of the entire ANI parser. The callgraph of the 47 `user32.dll` functions is shown in Fig. 1. The functions are grouped depending on the architectural component of the parser to which they belong. Note that there is no recursion in this callgraph.

In this section, we describe how we proved memory safety of the ANI parser using compositional exhaustive testing. Our verification results were obtained with a 32bit Windows 7 version of the parser and are presented in three stages.

5.1 Stage 1: Bottom-Up Strategy

For verifying the ANI parser, we started with a bottom-up strategy with respect to the callgraph of Fig. 1. We wanted to know how many functions of a real code base can be proven memory safe for any calling context by simply using exhaustive path enumeration. Our setup for this verification strategy consisted in attempting to verify each `user32.dll` function (one at a time) using MicroX with SAGE starting from the bottom of the callgraph. If all execution paths of the function were explored in a reasonable amount of time, i.e., less than 12 hours, and no bugs or other incompleteness-check violations were ever detected

[2] These percentages were obtained by comparing the number of constraints on symbolic values that were generated by SAGE for each of the 2 DLLs.

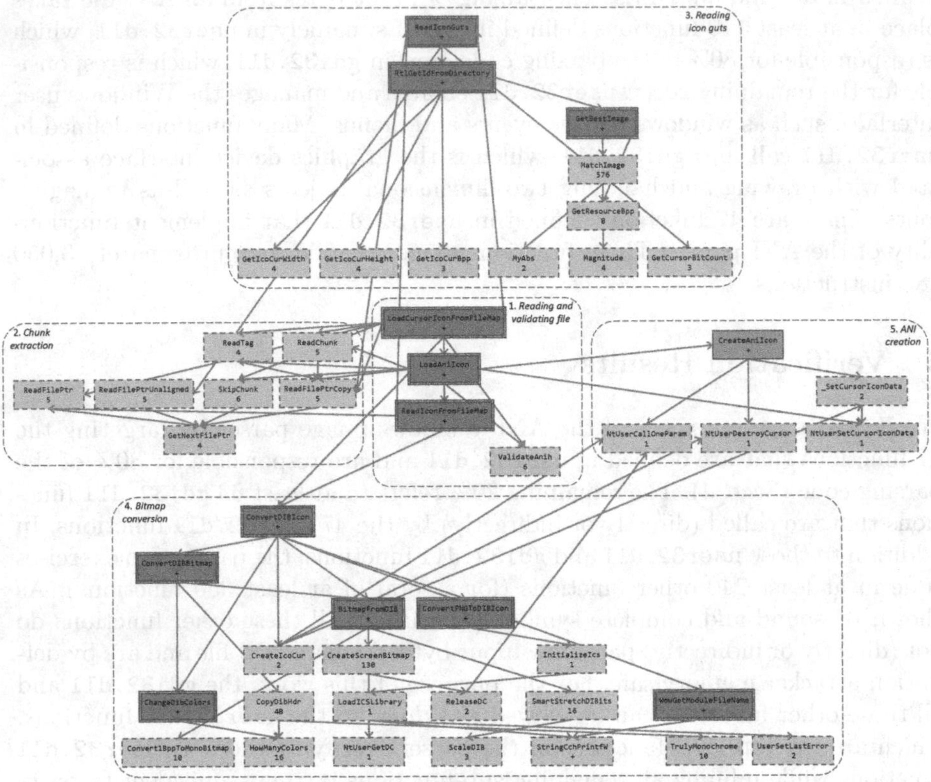

Fig. 1. The callgraph of the 47 **user32.dll** functions implementing the ANI parser core. Functions are grouped based on the architectural component of the parser to which they belong. The different shades and lines of the boxes denote the verification strategy we used to prove memory safety of each function. The boxes with the lighter shade and dotted lines indicate functions verified with the bottom-up strategy (Stage 1), the medium shade and single solid line functions verified by restricting the bounds of input-dependent loops (Stage 2), and the darker shade and double solid lines functions verified with the top-down strategy (Stage 3). Functions are annotated with the number of their execution paths. A + indicates that a function contains too many execution paths to be exhaustively enumerated within 12 hours without using additional techniques for controlling path explosion.

(Sect. 3.3), we marked the function as memory safe. To our surprise, 34 of the 47 functions shown in Fig. 1 could already be proven memory safe this way, and are shown with the lighter shade and dotted lines in the figure.

An exception was the `StringCchPrintfW` function of the *Bitmap conversion* component. This function writes formatted data to a specified string, which is stored in a destination buffer. Exploring all execution paths of function `StringCchPrintfW` that may be passed a destination buffer of any length and a format string with any number of format specifiers does not complete in 12 hours, and is actually very complex.

Inlining. To deal with this function, we just *inlined* it to each of its callers. Inlining a function means replacing the call sites of the function with the function body. In our context, inlining a function means that the function being inlined is no longer treated as an isolated unit that we attempt to verify for any (all) calling contexts, but instead, it is being included in the unit defined by its caller function(s) and proven only for the specific calling context defined in these caller function(s). For instance, function `LoadICSLibrary`, which takes no input arguments, calls function `StringCchPrintfW`. By inlining `StringCchPrintfW` to `LoadICSLibrary`, we can exercise the single execution path in `LoadICSLibrary` and prove attacker memory safety of both functions.

Verification Results. With the simple bottom-up strategy of this section, we were already able to prove attacker memory safety of 34 `user32.dll` functions out of 47, or 72% of the top-level functions of the ANI Windows parser. So far, we had to inline only one function, namely `StringCchPrintfW` to `LoadICSLibrary` of the *Bitmap conversion* component. The `gdi32.dll` functions (not shown in Fig. 1), which are called by the 47 `user32.dll` functions of Fig. 1, were also inlined (recursively) in those `user32.dll` functions. The boxes with the lighter shade and dotted lines of Fig. 1 represent the 34 functions that were verified with the bottom-up strategy. All these functions, except for those that were inlined, were verified in isolation for any calling context. This implies that all bounds for all loops (if any) in all those functions either do not depend on function inputs, or are small enough to be exhaustively explored within 12 hours. Recall that accesses to function input buffers are not yet proven memory safe (Sect. 3.2).

5.2 Stage 2: Input-Dependent Loops

For the remaining 13 `user32.dll` functions of the ANI parser, path explosion is too brutal and exhaustive path enumeration does not terminate in 12 hours. Therefore, during the second stage of the verification process, we decided to identify and restrict the bounds of *input-dependent loops* that might have been preventing us from verifying functions higher in the callgraph of the parser in Stage 1. We define an input-dependent loop as a loop whose number of iterations depends on bytes read from an ANI file, i.e., whole-program inputs. In contrast, when the number of iterations of a loop inside a function depends on function inputs that are not whole-program inputs, path explosion due to that loop can be eliminated by inlining that function to its caller(s).

Restricting Input-Dependent Loop Bounds. In order to control path explosion due to input-dependent loops, we manually *fixed the bounds*, i.e., the number of iterations, of those loops by assigning a concrete value to the program variable(s) containing the input bound(s). We extended MicroX for the user to easily fix the value of arbitrary x86 registers or memory addresses. Naturally, fixing an input value to a specific concrete value is like specifying an input

Table 1. All the input-dependent loop bounds fixed during the verification of the ANI parser. For each loop bound, the table shows the corresponding number of bytes in an ANI input file, the component of the parser containing loops with this bound (numbered as in Fig. 1), and the maximum value of the bound that we could verify in 12 hours.

Type of loop bound	**Component**	**Maximum loop bound**
Frames (4 bytes)	5	2^{32}
Steps (4 bytes)	5	2^{32}
Images/frame (2 bytes/frame)	3	1
File size	1	110

precondition, and the verification of memory safety becomes restricted to calling contexts satisfying that precondition.

As an example, consider function `CreateAniIcon` of the *ANI creation* component of the parser. `CreateAniIcon` calls functions `NtUserCallOneParam` and `NtUserDestroyCursor`, which have one execution path each, as well as function `_SetCursorIconData`, which has two execution paths as shown in Fig. 1. Despite the very small number of paths in its callees, function `CreateAniIcon` contains too many paths to be explored in 12 hours, which is indicated by the + in Fig. 1. This path explosion is due to two input-dependent loops inside that function. By fixing the bounds of these loops to any value from 1 to 2^{32}, the number of execution paths in the loops of function `CreateAniIcon` is always 4. Thus, we can prove memory safety of `CreateAniIcon` for any such fixed number of iterations of these loops.

Verification Results. During this stage of the verification process, we proved memory safety of only one additional `user32.dll` function of the ANI parser, namely `CreateAniIcon`. The box in Fig. 1 with the medium shade and single solid line represents function `CreateAniIcon` that was verified in Stage 2.

Tab. 1 presents a complete list of the input-dependent loop bounds that we fixed during the entire verification of the ANI parser. As described above, to verify memory safety of function `CreateAniIcon` of the *ANI creation* component (component 5 of Fig. 1), we had to fix two input-dependent loops using two whole-program input parameters (namely, frames and steps). In the remainder of this work (Sect. 5.3), we also had to fix two other whole-program input parameters to control a few other input-dependent loops. First, in the *Reading icon guts* component (component 3 of Fig. 1), there are three other input-dependent loops, located in functions `ReadIconGuts` and `GetBestImage`. The number of iterations of all those loops depends on the number of images contained in each icon, which corresponds to 2 bytes per frame of an ANI file. (A single icon may consist of multiple images of different sizes and color depths.) To limit path explosion due to those three loops, we had to fix the number of images per icon of the animated cursor to a maximum of 1. Second, in the *Reading and validating file* component

(component 1 of Fig. 1), there are two input-dependent loops, located in functions `LoadCursorIconFromFileMap` and `LoadAniIcon`, whose number of iterations depends on the size of the input file, which we had to restrict to a maximum of 110 bytes.

It is perhaps surprising that the number of input-dependent loop bounds in the entire parser is limited to a handful of input parameters read from an ANI file, for a total of around 10 bytes (plus the input file size) as shown in Tab. 1.

5.3 Stage 3: Top-Down Strategy

For the remaining 12 `user32.dll` functions still to be verified in the higher-level part of the callgraph of Fig. 1, path explosion was still too severe even after using inlining and fixing input-dependent loops. Therefore, we adopted a different, top-down strategy using sub-function summaries in order to prove memory safety compositionally as described in Sect. 2.2 and 3.

Summarization. As we explained earlier, summarizing sub-functions can alleviate path explosion in those sub-functions at the expense of computing re-usable logic summaries that capture function pre- and postconditions expressed in terms of function inputs and outputs, respectively. For this trade-off to be attractive, it is therefore best to summarize sub-functions (1) that contain many execution paths and (2) whose input/output interfaces with respect to higher-level functions are not too complex so that the logic encoding of their summaries remains tractable. Moreover, to prove memory safety of a sub-function with respect to its input buffers, all bounds-checking constraints inside that sub-function must be included in the precondition of its summary (Sect. 3.2).

Verification Results. To verify the remaining 12 top-level `user32.dll` functions, we manually devised the following summarization strategy based on the previous data about the numbers of paths in verified sub-functions (i.e., the numbers of paths in the boxes of Fig. 1) and by examining the input/output interfaces of the remaining functions. Specifically, we verified one by one the top-level function of each remaining component of the parser, namely function `ReadIconGuts` of the *Reading icon guts* component, `ConvertDIBIcon` of the *Bitmap conversion* component, and `LoadCursorIconFromFileMap` of the *Reading and validating file* component as follows (since the *Chunk extraction* and *ANI creation* components had already been verified during the previous stages).

Verification of `ReadIconGuts`. (*Reading icon guts* component) We fixed the bounds of the input-dependent loops of this component to a single loop iteration (Tab. 1) as discussed in Sect. 5.2, and summarized function `MatchImage`. This function only returns an integer (a "score") that does not influence the control-flow execution of its caller `GetBestImage` for one loop iteration, so its visible postcondition $post_f$ is very simple. Moreover, `MatchImage` takes only one buffer as input, therefore the precondition of its summary includes only bounds-checking constraints for that buffer. In its caller `GetBestImage`, the size of this buffer is always constant and equal to the size of a structure, so `MatchImage` is attacker memory safe. Overall, when restricting the bounds of the input-dependent loops in the *Reading icon guts* component, summarizing `MatchImage`, and inlining all the other functions below it in the callgraph, `ReadIconGuts` contained 468 execution paths that are explored by our tools in 21m 53s.

Verification of `ConvertDIBIcon`. (*Bitmap conversion* component) In a similar way, we verified this function after summarizing sub-function `CopyDibHdr`, whose summarization is also tractable in practice (details not shown here). After summarization, `ConvertDIBIcon` contains 28 execution paths exercised in 1m 58s. Note that, in the *Bitmap conversion* component, there are no input-dependent loops; although sub-function `ConvertPNGToDIBIcon` has loops whose numbers of iterations depend on this function's inputs and therefore could not be verified in isolation, inlining it to its caller `ConvertDIBIcon` eliminated this source of path explosion and it was then proven to be attacker memory safe.

Verification of `LoadCursorIconFromFileMap`. (*Reading and validating file* component) This is the very top-level function of the parser and the final piece of the verification puzzle. Since this final step targets the verification of the entire parser, it clearly requires the use of summarization to alleviate path explosion.

Fortunately, and perhaps surprisingly, after closely examining the implementation of the ANI parser's components, we realized that it is common for their output to be a single "success" or "failure" value. In case "failure" is returned, the higher-level component typically terminates. In case "success" is returned, the parsing proceeds but without reading any other sub-component outputs and with reading other higher-level inputs (such as other bytes that follow in the input file), i.e., completely independently of the specific path taken in the sub-component being summarized. Therefore, the visible postcondition of function summaries with such interfaces is very simple: a success/failure value. This is the case for the top-level functions of the lower-level components *Reading icon guts*, *Bitmap conversion*, and *ANI creation*. This was not the case for the *Chunk extraction* component, which mainly consists of auxiliary functions but does not significantly contribute to path explosion and was not summarized.

More specifically, for the verification of `LoadCursorIconFromFileMap`, we used three summaries for the following top-level functions of sub-components:

- `ReadIconGuts`, which returns a pointer to a structure that is checked for nullness in its callers. Then, caller `LoadCursorIconFromFileMap` returns null when this pointer is null. In caller `ReadIconFromFileMap`, in case the pointer is non-null, it is passed as argument to `ConvertDIBIcon`, which has already been verified for any calling context as described above.
- `ConvertDIBIcon`: case similar to `ReadIconGuts`.
- `CreateAniIcon`, which also returns a pointer to a structure. If this pointer is null, the parser fails and caller `LoadAniIcon` emits an error message:

  ```
  if (frames != 0) ani = CreateAniIcon(...);
  if (ani == NULL) EMIT_ERROR("Invalid icon");
  ```

  Otherwise, the pointer is returned by `LoadAniIcon` and subsequently by the top-level function of the parser.

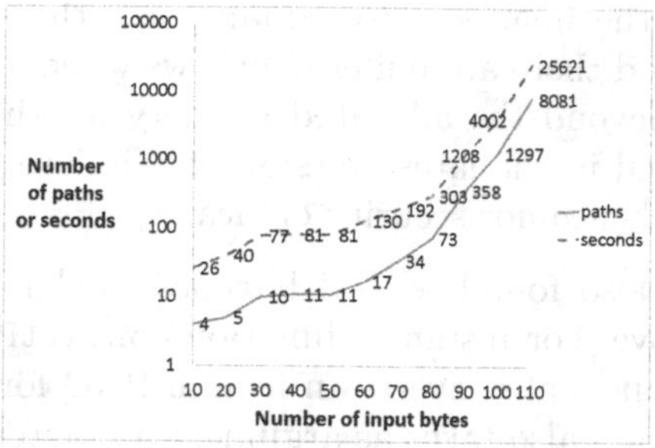

Fig. 2. The number of execution paths in the top-level function `LoadCursorIconFromFileMap` of the ANI parser and the time (in seconds) it takes to exercise these paths versus the number of input bytes when summarizing components *Reading icon guts*, *Bitmap conversion*, and *ANI creation*

Function `LoadCursorIconFromFileMap` also has an input-dependent loop whose number of iterations depends on the size of the input file being read and containing the ANI file to be parsed. By summarizing the top-level function of the above three lower-level components and fixing the file size, we were able to prove memory safety of the parser up to a file size of 110 bytes in less than 12 hours. Fig. 2 shows the number of execution paths in the parser as well as the time it takes to explore these paths when summarizing components *Reading icon guts*, *Bitmap conversion*, and *ANI creation* and controlling the file size.

6 Memory-Safety Bugs

In reality, the verification of the ANI Windows parser was slightly more complicated than presented in the previous section because the ANI parser is actually *not memory safe*! Specifically, we found three types of memory-safety violations during the course of this work:

- real bugs (fixed in the latest version of Windows),
- harmless bugs (off-by-one non-exploitable buffer overflows),
- code parts not memory safe by design.

We briefly discuss each of these memory-safety violations. Details are omitted on purpose.

Real Bugs. We found several buffer overflows all related to the same root cause. Function `ReadIconGuts` of the *Reading icon guts* component allocates memory for storing a single icon extracted from the input file and returns a pointer to this memory. The allocated memory is then cast to a structure, whose fields are read for accessing sub-parts of the icon, such as its header. However, the size of an icon, and therefore the size of the allocated memory, depends on the (untrusted) declared size of the images that make up the icon. These sizes are declared in the ANI file and might not correspond to the actual image sizes. Consequently, if the declared size of the images is too small, then the size of the allocated memory is too small, and there are buffer overflows when accessing the fields of the structure located beyond the allocated memory for the icon. These buffer overflows have been fixed in the latest version of Windows, but are believed to be hard to exploit and hence not security critical.

Harmless Bugs. We also found several harmless buffer overflows related to the bugs described above. For instance, function `ConvertPNGToDIBIcon` of the *Bitmap conversion* component converts an icon in PNG format to DIB (Device Independent Bitmap), and also takes as argument a pointer to the above structure for the icon. To determine whether an icon is in PNG format, `ConvertPNGToDIBIcon` checks whether the icon contains the 8-byte PNG signature. However, the allocated memory for the icon may be smaller than 8 bytes, in which case there can be a buffer overflow. Still, on Windows, every memory allocation (call to `malloc`) always results in the allocation of a reserved memory block of at least 8 bytes. So technically, accessing any buffer `buf` of size less than 8 up to `buf+7` bytes is not a buffer overflow according to the Windows runtime environment—such buffer overflows are harmless to both reliability and security.

Code Parts Not Memory Safe by Design. Finally, we found memory-safety violations that were expected and caught as runtime exceptions using `try/except` statements. For instance, `CopyDibHdr` of the *Bitmap conversion* component copies and converts an icon header to a common header format. The size of the memory that is allocated in `CopyDibHdr` for copying the icon header depends on color information defined in the header itself. This color information is read from the input file, and is therefore untrusted. Specifically, it can make the parser allocate a huge amount of memory, which is often referred to as a *memory spike*. Later, the actual header content is copied into this memory. To check whether the declared size matches the actual size, `CopyDibHdr` uses a `try` statement to probe the icon header in chunks of 4K bytes, i.e., the minimum page size, to ensure that the memory is readable and properly initialized. While probing the icon header inside the `try` statement, the parser may access unallocated memory beyond the bounds of the header, which is a memory-safety violation. However, this violation is expected to be caught in an `except` statement, which aborts parsing in higher-level functions.

The verification results of Sect. 5 were obtained after fixing or ignoring the memory-safety bugs discussed in this section. Those results are therefore sound only with respect to these additional assumptions.

7 Other Related Work

Traditional *interactive* program verification, based on static program analysis, verification-condition generation, and theorem proving, provides a broader framework for proving more complex properties of a larger class of programs but at the expense of more work from the user. For instance, the VCC [12] project verified the *functional correctness*, including memory safety and race freedom, of the Microsoft Hyper-V hypervisor [27], a piece of concurrent software (100K lines of C, 5K lines of assembly), and required more than 13.5K lines of source-code annotations for specifying contracts, loop invariants, and ghost state in about 350 functions by a team of more than 10 people and over a period of several years. As another impressive example, the seL4 project [25] designed and verified the C code of a microkernel using the interactive theorem prover Isabelle/HOL [31] and requiring about 200K lines of Isabelle scripts and 20 years of research in developing and automating the proofs. Also recently, Typed Assembly Language [29] (TAL) and the Boogie program verifier [4] were used to prove type and memory safety of (part of) the Verve operating system [37] (a total of 20 functions implemented in approximately 1.5K lines of x86 assembly), manually annotated with pre-/postconditions, loop invariants, and external function stubs for a total of 1,185 lines of annotations in about nine months of work.

In contrast, our verification project required only three months of work, no program annotations, no static program analysis, and no external function stubs, although our scope was more focused (attacker memory safety only), our application domain was different (sequential image parser versus concurrent/reactive operating-system code), and we did require several key manual verification steps, including fixing a few input-dependent loop bounds, as discussed in Sect. 5. Note that our purely dynamic techniques and x86-based tools can handle ANI x86 code patterns such as stack-modifying compiler-injected code for structured exception handling (SEH prologue and epilogue code for `try/except` statements) and stack-guard protection, which most static-analysis tools cannot handle.

Static-analysis-based software model checkers, like SLAM [3], BLAST [23], and Yogi [32], can *automatically* prove control-oriented API properties of specific classes of programs (specifically, device drivers). These tools rely on (predicate) abstraction in order to scale, and are not engineered to reason precisely about pointers, memory alignment, and aliasing. They were not designed and cannot be used as-is for proving (attacker) memory safety of an application as large and complex as the ANI Windows parser.

SAT/SMT-based bounded model checkers, as CBMC [11], are another class of static-analysis tools for automatic program verification. For loop-free programs and when symbolic execution has perfect precision, the program's logic representation generated by such model checkers is similar to verification-condition generation and captures both data and control dependencies on all program variables, which is similar to *eagerly* summarizing (as in Sect. 2.2) *every* program block and function. Even excluding all loops, such a monolithic whole-program logic encoding would not scale to accurately represent the entire ANI parser.

As shown in Sect. 5, systematic dynamic test generation also does not scale to the entire ANI parser without the selective use of function summarization and fixing a few input-dependent loop bounds. These crucial steps were performed manually in our work. Algorithms and heuristics for *automatic* program summarization have been proposed before [15,1,26] as well as other closely related techniques [5,28] and heuristics [21], which can be viewed as approximations of sub-program summarization. However, none of this prior work on automatic summarization has ever been applied to *verify* an application as large and complex as the parser considered here.

We emphasize that we are not aware of *any* automatic tool that, today, could prove (attacker) memory safety of an application like the ANI parser. We do not know which parts of the ANI code are in the subset of C for which tools like CCured [30] or Prefix [7] are sound, or how many memory-safety checks could be removed in those parts with such a sound static analysis. However, we do know that Prefix was run on this code for years, yet bugs remained, which is precisely why fuzzing is performed later [6].

Proving *attacker memory safety*, even more so *compositionally*, is novel: we prove that an attacker cannot trigger buffer overflows, but ignore other buffer overflows (for instance, due to the failure of trusted system calls). This requires a whole-program taint analysis to focus on what the attacker can control, performed using symbolic execution and the top-down strategy of Sect. 5.3. In contrast, other approaches like verification-condition generation, bounded model checking or traditional static analysis lack this global taint view and treat all program statements alike, without prioritizing the analysis towards parts closest to the attack surface, which hampers scalability and relevance to security.

8 Concluding Remarks

We showed how to prove attacker memory safety of an entire operating-system image parser using compositional exhaustive testing, i.e., no static analysis whatsoever. These results required a high-level of automation in our tools and verification process although key steps were performed manually, like fixing input-dependent loop bounds, guiding the summarization strategy, and fixing and avoiding memory-safety violations. Also, the scope of our work was only to prove attacker memory safety, not general memory safety or functional correctness, and the ANI parser is a purely sequential program. Finally, the verification guarantees provided by our work are valid only with respect to some important assumptions we had to make, mostly regarding input-dependent loop bounds. Overall, after this work, we are now confident that the presence of any remaining security-critical (i.e., attacker-controllable) buffer overflows in the ANI Windows parser is unlikely, but those conclusions are subject to the assumptions we made.

Here are some interesting findings that we did not expect:

- many ANI functions are loop free and were easy to verify (Sect. 5.1);
- all the input-dependent loops in the entire ANI parser are controlled by the values of about 10 bytes only in any ANI file plus the file size (Sect. 5.2);
- the remaining path explosion can be controlled by using only 5 function summaries with very simple interfaces (Sect. 5.3).

Our work suggests future directions for automating further several of the steps that were done manually (e.g., dealing with few but critical input-dependent loops and program decomposition at cost-effective interfaces). Perhaps future tools will perform those steps intelligently and automatically.

References

1. Anand, S., Godefroid, P., Tillmann, N.: Demand-driven compositional symbolic execution. In: Ramakrishnan, C.R., Rehof, J. (eds.) TACAS 2008. LNCS, vol. 4963, pp. 367–381. Springer, Heidelberg (2008)
2. Artzi, S., Kiezun, A., Dolby, J., Tip, F., Dig, D., Paradkar, A.M., Ernst, M.D.: Finding bugs in web applications using dynamic test generation and explicit-state model checking. TSE 36, 474–494 (2010)
3. Ball, T., Rajamani, S.K.: The SLAM toolkit. In: Berry, G., Comon, H., Finkel, A. (eds.) CAV 2001. LNCS, vol. 2102, pp. 260–264. Springer, Heidelberg (2001)
4. Barnett, M., Chang, B.-Y.E., DeLine, R., Jacobs, B., Leino, K.R.M.: Boogie: A modular reusable verifier for object-oriented programs. In: de Boer, F.S., Bonsangue, M.M., Graf, S., de Roever, W.-P. (eds.) FMCO 2005. LNCS, vol. 4111, pp. 364–387. Springer, Heidelberg (2006)
5. Boonstoppel, P., Cadar, C., Engler, D.: RWset: Attacking path explosion in constraint-based test generation. In: Ramakrishnan, C.R., Rehof, J. (eds.) TACAS 2008. LNCS, vol. 4963, pp. 351–366. Springer, Heidelberg (2008)
6. Bounimova, E., Godefroid, P., Molnar, D.A.: Billions and billions of constraints: Whitebox fuzz testing in production. In: ICSE, pp. 122–131. ACM (2013)
7. Bush, W.R., Pincus, J.D., Sielaff, D.J.: A static analyzer for finding dynamic programming errors. SPE 30, 775–802 (2000)
8. Cadar, C., Dunbar, D., Engler, D.R.: KLEE: Unassisted and automatic generation of high-coverage tests for complex systems programs. In: OSDI, pp. 209–224. USENIX (2008)
9. Cadar, C., Engler, D.: Execution generated test cases: How to make systems code crash itself. In: Godefroid, P. (ed.) SPIN 2005. LNCS, vol. 3639, pp. 2–23. Springer, Heidelberg (2005)
10. Cadar, C., Ganesh, V., Pawlowski, P.M., Dill, D.L., Engler, D.R.: EXE: Automatically generating inputs of death. In: CCS, pp. 322–335. ACM (2006)
11. Clarke, E.M., Kroening, D., Yorav, K.: Behavioral consistency of C and Verilog programs using bounded model checking. In: DAC, pp. 368–371. ACM (2003)
12. Cohen, E., Dahlweid, M., Hillebrand, M., Leinenbach, D., Moskal, M., Santen, T., Schulte, W., Tobies, S.: VCC: A practical system for verifying concurrent C. In: Berghofer, S., Nipkow, T., Urban, C., Wenzel, M. (eds.) TPHOLs 2009. LNCS, vol. 5674, pp. 23–42. Springer, Heidelberg (2009)
13. de Moura, L., Bjørner, N.S.: Z3: An efficient SMT solver. In: Ramakrishnan, C.R., Rehof, J. (eds.) TACAS 2008. LNCS, vol. 4963, pp. 337–340. Springer, Heidelberg (2008)
14. Elkarablieh, B., Godefroid, P., Levin, M.Y.: Precise pointer reasoning for dynamic test generation. In: ISSTA, pp. 129–140. ACM (2009)
15. Godefroid, P.: Compositional dynamic test generation. In: POPL, pp. 47–54. ACM (2007)
16. Godefroid, P.: Micro execution. In: ICSE, pp. 539–549. ACM (2014)
17. Godefroid, P., Kinder, J.: Proving memory safety of floating-point computations by combining static and dynamic program analysis. In: ISSTA, pp. 1–12. ACM (2010)
18. Godefroid, P., Klarlund, N., Sen, K.: DART: Directed automated random testing. In: PLDI, pp. 213–223. ACM (2005)
19. Godefroid, P., Lahiri, S.K., Rubio-González, C.: Statically validating must summaries for incremental compositional dynamic test generation. In: Yahav, E. (ed.) SAS 2011. LNCS, vol. 6887, pp. 112–128. Springer, Heidelberg (2011)

20. Godefroid, P., Levin, M.Y., Molnar, D.A.: Active property checking. In: EMSOFT, pp. 207–216. ACM (2008)
21. Godefroid, P., Levin, M.Y., Molnar, D.A.: Automated whitebox fuzz testing. In: NDSS, pp. 151–166. The Internet Society (2008)
22. Godefroid, P., Luchaup, D.: Automatic partial loop summarization in dynamic test generation. In: ISSTA, pp. 23–33. ACM (2011)
23. Henzinger, T.A., Jhala, R., Majumdar, R., Sutre, G.: Lazy abstraction. In: POPL, pp. 58–70. ACM (2002)
24. Howard, M.: Lessons learned from the animated cursor security bug (2007), `http://blogs.msdn.com/b/sdl/archive/2007/04/26/lessons-learned-from-the-animated-cursor-security-bug.aspx`
25. Klein, G., Elphinstone, K., Heiser, G., Andronick, J., Cock, D., Derrin, P., Elkaduwe, D., Engelhardt, K., Kolanski, R., Norrish, M., Sewell, T., Tuch, H., Winwood, S.: seL4: Formal verification of an OS kernel. In: SOSP, pp. 207–220. ACM (2009)
26. Kuznetsov, V., Kinder, J., Bucur, S., Candea, G.: Efficient state merging in symbolic execution. In: PLDI, pp. 193–204. ACM (2012)
27. Leinenbach, D., Santen, T.: Verifying the Microsoft Hyper-V hypervisor with VCC. In: Cavalcanti, A., Dams, D.R. (eds.) FM 2009. LNCS, vol. 5850, pp. 806–809. Springer, Heidelberg (2009)
28. Majumdar, R., Xu, R.-G.: Reducing test inputs using information partitions. In: Bouajjani, A., Maler, O. (eds.) CAV 2009. LNCS, vol. 5643, pp. 555–569. Springer, Heidelberg (2009)
29. Morrisett, J.G., Walker, D., Crary, K., Glew, N.: From system F to typed assembly language. In: POPL, pp. 85–97. ACM (1998)
30. Necula, G.C., McPeak, S., Weimer, W.: CCured: Type-safe retrofitting of legacy code. In: POPL, pp. 128–139. ACM (2002)
31. Nipkow, T., Paulson, L.C., Wenzel, M.: Isabelle/HOL. LNCS, vol. 2283. Springer, Heidelberg (2002)
32. Nori, A.V., Rajamani, S.K.: An empirical study of optimizations in YOGI. In: ICSE, pp. 355–364. ACM (2010)
33. Sen, K., Agha, G.: CUTE and jCUTE: Concolic unit testing and explicit path model-checking tools. In: Ball, T., Jones, R.B. (eds.) CAV 2006. LNCS, vol. 4144, pp. 419–423. Springer, Heidelberg (2006)
34. Song, D., et al.: BitBlaze: A new approach to computer security via binary analysis. In: Sekar, R., Pujari, A.K. (eds.) ICISS 2008. LNCS, vol. 5352, pp. 1–25. Springer, Heidelberg (2008)
35. Sotirov, A.: Windows animated cursor stack overflow vulnerability (2007), `http://www.offensive-security.com/os101/ani.htm`
36. Tillmann, N., de Halleux, J.: Pex–White Box Test Generation for .NET. In: Beckert, B., Hähnle, R. (eds.) TAP 2008. LNCS, vol. 4966, pp. 134–153. Springer, Heidelberg (2008)
37. Yang, J., Hawblitzel, C.: Safe to the last instruction: Automated verification of a type-safe operating system. In: PLDI, pp. 99–110. ACM (2010)

Automatic Inference of Heap Properties Exploiting Value Domains

Pietro Ferrara[1], Peter Müller[2], and Milos Novacek[2]

[1] IBM Thomas J. Watson Research Center, USA
pietroferrara@us.ibm.com
[2] Department of Computer Science, ETH Zurich, Switzerland
{peter.mueller,milos.novacek}@inf.ethz.ch

Abstract. Effective static analyses of heap-manipulating programs need to track precise information about the heap structures and the values computed by the program. Most existing heap analyses rely on manual annotations to precisely analyze general and, in particular, recursive, heap structures. Moreover, they either do not exploit value information to obtain more precise heap information or require more annotations for this purpose. In this paper, we present a combined heap and value analysis that infers complex invariants for recursive heap structures such as lists and trees, including relations between value fields of heap-allocated objects. Our analysis uses a novel notion of edge-local identifiers to track value information about the source and target of a pointer, even if these are summary nodes. With each potential pointer in the heap, our analysis associates value information that describes in which states the pointer may exist, and uses this information to improve the precision of the analysis by pruning infeasible heap structures. Our analysis has been implemented in the static analyzer Sample; experimental results show that it can automatically infer invariants for data structures, for which state-of-the-art analyses require manual annotations.

1 Introduction

Effective static analyses of heap-manipulating programs need to track precise information about the heap structures and the values computed by a program. Heap and value information is not independent: heap information determines which locations need to be tracked by a value analysis, and information about value fields may be useful to obtain more precise heap information, for instance, to rule out certain forms of aliasing. Moreover, many interesting invariants of heap-manipulating programs combine heap and value information such as the invariant that a heap structure is a sorted linked list.

Despite these connections, heap and value analyses have often been treated as orthogonal problems. Some existing heap analyses such as TVLA [18] rely on manual instrumentation to infer invariants that combine heap and value information. However, TVLA does not support general value domains, which limits, for instance, arithmetical reasoning. Recent work addresses this issue by combining TVLA with value domains, but still requires the user to provide predicates

D. D'Souza et al. (Eds.): VMCAI 2015, LNCS 8931, pp. 393–411, 2015.

to track and exchange information between the heap and value domains [21], or is not able to track complex invariants over recursive data structures [14]. Chang and Rival [5] present an efficient inference for combined heap and value invariants, which also relies on user-provided predicates. Other analyses do not require manual annotations [2,3], but are specific to programs that manipulate certain data structures such as singly-linked lists.

In this paper, we present a combined heap and value analysis—expressed as an abstract interpretation [8]—that infers complex invariants of heap structures. It is automatic in the sense that it uses only the information included in the program, without relying on manual annotations. Our analysis uses a graph-based abstraction of heaps, where each edge in the graph represents a *potential* pointer in the concrete heap. Each edge is associated with an abstract value state that characterizes in which concrete states this pointer might actually exist. The value states on the edges allow our analysis to represent disjunctive information in a single heap graph (like the bracketing constraints in Dillig et al.'s Fluid Updates [10]). They are also used to improve the precision of the analysis when value information implies that certain pointer chains cannot exist in concrete heaps. Our analysis can be instantiated with different value domains to obtain different trade-offs between precision and efficiency.

Like many heap analyses, we use summary nodes to abstract over sets of concrete objects. A key innovation of our analysis is to introduce *edge-local identifiers* for the source and target of each edge in the heap graph. An edge-local identifier represents a field of one particular concrete object, even when the object is abstracted by a summary node. By having identifiers per edge, the value analysis may relate the fields of the source and the target of a concrete pointer and, thus, track inductive invariants such as the sortedness of a linked list.

Example. Method increasingList in Fig. 1 creates and returns a linked list. If parameter v is non-positive, the list is empty, that is, result is null (invariant I1). Otherwise, the list satisfies the following properties: it is non-empty, that is, the result is non-null (I2), the first node has value 0 (I3), the values of all other nodes are one larger than their predecessor's (I4), and the value of the last node is v − 1 (I5). Note that these invariants imply that the list is acyclic and has v nodes.

```
1  Node increasingList (int v) {
2    Node result = null;
3    int i = v;
4    while (i > 0) {
5      Node p = new Node();
6      p.next = result;
7      p.val = i − 1;
8      result = p;
9      i = i − 1;
10   }
11   return result;
12 }
```

Fig. 1. Running example

Fig. 2 shows the abstract state that our analysis infers at the end of method increasingList. Here, we use a numerical domain such as Polyhedra [9] or Octagon [22] for the abstract states associated with each edge in the graph. The figure shows the relevant constraints from these states. They are expressed in terms of parameter v and the edge-local identifiers (Src, val) and (Trg, val), which refer to the val field of the source and target of a pointer, respectively.

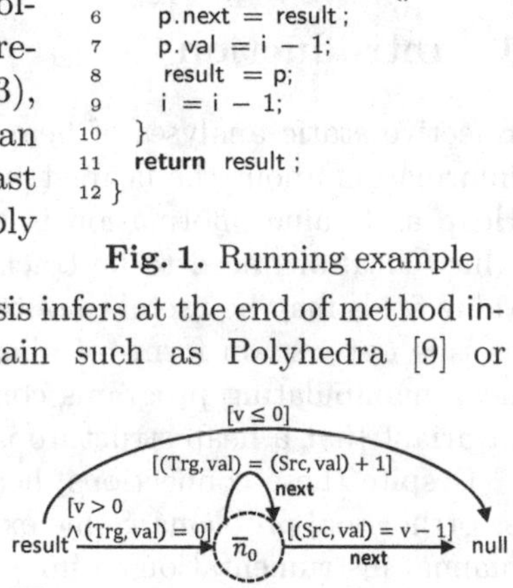

Fig. 2. The abstract heap state inferred at line 11 of Fig. 1

The abstract state reflects the five invariants stated above. Variable result is null if the constraints on the corresponding edge hold, that is, if v is non-positive (I1). Otherwise, result points to the summary node $\overline{n}_0$, which implies that it is non-null (I2). This example illustrates that our analysis represents disjunctive information in a single graph: both possible values of result are represented by the same graph, and we use value information to determine the states in which each pointer may exist. The constraint $(\mathsf{Trg}, \mathsf{val}) = 0$ on the edge from result to the summary node $\overline{n}_0$ expresses that the first list node has value 0 (I3). Note that the edge-local identifier allows us to express properties of a single object, even if it is abstracted by a summary node. The same feature is used in the constraint $(\mathsf{Trg}, \mathsf{val}) = (\mathsf{Src}, \mathsf{val}) + 1$ on the edge from $\overline{n}_0$ to itself to express invariant I4. Finally, the constraint $(\mathsf{Src}, \mathsf{val}) = \mathsf{v} - 1$ on the edge from $\overline{n}_0$ to null expresses that the last list node has value $\mathsf{v} - 1$ (I5). All five invariants are inferred automatically by our analysis without manual annotations.

Outline. Sec. 2 defines the language and the concrete domain. Sec. 3 formalizes the abstract domain, while Sec. 4 defines the abstract semantics. Sec. 5 reports the experimental results, Sec. 6 discusses related work, and Sec. 7 concludes.

2 Programming Language and Concrete Domain

We present our analysis for the small object-based language in Fig. 3. To simplify the formalization, we model local variables as fields of a special object $\Im$, that is, treat local variables as heap locations. We distinguish *reference field* and *value field* access expressions rAE and vAE, depending on the type of the accessed field. A reference expression rexp may be null, a reference field access expression, or an object creation. A value expression vexp may be a literal, a value field access expression, or a binary expression. Since the treatment of loops and conditionals is standard, the only relevant statements in ST are value and reference assignments.

$$
\begin{aligned}
\mathsf{rAE} &::= \Im.\mathsf{f_r} \mid \mathsf{rAE.f_r} \\
\mathsf{vAE} &::= \Im.\mathsf{f_v} \mid \mathsf{rAE.f_v} \\
\mathsf{rexp} &::= \mathsf{null} \mid \mathsf{rAE} \mid \mathsf{new\ C} \\
\mathsf{vexp} &::= \mathsf{n} \mid \mathsf{vAE} \mid \mathsf{vexp}\ \langle \mathsf{op} \rangle\ \mathsf{vexp} \\
\mathsf{op} &::= + \mid - \mid * \mid \cdots \\
\mathsf{ST} &::= \mathsf{rAE} = \mathsf{rexp} \mid \mathsf{vAE} = \mathsf{vexp}
\end{aligned}
$$

Fig. 3. Expressions and statements

In the concrete domain, we partition the content of heap locations into values and references. Let Ref be the set of concrete references (objects and null), with $\Im, \mathsf{null} \in \mathsf{Ref}$, and let Val be the set of values. Let $\mathsf{Field_{Ref}}$ and $\mathsf{Field_{Val}}$ be finite sets of reference and value fields, respectively. An execution state consists of a *value store* and a *reference store*. We model a value store as a partial map in $\mathsf{Store_{Val}} = (\mathsf{Ref} \setminus \{\mathsf{null}\}) \times \mathsf{Field_{Val}} \rightharpoonup \mathsf{Val}$ and a reference store as a partial map in $\mathsf{Store_{Ref}} = (\mathsf{Ref} \setminus \{\mathsf{null}\}) \times \mathsf{Field_{Ref}} \rightharpoonup \mathsf{Ref}$. For each reference in their domain, these maps contain an entry for every field. We will refer to entries in a reference store as *concrete edges*. We define the set of all concrete states (*concrete heaps*) as $\Sigma = \mathsf{Store_{Ref}} \times \mathsf{Store_{Val}}$.

3 Abstract Domain and Operators

In this section, we present the abstract domain, the concretization function, as well as join and widening operators.

3.1 Abstract Domain

Let $\overline{\mathsf{Ref}}$ be the set of *abstract references* (or *abstract nodes*) with $\Im, \mathsf{null} \in \overline{\mathsf{Ref}}$ (that is, we overload the symbols $\Im$ and null to denote both concrete and abstract references). Each abstract node $\overline{n} \in \overline{\mathsf{Ref}}$ represents either a single concrete non-null reference (*definite node*), or a non-empty set of concrete non-null references (*summary node*) with $\Im$ and null being definite nodes. The functions in $\mathsf{IsSummary} = \overline{\mathsf{Ref}} \rightarrow \{\mathsf{true}, \mathsf{false}\}$ define whether a node is a summary node.

An *abstract reference store* in $\overline{\mathsf{Store}_{\mathsf{Ref}}} = \mathcal{P}((\overline{\mathsf{Ref}} \setminus \{\mathsf{null}\}) \times \mathsf{Field}_{\mathsf{Ref}} \times \overline{\mathsf{Ref}})$ represents possible pointers between abstract nodes through reference fields. It can be interpreted as a directed graph where edges are labeled with a field name. Hence, we will refer to members of the abstract reference store as *abstract edges*. For an abstract edge $\overline{n}_1 \xrightarrow{f_r} \overline{n}_2$, we will refer to $\overline{n}_1$ as the *source* and to $\overline{n}_2$ as the *target* of the edge.

Our heap analysis is parameterized by an *abstract value domain* $\overline{\mathsf{V}}$, which tracks information about value fields, for instance, relations among numerical values. Each abstract edge is associated with an abstract value state (*abstract condition*) via a map in $\overline{\mathsf{Cond}} = (\overline{\mathsf{Ref}} \setminus \{\mathsf{null}\}) \times \mathsf{Field}_{\mathsf{Ref}} \times \overline{\mathsf{Ref}} \rightarrow \overline{\mathsf{V}}$. The abstract condition of an abstract edge approximates the concrete value stores in which the edge exists. That is, our abstract domain tracks disjunctive information by having several edges with the same source and field, and associating them with different abstract conditions.

Abstract value states in $\overline{\mathsf{V}}$ refer to memory locations via *abstract identifiers* $\overline{\mathsf{ID}} = \overline{\mathsf{Loc}} \cup \overline{\mathsf{EId}}$ where $\overline{\mathsf{Loc}} = (\overline{\mathsf{Ref}} \setminus \{\mathsf{null}\}) \times \mathsf{Field}_{\mathsf{Val}}$ and $\overline{\mathsf{EId}} = \{\mathsf{Src}, \mathsf{Trg}\} \times \mathsf{Field}_{\mathsf{Val}}$. An identifier $(\overline{n}, f_v) \in \overline{\mathsf{Loc}}$ represents the value field f_v of the concrete references abstracted by the node $\overline{n}$. *Edge-local identifiers* $(\mathsf{Src}, f_v), (\mathsf{Trg}, f_v) \in \overline{\mathsf{EId}}$ represent the value field f_v of the *single* concrete *source* or *target* reference of the concrete edges represented by an abstract edge. They track relations between the value fields of adjacent references in concrete heaps, which allows us to infer precise invariants on summary nodes. For instance, the constraint $(\mathsf{Src}, \mathsf{val}) \leq (\mathsf{Trg}, \mathsf{val})$ in the abstract condition of an abstract edge $\overline{n} \xrightarrow{\mathsf{next}} \overline{n}$ expresses sortedness of the concrete list that is abstracted by the summary node $\overline{n}$.

We define the set of all abstract states (*abstract heaps*) as $\overline{\Sigma} = \overline{\mathsf{Store}_{\mathsf{Ref}}} \times \overline{\mathsf{Cond}} \times \mathsf{IsSummary}$.

Example. The abstract heap in Fig. 4 depicts the loop invariant of the program in Fig. 1. Many of the constraints are similar to the constraints in Fig. 2. In particular, combining the abstract heap for the loop invariant with the negation of the loop guard (that is, $\mathsf{i} \leq 0$) yields the information reflected in Fig. 2, for instance, that result is null iff $\mathsf{v} \leq 0$ and that the first list node has value 0.

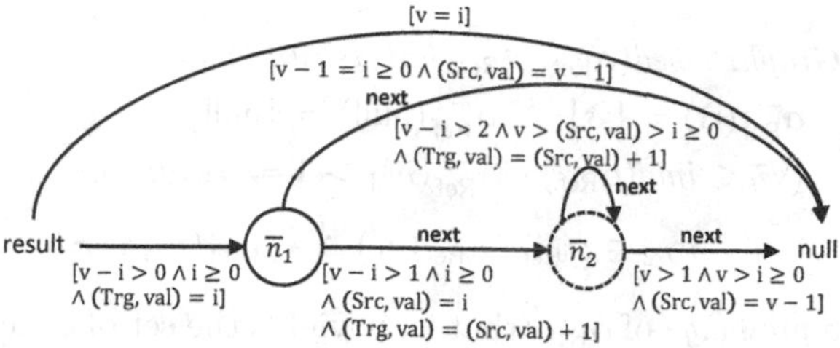

Fig. 4. The abstract heap representing the loop invariant at line 4 of the example in Fig. 1. Solid and dashed circles denote definite and summary nodes, respectively. Arrows depict abstract edges and are annotated with relevant constraints from their abstract conditions. To improve readability, we depict local reference variables as nodes and use local variables as identifiers in constraints, although the analysis models them as fields of $\Im$.

3.2 Concretization

In this section, we define the concretization function $\gamma : \overline{\Sigma} \to \mathcal{P}(\Sigma)$ that yields the set of concrete heaps represented by a given abstract heap.

We assume that our heap analysis is instantiated with a sound value analysis. Its concretization function $\gamma_{\overline{V}} : \overline{V} \to \mathcal{P}(\overline{\mathsf{ID}} \to \mathcal{P}(\mathsf{Val}))$ yields a set of maps from abstract identifiers to sets of concrete values. These maps yield sets of concrete values rather than single values since an abstract value state may contain identifiers for fields of summary nodes, and the value analysis alone cannot concretize them. Let *references*(st_{Ref}) be the set of concrete references of a given concrete reference store st_{Ref}, including $\Im$ and null. We define the concretization function γ of abstract heaps as:

$$(st_{\mathsf{Ref}}, st_{\mathsf{Val}}) \in \gamma(\overline{St}, \overline{con}, isSum) \Leftrightarrow \begin{pmatrix} \exists \alpha_{\mathsf{Ref}} \in (references(st_{\mathsf{Ref}}) \to \overline{\mathsf{Ref}}) \cdot \\ GraphEmbed(\alpha_{\mathsf{Ref}}, st_{\mathsf{Ref}}, (\overline{St}, isSum)) \wedge \\ ValueEmbed(\alpha_{\mathsf{Ref}}, (st_{\mathsf{Ref}}, st_{\mathsf{Val}}), \overline{con}) \end{pmatrix}$$

That is, a concrete heap $(st_{\mathsf{Ref}}, st_{\mathsf{Val}})$ is in the concretization of an abstract heap $(\overline{St}, \overline{con}, isSum)$ iff there exists an embedding α_{Ref} (a function from concrete references to abstract nodes) such that the *shape* and the *values* of the concrete heap can be embedded into the abstract heap. These embeddings are expressed via the predicates *GraphEmbed* and *ValueEmbed*, which are defined as follows.

GraphEmbed holds if a given concrete reference store matches the shape of a given abstract heap, ignoring the value information. This is the case if $\Im$ and null are the only concrete references that are abstracted to the abstract $\Im$ and null (1), if, whenever multiple concrete references are abstracted to a single abstract reference, that abstract reference is a summary node (2), and if every concrete edge is represented by an abstract edge in the abstract heap (3). Note that this abstract edge is unique since α_{Ref} is a function:

$$\begin{aligned}
&\mathit{GraphEmbed}(\alpha_{\mathsf{Ref}}, st_{\mathsf{Ref}}, (\overline{St}, \mathit{isSum})) \Leftrightarrow \\
&\quad \alpha_{\mathsf{Ref}}^{-1}(\Im) = \{\Im\} \ \wedge \ \alpha_{\mathsf{Ref}}^{-1}(\mathsf{null}) = \{\mathsf{null}\} \ \wedge && (1)\\
&\quad (\forall \overline{n} \in \mathit{img}(\alpha_{\mathsf{Ref}}) \cdot |\alpha_{\mathsf{Ref}}^{-1}(\overline{n})| > 1 \Rightarrow \mathit{isSum}(\overline{n})) \ \wedge && (2)\\
&\quad \forall r_1 \xrightarrow{f_r} r_2 \in st_{\mathsf{Ref}} \cdot \alpha_{\mathsf{Ref}}(r_1) \xrightarrow{f_r} \alpha_{\mathsf{Ref}}(r_2) \in \overline{St} && (3)
\end{aligned}$$

where $\alpha_{\mathsf{Ref}}^{-1}$ is the *preimage* of α_{Ref} (that is, it yields the set of concrete references abstracted by a given abstract reference).

ValueEmbed expresses that, for a given concrete reference store st_{Ref}, the value store st_{Val} matches all relevant abstract conditions in the abstract heap. Here, an abstract condition is *relevant* if it is associated with an abstract edge that corresponds to a concrete edge in st_{Ref}. In the definition below, we relate the concrete value store st_{Val} to each relevant abstract condition via a map s from abstract identifiers to sets of concrete values. For each concrete edge $r_1 \xrightarrow{f_r} r_2$ in the concrete reference store st_{Ref}, there is a map s in the concretization of the abstract condition of the corresponding abstract edge (4). The map s may constrain a concrete location (r, f_v) in three ways: via the abstract identifier $(\alpha_{\mathsf{Ref}}(r), f_v)$, via the edge-local identifier (Src, f_v) if r is the source of the concrete edge, that is, $r = r_1$, and via the edge-local identifier (Trg, f_v) if r is the target of the concrete edge, that is, $r = r_2$. In all three cases, the map s must yield a set that contains the value v stored in the concrete value store for (r, f_v) (5). Finally, any concrete value store matches the relevant abstract conditions only if the conditions do not contradict each other, even on abstract locations that are not included in a given concrete heap. To ensure there are no such contradictions, s must be in the concretization of *all* relevant conditions, ignoring edge-local identifiers, which may denote different locations for different abstract edges. We use the operator $\downarrow_{\overline{\mathsf{Loc}}}$ to project to the identifiers in $\overline{\mathsf{Loc}}$, that is, to remove edge-local identifiers (6).

$$\begin{aligned}
&\mathit{ValueEmbed}(\alpha_{\mathsf{Ref}}, (st_{\mathsf{Ref}}, st_{\mathsf{Val}}), \overline{con}) \Leftrightarrow \\
&\forall r_1 \xrightarrow{f_r} r_2 \in st_{\mathsf{Ref}} \cdot \exists s \in \gamma_{\overline{\mathsf{V}}}(\overline{con}(\alpha_{\mathsf{Ref}}(r_1) \xrightarrow{f_r} \alpha_{\mathsf{Ref}}(r_2))) \cdot && (4)\\
&\qquad \forall ((r, f_v) \mapsto v) \in st_{\mathsf{Val}} \cdot \begin{pmatrix} v \in s(\alpha_{\mathsf{Ref}}(r), f_v) \wedge \\ r = r_1 \Rightarrow v \in s(\mathsf{Src}, f_v) \wedge \\ r = r_2 \Rightarrow v \in s(\mathsf{Trg}, f_v) \end{pmatrix} \wedge && (5)\\
&\qquad s \downarrow_{\overline{\mathsf{Loc}}} \in \gamma_{\overline{\mathsf{V}}}\left(\bigsqcap_{r_1' \xrightarrow{f_r'} r_2' \in st_{\mathsf{Ref}}} \left(\overline{con}(\alpha_{\mathsf{Ref}}(r_1') \xrightarrow{f_r'} \alpha_{\mathsf{Ref}}(r_2')) \downarrow_{\overline{\mathsf{Loc}}} \right) \right) && (6)
\end{aligned}$$

Example. Fig. 5 shows the reference and value stores of two concrete heaps. The heap of the left) is in the concretization of the abstract heap in Fig. 2. For the embedding $\alpha_{\mathsf{Ref}} = [\Im \mapsto \Im, \mathsf{null} \mapsto \mathsf{null}, r_1 \mapsto \overline{n}_0, r_2 \mapsto \overline{n}_0]$, *GraphEmbed* holds since $\overline{n}_0$ is a summary node and all three concrete edges have corresponding abstract edges. *ValueEmbed* also holds since the concrete value store satisfies

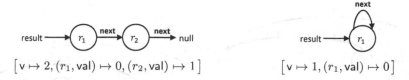

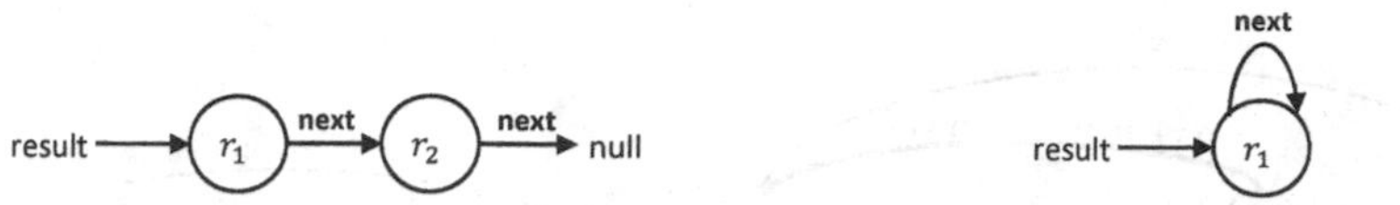

$[\mathsf{v} \mapsto 2, (r_1, \mathsf{val}) \mapsto 0, (r_2, \mathsf{val}) \mapsto 1]$ $[\mathsf{v} \mapsto 1, (r_1, \mathsf{val}) \mapsto 0]$

Fig. 5. Concrete heaps, consisting of a reference store, displayed on top, and a value store, displayed underneath. The heap on the left is in the concretization of the abstract heap in Fig. 2, whereas the heap on the right is not because it violates the condition that list nodes store increasing values.

the three relevant abstract conditions, and these conditions do not contradict each other.

In contrast, the heap on the right is *not* in the concretization of the abstract heap in Fig. 2. The graph embedding forces the embedding to be $\alpha_{\mathsf{Ref}} = [\Im \mapsto \Im, \mathsf{null} \mapsto \mathsf{null}, r_1 \mapsto \overline{n}_0]$. Therefore, both edge-local identifiers $(\mathsf{Src}, \mathsf{val})$ and $(\mathsf{Trg}, \mathsf{val})$ on the abstract edge from $\overline{n}_0$ to $\overline{n}_0$ correspond to (r_1, val), such that there is no value for (r_1, val) that satisfies the constraint $(\mathsf{Trg}, \mathsf{val}) = (\mathsf{Src}, \mathsf{val}) + 1$. In other words, any map s in the concretization of this constraint assigns different values to these edge-local identifiers and, thus, does not satisfy condition (5).

3.3 Join

The *join* operator $\sqcup_{\overline{\Sigma}}$ first computes an abstract reference store for the joined heaps and then the abstract conditions for the edges in this store.

Abstract Reference Store. An abstract heap can be viewed as a directed graph in which vertices are labeled as $\Im$, null, definite node other than $\Im$ and null, or summary node; edges are labeled with reference fields. The vertex labels are used to avoid matching nodes in two heaps that cannot correspond (for instance, a summary node and a definite node). A *labeled heap graph* is a triple $g = (V, E, \eta) \in \mathsf{Graph}$, where $V \subseteq \overline{\mathsf{Ref}}$ is a set of vertices, $E \subseteq V \times \mathsf{Field}_{\mathsf{Ref}} \times V$ is a set of edges labeled with a reference field, and $\eta : V \to \{\Im, \mathsf{Null}, \mathsf{Def}, \mathsf{Sum}\}$ is a labeling function on vertices. We assume a *strict total order* $<_{\mathsf{G}}$ on graphs that ensures in particular that $g_1 <_{\mathsf{G}} g_2$ if g_1 has fewer vertices than g_2 or the same number of vertices but fewer edges.

To improve performance, we define the join of two abstract reference stores such that it minimizes the size of the resulting store. Its structure is the minimum common supergraph of the two joined stores. Let g_1 and g_2 be graphs. Graph g is a *common supergraph* of g_1 and g_2 iff g_1 and g_2 are subgraph isomorphic to g with the isomorphisms $\mathcal{I}_1$ and $\mathcal{I}_2$, respectively. We call g the *minimum common supergraph* (MCS) of g_1 and g_2 if there exists no other common supergraph that is smaller in the ordering $<_{\mathsf{G}}$. The procedure $MCS(g_1, g_2)$ yields the (unique) minimum common supergraph g of g_1 and g_2 as well as the corresponding subgraph isomorphisms $\mathcal{I}_1$ and $\mathcal{I}_2$ between g_1 and g, and g_2 and g, respectively. The problem of computing MCS can be reduced to the well-studied problem

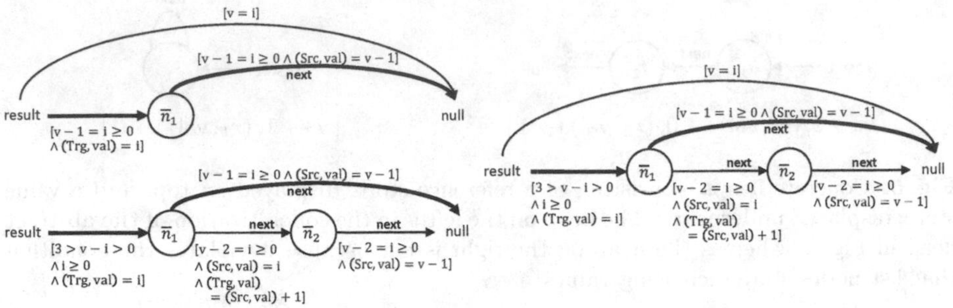

Fig. 6. The abstract heap graphs on the left occur before and after the second iteration of the fixed-point computation of the loop invariant (line 4) in Fig. 1. Joining them results in the heap on the right. Bold arrows indicate edges of the maximum common subgraph.

of finding the maximum common subgraph [4]. See the accompanying technical report [15] for the definitions of graph/subgraph isomorphism and maximum common subgraph. Intuitively, we can compute $(g, \mathcal{I}_1, \mathcal{I}_2) = MCS(g_1, g_2)$ by "gluing" to the maximum common subgraph of g_1 and g_2 those parts of g_1 and g_2 that are not in their maximum common subgraph.

Let Π : $\overline{\mathsf{Store}_{\mathsf{Ref}}} \times \mathsf{IsSummary} \rightarrow \mathsf{Graph}$ be a *bijective* function from abstract stores to heap graphs. The abstract store and the IsSummary function of the join of $(\overline{St}_1, \overline{con}_1, isSum_1)$ and $(\overline{St}_2, \overline{con}_2, isSum_2)$ are $(\overline{St}, isSum) = \Pi^{-1}(MCS(\Pi(\overline{St}_1, isSum_1), \Pi(\overline{St}_2, isSum_2)) \downarrow_1)$, where $\downarrow_1$ denotes projection of a tuple on the first component, that is, the graph returned by *MCS*. Note that $\Pi(\overline{St}, isSum)$ includes both $\Pi(\overline{St}_1, isSum_1)$ and $\Pi(\overline{St}_2, isSum_2)$. Hence, the abstract reference store $(\overline{St}, isSum)$ subsumes the abstract reference stores $(\overline{St}_1, isSum_1)$ and $(\overline{St}_2, isSum_2)$.

Example. Fig. 6 shows on the left the abstract heap graphs g_1 and g_2 before and after the second iteration of the fixed-point computation of the loop invariant (line 4) in Fig. 1, and their join g on the right. Besides the special nodes $\Im$ and null, the maximum common subgraph includes node $\overline{n}_1$ as well as the edges from result to $\overline{n}_1$ and from $\overline{n}_1$ to null. To this common subgraph, we add the remainder of g_1 (the edge from result to null) and the remainder of g_2 ($\overline{n}_2$ with its edges). Note that both g_1 and g_2 are subgraph isomorphic to g, where the isomorphism is the identity function.

Abstract Conditions. Consider an edge in the abstract store resulting from the join of two abstract heaps. We determine its abstract condition as follows. If the edge is in the maximum common subgraph of the joined heap graphs, its abstract condition is the join of the abstract conditions in the two heaps. Otherwise, the condition is the same as in the heap that contributed the edge, after applying the subgraph isomorphism.

As explained above, computing the minimum common supergraph $(g, \mathcal{I}_1, \mathcal{I}_2) = MCS(\Pi(\overline{St}_1, isSum_1), \Pi(\overline{St}_2, isSum_2))$ yields the subgraph isomorphisms $\mathcal{I}_1$ and $\mathcal{I}_2$ from $\Pi(\overline{St}_1, isSum_1)$ to g and from $\Pi(\overline{St}_2, isSum_2)$ to g, respectively.

We define the function $rename_{\mathsf{ISO}} : (\overline{\mathsf{Ref}} \rightarrow \overline{\mathsf{Ref}}) \times \overline{\mathbb{V}} \rightarrow \overline{\mathbb{V}}$ to rename the identifiers in $\overline{\mathsf{Loc}}$ of a given abstract value state according to an isomorphism. Using this renaming, we define the join operator $\sqcup_{\overline{\Sigma}} : \overline{\Sigma} \times \overline{\Sigma} \rightarrow \overline{\Sigma}$ as

$$(\overline{St}_1, \overline{con}_1, isSum_1) \sqcup_{\overline{\Sigma}} (\overline{St}_2, \overline{con}_2, isSum_2) = (\overline{St}, \overline{con}, isSum)$$

where:

$$\begin{aligned}
&(g, \mathcal{I}_1, \mathcal{I}_2) = MCS(\Pi(\overline{St}_1, isSum_1), \Pi(\overline{St}_2, isSum_2)) \wedge \\
&(\overline{St}, isSum) = \Pi^{-1}(g) \wedge \\
&\overline{con} = \left[\overline{e} \mapsto \overline{s} \;\middle|\; \overline{e} \in \overline{St} \wedge \overline{s} = \bigsqcup \left\{ \overline{s}' \;\middle|\; \begin{array}{l} \exists\, i \in \{1,2\} \cdot \exists\, (\overline{n}_1, f_r, \overline{n}_2) \in \overline{St}_i \cdot \\ \overline{e} = (\mathcal{I}_i(\overline{n}_1), f_r, \mathcal{I}_i(\overline{n}_2)) \wedge \\ \overline{s}' = rename_{\mathsf{ISO}}(\mathcal{I}_i, \overline{con}_i(\overline{n}_1, f_r, \overline{n}_2)) \end{array} \right\} \right]
\end{aligned}$$

Computing the maximum common subgraph is NP-complete; however, most code fragments change only small portions of the abstract heap. Our implementation exploits this fact to compute the isomorphisms incrementally, usually in linear time.

Example. Consider the edge from result to $\overline{n}_1$ in the heap on the right of Fig. 6, which is in the maximum common subgraph of the heaps on the left. Hence, its abstract condition is the join of the conditions for those heaps (assuming a relational numerical domain). Since the constraint $\mathsf{v}-1 = \mathsf{i}$ in the top left abstract heap implies the constraint $3 > \mathsf{v} - \mathsf{i} > 0$ in the lower heap, the latter constraint is tracked by the result of the join operation; the other constraints of the joined conditions are identical and, thus, carried over to the result. Conversely, the edges from result to null, from $\overline{n}_1$ to $\overline{n}_2$, and from $\overline{n}_2$ to null are not in the maximum common subgraph; their conditions come from the heap contributing the edges.

3.4 Widening

The above join operator does not guarantee the convergence of the analysis. In fact, the size of the abstract heap may grow at each application of join, and the abstract conditions may not stabilize. Therefore, we define a *widening* operator $\nabla_{\overline{\Sigma}} : \overline{\Sigma} \times \overline{\Sigma} \rightarrow \overline{\Sigma}$ that guarantees that the analysis reaches a fixed point in finite time (that is, terminates). In order to do so, the widening operator must bound the size of the abstract heap, which means that it has to merge nodes into summary nodes. This merging is controlled via a finite set of field access expressions $\mathcal{W}$, which is a parameter of the analysis and denotes references that the analysis should track separately. By default, $\mathcal{W}$ is the set of local reference variables, but it can be extended to any set of field access expressions if desired. For all examples in our evaluation (Sec. 5), the analysis uses the default.

We perform widening in two steps. First, in both input heaps, we merge nodes that (i) are denoted by the same set of field access expressions from $\mathcal{W}$, *and*

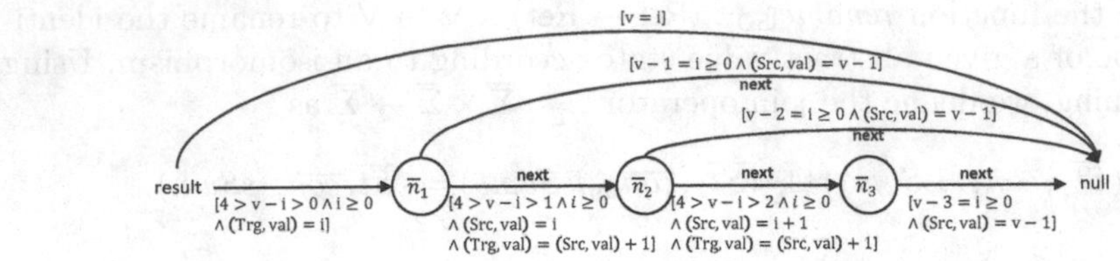

Fig. 7. Heap before the fourth iteration of the fixed-point computation of the loop invariant in Fig. 1.

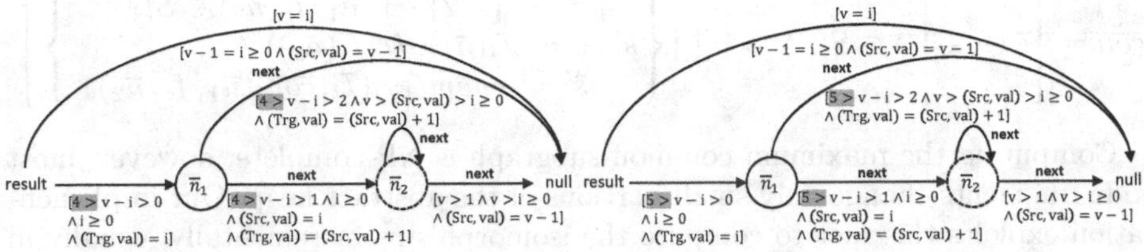

Fig. 8. Heaps with merged nodes before the fourth (left) and fifth (right) iteration of the fixed-point computation. The heaps differ only in the highlighted constraints.

(ii) are reachable (via some access path) from the same set of local variables. Second, if the two heaps are isomorphic, we apply edge-wise widening to the abstract conditions; otherwise, we join them. We refer the reader to our technical report [15] for more details and a complete formalization.

Example. Suppose we widen the abstract heap before the fourth iteration of the fixed-point computation for the loop in Fig. 1 with the heap before the fifth iteration. The abstract heap before the fourth iteration is displayed in Fig. 7; the heap before the fifth iteration looks similar, but has four definite nodes.

In the first step, widening merges nodes using the default $\mathcal{W} = \{\mathsf{result}\}$. In the heap from Fig. 7, we merge $\overline{n}_2$ and $\overline{n}_3$ into a single summary node $\overline{n}_2$ since they are (i) denoted by the same set of field access expressions from $\mathcal{W}$ (the empty set since result denotes neither $\overline{n}_2$ nor $\overline{n}_3$), and (ii) they are reachable from the same set of local variables ($\{\mathsf{result}\}$). However, $\overline{n}_1$ is denoted by a different set of field access expressions ($\{\mathsf{result}\}$), and therefore not merged with $\overline{n}_2$ and $\overline{n}_3$. The edges from $\overline{n}_2$ and $\overline{n}_3$ to null are also merged, and their conditions are joined. The resulting heap is shown on the left of Fig. 8. Merging nodes in the heap before the fifth iteration (not shown) results in the heap on the right of Fig. 8. Note that these heaps are isomorphic, that is, the heap shape has stabilized.

In the second step, since the heaps after merging are isomorphic, we apply edge-wise widening to the abstract conditions. This step removes the upper bound on $\mathsf{v} - \mathsf{i}$, but leaves all other constraints unaffected, that is, the abstract conditions have stabilized. The resulting heap is shown in Fig. 4; it represents the loop invariant of the program from Fig. 1.

4 Abstract Semantics

In this section, we formalize the semantics of reference and value assignments.

4.1 Reference Assignment

An abstract store includes disjunctive information. Therefore, for a reference assignment $\mathsf{p.f_r} = \mathsf{rhs}$, there may be several abstract references for the receiver p and the right-hand side rhs, which may be reached through different paths with different value conditions. The value states on the edges along each path specify the conditions under which p and rhs evaluate to a particular abstract reference. The abstract semantics for reference assignments adds an abstract edge for each possible combination of receiver p and right-hand side rhs, with an abstract condition that reflects when this combination exists.

The rule below formalizes reference assignments of the form $\mathsf{p.f_r} = \mathsf{rhs}$, where $\mathsf{p.f_r} \in \mathsf{rAE}$ and $\mathsf{rhs} \in \mathsf{rexp}$. Since we encode local variables as fields of a special reference $\Im$, the rule also covers assignments to those. It uses an auxiliary function $\overline{eval}_{\mathsf{rexp}}$ (defined in the technical report [15]), which takes a reference expression (or $\Im$) re and an abstract state $\overline{\sigma}$ and yields (a) a set NC of pairs, each consisting of an abstract reference to which re may evaluate in $\overline{\sigma}$ and the condition under which re may evaluate to this reference, and (b) a resulting abstract state, which is used to encode allocation, that is, when re contains new expressions.

$$(NC_{\mathsf{rhs}}, (\overline{St}_{\mathsf{rhs}}, \overline{con}_{\mathsf{rhs}}, isSum_{\mathsf{rhs}})) = \overline{eval}_{\mathsf{rexp}}(\mathsf{rhs}, \overline{\sigma}) \quad (1)$$
$$(NC_{\mathsf{p}}, \_) = \overline{eval}_{\mathsf{rexp}}(\mathsf{p}, (\overline{St}_{\mathsf{rhs}}, \overline{con}_{\mathsf{rhs}}, isSum_{\mathsf{rhs}})) \quad (2)$$
$$strong \iff \exists\, \overline{n} \in \overline{\mathsf{Ref}} \cdot (NC_{\mathsf{p}} = \{(\overline{n}, \_)\} \ \wedge\ \neg isSum_r(\overline{n})) \quad (3)$$
$$strong \Rightarrow (\overline{St} = \{(\overline{n}_1, f, \overline{n}_2) \in \overline{St}_{\mathsf{rhs}} \mid (\overline{n}_1, \_) \notin NC_{\mathsf{p}} \ \vee\ \mathsf{f_r} \neq f\}) \quad (4)$$
$$(\neg strong) \Rightarrow (\overline{St} = \overline{St}_{\mathsf{rhs}}) \quad (5)$$
$$\overline{con}_{asg} = \left[(\overline{n}_{\mathsf{p}}, \mathsf{f_r}, \overline{n}_{\mathsf{rhs}}) \mapsto (\mathsf{Trg}\,To\mathsf{Src}(\overline{s}_{\mathsf{p}}) \sqcap \overline{s}_{\mathsf{rhs}}) \,\middle|\, \begin{array}{l} (\overline{n}_{\mathsf{p}}, \overline{s}_{\mathsf{p}}) \in NC_{\mathsf{p}} \wedge \\ (\overline{n}_{\mathsf{rhs}}, \overline{s}_{\mathsf{rhs}}) \in NC_{\mathsf{rhs}} \end{array} \right] \quad (6)$$
$$\overline{St}' = \overline{St} \cup dom(\overline{con}_{asg}) \quad (7)$$
$$\overline{con}' = \overline{con}_{\mathsf{rhs}} \left[\overline{e} \mapsto \overline{s} \,\middle|\, \begin{array}{l} \overline{e} \in dom(\overline{con}_{asg}) \ \wedge\ (\overline{e} \notin \overline{St} \Rightarrow \overline{s} = \overline{con}_{asg}(\overline{e})) \ \wedge \\ (\overline{e} \in \overline{St} \Rightarrow \overline{s} = \overline{con}_{asg}(\overline{e}) \sqcup \overline{con}_{\mathsf{rhs}}(\overline{e})) \end{array} \right] \quad (8)$$
$$\overline{\langle \mathsf{p.f_r} = \mathsf{rhs}, \overline{\sigma} \rangle \to_{\overline{\Sigma}} (\overline{St}', \overline{con}', isSum_{\mathsf{rhs}})}$$

A reference assignment first evaluates rhs to obtain the possible abstract references for the right-hand side expression together with the corresponding conditions, as well as a successor state (1). The receiver p is evaluated in this successor state. Since it is side-effect free (see Fig. 3), we discard the state resulting from its evaluation (2). The analysis performs a strong update iff there is only one abstract reference $\overline{n}$ for the receiver, which is a definite node (3). In that case, the analysis removes all edges whose source is the receiver node and that are labeled with the assigned field $\mathsf{f_r}$ (4); otherwise, it performs a weak update, that is, retains all existing edges (5). To add the edges for all possible combinations

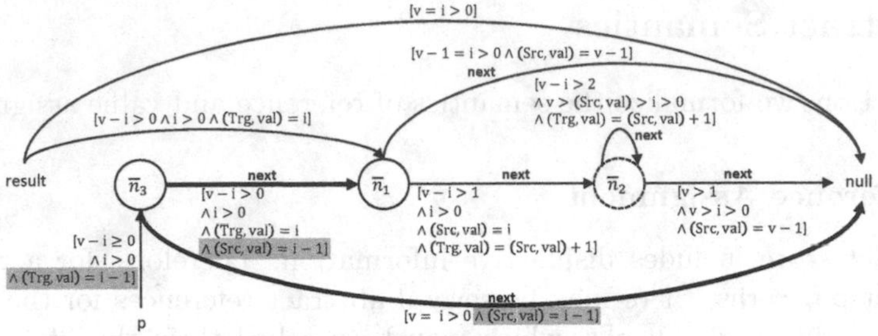

Fig. 9. The abstract heap after line 7 of the program in Fig. 1. The bold edges are added by the reference assignment in line 6; the highlighted constraints come from the value assignment in line 7.

of receivers and right-hand sides, we first create a map $\overline{con}_{asg}$ that maps each of the new edges to the abstract condition that describes when the particular combination exists, that is, the greatest lower bound of the conditions for choosing a particular abstract reference for the receiver and a particular abstract reference for the right-hand side, respectively (6). The only twist in this step is how to handle edge-local identifiers. The receiver is denoted by Trg in conditions on edges pointing to the receiver, but by Src in the new edges. Function Trg*To*Src performs this conversion. Since the map $\overline{con}_{asg}$ contains an entry for each new edge, we obtain the final abstract store by adding the domain of this map to the store constructed in step 4 or 5 (7). Finally, the abstract conditions are updated: For each new edge that is not present in the store before the reference assignment, we add the condition from $\overline{con}_{asg}$. For each edge that is already present (which may happen during a weak update), we join the condition from $\overline{con}_{asg}$ and the existing condition (8).

Example. Fig. 9 *without* the bold edges and the highlighted constraints, shows the abstract heap after line 5 in Fig. 1. It is obtained from the abstract heap in Fig. 4 (the loop invariant) by (i) assuming the loop guard ($\mathsf{i} > 0$) in all abstract conditions and (ii) applying the abstract semantics of the statement Node p = new Node() (line 5), which introduces the definite node $\overline{n}_3$. (Its next field initially points to null, which is not shown in the figure.) We will now illustrate the abstract semantics of the reference assignment p.next = result (line 6).

The right-hand side of the assignment, result, evaluates to null or to $\overline{n}_1$ (point (1) of of the rule above). Since the receiver p evaluates to a single definite node $\overline{n}_3$ (2), we perform a strong update (3). The strong update removes all out-edges of $\overline{n}_3$ labeled with next (4) and introduces new edges for all combinations of abstract references for the receiver and for the right-hand side, that is, edges from $\overline{n}_3$ to null and from $\overline{n}_3$ to $\overline{n}_1$ (7). These edges are shown in bold in Fig. 9. The former edge exists if the right-hand side (result) evaluates to null, that is, if $\mathsf{v} = \mathsf{i} > 0$; the latter exists if result evaluates to $\overline{n}_1$, that is, if $\mathsf{v} - \mathsf{i} > 0 \wedge \mathsf{i} > 0 \wedge (\mathsf{Trg}, \mathsf{val}) = \mathsf{i}$ (6). These constraints are the abstract conditions of the new edges (8), as shown in Fig. 9 (still ignoring the highlighted constraints, which will be discussed later).

4.2 Value Assignment

Like the semantics of reference assignments, the abstract semantics of a value assignment $\mathsf{p.f_v} = \mathsf{rhs}$ (where $\mathsf{p.f_v} \in \mathsf{vAE}$ and $\mathsf{rhs} \in \mathsf{vexp}$) needs to consider each possible combination of evaluations for the receiver p and for the right-hand side rhs. For each combination, it updates all abstract conditions in the abstract store to reflect the assignment and the conditions under which the combination exists. The following rule formalizes this intuition.

$$\frac{\begin{array}{rr} \overline{S} = \overline{eval}_{\mathsf{vexp}}(\mathsf{rhs}, (\overline{St}, \overline{con}, isSum)) & (1) \\ (NC_{\mathsf{p}}, \_) = \overline{eval}_{\mathsf{rexp}}(\mathsf{p}, (\overline{St}, \overline{con}, isSum)) & (2) \\ \overline{con}' = update_{\overline{\mathsf{Cond}}}(\mathsf{rhs}, \mathsf{f_v}, NC_{\mathsf{p}}, \overline{S}, \overline{con}) & (3) \end{array}}{\langle \mathsf{p.f_v} = \mathsf{rhs}, (\overline{St}, \overline{con}, isSum)\rangle \rightarrow_{\overline{\Sigma}} (\overline{St}, \overline{con}', isSum)}$$

Each way of evaluating the right-hand side expression rhs, if it contains a field access, chooses a path through the abstract store. The abstract conditions of the edges along a path describe when this path may be chosen. Function $\overline{eval}_{\mathsf{vexp}}$ (defined in our technical report [15]) yields the set $\overline{S}$ of conditions (value states) that describe each way of evaluating rhs (1). Analogously to step 2 of reference assignment, we evaluate the receiver expression p to obtain the possible receiver references, each with a condition under which p may evaluate to this reference (2). We use the function $update_{\overline{\mathsf{Cond}}}$ (defined in our technical report [15]) to reflect the value assignment in the value states of all edges in the abstract store (3). This function considers all possible combinations of receiver reference (obtained from NC_{p}) and value state for a particular way of evaluating the right-hand side expression (from $\overline{S}$). For each of them, it propagates the value information that has to hold when this combination is chosen to the conditions of each edge in the abstract store and applies the assignment operation of the value domain. The condition of each edge in the abstract store is then defined to be the join of the conditions obtained for all ways of executing the value assignment.

Example. Fig. 9 *without* the highlighted constraints shows the abstract heap after line 6 in Fig. 1. The highlighted constraints are introduced by the abstract semantics of the statement p.val = i - 1 (line 7). There is only one way to evaluate the right-hand side expression. Therefore, $\overline{eval}_{\mathsf{vexp}}$ yields a singleton set (point (1) of the rule above). This set contains the condition $\mathsf{v} - \mathsf{i} \geq 0 \wedge \mathsf{i} > 0$, which holds in each concrete heap (otherwise there would be no value for result). Similarly, the receiver expression p evaluates to a single node, $\overline{n}_3$, under the same condition (2). This condition must be satisfied in order to be able to perform the assignment. Therefore, we conjoin it to each abstract condition in the store (which has no effect in this example), and then assign $\mathsf{i} - 1$ to $(\overline{n}_3, \mathsf{val})$ since p evaluates to $\overline{n}_3$ (3). Moreover, since $\overline{n}_3$ is the target of the edge from p to $\overline{n}_3$, we also add the constraint $(\mathsf{Trg}, \mathsf{val}) = \mathsf{i} - 1$ for the edge-local identifier to the condition on this edge, and analogously for $(\mathsf{Src}, \mathsf{val})$ on both out-edges of $\overline{n}_3$ (3).

Table 1. Analysis times (in seconds) of classes implementing different data structures when instantiating the analysis with the Octagon and Polyhedra value domains. For each class, we inferred an object invariant by computing a fixed point over all its methods.

Data Structure	Operations	Octa.	Poly.	Data Structure	Operations	Octa.	Poly.
SortedSLL	constructor insertKey deleteKey findKey deepCopy	1.24	1.82	BST	constructor insertKey findKey	1.96	2.43
SortedDLL	constructor insertKey deleteKey findKey deepCopy	1.91	2.83	NodeCachingSLL	constructor add remove findKey	0.87	1.04
				PersonAndAccount	withdraw deposit changeInterest	0.38	0.43

5 Experimental Results

We implemented our analysis in the static analyzer Sample and applied it to Scala implementations of typical list and tree operations (some of which we took from the literature [5,7,14]), operations on nested recursive data structures (such as lists of lists), and a simple aggregate structure [12]. We performed the experiments on an Intel Core i7-Q820 CPU (1.73GHz, 8GB) running the 64-bit version of Ubuntu 14.04. We instantiated our analysis with the Octagon [22] and Polyhedra [9] value domains implemented in Apron [17]. We used the default widening parameter, that is, $\mathcal{W}$ is the set of local reference variables. There were no manual annotations for any of the benchmarks.

Inference of Object Invariants. Tab. 1 reports the analysis times (the average of 10 runs) for implementations of five different data structures. We instantiated Logozzo's framework [19] with our analysis to infer object invariants for each data structure by computing a fixed point over all its operations.

SortedSLL implements a sorted singly-linked list (SLL). The inferred object invariant expresses that the values stored in the list nodes are non-decreasing.

SortedDLL implements a sorted doubly-linked list (DLL). Our analysis infers sortedness in both directions, that is, via the next and prev fields. However, the analysis cannot infer the structural invariant of doubly-linked lists $n.\mathsf{next} \neq \mathsf{null} \Rightarrow n = n.\mathsf{next.prev}$ because it has no way of relating the concrete references of the two edges $\overline{n} \xrightarrow{\mathsf{next}} \overline{n}$ and $\overline{n} \xrightarrow{\mathsf{prev}} \overline{n}$ for the summary node $\overline{n}$.

BST implements a binary search tree. The analysis infers both the value and the shape information of a BST data structure. Our implementation stores the infimum and supremum of all keys of a sub-tree in its root. This information allows our analysis to relate the value stored in the root to the values in the left and right sub-trees, and, thus, to infer that the shape is a tree, that is, loop-free and not a general DAG. We omitted method deleteKey because our analysis is not able to infer that replacing the deleted key with the next smallest key preserves sortedness; it does, however, infer that the tree shape is preserved.

Table 2. Analysis times (in seconds) for single operations on different data structures when instantiating the analysis with the Octagon and Polyhedra value domains. The first 4 operations work on singly-linked lists (SLL) and doubly-linked lists (DLL). The fifth operation works on lists of singly-linked lists that store values. The last operation transforms an SLL to a binary search tree.

Operation	Octa.	Poly.
insertionSort	0.43 - SLL 0.72 - DLL	0.48 - SLL 0.85 - DLL
partitionWithKey	0.32 - SLL 0.48 - DLL	0.34 - SLL 0.55 - DLL
createListOfZerosAndSum	0.22 - SLL 0.39 - DLL	0.23 - SLL 0.43 - DLL
increasingList	0.28 - SLL 0.41 - DLL	0.31 - SLL 0.50 - DLL
sortListOfListsOfValues	1.45	1.88
listToBST	1.03	1.21

NodeCachingSLL implements an acyclic SLL that maintains a cache of node objects to reduce object creation and garbage collection. The inferred object invariant expresses that the list and the cache are disjoint and that the size of the cache is between 0 and maximumCacheSize. Moreover, we inferred that the addKey method creates a new object only if the cache is empty. Every node of the list stores the length of the list rooted at the node. This information lets our analysis infer that the list and its cache are acyclic, which is needed to infer disjointness of the list and the cache. The latter step required materialization, that is, splitting a definite node off a summary node, which is supported by our implementation, but not explained in this paper.

Besides the object invariants for these four classes, our analysis infers that the result of method findKey is either null or has the value of the given key. This postcondition is inferred even if the result is represented by a summary node.

PersonAndAccount implements an aggregate data structure similar to the example from a paper on the verification of object invariants [12]. The analysis infers combined shape and value invariants, for instance, that Account and Person objects reference each other, the sum of the account balance and person's salary is positive, and the interest rate of the account is always non-negative.

Inference of Method Postconditions. Tab. 2 reports the analysis times of individual operations on different data structures. The initial abstract states and the abstract heaps that represent the arguments to the operations contain only information that is provided by the static types; no annotations were used. The first four operations manipulate singly and doubly-linked lists. insertionSort takes an unsorted list of values and sorts it. The analysis infers that the result is a sorted list. partitionWithKey takes a list of values and a key, and creates two new lists such that the keys in one are less than or equal to the given key, and the keys in the other are greater. The analysis infers this value property and that the resulting lists are disjoint. createListOfZerosAndSum creates a list of zeros and subsequently traverses the list and sums up the values. The analysis infers that the result is a list of zeros, and the sum of the values is zero. increasingList is the method from Fig. 1, with an analogous implementation for DLLs. The analysis infers the heap in Fig. 2 (and an analogous heap for DLLs).

The last two operations of Tab. 2 demonstrate that the analysis is able to infer non-trivial shape and value properties for programs manipulating nested recursive data structures or a combination of different data structures. sortListOfListsOfValues takes a singly-linked list of SLLs that store values, and sorts each of the lists. The analysis infers that the result is a list of sorted SLLs. listToBST takes an SLL of values and creates a binary search tree out of it, without using the methods of the BST class discussed above. The analysis infers that the result is a binary search tree.

Discussion. The analysis times in Tab. 1 and Tab. 2 demonstrate the efficiency of our analysis. For all our benchmark classes, the fixed point over all their methods was computed within 3 seconds when using the Polyhedra domain. When instantiated with a more efficient but less precise value domain, the efficiency of the analysis increases, as illustrated by the usage of the Octagon domain.

Our experiments demonstrate that our analysis can infer invariants that combine shape and value information in interesting ways, for instance, sortedness of lists and trees, or invariants that relate the states of different objects in an aggregate structure. Our analysis leverages data stored in value fields, such as the infimum and supremum in the BST class discussed above, to obtain more precise shape information. As future work, we plan to rely less on such fields by tracking additional abstract conditions (such as injectivity of references) on edges and by generalizing edge-local identifiers to reference fields.

6 Related Work

Dillig et al. [10,11] present a precise content analysis for arrays and containers, in which heap edges are qualified by logical constraints over indexes into a container. This idea inspired our approach of tracking disjunctive information via the value states associated with edges in the heap. Our analysis uses generic value domains instead of logical constraints and can therefore be instantiated with different levels of precision and efficiency. Moreover, it uses edge-local identifiers instead of indexes, which allows us to express constraints on arbitrary nodes (especially summary nodes) in the heap, not only on indexed structures such as arrays and containers. Whereas Dillig et al. concentrate on clients of arrays and containers, our analysis targets arbitrary heap-manipulating programs including implementations of containers.

Similarly to our work, Bouajjani et al. [2,3] introduce a static analysis that automatically infers combined shape and numerical invariants and is parametric in the underlying value domain. The main difference is that their technique is specific to programs that manipulate singly-linked lists of values. For such data structures Bouajjani et al.'s approach is more powerful since it can relate an arbitrary number of successive positions in a list. In contrast, the aim of our analysis is to be applicable to general heap-manipulating programs.

Sagiv et al. [23] introduce a shape analysis in which invariants are expressed in 3-valued first order logic with transitive closure (FOLTC). These invariants may combine shape and value constraints. The analysis requires user-supplied predicates, whereas our analysis does not need manual annotations; it represents a state by a set of logical structures, whereas our analysis maintains a single abstract heap, reducing the number of nodes and edges, and therefore the complexity of the overall analysis. The merging of nodes in our widening operator can be viewed as a special case of canonical abstractions.

McCloskey et al. [21] propose a framework for combining shape and numerical domains (encoded as predicates in FOLTC) in a generic way. However, users have to supply shared predicates via which the domains communicate and which usually resemble the properties one wants to prove. In contrast, our analysis can be parametcrized by arbitrary value domains without any manual overhead.

Ferrara et al. [13,14] and Fu [16] combine different heap and value analyses. Whereas their work represents a state as a heap abstraction and a single value state, our analysis attaches a value state to each edge in the heap abstraction, allowing for a precise tracking of disjunctive information. Moreover, in the value states of Ferrara et al.'s and Fu's work, different heap identifiers represent disjoint portions of the heap. This is not the case for our edge-local identifiers, which refer to memory locations already represented by abstract identifiers and which enable a precise treatment of summary nodes.

Chang et al. [7] introduce a shape analysis based on user-supplied invariants that describe data structures such as lists and trees. These invariants are used to abstract over a potentially unbounded number of concrete references. Chang and Rival [5,6] extend this work and present a framework for combining shape and numeric abstractions into a single domain. Their approach enables the precise and modular analysis of heap and numeric invariants, but relies on user-supplied properties, whereas our analysis does not require manual annotations.

Abdulla et al. [1] introduce a fully automatic analysis of dynamically-allocated heap data structures. They abstract heaps as forest automata, extended by constraints on the values stored in heap nodes. While the analysis precisely tracks shape information, the value constraints can represent only a fixed set of ordering relations. For instance, they cannot express invariant I4 of our running example (see introduction). Moreover, our analysis can be parametrized with different value domains, allowing for different trade-offs between precision and efficiency.

Marron et al. [20] introduce heap abstractions that are similar to the graphs representing abstract heaps in our work. In fact, the formalization of the concretization function in Sec. 3.2 is inspired by their work. However, there are important technical differences. In particular, Marron et al.'s analysis maintains a normal form, which makes their lattice finite, but loses information when merging two heap graphs. In contrast, we deal with an infinite lattice, but preserve some of this information. Moreover, Marron et al.'s heap graphs track specific aliasing predicates (such as injectivity of fields or tree shapes), but no value information. Finally, the purpose of their work is to provide a high-level abstraction of *concrete* runtime heaps, whereas we propose an abstract domain and an abstract semantics for a static code analysis.

7 Conclusion

In this paper, we have presented a static analysis that infers complex invariants combining shape and value information. The analysis is parametric in the underlying value domain, allowing for different trade-offs between precision and efficiency. A key innovation of our analysis is the introduction of edge-local identifiers to track value information about the source and target of a pointer, which allows it to infer inductive invariants such as sortedness of a linked list. The analysis has been implemented in the static analyzer Sample. Our experiments demonstrate its effectiveness.

As future work, we plan to generalize the abstract conditions associated with abstract edges to track richer information. Supporting reference equalities and inequalities would allow our analysis to infer more structural invariants such as the invariant of a doubly-linked list. Supporting regular expressions over field names as additional abstract identifiers would allow the analysis to infer global properties.

Acknowledgments. We are grateful to Uri Juhasz and Alexander Summers for numerous discussions, to John Boyland for helpful comments on a draft of this paper, and to Severin Heiniger for his contributions to the implementation. We would like to thank the anonymous reviewers for the useful feedback.

References

1. Abdulla, P.A., Holík, L., Jonsson, B., Lengál, O., Trinh, C.Q., Vojnar, T.: Verification of heap manipulating programs with ordered data by extended forest automata. In: Van Hung, D., Ogawa, M. (eds.) ATVA 2013. LNCS, vol. 8172, pp. 224–239. Springer, Heidelberg (2013)
2. Bouajjani, A., Drăgoi, C., Enea, C., Sighireanu, M.: On inter-procedural analysis of programs with lists and data. In: PLDI. ACM (2011)
3. Bouajjani, A., Drăgoi, C., Enea, C., Sighireanu, M.: Abstract domains for automated reasoning about list-manipulating programs with infinite data. In: Kuncak, V., Rybalchenko, A. (eds.) VMCAI 2012. LNCS, vol. 7148, pp. 1–22. Springer, Heidelberg (2012)
4. Bunke, H., Jiang, X., Kandel, A.: On the minimum common supergraph of two graphs. Computing 65(1), 13–25 (2000)
5. Chang, B.-Y.E., Rival, X.: Relational inductive shape analysis. In: POPL. ACM (2008)
6. Chang, B.-Y.E., Rival, X.: Modular construction of shape-numeric analyzers. In: David A. Schmidt's 60th Birthday Festschrift. EPTCS (2013)
7. Chang, B.-Y.E., Rival, X., Necula, G.C.: Shape analysis with structural invariant checkers. In: Riis Nielson, H., Filé, G. (eds.) SAS 2007. LNCS, vol. 4634, pp. 384–401. Springer, Heidelberg (2007)

8. Cousot, P., Cousot, R.: Abstract interpretation: a unified lattice model for static analysis of programs by construction or approximation of fixpoints. In: POPL. ACM (1977)
9. Cousot, P., Halbwachs, N.: Automatic discovery of linear restraints among variables of a program. In: POPL. ACM (1978)
10. Dillig, I., Dillig, T., Aiken, A.: Fluid updates: Beyond strong vs. Weak updates. In: Gordon, A.D. (ed.) ESOP 2010. LNCS, vol. 6012, pp. 246–266. Springer, Heidelberg (2010)
11. Dillig, I., Dillig, T., Aiken, A.: Precise reasoning for programs using containers. In: POPL. ACM (2011)
12. Drossopoulou, S., Francalanza, A., Müller, P., Summers, A.J.: A unified framework for verification techniques for object invariants. In: Vitek, J. (ed.) ECOOP 2008. LNCS, vol. 5142, pp. 412–437. Springer, Heidelberg (2008)
13. Ferrara, P.: Generic combination of heap and value analyses in abstract interpretation. In: McMillan, K.L., Rival, X. (eds.) VMCAI 2014. LNCS, vol. 8318, pp. 302–321. Springer, Heidelberg (2014)
14. Ferrara, P., Fuchs, R., Juhasz, U.: TVAL+: TVLA and value analyses together. In: Eleftherakis, G., Hinchey, M., Holcombe, M. (eds.) SEFM 2012. LNCS, vol. 7504, pp. 63–77. Springer, Heidelberg (2012)
15. Ferrara, P., Müller, P., Novacek, M.: Automatic inference of heap properties exploiting value domains. Technical Report 794, ETH Zurich (2013)
16. Fu, Z.: Modularly combining numeric abstract domains with points-to analysis, and a scalable static numeric analyzer for Java. In: McMillan, K.L., Rival, X. (eds.) VMCAI 2014. LNCS, vol. 8318, pp. 282–301. Springer, Heidelberg (2014)
17. Jeannet, B., Miné, A.: APRON: A library of numerical abstract domains for static analysis. In: Bouajjani, A., Maler, O. (eds.) CAV 2009. LNCS, vol. 5643, pp. 661–667. Springer, Heidelberg (2009)
18. Lev-Ami, T., Sagiv, M.: TVLA: A system for implementing static analyses. In: Palsberg, J. (ed.) SAS 2000. LNCS, vol. 1824, pp. 280–302. Springer, Heidelberg (2000)
19. Logozzo, F.: Automatic inference of class invariants. In: Steffen, B., Levi, G. (eds.) VMCAI 2004. LNCS, vol. 2937, pp. 211–222. Springer, Heidelberg (2004)
20. Marron, M., Sánchez, C., Su, Z., Fähndrich, M.: Abstracting runtime heaps for program understanding. IEEE Trans. Software Eng. 39(6), 774–786 (2013)
21. McCloskey, B., Reps, T., Sagiv, M.: Statically inferring complex heap, array, and numeric invariants. In: Cousot, R., Martel, M. (eds.) SAS 2010. LNCS, vol. 6337, pp. 71–99. Springer, Heidelberg (2010)
22. Miné, A.: The octagon abstract domain. Higher Order Symbol. Comput. (2006)
23. Sagiv, M., Reps, T., Wilhelm, R.: Parametric shape analysis via 3–valued logic. In: POPL. ACM (1999)

Dependent Array Type Inference from Tests

He Zhu[1], Aditya V. Nori[2], and Suresh Jagannathan[1]

[1] Purdue University
[2] Microsoft Research

{zhu,suresh}@cs.purdue.edu, adityan@microsoft.com

Abstract. We present a type-based program analysis capable of inferring expressive invariants over array programs. Our system combines dependent types with two additional key elements. First, we associate dependent types with effects and precisely track effectful array updates, yielding a sound flow-sensitive dependent type system that can capture invariants associated with side-effecting array programs. Second, without imposing an annotation burden for quantified invariants on array indices, we automatically infer useful array invariants by initially guessing very coarse invariant templates, using test suites to exercise the functionality of the program to faithfully instantiate these templates with more precise (likely) invariants. These inferred invariants are subsequently encoded as dependent types for validation. Experimental results demonstrate the utility of our approach, with respect to both expressivity of the invariants inferred, and the time necessary to converge to a result.

1 Introduction

A program invariant describes valid behaviors a program is expected to produce, and can often be derived by a fixpoint construction over an over-approximation of program states [4]. However, applying such a strategy to discover useful properties of values stored in unbounded collections of heap cells is nontrivial.

Dependent type systems [22,17] have been proven to be successful in automated verification of complex invariants for data structures, even when there are an unbounded number of heap locations under consideration [23]. In these systems, decidability is achieved, however, at the loss of flow-sensitivity, i.e., a strong update to a concrete location (e.g. a single array cell) must be subsumed by the whole data structure (e.g. the whole array). As a result, it is not obvious how existing dependent type systems can be extended to verify useful functional properties (e.g. *a sorting procedure will sort only a part of the elements in an input array*) that are beyond the scope of global invariants (e.g. a general memory safety properties).

In this paper, we address these issues by introducing a new dependent type system for array programs that can discharge complex flow-sensitive array invariants naturally characterized in terms of quantifiers on array indices. The dependent type system is effectful because it can tolerate side-effecting array updates. Built on top of a standard type system, our system refines basic type

D. D'Souza et al. (Eds.): VMCAI 2015, LNCS 8931, pp. 412–430, 2015.

with a type refinement predicate that captures precise properties of the values defined by the type. Importantly, to verify flow-sensitive invariants, type refinements may be quantified. This is crucial, as strong updates in a procedure may only update a subset of the array.

Rather than requiring users to annotate types with refinements, our approach attempts to learn quantified array invariants. Although significant advances have been made in recent years to allow useful array invariants to be inferred automatically, prior approaches either (a) require a predefined fixed or parameterized partition of array indices [10,14], (b) entail sophisticated reasoning over quantified abstract domains [12], or (c) rely on powerful theorem provers to provide predicates [1,2,15,18,20,24] (as *interpolants*) that may hold on the program in general. We consider the problem from a different perspective, based on the expectation that useful array invariants should be observable from test runs. By summarizing or generalizing the properties that hold in all such runs, we can construct a set of candidates or likely invariants. We then lift these presumed invariants to our dependent type system for validation.

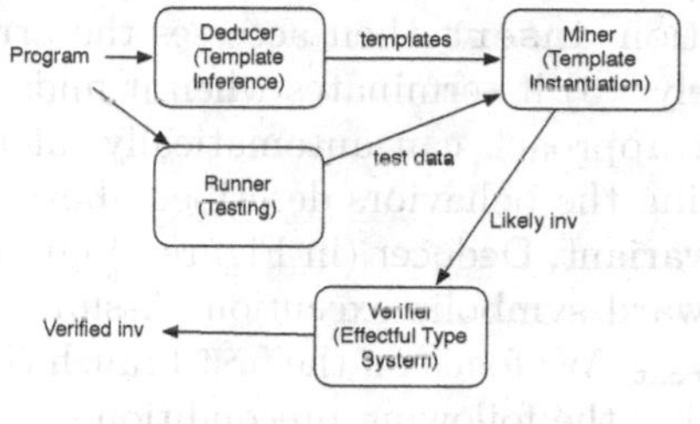

Fig. 1. Framework

The framework of our approach is outlined in Figure 1 : (I) a Deducer initially guesses coarse templates for the invariants; (II) a Runner then runs the subject program through simple random test suites; (III) a Miner generates a constraint system by substituting the variables in the template with concrete values from test runs; (IV) a Verifier validates the likely dependent types derived from the solution of the constraint system.

Our technique is *compositional*—invariants are inferred for each procedure without the need for additional context information about callers and callees. It is *lightweight* because the constraint system from which program invariants are inferred is obtained from concrete program states and not limited by a specific abstract domain construction; experimental results also indicate that the approach allows fast convergence from a *likely* to a *provable* invariant. Our paper thus makes the following contributions:

1. We propose a novel data driven algorithm to infer array invariants that leverages observations from test cases to guide inference.
   - Avoiding the high cost of inferring exact array invariants, our approach initially guesses coarse invariant *templates*, at the expense of precision.
   - We train the template with concrete program states collected from test runs to instantiate it to likely invariants, recovering precision.
2. We integrate our technique within a new effectful dependent type system that can be used to automatically validate the correctness of the likely invariants.

2 Overview

We use the inner loop of the classic *insertion-sort* program shown in Figure 2 to illustrate and motivate our approach. Figure 2 visualizes the execution of

```
let rec insert i j a =
  if (i >= 0 and a[i] > a[j])
  then
L1: let _ = a[i+1] := a[i] in
      insert (i-1) j a
  else i+1

(* assume j > 0 *)
let _ = insert (j-1) j a
```

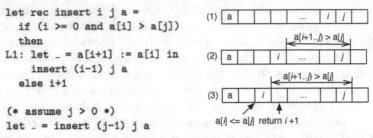

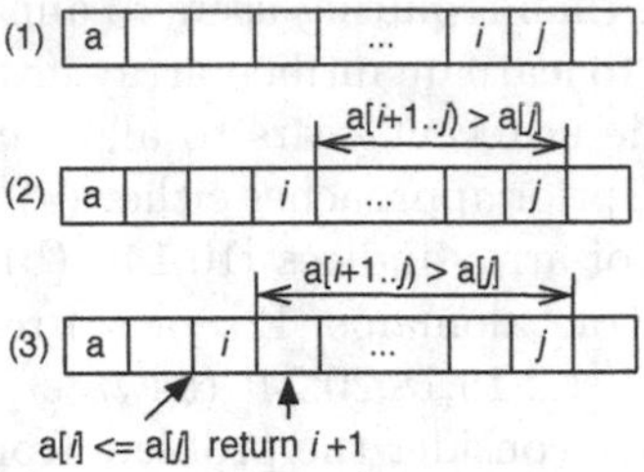

Fig. 2. Inner array insertion-sort program

the recursive function `insert`: (1) initially parameter `i` is set to the index of the left adjacent element of a[j]; (2) function `insert` then accesses the array elements with indices less than `j` iteratively; (3) it terminates when it finds an element that is no greater than a[j]. Our approach can automatically infer a useful dependent type for `insert`, capturing the behaviors described above.

Instead of directly inferring an exact invariant, Deducer (in Figure 1) guesses the invariant's template based on a backward symbolic execution. Assume we infer that the postcondition of `insert` is $\varphi_{\mathtt{post}}$. We focus on the first branch (L1) and unwind the recursion only once, deriving the following precondition,

$$\varphi_{\mathtt{pre}} \equiv \exists \mathtt{a}'. [\mathtt{a}'/\mathtt{a}]\varphi_{\mathtt{post}} \wedge ((\mathtt{i} >= 0 \wedge \mathtt{a}[\mathtt{i}] > \mathtt{a}[\mathtt{j}] \wedge$$
$$\forall \mathtt{a_0}.((\mathtt{a_0} = \mathtt{i}+1 \Rightarrow \mathtt{a}'[\mathtt{i}+1] = \mathtt{a}[\mathtt{i}]) \wedge (\mathtt{a_0} \neq \mathtt{i}+1 \Rightarrow \mathtt{a}'[\mathtt{a_0}] = \mathtt{a}[\mathtt{a_0}])) \wedge ...) \vee ...)$$

where $\mathtt{a_0}$ is a special universal variable and we use $\mathtt{a}'$ to refer to a in the state after the update. Note that the precondition provides information about how array elements are manipulated by a procedure. In particular, $\varphi_{\mathtt{pre}}$ reflects the fact that the $(\mathtt{i})^{\mathtt{th}}$ element of a is moved to its right position if it is greater than the $(\mathtt{j})^{\mathtt{th}}$ element in `insert`. It is unclear, however, how to generalize this condition, which defines only an under-approximation of the desired invariant.

Nonetheless, it is possible to guess that a general invariant may be in the shape of the predicate $\mathtt{a}[\mathtt{i}] > \mathtt{a}[\mathtt{j}]$ from $\varphi_{\mathtt{pre}}$. Based on the assumption that array invariants are typically universally quantified on array indices, we infer the following form for a valid invariant:

$$\forall \mathtt{a_0}.\ 0 \leq \mathtt{a_0} < \chi_1(\bar{x}) \Rightarrow \mathtt{a}[\mathtt{a_0}; \chi_2(\bar{x})] > \mathtt{a}[\chi_3(\bar{x})]\}$$

where $\bar{x} = \{\mathtt{i}, \mathtt{j}\}$ is used to denote all the scalar parameters of `insert` and $\chi(\bar{x}) = \bar{c} * \bar{x}$ represents a parameterized linear expression over $\bar{x}$ ($\bar{c}$ are unknown coefficients). This predicate abstracts a relation to describe how `insert` (iterating over `i`) might maintain an invariant over array a. In this formula, $\mathtt{a}[\mathtt{a_0}; \chi_2(\bar{x})]$ is universally quantified on the special variable $\mathtt{a_0}$ which is bounded by $\chi_1(\bar{x})$.

Obviously, concrete program states collected from test runs must satisfy the guessed invariant template in terms of insert's preconditions (and postconditions). To generate such states, Runner calls the array *insertion-sort* program with a randomly generated array. We dump the input/output values of insert as its concrete pre- and post-states. For each pre-state, we substitutes the variables in the template with their values in this concrete state, deriving some constraints. Thus we obtain a linear constraint system over the unknown coefficients. Using an SMT solver, Miner is able to instantiate the template to the following likely invariant (precondition):

$$\forall a_0.\ 0 \leq a_0 < j - i - 1 \Rightarrow a[a_0 + i + 1] > a[j]$$

Note that this likely invariant is obtained by exploiting the local states of insert solely. Not all instantiations are real invariants; spurious instantiations coincide with properties exposed by particular test cases but do not hold in general. Verifier validates whether a likely invariant generalizes by encoding the invariant into a dependent type system (covered in Section 4). Dependent type constraints are solved via an abstract interpretation to yield valid types (whose type refinements are a conjunction of the predicates from the likely invariants) for the program. We delay details of how the above invariant can be validated to Example 2.

Applying all these steps (with a similar inference step for deriving the postcondition), we are able to associate the following non-trivial type to insert:

$$\begin{aligned}&\mathtt{i} : \mathtt{int} \rightarrow \mathtt{j} : \mathtt{int} \rightarrow \mathtt{a} : \{\mathsf{array} \mid \forall \nu_0.\ 0 \leq \nu_0 < \mathtt{j} - \mathtt{i} - 1 \Rightarrow \nu[\nu_0 + \mathtt{i} + 1] > \nu[\mathtt{j}]\}\\ &\rightarrow \mathtt{ret} : \mathsf{int}/[\mathtt{a} : \{\mathsf{array} \mid \forall \nu_0.\ 0 \leq \nu_0 < \mathtt{j} - \mathtt{ret} \Rightarrow \nu[\nu_0 + \mathtt{ret}] > \nu[\mathtt{j}]\}]\end{aligned}$$

where the special variable ν is used to denote the value of term a in its corresponding type refinement predicate (we ignore the dependent type for i and j for simplicity). If ν refers to an array, then ν_0 denotes its first subscript. This type specifies that, in insert, the array elements in $a[i + 1, \cdots, j - 1]$ are greater than $a[j]$; and produces as a side-effect that, the elements in $a[ret, \cdots, j - 1]$ are greater than $a[j]$ where ret denotes the return value (in Section 7, we discuss how the predicates over a and a′ in $\varphi_{\mathtt{pre}}$ are also exploited to deduce a universally existentially quantified ($\forall\exists$) invariant capable of proving preservation property).

3 Language

In the rest of the paper, we focus on single-dimensional arrays for simplicity; our approach can be naturally extended to handle multi-dimensional cases.

We formalize our ideas in the context of a call-by-value variant of the λ-calculus with support for dependent types. The syntax of the language is shown in Figure 3. Typically a is only bound to arrays and x and y are usually bound to both *scalar* variables, drawn from some non-array base type, and arrays. Predicates (p) are Boolean expressions built from a predefined set ($\mathcal{Q}$) of first-order relational operators (functions); the arguments to these operators are restricted to simple expressions - variables, constants, or array expressions and arithmetic

$$x, y \in \mathsf{Var} \quad a \in \mathsf{Arr} \quad c \in \mathsf{Constant} ::= 0, \ldots, \mathsf{true}, \mathsf{false} \quad B \in \mathsf{Base} ::= \mathsf{int} \mid \mathsf{bool} \mid \mathsf{array}$$
$$\tau \in \mathsf{Monotype} ::= B \mid \tau \to \tau \quad P \in \mathsf{DepType} ::= \{\nu : B \mid r\}/T \mid \{x : P \to P\}$$
$$r \in \mathsf{Refinement} ::= \kappa \mid p \quad T \in \mathsf{EffType} ::= (x : \{\nu : B \mid r\}/[\,]); T \mid [\,]$$
$$p \in \mathsf{Predicate} ::= p \text{ and } p \mid p \text{ or } p \mid \mathcal{Q}(s, \ldots, s) \quad \mathcal{Q} \in \{>=, >, \cdots\}$$
$$s \in \mathsf{SimpleExp} ::= \nu_0 \mid \nu \mid x \mid a \mid c \mid s \text{ op } s \mid a[s] \quad \mathsf{op} \in \{+, -, \cdots\}$$
$$e ::= s \mid a[s] := s \mid \lambda x.e \mid \text{if } p \text{ then } e \text{ else } e \mid \text{let } x = e \text{ in } e \mid e\ x$$

Fig. 3. Syntax

compositions of such expressions; a type refinement (r) is either a type refinement variable (κ) that represents an unknown type refinement or a concrete predicate (p). Instantiation of the type refinement variables to concrete predicates takes place through the type refinement algorithm described in Section 5.

Our language supports a small set of base types (B), monotypes (τ) and dependent types (P) that include dependent base types and dependent function types. A *dependent base type* is written $\{\nu : B| r\}/ T$. B is a base type, such as int or bool, and r is called a *type refinement* that constrains the value defined by the type. Effect type T is a sequence of dependent types binding to side-effecting arrays, conservatively approximating the side-effects an expression may produce. These bindings have no further effect, i.e., effect types are not nested. In the following, we will often omit the declaration of ν or T if it is empty for simplicity. For example, the expression (let _ $= a[x] := 1$ in 0) where x is an integer, has type $\{\{\mathsf{int} \mid \nu = 0\}/T_{ex}\}$ where

$$T_{ex} \equiv \{a : \{\mathsf{array}|\forall \nu_0.\ (\nu_0 = x \Rightarrow \nu\ [\nu_0] = 1) \wedge (\nu_0 \neq x \Rightarrow \nu\ [\nu_0] = a\ [\nu_0])\}\}$$

This type reflects that the expression yields 0, but additionally has a side-effect that updates the xth element of array a to 1. When this effect is merged with the type environment of this expression (detailed in Section 4), the array a inside the type refinement will be modified to refer to the old array before the update.

A *dependent function type* is written $\{x : P_x \to P\}$[1] where the argument x is constrained by the dependent type P_x, and the result type is specified by P. For instance, $\{a : \mathsf{array} \to x : \{\nu : \mathsf{int} \mid \nu > 0\} \to \{\nu\ : \mathsf{int} \mid \nu > x\}/T_{ex}\}$ specifies the function that given a positive integer returns an integer greater than x, that also raises a side-effect captured by T_{ex}.

Unknown type refinements for array type parameters and return value ($\bar{a}$) of a function are instantiations from a *general template* that is created for each array a_i ($a_i \in \bar{a}$ and the syntactic sugar $\bar{a}[a_{i0}; \bar{x}]$ denotes an arbitrary array expression whose array indices are arithmetic compostions from variables in $[|a_{i0}; \bar{x}|]$):

$$I \equiv \forall a_{i0}.0 \leq a_{i0} < \varphi_i(\bar{x}) \Rightarrow (\bigwedge_{a_j \in \{\bar{a}/a_i\}} \varphi_j(\bar{x}) \leq \psi_j(\bar{x}) < \varphi'_j(\bar{x})) \Rightarrow \mathcal{Q}(\bar{a}[a_{i0}; \bar{x}], \bar{x})$$

[1] Although side-effects can be associated to closures (function typed), we disallow it in the paper to keep simplicity but implement it in our tool (Section 8).

where a_{i0} represents the single subscript of array a_i, $\varphi_i(\bar{x})$ is an arithmetic expression over non-array base type parameters, serving as an upper bound for a_{i0}, and $\mathcal{Q}(\bar{a}[a_{i0}; \bar{x}], \bar{x})$ is a predicate (drawn from the language of linear arithmetic and uninterpreted functions) over array expressions $\bar{a}[a_{i0}; \bar{x}]$ and all scalars parameters $\bar{x}$ of the function. The second implication condition naturally bounds the array index for arrays other than a_i. To translate an instantiation of the template into a type refinement, we simply perform the substitution $[\nu/a_i][\nu_0/a_{i0}]I$, which can be embedded into the dependent type of a_i (e.g., see the type of `insert` in Section 2).

4 Dependent Type System for Arrays

Figure 4 defines dependent type inference rules; these rules are adapted from [22], generalized to deal with array update effects. Syntactically, $\Gamma \vdash e : P$ states that expression e has dependent type P under type environment Γ, which is a sequence of type bindings $x : P$ and guard predicates p. The former are standard; the latter capture path-sensitivity of program branches, following [22].

As in [22], the built-in units of function such as $+, -$ are encoded as constants which have predefined dependent types that capture their semantics. In this paper we are particularly interested in array updates as side-effects and we encode array update function $a[x] := y$ as *primitive constant*. Its type is given as:

$$\begin{array}{l}\Gamma \vdash (a[x] := y) : \{a : \mathsf{array} \rightarrow x : \mathsf{int} \rightarrow y : \mathsf{int} \rightarrow \\ \mathsf{unit}/[a : \{\mathsf{array} | \forall \nu_0.\ (\nu_0 = x \Rightarrow \nu[\nu_0] = y) \wedge (\nu_0 \neq x \Rightarrow \nu[\nu_0] = a[\nu_0])\}]\}\end{array}$$

Before describing the key components of the type system, we introduce some auxiliary functions. We define $\mathtt{mod}(\Gamma, e)$ as the function that returns all the arrays bound in Γ that have array updates inside e. Firstly, $\mathtt{mod}(\Gamma, a[x] := y) = a$. The other cases are simply recursively defined. Additionally, function $\mathtt{Eff}(P)$ returns the effect of dependent type P (a function definition given as a lambda expression does not produce side-effects). Function $\mathtt{Ty}(P)$ erases the effects for base dependent types. We use *dom*(T) to return the keys of the bindings of effect T.

$$\begin{array}{ll}\mathtt{Eff}(\{\nu : B \mid p\} \;/\; T) = T & \mathtt{Eff}(\{x : P \rightarrow P\}) = [\,] \\ \mathtt{Ty}(\{\nu : B \mid p\} \;/\; T) = \{\nu : B \mid p\} \;/\; [\,] & \mathtt{Ty}(\{x : P \rightarrow P\}) = \{x : P \rightarrow P\}\end{array}$$

Well-Formedness Judgement. These rules are of the form $\Gamma @ \mathtt{modset} \vdash P$, and check if dependent type P is well defined under type environment Γ, which is extended with a set of arrays (`modset`) that may be updated by this type's underlying expression. Rule WF_Base firstly checks that the type refinement p of a dependent base type does not refer to program variables that escape from its type environment Γ, i.e, p is a well defined predicate. Secondly we enforce that all the side-effects raised by an expression must be captured by its type by checking that the keys of the binding in its effect T must contain `modset` and that T

$$\frac{\Gamma;\nu : B \vdash p : \mathsf{bool} \quad \mathtt{modset} \subseteq dom(T) \quad \Gamma \vdash T}{\Gamma @ \mathtt{modset} \vdash \{\nu : B|p\}/T} \ \mathsf{WF\_Base}$$

$$\frac{\Gamma; x : P_x @ \mathtt{modset} \vdash P}{\Gamma @ \mathtt{modset} \vdash x : P_x \to P} \ \mathsf{WF\_Fun} \qquad \frac{\forall\{a : P\} \in T.\ \Gamma @[\,] \vdash P}{\Gamma \vdash T} \ \mathsf{WF\_Eff}$$

$$\frac{\Gamma; x : P_x \vdash e : P_e \quad \Gamma; x : P_x \vdash P_e <: P}{\Gamma \vdash \lambda x.e : \{x : P_x \to P\}} \ \mathsf{Fun}$$

$$\frac{\Gamma \vdash e : \{x : P_x \to P\} \quad \Gamma \vdash y : P'_x \quad \Gamma \vdash P'_x <: P_x}{\Gamma \vdash e\ y : [y/x]P} \ \mathsf{App}$$

$$\frac{\begin{array}{c}\Gamma \vdash e_1 : P' \quad \Gamma @\{\mathtt{mod}\,(\Gamma, e_1) \cup \mathtt{mod}\,(\Gamma, e_2)\} \vdash P \\ \theta = \{[\widetilde{y}/y] \mid y \in dom(\mathtt{Eff}\,(P'))\} \\ \theta(\Gamma; x : \mathtt{Ty}\,(P'); \mathtt{Eff}\,(P'); \forall y \in dom(\mathtt{Eff}\,(P')).\widetilde{y} : \Gamma(y)) \vdash e_2 : P\end{array}}{\Gamma \vdash \mathtt{let}\ x = e_1\ \mathtt{in}\ e_2 : P} \ \mathsf{Let}$$

$$\frac{\Gamma \vdash p : \mathsf{bool} \quad \Gamma; p \vdash e_2 : P \quad \Gamma; \neg p \vdash e_3 : P \quad \Gamma @\{\mathtt{mod}\,(\Gamma, e_1) \cup \mathtt{mod}\,(\Gamma, e_2)\} \vdash P}{\Gamma \vdash \mathsf{if}\ p\ \mathtt{then}\ e_1\ \mathtt{else}\ e_2 : P} \ \mathsf{If}$$

$$\frac{\langle \Gamma \rangle \wedge \langle \nu : r_1 \rangle \Rightarrow \langle \nu : r_2 \rangle \quad \Gamma \vdash T_1 <: T_2}{\Gamma \vdash \{\nu : B|r_1\}/T_1 <: \{\nu : B|r_2\}/T_2} \ \mathsf{Sub\_Base}$$

$$\frac{\Gamma \vdash P'_x <: P_x \quad \Gamma; x : P'_x \vdash P <: P'}{\Gamma \vdash \{x : P_x \to P\} <: \{x : P'_x \to P'\}} \ \mathsf{Sub\_Fun}$$

$$\frac{dom(T_1) \subseteq dom(T_2) \quad \forall\{a : P\} \in T_2.\ \Gamma; T_1 \vdash a : P}{\Gamma \vdash T_1 <: T_2} \ \mathsf{Sub\_Eff}$$

Fig. 4. Typing rules

is well-formed. Rule WF_Fun and WF_Eff define well-formedness conditions for functions and effects, resp.

Type Judgements. The typing rules state how an expression e can be dependently typed. Rules Fun and App are standard. As in [22], our approach requires the need for *pending substitutions* because the dependent type of a function application is derived by substituting all the formal argument x in the output by the actual y. It is formally defined as $\theta ::= [y/x]; \theta \mid [\,]$. Pending substitution for base dependent type is defined as $\theta(\{\nu : B \mid p\} \ / \ T) = \{\nu : B \mid \theta p\} \ / \ \theta T$. where $\theta T = \{\theta x : \theta P \mid x : P \in T\}$. Note that we push pending substitution to effects. Pending substitution for functional types are trivially recursively defined.

In rule Let, the well-formedness condition checks that the effect of the entire Let-expression subsumes all the effects produced by e_1 and e_2. When typing expression e_2, we require that the side-effects of e_1 must refresh e_2's typing environment for soundness (Ty(P') resets P''s effects to empty). Note that $\Gamma; T$ means Γ is merged with the effects T: for each binding $x : P \in T$, we substitute the original binding to x in Γ with P. However, the original binding is not simply discarded. If y is an array which could be updated by e_1 (witnessed by its type's effect), its original dependent type recorded in Γ is re-associated to a $\widetilde{y}$. Intuitively, we use $\widetilde{\mathrm{y}}$ to refer to y in the state before the update. This relieves typing burden because now the array y after the update can refer to its original version $\widetilde{y}$ for the elements that are not changed. To retain soundness, the appearance of y in the type refinement predicates of the dependent types bound to Γ must be substituted with $\widetilde{y}$. This is achieved by performing environment substitution θ as defined in the rule. Formally, $\theta\Gamma = \{x : \theta P | x : P \in \Gamma\}$. Rule `If` is standard except we require that all the effects made by its subexpressions must be subsumed by the effect of the entire `If`-expression.

Subtype Judgement. This class of rules checks at each call site that the actual arguments satisfy the precondition of the called function and verify, at each definition site, that the return value establishes the desired postcondition. Rule `Sub_Base` checks whether a dependent type subtypes another dependent type for based typed expression. The premise check requires the conjunction of environment formula $\langle\Gamma\rangle$ and $\langle\nu : r_1\rangle$ implies $\langle\nu : r_2\rangle$. Our encoding of $\langle\Gamma\rangle$ (or $\langle\nu : r_1\rangle$ and $\langle\nu : r_2\rangle$) as a first order logic formula is inspired by [22]:

$$\bigwedge\{p \mid p \in \Gamma\} \wedge \bigwedge\{[x/\nu][x_0/\nu_0]r \mid x : \{\nu : B \mid r\}/T \in \Gamma\} \qquad (\varrho)$$

For example, consider typing an expression e when it is enclosed in a statement `let _` $= A[x] := y$ `in` e. According to rule App and Let, the type environment of e is $[\widetilde{A}/A](A : \{\forall\nu_0.\ (\nu_0 = x \Rightarrow \nu[\nu_0] = y) \wedge (\nu_0 \neq x \Rightarrow \nu[\nu_0] = A[\nu_0])\}; \widetilde{A} : \{\Gamma(a)\})$ where $\widetilde{A}$ is a copy of the original array. The encoding for A according to (ϱ) is

$$A : [A/\nu][A_0/\nu_0]\{\mathsf{array}|\forall\nu_0.\ (\nu_0 = x \Rightarrow \nu[\nu_0] = y) \wedge (\nu_0 \neq x \Rightarrow \nu[\nu_0] = \widetilde{A}[\nu_0])\}$$

This illustrates the fact the array update application $A[x] := y$ produces as a side-effect, an update to the $x^{\mathtt{th}}$ element of the array; the other elements of the array are not changed and hence refer to the original array which is remembered by the type system as $\widetilde{A}$. This kind of embedding aims to strengthen the antecedent of the implication and is conservative [22]. Rule `Sub_Fun` is again standard, and rule `Sub_Eff` checks wether two effects are subtyped. Arrays bound in T_1 should be subsumed by that in T_2; subtype checking is reduced to dependent type checking $\Gamma; T_1 \vdash a : P$ for each array a bound in T_2.

Features. Our analysis has several notable characteristics. First, by piggybacking type refinements (which are inferred using the techniques described in Section 5) on top of standard type inference, we can use abstract interpretation (in the form of liquid type inference [22]) to verify array properties. Thus, our technique reduces static analysis for arrays to a Boolean fixpoint computation. Unlike a theorem prover based approach which must generate suitable predicates on the fly, our type system ensures termination. A detailed comparison with related work is summarized in Section 9. Our type system maintains precision in the face of array updates by using case splits on array indices; to avoid case explosion, we exploit the natural function summarization that is expressed by a function type signature.

5 Array Type Refinements Inference

In this section we show how type refinements in dependent types can be automatically inferred from tests. Specifically, we infer a dependent function type for each function by inferring the function's precondition and postcondition. Our type refinement inference is compositional, i.e., we generate likely array invariants for a function, independent of its caller and callee.

5.1 Template Generation

As we have discussed in Section 2, our inference starts from a symbolic analysis analogous to weakest precondition generation wp. We guess invariant templates for each function according to its wp. Our wp algorithm simply pushes postconditions backward, substituting terms for values in the presumed postcondition based on the structure of the predicate used to generate the precondition.

$$
\begin{aligned}
\mathsf{wp}(e,\phi) = \ & \mathsf{case}\ e\ \mathsf{of} \\
& \mid \mathtt{if}\ p\ \mathtt{then}\ e_1\ \mathtt{else}\ e_2 \rightarrow (p \wedge \mathsf{wp}(e_1,\ \phi)) \vee (\neg p \wedge \mathsf{wp}(e_2,\ \phi))) \\
& \mid \mathtt{let}\ x\ =\ e_1\ \mathsf{in}\ e_2 \rightarrow \mathsf{wp}(e_1,\ [\nu/x]\mathsf{wp}(e_2,\phi))) \\
& \mid (\lambda x.e)\ y \rightarrow [y/x]\mathsf{wp}(e,\ \phi) \\
& \mid e\ y \rightarrow \mathsf{wp}((\lambda x.e')\ y,\ \phi) \quad \text{(where } e \text{ can be deferred to } \lambda x.e'\text{)} \\
& \mid a[s_1] := s_2 \rightarrow \exists a'.\ \phi[a'/a] \wedge \\
& \qquad \{\forall a_0.\ (a_0 = s_1 \Rightarrow a'[s_1]\ \{\geq,\ \leq\}\ s_2) \wedge (a_0 \neq s_1 \Rightarrow a'[a_0] = a[a_0])\} \\
& \mid s \rightarrow [s/\nu]\phi
\end{aligned}
$$

To invoke wp, we initially supply true as the ϕ argument. Notably, during the process, it is refined to capture all the array reads and updates through `if` cases and array update cases of the rules. However this wp definition does not terminate for recursive functions. Since our aim is to guess coarse templates of array invariants, we simply bound the number of times a recursive function call is unrolled (at most 2 in our experiments). When wp has just traversed a function f, our system remembers the immediate result as f's weakest precondition and can later retrieve it using wp(f). As stated in Section 2, wp reflects under-approximative information about how array elements are manipulated by a procedure. Our inference principle is that, while information implied in wp is under-approximate, if encoded into a template, can nonetheless be potentially generalized by running tests for instantiation.

We supply the weakest precondition wp(f) of a function f to our template generation algorithm, `guessT` in Figure 5, which outputs a set of invariant templates for f. We define `scalar`(f) as the *scalar* parameters and return value of function f, and `scalar`(p) as the scalar variables used in a predicate p. Similarly, `scalar`(s) returns the scalar variables used in a simple expression s. For readability, we define that notation $s \not\equiv s_i$ is true if and only if `scalar`(s) $\cap$ `scalar`(s_i) $= \emptyset$.

`let guessT` f wp `=`
 `foreach atomic predicate` $(p$ `as` $\mathcal{Q}(\bar{a}[\_];\bar{x}))$ `in` wp
`L: foreach` $a_i[s_i]$ `in` p
    `let` a_{i_0} `= create_var "`a_{i_0}`" in`
    `let` b `=` $\chi(\texttt{scalar}(f))$ `in`
    `output "`
    $\forall a_{i_0}.\ 0 \leq a_{i_0} < \texttt{b} \Rightarrow$
      $\{\bigwedge_{\substack{a[s]\in p\\ a\neq a_i \wedge s \not\equiv s_i}} \begin{array}{c}\chi(\texttt{scalar}(f)/\texttt{scalar(p)}) \leq \chi(\texttt{scalar}(f) \cup \texttt{scalar(p)}) \\ < \chi(\texttt{scalar}(f)/\texttt{scalar(p)})\end{array}\} \Rightarrow$
        $\mathcal{Q}(a_i[a_{i_0};\texttt{scalar}(f)];\ (a[\chi(a_{i_0};\texttt{scalar}(f))] \mid a[s]\in p \wedge a\neq a_i \wedge \neg(s \not\equiv s_i));$
                        $(a[\chi(\texttt{scalar}(f))] \mid a[s]\in p \wedge a\neq a_i \wedge (s \not\equiv s_i));\ \bar{x})$`"`

Fig. 5. Array Invariant Template Inference

In `guessT`, our algorithm traverses `wp` and generates invariant templates (defined in Section 3) for each of its simple relational predicates $\mathcal{Q}(\bar{a}[\_];\bar{x})$), denoted as p, if it ranges over some array expression $\bar{a}[\_]$. Inside the loop at location L, for each array expression $a_i[s_i]$, we create a universal variable a_{i0} and its upper bound as $\chi(\texttt{scalar}(f))$ for array a_i. Suppose $\bar{v}$ is a set of scalar variables. $\chi(\bar{v})$ is an arithmetic template over $\bar{v}$: $c_1 * v_1 + \cdots + c_n * v_n + c_0$, with coefficients $c_i (0 \leq i < n)$ as integer variables. Arrays other than a_i are also required to be accordingly bounded (intuitively corresponding to an array index partition) as the algorithm shows (the set minus operation used in these lower- and upper-bounds simply helps avoid considering uninteresting invariants).

Our algorithm then infers appropriate index templates over f's scalar variables for each array expression $a[s]$ in p, while it maintains the main shape of p. If an array expression $a[s]$ is exactly $a_i[s_i]$ or it happens to share some scalar variables with $a_i[s_i]$ in their subscripts, we create its index template, applying χ over the special universal variable a_{i_0} and the scalar parameters defined in $\texttt{scalar}(f)$. Otherwise, s and s_i have disjoint scalar variables; the index of a is transformed to an index template over $\texttt{scalar}(f)$ only.

Example 1. Consider the `insert` procedure in Figure 2. The weakest precondition of `insert`, `wp(insert)`, defines a simple predicate: $\texttt{p}_1 \equiv \texttt{a}[\texttt{i}] > \texttt{a}[\texttt{j}]$. Inside the loop at L, assume array expression a[i] is picked. To infer a precondition, the type signature of `insert` reveals that $\texttt{scalar(insert)} = \{\texttt{i},\texttt{j}\}$. So $\texttt{p}_1$ is parameterized to $\texttt{a}[\chi_2(\texttt{a}_0,\texttt{i},\texttt{j})] \leq \texttt{a}[\chi_3(\texttt{i},\texttt{j})]$ as a template and the universal variable $\texttt{a}_0$ is accordingly bounded by $\chi_1(\texttt{i},\texttt{j})$. The final template is:

$$\forall \texttt{a}_0.\ 0 \leq \texttt{a}_0 < \chi_1(\texttt{i},\texttt{j}) \Rightarrow \{\texttt{a}[\chi_2(\texttt{a}_0,\texttt{i},\texttt{j})] \leq \texttt{a}[\chi_3(\texttt{i},\texttt{j})]\}$$

5.2 Program Sampling

We train the invariant templates of a function using its concrete program states collected from test runs. To this end we instrument the entry and exit of function bodies to dump values of function parameters and returns into a log-file, as pre- and post-states of the corresponding function resp. The format of a concrete program state is as follows.

$$V\ x = \begin{cases} u & \leftarrow \textsf{type(x)} = \textsf{int}\ \textit{or}\ \textsf{bool} \\ [|0 : u_0, 1 : u_1, \cdots|] & \leftarrow \textsf{type(x)} = \textsf{Array} \end{cases}$$

If a variable x is scalar, V maps it to the corresponding scalar value, u, sampled in the log file. Otherwise if x is of array type, V maps it to a record where each array element is indexed by its corresponding array subscript. We can use $V\ x\ j$ to retrieve the jth element (u_j) of the array x. The program may be run with multiple tests so we collect a set of pre- or post-states Vs.

5.3 Template Instantiation

With an invariant template and a set of program states Vs, we build a constraint system to find all valid template instantiations that fit the concrete states. For each state $V \in V$s, four constraints are generated. The first one constrains the array content for all array $\bar{a}$, which is encoded as

$$\bigwedge_{0 \le i < |\bar{a}|} \ \bigwedge_{0 \le k < \texttt{Array.length}\,(a_i)} a_i[k] = V\ a_i\ k$$

The second constraint enforces that the requirement that an instantiation should be invariant for all the elements in array a_i:

$$\bigwedge_{0 \le k < \texttt{Array.length}\,(a_i)} [k/a_{i0}][V\ \bar{x}/\bar{x}] \begin{array}{l}(0 \le a_{i0} < \varphi_i(\bar{x})) \Rightarrow (\bigwedge_{a_j \in \{\bar{a}/a_i\}} (\varphi_j(\bar{x}) \le \psi_j(\bar{x}) \\ \quad < \varphi'_j(\bar{x}))) \Rightarrow \mathcal{Q}(\bar{a}[a_{i0}; \bar{x}], \bar{x})\end{array}$$

In the first substitution, since a_{i0} is bounded by $\texttt{Array.length}\,(a_i)$ and must be no less than 0, we instantiate it to each possible value $k \in [0, \texttt{Array.length}\ A)$. In the second substitution, we replace scalar variables $\bar{x}$ by $V\ \bar{x}$. As an implication with a `false` premise is always an invariant, albeit useless, the third constraint guarantees the integrity of instantiated invariants:

$$0 \le \varphi_i(\bar{x}) \le \texttt{Array.length}\,(a_i) \wedge \bigwedge_{a_j \in \{\bar{a}/a_i\}} 0 \le \varphi_j(\bar{x}) \le \varphi'_j(\bar{x}) \le \texttt{Array.length}\,(a_j)$$

The fourth constraint aims to rule out array bound exceptions. Index expressions, after instantiation, must respect array length and be positive.

$$\bigwedge_{a[\chi] \in \mathcal{Q}(\bar{a}[a_{i0}; \bar{x}], \bar{x})} 0 \le \chi < \texttt{Array.length}(a)$$

These rules help to shrink the search space for likely invariants into a subset of those syntactically restricted by the template. To avoid over-fitting, we further require that all the coefficients must fall into the interval $[-d, d]$ where d is the maximum known constant in the function where the template is inferred. We feed all $4|V\mathrm{s}|$ constraints to a decision procedure to find all the valid assignments for the unknown coefficients.

6 Array Type Refinements Checking

Inferred invariants are not guaranteed to generalize. We lift likely invariants into dependent types, which are subsequently validated through the type system introduced in Section 4. Initially we represent dependent base type as standard base type extended with a type refinement variable κ indicating an unknown type refinement. The dependent type P for an expression e must over-approximate e's side-effects. To generate the effect T for e, for all the arrays $x \in \mathtt{mod}(\Gamma, e)$ where Γ is the type environment for e, we call an auxiliary function $\mathtt{Push}(P, x : P_x)$ where P_x is a dependent type for x with unknown type refinement. This function pushes the effect to the right position in P; its definition is given as

$$\mathtt{Push}(\{\{\nu : B \mid p\} \;/\; T\}, T') = \{\{\nu : B \mid p\} \;/\; T; T'\}$$
$$\mathtt{Push}(\{x : P_1 \to P_2\}, T') = \{x : P_1 \to \mathtt{Push}(P_2, T')\}$$

This process is performed before the generation of type constraints.

Type constraints over unknown type refinement variables that capture the subtyping relations between the types of various subexpressions are generated by traversing the program expression in a syntax-directed manner, applying the typing rules in Figure 4. We prove (see [30]) that the generated type constraints are solvable if and only if a valid type derivation exists. In our system, the type refinements for arrays are automatically inferred from test runs and are initially associated to all the unknown type refinement variables for array types. The type checker enumerates all possible solutions following the strategy in [22]. Notably, the type inference is abstracted into an abstract interpretation infrastructure [4]. Specifically, we solve these type constraints by iteratively removing the type refinements for unknown type refinement variables that prevent a type constraint from being satisfied using a decision procedure (an SMT solver) for the implication check in the subtyping rule shown in Figure 4.

Example 2. Consider the `insert` function in Figure 2. Refining `insert`'s standard type, we initially generate its dependent type with unknown type refinement variables: $\{\mathtt{i} : \{\mathtt{int}|\kappa_i\} \to \mathtt{j} : \{\mathtt{int}|\kappa_j\} \to \mathtt{a} : \{\mathtt{array}|\kappa_a\} \to \mathtt{ret} : \{\mathtt{int}|\kappa_{ret}\}/[a : \{\mathtt{array}|\kappa_a^{\mathtt{Eff}}\}]\}$. The variable $\kappa_a^{\mathtt{Eff}}$ represents the effect this function makes; syntactic sugar `ret` represents the return value. According to type checking rule Let, the effect of the `let` expression in `if` branch must be merged with the type environment for the locally-bound subexpressions. Thus, we generate a constraint:

$$\cdots ; \tilde{\mathtt{a}} : \kappa_a; i >= 0; \tilde{\mathtt{a}}[\mathtt{i}] > \tilde{\mathtt{a}}[\mathtt{j}] \vdash \{\forall \mathtt{a_0}.((\mathtt{a_0} = \mathtt{i} + 1 \Rightarrow \mathtt{a}[\mathtt{i} + 1] = \tilde{\mathtt{a}}[\mathtt{i}])$$
$$\wedge (\mathtt{a_0} \neq \mathtt{i} + 1 \Rightarrow \mathtt{a}[\mathtt{a_0}] = \tilde{\mathtt{a}}[\mathtt{a_0}]))\} <: [\mathtt{i} - 1/\mathtt{i}]\kappa_a$$

from the call to `insert` that forces the actual array `a` passed in at the callsite to be a subtype of the formal of `insert`, according to rule App. Note that $\tilde{\mathtt{a}}$ denotes the old array before the update operation, in the type environment. Instantiating κ_a to the likely invariant inferred in Section 2 and executing the implication check in rule Sub_Base for subtyping would yield a verification condition, whose validity implies the invariant's correctness.

However, such implication checks are quantified formulae which are generally undecidable. The reason is that SMT solvers do not support quantifier instantiation for formulae of arbitrary structure. Our approach provides a heuristic wrapper to SMT solvers, similar to [28]. For a formula given as an universally quantified array invariant, we instantiate its universal variable with all the array accessing indices collected from the program. This mechanism is conservative because all such formulae are quantified over array indices, and is also sound. If a formula is also existentially quantified, we instantiate its existential with a fresh variable which is again matched to other corresponding universally quantified formulae.

7 Extensions

The template (over array and scalar variables) produced from Figure 5 covers a fairly general family of properties and is expressive enough to infer array invariants over an unbounded number of array elements. A natural question to ask is how we might judge the quality or usefulness of the invariants?

To show usefulness, we propose to use the inferred invariants to prove two important classes of program specifications: those that reflect sorting properties, and those that preserve the elements of the input. However, specifying suitable sorting and preservation invariants within a proper array bound requires array-specific domain knowledge. Instead, we equip our system with two built-in very simple templates for capturing sorting and preservation and use tests to instantiate such two specifications.

Array Sorting Invariants. The following template allows our system to infer an array sorting invariant for an arbitrary array a:

$$\forall \mathsf{a}_0.\ \chi(\bar{x}) \leq \mathsf{a}_0 < \chi'(\bar{x}) \Rightarrow \mathsf{a}[\mathsf{a}_0]\ \{\leq, \geq\}\ \mathsf{a}[\mathsf{a}_0 + 1]$$

Array Preservation Invariants. We are also interested in discovering and verifying properties like: "After sorting, the output array a_i preserves all the set of elements from the input array a_j". To this end, the postcondition of a function must be both universally and existentially quantified, and be able to refer to the state of the array a_j at the beginning of the function, which we denote as $\widetilde{a_j}$:

$$\forall a_{j0}.\exists a_{i0}.\ 0 \leq a_{j0} < \chi_j(\bar{x}) \Rightarrow 0 \leq a_{i0} < \chi_i(\bar{x}) \wedge (\widetilde{a_j}[\chi'_j(a_{j0}; \bar{x})] = a_i[\chi'_i(a_{i0}; \bar{x})])$$

where a_{i0} in this case is existentially quantified while another special variable a_{j0} for $\widetilde{a_j}$ (a_j may or may not equal to a_i) is universally quantified. An instantiation of this template yields a preservation invariant: for all the set of array elements (in some scope) in $\widetilde{a_j}$, they are preserved in a_i. Such templates can be created when we detect an array update involving two arrays during the process of generating the weakest precondition.

To deal with this extension, our template instantiation algorithm in Section 5 needs to be sightly extended. A concrete state logged in a file must include both $\bar{a}$ and $\tilde{\bar{a}}$ (the array at the beginning of the function) when trying to infer a function's post-condition. Specifically, for a $\forall\exists$ template and a set of program state Vs, for each state $V \in Vs$, we again generate four similar constraints.

$$\begin{cases} 1. \bigwedge_{0 \le k < \texttt{Array.length}(a_i)} a_i[k] = V\ a_i\ k \wedge \bigwedge_{0 \le k < \texttt{Array.length}(\widetilde{a_j})} \widetilde{a_j}[k] = V\ \widetilde{a_j}\ k \\ 2.\ 0 \le \chi_j(x) \le \texttt{Array.length}(\widetilde{a_j}) \wedge 0 \le \chi_i(x) \le \texttt{Array.length}(a_i) \\ 3.\ 0 \le \chi_j'(a_{j0}; \bar{x}) < \texttt{Array.length}(\widetilde{a_j}) \wedge 0 \le \chi_i'(a_{i0}; \bar{x}) < \texttt{Array.length}(a_i) \\ 4. \bigwedge_{0 \le k < \texttt{Array.length}(a_j)} [k/a_{j0}][ex/a_{i0}][V\ \bar{x}/\bar{x}] \\ \qquad 0 \le a_{j0} < \chi_j(\bar{x}) \Rightarrow 0 \le a_{i0} < \chi_i(\bar{x}) \wedge (\widetilde{a_j}[\chi_j'(a_{j0}; \bar{x})] = a_i[\chi_i'(a_{i0}; \bar{x})]) \end{cases}$$

The first three constraints are self-explanatory. The fourth constraint enforces that an (instantiated) invariant must hold for all the possible values of the universal variable a_{j0}. It also requires the solver to present a witness for the existential variable a_{i0} for each possible value of a_{j0} (ex is always a fresh variable).

8 Experimental Results

We have implemented our method [2] and evaluated it using benchmarks from recent related work [7,19]. We additionally infer invariants for *binarysearch*, *quicksort-inner* and the complete *mergesort* (see a detailed case study in [30]) and *insertionsort* programs. The results are summarized in Table 1. For the sorting programs, we try to infer and prove the sorted-ness of the result. For each of these benchmarks, our system successfully finds the desired pre- and post-conditions. In the table, we record the number of likely invariants and the time spent in invariant generation as gen_inv and inv_time, resp.; columns inv and vc_time represents the number of validated invariants and the time for validation. Columns tests refers to the number of tests (array input are randomly generated) needed to converge. In the experiment, we keep the size of input arrays to be a small value, either 4 or 5, to refute over-fitting invariants and achieve efficiencies. Notably, we use exactly *the same test suites* for the classic array sorting benchmarks. Compared to [7,19], our primary point of distinction is the use of test runs to infer array invariants and the absence of any requirement to annotate post-conditions, which are now inferred; the overall execution time of our implementation just slightly increases compared to [7], although we require much less annotations. A subset of our benchmarks can be verified via the system presented in [12], that extends abstract interpretation with a quantified abstract domain; like our technique, [12] also does not assume predefined predicates and annotated post-conditions. With the invariants inferred from a small set of tests, our approach can (significantly) more quickly converge to a solution compared to [12], which only relies on static semantics. Subsequent work [28] improves on [12], achieving results similar to ours, but at the cost of requiring programmers to explicitly specify a set of predicates and templates from which invariants are composed.

We also evaluated how increasing tests can affect the performance of our tool by tuning the number of test cases for *insertion-sort-full* in Table 2. It

[2] webpage: `https://www.cs.purdue.edu/homes/zhu103/asolve/index.html`

Table 1. ∀ invariant results

Benchmarks	gen_inv	inv	tests	inv_time	vc_time	total_time
parlindrome[19]	4	4	1	1.22s	0.13s	1.50s
seq-init[19]	2	2	1	0.33s	0.22s	0.71s
max-and-min[19]	4	4	1	0.27s	0.94s	1.78s
first-occur[19]	5	5	2	0.54s	0.59s	1.59s
sum-pair[19]	23	5	2	9.02s	1.63s	11.22s
array-init[7]	7	7	1	0.16s	0.25s	0.61s
array-reverse[7]	4	4	1	0.80s	0.36s	1.40s
array-copy[7]	7	7	1	0.46s	0.36s	1.05s
array-find[7]	2	2	1	0.10s	0.22s	0.45s
array-difference[7]	7	7	2	1.32s	0.76s	2.52s
binarysearch	8	5	2	0.95s	1.00s	2.46s
bubblesort-inner[7]	7	3	3	2.68s	1.40s	4.61s
selection-sort-inner[7]	6	4	3	3.03s	0.84s	4.36s
quick-sort-inner	12	8	2	2.58s	3.86s	7.26s
insert-sort-inner	8	3	2	0.66s	0.78s	1.76s
merge-sort-full	36	32	1	26.66s	22.66s	52.12s

Table 2. Increasing the number of tests for verifying insertion-sort-full

Benchmarks	gen_inv	inv	tests	inv_time	vc_time	total_time
insert-sort-full	20	9	1	3.57s	2.20s	6.43s
insert-sort-full	14	9	2	4.07s	1.83s	6.60s
insert-sort-full	12	9	3	4.34s	1.74s	6.83s
insert-sort-full	≤12	9	≥4	≥6.37s	≤1.79s	≥8.96s

can be seen that although increasing tests could reduce the number of false invariants generated (the verification time reduces correspondingly), the time spent in inference grows. Based on our experience, the number of tests never needs to be greater than a small number (2 or 3 in our experiments). Indeed, our experiments provide evidence to our claim that a simple random test suite suffices to infer very complex array invariants. Finally we show the result of applying our tool to infer preservation (∀∃) properties in Table 3.

Limitations. We briefly comment some limitations of our approach. First, the search space for array invariant is restricted by the shape of the general templates defined in Section 3, and can only discover program invariants that reside within this space. For example, our technique cannot find array invariants that express properties related to non-contiguous partitions of the array. Secondly, invariants discovered from the general template may sometimes be redundant. The reason is that discovered array invariants are all universally quantified. Adjusting the bound for universally quantified variables and the array indices computed from these variables accordingly may generate array invariants with different surface-level descriptions that have the same intension. Our approach bounds the value

Table 3. ∀∃ invariant results

Benchmarks	gen_inv	inv	tests	inv_time	vc_time	total_time
selection-sort	3	3	1	0.27s	1.41s	2.44s
bubble-sort	3	3	1	0.27s	1.68s	2.76s
quick-sort	9	8	1	1.31s	5.89s	9.05s

constants used by the general template to reduce the likelihood of redundant invariants. In future work, we plan to exploit deeper semantic approaches to filter redundant invariants.

9 Related Work and Conclusion

The idea of using a dependent type system to verify data structures is well studied. LIQUIDTYPE [22] infers sound dependent types whose type refinements are conjunctions over atomic predicates presented from programmers. This approach can prove complex invariants over data structures [16], and has been extended to support abstract type refinements [29], which allows dependent types to be parametrized over type refinements. The ability to infer and verify flow-sensitive properties (for array programs) distinguishes our approach from these efforts.

Abstract interpretation [4] has long been used to infer array invariants. In [10] and its subsequent work [14], invariants are discovered based on an abstract interpretation over abstract values associated with each symbolic array partition. To overcome the problem that array indices can only be quantified over intervals from a fixed partition, [12] introduces quantified abstract domains and infers more general array properties of the form $\forall \texttt{l}.\varphi(\texttt{l}) \Rightarrow \psi(\texttt{a[l]}\cdots)$. However, abstract interpretation becomes difficult because φ must be under-approximated and it also requires programmers to provide templates for the invariants to be inferred. To overcome these difficulties, a similar but more scalable framework for array programs is presented in [5]. With parameterized bound expressions, arrays are automatically divided and each segment can be uniformly abstracted; such analyses are then combined via a reduced product with existing analyses for scalars. Our approach, in contrast, does not require array divisions and a fixed set of predicates in advance. Another dedicated array program analysis, fluid update [8], also avoids explicit array index partition. It also models array as an abstract location quantified by its index. To avoid the need for explicit array partitions, it retains both over- and under-approximative information of array updates, blurring the boundary of strong and weak updates. In contrast to our approach (dedicated to discovering complex invariants about unbounded array elements), their focus is on unified pointer, scalar and array reasoning.

Theorem provers have also been used for discovering invariants for array programs. Some approaches follow a counterexample guided abstraction refinement paradigm to extract information from spurious error paths about the range of array indices over which a universally quantified property may hold, or derive array entries that violate an assertion from which predicates that may hold in unbounded intervals are then inferred [1,15,18,20,24]. Similar to our technique, these approaches are flexible because they do not assume a finite set of abstractions fixed in advance but generate suitable assertions on the fly. In contrast, our technique does not rely on program assertions or spurious program paths, and can infer likely program invariants before verification. Other techniques attempt to solve for unknown relations such as loop invariants that occur in verification conditions. This line of work has also been applied to array program in [2] by extending Horn solver to handle quantified predicates. Constraint-based invariant generation [3] is similarly adopted for discovering and verifying universally quantified properties over array variables. For example, a CLP program transformation [11] has been extended to handle array manipulating program in [7]. This work generates a set of verification conditions expressed as CLP (Array) program whose satisfiability implies that the program specification is proved. In [19], by means of Farkas' Lemma, the problem of discovering loop invariants is transformed into a satisfiability problem over the constraints generated from array programs. In contrast to these efforts, our approach builds simple constraints over concrete program states and hence is agnostic to specific program instructions so that it does not rely on the power of specialized theorem provers.

Our approach is inspired by the idea of using tests to improve the precision and efficiency of program analysis. Daikon [9] uses conjunctive template to find invariants, from configurations recorded along test runs. One of its extension in [21] uses equation solving to find array invariant but does not support implication and quantification. In contrast, we search quantified array invariants that allows implication (disjunction). In [6], since invariants are produced from symbolic execution of program paths that the concrete tests satisfy during their executions, the relevance of the generated invariants is increased compared to Daikon. In [13], the information obtained from static abstract interpretation is combined with that from tests to strengthen the ability of invariant generators but it does not consider quantified invariants. We are also inspired by recent interest in using machine learning to infer loop invariants. Compared to learning algorithms that synthesize program invariants in terms of classifiers distinguishing good and bad program samples [27,26,25], we search invariants from a broader program space since the typical learning techniques only search for invariants bounded by annotated assertions; we are unaware of prior learning based approaches capable of handling array programs as complex as the ones we have considered.

Conclusion. This paper presents a compositional and lightweight invariant inference technique that uses test runs to infer quantified array invariants. Our technique builds a constraint system for inferring array invariants on top of concrete program states. All likely flow-sensitive invariants inferred are validated by our dependent type system that allows side-effecting array updates. Experimental results demonstrate the practicality and expressivity of our approach.

References

1. Alberti, F., Bruttomesso, R., Ghilardi, S., Ranise, S., Sharygina, N.: SAFARI: SMT-based abstraction for arrays with interpolants. In: Madhusudan, P., Seshia, S.A. (eds.) CAV 2012. LNCS, vol. 7358, pp. 679–685. Springer, Heidelberg (2012)
2. Bjørner, N., McMillan, K., Rybalchenko, A.: On solving universally quantified horn clauses. In: Logozzo, F., Fähndrich, M. (eds.) SAS 2013. LNCS, vol. 7935, pp. 105–125. Springer, Heidelberg (2013)
3. Colón, M.A., Sankaranarayanan, S., Sipma, H.B.: Linear invariant generation using non-linear constraint solving. In: Hunt Jr., W.A., Somenzi, F. (eds.) CAV 2003. LNCS, vol. 2725, pp. 420–432. Springer, Heidelberg (2003)
4. Cousot, P., Cousot, R.: Abstract interpretation: A unified lattice model for static analysis of programs by construction or approximation of fixpoints. In: POPL (1977)
5. Cousot, P., Cousot, R., Logozzo, F.: A parametric segmentation functor for fully automatic and scalable array content analysis. In: POPL (2011)
6. Csallner, C., Tillmann, N., Smaragdakis, Y.: Dysy: Dynamic symbolic execution for invariant inference. In: ICSE (2008)
7. De Angelis, E., Fioravanti, F., Pettorossi, A., Proietti, M.: Verifying array programs by transforming verification conditions. In: McMillan, K.L., Rival, X. (eds.) VMCAI 2014. LNCS, vol. 8318, pp. 182–202. Springer, Heidelberg (2014)
8. Dillig, I., Dillig, T., Aiken, A.: Fluid updates: Beyond strong vs. Weak updates. In: Gordon, A.D. (ed.) ESOP 2010. LNCS, vol. 6012, pp. 246–266. Springer, Heidelberg (2010)
9. Ernst, M.D., Perkins, J.H., Guo, P.J., McCamant, S., Pacheco, C., Tschantz, M.S., Xiao, C.: The daikon system for dynamic detection of likely invariants. Sci. Comput. Program., 35–45 (December 2007)
10. Gopan, D., Reps, T.W., Sagiv, S.: A framework for numeric analysis of array operations. In: POPL (2005)
11. Grebenshchikov, S., Gupta, A., Lopes, N.P., Popeea, C., Rybalchenko, A.: HSF(C): A software verifier based on horn clauses - (competition contribution). In: Flanagan, C., König, B. (eds.) TACAS 2012. LNCS, vol. 7214, pp. 549–551. Springer, Heidelberg (2012)
12. Gulwani, S., McCloskey, B., Tiwari, A.: Lifting abstract interpreters to quantified logical domains. In: POPL (2008)
13. Gupta, A.K., Majumdar, R., Rybalchenko, A.: From tests to proofs. International Journal on Software Tools for Technology Transfer (2013)
14. Halbwachs, N., Péron, M.: Discovering properties about arrays in simple programs. In: PLDI (2008)
15. Jhala, R., McMillan, K.L.: Array abstractions from proofs. In: Damm, W., Hermanns, H. (eds.) CAV 2007. LNCS, vol. 4590, pp. 193–206. Springer, Heidelberg (2007)
16. Kawaguchi, M., Rondon, P., Jhala, R.: Type-based data structure verification. In: PLDI (2009)
17. Kawaguchi, M., Rondon, P.M., Jhala, R.: Dsolve: Safety verification via liquid types. In: Touili, T., Cook, B., Jackson, P. (eds.) CAV 2010. LNCS, vol. 6174, pp. 123–126. Springer, Heidelberg (2010)
18. Kovács, L., Voronkov, A.: Finding loop invariants for programs over arrays using a theorem prover. In: Chechik, M., Wirsing, M. (eds.) FASE 2009. LNCS, vol. 5503, pp. 470–485. Springer, Heidelberg (2009)

19. Larraz, D., Rodríguez-Carbonell, E., Rubio, A.: SMT-based array invariant generation. In: Giacobazzi, R., Berdine, J., Mastroeni, I. (eds.) VMCAI 2013. LNCS, vol. 7737, pp. 169–188. Springer, Heidelberg (2013)
20. McMillan, K.L.: Quantified invariant generation using an interpolating saturation prover. In: Ramakrishnan, C.R., Rehof, J. (eds.) TACAS 2008. LNCS, vol. 4963, pp. 413–427. Springer, Heidelberg (2008)
21. Nguyen, T., Kapur, D., Weimer, W., Forrest, S.: Using dynamic analysis to discover polynomial and array invariants. In: ICSE (2012)
22. Rondon, P.M., Kawaguchi, M., Jhala, R.: Liquid types. In: PLDI (2008)
23. Rondon, P.M., Kawaguchi, M., Jhala, R.: Low-level liquid types. In: POPL (2010)
24. Seghir, M.N., Podelski, A., Wies, T.: Abstraction refinement for quantified array assertions. In: Palsberg, J., Su, Z. (eds.) SAS 2009. LNCS, vol. 5673, pp. 3–18. Springer, Heidelberg (2009)
25. Sharma, R., Aiken, A.: From invariant checking to invariant inference using randomized search. In: Biere, A., Bloem, R. (eds.) CAV 2014. LNCS, vol. 8559, pp. 88–105. Springer, Heidelberg (2014)
26. Sharma, R., Gupta, S., Hariharan, B., Aiken, A., Nori, A.V.: Verification as learning geometric concepts. In: Logozzo, F., Fähndrich, M. (eds.) SAS 2013. LNCS, vol. 7935, pp. 388–411. Springer, Heidelberg (2013)
27. Sharma, R., Nori, A.V., Aiken, A.: Interpolants as classifiers. In: Madhusudan, P., Seshia, S.A. (eds.) CAV 2012. LNCS, vol. 7358, pp. 71–87. Springer, Heidelberg (2012)
28. Srivastava, S., Gulwani, S.: Program verification using templates over predicate abstraction. In: PLDI (2009)
29. Vazou, N., Rondon, P.M., Jhala, R.: Abstract refinement types. In: Felleisen, M., Gardner, P. (eds.) ESOP 2013. LNCS, vol. 7792, pp. 209–228. Springer, Heidelberg (2013)
30. Zhu, H., Nori, A.V., Jagannathan, S.: Dependent array type inference from tests. Tech. rep., Purdue Univsersity (2014), `https://www.cs.purdue.edu/homes/zhu103/asolve/asolvetech.pdf`

A Hierarchy of Proof Rules for Checking Differential Invariance of Algebraic Sets*

Khalil Ghorbal[1], Andrew Sogokon[2], and André Platzer[1]

[1] Carnegie Mellon University, Computer Science Department, Pittsburgh, PA, USA
{kghorbal,aplatzer}@cs.cmu.edu
[2] University of Edinburgh, LFCS, School of Informatics, Edinburgh, Scotland, UK
a.sogokon@sms.ed.ac.uk

Abstract This paper presents a theoretical and experimental comparison of sound proof rules for proving invariance of algebraic sets, that is, sets satisfying polynomial equalities, under the flow of polynomial ordinary differential equations. Problems of this nature arise in formal verification of continuous and hybrid dynamical systems, where there is an increasing need for methods to expedite formal proofs. We study the trade-off between proof rule generality and practical performance and evaluate our theoretical observations on a set of heterogeneous benchmarks. The relationship between increased deductive power and running time performance of the proof rules is far from obvious; we discuss and illustrate certain classes of problems where this relationship is interesting.

1 Introduction

In safety verification of dynamical systems, either purely continuous or hybrid [22,29], one is typically concerned with ensuring that by initializing a system in some set of states $X_0 \subseteq X$ (where X is the state space), the system will never evolve into an unsafe state (belonging to some $X_u \subseteq X$). When the system is given by ordinary differential equations $\dot{\boldsymbol{x}} = \boldsymbol{p}(\boldsymbol{x})$, one may attempt to solve this problem by showing that the solution to the initial value problem, for any initial value $\boldsymbol{x}_0 \in X_0$, cannot enter the unsafe region; that is, $\boldsymbol{x}(\boldsymbol{x}_0, t) \notin X_u$ for all $t \geq 0$, where $\boldsymbol{x}(\boldsymbol{x}_0, t)$ is the state of the system at time t w.r.t. the initial value $\boldsymbol{x}_0$. This safety verification problem is equivalent to showing that the intersection of the reachable set $\{\boldsymbol{x}(\boldsymbol{x}_0, t) \in X \mid t \geq 0\}$ with the set of unsafe states is empty. However, solutions to ordinary differential equations will rarely be available in closed form; and even when they are, will often be much more complicated than the differential equations themselves. Instead, it is possible to work with the differential equations *directly* [26,21,23,29].

A fundamental notion in safety verification is that of an *invariant set*. In fact, exact reachable sets of any given state $\boldsymbol{x}_0$ of the system are the *smallest* invariant sets one can hope to find that include $\boldsymbol{x}_0$. However, obtaining and working with exact descriptions of

* This material is based upon work supported by the National Science Foundation (NSF) under NSF CAREER Award CNS-1054246, NSF EXPEDITION CNS-0926181, NSF CNS-0931985, by DARPA under agreement number FA8750-12-2-029, as well as the Engineering and Physical Sciences Research Council (UK) under grant EP/I010335/1.

D. D'Souza et al. (Eds.): VMCAI 2015, LNCS 8931, pp. 431–448, 2015.

reachable sets is not always practical or even possible. This does not mean that system safety cannot be established by other means - if one finds a *larger* invariant set, $I \subseteq X$, with a simpler (perhaps algebraic) description which contains the reachable set and does not itself intersect the set of unsafe states (i.e. $I \cap X_u = \emptyset$), then one can soundly conclude that the system is safe. In this paper, we focus on checking whether a given set is an *invariant region* from which no system trajectory can escape.

Hybrid systems verification completely reduces to questions about invariant regions [20,22]. We focus on the important case where the invariant regions are algebraic sets, i.e. can be defined by polynomial equations. Many sound proof rules already exist for deciding invariance properties of algebraic sets. However, in order to identify a good trade-off, it is crucial to study the relationship between the deductive power and the practical running time performance of these proof rules.

Contributions. (**I**) We theoretically compare the deductive power of 7 different proof rules for checking invariance properties of algebraic sets under the flow of polynomial ordinary differential equations. Further, we assess the practical utility of each of these rules in order to identify a good trade-off between generality and running time performance. (**II**) We investigate the effect of *square-free reduction* on both the deductive power and the computational complexity of the proof rules. (**III**) We assess the practical proof rule performance on a heterogeneous set of 75 benchmarks. We demonstrate the counter-intuitive fact that square-free reduction does not necessarily improve the computational efficiency of certain proof rules and explore interesting connections between the deductive power and the practical running time performance that we observe for the proof rules.

Content. In Section 2, we recall some basic definitions and concepts that will be used throughout the paper. We then introduce (in Section 3) two proof rules that serve as extensions of Lie's criterion for equational invariants. In Section 4, we compare the deductive power of the proof rules. The benefits and drawbacks of performing square-free reduction as a pre-processing step are investigated in Section 5. In Section 6, we present the set of benchmarks and our experimental results. We finally discuss other related work in Section 7 before concluding. All proofs, as well as more detailed results from running our benchmarks, can be found in the companion technical report [10].

2 Preliminaries

We consider autonomous[1] polynomial vector fields (see Def. 1 below).

Let $\boldsymbol{x} = (x_1, \ldots, x_n) \in \mathbb{R}^n$, and $\boldsymbol{x}(t) = (x_1(t), \ldots, x_n(t))$, where $x_i : \mathbb{R} \to \mathbb{R}$, $t \mapsto x_i(t)$. The ring of polynomials over the reals will be denoted by $\mathbb{R}[x_1, \ldots, x_n]$.

Definition 1 (Polynomial Vector Field). *Let* p_i, $1 \leq i \leq n$, *be multivariate polynomials of the polynomial ring* $\mathbb{R}[\boldsymbol{x}]$. *A* polynomial vector field, **p**, *is an explicit system of ordinary differential equations with polynomial right-hand side:*

[1] That is, the rate of change of the system over time depends only on the system's state, not on time. Non-autonomous systems with polynomial time-dependence can be made autonomous by adding an extra clock variable that reflects the progress of time.

$$\frac{dx_i}{dt} = \dot{x}_i = p_i(\boldsymbol{x}), \quad 1 \leq i \leq n \ . \tag{1}$$

Since polynomial functions are smooth (C^∞, i.e. they have derivatives up to any order), they are locally Lipschitz-continuous. By the Cauchy-Lipschitz theorem (a.k.a. Picard-Lindelöf) [14], there exists a unique maximal solution to the initial value problem ($\dot{\boldsymbol{x}} = \boldsymbol{p}$, $\boldsymbol{x}(0) = \boldsymbol{x}_0$) defined for t in some nonempty open interval.

For $h \in \mathbb{R}[x_1 \ldots, x_n]$, if $h(\boldsymbol{x}(t)) = 0$ for all $t \geq 0$, we say that the equation $h = 0$ is a *(positive) invariant* under the flow of $\boldsymbol{p}$. In differential dynamic logic [20], invariance of $h = 0$ is semantically equivalent to the validity of the following formula:

$$(h = 0) \rightarrow [\dot{\boldsymbol{x}} = \boldsymbol{p}](h = 0) \tag{2}$$

Geometrically, the equation $h = 0$ represents the set of real roots of h. Such a set is known as *real algebraic set* or a *real variety* and will be henceforth denoted by $V_{\mathbb{R}}(h)$. Algebraic sets are intimately related to sets of polynomials with special algebraic properties called *ideals*. Ideals are closed under addition and external multiplication; that is, if I is an ideal, then for all $h_1, h_2 \in I$, the sum $h_1 + h_2 \in I$; and if $h \in I$, then, $qh \in I$, for all $q \in \mathbb{R}[x_1 \ldots, x_n]$. To say that the real variety $V_{\mathbb{R}}(h)$ of the ideal *generated by* h is invariant under the flow of the vector field $\boldsymbol{p}$ is equivalent to the statement that the equation $h = 0$ is invariant.

We will use ∇h to denote the gradient of $h : \mathbb{R}^n \rightarrow \mathbb{R}$, that is the vector of its partial derivatives $(\frac{\partial h}{\partial x_1}, \ldots, \frac{\partial h}{\partial x_n})$. The *Lie derivative* of h along the vector field $\boldsymbol{p}$ gives the rate of change of h along the flow of $\dot{\boldsymbol{x}} = \boldsymbol{p}(\boldsymbol{x})$ and is formally defined as the scalar product of ∇h and $\boldsymbol{p}$.

$$\mathfrak{L}_{\boldsymbol{p}}(h) \overset{\text{def}}{=} \nabla h \cdot \boldsymbol{p} \ . \tag{3}$$

Higher-order Lie derivatives are defined recursively as $\mathfrak{L}_{\boldsymbol{p}}^{(k+1)}(h) = \mathfrak{L}_{\boldsymbol{p}}(\mathfrak{L}_{\boldsymbol{p}}^{(k)}(h))$, with $\mathfrak{L}_{\boldsymbol{p}}^{(0)}(h) = h$.

We now recall five important proof rules for checking invariance of polynomial equalities, or equivalently the validity of Eq. (2). In Fig. 1, $\text{DI}_=$ shows the differential invariant [21] proof rule restricted to handling equalities. The condition imposed by the premise of $\text{DI}_=$ is sufficient, but not necessary; it characterizes polynomial invariant functions. The premise of the Polynomial-scale consecution proof rule [26], P-c in Fig. 1, requires $\mathfrak{L}_{\boldsymbol{p}}(h)$ to be in the ideal generated by h. The condition is also only sufficient (but is particularly suitable for *generating* invariant varieties [16]). We also consider the constant-scale consecution proof rule [26,29], denoted by C-c. The premise of proof rule C-c requires that $\mathfrak{L}_{\boldsymbol{p}}(h) = \lambda h$, where λ is a scalar, not a polynomial as in P-c. It is therefore a simple special case of P-c. When $\lambda = 0$, one obtains the premise of the proof rule $\text{DI}_=$. It is worth noting that P-c, including its special case C-c, was mentioned as early as 1878 [5] and used extensively in the study of integrability of dynamical systems, where they are known as *second integrals* [12, Chapter 2]. It serves as a natural extension to invariant functions, also known as *first integrals*, which are covered by the proof rule $\text{DI}_=$. The proof rule Lie gives Lie's criterion [13,19] for invariance of $h = 0$; this proof rule will be discussed in more depth and extended to handle tricky cases in Section 3. The last rule, DRI in Fig. 1, was recently introduced and characterizes (i.e. gives necessary and sufficient conditions for) invariant varieties under the flow

$$(\mathrm{DI}_=)\frac{\mathfrak{L}_{\boldsymbol{p}}(h) = 0}{(h = 0) \to [\dot{\boldsymbol{x}} = \boldsymbol{p}](h = 0)} \qquad (\text{C-c})\frac{\exists \lambda \in \mathbb{R},\ \mathfrak{L}_{\boldsymbol{p}}(h) = \lambda h}{(h = 0) \to [\dot{\boldsymbol{x}} = \boldsymbol{p}](h = 0)}$$

$$(\text{Lie})\frac{h = 0 \to (\mathfrak{L}_{\boldsymbol{p}}(h) = 0 \wedge \nabla h \neq \mathbf{0})}{(h = 0) \to [\dot{\boldsymbol{x}} = \boldsymbol{p}](h = 0)} \qquad (\text{P-c})\frac{\mathfrak{L}_{\boldsymbol{p}}(h) \in \langle h \rangle}{(h = 0) \to [\dot{\boldsymbol{x}} = \boldsymbol{p}](h = 0)}$$

$$(\text{DRI})\frac{h = 0 \to \bigwedge_{i=0}^{N-1} \mathfrak{L}_{\boldsymbol{p}}^{(i)}(h) = 0}{(h = 0) \to [\dot{\boldsymbol{x}} = \boldsymbol{p}](h = 0)}$$

Fig. 1. Proof rules for checking the invariance of $h = 0$ w.r.t. $\boldsymbol{p}$: $\mathrm{DI}_=$ [23, Theorem 3], C-c and P-c [26, Lemma 2], Lie [19, Theorem 2.8], DRI [9, Theorem 2]

of polynomial vector fields [9]. The number N in DRI is the maximum length of the ascending chain of polynomial ideals $\langle h \rangle \subset \langle h, \mathfrak{L}_{\boldsymbol{p}}(h) \rangle \subset \langle h, \mathfrak{L}_{\boldsymbol{p}}(h), \mathfrak{L}_{\boldsymbol{p}}^{(2)}(h) \rangle \subset \cdots$, which is finite and computable [9].

3 Lie's Criterion

One immediate (and somewhat embarrassing) deficiency of the proof rule Lie (Fig. 1) is its inability to prove invariance properties for isolated points (e.g. system equilibria) for the simple reason that a description of such a point $\boldsymbol{a} = (a_1, \dots, a_n) \in \mathbb{R}^n$ is (when $n > 1$) given by the sum-of-squares equation $h(\boldsymbol{x}) = (x_1 - a_1)^2 + \cdots + (x_n - a_n)^2 = 0$. This sum-of-squares polynomial h is *positive-definite*, i.e. $h(\boldsymbol{a}) = 0$ and $h(\boldsymbol{x}) > 0$ for all $\boldsymbol{x} \in \mathbb{R}^n \setminus \{\boldsymbol{a}\}$. Positive definite functions have vanishing gradient at their minima, in this case $\boldsymbol{a}$, and thus the formula $h = 0 \to \nabla h = \mathbf{0}$ holds. This violates the regularity condition in the premise of the proof rule Lie, namely:

$$h = 0 \longrightarrow \nabla h \neq \mathbf{0} \ . \tag{4}$$

In fact, $h = 0 \to \mathfrak{L}_{\boldsymbol{p}}(h) = 0$ is a necessary condition when $h = 0$ is an invariant equation. Note that simply removing Eq. (4) from the premise of the proof rule Lie is unsound (see e.g. [23]); that is, the condition $h = 0 \to \mathfrak{L}_{\boldsymbol{p}}(h) = 0$ alone is insufficient to prove the invariance property for $h = 0$. Unsoundness in the above naïve attempt at a generalization is a consequence of *singularities* that may be present in the variety $V_{\mathbb{R}}(h)$. Singularities of $V_{\mathbb{R}}(h)$ are points $\boldsymbol{x} \in V_{\mathbb{R}}(h)$ where the gradient of h vanishes, i.e. $\nabla h(\boldsymbol{x}) = \mathbf{0}$.

Definition 2 (Singular Locus). *Let $h \in \mathbb{R}[x_1, \dots, x_n]$, the* singular locus *of $h = 0$, henceforth denoted* $\mathrm{SL}(h)$*, is the set of singular points, that is, points $\boldsymbol{x}$ satisfying*

$$h = 0 \wedge \frac{\partial h}{\partial x_1} = 0 \wedge \cdots \wedge \frac{\partial h}{\partial x_n} = 0 \ .$$

Points that are not singular are called regular. At singular points, the Lie derivative of h along any vector field is $\mathbf{0} \cdot \boldsymbol{p} = 0$. To avoid these degenerate cases, the regularity condition (Eq. (4)) rules out singularities altogether. In the next section we present two extensions of Lie's criterion that, in a similar vein to [27], partially overcome the strong regularity condition by treating the points on the singular locus separately.

3.1 Handling Singularities

Equilibria are points in the state space where the vector field vanishes ($\boldsymbol{p} = \mathbf{0}$) so that there is no motion. However, as seen above, Lie's criterion cannot generally be applied to prove invariance properties of isolated equilibria because their description involves singularities. One simple way to resolve this issue is to drop the non-vanishing gradient condition and replace it with the proviso that there be no flow (that is $\boldsymbol{p} = \mathbf{0}$) in the variables of the invariant candidate on the singular locus; this will allow singularities in the invariant candidate and will provide a *sound* proof method in which there is no need to check for non-vanishing gradient. Below we present two extensions to the proof rule Lie and justify their soundness after recalling some basic geometric notions.

Definition 3 (Lie°: Lie **+ Equilibria).**

$$(\text{Lie}^\circ)\frac{h = 0 \to \left(\mathfrak{L}_{\boldsymbol{p}}(h) = 0 \wedge \left(\text{SL}(h) \to \bigwedge_{x_i \in \text{vars}(h)} p_i = 0\right)\right)}{(h = 0) \to [\dot{\boldsymbol{x}} = \boldsymbol{p}](h = 0)},$$

where vars(h) *denotes the set of state variables* x_i *occurring in the polynomial* h.

The Lie° proof rule can be generalized further at the expense of adding an extra variable by replacing the "no flow" condition ($p_i = 0$) for points on the singular locus with $\forall \lambda.\ h(\boldsymbol{x} + \lambda \boldsymbol{p}(\boldsymbol{x})) = 0$, where λ is a fresh symbol.

Definition 4 (Lie*: Lie **+ Vanishing Sub-tangent).**

$$(\text{Lie}^*)\frac{h = 0 \to \left(\mathfrak{L}_{\boldsymbol{p}}(h) = 0 \wedge (\text{SL}(h) \to h(\boldsymbol{x} + \lambda \boldsymbol{p}) = 0)\right)}{(h = 0) \to [\dot{\boldsymbol{x}} = \boldsymbol{p}](h = 0)}.$$

To prove soundness of Lie° and Lie*, we use a result about positive invariance of closed sets under locally Lipschitz-continuous vector fields, known as the Nagumo theorem [18,30, Chapter 10, XV–XVI, pp. 117-119], which gives a powerful (but generally intractable) geometric characterization of positively invariant closed sets. The notion of positive invariance of the equation $h = 0$ from Section 2 generalizes to an arbitrary set.

Definition 5 (Invariant Sets). *A set S is* positively (negatively) invariant *under the flow of $\dot{\boldsymbol{x}} = \boldsymbol{p}$ if for all $\boldsymbol{x}_0 \in S$ we have $\boldsymbol{x}(\boldsymbol{x}_0, t) \in S$ for all $t \geq 0$ ($t \leq 0$), where $\boldsymbol{x}(\boldsymbol{x}_0, t)$ is the solution of the initial value problem ($\dot{\boldsymbol{x}} = \boldsymbol{p}, \boldsymbol{x}(0) = \boldsymbol{x}_0$). A set S is* bi-invariant *if it is both positively and negatively invariant.*

Nagumo's theorem needs the geometric notion of sub-tangential vectors to a set.

Definition 6 (Sub-tangent vector). *A vector $\boldsymbol{v} \in \mathbb{R}^n$ is sub-tangential to a set S at $\boldsymbol{x} \in S$ if*

$$\liminf_{\lambda \to 0^+} \frac{\text{dist}\,(S, \boldsymbol{x} + \lambda \boldsymbol{v})}{\lambda} = 0,$$

where dist *denotes the Euclidean set distance, i.e.* $\text{dist}(S, \boldsymbol{x}) \equiv \inf_{\boldsymbol{y} \in S} \|\boldsymbol{x} - \boldsymbol{y}\|$.

Theorem 1 (Nagumo Theorem). *Given a continuous system $\dot{\boldsymbol{x}} = \boldsymbol{p}(\boldsymbol{x})$ and assuming that solutions exist and are unique inside some open set $O \subseteq \mathbb{R}^n$, let $S \subset O$ be a closed set. Then, S is* positively invariant *under the flow of the system if and only if $\boldsymbol{p}(\boldsymbol{x})$ is sub-tangential to S for all $\boldsymbol{x} \in \partial S$, where ∂S is the boundary of S.*

Let us observe that given $\boldsymbol{x} \in \partial S$, if $\boldsymbol{x} + \lambda \boldsymbol{p}(\boldsymbol{x}) \in S$ for all $\lambda \in \mathbb{R}$, then dist $(S, \boldsymbol{x} + \lambda \boldsymbol{p}(\boldsymbol{x})) = 0$ and $\boldsymbol{p}(\boldsymbol{x})$ is sub-tangential to S at $\boldsymbol{x}$. This observation is important for algebraic sets, for which $\partial S = S$, and the condition $\boldsymbol{x} + \lambda \boldsymbol{p}(\boldsymbol{x}) \in S$ translates to $h(\boldsymbol{x} + \lambda \boldsymbol{p}(\boldsymbol{x})) = 0$. This is the main idea behind the soundness of the proof rule Lie* (see [10] for the detailed proof).

Proposition 1. *The proof rule* Lie* *is sound.*

The case $\boldsymbol{p}(\boldsymbol{x}) = 0$ for all $\boldsymbol{x}$ in the singular locus is a special case of the proof rule Lie*. Therefore, the soundness of Lie° is an immediate corollary of Prop. 1.

Corollary 1. *The proof rule* Lie° *is sound.*

4 Proof Rules: Hierarchy and Complexity

In this section, we compare the deductive power of the existing (Fig. 1) and the newly-introduced proof rules (Lie° and Lie* in Section 3) for checking the invariance of algebraic sets. This study should be complemented by another comparison that considers the interaction between the different proof rules in the context of a formal proof system in a similar vein to [24]. We leave this for future work.

Given two proof rules (let us call them R_1 and R_2) featuring the same conclusion $((h = 0) \longrightarrow [\dot{\boldsymbol{x}} = \boldsymbol{p}](h = 0))$, we will say that R_2 generalizes R_1 and write $R_2 \succcurlyeq R_1$ (or $R_1 \preccurlyeq R_2$), if the premise of R_1 implies the premise of R_2. That is, if R_1 proves that $h = 0$ is an invariant, then so does R_2. If $R_1 \preccurlyeq R_2$ and $R_1 \succcurlyeq R_2$, we say that R_1 and R_2 are equivalent, and denote this by $R_1 \sim R_2$. Likewise, $R_1 \not\preccurlyeq R_2$ (or $R_2 \not\succcurlyeq R_1$) denotes that R_1 is not generalized by R_2. We also write $R_1 \prec R_2$ when $R_1 \preccurlyeq R_2$ and $R_1 \not\succcurlyeq R_2$. That is, the rule R_2 *increases* the deductive power of R_1.

It is easy to see that the order $\preccurlyeq$ is a partial order (with $\sim$ acting as equality): it is reflexive, $R \preccurlyeq R$ (the premise of R implies itself); it is anti-symmetric (by definition), and transitive: if $R_1 \preccurlyeq R_2$ and $R_2 \preccurlyeq R_3$, then the premise of R_1 implies the premise of R_3 by transitivity of the implication, so $R_1 \preccurlyeq R_3$. Finally, If $R_1 \not\preccurlyeq R_2$ and $R_1 \not\succcurlyeq R_2$, we will write $R_1 \prec\succ R_2$ and say that the proof rules R_1 and R_2 are *incomparable*. This means that for both R_1 and R_2 there are problems that one rule can prove and the other cannot. In the sequel, we use the partial order $\preccurlyeq$ to illustrate the lattice structure of the proof rules under consideration. In Section 4.2 we discuss the computational complexity of the conditions appearing in their premises.

4.1 Hierarchy

We use the partial order ($\preccurlyeq$) to compare the deductive power of all considered proof rules $\{\mathrm{DI}_=, \text{C-c}, \text{P-c}, \text{Lie}, \text{Lie}^\circ, \text{Lie}^*, \text{DRI}\}$. For convenience, the propositions of this

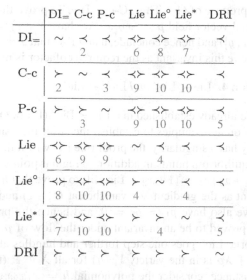

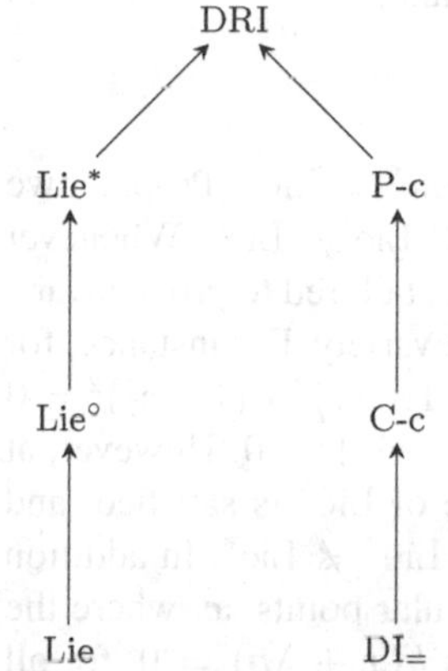

Fig. 2. Hasse diagram. An arrow $R_1 \rightarrow R_2$ means $R_1 \prec R_2$, all other non depicted links mean ($\prec\succ$).

	$DI_=$	C-c	P-c	Lie	Lie°	Lie*	DRI
$DI_=$	$\sim$	$\prec$ 2	$\prec$	$\prec\succ$ 6	$\prec\succ$ 8	$\prec\succ$ 7	$\prec$
C-c	$\succ$ 2	$\sim$	$\prec$ 3	$\prec\succ$ 9	$\prec\succ$ 10	$\prec\succ$ 10	$\prec$
P-c	$\succ$	$\succ$ 3	$\sim$	$\prec\succ$ 9	$\prec\succ$ 10	$\prec\succ$ 10	$\prec$ 5
Lie	$\prec\succ$ 6	$\prec\succ$ 9	$\prec\succ$ 9	$\sim$	$\prec$ 4	$\prec$	$\prec$
Lie°	$\prec\succ$ 8	$\prec\succ$ 10	$\prec\succ$ 10	$\succ$ 4	$\sim$	$\prec$ 4	$\prec$
Lie*	$\prec\succ$ 7	$\prec\succ$ 10	$\prec\succ$ 10	$\succ$	$\succ$ 4	$\sim$	$\prec$ 5
DRI	$\succ$	$\succ$	$\succ$	$\succ$	$\succ$	$\succ$	$\sim$

Fig. 3. Comparison matrix of the deductive power of {$DI_=$, C-c, P-c, Lie, Lie°, Lie*, DRI}. The numbers refer to the propositions.

section are summarized in the comparison matrix (Fig. 3). For instance, Prop. 6 proves that $DI_= \prec\succ$ Lie. Cells without numbers are proved by transitivity of the partial order. For instance, $DI_= \prec$ DRI can be proved using $DI_= \prec$ C-c (Prop. 2) and C-c $\prec$ P-c (Prop. 3) and P-c $\prec$ DRI (Prop. 5). The Hasse diagram (Fig. 2) gives the lattice structure where arrows represent strictly increasing deductive power; every missing edge in the graph represents $\prec\succ$, as shown in the comparison matrix.

We begin by comparing Darboux-based proof rules, i.e. {$DI_=$, C-c, P-c} and then proceed to the Lie-based proof rule family, i.e. {Lie, Lie°, Lie*}. Next, we demonstrate the deductive superiority of the necessary and sufficient conditions in the premise of the proof rule DRI. Finally, we establish that Darboux-based proof rules and Lie-based proof rules form two *distinct* proof rule families; that is, any proof rule from one family is deductively incomparable to any proof rule from the other family.

Proposition 2. $DI_= \prec$ C-c.

Proof. The premise of the rule C-c requires the existence of some $\lambda \in \mathbb{R}$, such that $\mathfrak{L}_{\boldsymbol{p}}(h) = \lambda h$. In particular, $\lambda = 0$ gives the premise of $DI_=$. Thus, $DI_= \preccurlyeq$ C-c. To see that $DI_= \not\succcurlyeq$ C-c, consider the one-dimensional vector field $\boldsymbol{p} = (x)$, we have $\mathfrak{L}_{\boldsymbol{p}}(x) = 1x$, and hence C-c ($\lambda = 1$) concludes that $x = 0$ is an invariant. However, $DI_=$ cannot prove the invariance of $x = 0$ because x is not a conserved quantity in the system. □

Proposition 3. C-c $\prec$ P-c.

Proof. The premise of the rule P-c requires the existence of some $\alpha \in \mathbb{R}[\boldsymbol{x}]$, such that $\mathfrak{L}_{\boldsymbol{p}}(h) = \alpha h$ (equivalently, $\mathfrak{L}_{\boldsymbol{p}}(h) \in \langle h \rangle$). In particular, the constant polynomial gives the premise of C-c. Thus, C-c $\preccurlyeq$ P-c. To prove that C-c $\not\succcurlyeq$ P-c, consider he two-dimensional vector field $\boldsymbol{p} = (xy, x)$, we have $\mathfrak{L}_{\boldsymbol{p}}(x) = xy$ (or equivalently $\mathfrak{L}_{\boldsymbol{p}}(x) \in \langle x \rangle \subset \mathbb{R}[x, y]$) and hence conclude, using P-c, that $x = 0$ is an invariant. However, C-c fails to prove this invariant as the required cofactor is not a scalar. □

Proposition 4. Lie $\prec$ Lie° *and* Lie° $\prec$ Lie*.

Proof. We already established that Lie $\preccurlyeq$ Lie° (Prop. 1) and Lie° $\preccurlyeq$ Lie* (Prop. 1); we give two counterexamples to establish the strict inclusion. (**I**) Lie $\not\succcurlyeq$ Lie°. Whenever the variety has a singularity, the proof rule Lie will fail. Lie° is tailored to prove invariance of equilibrium points in addition to regular points of the variety. For instance, for $\boldsymbol{p} = ((-1+x_1)x_2, x_2(1+x_2))$, Lie fails to prove that $h = (-1+x_1)^2+(1+x_2)^2 = 0$ is invariant as the gradient ∇h vanishes at $(1, -1)$ and $h((1, -1)) = 0$. However, at $(1, -1)$ we also have $p_1 = p_2 = 0$, and hence the premise of Lie° is satisfied, and $h = 0$ is proved to be an invariant under the flow of $\boldsymbol{p}$. (**II**) Lie° $\not\succcurlyeq$ Lie*. In addition to equilibria, Lie* goes one step further and handles all singular points, $\boldsymbol{x}$, where the vector $\boldsymbol{x} + \lambda \boldsymbol{p}$ is in the variety $V_{\mathbb{R}}(h)$ for all $\lambda \in \mathbb{R}$ (that is $h(\boldsymbol{x} + \lambda \boldsymbol{p}) = 0$, for all λ). For instance, consider the polynomial $h = x_1x_2x_3$, its singular locus is given by the three axes $x_1 = x_2 = 0$, $x_1 = x_3 = 0$ and $x_2 = x_3 = 0$. For the vector field $\boldsymbol{p} = (x_1, x_2, x_3)$, the equilibrium point is at the origin $(0, 0, 0)$, which obviously does not contain the entire singular locus of h. Thus, Lie° fails but Lie* succeeds because $h(\boldsymbol{x} + \lambda \boldsymbol{p}) = 0$ when $\boldsymbol{x}$ is a point of one of the axes. □

Proposition 5. P-c $\prec$ DRI *and* Lie* $\prec$ DRI.

Proof. DRI is both necessary and sufficient [9], so we know that P-c $\preccurlyeq$ DRI and Lie* $\preccurlyeq$ DRI. To prove the claim it is left to show that (**I**) P-c $\not\succcurlyeq$ DRI. Consider the following two-dimensional vector field: $\boldsymbol{p} = ((-1 + x_1)(1 + x_1), (-1 + x_2)(1 + x_2))$. The candidate invariant (given by the roots of the Motzkin polynomial) $h = 1-3x_1^2x_2^2+x_1^4x_2^2+x_1^2x_2^4 = 0$ cannot be proved using P-c, as $\mathfrak{L}_{\boldsymbol{p}}(h) \notin \langle h \rangle$. However, the invariance property may be proved using DRI. For this, we need to consider the second-order Lie derivative of h and we prove that $\mathfrak{L}_{\boldsymbol{p}}^{(2)}(h) \in \langle h, \mathfrak{L}_{\boldsymbol{p}}(h) \rangle$. Thus, the premise of DRI holds for $N = 2$. (**II**) Lie* $\not\succcurlyeq$ DRI. Consider the following three-dimensional vector field $\boldsymbol{p} = (-x_2+x_1(1-x_1^2-x_2^2), x_1+x_2(1-x_1^2-x_2^2), x_3)$. We want to prove that $h = (-1+x_1^2+x_2^2)^2+x_3^2 = 0$ is an invariant. In this case, the variety $V_{\mathbb{R}}(h)$ is exactly equal to the singular locus of h which is the two-dimensional unit circle $-1 + x_1^2 + x_2^2 = 0$. However, at all points of this unit circle, the vector field $\boldsymbol{p}$ is equal to $(-x_2, x_1, 0) \neq 0$, which prevents us from using Lie* (because $h((x_1, x_2, 0) + \lambda(-x_2, x_1, 0)) \neq 0$ for some $\lambda \in \mathbb{R}$). The rule DRI proves the invariance of $h = 0$ with $N = 2$. □

To appreciate the difference between $\text{DI}_=$ and Lie, let us note that while the condition in the premise of $\text{DI}_=$ may seem strong (i.e. too conservative), singularities in the invariant candidate do not present a problem for $\text{DI}_=$, whereas the premise of Lie rules out such candidates altogether (see Fig. 4). Indeed, the proof rule Lie cannot prove that $0 = 0$ (the whole space is invariant), whereas this is the most trivial case for $\text{DI}_=$.

Proposition 6 ($\text{DI}_=$ **and** Lie **are incomparable.**). $\text{DI}_= \prec\succ$ Lie.

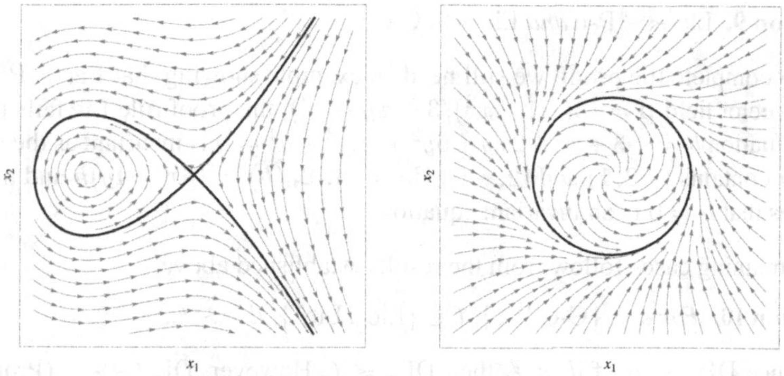

Fig. 4. The invariance of the variety $V_{\mathbb{R}}(x_1^2+x_1^3-x_2^2)$ (**left**) provable using $\mathrm{DI}_=$ (but not Lie since $(0,0)$ is a singular point) and a smooth invariant limit cycle $V_{\mathbb{R}}(x_1^2+x_2^2-1)$ (**right**) provable using Lie (but not $\mathrm{DI}_=$ since it is not an invariant function)

Proof. (I) $\mathrm{DI}_= \not\preccurlyeq$ Lie. For the vector field $\boldsymbol{p} = (-2x_2, -2x_1 - 3x_1^2)$, the equation $x_1^2 + x_1^3 - x_2^2 = 0$ is provable with $\mathrm{DI}_=$ but not Lie, see Fig. 4 (left). (II) $\mathrm{DI}_= \not\succcurlyeq$ Lie. For the vector field $\boldsymbol{p} = (x_1 - x_1^3 - x_2 - x_1x_2^2, x_1 + x_2 - x_1^2x_2 - x_2^3)$, the invariance of the limiting cycle $x_1^2 + x_2^2 - 1 = 0$ is provable with Lie but not $\mathrm{DI}_=$, see Fig. 4 (right). □

We now prove that Lie-based proof rules {Lie, Lie°, Lie*}, and Darboux-based proof rules $\{\mathrm{DI}_=, \text{C-c}, \text{P-c}\}$ are two distinct families of proof rules; that is, any Lie-based proof is deductively incomparable to any Darboux-based proof rule. The following lemma follows from the transitivity of the partial order.

Lemma 1. *If $R_1 \preccurlyeq R_2$ and $R_3 \prec\succ R_1$, then $R_2 \not\preccurlyeq R_3$.*

Proof. Consider three proof rules R_1, R_2 and R_3. If $R_2 \preccurlyeq R_3$, using $R_1 \preccurlyeq R_2$, one gets by transitivity $R_1 \preccurlyeq R_3$, which contradicts the assumption $R_3 \prec\succ R_1$.

Proposition 7. $\mathrm{DI}_= \prec\succ$ Lie*.

Proof. Since Lie $\preccurlyeq$ Lie° (Prop. 1) and Lie° $\preccurlyeq$ Lie* (Prop. 1), then Lie $\preccurlyeq$ Lie*. By Lem. 1, from Lie $\preccurlyeq$ Lie* and $\mathrm{DI}_= \prec\succ$ Lie (Prop. 6), we get Lie* $\not\preccurlyeq \mathrm{DI}_=$. The following example proves that $\mathrm{DI}_= \not\preccurlyeq$ Lie*: Consider the three-dimensional vector field $\boldsymbol{p} = (x_2, -x_1, 0)$. The invariance of the equation $x_3^2 + (-1 + x_1^2 + x_2^2 + x_3^2)^2 = 0$ cannot be established using Lie* (the singular locus is a circle in $\mathbb{R}^3$), but is easily provable using $\mathrm{DI}_=$ as $\mathfrak{L}_{\boldsymbol{p}}(h)$ vanishes. □

Proposition 8. $\mathrm{DI}_= \prec\succ$ Lie°.

Proof. By Lem. 1, from Lie $\preccurlyeq$ Lie° (Prop. 1) and $\mathrm{DI}_= \prec\succ$ Lie (Prop. 6), we get Lie° $\not\preccurlyeq$ $\mathrm{DI}_=$. On the other hand, if $\mathrm{DI}_= \preccurlyeq$ Lie° then, by transitivity $\mathrm{DI}_= \preccurlyeq$ Lie* (since Lie° $\preccurlyeq$ Lie* by Prop. 1), which contradicts $\mathrm{DI}_= \prec\succ$ Lie* (Prop. 7). Thus, $\mathrm{DI}_= \not\preccurlyeq$ Lie°, and the proposition follows. □

Similarly, by substituting $\mathrm{DI}_=$ by Lie, Lie* by P-c, and Lie° by C-c in Prop. 7 and Prop. 8 as well as their respective proofs, we show that:

Proposition 9. Lie $\prec\succ$ P-c *and* Lie $\prec\succ$ C-c.

Proof. To complete the proof, we still need an example showing that Lie $\not\preccurlyeq$ P-c. Consider the vector field $\boldsymbol{p} = (3(-4+x^2), 3+xy-y^2)$, the proof rule Lie fails to prove that the equation $h = -3+x^2+2xy+6y^2+2xy^3+y^4 = 0$ is invariant as the singular locus of h contains $(-2,1)$ and $(2,-1)$. However, $\mathfrak{L}_{\boldsymbol{p}}(h) = (6x-4y)h$ and therefore P-c proves that $h = 0$ is an invariant equation. □

The remaining cases follow from the results established above.

Proposition 10. *For* $d \in \{\text{C-c}, \text{P-c}\}$, $\ell \in \{\text{Lie}^\circ, \text{Lie}^*\}$, $d \prec\succ \ell$.

Proof. Since $\text{DI}_= \prec d$, if $d \preccurlyeq \ell$, then $\text{DI}_= \preccurlyeq \ell$. However, $\text{DI}_= \prec\succ \ell$ (Prop. 7 and Prop. 8). Thus $d \not\preccurlyeq \ell$. Similarly, since $l \succ$ Lie, if $d \succcurlyeq \ell$, then $d \succcurlyeq$ Lie which contradicts $d \prec\succ$ Lie (Prop. 9). Hence $d \not\succcurlyeq \ell$ and the proposition follows. □

Remark 1. Provided the invariant candidate has no singular points, Lie's criterion is known to be both necessary and sufficient to prove invariance properties of level sets [19, Theorem 2.8]. Also, $\text{DI}_=$ characterizes invariant functions [23] but not all invariant equations. On the other hand, for algebraic differential equations, the differential radical criterion in DRI fully characterizes all invariant algebraic sets [9]. Thus, as established in Prop. 5, DRI increases the deductive power of both Darboux-based rules $\{\text{DI}_=, \text{C-c}, \text{P-c}\}$ and Lie-based rules $\{\text{Lie}, \text{Lie}^\circ, \text{Lie}^*\}$, which form different families.

4.2 Complexity

While decidable [28], the complexity of real quantifier elimination is doubly exponential in the number of quantifier alternations [6]. Most existing implementations of real quantifier elimination procedures are based on cylindrical algebraic decomposition (CAD) [2,3], which has doubly-exponential running time in the number of variables.

The purely existential fragment of real quantifier elimination has been shown to exhibit singly exponential time complexity in the number of variables [1]. However, in practice this has not yet led to an efficient decision procedure, so typically it is much more efficient to use CAD. Theoretically, the best bound on the complexity of deciding a sentence in the universal theory of $\mathbb{R}$ is given by $(sd)^{O(n)}$, where s is the number of polynomials in the formula, d their maximum degree and n the number of variables [1].

The premises of rules $\text{DI}_=$, Lie, Lie°, Lie^* are universally quantified sentences in the theory of real arithmetic. One sees from the expression for the complexity bound that it is important for these rules to keep the number of variables low and also that it is desirable to work with polynomials of low degree. In this respect, we would anticipate the rule Lie^* to incur a performance penalty from introducing a fresh variable.

C-c and P-c involve reasoning about multivariate polynomial ideal membership, which is an EXPSPACE-complete problem over $\mathbb{Q}$ [17]. Gröbner basis algorithms allow us to perform membership checks in ideals generated by multivariate polynomials. Significant advances have been made in algorithms for computing Gröbner bases [8] which in practice can be expected to perform very well.

The premise of DRI may be decided using a real quantifier elimination procedure, like any other first-order sentence in the theory of real arithmetic. However, in order to obtain the bound N on the order of the Lie derivatives, one is also required to check for polynomial ideal membership at least $N-1$ times.

5 Square-Free Reduction

In this section we assess the utility of performing square-free reduction of invariant candidates as a means of (i) increasing the deductive power of Lie-based proof rules and (ii) simplifying problems passed to decision procedures for real arithmetic.

5.1 Square-Free Reduction with Lie-Based Proof Rules

While Lie uses a powerful criterion that captures a large class of practically relevant invariant sets, it will fail for some seemingly simple invariant candidates. For instance, the condition in the premise of Lie will not hold when the goal is to prove that $h = x^2 - 6x + 9 = 0$ is invariant, no matter what vector field one considers. The reason for this is simple: $x^2 - 6x + 9$ factorizes into $(x-3)^2$. The problem here lies in the polynomial h itself, rather than the real variety $V_{\mathbb{R}}(h)$. In fact, $V_{\mathbb{R}}(h)$ is exactly the singular locus of h and the proof rule Lie fails because *all* points inside $V_{\mathbb{R}}(h)$ are singular points. More generally, the chain rule implies $\nabla h^k \cdot \boldsymbol{p} = kh^{k-1}\nabla h \cdot \boldsymbol{p}$, which has the consequence that any polynomial h which is not square-free will have vanishing gradient at the real roots of factors with multiplicity greater than 1.

One can eliminate such annoying instances by reducing h to square-free form, which is a basic pre-processing step used in computer algebra systems. The square-free reduction of a polynomial h may be computed efficiently as follows:

$$\mathrm{SF}(h) = \frac{h}{\gcd\left(h, \frac{\partial h}{\partial x_1}, \ldots, \frac{\partial h}{\partial x_n}\right)}. \tag{5}$$

Intuitively, in performing square-free reduction we hope to shrink the singular locus of the original polynomial. If $\mathrm{SL}(\mathrm{SF}(h))$ is the empty set (which is the case for $h = x^2 - 6x + 9$ in the example given above), the proof rule Lie applies to $\mathrm{SF}(h)$ but not to h. In general, $\mathrm{SF}(h)$ may satisfy the assumptions of the proof rules Lie° or Lie*, where h fails to do so. It is always sound to conclude that $h = 0$ is invariant from the knowledge that $\mathrm{SF}(h) = 0$ is invariant, since real varieties remain unaltered under square-free reduction of their defining polynomials [4], i.e. $V_{\mathbb{R}}(h) \equiv V_{\mathbb{R}}(\mathrm{SF}(h))$, thus replacing h with $\mathrm{SF}(h)$ in the premise of Lie, Lie° and Lie* remains sound and enlarges the class of polynomials that these proof rules can work with.

Proposition 11. *For all* $\ell \in \{\text{Lie}, \text{Lie}^{\circ}, \text{Lie}^{*}\}$, $\ell \prec \mathrm{SF}\,\ell$.

This result is unsurprising when one understands that Lie-based proof rules use geometric concepts to prove invariance properties of sets. In fact, the square-free reduction removes some purely algebraic oddities that prevent the geometric condition from holding true when checked syntactically by a machine.

In addition to increasing the deductive power, the square-free reduction reduces the total degree of the polynomial in the invariant candidate and hence serves to reduce the complexity of deciding the conditions in the premise (see Section 4.2). In our implementation, we adopt the convention that invariant candidates supplied to Lie and its generalizations are square-free reduced in a pre-processing step.

5.2 Square-Free Reduction with Darboux-Based Proof Rules

Unlike Lie-based proof rules, it is perhaps surprising that using square-free reduction as a pre-processing step for the proof rules $\text{DI}_=$ and C-c, denoted $\text{SFDI}_=$ and SFC-c respectively, does *not*, in general, increase the deductive power.

Proposition 12. $\text{DI}_= \prec\succ \text{SFDI}_=$.

Proof. (**I**) $\text{DI}_= \not\prec \text{SFDI}_=$. The polynomial $h = x^2y$ is an invariant function for the vector field $\mathbf{p} = (x^2, -2xy)$, thus $\text{DI}_=$ proves the invariance of $h = 0$. However, $\text{SF}(h)$ is not an invariant function for the same vector field, since $\mathfrak{L}_{\mathbf{p}}(\text{SF}(h)) = \mathfrak{L}_{\mathbf{p}}(xy) = -x^2y \neq 0$, thus $\text{SFDI}_=$ fails to prove the invariance of $h = 0$. (**II**) $\text{SFDI}_= \not\prec \text{DI}_=$. Similarly, the polynomial $h = xy$ is an invariant function for the vector field $\mathbf{p} = (x, -y)$, thus $\text{SFDI}_=$ proves the invariance of $x^2y = 0$, since $\text{SF}(x^2y) = h$. However, $\text{DI}_=$ fails to prove the invariance of $x^2y = 0$, because $\mathfrak{L}_{\mathbf{p}}(x^2y) = x^2y \neq 0$. □

Prop. 12 may at first seem counter-intuitive. However, the criterion in the premise of $\text{DI}_=$ is different in that it proves that the candidate h is an *invariant function*. In performing square-free reduction on h, one in general obtains a different function, $\text{SF}(h)$, which need not be conserved in the system if h is conserved or, conversely, may be conserved even if h is not.

The same observation holds for C-c as the SF reduction does not preserve the constant rate exponential decrease (or increase).

Proposition 13. C-c $\prec\succ$ SFC-c.

Proof. (**I**) C-c $\not\prec$ SFC-c. The proof rule C-c proves the invariance of $h = x^2y = 0$ for the vector field $\mathbf{p} = (x^2, y(1-2x))$ as $\mathfrak{L}_{\mathbf{p}}(h) = 1h$. However, C-c cannot prove $\text{SF}(h) = 0$, since $\mathfrak{L}_{\mathbf{p}}(\text{SF}(h)) = \mathfrak{L}_{\mathbf{p}}(xy) = (1-x)\,\text{SF}(h)$. (**II**) SFC-c $\not\prec$ C-c. For the same h, C-c proves the invariance of $\text{SF}(h) = 0$ for the vector field $\mathbf{p} = (x^2, y(1-x))$ as $\mathfrak{L}_{\mathbf{p}}(\text{SF}(h)) = \mathfrak{L}_{\mathbf{p}}(xy) = 1\,\text{SF}(h)$. However, without the SF reduction C-c alone fails to prove the invariance of $h = 0$ for the considered $\mathbf{p}$, as $\mathfrak{L}_{\mathbf{p}}(h) = (x+1)h$. □

After Prop. 12 and 13, one expects P-c to be incomparable with its square-free counterpart. Surprisingly, the proof rules P-c and SFP-c (which applies P-c after the square-free reduction) are in fact equivalent. This follows from the fact that a polynomial is Darboux for a vector field $\mathbf{p}$ if and only if all its factors are also Darboux for the same vector field. Our findings are stated in Prop. 14 and its corollary Prop. 15 (both proofs are available in the report [10]).

Proposition 14. *Let $h = q_1^{m_1} \cdots q_r^{m_r}$ denote the decomposition of the polynomial h into irreducible (over the reals) factors, q_i. Then, h is Darboux for* **p** *if and only if, for all i, q_i is Darboux for* **p**.

Proposition 15. P-c $\sim$ SFP-c.

Remark 2. The condition $\mathfrak{L}_{\mathbf{p}}(p) \in \langle \text{SF}(p) \rangle$ is not sufficient to prove the invariance of $p = 0$. It is therefore an unsound proof rule. Consider the polynomial $p = (-1 + x^2)^2$ and the 1-dimensional vector field $\dot{x} = x$. Although $\mathfrak{L}_{\mathbf{p}}(p) = 4(-1+x^2)x^2 \in \langle -1 + x^2 \rangle = \langle \text{SF}(p) \rangle$, the equation $p = 0$ is not invariant, however, because $x(t) = \pm e^t$. Notice that the proof rule P-c (with or without the square-free reduction) is unable to prove or disprove the invariance of $p = 0$.

5.3 Square-Free Reduction On Differential Radical Invariants (DRI)

Square-free reduction cannot increase the deductive power of the proof rule DRI because its premise is necessary and sufficient to prove invariance of real algebraic sets, which is unaffected by applying SF reduction. However, the computational impact of using square-free reduction with DRI remains an interesting question. Empirically, we observed a better performance of DRI when the SF reduction is applied first. In addition to lowering the degrees of the involved polynomials (as it did for Lie-based proof rules), we observed that the order N_{SF} for $\text{SF}(h)$ is always lower than the order N for h. We, therefore, conjecture $N_{\text{SF}} \leq N$. However, we identified an example for which square-free reduction resulted in a significant ($\times 100$) computational overhead (see [10, Section 5.3]) due to the ideal membership checking (which we perform using Gröbner bases with reverse lexicographic monomial ordering). In our implementation of DRI, called DRI_{opt} in the sequel, we use the square-free reduction only as a pre-processing step for the quantifier elimination problems in the premise of DRI.

Remark 3. Notice that Prop. 14 does not have an analogue for DRI. In other words, if a polynomial equation $h = 0$ is invariant for $\boldsymbol{p}$, its irreducible factors need not define invariant equations themselves. Geometrically, this means that if a variety is invariant under the flow of $\boldsymbol{p}$, its irreducible components need not be invariants under the flow of $\boldsymbol{p}$. For instance, consider the irreducible polynomials $q_1 = y-1$ and $q_2 = x^2+(y-1)^2$. The equation $q_1q_2 = 0$ which is equivalent to $y = 1$, is invariant for $\boldsymbol{p} = (1, 0)$, since the premise of the proof rule DRI holds true for $N = 3$. However, the equation $q_2 = 0$, which is equivalent to $x = 0 \wedge y = 1$, is not an invariant equation for $\boldsymbol{p}$.

6 Experimental Comparison

We empirically compare the running time performance of all the proof rules discussed in this paper on a heterogeneous collection of 76 invariant varieties (available in [10]). The examples we used originate from a number of sources—many come from textbooks on Dynamical Systems; some from the literature on formal verification of hybrid systems; others have been hand-crafted to exploit sweetspots of certain proof rules. In this section, the prefix SF is implicit for all Lie-based proof rules. We consider 4 equally sized classes of invariant sets: (1) 24 smooth invariants, where Lie is both necessary and sufficient, (2) 17 isolated equilibria as trivial (for humans, not machines) equational invariants for which both Lie° and Lie* provide necessary and sufficient conditions, (3) 17 other singularities and high integrals, (4) 18 functional invariants, where $\text{DI}_=$ is necessary and sufficient. The most interesting experimental question we seek to address here is whether the greater generality of the more deductively powerful proof rules also comes at a substantially higher computational cost when assessed across the entire spectrum of examples. As a complement to the theoretical deductive power relationships between the different proof rules (Section 4), we also seek to identify some nuances in the complexity of the conditions in the premises, which the coarse-grained complexity bounds miss, being highly sensitive to the number of variables.

From our experiments it emerges that the proof rules exhibit different (and at times surprising) trade-offs between generality and efficiency. Figure 5 compares the number

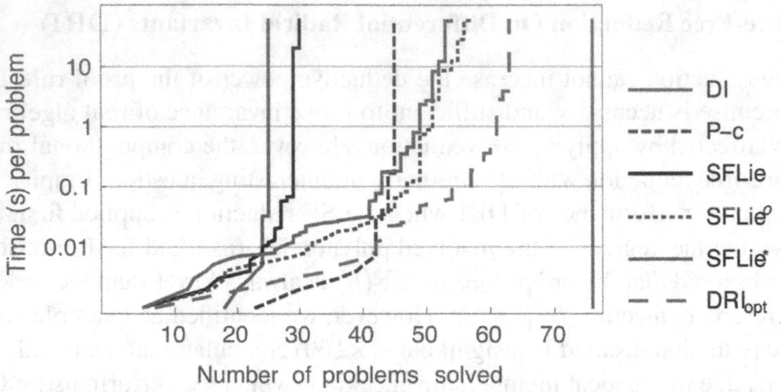

Fig. 5. Experimental performance of proof rules: problems solved per time (log scale)

of invariant varieties that each rule could prove within 60 seconds. The vertical axis shows cumulative time spent on the problems. All runs were performed on an Intel Core i5 1.7GHz machine with 4Gb RAM. Generally, we observe DRI performing very well across the entire spectrum of problem classes. This is very encouraging, but also at first sight appears to defy intuition since it implies that one does not necessarily sacrifice performance when opting to use a more deductively powerful rule. In this graph, we also see that overall Lie° appears to offer an interesting compromise between deductive power and efficiency—it is able to prove a significant body of problems that are out of scope for Lie, while avoiding the complexity penalty which affects Lie* (due to introducing an extra variable).

A more careful analysis of the benchmarks reveals interesting relationships that are obscured in the "big picture"; to see them, one needs to consider the individual classes of invariants for which some of the sufficient conditions in the rules are in fact *necessary and sufficient*. Together with DRI, this yields two *decision procedures* for each class and allows us to focus only on running time performance and assess practicality of proof rules. In Fig. 6, we observe the rules Lie° and Lie* performing very well in proving invariance of isolated equilibria. This is to be expected as Lie° in particular was formulated with this problem class in mind. It is interesting that DRI remains highly competitive here; though its performance is slightly poorer in our set of benchmarks.

It is clear that because proof rules Lie° and Lie* generalize Lie, they will be able to prove every problem in the smooth invariant benchmarks. The running time performance of the three rules is almost identical, with Lie offering a slight speed-up over its generalizations. The premises of Lie° and Lie* impose conditions on states in the singular locus, which is the empty set for smooth invariants; this, in practice, appears to be slightly more expensive than checking an equivalent property that the gradient is non-vanishing on the variety (as in the premise of Lie).

The proof rules $DI_=$ and P-c, corresponding to conditions with historical origins in the study of integrability of dynamical systems, can be seen to perform very well in proving functional invariants, while performing very poorly in benchmarks for isolated equilibria. In proofs of smooth invariants their behaviour is radically different, with $DI_=$ proving only a handful of examples and P-c succeeding in proving most of the

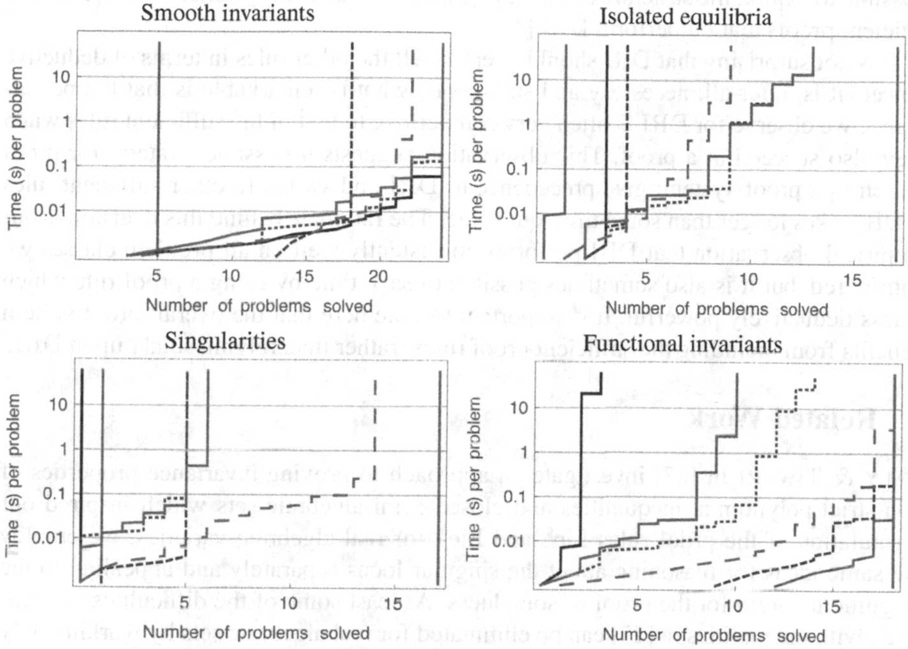

Fig. 6. Number of problems solved per class (log scale)

problems very efficiently. This can be explained by the fact that P-c generalizes $\mathrm{DI}_=$ and is therefore more deductively powerful. P-c appears slightly slower at proving functional invariants, but shows very impressive running time performance for some problems from the smooth invariant benchmarks, where it is the fastest proof rule for many of problems where it succeeds. Comparing running time performance with DRI, we see that DRI is only slightly slower at proving functional invariants than $\mathrm{DI}_=$ and P-c. Again, the performance gap between DRI and the two rules appears to be insignificant for most problems. Theoretically, when P-c proves an invariant, DRI applies conditions that are identical to the premise of P-c. Hence, although DRI is a generalization, this does not come at a significant extra cost for the classes where P-c shows good running time performance. The slightly greater running time of DRI compared to that of P-c can be accounted for by the fact that in our implementation DRI computes the Gröbner basis for *every* order N including for $N = 1$ where such computation is unnecessary.

For functional invariants $\mathrm{DI}_=$ benefits from the fact that the condition in its premise, which requires to show that the Lie derivative evaluates to zero everywhere, is equivalent to showing that the Lie derivative is the zero polynomial, which can be checked very efficiently by symbolic computation, without a decision procedure for real arithmetic.

In the examples featuring singularities and high integrals in the benchmarks we see DRI as the clear winner, simply because there was no other rule that was tailored to work on this class. Indeed, the structure of these invariant sets can be rather involved, making it difficult to characterize in a single proof rule; however, sometimes it is possible to exploit the structure of high integrals inside a proof system and arrive at very efficient proofs that outperform DRI [11].

It is not surprising that DRI should overtake all the other rules in terms of deductive power (it is, after all, necessary and sufficient); what is remarkable is that the performance we observe for DRI is often very competitive to that of the sufficient rules when they also succeed at a proof. This observation suggests a possible strategy for proof search in a proof system: give precedence to DRI and switch to other sufficient rules if DRI takes longer than some time-out value. The rationale behind this decision is our empirical observation that DRI performs consistently well on all problem classes we considered, but it is also sometimes possible to save time by using a proof rule which is less deductively powerful. It is important to note here that the overall proof system benefits from including the sufficient proof rules, rather than relying solely upon DRI.

7 Related Work

TALY & TIWARI in [27] investigate an approach to proving invariance properties of non-strict polynomial inequalities and closed semi-algebraic sets which inspired our formulation of the proof rules Lie$^\circ$ and Lie* for real algebraic varieties; we employ the same ideas for reasoning about the singular locus separately and appealing to the Nagumo theorem for the proof of soundness. At least some of the difficulties encountered with inequalities in [27] can be eliminated for real algebraic sets by working only with square-free reduced polynomials; a reduction we perform as a pre-processing step. Indeed, in [27] the authors provide a simple example in which an invariant polynomial equality is encoded as a polynomial inequality of the form $h^2 \leq 0$ (over the reals this is equivalent to $h^2 = 0$) which falls out of scope of their proof rules. Square-free reduction may be extended to polynomial inequalities using order parity decomposition [7] and makes progress possible on similar problems.

The deductive power of the proof rule DI (which generalizes $\mathrm{DI}_=$ to semi-algebraic sets) combined with other proof rules (such as differential cut or differential weakening) have been investigated in [24]. In this work, we focus on sound proof rules for checking invariance properties of algebraic sets and investigate their deductive power as well as their practical efficiency. To our knowledge, this is the first attempt to structure and empirically compare the performance of the proof rules we considered.

8 Conclusions and Future Work

We have theoretically and empirically compared proof rules for checking invariance properties of real algebraic sets in polynomial vector fields. Our work investigated an important aspect of deductive safety verification of continuous and hybrid dynamical systems. Namely, given the abundance of existing sufficient conditions for invariant equations ($\mathrm{DI}_=$, C-c and P-c, Lie), in addition to the extensions of Lie's criterion, Lie$^\circ$ and Lie*, and the recently developed *necessary and sufficient* conditions for real algebraic invariants (DRI [9]), it is crucial to know whether the gains in deductive power come at the price of greater computational complexity and poor running time performance that would hinder practical applications. The work presented in this paper leads us to arrive at the following conclusions:

- Empirically, we observe that the most deductively powerful rule (DRI) performs very well in checking invariance of polynomial equalities.
- P-c is made redundant by DRI (DRI strictly increases the deductive power of P-c while being equally efficient).
- Reducing polynomials to square-free form is always of benefit to the proof rule Lie and its generalizations, where it yields improvements in both the deductive power and the running time performance.
- We proved that combining SF with the proof rules $DI_=$ and C-c yields new *incomparable* proof rules, whereas SF with P-c is as powerful as P-c alone.
- Performing square-free reduction of an invariant candidate may introduce a performance penalty for DRI and therefore cannot be regarded as an optimization.

It is our hope to extend this work to similarly study proof methods for invariance of semi-algebraic sets in polynomial vector fields. This problem is of fundamental importance to verification of continuous and hybrid systems [20,22] and a better understanding of the factors affecting proof rule efficiency has the potential to be of considerable practical utility. There are currently three available methods that have been proposed for checking invariance of semi-algebraic sets: the method of differential invariants due to Platzer [25], a characterization of invariant semi-algebraic sets due to Liu et al. [15] and a method for closed semi-algebraic sets based on the Nagumo theorem proposed by Taly & Tiwari [27]. The latter approach can unfortunately be shown to be unsound (we identify the problem in [10, Appendix B]); however, this deficiency can be fixed. It would be very interesting to extend the work presented in this paper to investigate the relationship between deductive power and running time performance in the aforementioned methods. We leave this for future work.

Acknowledgments. The authors would like to thank Dr. Ashish Tiwari at SRI International for his kind and informative response to our technical queries and extend special thanks to Dr. Paul B. Jackson at the LFCS, University of Edinburgh, for his valuable help in improving the manuscript.

References

1. Basu, S., Pollack, R., Roy, M.F.: On the combinatorial and algebraic complexity of quantifier elimination. J. ACM 43(6), 1002–1045 (1996)
2. Collins, G.E.: Hauptvortrag: Quantifier elimination for real closed fields by cylindrical algebraic decomposition. In: Brakhage, H. (ed.) GI-Fachtagung 1975. LNCS, vol. 33, pp. 134–183. Springer, Heidelberg (1975)
3. Collins, G.E., Hong, H.: Partial cylindrical algebraic decomposition for quantifier elimination. J. Symb. Comput. 12(3), 299–328 (1991)
4. Cox, D.A., Little, J., O'Shea, D.: Ideals, Varieties, and Algorithms - an introduction to computational algebraic geometry and commutative algebra, 2nd edn. Springer (1997)
5. Darboux, J.G.: Mémoire sur les équations différentielles algébriques du premier ordre et du premier degré. Bulletin des Sciences Mathématiques et Astronomiques 2(1), 151–200 (1878), `http://eudml.org/doc/84988`
6. Davenport, J.H., Heintz, J.: Real quantifier elimination is doubly exponential. J. Symb. Comput. 5(1/2), 29–35 (1988)
7. Dolzmann, A., Sturm, T.: Simplification of quantifier-free formulas over ordered fields. Journal of Symbolic Computation 24, 209–231 (1995)

8. Faugère, J.C.: A new efficient algorithm for computing Gröbner bases without reduction to zero (F5). In: ISSAC, pp. 75–83. ACM, New York (2002)
9. Ghorbal, K., Platzer, A.: Characterizing algebraic invariants by differential radical invariants. In: Ábrahám, E., Havelund, K. (eds.) TACAS 2014. LNCS, vol. 8413, pp. 279–294. Springer, Heidelberg (2014)
10. Ghorbal, K., Sogokon, A., Platzer, A.: A hierarchy of proof rules for checking differential invariance of algebraic sets. Tech. Rep. CMU-CS-14-140, School of Computer Science, Carnegie Mellon University, Pittsburgh, PA (November 2014), `http://reports-archive.adm.cs.cmu.edu/anon/2014/abstracts/14-140.html`
11. Ghorbal, K., Sogokon, A., Platzer, A.: Invariance of conjunctions of polynomial equalities for algebraic differential equations. In: Müller-Olm, M., Seidl, H. (eds.) SAS 2014. LNCS, vol. 8723, pp. 151–167. Springer, Heidelberg (2014)
12. Goriely, A.: Integrability and Nonintegrability of Dynamical Systems. Advanced series in nonlinear dynamics. World Scientific (2001)
13. Lie, S.: Vorlesungen über continuierliche Gruppen mit Geometrischen und anderen Anwendungen. Teubner, Leipzig (1893)
14. Lindelöf, E.: Sur l'application de la méthode des approximations successives aux équations différentielles ordinaires du premier ordre. Comptes rendus hebdomadaires des séances de l'Académie des sciences 116, 454–458 (1894)
15. Liu, J., Zhan, N., Zhao, H.: Computing semi-algebraic invariants for polynomial dynamical systems. In: EMSOFT, pp. 97–106. ACM (2011)
16. Matringe, N., Moura, A.V., Rebiha, R.: Generating invariants for non-linear hybrid systems by linear algebraic methods. In: Cousot, R., Martel, M. (eds.) SAS 2010. LNCS, vol. 6337, pp. 373–389. Springer, Heidelberg (2010)
17. Mayr, E.W.: Membership in polynomial ideals over Q is exponential space complete. In: Cori, R., Monien, B. (eds.) STACS 1989. LNCS, vol. 349, pp. 400–406. Springer, Heidelberg (1989)
18. Nagumo, M.: Über die Lage der Integralkurven gewöhnlicher Differentialgleichungen. Proceedings of the Physico-Mathematical Society of Japan 24, 551–559 (1942) (in German)
19. Olver, P.J.: Applications of Lie Groups to Differential Equations. Springer (2000)
20. Platzer, A.: Differential dynamic logic for hybrid systems. J. Autom. Reasoning 41(2), 143–189 (2008)
21. Platzer, A.: Differential-algebraic dynamic logic for differential-algebraic programs. J. Log. Comput. 20(1), 309–352 (2010)
22. Platzer, A.: The complete proof theory of hybrid systems. In: LICS, pp. 541–550. IEEE (2012)
23. Platzer, A.: A differential operator approach to equational differential invariants - (invited paper). In: Beringer, L., Felty, A. (eds.) ITP 2012. LNCS, vol. 7406, pp. 28–48. Springer, Heidelberg (2012)
24. Platzer, A.: The structure of differential invariants and differential cut elimination. Logical Methods in Computer Science 8(4), 1–38 (2012)
25. Platzer, A., Clarke, E.M.: Computing differential invariants of hybrid systems as fixedpoints. In: Gupta, A., Malik, S. (eds.) CAV 2008. LNCS, vol. 5123, pp. 176–189. Springer, Heidelberg (2008)
26. Sankaranarayanan, S., Sipma, H.B., Manna, Z.: Constructing invariants for hybrid systems. Form. Methods Syst. Des. 32(1), 25–55 (2008)
27. Taly, A., Tiwari, A.: Deductive verification of continuous dynamical systems. In: FSTTCS. LIPIcs, vol. 4, pp. 383–394 (2009)
28. Tarski, A.: A decision method for elementary algebra and geometry. Bull. Amer. Math. Soc. 59 (1951)
29. Tiwari, A.: Abstractions for hybrid systems. Form. Methods Syst. Des. 32(1), 57–83 (2008)
30. Walter, W.: Ordinary Differential Equations. Springer, New York (1998)

Effective Abstractions for Verification under Relaxed Memory Models

Andrei Dan[1], Yuri Meshman[2], Martin Vechev[1], and Eran Yahav[2]

[1] ETH Zurich
[2] Technion

Abstract. We present a new abstract interpretation based approach for automatically verifying concurrent programs running on relaxed memory models.

Our approach is based on three key insights: (i) behaviors of relaxed models (e.g. TSO and PSO) are naturally captured using explicit encodings of *store buffers*. Directly using such encodings for program analysis is challenging due to *shift operations* on buffer contents that result in significant loss of analysis precision. We present a new abstraction of the memory model that eliminates expensive shifting of store buffer contents and significantly improves the precision and scalability of program analysis, (ii) an encoding of store buffer sizes that leverages knowledge of the abstract interpretation domain, further improving analysis precision, and (iii) a source-to-source transformation that realizes the above two techniques: given a program P and a relaxed memory model M, it produces a new program P_M where the behaviors of P running on M are over-approximated by the behavior of P_M running on sequential consistency (SC). This step makes it possible to directly use state-of-the-art analyzers under SC.

We implemented our approach and evaluated it on a set of finite and infinite-state concurrent algorithms under two memory models: Intel's x86 TSO and PSO. Experimental results indicate that our technique achieves better precision and efficiency than prior work: we can automatically verify algorithms with fewer fences, faster and with lower memory consumption.

1 Introduction

To improve performance, modern hardware architectures support relaxed memory models. A relaxed memory model allows the underlying architecture to reorder memory operations and execute them non-atomically. As a result, a concurrent program can have additional behaviors that would not be possible to obtain under the intuitive, sequentially consistent setting [16]. These additional relaxed behaviors complicate the task of reasoning about the correctness of the program, manually and automatically.

This necessitates the development of new, scalable and precise analysis techniques for automatic verification of (potentially infinite-state) concurrent programs running on relaxed memory models. Automatic verification in this setting is a challenging problem as the relaxed memory model can significantly increase the number and diversity of new behaviors, which in turn affects the overall precision and scalability of the analysis.

Our Approach. We present a new analysis system for verifying concurrent programs running on relaxed memory models such as Intel's x86 TSO and PSO buffered memory models. Our system builds upon three core concepts:

D. D'Souza et al. (Eds.): VMCAI 2015, LNCS 8931, pp. 449–466, 2015.

First, we present a new abstraction that eliminates some of the expensive work in managing the store buffers required by the memory model, thus significantly reducing the analysis effort and improving its precision. This abstraction is also directly applicable and useful for other verification frameworks, both finite and infinite-state (e.g., bounded model checking, abstract interpretation and predicate abstraction).

Second, we show how to leverage knowledge of the particular program analysis used in this work (abstract interpretation with numerical domains) by encoding the size of the store buffers in a way that reduces the loss of precision under that abstract domain.

Third, we address the problem of building a robust analyzer that incorporates the above two concepts. We present a source-to-source transformation that enables direct reuse of program analyzers under sequential consistency for verifying concurrent programs running on relaxed memory models. That is, given a program P, a specification S and a memory model M, the transformation automatically constructs a new program P_M such that if $P_M \models_{SC} S$ then $P \models_M S$. The program P_M contains *an abstraction of the relaxed behaviors induced by* M, thereby ensuring soundness of the approach.

While prior works [10,3,18] also suggest source-to-source transformations, we show experimentally that our approach is more precise and efficient: it enables verification of (infinite-state) concurrent algorithms that prior work cannot, and for programs where prior work succeeds, our approach is faster and requires less memory.

In addition to presenting the above techniques (useful for both finite and infinite-state verification), this work represents one of the few studies on using abstract interpretation for verifying properties of infinite-state concurrent programs running on relaxed memory models and what's more, our approach requires no user annotations.

Main Contributions. The main contributions of this paper are:

- A new abstraction for the store buffers of the memory model that eliminates expensive shifting of buffer contents. This abstraction reduces the workload on subsequent program analyzers and improves their scalability and precision.
- A source-to-source transformation that realizes the new abstraction (and the memory model effects), producing a program that can be soundly analyzed with verifiers for sequential consistency. The translation also leverages knowledge of the underlying abstract domain in order to encode the size of the store buffers in a way which reduces the overall loss of analysis precision.
- A complete implementation of the approach integrated with CONCURINTERPROC [12], a tool based on abstract interpretation [8] with numerical abstract domains that can analyze infinite-state concurrent programs under sequential consistency.
- A thorough empirical evaluation on a range of challenging concurrent algorithms. Experimental results indicate that our technique is superior in both precision and efficiency to prior work and enables verification, for the first time, of several concurrent algorithms running on Intel's x86 TSO and PSO memory models.

2 Overview

In this section we illustrate our approach on a running example. The goal of this section is to give some intuition about and informal understanding of the work. Full formal details are provided in later sections.

```
        initial values: X=0  Y=0
Thread 1:                      Thread 2:

1: X = 1                       1: Y = 1
2: a = Y                       2: b = X
3: X = a + 1                   3: Y = b + 1
4: fence                       4: fence
5:                             5:
```

$$\text{Spec:}\ ((pc_1 = 5) \wedge (pc_2 = 5)) \Rightarrow (X + Y \geq 2)$$

Fig. 1. Example program

To understand our approach, consider the concurrent program shown in Fig. 1. It consists of two threads that share the integer variables `X` and `Y` (variables `a` and `b` are local to each thread). The figure also shows an assertion which holds once both threads have completed their execution, namely that `X + Y` $\geq$ 2. Our objective is to verify that the program satisfies this assertion under relaxed memory models such as Intel's x86 TSO and PSO.

2.1 Relaxed Behaviors

In the example in Fig. 1, Thread 1 can execute the statements at labels `1` and `2` in the opposite order. Similarly, Thread 2 can execute the statements at labels `1` and `2` in the opposite order due to the nature of relaxed memory models such as TSO. Relaxed models such as TSO allow program statements to be executed out of order, resulting in behaviors not possible under sequential consistency. Under TSO, a store and a load (by the same thread) accessing different memory locations are allowed to be reordered. Therefore after both threads execute the statements at the labels `1` and `2`, one can end up in a state where the state is `X = Y = 0`. This state is impossible to obtain under sequential consistency (SC), yet is allowed under TSO. Weaker models such as PSO allow not only the reordering of store and load instructions but even the reordering of two stores (if they access different memory locations). In general, such reorderings are possible because the processor maintains store buffers per each thread, and delays expensive writes to shared memory. For instance, in Intel's x86 TSO, every thread updates a FIFO store buffer where the thread enqueues its shared memory writes and the memory sub-system dequeues these buffered writes (in the order of least recent write first) non-deterministically and updates shared memory.

2.2 SC Equivalence vs. Flexible Safety Specifications

When considering the problem of verifying programs running on relaxed models, there are two general choices for how we select the safety property to be verified, each influencing the design of the analysis abstraction. One direction is to develop analyzers that try to prove and (if need to) enforce that the relaxed program produces results equivalent to the sequentially consistent program (and, if not equivalent, to insert fences that make it so). This line of work was pioneered by Shasha and Snir [22], with various works later improving on the precision of the analysis and fence inference [23,2].

Another direction, and the one pursued in this paper, is to develop analyzers which can enforce arbitrary safety properties, not only equivalence. This is advantageous for two reasons:

(i) the relaxed program might produce behaviors which are valid yet do not exist under SC, and enforcing equivalence leads to generation of redundant fences. To illustrate this point, consider the program in Fig. 1. As mentioned before, the state `X = Y = 1` is reachable under TSO at the end of the program. This state is impossible to reach under SC. If we aim to achieve SC equivalence, additional `fence` statements should be inserted in the program to prevent re-orderings that lead to this state. If we focus on ensuring the safety specification, only the current fences at labels `4` in the two threads are sufficient for verification; and

(ii) even if equivalence is the right specification, it may be difficult to produce an analysis that can prove equivalence; writing a more program specific, flexible safety property (which enforces the same constraints) may be easier to verify. We illustrate this point in Section 6: we show that [2] produces redundant fences, which our analysis avoids.

2.3 Our Approach

We now discuss the flow taken in this work. For ease of presentation, we directly present the source-to-source transformation with the abstraction embedded into that transformation.

Step 1: Buffer analysis A preliminary step of our approach is a buffer-size analysis of the input program (recall that a buffer exists in each thread). This analysis outputs an over-approximation of the size of the write buffer at each point in the program. For our running example, the analysis determines that at line `1` (of both threads), the maximum write buffer size is 1, at line `3` the maximum buffer size is 2, and at line `5`, the maximum buffer size is 0 (due to `fence`).

Step 2: Abstraction and source-to-source transformation A key step of our approach is an abstraction that eliminates buffer shifting and a source-to-source transformation realizing that abstraction (we focus on presenting both together). Here, the write buffer of each thread is directly encoded into the source code of the target program. The transformation (with abstraction) proceeds by processing the original program in a statement by statement manner. In Fig. 2, we show the result of applying our transformation for TSO on the statements of Thread 1. We next informally discuss this procedure.

To encode the store buffers used by the relaxed memory model, we introduce two kinds of variables. An example of the first kind is $\mathtt{X_1t_1}$, which captures the value of the first write to shared variable `X` found in the buffer of thread $\mathtt{t_1}$. An example of the second kind is the boolean variable $\mathtt{flagX_1t_1}$, which denotes whether or not the first element of the write buffer of $\mathtt{t_1}$ stores a write to shared variable `X` (as in general the first write found in the buffer of thread $\mathtt{t_1}$ could be to some other shared variable).

Returning to our example, since the buffer is initially empty, the statement `X = 1` is translated to two updates. First, the new variable X_1t_1 is updated and set to `1`, and second, the boolean variable flagX_1t_1 is set to `true`.

However, simply updating the two newly generated variables is not enough because under TSO (and PSO), the memory sub-system can trigger a non-deterministic flush of a thread's store buffer at any point (the flush operation dequeues the least recent write in the buffer and updates shared memory with that write). To capture this behavior, we add a special flush code fragment after every program statement. Therefore, in our example, a flush is added after the statements at labels `1,2` and `3`. The flush code fragments following the statements at labels `1` and `2` are identical. The loop captures the non-deterministic effects of the flush semantics: either the flush takes place and the write stored in X_1t_1 is flushed to shared memory (and if so, the boolean variable flagX_1t_1 is reset to `false`), or the program continues with no changes.

Original statement:	Transformed statement:
X = 1	X_1t_1 = 1 flagX_1t_1 = **true**

flush	**while** random **do**
	  if flagX_1t_1 **then**
	    X = X_1t_1
	    flagX_1t_1 = **false**

a = Y	a = Y

flush	**while** random **do**
	  if flagX_1t_1 **then**
	    X = X_1t_1
	    flagX_1t_1 = **false**

X = a + 1	**if** flagX_1t_1 **then**
	  X_2t_1 = a + 1
	  flagX_2t_1 = **true**
	else
	  X_1t_1 = a + 1
	  flagX_1t_1 = **true**

flush	**while** random **do**
	  if flagX_1t_1 **then**
	    X = X_1t_1
	    flagX_1t_1 = **false**
	  else if flagX_2t_1 **then**
	    X = X_2t_1
	    flagX_2t_1 = **false**

fence	assume($\neg$ flagX_1t_1 $\wedge$ $\neg$ flagX_2t_1)

Fig. 2. The result of applying our transformation for TSO on Thread 1 from Fig. 1. The `flush` statements are not part of the program but need to be captured by the translation (and are inserted after every program statement).

Statement `a = Y` is translated without change as the buffer size analysis determines that `Y` is never written to by Thread 1 and hence the value is always read from shared memory (as opposed to the buffer).

Next, statement `X = a + 1` is translated. The generated code fragment first tests if flagX_1t_1 is set to `true`. This answers the question of whether the first position in the buffer is already taken. We need this test as it is statically unknown whether a non-deterministic flush has fired. Depending on the result of the test, we now know where to write the value `a + 1`. If the first position of the write buffer is occupied, `a + 1` is stored to the second element of the write buffer and the appropriate flag is set (i.e., $\texttt{flagX}_2\texttt{t}_1$ is set to `true`). Otherwise, we store the value `a + 1` to the first position in the buffer and set the appropriate flag.

We next generate the flush code fragment after the statement at label `3`. This flush code is slightly different than the previous two flush fragment because at this point in the translation, the buffer-size analysis indicates that the maximum possible buffer size is 2. Therefore, we need to dynamically check what the actual size of the buffer is and flush the appropriate entry. This can either be the variable $\texttt{X}_1\texttt{t}_1$ or the variable $\texttt{X}_2\texttt{t}_1$. Naturally, once the write to shared memory is completed, we set the corresponding auxiliary boolean variable accordingly: $\texttt{flagX}_1\texttt{t}_1$ or $\texttt{flagX}_2\texttt{t}_1$.

A key point is that we *do not* shift the store buffer contents on `flush` as a direct encoding of the memory model would do (and as previous approaches do ; see [10], [18]. Doing less work on a `flush` leads to more precise analysis and greater efficiency than prior work.

Finally, the fence statement at label `4` ensures that all writes before the fence are flushed to shared memory. An assume statement on both boolean variables captures this requirement.

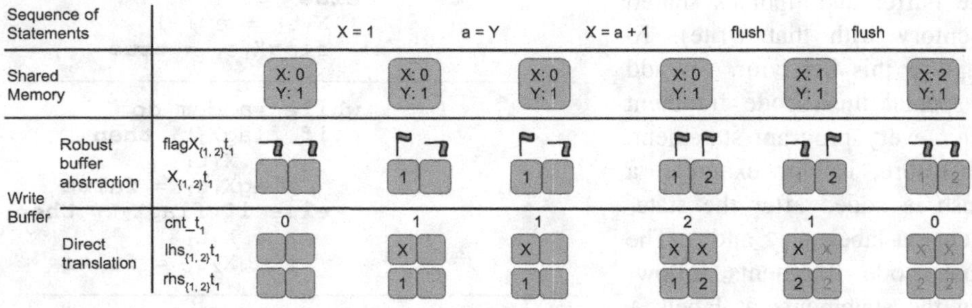

Fig. 3. The effect of a program trace on shared state and the state used by the two translations. The figure shows only statements of Thread 1 as well as flushes affecting Thread 1's write buffer.

An example trace. In Fig. 3 we illustrate how a particular program trace updates the shared memory and the newly generated variables. The first line of that figure shows the sequence of statements in the trace. The second line shows the shared memory state (before and after each statement is executed). The third line (titled "robust buffer abstraction") shows the values of the newly generated variables. Here, the first square box corresponds to $\texttt{X}_1\texttt{t}_1$ and the second square box corresponds to $\texttt{X}_2\texttt{t}_1$. Similarly, the first flag corresponds to $\texttt{flagX}_1\texttt{t}_1$ and the second flag to $\texttt{flagX}_2\texttt{t}_1$. If a flag is raised, it means the variable is set to `true`; otherwise it is set to `false`. For now we can ignore the fourth line (this is a previous transformation used by [10] and [18] and is discussed later in the paper in Section 4). The trace we show and discuss is:

(i) initially, $\texttt{flagX}_1\texttt{t}_1$ and $\texttt{flagX}_2\texttt{t}_1$ are set to `false` and shared variables `X` and `Y` contain 0;
(ii) thread 2 executes `Y = 1` and a flush updates `Y` in shared memory (the trace in Fig. 3 starts after this step);

(iii) thread 1 executes `X = 1` resulting in $\texttt{flagX}_1\texttt{t}_1$ being set to `true` and $\texttt{X}_1\texttt{t}_1$ containing the value 1;
(iv) thread 1 reads `a = Y`, obtaining the value 1 (Fig. 3 omits local variable a, so no changes are shown);
(v) thread 1 executes `X = a + 1` resulting in $\texttt{flagX}_2\texttt{t}_1$ being set to `true` and $\texttt{X}_2\texttt{t}_1$ containing the value 2 at which point we have two writes in the store buffer of Thread 1;
(vi) a flush of Thread 1's buffer results in $\texttt{X}_1\texttt{t}_1$'s value being written to shared memory setting `X` to 1 and $\texttt{flagX}_1\texttt{t}_1$ is set to `false` to mark that the flush completed;
(vii) a flush of Thread 1's buffer results in `X` being set to 2 in shared memory and in setting $\texttt{flagX}_2\texttt{t}_1$ to `false`;

Step 3: Program Analysis Once the translated (and potentially infinite-state) concurrent program is obtained, the final step is to analyze it and attempt to prove the property of interest. Any analysis can be used; in this work we chose logico-numerical abstract domains for the following reasons:(i) there are readily available tools that implement these domains (e.g., we use CONCURINTERPROC, which implements convex numerical domains combined with boolean values), allowing us to focus on the novel parts of the work, and (ii) our benchmarks manipulate numerical variables and the properties we prove depend only on such numerical manipulations. We do note, however, that our abstraction can be useful in any setting, not just that of abstract interpretation.

The resulting analysis outputs invariants for each pair of thread locations. For instance, at labels `5`, when both threads have completed, a fragment of the resulting invariant produced by the analysis is:

$$\neg\texttt{flagX}_1\texttt{t}_1 \wedge \neg\texttt{flagX}_2\texttt{t}_1 \wedge \texttt{X} \geq \texttt{X}_1\texttt{t}_1 \wedge \texttt{X}_1\texttt{t}_1 \geq 1 \wedge \ldots$$

This invariant contains both a boolean part, consisting of concrete values for the auxiliary variables $\texttt{flagX}_1\texttt{t}_1$ and $\texttt{flagX}_2\texttt{t}_1$, and a numerical part in the polyhedra numerical domain: $\texttt{X} \geq \texttt{X}_1\texttt{t}_1$ and $\texttt{X}_1\texttt{t}_1 \geq 1$.

Both auxiliary boolean variables are `false`, which corresponds to an empty write buffer for Thread 1. From the numerical inequalities, we conclude that $\texttt{X} \geq 1$. Similar constraints are obtained for the variables in Thread 2, allowing us to conclude that $\texttt{Y} \geq 1$. Thus, we can conclude that the specification $\texttt{X} + \texttt{Y} \geq 2$ holds when both threads terminate.

We note that for our running example, direct handling of write buffer contents as used in [18] fails to verify the specification, even though the program satisfies it. This is because a direct, shift-based handling causes precision loss during the analysis. In the next section, we formally present our abstraction and transformation, discuss how it compares to prior work, and show why it leads to more scalable and precise analysis.

3 Background

In this section we provide a brief review of previous direct encoding techniques as well as terms that will be useful for our new abstraction in Section 4.

3.1 Direct Source-to-Source Encoding

Let $Prog$ be the set of all programs, Rmm be the set of relaxed memory models (in this paper $Rmm = \{x86\ TSO, PSO\}$), and $\mathbb{N}$ the natural numbers. The translation mechanism can be seen as a function with the signature: $T : (Prog \times Rmm \times \mathbb{N}) \rightarrow Prog$ where $P \in Prog$ is an input program, $M \in Rmm$ is a relaxed memory model, and $b \in \mathbb{N}$ is a bound on the buffer size.

The meaning of buffer size bound b Key elements of the x86 TSO memory model (and the PSO memory model) are the store buffers found between each thread and shared memory. Given buffer size bound b, the output of the translation is a new program $P_M \in Prog$ where $P_M = T(P, M, b)$.

By construction, the behavior of P_M under sequential consistency semantics captures the behavior of P under the relaxed model M, with the exception of potentially overflowing the store buffer. That is, if during the execution of P_M an attempt is made to store more than b elements to the buffer, then the program P_M aborts.

If we manage to verify that P_M satisfies the specification (without aborting), we can guarantee that P satisfies the specification under the memory model M. If the program P_M aborts, we may have to refine our model and retry verification with a larger buffer size.

It is generally impossible to statically determine the maximal store buffer size reachable during a program execution. However, in practice, static analysis can over-approximate the maximal possible store buffer size. We distinguish two cases:(i) the over-approximated value is finite. In this case, the buffer size over-approximation is useful in optimizing the transformation procedure, and (ii) the over-approximated value is unbounded. In this case, the transformation has a fixed buffer bound defined by the user.

3.2 Direct Translation

We first discuss the intuitive, direct translation function which encodes the relaxed memory semantics into the program source code. This direct translation is used by prior works focusing on infinite-state verification [10,18]. We denote this translation by:

$$T_D : (Prog \times Rmm \times \mathbb{N}) \rightarrow Prog.$$

In the following, we use $Local$ to denote the set of local variables (per thread) and $Shared$ the set of global shared variables. Expressions, both numerical and boolean, can refer only to local variables. Statements can read and write global variables. We use $Stmt$ to denote all statements.

The translation encodes relaxed memory store buffers using temporary variables. For each statement of $P \in Prog$ we generate a code segment that captures the relaxed behavior of that statement. We define a transformation function at statement level:

$$[\![\,]\!] \in Stmt \times Thread \times \mathbb{N} \rightarrow Stmt.$$

The direct translation introduces new variables for capturing the effect of storing values into store-buffers instead of directly into main memory. For TSO (the translation for PSO is similar), the buffer is modeled with the following local variables:

- variable identifiers: lhs₁t, lhs₂t, ..., lhs$_b$t, where b is the maximum size of the buffer. The identifier of a global variable is an integer – it stores an index of the shared variable to be written to shared memory.
- buffer content values: $\texttt{rhs}_1\texttt{t}$, $\texttt{rhs}_2\texttt{t}$, ..., $\texttt{rhs}_b\texttt{t}$ – each stores the actual value to be written to shared memory.
- buffer counter: cnt_t takes values in the range $[0, b]$ – it stores the size of the buffer during execution.

$[\![X = r]\!]_b^t$

```
if (cnt_t=b)
  abort("overflow")

cnt_t = cnt_t+1
if (cnt_t=1)
  lhs1t = X
  rhs1t = r
...
if (cnt_t=b)
  lhsbt = X
  rhsbt = r
```

$[\![r = X]\!]_b^t$

```
if (cnt_t=n)∧
     (lhsbt=X)
  r = rhsbt
...
else if (cnt_t=n)∧
     (lhs1t=X)
  r = rhs1t
else
  r = X
```

$[\![flush]\!]_b^t$

```
while random do
  if (cnt_t>0)
   ▷ ∀ X ∈ Shared :
     if (lhs1t = X)
       X = rhs1t
   ▷ end
   if (cnt_t>1)
     lhs1t = lhs2t
     rhs1t = rhs2t
     ...
     if (cnt_t=b)
       lhs(b-1)t = lhsbt
       rhs(b-1)t = rhsbt
   cnt_t = cnt_t-1
   yield
```

$[\![fence]\!]_b^t$

```
assume
(cnt_t = 0)
```

Fig. 4. Direct TSO Translation Rules of T_D

Fig. 4 presents the rules of the direct translation. In the translation of each statement, the generated sequence of statements is atomic. An exception to that rule is the flush in which only the inside of the generated loop is atomic and context switches are allowed between the loop iterations.

Write to a global variable $[\![X = r]\!]_b^t$: the store to a global variable X first checks whether it can exceed the buffer bound b, and if so, the program aborts. Otherwise, the counter is incremented. The rest of the logic checks the value of the counter and updates the corresponding local variables. The global variable X is not updated and only local variables are modified.

Read from a global variable $[\![r = X]\!]_b^t$: the load from a global variable X checks the current depth of the buffer and then loads from the corresponding local variable. When the buffer is empty (i.e., cnt_t = 0), or the variable has no occurrences in the buffer, the load is performed directly from shared memory.

Fence statement $[\![fence]\!]_b^t$: the fence waits for the buffer to be empty before executing.

Flush procedure $[\![flush]\!]_b^t$: the flush procedure is translated into a non-deterministic loop (we use random). If the buffer counter is positive and the entry at position 1 in the buffer ($\texttt{lhs}_1\texttt{t}$) refers to X, then the write value at position 1 (i.e., $\texttt{rhs}_1\texttt{t}$) is stored in X. The contents of the local variables are then updated by shifting: the content of each

$x_{j+1}t$ is moved to its predecessor x_jt where $1 \leq j < b$. Finally, the buffer count is decremented.

To encode non-deterministic flushes of the memory sub-system, a flush procedure is added by the translation function to the output program. The role of the flush procedure is to soundly encode the possible non-deterministic flushes of the store buffer, triggered by the memory subsystem. Naively, a faithful translation of the flush action requires placing the flush code after *each* statement of the program that accesses shared memory. However, this can be optimized using a simple preliminary static analysis that finds cases where the store buffer is guaranteed to be empty (and thus no flush is needed), or guaranteed to be bounded by a fixed size (and thus the flush code can be simplified).

Trace Example. Returning to Fig. 3 of Section 2, the last row of the figure (titled "Direct translation") illustrates how a given trace is processed using the direct translation. The key here is the processing of the first `flush` statement, where the contents of the store buffer are explicitly shifted. As we will see next, such explicit shifting is in fact completely avoided by our new abstraction and subsequent translation.

Shortcomings of the Direct Translation. The main problem with the direct translation is that it performs operations that have a devastating effect on verification. Specifically: (i) the `flush` operation performs a shift of the array content, an operation that is *very costly* and makes it harder to track the relationships between values; (ii) the sizes of store buffers are tracked via numerical variables (i.e., `cnt_t`), the value of which may be lost under abstraction. As we show in Section 5, these shortcomings cause verification using direct translation to fail in more than 50% of our benchmarks, and to be costly for the remaining ones. In the next section, we present an abstraction and a translation which address these two shortcomings.

4 Abstraction-Guided Translation

We next present our new translation, which is based on a novel abstraction of the store buffers. We also contrast our approach with the direct encoding discussed earlier:

$$T_V : (Prog \times Rmm \times \mathbb{N}) \rightarrow Prog.$$

Our presentation focuses on the x86 TSO memory model (the details for PSO are similar). We first discuss the new abstraction, which eliminates shifting of values in the store buffers. Here, when an element is flushed from the buffer, the other elements maintain their position, significantly reducing the cost of the flush operation. This abstraction is generally applicable for any analysis. We then discuss an approach for replacing the counter variables that track the current size of the write buffers with boolean variables, which also improves precision when using abstract interpretation based analysis.

4.1 Robust Buffer Abstraction – Eliminating Buffer Shifting

The flush procedure appears at multiple places in the resulting program and hence its operation is critical to the overall precision and scalability of the analysis. As discussed earlier, the direct translation encodes a store buffer using two *bounded* arrays per thread

$[\![X = r]\!]_b^t$

```
if OR(b,t)
  abort("overflow")
else
if OR(b-1,t)
  X_bt = r
  flagX_bt = true
else
if OR(b-2,t)
  ...
else
  X_1t = r
  flagX_1t = true
```

$[\![r = X]\!]_b^t$

```
if (flagX_bt)
  r = X_bt
else
if (flagX_{b-1}t)
  ...
else
  r = X
```

$[\![flush]\!]_b^t$

```
while random do
  yield
  if (flagX_1t)
    X = X_1t
    flagX_1t = false
  else
  if (flagY_1t)
    Y = Y_1t
    flagY_1t = false
  else
  if (flagX_2t)
    ...
```

$[\![fence]\!]_b^t$

```
assume
(¬OR(b,t) ∧
 ... ∧
 ¬OR(1,t))
```

Fig. 5. Abstraction-guided translation rules (i.e. T_V) for TSO.

(i.e. `lhs` and `rhs`) and a counter. If the bound is reached during analysis, an overflow error is triggered and the analysis aborts. When this happens, the user may increase the buffer bound, transform the program using the new bound, and rerun the analysis on the newly obtained program. The flush routine in the direct translation is implemented using a non-deterministic loop. In the loop body, the first element in the store buffer (the oldest) is flushed to memory. Next, the remaining elements are *shifted* one position to the left in the buffer. An advantage of shifting is that it frees entries at the end of the arrays encoding the buffer, thus creating free space for buffering additional store operations.

Key Idea: Our observation is that we can handle the flush operation without shifting the array content, thus obtaining an abstraction (over-approximation) of the relaxed memory semantics. This approximation is sound (the proof is presented in Section 4.4) but may *introduce additional cases of overflow*. That is, if a program reaches an overflow when analyzed with our abstraction, it is possible that this overflow may not occur when using the direct, shifting encoding. However, we believe such situations are very rare in practice – in our evaluation in Section 5, no additional such overflows appeared in any of the benchmarks. We formally discuss how our abstraction is incorporated into the translation later in Section 4.3.

4.2 Replacing Counters with Boolean Flags

Another ingredient of our approach is leveraging properties of the underlying program analysis. Unlike the general abstraction above, here we discuss an optimization suitable for abstract interpretation based analysis with numerical domains.

The direct translation keeps designated counters to track the current position in store buffers. When using numerical abstract domains such as Octagon [19] and Polyhedra [9], the exact numerical value of a variable may be abstracted away at program join points. This abstraction, desirable in most cases, has negative effects when applied to key variables such as buffer counters. We would therefore like to keep the values of buffer counters even when different values for the count reach program join points.

Towards this, we use a logico-numerical domain, which combines a numerical domain and a logical domain that tracks boolean combinations of predicates. Rather than storing values of buffer counters as integers in the numerical part of the domain, we encode them using boolean variables in the logical part. This allows us to naturally maintain a disjunction of possible values for counters, without joining them. Using boolean variables to track buffer sizes therefore improves the precision of the analysis inside the flush procedure by differentiating cases where values of counter variables differ. This encoding can be viewed as a form of trace partitioning [20], where joins are delayed based on certain key values (in our case, the values of counter variables).

4.3 New Translation Rules

The source-to-source translation presented next incorporates both of the ideas described above. It replaces *cnt_t* counter variables with boolean variables. For each shared variable $\mathtt{X} \in \mathit{Shared}$, write buffer index $i \in [1, b]$, and thread identifier $t \in \mathit{Thread}$, a boolean variable $\mathtt{flagX}_i\mathtt{t}$ is added.

If $\mathtt{flagX}_i\mathtt{t}$ is `true`, then there is a shared variable `X` write in the thread t write buffer, to position i.

The x86 TSO memory model has a single write buffer per thread. This translates to the invariant: for a fixed $i \in [1, b]$ and a fixed $t \in \mathit{Thread}$, there exists at most one shared variable `X` such that $\mathtt{flagX}_i\mathtt{t}$ is `true`. In other words, at each location of the TSO buffer there is at most one shared variable write. We define the function:

$$\mathtt{OR(i,\ t)} = \vee_{X \in \mathit{Shared}}\ \mathtt{flagX}_i\mathtt{t}.$$

The function `OR(i, t)` returns `true` if there exists a write (to any shared variable) at the position i in the write buffer of thread t. The previously mentioned invariant means that at most one disjunct will be true in the formula above. Fig. 5 shows the rules of the abstraction-guided translation:

Write to a global variable $[\![X = r]\!]^t_b$: first checks if there is a write in the last element of the store buffer. If so, the analysis indicates an overflow and stops. If the store buffer is not yet full, the translation determines the highest index i in the buffer which is already occupied and places the current write at the position $i + 1$. Note that in each branch of the if-then-else statement, a boolean variable is modified. This enables the robust buffer abstraction (Sec. 4.1) and the boolean encoding of counters (Sec. 4.2).

Read from a global variable $[\![r = X]\!]^t_b$: searches in the store buffer for the most recent write to the shared variable `X` and returns that value. If there is no write to `X` in the store buffer, then the value is read from the shared memory.

Fence statement $[\![\mathit{fence}]\!]^t_b$: assumes that at this point the store buffer is empty – there are no pending writes.

Flush action $[\![\mathit{flush}]\!]^t_b$: searches for the least recent entry in the store buffer and writes it to the shared memory. As opposed to the direct encoding, the element at position 1 is not flushed *because the shifting procedure was removed.* To know which variable is the buffered write, case testing is performed.

The new translation extends naturally to a sequence of statements and to programs with n concurrent threads: $[\![P]\!]_b = [\![S]\!]^1_b \parallel \cdots \parallel [\![S]\!]^n_b$.

4.4 Soundness of the Robust Buffer Abstraction

We next prove that the RBA abstraction incorporated in the translation T_V is sound as it over-approximates the direct translation T_D. Given a program P, memory model M, and buffer bound b, $P^D = T_D(P, M, b)$ is the program that results from applying direct translation, and $P^V = T_V(P, M, b)$ is the result of the abstraction-guided translation.

D: direct translation domain.	**V: abstraction-guided translation.**
$[b]$ = value of $cnt\_t \in \{0 \dots b\}$	$(Shared \rightarrow Bool)$ = values of `flagXᵢt`
$Shared \times \mathbb{N}$ = values of $lhs_i t, rhs_i t$	$(Shared \rightarrow \mathbb{N})$ = values of `Xᵢt`
$B_t^D = [b] \times Seq_{\leq b}(Shared \times \mathbb{N})$	$B_t^V = Seq_{\leq b}(Shared \rightarrow (Bool \times \mathbb{N}))$

Fig. 6. Translation Domains

Fig. 6 summarizes the data structures needed to encode the write buffer of a thread t in the direct and abstraction-guided translations:

- B_t^D is the tuple containing the value of $cnt_t \in [b]$ and the sequence of pairs of values for $lhs_i \in Shared$ and $rhs_i t \in \mathbb{N}$, $i \in \{1 \dots b\}$.
- B_t^V is a sequence of elements which, for each shared variable $X \in Shared$, associate a tuple containing the boolean variable $\texttt{flagX}_i\texttt{t} \in B$ and the stored value $\texttt{X}_i\texttt{t} \in \mathbb{N}$.

Let $B^D = \{B_t^D | t \in Threads\}$ and $B^V = \{B_t^V | t \in Threads\}$ be the sets of values of all write buffers of the programs P^D and P^V.

We define the state of a translated program as the values of the shared variables, local variables, program counter, and auxiliary variables added by the translation: $\sigma = \langle Shared_\sigma, Local_\sigma, pc_\sigma, B \rangle$ or $\sigma = overflow$. B is either the direct translation buffer state B^D or the abstraction-guided translation buffer state B^V.

Definition 1 (Observable part of a state). *The observable part of a state includes: (i) the values of the shared variables, (ii) the values of the local variables, and (iii) the values and order between elements of the* non-empty section *of the buffer.*

For T_D, the observable part of the state contains the values of the shared and local variables and the values of lhs_i and rhs_i for $i \in [1 \dots cnt\_t]$. Similarly, for T_V, the observable part of the state contains the values of the shared and local variables and the values of $\texttt{X}_i\texttt{t}$ for i and t, where $\texttt{flagX}_i\texttt{t}$ is *true*.

Definition 2 (Equivalent states). *Two states σ^D and σ^V are equivalent if their observable parts correspond (the global and local variables have the same values and the buffers B^D and B^V denote the same buffer content).*

We define the transitions between two states (σ_i, σ_{i+1}) for transformed programs as the translation rule (Fig. 4 or Fig. 5) corresponding to the transition in the original program P. A trace of a program is represented as a sequence of states $\pi = \sigma_1 \dots \sigma_n$.

Theorem 1 (The RBA abstraction used in T_V is sound). *For any trace $\pi^D = \sigma_1^D \dots \sigma_s^D$ of P^D of finite length s, there exists a corresponding trace $\pi^V = \sigma_1^V \dots \sigma_s^V$ of T^V, such that for all $i \in \{1 \dots s\}$, σ_i^V and σ_i^D are equivalent or σ_i^V is overflow.*

Proof. The proof is by induction on the length of π^D.

First, we show how to build the trace π^V. Given $\pi^D = \sigma_1^D \ldots \sigma_s^D$, the transition $(\sigma_i^D, \sigma_{i+1}^D)$ for $i \in [1 \ldots s-1]$ is a rule in Fig. 4, corresponding to the translation of an instruction in program P. We construct π^V by applying at each step $(\sigma_i^V, \sigma_{i+1}^V)$ the corresponding rule from Fig. 5.

Next, we prove that π^V and π^D have equivalent states.

Base case: for $i = 1$, in the initial state, all write buffers are empty, the shared variables have their initial values, and the local variables are not yet declared. Thus, states σ_1^V and σ_1^D are equivalent.

Induction step: for $i > 1$, we assume that the states σ_i^V and σ_i^D are equivalent or σ_i^V is overflow. If σ_i^V is overflow, then σ_{i+1}^V is also overflow (by convention, an overflow state cannot be changed).

If σ_i^V is not overflow, then the states σ_i^V and σ_i^D are equivalent (by the induction assumption). Our construction applies the transition $(\sigma_i^D, \sigma_{i+1}^D)$ as defined by the rules in Fig. 4 and the corresponding transition $(\sigma_i^V, \sigma_{i+1}^V)$ as defined by Fig. 5. We now show that σ_{i+1}^D and σ_{i+1}^V are equivalent or σ_{i+1}^V is overflow via case splitting on the transition type:

- `store`: write to a global variable $[\![\mathrm{X} = \mathrm{r}]\!]_b^t$. Here, the local and shared variables remain unchanged. From the induction assumption σ_i^D and σ_i^V, buffers hold the same values in the same order. From the assumption $\sigma_i^D \neq overflow$ and from the definition of `store`, we have that buffer content in σ_i^D and σ_i^V is the same or σ_{i+1}^V will reach overflow.
- `load`: read from a global variable $[\![\mathrm{r} = \mathrm{X}]\!]_b^t$. Here, the buffer contents are unchanged. The shared variables are also unchanged. From the induction assumption and the definition of `load` we have that the values of r for σ_{i+1}^D and for σ_{i+1}^V are the same.
- `fence`: fence statement $[\![\mathrm{fence}]\!]_b^t$. Here, the transition assumes that at this point the store buffers are empty for both translations. The states do not change and the assumption on σ_i^D and σ_i^V propagates to the states σ_{i+1}^D and σ_{i+1}^V.
- `flush`: flush action $[\![\mathrm{flush}]\!]_b^t$. Here, the local variables are unchanged. From the induction assumption, the buffers of σ_i^D and σ_i^V hold the same values in the same order, i.e., the same least recent element in the buffer will be flushed to main memory for σ_{i+1}^D and σ_{i+1}^V.

This concludes the proof of Theorem 1 that T^V is an over-approximation of T^D and the RBA abstraction is sound. This also means that even if the trace π^D does not reach an overflow, the corresponding trace π^V may result in overflow.

5 Evaluation

We implemented our approach and evaluated it on a range of challenging concurrent algorithms. We then compared its performance with the direct transformation discussed earlier [18]. All our experiments ran on an Intel(R) Xeon(R) 2.13 GHz server with 250 GB RAM. To perform the analysis, we used CONCURINTERPROC [12], a tool based on the APRON library [13], which supports various numerical abstract domains. We relied on the Z3 [11] SMT solver to check that the inferred invariants imply the specification.

Table 1. Verification results comparing our new transformation with prior work [18]

Program	Model	Number fences	Abstraction-guided translation Time (sec)	Abstraction-guided translation Memory (MB)	Direct translation [18] Time (sec)	Direct translation [18] Memory (MB)
Abp	TSO	0	5	189	14	352
	PSO	0	6	167	12	222
Bakery	TSO	4	1148	4749	-	-
	PSO	4	3429	10951	-	-
Concloop	TSO	2	8	547	18	891
	PSO	2	6	504	23	783
Dekker	TSO	6	227	2233	-	-
	PSO	4	121	1580	-	-
Kessel	TSO	4	14	357	15	424
	PSO	4	6	198	80	628
Loop2 TLM	TSO	2	66	2234	-	-
	PSO	2	36	1650	-	-
Peterson	TSO	2	89	1549	-	-
	PSO	4	20	901	331	2280
Pgsql	TSO	3	282	1727	-	-
	PSO	1	55	758	-	-
Queue	TSO	1	1	101	1	115
	PSO	1	1	108	1	106
Sober	TSO	2	30	1784	-	-
	PSO	3	148	263	215	3499
Szymanski	TSO	3	1066	3781	-	-
	PSO	4	507	2076	-	-
Chase-Lev WSQ	TSO	2	17	550	-	-
	PSO	4	9	520	10	528
THE WSQ	TSO	4	125	1646	-	-
	PSO	4	391	2338	-	-

The verification procedure has three steps:

(i) Applying the transformation on program P, obtaining a new program P_M.
(ii) Running CONCURINTERPROC on that transformed program.
(iii) Using Z3 to check whether the inferred invariants satisfy the specification.

The above procedure is repeated until it is no longer possible to further reduce the number of fences in the algorithm. We evaluated our approach on 13 concurrent algorithms, out of which 5 are infinite-state. The safety specifications are either mutual exclusion or reachability invariants involving labels of different threads.

Our main goal was to study the Abstraction-guided translation precision and efficiency gains (i.e. memory consumption, speed) compared to the direct translation [18], while using the same analysis tool (in this case CONCURINTERPROC) to verify the output programs. Where applicable, we also discuss how our work compares to other works that are state of the art(here and in Section 6). Table 1 summarizes our experimental results for both the x86 TSO and PSO memory models.

The minimal number of fences necessary to verify each algorithm are shown in column 3 of Table 1. The time and memory resources used by the analysis are shown for both the new transformation (in columns 4 and 5 of the table) and the previous transformation (in columns 6 and 7). We observe two trends:

- For Bakery, Dekker, Loop2-TLM, Pgsql, Szymanski and THE WSQ, the new transformation verifies the program with strictly fewer fences than the direct translation. The dash indicates that verification failed (out of memory or timeout) for those placements (or their subsets) using the direct translation.
- For the rest of the benchmarks, the direct translation was successful in verifying the same fence placement as our new translation. But in all those cases the time and memory consumption were better using the new translation, and in some instances (e.g., Sober) memory consumption was reduced by 10x.

Comparison to other work. Recent work [2] infers fences such that the program under the relaxed model is equivalent to SC – recall that we discussed such approaches as one of two general approaches in Section 3. Although scalable, the authors' abstraction tends to lead to significant precision loss, thus inserting redundant fences. For instance, in Lamport's Bakery under TSO, their abstraction inserts 8 fences, compared to 4 fences inserted by our analysis. This precision loss is observed also for other mutual exclusion algorithms such as Peterson under TSO (3 vs. 2 fences) and Szymansky under TSO (8 vs. 3 fences).

Another line of work [3] also produces an SC program from the original program and the relaxed memory model semantics. The work uses testing to find bugs in many litmus tests and algorithms (e.g., Bakery, Peterson, Dekker, Szymanski), but does not actually perform verification on any of them. Nor does it address the problem of how the proposed translation would affect infinite-state verification. For instance, when we tried [3] even on a few small examples, the resulting SC program used many more auxiliary boolean variables than our translation (e.g., 40 vs. 8). Note that even a small increase in the number of boolean variables quickly leads to state explosion (more disjunctions) in the program analysis. This is also confirmed by our experiments with CONCURINTERPROC, where, for instance, any program with more than 40 boolean variables could not be verified due to state explosion.

Summary of Results. In summary, for each program, our new transformation enables verification with a lower or equal number of fences compared to the direct translation. The new transformation also leads to a more efficient (in space and time) subsequent analysis of the resulting program. Based on our experimental results, we believe that our new abstraction-gudied transformation is a key building block in automating verification of both finite and infinite-state concurrent programs on relaxed memory models.

6 Related Work

We next discuss some additional work most closely related to ours. Over the last few years there has been significant interest in ensuring correctness (via synthesis and verification) of concurrent programs running on relaxed memory models. Most of the research has so far considered only finite-state programs [5,6,7,14,15,17]. (Some of these papers however, do handle specific kinds of infinite-state problems, such as unbounded store buffers, but where all shared variables range over finite domains). Some recent works also handle infinite-state programs [1,2,10,18,21].

One approach to handling relaxed memory models is to encode the effect of the model directly into the program and then analyze the resulting program using tools that work for sequential consistency (e.g., [3,4,10]). We follow the same general idea. The main contribution of our work is a new abstraction and a transformation which improves the precision and efficiency of the resulting program analysis. For instance, as we showed in the paper, using the direct encoding as in [18] will result in significant loss of precision and efficiency (i.e., failure to verify correct programs). Abdulla et al. [1] explore online predicate abstraction for handling infinite-state verification while Dan et al. [10] also explore predicate abstraction but this time based on offline analysis of boolean programs. Technically, these works are quite different from ours since: (i) they both use direct encoding and also (ii) they both use predicate abstraction which, even with abstraction refinement, tends to require manually supplied predicates. In contrast, we provide a new robust abstraction of the store buffers and explore the application of numerical abstract domains that do not require manual annotations. We also provide a more comprehensive experimental study than either of aforementioned works (we consider x86 TSO, as well as the more relaxed PSO model and a range of challenging concurrent algorithms). For the common benchmarks, [1] and our approach achieve comparable results. A possible limitation of this work is locked writes, meaning that fences are generated immediately following a write to shared memory. Our tool is more flexible since fences can be placed at any label. We again note that the robust buffer abstraction (RBA) proposed in this work can be immediately useful with predicate abstraction as well. In the work of [21], arbitrary safety properties are not taken into account. This work supports two fence removal optimizations (for TSO), which are not enough to eliminate redundant fences. We applied their optimizations on a few of our benchmarks and, unfortunately, it failed to remove redundant fences (e.g., in the Chase WSQ algorithm).

7 Conclusion

We proposed a new approach for verifying concurrent programs on relaxed memory models. Our approach consists of a robust abstraction of the store buffers, an encoding of the store buffer sizes that leverages the underlying abstract domains, and a source to source translation that encodes relaxed memory model semantics into the target program, thereby enabling the use of existing verification tools for sequential consistency.

We implemented our approach and evaluated it on a set of finite and infinite-state concurrent algorithms using an existing state-of-the art abstract interpretation engine. Our experimental results demonstrate that the overall system is superior to prior work in terms of precision and performance, enabling verification of concurrent algorithms on both x86 TSO and PSO memory models not possible before.

References

1. Abdulla, P.A., Atig, M.F., Chen, Y.-F., Leonardsson, C., Rezine, A.: Automatic fence insertion in integer programs via predicate abstraction. In: Miné, A., Schmidt, D. (eds.) SAS 2012. LNCS, vol. 7460, pp. 164–180. Springer, Heidelberg (2012)
2. Alglave, J., Kroening, D., Nimal, V., Poetzl, D.: Don't sit on the fence - a static analysis approach to automatic fence insertion. In: Biere, A., Bloem, R. (eds.) CAV 2014. LNCS, vol. 8559, pp. 508–524. Springer, Heidelberg (2014)

3. Alglave, J., Kroening, D., Nimal, V., Tautschnig, M.: Software verification for weak memory via program transformation. In: Felleisen, M., Gardner, P. (eds.) ESOP 2013. LNCS, vol. 7792, pp. 512–532. Springer, Heidelberg (2013)
4. Atig, M.F., Bouajjani, A., Parlato, G.: Getting rid of store-buffers in TSO analysis. In: Gopalakrishnan, G., Qadeer, S. (eds.) CAV 2011. LNCS, vol. 6806, pp. 99–115. Springer, Heidelberg (2011)
5. Bouajjani, A., Derevenetc, E., Meyer, R.: Checking and enforcing robustness against TSO. In: Felleisen, M., Gardner, P. (eds.) ESOP 2013. LNCS, vol. 7792, pp. 533–553. Springer, Heidelberg (2013)
6. Burckhardt, S., Musuvathi, M.: Effective program verification for relaxed memory models. In: Gupta, A., Malik, S. (eds.) CAV 2008. LNCS, vol. 5123, pp. 107–120. Springer, Heidelberg (2008)
7. Burnim, J., Sen, K., Stergiou, C.: Testing concurrent programs on relaxed memory models. In: ISSTA 2011 (2011)
8. Cousot, P., Cousot, R.: Abstract interpretation: A unified lattice model for static analysis of programs by construction of approximation of fixed points. In: POPL 1977 (1977)
9. Cousot, P., Halbwachs, N.: Automatic discovery of linear restraints among variables of a program. In: POPL 1978 (1978)
10. Dan, A.M., Meshman, Y., Vechev, M., Yahav, E.: Predicate abstraction for relaxed memory models. In: Logozzo, F., Fähndrich, M. (eds.) SAS 2013. LNCS, vol. 7935, pp. 84–104. Springer, Heidelberg (2013)
11. de Moura, L., Bjørner, N.S.: Z3: An efficient SMT solver. In: Ramakrishnan, C.R., Rehof, J. (eds.) TACAS 2008. LNCS, vol. 4963, pp. 337–340. Springer, Heidelberg (2008)
12. Jeannet, B.: Relational interprocedural verification of concurrent programs. Software and System Modeling 12(2), 285–306 (2013)
13. Jeannet, B., Miné, A.: APRON: A library of numerical abstract domains for static analysis. In: Bouajjani, A., Maler, O. (eds.) CAV 2009. LNCS, vol. 5643, pp. 661–667. Springer, Heidelberg (2009)
14. Kuperstein, M., Vechev, M., Yahav, E.: Automatic inference of memory fences. In: FMCAD 2010 (2010)
15. Kuperstein, M., Vechev, M., Yahav, E.: Partial-coherence abstractions for relaxed memory models. In: PLDI 2011 (2011)
16. Lamport, L.: How to make a multiprocessor computer that correctly executes multiprocess programs. IEEE Trans. Comput. 28(9), 690–691 (1979)
17. Linden, A., Wolper, P.: An automata-based symbolic approach for verifying programs on relaxed memory models. In: van de Pol, J., Weber, M. (eds.) SPIN 2010. LNCS, vol. 6349, pp. 212–226. Springer, Heidelberg (2010)
18. Meshman, Y., Dan, A., Vechev, M., Yahav, E.: Synthesis of memory fences via refinement propagation. In: Müller-Olm, M., Seidl, H. (eds.) SAS 2014. LNCS, vol. 8723, pp. 237–252. Springer, Heidelberg (2014)
19. Miné, A.: The octagon abstract domain. Higher Order Symbol. Comput. 19(1), 31–100 (2006)
20. Rival, X., Mauborgne, L.: The trace partitioning abstract domain. ACM Trans. Program. Lang. Syst. 29(5), 26 (2007)
21. Sevcík, J., Vafeiadis, V., Nardelli, F.Z., Jagannathan, S., Sewell, P.: Compcerttso: A verified compiler for relaxed-memory concurrency. J. ACM 60(3), 22 (2013)
22. Shasha, D., Snir, M.: Efficient and correct execution of parallel programs that share memory. ACM Trans. Program. Lang. Syst. 10(2), 282–312 (1988)
23. Sura, Z., Fang, X., Wong, C.-L., Midkiff, S.P., Lee, J., Padua, D.: Compiler techniques for high performance sequentially consistent java programs. In: PPoPP 2005 (2005)

Author Index